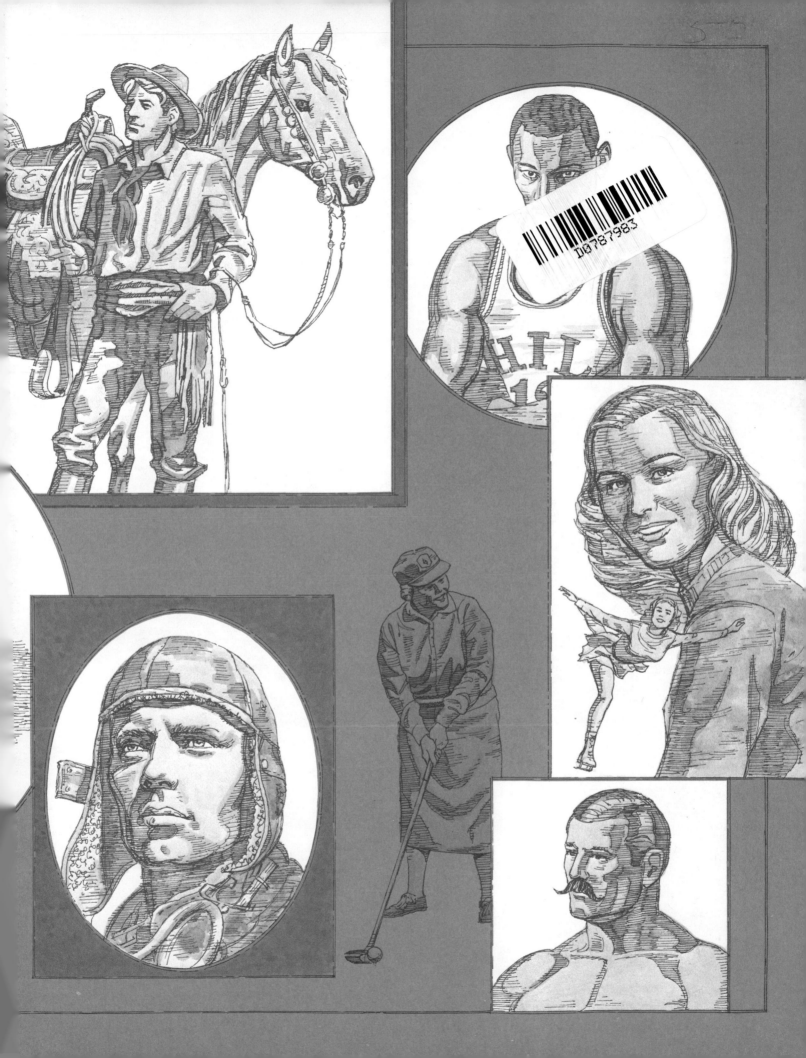

THE
HALLS OF FAME

THE
HALLS OF FAME

Featuring Specialized Museums of Sports, Agronomy, Entertainment and the Humanities

EDITED BY

Thomas C. Jones

IN COLLABORATION WITH

Buck Dawson

Assisted by Harriet Helmer and Al Josephson

Watercolor Illustrations by Kay Smith

Published by J. G. FERGUSON PUBLISHING COMPANY / CHICAGO

BOUND IN HANDICRAFTED MISSION LEATHER BY BROWN & BIGELOW, ST. PAUL, MINNESOTA

INTRODUCTION

One of the relatively new tourist attractions in the United States and Canada is the *Hall of Fame*. There are various reasons for the rapid growth of this kind of museum, but perhaps the most important is the burgeoning of all forms of entertainment. Every sport has expanded greatly and more people than ever before are interested in following the heroes of athletics, amateur and professional. The museums devoted to the achievements of sports and entertainment personalities and important leaders, and the growth and changes of each activity, are all a part of a national feeling of nostalgia.

Many spectators have been introduced to such sports as track, gymnastics, swimming, rowing, amateur boxing and wrestling, skiing, and figure skating through the televising of the Olympic games. These quadrennial games have generated a general awareness of the drama of sport and the personalities connected with it. In the past, this devotion to the performing heroes existed in a more limited way.

The first hall of fame, founded in 1900, was dedicated to the great individuals who contributed in some way to the establishment and growth of the United States of America. This is the Hall of Fame for Great Americans, established on the heights that commanded the Hudson River in the Revolutionary War which became the campus of New York University in the Bronx borough of New York City. The campus is now that of Bronx Community College.

At the Helms Athletic Foundation, now the Citizens Savings Foundation, in Los Angeles, California, a general Sports Hall of Fame dates back to 1936. The prestigious Baseball Hall of Fame in Cooperstown, New York, was established in approximately the same years, the first selections being made in 1936. Another hall of fame that dates back many years is Statuary Hall in the Capitol, Washington, D.C. This is the only collection of statuary devoted to individuals honored by the separate states and it represents a wide range of public personalities spanning all the years of American history.

Revolutionary changes in American life

Following World War II, with the advent of television, the great expansion of travel in all forms of transportation, the shorter hours of the workday and the benefit of paid vacations for millions of workers, there was a greatly increased interest in all kinds of sports and various other forms of entertainment. Electronic instruments, such as guitars and microphones controlled by a panel where tones could be greatly amplified and mixed to create pleasing and unusual sounds audible to large crowds, helped establish many entertainers performing before thousands of fans at state fairs and other outdoor and indoor arenas.

The revolution in electronics for the performer was paralleled by the new and more sophisticated receivers of entertainment in the form of portable radios, car radios, record players, color television and various sound track systems, all of which contributed to the popularity of many stars who received wide exposure.

The great growth in country and western entertainers occurred through these new mechanical wonders. In the days of radio, the "Barn Dance" and the "Grand Ole Opry" popularized many of these stars. However, since the 1950s, this form of entertainment has become one of the giants of the music industry. Nashville, the capital of country music, honored this lively and popular form of entertainment by establishing the Country Music Hall of Fame and Museum, which annually shows its hospitality to more than a half million fans.

The quality of most halls of fame speaks for itself. As with all museums, there are great variations in size and investment in these attractions. Many are new and still in the developmental stage. Even in the newest and smaller halls of fame, there are numerous features of interest unique to the sport or activity being covered. Some have proven to be so popular it has been necessary to expand the facilities. A few of the establishments have temporary buildings that serve to house the accumulated treasures pending completion of new building construction. Notwithstanding the varying size and number of years of existence of these institutions, each is worth the effort of a visit by any traveler with even a remote interest in the sport, entertainment, or historical subjects represented.

What is a Hall of Fame?

Buck Dawson of the International Swimming Hall of Fame, who cooperated so wholeheartedly in this project to publish a detailed *Halls of Fame* book, expresses his philosophy concerning these museums as follows:

A hall of fame is a museum with a personality. Whereas an anthropological museum deals in the composite man, a hall of fame deals in specific men and women—personalities whose talent and achievement express biographically the dramatic episodes displayed in the hall of fame. Hence, it is a living museum, even though some of the honorees are deceased. It tells the story of measured accomplishment in terms of the talented heroes who were the high achievers in the activity honored, be it music, theater or sport. The story of baseball is told through the anecdotes of Wee Willie Keeler, who "hit 'em where they ain't," Ted Williams, Babe Ruth and Ty Cobb. The statistics and rules of the game and the equipment of the game are all secondary to the personalities who played this game.

The Swimming Hall of Fame's big three are the great swimmers who made it even bigger in show business—Johnny Weissmuller as "Tarzan," Buster Crabbe as "Flash Gordon," "Buck Rogers" and "Billy the Kid," and Eleanor Holm, New York World's Fair Aquacades star. Unlike other movie stars, these three are Olympic champions, an uncommon blending of the real and the unreal that is life.

The Movie Stars Hall of Fame recognizes Gene Autry and John Wayne along with swimmers Weissmuller and Esther Williams. The Cowboy Hall of Fame recognizes cowboy actors Autry, Wayne and Crabbe, along with Walter Brennan, Joel McCrea, Roy Rogers and others. Real cowboys? No, real personalities! These actors made cowboys a part of everybody's daily life. They made the cowboy fans who now want to come and see the real cowboys at the Cowboy Hall of Fame. Just as movie cowboys bring people to see real cowboys, so the Cowboy Hall of Fame brings people to see the Hall of Fame's Museum of Western Heritage. Western artists Remington and Russell are

Cowboy Hall of Fame personalities. There are Remingtons in other art museums, but at the Cowboy Hall of Fame, the artist's work is depicted through his experience in the nineteenth century West. This again is what distinguishes between a hall of fame and other types of museums.

And why not? Most of us are interested in people. Certainly, Michelangelo and Leonardo da Vinci live on through their art, but their lives were dramatic enough to live on as best-selling biographies. Bringing it up to the present, which is what most halls of fame do, what hall of fame buff would deny as much interest in writer Ernest Hemingway's life as in what he has written?

We asked some students on the beach in Fort Lauderdale if they wanted to see a museum and the answer was "No." We asked if they wanted to see a hall of fame and the answer was "Maybe." We asked if they wanted to see Johnny Weissmuller and the answer was "Yes, where is he?" For these sun worshipers, at least, halls of fame must come to life through personalities. How do we do this? With movie stars, jazz musicians and country music singers, it is easy. We show Humphrey Bogart on film kissing Ingrid Bergman in "Casablanca" and he lives and the Movie Stars Hall of Fame museum lives with him because the viewers like to "Play It Again, Sam." This is also true with Caruso's singing or Bix Beiderbeck playing trumpet on an old record retaped and played in front of a wax figure of what these personalities looked like those many years ago.

For sports halls of fame, it may not be so easy. Nothing becomes history faster than a good race, yet nothing is quite as real as a measured moment in sport. Likewise, our greatest peacetime heroes are the persons who make those moments worth remembering. Sports stars have short careers, and halls of fame have the responsibility of preserving these people at their particular moments of triumph. At the great moment, a sports hero is larger than life, so the Swimming Hall of Fame has its honorees depicted larger than life in twelve-foot-high photo murals that the sports fan can look up to.

At the Citizens Savings (formerly Helms) Hall of Fame, the great moments are made real by a talk with the curator, Bill Schroeder, who was there when most of it happened or else he personally knows almost everyone who made it happen. At the Tennis Hall of Fame, in the picturesque old Newport Casino, the viewer sees a picture of a great amateur tennis player of the 1920s and then he reads the bottom line and calls his wife. "Hey, Mabel, look here—this old guy is Merv Griffin's uncle."

There is a hall of fame for the great cowboys, another for the great circus performers, and still another honoring police and law men. If you are a real sports fan, you will take your hall of fame seriously as a shrine. The Basketball Hall of Fame is so shrinelike that each honoree is depicted on a stained glass window. There is a dignity to halls of fame, but also a sense of humor, and sometimes even a touch of irony needs expression, like the little kid who pleaded, "Say it ain't so, Joe," to his hero, Shoeless Joe Jackson after the 1919 Chicago Black Sox scandal.

The hall of famers in sport, music and acting are people fortunate enough to have a special talent which we can envy and admire. They took the risk and were ready when their big chances came. A Boxing Hall of Fame visitor might say to his buddy, "I saw Sugar Ray the night he knocked out Randy Turpin at the Polo Grounds." Every fan can find something from his own youth in a hall of fame. "Hey, Harriet, look here. I knew that guy—he ran against my brother at the Penn Relays."

Halls of fame are a recent North American phenomenon, beginning with Baseball at Cooperstown and Helms in Los Angeles in the early 1930s. The idea has spread.

An apology

In this compilation of more than forty chapters, each covering a separate hall of fame, there is a wide variation in subject treatment. This is necessitated by the nature of the activity or sport, the materials furnished by the institution, the number of honorees, the focus on the qualifications for being honored, and the practical limitations of space. For example, a swimmer is honored because of his performances in specific events. Training for the record-breaking performances took years, but the hall of fame honors the swimmer for his race against the stopwatch and other competition, and that is how his attainment appears in the summary of why he or she was elected to the hall of fame.

On the other hand, the career of a horse trainer, a jockey, or a baseball or football player usually spans from ten to thirty years, and the election to the hall of fame results from consistently outstanding performances over a period of years. In these cases, the biographical treatment of the hall of fame member is necessarily more detailed.

Of the forty-odd chapters honoring particular halls of fame, thirty represent sports. It is true that athletics, by their very nature, peculiarly lend themselves to this manner of honoring past stars. However, there are many halls of fame in professions that are growing in importance and public interest, as well as local and state halls of fame honoring athletes and public figures, which might well deserve to be included in a work of this type at some future date.

We have attempted to list all the halls of fame, professional and otherwise, in the last pages of this volume, but feel certain that we have inadvertently omitted some. We apologize in advance where this has occurred and suggest that you notify the publisher, so that in future editions, additions and changes can be made to correct and update the volume.

Thomas C. Jones, Editor

ACKNOWLEDGMENTS

No reference work of this size and diversity can be assembled without the cooperation and dedication of many people and organizations. This is particularly true when there are forty-four chapters as unrelated as the Country Music Hall of Fame and the Canadian Hockey Hall of Fame, or the National Cowboy Hall of Fame and the International Swimming Hall of Fame. Every chapter required the cooperation of the administrative staff of each museum in sending photographs and information about the special attractions and unique exhibits that make its hall of fame interesting to the public. In several instances, staff members of museums wrote the articles for their chapters. These are duly noted with by-lines. We do not have space to name all of the individuals who have cooperated personally, but we are grateful indeed to the many who have helped us complete a big, expensive project that we think makes a contribution to a previously neglected subject area.

It is entirely fitting that the original sponsor of this project in support of the publisher be the remembrance advertising firm of Brown & Bigelow of Saint Paul, Minnesota. They have been interested in halls of fame for years and, in fact, gave to the Baseball Hall of Fame the series of original calendar paintings featuring baseball scenes by Norman Rockwell. This book has been in the planning and developmental process for about three years, dating back to 1974, as a sequel to the bicentennial series developed by the same team of editors, artists, printers and binders for initial publication in genuine leather bindings exclusively by Brown & Bigelow.

The popularity of the hall of fame type museum is attested to by the number of new ones that are under construction or proposed. It is possible that important and worthy institutions of this nature have been omitted. We think we have covered all general sports halls of fame, including those where the ground has just been broken and the scheduled completion is within the next eighteen months. All general halls of fame of national interest have been included. Specialized halls of fame with a national audience, such as Country Music, National Cowboy and Western Heritage, the Agricultural Hall of Fame, and others are in the book because they are important museums that deserve to be better known throughout the country. We included six Canadian sports halls of fame because of the mutuality of interest in Canadian and American sports.

There are excellent professional halls of fame and many local, college, military unit, and state halls of fame that have been omitted. The list of other halls of fame in the closing pages of this volume is by no means complete. It is offered for the convenience of hall of fame buffs or others who wish to have the information.

Without the months of untiring and dedicated efforts of the immediate staff assistants, the book could not have been completed. This is especially true of Al Josephson, designer and assistant editor, who is responsible for assembling the thousands of facts, dates, photos, biographies, and articles that constitute the end product. Harriet Helmer, editorial assistant, has filtered from the reams of raw material the inaccuracies, inconsistencies, and miscellaneous errors that are inevitable in a work of this nature. My secretary, Alberta Hutman, has patiently handled the great mass of material accumulated during the course of production. The Chicago area based firm of Photopress, Inc., with Don Vendl as account man, deserves great credit for its willingness to permit the space and time required to assemble the material and lithograph it as soon as the mechanicals came out of the art department. Other vital elements of the production team are Jim Fox and Dorothy Hays of the Clarinda Company, typesetters, Bill Currie of G & R Typesetting Company, and Jim Stewart of the Engdahl Company, bookbinders.

This is the fourth major publication in which the brilliant watercolor paintings of Chicago artist Kay Smith have been featured to supplement the black and white and other color illustrations. Some halls of fame can be more effectively portrayed through the artistic eye of a painter than through photography. Where we felt this was true, we commissioned the artist to do a painting on the scene. The results speak for themselves in the eighteen subjects she painted plus a painting and sketches of Secretariat, the super horse. We selected this great champion as the top performer of the last quarter-century. We are grateful to Seth Hancock of Claiborne Farm for allowing Kay Smith to paint the Triple Crown winner, and we thank Anna Bishop for making the arrangements for her to do so.

In the very necessary work of contacting and encouraging members of the Association of Sports Halls of Fame to cooperate in this project, we have had the help of Buck Dawson, Mary Church, and other staff members of the International Swimming Hall of Fame. This has been a most important factor in the final result.

Finally, we thank every organization that sent material to be used in this publication and apologize to those who graciously sent material, but whose hall of fame was omitted from the book. There was just not enough space to include every institution this time. Perhaps a supplementary edition can include all the others if the idea proves to be popular.

Thomas C. Jones, Editor

CONTENTS

SPORTS HALLS OF FAME IN CANADA

OTHER HALLS OF FAME

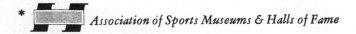 * *Association of Sports Museums & Halls of Fame*

LIST OF COLOR ILLUSTRATIONS

The beautiful Greek Exedra erected as a memorial to Louis Chevrolet and other pioneers of the automobile industry situated near the southwest corner of the Hall of Fame. In addition to the magnificent bust of Louis Chevrolet there are four historical bronze panels depicting four of Chevrolet's major accomplishments.

They show:
• Chevrolet's 1923 Barber-Warnock Fronty Ford at the Indianapolis Motor Speedway with Henry Ford at the wheel and Louis standing alongside, flanked by Barney Oldfield and Harvey Firestone.
• Louis and W. C. Durant, founder of General Motors, with the first Chevrolet passenger car in 1911.
• Chevrolet's first winning car at Indianapolis, driven to victory in 1920 by brother Gaston, with four Speedway pioneers in the background—Carl G. Fisher, James A. Allison, L. H. Trotter, and T. E. (Pop) Myers.
• Chevrolet's second Indianapolis winner, driven by Tommy Milton in 1921, with Capt. E. V. Rickenbacker, Col. A. W. Herrington, Louis Schwitzer and C. W. Van Ranst.

— All photographs in this chapter, courtesy Indianapolis Motor Speedway

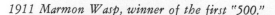

THE AUTO RACING HALL OF FAME AND MUSEUM

Speedway, Indiana

This very impressive and exciting museum was opened April 5, 1976, after years of planning and preparation. Auto racing's Hall of Fame was established in 1952 by members of the American Automobile Association in cooperation with the Edison Institute of the Ford Foundation with three main objectives. These were: (1) perpetuating the names and memories of outstanding racing personalities; (2) demonstrating racing's contributions to the development of the automobile industry; and (3) portraying the impact of those contributions on the American way of life.

Although the early efforts of the committee to acquire memorabilia for the Hall of Fame met with little success, they did select with the help of race historians, media representatives, and others identified with racing,

1911 Marmon Wasp, winner of the first "500."

an original Hall of Fame drawn from driver, mechanic, car owner, promoter, official, and manufacturer. The first ballot in 1952 was limited to men active prior to 1911 and the following ten were chosen: Louis Chevrolet, Bert Dingley, Harvey Firestone, Sr., Carl G. Fisher, Henry Ford, Ray Harroun, Barney Oldfield, William K. Vanderbilt, Fred J. Wagner, and T. E. (Pop) Myers.

In 1953 and '54 out of thirty-three nominees of men active in racing prior to 1920 seven were elected to the Racing Hall of Fame: Bob Burman, Earl Cooper, Ralph DePalma, Tommy Milton, Ralph Mulford, Dario Resta, and Eddie Rickenbacker.

After this, the AAA withdrew its support from racing in general including the Racing Hall of Fame project.

In 1956 Indianapolis Speedway President Tony Hulman created a museum for automobile racing on the Speedway grounds and formed the Indianapolis Motor Speedway Foundation Inc., a non-profit organization to administer all museum affairs.

The many visitors to the museum indicated great regret that the Hall of Fame idea had been abandoned by its founders. The momentum to reinstate the Hall of Fame became so pervasive that in 1961 the Speedway Foundation with AAA approval and the cooperation of the Ford Museum, Dearborn, Michigan, placed in operation a plan to reorganize the Hall of Fame.

A committee of 100 qualified individuals was formed to nominate and vote on additional candidates annually, beginning in 1962, subject to two basic requirements, (1) a waiting period of at least 20 years from the date

Starting lineup for the first Indianapolis 500-mile race May 30, 1911.

Tommy Milton, winner of the 1921 "500", with Barney Oldfield and Louis Chevrolet to the right of the driver.

of any individual's first active participation in the sport before his name could be placed on the ballot, and approval by 75 per cent or more of the 100 members of the selection committee for enshrinement.

The selection committee voting on the candidates each year consists of all living Hall of Fame members: drivers, mechanics, and race officials from all eras of racing, members of the Speedway Foundation's board of directors; press-TV-radio representatives, race historians, and representatives of accessory companies associated with the sport.

The Hall of Fame and Museum appeals to all ages of visitors because of the great variety of displays related to every phase of automobile and racing history, with which most visitors have to some degree had exposure since the earliest years of childhood.

The extensive collections include many famous car models of the past such as nineteen classic and antique passenger cars, forty-one historic race cars including several "500" winners and a number of race engines such as two Millers, one Meyer Drake Offenhauser, one Foyt, one Ford and one Monroe-Frontenae.

Dozens of trophies are on display along with hundreds of historical photos and racing memorabilia.

The museum is immaculate in all aspects and it is comfortable and pleasant with ample parking areas. The displays afford an easy opportunity to examine the most intricate details of the classic cars and famous racers. There is an active gift shop and lunch facility.

A feature of the exterior is the fountain in the shape of a wheel. The hub is formed by the main column of water. Circling this are three rows of pipes each with eleven spigots symbolic of the thirty-three starters in the "500".

MEMBERS

JAMES A. ALLISON (promoter), one of the four founders of the Indianapolis Motor Speedway, was a major factor in the track's successful operation because of his sound business judgment. He succeeded Carl G. Fisher as Speedway president and assumed complete charge of the "500" when Fisher began to lose interest in racing after World War I while developing Miami Beach as a winter resort. Allison also was intensely interested in engine development and he formed the Allison Engineering Company — now the Allison Division of General Motors — to stimulate the building of better race cars with which to repel the European challenge to American supremacy.

TONY BETTENHAUSEN (driver) scored victories in 21 big car championship events and won the national title in 1951 as well as in 1958. He also was runnerup for the crown in 1959, when he drove five different cars on the championship circuit. Although Tony announced his retirement as an active driver on two occasions because of injuries, his career spanned the 23-year period from 1938 until his death in a 1961 racing accident. He participated in 14 Indianapolis 500-mile races, making his best showing by placing second in 1955; and was a top-flight contender, consistently, on dirt as well as on pavement.

GEORGE BIGNOTTI (mechanic) who came to the Indianapolis Motor Speedway as a crew member for the first time in 1954, has more USAC championship victories to his credit than any other chief mechanic. He started the 1975 season with a total of 68 such triumphs, including nine in 500-mile events. His six Indianapolis wins were scored by A. J. Foyt in 1961 and 1964, Graham Hill in 1966, Al Unser in 1970 and 1971, and Gordon Johncock in 1973. Joe Leonard and Wally Dallenbach won for him at Ontario in 1971 and 1973, respectively; and Leonard also drove a car prepared by Bignotti to victory at Pocono in 1972. Seven USAC national driving championships (four by Foyt, two by Leonard and one by Unser) also have been won in George's cars.

JIMMY BRYAN (driver), recognized universally as one of the sport's greatest dirt-track drivers, gained additional renown by scoring impressive victories on the paved courses at Indianapolis and Monza (Italy). He won the national driving championship three times — in 1954, 1956 and 1957 — and was second in the final standing for 1955. At one stage during this four-year period he won seven consecutive dirt track championship races. He scored his Indianapolis "500" triumph in 1958, after finishing second once and third once in earlier attempts. He won the first Monza "500" in 1957 and finished second in a similar event on the same course one year later.

BOB BURMAN (driver) tested cars for Buick as early as 1903 and ranked among the nation's top-flight drivers from 1906 until his death in a 1916 crash at Corona, Cal. Although he competed successfully in most of the major championship events on all types of race courses — including the board tracks at Chicago and New York — he gained his greatest fame in a series of record runs, 24-hour events, match races and exhibition appearances against such rivals as Barney Oldfield, Ralph DePalma, Earl Cooper and Louis Disbrow. In 1911, on the sand at Daytona Beach, Burman shattered Oldfield's land speed record by more than 10 miles an hour by averaging 141.732 for the measured mile at the wheel of the same Benz Oldfield had used to set a record a year earlier.

GASTON CHEVROLET (driver) left France as a young man to join his two older brothers in the United States and he began to attract attention by finishing well in four 1917 races, including a 250-mile event on the boards at Cincinnati. Following a 12-months suspension by the AAA Contest Board for participating in unsanctioned events, he drove at Indianapolis in 1919 for the first time and placed 10th in a Chevrolet Frontenac. Later in the same season he scored three important board track victories, two at Sheepshead Bay and

*Speedway President Carl G. Fisher's
1911 Stoddard-Dayton official pace car.*

Passing the grandstand in the first "500" showing the drivers and mechanics as they round the first turn, Louis Disbrow in the number 5 Pope-Harford, Joe Jagersberger's number 8 Case and Will Jones number 9 Case.

one at Uniontown. He won the 1920 Indianapolis race in a Chevrolet Monroe and was at the peak of his career when he suffered fatal injuries in a crash at Beverly Hills.

LOUIS CHEVROLET (driver and car builder) came to this country from France in 1905 to work as a mechanic for a New York importer of European cars and started his racing career five years later by driving a Fiat to victory in a three-mile race against Barney Oldfield and Walter Christie. Louis, the oldest of three brothers, also drove for Buick and several other manufacturers before building his own cars, which scored many notable victories including the Indianapolis "500" in 1920 (a Monroe, driven by brother Gaston) and 1921 (a Frontenac driven by Tom Milton). As a driver until 1923, Louis won the 395-mile 1909 Cobe Trophy Road Race and many important events on the board speedways at Uniontown, Chicago, Cincinnati and Sheepshead Bay.

EARL COOPER (driver and engineer) became a consistent winner in 1913, for Stutz, after five years of moderate success with other makes of cars on the Pacific Coast. He was particularly outstanding in road course events during the early part of his career, winning races of more than 300 miles duration at Santa Monica, Corona, Elgin and Point Loma. Later he enjoyed almost equal success on the board tracks, scoring major victories as late as 1926 during a driving career interrupted twice by decisions to retire. He won the AAA national driving titles in 1913, 1915 and 1917 and built Miller-powered race cars for Studebaker as well as Marmon.

BILL CUMMINGS (driver) moved up from the half-mile dirt tracks to AAA championship competition in 1930 and compiled an enviable record annually until he crashed to his death in a 1938 highway accident on wet pavement. He drove in nine consecutive Indianapolis races, setting a new record of 104.863 miles an hour to win the 1934 event and collecting enough points at other tracks to capture the national driving title that season. He finished sixth or better in three other starts at "Indy" and won the pole position in the "500" starting lineup twice. He placed seventh in the 1936 International road race at Roosevelt Raceway and scored one or more victories in championship events on five of the nation's one-mile dirt tracks.

RALPH De PALMA (driver and engineer) came to the United States in 1893, when only 10 years old, and started his successful racing career in 1903. He scored one or more victories on almost every major race course operated under AAA Contest Board sanction and was crowned National champion in 1912 and 1914. He drove in 10 Indianapolis events, winning in 1915, and still holds the distinction of having led the "500" for more laps than any other participant (613). He also campaigned successfully in Europe and helped design and build the Packard V-12 which he drove to a new land speed record of 149.87 miles an hour on the measured mile at Daytona Beach in 1919.

PETER De PAOLO (driver) joined his uncle Ralph DePalma as riding mechanic immediately after World War I and made his first appearance in competition at the wheel of a race car in 1922. He earned a place on the Duesenberg factory team in 1924 and became the first Indianapolis driver to exceed the 100-mile-an-hour mark by averaging 101.13 for Duesenberg one year later. He also scored important victories on the board tracks at Fresno, Altoona, Laurel, Rockingham and Miami and competed with distinction in grand prix events on two trips to Europe. He won the AAA National driving championship twice, in 1925 and 1927, and placed third in the 1926 point standing behind Harry Hartz and Frank Lockhart.

BERT DINGLEY (driver) earned national recognition as early as 1905 as a member of The Pope Toledo team by defeating all rivals for the right to represent the United States in the second Vanderbilt Cup Race; and he compiled an enviable record annually until he suffered serious injuries in a 1914 race at Tacoma, Wash. In 1909 he was hailed as the American Automobile Association's national champion as the result of a consistent performance which included victories (for Chalmers) in the San Francisco-to-Portland road race and the 202-mile Santa Monica road race. In six other major starts that season he also placed second twice, third once and fourth once.

AUGUST DUESENBERG (engineer), remained in the shadow of his older brother (Fred) for most of his career, but contributed his full share of ideas and effort to the development of the early Mason race cars and the splendid creations which carried the Duesenberg name to repeated victories for more than 20 years beginning in 1914. He was particularly interested in the development of smaller racing engines and he ultimately assumed complete responsibility for Duesenberg's racing activities as Fred devoted increasing attention to corporate affairs. "Augie" also designed and built the Duesenberg car in which a Cummins Diesel engine was used for the first non-stop performance by an Indianapolis 500-mile race participant.

*Peter DePaolo in Duesenberg, winner of the 1925 "500"
at an average speed of 101.13 miles per hour.*

FRED DUESENBERG (engineer) believed in proving the speed and durability of his products in competition; and the Duesenberg entries provided the principal opposition for the Miller Specials in the championship events of the 1920's. During that decade at Indianapolis, for example, Duesenberg won in 1924, 1925 and 1927 while finishing second or third in four of the other seven "Indy" events. A Duesenberg driven by Pete DePaolo was the first "500" winner at better than 100 miles an hour. Tommy Milton drove a Duesenberg to a new land speed record of 156.046 miles an hour for the measured mile at Daytona Beach in 1920 and Jimmy Murphy drove a Duesenberg to an impressive victory in the 1921 French Grand Prix.

HARVEY FIRESTONE, Sr. (industrialist) was quick to recognize Speedway racing, at the time of its inception, as an outdoor laboratory and proving ground for automotive products. He welcomed competition and risked the future of the young Firestone company on its ability to build better and safer tires for the racing fraternity in order to emphasize the quality of its passenger car tires. Firestone tires won the first Indianapolis 500-mile race and they have continued to win the great majority of championship events since that time. The company's racing division which he established, also has been an important factor in the sport's steadily growing popularity.

CARL G. FISHER (driver and promoter) helped popularize the automobile during the industry's pioneer era by competing against Barney Oldfield and other drivers in a series of lucrative exhibition events on the half-mile county fair tracks of the mid-west for a four-year period beginning in 1902. He urged automobile manufacturers repeatedly to support plans for speedways, where they could prove the reliability of their products in competition; and, when his efforts along that line proved unproductive, he persuaded three business associates to join him in the construction of the Indianapolis Motor Speedway, serving as president from its inception until after the 1923 event.

1914 Delage, winner of the fourth "500'.

HENRY FORD (driver and car owner) was the first American to establish a land speed record when he drove his Ford 999 race car at 91.370 miles an hour over a measured mile course on the frozen surface of Lake St. Clair near Detroit, surpassing the mark of 84.730 mph recorded a few months earlier by Arthur Duray of France. Ford also participated successfully in races at other locations in this country during the first five years of the 20th century as a driver and car owner. He repeatedly relied on racing as an important factor in the Ford Motor Company's sales promotion program and was represented by a team of cars in the Indianapolis 500-mile event as late as 1935.

RAY HARROUN (driver and engineer) participated in almost every major automobile race during a six-year period beginning in 1905 and climaxed his driving career with a victory in the inaugural Indianapolis 500-mile event on May 30, 1911, at the wheel of a six-cylinder Marmon. His 1910 record, when he won the National driving championship, included two important victories on the Plays del Rey board track in California and additional triumps of major importance in 200-mile races at Atlanta, Georgia, and on the Indianapolis Motor Speedway. After retiring as a driver, Harroun designed race cars for the Maxwell Company, including one which ran on kerosene and was driven to ninth place by Will Carlson at Indianapolis in 1914.

HARRY HARTZ (driver and car owner) ranks among the most consistent race participants of all time. He won the National championship in 1926 and scored major victories on the board tracks at Fresno, Culver City and Atlantic City. In five consecutive years at the Indianapolis Motor Speedway, beginning in 1922, he scored three seconds and two fourths. He also participated in many stock car speed and endurance runs. After retiring as a driver, he enjoyed exceptional success as a car owner, preparing the Miller-Hartz Specials which Billy Arnold and Fred Frame drove to their impressive "500" victories in 1930 and 1932, respectively.

EDDIE HEARNE (driver) ranked among the stars of racing's pioneer days and still was a consistent winner as late as 1923. Prior to the first "500" in 1911, Hearne participated in seven free-for-all races at the Indianapolis Motor Speedway, ranging up to distances of 100 miles, and won five of them. He won a 200-mile road race at Cincinnati in 1911 and finished second in the Savannah Grand Prix the same year. After participating in the first two Indianapolis Memorial Day Classics, Hearne retired from the sport, but returned to active competition following World War I and finished second to Howdy Wilcox in the 1919 Indianapolis event. He also placed third in 1922 and fourth in 1923, the year in which he won the national title by scoring important victories on the board tracks.

HARRY "COTTON" HENNING (mechanic and car owner) served as crew chief for many drivers who scored important victories with his equipment on all types of race courses for more than a quarter of a century beginning in the early 1920's. During his career he enjoyed equal success with Duesenberg, Miller, Maserati and Offenhauser engines. His winners in the Indianapolis 500-mile race included Pete DePaolo in 1925, Bill Cummings in 1934, and Wilbur Shaw in 1939 and 1940. He became a car owner after World War II and Ted Horn finished third and fourth for him at "Indy" in 1947 and 1948, respectively.

RALPH HEPBURN (driver) participated in 15 Indianapolis 500-mile races over a period of more than two decades, gaining the unique distinction of leading the field for several laps on his rookie appearance in 1925 and in his final "Indy" effort in 1946. He ran at the head of the pack again during part of the 1937 race and figures in the closest finish ever recorded at "Indy," trailing Race Winner Wilbur Shaw across the line by the slim margin of only 2.16 seconds. Hepburn also placed third in 1931, fourth in 1941 and fifth in 1935 while earning high ranking among the all-time Indianapolis mileage leaders. In the first race after World War II he set new one-lap and four-lap records in a front-drive Novi Special.

Starting lineup for the 1923 Indianapolis race.

TED HORN (driver) won important races on almost every track in operation during his era except at Indianapolis; and his "500" record is unequalled for consistency. It shows that he finished fourth or better in nine straight events on the big two-and-a-half-mile oval, beginning in 1936. He was second once and third four times. He also was the pole position winner in 1947 and, in three of his "Indy" races, he led the field part of the time. Horn enjoyed even greater success on the dirt tracks and won the national title for three straight years, beginning in 1946, after finishing fourth or better in the final point standing on five previous occasions.

ANTON HULMAN (promoter) purchased the Indianapolis Motor Speedway after World War II and restored the annual 500-mile race to its rightful International prominence. In addition to transforming the track's aging facilities into structures of magnificent permanence, he increased prize money for the annual 500-mile race from a previous "high" of $96,250 to an all-time peak of $1,015,686 in 1974. He also guided the sport through its difficult transition period from AAA to USAC supervision, established the Speedway museum on a non-profit basis and served effectively as racing's "good will ambassador" on trips to Canada, Mexico, Japan and many European countries.

23

FRANK LOCKHART (driver and engineer) flashed into prominence with an impressive victory at Indianapolis in 1926 and led the field again for the first 91 laps the following year, after setting a new qualifying record of 120.1 miles an hour in a Miller Special with the help of a patented intercooler which he had developed. He also scored important triumphs on the board tracks at Fresno, Charlotte, Altoona and Rockingham and established an amazing one-lap record of 147.7 miles an hour on the Atlantic City board Speedway. Driving a Miller-powered Stutz Blackhawk Special of distinctive design at Daytona Beach in 1928, he averaged 207.552 for the measured mile but crashed to his death later the same day because of a tire failure.

JEAN MARCENAC (mechanic) came to the United States from Europe soon after World War I and quickly established himself as one of the most respected and successful individuals in his field for a career which spanned more than 40 years. During one six-year period beginning in 1927, his cars won four Indianapolis 500-mile races: George Souders in 1927, Ray Keech in 1929, Billy Arnold in 1930 and Fred Frame in 1932. Cars prepared by Marcenac also scored victories on most of the nation's other major tracks, and, after World War II, he worked on the supercharged Novi Specials which set several records at Indianapolis.

REX MAYS (driver) became the third man in racing history to win two consecutive national championships, accomplishing that feat in 1940 and 1941. Although never a "500" winner, he led the field on one or more occasions in nine of the twelve Indianapolis events in which he participated; and only A. J. Foyt, Jr. can duplicate his record of earning the No. 1 starting position four times at Indianapolis, where he finished second to Wilbur Shaw in 1940 and second to Mauri Rose in 1941. Mays also scored many victories on the one-mile dirt tracks and was the first American to finish the 1937 International road race at Roosevelt Raceway in competition with Europe's best cars and drivers.

LOUIS MEYER (driver and engineer) competed successfully in major events for 12 full seasons, beginning in 1927. He earned the enviable distinction of being the first three-time Indianapolis winner with victories in 1928, 1933 and 1936; and captured the National driving title in 1928, 1929, and 1933. His record also includes victories in three 300-mile events on the boards at Altoona and several on the nation's one-mile dirt tracks. After World War II, and following his retirement as a driver in 1939, he went into

Lou Meyer, driver, and Lawson Harris, mechanic, in the 1936 winner of the "500." Meyer was also the first three-time winner at Indianapolis.

partnership with Dale Drake and built the Offenhauser engines which powered 18 consecutive winning cars at Indianapolis beginning in 1947.

HARRY MILLER (engineer) developed the Miller engine and later built complete Miller-engine race cars which eventually out-performed all rivals on most of the nation's race courses. Miller engines won more major events than any other power plant in racing history and the dominant four-cylinder Offenhauser engine, built by the Meyer-Drake Company, evolved directly from Miller's earlier straight-eight design. He built rear-drive and front-drive cars with equal success during the 1920's and also designed a rear-engine four-wheel drive race car during the late 1930's.

TOMMY MILTON (driver, engineer and official) gained his early experience on the dirt tracks of the Midwest, beginning in 1914, and became one of America's all-time top-flight drivers during the "boom years" of the sport following World War I. Equally successful on paved tracks and board tracks, he was the first driver to win the AAA national championship for two consecutive years (1920 and 1921) and the first to win two Indianapolis 500-mile races (1921 and 1923). He helped design and build a twin-engine Duesenberg which he drove to a new record of 156.046 for the measured mile at Daytona Beach in 1920 and served as chief steward of the "500" for four years.

LOU MOORE (driver and car owner) started in nine Indianapolis events, was on the pole once and led the field on two different occasions. He finished second once and third twice. His championship victories included races at Altoona, Woodbridge and Syracuse. He owned the 1938 winning car driven by Floyd Roberts and, after World War II, Moore built and owned the Blue Crown Spark Plug Specials in which Rose and Bill Holland dominated the "500" for three straight years beginning in 1947. Rose won in 1947 and 1948, with Holland second both times. Holland won in 1949 and finished second again in 1950.

RALPH MULFORD (driver) raced from 1907 through 1925 and—despite his steadfast policy of never competing on Sunday—compiled an impressive list of victories in all types of competition. He dominated the early 24-hour events for Lozier and excelled in the longer road races of his time, winning the 1910 Elgin event and the 1911 Vanderbuilt Cup Race at Savannah. He also placed second in the 1911 Indianapolis "500" and finished the season as the AAA national champion. His performance on the board tracks included a victory in the 300-mile inaugural race at Des Moines for Duesenberg and he continued to win on the boards after World War I while also setting new stock car records for Hudson and Chandler.

JIMMY MURPHY (driver) is the only American ever to win the French Grand Prix. He accomplished the feat with a Duesenberg in 1921 and won the Indianapolis "500" the following year at a record-breaking average speed of 94.48 miles an hour. He also was the National driving champion in 1922 and again in 1924. Major victories scored by Murphy during the five-year period beginning in 1920, after an apprenticeship as Tom Milton's riding mechanic, included three at Beverly Hills, three at Altoona, two at Fresno, one at Cotati and one at Kansas City. In addition to his 1922 Indianapolis victory, he also finished third in the "500" twice and fourth once.

THEODORE E "POP" MYERS (race promoter and official) earned an important niche in the history and tradition of automobile racing by devoting the last 40-plus years of his life unselfishly to the improvement of the sport in general and the Indianapolis 500-mile race in particular. He joined the staff of the Indianapolis Motor Speedway in 1910, prior to the first "500" and served with distinction as vice-president as well as general manager under all three regimes of track ownership. He made three trips to Europe as a "Good Will Ambassador" for the American racing fraternity and served for many years as a member of the AAA Contest Board.

BARNEY OLDFIELD (driver) began making his name synonymous with automobile racing as early as 1902 and became one of the most famous and picturesque figures of the pioneer era with such cars as Ford's 999, the Winton Bullet, the Peerless Green Dragon, the Blitzen Benz and the front-wheel-drive Christie. Although devoting most of his time to a series of "barnstorming" appearances on the nation's smaller dirt tracks he also drove in several major championship events for Fiat, Mercer, Maxwell, Stutz and other manufacturers with considerable success before retiring as a driver in 1918. Early in 1910 he averaged 131.724 miles an hour in a Benz on the sand at Daytona Beach to surpass the world's land speed record for a measured mile by more than four miles an hour.

DARIO RESTA (driver) born in England of Italian parents, brought a Peugeot to the United States in 1915, after competing successfully in European events since 1909, and scored an impressive number of victories for two straight seasons against the nation's best cars and drivers. His 1915 record included triumphs in the American Grand Prix and the Vanderbilt Cup race as well as in featured board track events at Chicago and Sheepshead Bay. During the following season he won the Vanderbilt Cup Race again, the annual Indianapolis race (cut to 300 miles that year) and additional major events on board speedways to capture the AAA national championship.

EDWARD V. RICKENBACKER (driver, promoter and official) started his racing career in 1910, participated in the 1911 inaugural Indianapolis "500" in a relief role and began to attract national attention in 1914 with a series of important dirt track victories followed by additional triumphs on the new board speedways of that era. He won renown during World War I as America's "Ace of Aces" and, in the summer of 1927, headed a group of investors who purchased the Indianapolis Motor Speedway and established him as its president. He guided the "500" through the economic difficulties of the 1930s and served as chairman of the AAA Contest Board for several years before selling the Speedway to Anton Hulman, Jr., in November of 1945.

Mauri Rose seated in a Blue Crown Special, winner in 1947 and 1948.

MAURI ROSE (driver) is the only multiple winner at Indianapolis to score victories both before and after the four-year break in racing activity caused by World War II. He won the AAA national driving title in 1936 and received the checkered flag at Indianapolis for the first time in 1941. After starting on the pole in his own car, which developed mechanical trouble, he took over a car started by Floyd Davis and came from far behind to win. Rose also drove a Blue Crown Special to victory without relief in 1947 and again in 1948. He placed fourth or better in four other Indianapolis events and was the first American to finish the 1936 Vanderbilt Cup race on Long Island.

WILBUR SHAW (driver and promoter) won six 100-mile championship events in a single season as early as 1929 and reached the peak of his competitive career during the 10-year period beginning in 1931. He won at Indianapolis in 1937, 1939, and 1940, duplicating Louis Meyer's three "500" triumphs and becoming the first driver to win consecutive Indianapolis races. He also finished second three times at "Indy" and was the race leader at some stage of seven of the 14 Indianapolis events in which he participated. He was the National driving champion twice, in 1937 and 1939; and, after persuading Tony Hulman to buy the Indianapolis Motor Speedway in 1945, Shaw served as its president and general manager until his death in a 1954 airplane accident.

HARRY STUTZ (engineer) became associated with racing by organizing the Marion team and, beginning in 1911, he designed and built the Stutz cars which competed successfully in the nation's outstanding events for a period of eight years. With Earl Cooper and Gil Anderson doing most of the driving, Stutz scored repeated victories in the Elgin road races and won important events on the road courses at Santa Monica, Corona and Point Loma. Stutz cars won the 1915 Minneapolis 500-mile race and major events on the board tracks at Sheepshead Bay and Chicago while also finishing well in all of the first five Indianapolis races. In addition, after selling the original company, Stutz sponsored the Miller-engine car which Tommy Milton drove to victory at "Indy" in 1923.

WILLIAM K. VANDERBILT (race driver and promoter) provided tremendous stimulation for the young automobile industry by sponsoring the series of famous Vanderbilt Cup races beginning in 1904. Prior to that time, however, he had earned recognition as an outstanding driver of International caliber by scoring several noteworthy victories and finishing third against top-flight European competition in the 318-mile International Circuit des Ardenness (France) in 1902. He also broke Henry Ford's 999 land speed record for the measured mile by averaging 92.307 on the sand at Daytona Beach in January of 1904 at the wheel of a Mercedes.

BILL VUKOVICH (driver), who concentrated most of his racing efforts on the "500" after winning the 1951 AAA national midget championship, is one of only four drivers to score two consecutive victories at the Indianapolis Motor Speedway. In 1953 he won the pole position with a speed of 138.392 miles an hour and led the field on a terribly hot Race Day for all but five laps to win impressively. One year later he started in 19th place and set a new race record of 130.84 M.P.H. He also led most of the way in 1952, before being eliminated by steering gear failure with only nine laps to go; and, in 1955, he was out in front again on his way to an unprecedented third straight victory when he crashed to his death in an accident involving slower cars on the track.

FRED WAGNER (race official) was almost as well known by the racing fans of his era as any prominent driver. During a career which started in 1899 and spanned more than three decades, he served as official starter for most of the important championship events on all types of race courses, commanding fees up to $1,000 a day by virtue of his colorful and capable performances. He set the standards for other officials to follow: his showmanship contributed to the steadily growing popularity of the sport, and his sound advice on all matters pertaining to racing was sought by promoters and participants alike.

Wilbur Shaw, winner of the "500" in 1937, 1939 and 1940.

Johnny Rutherford on an 18-second pit stop for tires and fuel.

HOWARD WILCOX (driver) participated in the 1909–1910 Indianapolis Speedway events and figured prominently in all of the first eleven 500-mile races finishing in the first 10 four times before winning the event in 1919. Another of his outstanding victories was scored in the American Grand Prix at Santa Monica in 1916, when he averaged 85.59 miles an hour for the 403-mile event. Wilcox also was outstanding on the board tracks during the early 1920's and served as a relief driver—after his own car had been eliminated by mechanical trouble—to help Tommy Milton win the Indianapolis "500" in 1923.

Bergere and Dawson elected in 1976

CLIFF BERGERE (driver) participated in 16 Indianapolis 500-mile races and has driven more miles (6,130) in competition at Indianapolis than any other driver in the history of the track, except A. J. Foyt, who surpassed Bergere's mark in 1975. Cliff led the field on three different occasions (1941, 1946, and 1947) won the pole position in 1946, placed among the first ten eight times and finished third twice. He also was the first driver to go the full distance in a conventional race car (1941 when he finished fifth) without making a pit stop.

Joe Dawson wins second "500" in 1912.

JOE DAWSON (driver and official) is remembered best for winning the 1912 Indianapolis "500" in a National. As a member of the Marmon Team headed by Ray Harroun, however, he won several short-distance races on the Indianapolis track and at Atlanta in 1910; and also finished second in the Vanderbilt Cup race that year, only 26 seconds behind the winner. He placed fifth in the 1911 Indianapolis 500 and won it in 1912. He retired in 1914, but was appointed to the AAA Contest Board in the 20's and served with great distinction until his death shortly after World War II.

LATER SCENES OF "500" RACES

(Above) A. J. Foyt winner in 1957.

(At left) Sam Hanks winner in 1957.

(Below) Al Unser winner in 1971.
(At bottom of page) Johnny Rutherford passing Wally Dallenbach in the 1976 race.

(Above) The National
Baseball Hall of Fame
and Museum, Inc.
Cooperstown, New York

(At right)
The library of
the Baseball Hall
of Fame complex.
— Photo by Frank Rollins

THE BASEBALL HALL OF FAME AND MUSEUM

Cooperstown, New York

Major league baseball in its seventieth year voted to explore the history of the game. They concluded that the first traces of the modern game appeared on a farm in Cooperstown, New York in 1839.

In Central New York State seventy miles west of Albany, forty-five miles east of Utica, 100 miles east of Syracuse and twenty-three miles north of Oneonta, Cooperstown was founded by wealthy landowner Judge William Cooper – father of James Fenimore Cooper, American novelist remembered for his stories of central New York, *The Leatherstocking Tales, The Last of the Mohicans, The Deerslayer, The Spy* and many others. It is fitting that such a revered game as baseball should have had its origin in such a truly American setting.

The first step in establishing this baseball shrine was to build Doubleday Field on the farm lot where youths first played the game in 1839. The first game in the stadium was played in 1920 in dedication ceremonies attended by many prominent baseball figures and other dignitaries and fans.

A baseball said to be ninety years old, pictures of Civil War prisoners playing baseball and a Currier and Ives print of an 1846 baseball game at Hoboken, New Jersey, attracted interest in the Cooperstown library. This stimulated Stephen C. Clark of Cooperstown and Ford C. Frick, President of the National League, to work on the establishment of a baseball museum. Then the idea of a Hall of Fame was added. The members of the Hall of Fame were to be elected by the Baseball Writers Association of America.

The First Election in 1936

The first election was held in 1936 and the first honorees were Ty Cobb, Walter Johnson, Christy Mathewson, Babe Ruth and Honus Wagner. Since that first election there have been 157 players, managers, umpires and owners honored by induction into the Hall of Fame.

The National Baseball Hall of Fame and Museum building was dedicated June 12, 1939, with eleven living members present including Cy

— Photo by Frank Rollins

—Unless indicated otherwise all photographs in this chapter courtesy Baseball Hall of Fame and Museum

31

Young, Connie Mack, Ty Cobb, Honus Wagner, Napoleon Lajoie, Eddie Collins, Walter Johnson, Tris Speaker, Grover Cleveland Alexander, Babe Ruth and George Sisler, as well as widows of former stars, thirty-two active players, and Postmaster General James A. Farley, who presented baseball's centennial stamp.

Additions to the building were dedicated in 1950, 1958 and a separate library in 1968.

Other dignitaries at the dedication ceremonies were Kenesaw M. Landis, executives of the various American and National League clubs, a hundred newspaper and magazine reporters and many radio and news reel reporters and photographers, Mrs. John McGraw and Mrs. Christy Mathewson, widows of former baseball starts, and Lt. Daniel C. Doubleday for whom the Field is named and who is credited with starting organized baseball.

The day the museum opened, two players representing each major league club chose up sides, the two leagues intermixed, homespun style, and played a game enjoyed by all. Six of the men who played in that first game were later enshrined in the Hall of Fame.

Since then, beginning in 1940, big league teams have taken turns being scheduled annually at Doubleday Field on installation day, except for one year in World War II.

On Hall of Fame Day new members are inducted into the Hall of Fame in morning exercises on the porch of the library, a beautiful setting in the courtyard formed by the buildings. The baseball commissioner presides with a welcoming message from the president of the Hall of Fame. Both league executives and representatives of all the teams in the American and National leagues are present along with members of the media and fans. Following the induction, the big event is the game played on Doubleday Field where it all began in 1839.

An Impressive Museum

Cooperstown and the surrounding villages and towns are all charming and in themselves well worth the effort of a visit. Lake Otsego, where James Fenimore Cooper had visions of the Last of the Mohicans, is a perfect setting as a reflecting pool for this delightful historic New York community.

The museum itself is very impressive and has hundreds of attractions to thrill every visitor from the wife who casually accompanies a family of enthusiastic young players and a husband fan, who collected baseball cards as a kid, to the most avid expert who knows them all, their averages, whom they played for, what position, and the legendary stories of these stars of the past whose feats are preserved for posterity through this excellent shrine.

This is baseball's trophy shelf, but it is a lot more than that. No ball game is wafted away by the breezes of time. A report of every contest is kept in the files at Cooperstown. When a no-hit game is pitched, it automatically is honored here.

The Babe Ruth locker from Yankee Stadium as it appears in the Ruth niche in the museum.

The famous Indianapolis Motor Speedway track where the "Indy 500" is contested each
Memorial Day weekend shown here at the beginning of a race with the thirty-three racers
lined up behind the pace car with the pits on the right in front of the judges tower
and the infield stand.

(on following page)
The Hall of Fame of Auto Racing at Speedway, Indiana showing the parking areas,
fountains and the Louis Chevrolet Memorial in the form of a Greek Exedra
at the left with the track in the background. The very attractive new building
has displays that will interest every visitor because of their variety and appeal
to all ages of viewers.

FROM A WATERCOLOR PAINTING BY KAY SMITH

*Some of the classic and antique passenger cars on display in the Indianapolis
Motor Speedway's new Hall of Fame. In the foreground is a four-cylinder 1914 Stutz.
The white car next to it is a six-cylinder 1914 Marmon. Behind the Stutz is
Augie Duesenberg's personal car: a 1927 eight-cylinder Duesenberg roadster.*

Some other famous race cars on view in the Indianapolis Motor Speedway's new Hall of Fame. Car No. 34 is a 1909 Buick which Louis Chevrolet drove at the Indianapolis Motor Speedway prior to the first 500-mile race in 1911. Car No. 12 is the eight-cylinder Duesenberg which Jimmy Murphy drove to victory in the 1921 French Grand Prix.

Doubleday Field,
a few blocks from the
Baseball Hall of Fame,
Cooperstown, New York,
where the annual
Hall of Fame game
is played every August.

FROM A
WATERCOLOR PAINTING
BY KAY SMITH

The Naismith Memorial Basketball Hall of Fame in Springfield, Massachusetts where in the winter of 1891, James Naismith invented an indoor game that was vigorous and challenging and yet safe enough to play indoors, the game that came to be known as basketball. The Hall of Fame is a fascinating museum that recalls many of the players, teams, and games of the past that brought never-to-be-forgotten thrills.

It is the oldest one-sport Hall of Fame where young and old can hear the voices, see the movies and photographs of historic games and the players.

The museum on four large floors, including the Presidents' and Babe Ruth wings, provides display space for exhibits that show the game as it was and as it is. The impressive Hall of Fame itself with its high ceilings affords space for the plaques of the honorees appropriately displayed.

People who enjoy nostalgia will find a great variety of relics of the past. There are lockers and ball park seats from old stadiums that have become the victims of time. Old gloves and uniforms of yesterday's performers will bring back many fond memories to the older visitors.

You should see the middle-aged visitors touch their toes on the home plate that was pried from the hallowed turf of Ebbets Field after the final game in 1957. They will be amazed to see the bottle bat from 1920 with which Heinie Groh hit .300. There is the rubber sleeve Sandy Koufax used to soak his arm in after a game, and Christy Mathewson's flannel sleeves removable from the uniform to be buttoned on to another uniform the next day and his Bible and set of checkers. There is a slab of slippery elm such as Burleigh Grimes chewed when the spit ball was legal, and finally for the Chicago fans there is a Comiskey Park sign that hung on the front of the elevated trains.

But this is not a hallowed tomb of yesterday's exploits. Hank Aaron's souvenirs and Roberto Clemente's bat that hit his 3000 hits are here along with mementoes of Willie Mays, Mickey Mantle, Roger Maris,

Members of the Hall of Fame who attended the annual game at Doubleday Field August 18, 1975.
They are from left to right: Ralph Kiner, Judy Johnson, Billy Herman, Earl Averill, Stan Coveleski, Burleigh Grimes, Charles Gehringer, Bill Terry, Joe Cronin, Bob Feller, Eddie Rousch, Lloyd Waner, Waite Hoyt, Rube Marquard, Buck Leonard, Monte Irvin, George Kelly, Cool Papa Bell, Jocko Conlan and Roy Campanella.

Jim Konstanty, the most valuable player in the National League in 1950, views the model of the late Roberto Clemente together with the display case of mementos of the great Clemente career. — Photo by Frank Rollins

Brooks Robinson, Harmon Killebrew, Bob Gibson, Billy Williams, Nate Colbert, Hoyt Wilhelm, Walter Alston, Jim Gilliam, Denny McLain, Cesar Futierrez, Maury Wills, Sandy Koufax, and hundreds of others. Part of the evolution of the game is shown dramatically with the display of Dan Brouthers' nineteenth century wagon tongue that he issued as a bat alongside Frank Robinson's whiplike 1971 model.

Visitors are attracted by many different things. The points of interest here are endless. The actual base that Lou Brock stole in 1974 setting the all time single season record of 105 is on display. Al Kaline's 3000th hit bat, the ball with which Bob Gibson struck out his 3,000th batting victim, Frank Robinson's first lineup card as negro playing manager, Rollie Fingers's jersey and Dick Green's glove directly from the Oakland Athletics World Championship locker room and souvenirs of Nolan Ryan's four no-hitters.

Contrasting with these newer relics of the game there are an 1839 baseball, the original manuscript of *Take Me Out To the Ball Game,* Babe Ruth's 60th and Roger Maris' 61st bats, Honus Wagner's and other lockers, Cy Young's glove, Ty Cobb's shoes — a file on every major league player since 1871, a hundred thousand photographs plus movies and recordings.

The National Baseball Library is a separate building where throughout the summer motion pictures of famous games and players are shown on regular schedules. It is dedicated to the communications of baseball — writing, photography, art and broadcasting. The Brown and Bigelow collection of Norman Rockwell paintings of baseball scenes is displayed along with a collection of books, magazines, guides, newspapers, microfilm and almost every conceivable record of the game.

There is something for everyone in Cooperstown and it is not necessary to be a baseball fan to enjoy the visit.

MEMBERS OF THE HALL OF FAME

GROVER CLEVELAND ALEXANDER—Great National League pitcher for two decades with Phillies, Cubs and Cardinals starting in 1911. Won 1926 World Championship for Cardinals by striking out Lazzeri with bases full in final crisis at Yankee Stadium. (Elected 1938)

ADRIAN CONSTANTINE ANSON (Cap)—Greatest hitter and greatest National League player-manager of 19th century. Started with Chicago in National League's first year, 1876. Chicago manager from 1879 to 1897, winning 5 pennants. Was .300 class hitter 20 years, batting champion 4 times. (Elected 1939)

LUCIUS BENJAMIN APPLING (Luke)—Chicago A.L. 1930–1950. A.L. batting champion in 1936 and 1943. Played 2218 games at shortstop for major league mark. Had 2749 hits. Lifetime batting average of .310. Led A.L. in assists 7 years. Holds A.L. record for chances accepted by shortstop 11,569. (Elected 1964)

HOWARD EARL AVERILL (Rock)—Cleveland A.L. Detroit A.L. Boston N.L. 1929–1941. Compiled .318 career batting average and hit 238 home runs. Twice made more than 200 hits in season, pacing league with 232 in 1936. Drove in 100 or more runs five times. Rapped four homers, three consecutively in first game and batted in 11 runs in 1930 twin-bill. (Elected 1975)

JOHN FRANKLIN BAKER—Philadelphia A.L. 1908–1914. New York A.L. 1916–1922. Member of Connie Mack's famous $100,000 infield. Led American League in home runs 1911–12–13, tied in 1914. Won two World Series games from Giants in 1911 with home runs, thus getting name "Home Run" Baker. Played in six World Series, 1910–11–13–14–21–22. (Elected 1955)

DAVID JAMES BANCROFT (Beauty)—Philadelphia N.L. New York N.L. Boston N.L. Brooklyn N.L. 1915–1930. Set major league record for chances handled by a shortstop in a season—984 in 1922. Led league in putouts for shortstops in 1918–1920–1921–1922. Hit .319 in 1921, .321 in 1922 and .304 in 1923 with New York Giants. Hit .319 in 1925 and .311 in 1926 with Boston. Player-manager of Braves 1924–1927. (Elected 1971)

EDWARD GRANT BARROW—Club executive, manager, league president in minors and majors from 1894 to 1945. Converted Babe Ruth from pitcher to outfielder as manager of Boston A.L. in 1918. Discovered Honus Wagner and many other great stars. Won World Series in 1918. Built New York Yankees into outstanding organization in baseball as business manager from 1920 to 1945, winning 14 pennants, 10 World Series. (Elected 1953)

GROVER CLEVELAND ALEXANDER

JACOB PETER BECKLEY (Old Eagle Eye)—1888–1907. Famed National League slugger made 2930 hits for lifetime .309 batting average. Holds record in majors for first base: for chances accepted 25,000, most putouts 23,696, most games 2368. Played 20 seasons with Pittsburgh, New York, Cincinnati and St. Louis. (Elected 1971)

JAMES THOMAS BELL (Cool Papa)—Negro Leagues 1922–1950. Combined speed, daring and batting skill to rank among best players in negro leagues. Contemporaries rated him fastest man on base paths. Hit over .300 regularly, topping .400 on occasion. Played 29 summers and 21 winters of professional baseball. (Elected 1974)

CHARLES ALBERT BENDER (Chief)—Philadelphia A.L. 1903–1914. Philadelphia N.L. 1916–1917. Chicago A.L. 1925. Famous Chippewa Indian. Won over 200 games. Pitched for Athletics in 1905–1910–1911–1913–1914 World Series. Defeated N.Y. Giants 3–0 for A's only victory in 1905. First pitcher in World Series of 6 games (1911) to pitch 3 complete games.

CHARLES ALBERT BENDER

Pitched no-hit game against Cleveland in 1910. Highest A.L. percentages in 1910–1911–1914. (Elected 1953)

LAWRENCE PETER BERRA (Yogi) — New York A.L. 1946–1963. New York N.L. 1965. Played on more pennant-winners (14) and World Champions (10) than any player in history. Had 358 home runs and lifetime .285 batting average. Set many records for catchers, including 148 consecutive games without an error. Voted A.L. most valuable player 1951–54–55. Managed Yankees to pennant in 1964. (Elected 1972)

JAMES LEROY BOTTOMLEY (Sunny Jim) — St. Louis N.L. Cincinnati N.L. St. Louis A.L. 1922–1937. Superb clutch hitter. Drove in 100 or more runs six years in row, 1924–1929, leading league twice. Established record by batting in 12 runs in one game. Most valuable player 1928. Hit seven homers in span of five games in 1929. Had lifetime .310 batting average. (Elected 1974)

LOUIS BOUDREAU — Cleveland A.L. 1938–1950. Boston A.L. 1951–1952. Led A.L. shortstops in fielding eight seasons. Set major loop mark for double plays by shortstop (134) and won batting title 1944. Paced A.L. in doubles three times. Most valuable player 1948, when he batted .355 to lead Indians to pennant as player-pilot. Lifetime batting average .295. (Elected 1970)

ROGER BRESNAHAN — Battery mate of Christy Mathewson with the New York Giants, he was one of the game's most natural players and might have starred at any position. The "Duke of Tralee" was one of the few major league catchers fast enough to be used as a leadoff man. (Elected 1945)

DENNIS BROUTHERS (Dan) — Hard-hitting first baseman of eight major league clubs, he was part of the original "Big Four" of Buffalo. Traded with other members of that combination to Detroit, he hit .419 as the city won its only National League Championship in 1887. (Elected 1945)

MORDECAI PETER BROWN (Three-Fingered) — Member of Chicago N.L. championship team of 1906, 1907, 1908, 1910. A right-handed pitcher, he won 239 games during major league career that also included St. Louis and Cincinnati N.L. and clubs in F.L. First major leaguer to pitch four consecutive shutouts, achieving this feat on June 13, June 25, July 2 and July 4 in 1908. (Elected 1949)

HON. MORGAN G. BULKELEY — First president of the National League and a leader in its organization in 1876 which laid the foundation of the national game for posterity. (Elected 1937)

JESSE C. BURKETT — Batting star who played outfield for the New York, Cleveland and St. Louis N.L. teams and the St. Louis and Boston A.L. teams. Shares with Rogers Hornsby and Ty Cobb the record of hitting .400 or better the most times. Accomplished this on three occasions. Topped the N.L. in hitting three times, batting over .400 to gain the championship in 1895 and 1896. (Elected 1946)

ROY CAMPANELLA (Campy) — Brooklyn N.L. 1948–1957. Most valuable player N.L. 1951–1953–1955. Established records for catchers: most home runs in a season 41, most runs batted in 142. Set N.L. record for chances accepted by catchers for most consecutive years 6, tied record for most years in putouts 6, caught 100 or more games for most consecutive years 9. Led in fielding average for catchers 1949–1952–1953–1957. (Elected 1969)

MAX GEORGE CAREY — Pittsburgh N.L. 1910–1926, 1930. Brooklyn N.L. 1926–1929, 1932–1933. Holds National League records for outfielders: games played, 2421; putouts, 6363; assists, 339; total chances, 6702. Modern league record for most stolen bases, 738. Major league record for

A medal honoring Dan Brouthers.

most years leading league in stolen bases, 10. Batting average .285 for 20 seasons. In 1922, 51 stolen bases in 53 attempts. (Elected 1961)

ALEXANDER JOY CARTWRIGHT, JR. – The "Father of Modern Baseball" set bases 90 feet apart, established 9 innings as game and 9 players as team. Organized the Knickerbocker Baseball Club of New York in 1845. Carried baseball to Pacific coast and Hawaii in pioneer days. (Elected 1938)

HENRY CHADWICK – Baseball's preeminent pioneer writer for half a century. Inventor of the box score. Author of the first rule book in 1858. Chairman of Rules Committee in first nationwide baseball organization. (Elected 1938)

MAX GEORGE CAREY   FRANK LEROY CHANCE

FRANK LEROY CHANCE – Famous leader of Chicago Cubs. Won pennant with Cubs in first full season as manager in 1906. That team compiled 116 victories unequaled in major league history. Also won pennants in 1907, 1908, and 1910 and World Series winner in 1907 and 1908. Started with Chicago in 1898. Also manager New York A.L. and Boston A.L. (Elected 1946)

OSCAR McKINLEY CHARLESTON – Negro Leagues 1915–1944. Rated among all-time greats of negro leagues. Versatile star batted well over .300 most years. Speed, strong arm and fielding instincts made him standout center fielder. Later moved to first base. Also managed several teams during 40 years in negro baseball. (Elected 1976)

JOHN DWIGHT CHESBRO (HAPPY JACK) – Famed pitcher who led both leagues in percentage – National League in 1902; American League in 1904. Served with Pittsburgh N.L. and the New York and Boston A.L. Won 41 games, tops in majors, in 1904 and during big league career compiled 192 victories while losing only 128. (Elected 1946)

FRED CLARKE – The first of the successful "boy managers," at twenty-four he piloted Louisville's Colonels in the National League. Won 4 pennants for Pittsburgh and a World Championship in 1909. Starred as an outfielder for 22 seasons. (Elected 1945)

JOHN GIBSON CLARKSON – Worcester, N.L. 1882. Chicago N.L. 1884–87. Boston, N.L. 1888–92. Cleveland, N.L. 1892–94. Pitched 4 to 0 no-hit game against Providence in 1885. Won 328 lost 175 Pct .652 led league with 53 victories in 1885 (including 10 shutouts) 38 in 1887, 49 in 1888 and 49 in 1889. Had 2013 strikeouts in 4514 innings. (Elected 1963)

ROBERTO WALKER CLEMENTE – Pittsburgh N.L. 1955–1972. Member of exclusive 3000-hit club. Led National League in batting four times. Had four seasons with 200 or more hits while posting lifetime .317 average and 240 home runs. Won most valuable player award 1966. Rifle-armed defensive star set N.L. mark by pacing outfielders in assists five years. Batted .362 in two World Series, hitting in all 14 games. (Elected 1973)

Ty Cobb

CHARLES A. COMISKEY

TYRUS RAYMOND COBB—Detroit—Philadelphia, A.L. 1905–1928. Led American League in batting twelve times and created or equaled more major league records than any other player. Retired with 4191 major league hits. (Elected 1936)

GORDON COCHRANE (Mickey)—Philadelphia A.L. 1925–1933. Detroit A.L. 1934–1937. Fiery catcher compiled a notable record both as a player and manager. The spark of the Athletics' championship teams of 1929–30–31, had an average batting mark of .346 for those three years. Led Detroit to two league championships and a World Series title in 1935. (Elected 1947)

EDWARD TROWBRIDGE COLLINS—Chicago—Philadelphia A.L. 1906–1930. Famed as batsman, base runner and second baseman, and also as field captain. Batted .333 during major league career. Second only to Ty Cobb in modern base stealing. Made 3313 hits in 2826 games. (Elected 1939)

JAMES COLLINS—Considered by many the game's greatest third baseman, he revolutionized style of play at that bag. Led Boston Red Sox to first World Championship in 1903. A consistent batter, his defensive play thrilled fans of both major leagues. (Elected 1945)

EARLE BRYAN COMBS—New York Yankees 1924–1935. Lead-off hitter and center fielder of Yankee champions of 1926–27–28–32. Lifetime batting average .325. 200 or more hits three seasons. Led league with 231 hits in 1927 while batting .356. Paced A.L. in triples three times and twice led outfielders in putouts. Batted .350 in four World Series. (Elected 1970)

CHARLES A. COMISKEY (The Old Roman)—Started 50 years of baseball as St. Louis Browns' first baseman in 1882 and was first man at this position to play away from the bag for batters. As Browns' manager, captain and player, won 4 straight American Association pennants starting in 1885. World champions first 2 years. Owner and president Chicago White Sox 1900 to 1931. (Elected 1939)

JOHN BERTRAND CONLAN (Jocko)—Umpire National League 1941–1965. Sunny disposition, accuracy and hustle earned him rating as standout umpire and he won respect of players and managers with his fairness. Only arbiter to work in each of first four N.L. pennant playoffs. Chosen for six World Series and six All-Star games. (Elected 1974)

THOMAS HENRY CONNOLLY—Umpire National League 1898–1899. American League 1901–1953. Officiated in first A.L. game in Chicago, 1901. Umpired in eight World Series, including the first one in 1903 and in games when Boston, New York and Philadelphia parks were dedicated. Named chief of A.L. staff in 1931. Born in England, he became a professional umpire in 1894. (Elected 1953)

ROGER CONNOR—Troy N.L. New York N.L. New York P.L. Philadelphia N.L. St. Louis N.L. 1880–1897. Power-hitting star of dead-ball era. Set career home run record for 19th century players. Won league batting championship in 1885 and hit .300 or better 12 times. Hit three homers in a game in 1888 and made six hits in six at-bats in a game in 1895. (Elected 1976)

STANLEY ANTHONY COVELESKI—Philadelphia A.L. 1912. Cleveland A.L. 1916–1924. Washington A.L. 1925–1927. New York A.L. 1928. Star pitcher with a record of 214 wins, 141 losses, average .603, E.R.A. 2.88. Won 20 or more games in 5 seasons. Won 13 straight games in 1925. Pitched and won 3 games for Cleveland in 1920 World Series with E.R.A. 0.67. (Elected 1969)

SAMUEL EARL CRAWFORD (Wahoo Sam)—Cincinnati N.L. 1899–1902. Detroit A.L. 1903–1917. Had lifetime record of 2964 hits, batting average of .309. Played 2505 games. Holds major league record for most triples, 312. League leader one or more seasons in doubles, triples, runs batted in, runs scored, chances accepted, home runs (N.L. 1901 – A.L. 1908) and total bases (N.L. 1902 – A.L. 1913). (Elected 1957)

JOSEPH EDWARD CRONIN – Pittsburgh N.L. 1926 – 1927. Washington A.L. 1928 – 1934. Boston A.L. 1935 – 1945. Named all-star shortstop seven seasons. Most valuable player A.L. 1930. Led A.L. shortstops in fielding 1931 – 1932. Most putouts and double plays 1930 – 31 – 32. Lifetime batting average .302. Won pennant in 1933 in first season as manager Washington A.L. at age 26. Traded to Boston 1934 for reported record price of $250,000. (Elected 1956)

W. A. CUMMINGS (Candy) – Pitched first curve ball in baseball history. Invented curve as amateur ace of Brooklyn Stars in 1867. Ended long career as Hartford pitcher in National League's first year 1876. (Elected 1939)

HAZEN SHIRLEY CUYLER (Kiki) – Pittsburgh N.L. 1921 – 1927. Chicago N.L. 1928 – 1935. Cincinnati N.L. 1935 – 1937. Brooklyn N.L. 1938. Led N.L. in stolen bases 1926 – 1928 – 1929 – 1930. Batted .354 in 1924, .357 in 1925, .360 in 1929, .355 in 1930. Lifetime total 2299 hits, batting average .321. Named to All-Star team in 1925. (Elected 1968)

JAY HANNA DEAN (Dizzy) – St. Louis N.L. 1932 – 1937. Chicago N.L. 1938 – 1941. One of four N.L. pitchers to win 30 or more games under modern regulations. Pitched in 1934 (St. Louis) 1938 (Chicago) World Series. Led league in strikeouts 1932 – 33 – 34 – 35. Single game record with 17, July 30, 1933. First pitcher to make two hits in one inning in World Series. Most valuable N.L. player in 1934. (Elected 1953)

ED DELAHANTY – One of the game's greatest sluggers. Led National League hitters in 1899 with an average of .408 for Philadelphia; American League batters in 1902 with a mark of .376 for Washington. Made 6 hits in 6 times at bat twice during career and once hit 4 home runs in a game. (Elected 1945)

WILLIAM MALCOLM DICKEY – New York A.L. 1928 – 1946. Set record by catching 100 or more games 13 successive seasons. Played with Yankees, champions of 1932 – 36 – 37 – 38 – 39 – 41 – 42 – 43, when club won 7 World Series titles. Holds numerous World Series records for catchers, including most games, 38. Played on 8 All-Star teams from 1932 to 1946. Lifetime batting average of .313 in 1789 games. (Elected 1954)

JOSEPH PAUL DI MAGGIO – New York A.L. 1936 – 1951. Hit safely in 56 consecutive games for major league record 1941. Hit 2 home runs in one inning 1936. Hit 3 home runs in one game (3 times). Holds numerous batting records. Played in 10 World Series (51 games) and 11 All-Star games. Most valuable player A.L. 1939, 1941, 1947. (Elected 1955)

JOSEPH PAUL DI MAGGIO

HUGH DUFFY – Brilliant as a defensive outfielder for the Boston Nationals, he compiled a batting average in 1894 which was not to be challenged in his lifetime – .438. (Elected 1945)

WILLIAM GEORGE EVANS – Umpire and executive employed by American League in 1906 at age 22, making him youngest umpire ever in majors. Served on A.L. staff through 1927. Officiated in six World Series. General manager of Cleveland Indians 1927 – 1935. Farm director of Boston Red Sox 1936 – 1940. President of Southern Association 1942 – 1946. General manager of Detroit Tigers 1947 – 1951. (Elected 1973)

JOHN JOSEPH EVERS (The Trojan) – Middleman of the famous double play combination of Tinker to Evers to Chance. With the pennant winning Chicago Cubs of 1906 – 07 – 08 – 10 and with the Boston Braves' miracle team of 1914. Voted most valuable player in N.L. in 1914. Served as player, coach and manager in big leagues and as a scout from 1902 through 1934. Shares record for making most singles in four-game World Series. (Elected 1946)

WM. B. EWING (Buck)—Greatest 19th century catcher. Giant in stature and Giant captain of New York's first National League champions 1888 and 1889. Was genius as field leader, unsurpassed in throwing to bases, great long-range hitter. National League career 1881 to 1899 Troy, New York Giants and Cleveland; Cincinnati manager. (Elected 1939)

URBAN CLARENCE FABER—Chicago A.L. 1914–1933. Durable right-hander who won 253, lost 211, E.R.A. 3.13 games in two decades with White Sox. Victor in 3 games of 1917 World Series against Giants. Won 20 or more games in season four times, three in succession. (Elected 1964)

ROBERT WILLIAM ANDREW FELLER—Cleveland A.L. 1936–1941, 1945–1956. Pitched 3 no-hit games in A.L., 12 one-hit games. Set modern strikeout record with 18 in game, 348 for season. Led A.L. in victories 6 (one tie) seasons. Lifetime record: won 266, lost 162, P.C. .621, E.R.Average 3.25, struck out 2581. (Elected 1962)

ELMER HARRISON FLICK—Philadelphia N.L. 1898–1902. Cleveland A.L. 1902–1910. Outfielder who batted .378 for 1900 Phillies. Left lifetime mark of .315 for 13 seasons. A.L. batting champion in 1905. Led A.L. in triples 1905–1906–1907 and in steals 1904, tying for leadership again in 1906. (Elected 1963)

EDWARD CHARLES FORD (Whitey)—New York A.L. 1950–1967. Posted best winning percentage—.690—among twentieth century pitchers with 200 or more decisions. Had 236 victories and 106 losses. Lifetime earned-run average 2.74. Paced A.L. in victories and winning Pct. three times and in earned-run average and shutouts twice. Won Cy Young Award in 1961. Set World Series standards for games pitched 22; innings 146; wins 10 and strike-outs 94, and with 33²/₃ consecutive scoreless innings. (Elected 1974)

JAMES E. FOXX (Jimmy)—Philadelphia A.L. 1926–1935. Boston A.L. 1936–1942. Chicago N.L. 1942–1944. Philadelphia N.L. 1945. Noted for his batting, particularly as a home run hitter. Collected 534 home runs in 2317 games. Had a lifetime batting average of .325 and, in three World Series, compiled a mark of .344. Appeared in seven All-Star games in which he batted .316. Played first and third bases and also was a catcher. (Elected 1951)

FORD CHRISTOPHER FRICK—Sportswriter, sportscaster. Founder of Baseball Hall of Fame. President of National League 1934–1951. Commissioner of Baseball 1951–1965. (Elected 1970)

FRANK FRISCH—New York N.L. 1919–1926. St. Louis N.L. 1927–1938. Pittsburgh N.L. 1940–1946. Jumped from college to the majors. The "Fordham Flash" was an outstanding infielder, base runner and batter. Had a lifetime batting mark of .316. Holds many records. Played in 50 World Series games. Managed St. Louis from 1933 through 1938 and won World Series in 1934. Managed Pittsburgh from 1940 through 1946. (Elected 1947)

JAMES F. GALVIN (Pud)—St. Louis N.A. 1875. Buffalo N.L. 1879–1885. Pittsburgh A.A. 1885–1886. Pittsburgh N.L. 1887–1889; 1891–1892. Pittsburgh P.L. 1890. St. Louis N.L. 1892. Won 365 games. Lost 311. When elected only four pitchers had won more games. Pitched no-hit games in 1880 and 1884. Pitched 649 complete games. (Elected 1965)

HENRY LOUIS GEHRIG—New York Yankees 1923–1939. Holder of more than a score of major and American League records, including that of playing 2130 consecutive games. When he retired in 1939, he had a lifetime batting average of .340. (Elected 1939)

CHARLES L. GEHRINGER—Second baseman with Detroit A.L. from 1925 through 1941 and coach in 1942. Compiled lifetime batting average of

ROBERT WILLIAM ANDREW FELLER

HENRY LOUIS GEHRIG

The gallery of plaques honoring the members of the Hall of Fame. — Photo by Frank Rollins

.321. In 2323 games collected 2839 hits. Named most valuable player in A.L. in 1937. Batted .321 in World Series competition and had a .500 average for six All-Star games. (Elected 1949)

JOSHUA GIBSON (Josh) — Negro Leagues 1930–1946. Considered greatest slugger in negro baseball leagues. Power-hitting catcher who hit almost 800 home runs in league and independent baseball during his 17-year career. Credited with having been Negro National League batting champion in 1936–38–42–45. (Elected 1972)

VERNON LOUIS GOMEZ (Lefty) — New York A.L. 1930–1942. Washington A.L. 1943. Won 20 or more games four times in helping Yankees to win seven pennants. Led A.L. with 26–5 record, 2.33 earned-run average in 1934 and with 21 victories and 2.33 E.R.A. in 1937. Paced A.L. in winning Pct. twice, strikeouts three times. Set World Series mark by winning 6 games without a loss. (Elected 1972)

LEON ALLEN GOSLIN (Goose) — Washington A.L. 1921–1930, 1933, 1938. St. Louis A.L. 1930–1932. Detroit A.L. 1934–1937. Batted .344 in 1924, .334 in 1925, .354 in 1926, .334 in 1927. Led A.L. in batting in 1928 with .379 average. Runs batted in for 1924–129. Hit .300 or better 11 years. Lifetime total of 2735 hits, batting average .316. Made 37 hits in 5 World Series. (Elected 1968)

HENRY BENJAMIN GREENBERG — Detroit A.L. 1933–1946. Pittsburgh N.L. 1947. One of baseball's greatest right-handed batters. Tied for most home runs by right-handed batter in 1938–58, most runs batted in 1935–37–40–46, and home runs 1938–40–46. Won 1945 pennant on last day of season with grand slam home run in 9th inning. Played in 4 World Series, 2 All-Star games. Most valuable A.L. player twice, 1935–1940. Lifetime batting average .313. (Elected 1956)

CLARK C. GRIFFITH — Associated with major league baseball for more than 50 years as a pitcher, manager and executive. Served as a member of the Chicago and Cincinnati teams in the N.L. and the Chicago, New York and Washington clubs in the A.L. Compiled more than 200 victories as a pitcher, manager of the Cincinnati N.L. and Chicago, New York and Washington A.L. teams for 20 years. (Elected 1946)

Rogers Hornsby

CHARLES LEO (GABBY) HARTNETT

BURLEIGH ARLAND GRIMES—1916–1934. One of the great spitball pitchers. Won 270 games, lost 212 for 7 major league clubs. Five 20-victory seasons. Won 13 in row for Giants in 1927. Managed Dodgers in 1937 and 1938. Lifetime E.R.A. 3.52. (Elected 1964)

ROBERT MOSES GROVE—Philadelphia A.L. 1925–1933. Boston A.L. 1934–1941. Winner of 300 games in the majors over a span of 17 years. Led A.L. in strikeouts seven consecutive seasons. Won 20 or more games eight seasons. In 1931, while winning 31 games and losing 4, compiled a winning streak of 16 straight. Won 79 games for the three-time pennant winning Athletics team of 1929–30–31. (Elected 1947)

CHARLES JAMES HAFEY (Chick)—St. Louis N.L. 1924–1931. Cincinnati N.L. 1932–1937. Great outfielder who compiled .317 lifetime batting average. Leading hitter of N.L. with .349 in 1931. Batted .329 or better six consecutive years. Equaled league record of ten hits in succession in 1929. Lifetime fielding average .971. (Elected 1971)

JESSE JOSEPH HAINES (Pop)—Cincinnati N.L. 1918. St. Louis N.L. 1920–1937. Durable right-hander won 210 games, lost 158–all in his 18 years with Cardinals. Gained 20-victory class three times. Tossed 5–0 no-hitter vs. Boston in 1924. Defeated Yankees twice in 1926 World Series. Led N.L. in complete games 25, shutouts 6, while posting 24–10 record, 1927. (Elected 1970)

WILLIAM R. HAMILTON—Philadelphia N.L. 1890–1895. Boston N.L. 1896–1901. Holds records for single season: runs scored, 196 in 1894, stolen bases, 115 in 1891. Lifetime total stolen bases, 937. Batted .395 in 1893, .399 in 1894, .393 in 1895. Led National League in 1891 with .338 average. Lifetime batting average of .344. Scored 100 or more runs during 10 seasons. (Elected 1961)

WILLIAM HARRIDGE—President of American League 1931–1958 after serving as secretary of league 1927–1931 and secretary to A.L. president 1911–1927. Chairman of American League Board of Directors 1958–1971. (Elected 1972)

STANLEY RAYMOND HARRIS (Bucky)—Served 40 years in majors as player, manager and executive, including 29 as pilot. Slick second sacker earned tag of "Boy Wonder" by guiding Washington to 1924 world title as a 27-year-old in debut as player-pilot. Won A.L. flag again in 1925. Led Yankees to 1947 pennant. Also managed Detroit, Boston Red Sox and Philadelphia Phillies. (Elected 1975)

CHARLES LEO HARTNETT (Gabby)—Chicago N.L. 1922–1940. New York N.L. 1941. Caught 100 or more games per season for 12 years, eight in succession, 1930 to 1937, for league record. Set mark for consecutive chances for catcher without error, 452 in 1933–34. Highest fielding average for catcher in 100 or more games in 7 seasons; most putouts N.L. 7292; most chances accepted N.L. 8546. Lifetime batting average .297. (Elected 1955)

HARRY EDWIN HEILMANN—Detroit A.L. Cincinnati N.L. 1916–1932. Right-handed hitting outfielder and first baseman. Won American League batting championship four times 1921–23–25 and 1927. In 1923 batted .403. Collected 2660 hits and 183 home runs in 2146 major league games. Had lifetime batting average of .342 and fielding mark of .975. (Elected 1952)

WILLIAM JENNINGS HERMAN (Billy)—Chicago, Brooklyn, Boston, Pittsburgh N.L. 1931–1947. Master of hit-and-run play owned .304 lifetime batting average. Made 200 or more hits in season three times. Led league in hits 227 and doubles 57 in 1935. Set major league record for second basemen with five seasons of handling 900 or more chances and N.L. mark of 466 putouts in 1933. Led loop keystoners in putouts seven times. (Elected 1975)

HARRY BARTHOLOMEW HOOPER — Boston A.L. 1909–1920. Chicago A.L. 1921–1925. Leadoff hitter and right fielder of 1912–15–16–18 World Champion Red Sox. Noted for speed and strong arm. Collected 2466 hits for .281 career average. Had 3981 putouts and 344 assists. Lifetime fielding average .966. (Elected 1971)

ROGERS HORNSBY — National League batting champion 7 years 1920–1925; 1928. Lifetime batting average .358, highest in National League history. Hit .424 in 1924, 20th century major league record. Manager 1926 World Champion St. Louis Cardinals. Most valuable player 1925 and 1929. (Elected 1942)

WAITE CHARLES HOYT (Schoolboy) — New York Yankee pitcher 1921–1930. Lifetime record: 237 games won, 182 games lost, .566 average, earned run average 3.59. Pitched three games in 1921 World Series and gave no earned runs. Also pitched for Boston, Detroit and Philadelphia A.L. and Brooklyn, New York and Pittsburgh N.L. (Elected 1969)

ROBERT CAL HUBBARD — Umpire, American League 1936–1951. One of the most respected, efficient and authoritative umpires in history of majors. Gentle giant boasted special knack for dealing with situations on field. Worked four World Series and three All-Star games. Served as league's assistant umpire supervisor in 1952 and as umpire supervisor from 1953 to 1969. (Elected 1976)

CARL HUBBELL — New York N.L. 1928–1943. Hailed for impressive performance in 1934 All-Star game when he struck out Ruth, Gehrig, Foxx, Simmons and Cronin in succession. Nicknamed "Giants' Meal Ticket." Won 253 games in majors, scoring 16 straight in 1936. Compiled streak of 46⅓ scoreless innings in 1933. Holder of many records. (Elected 1947)

MILLER JAMES HUGGINS — 1904–1929 manager of St. Louis Cardinals and New York Yankees. Led Yankees to 6 pennants in 1921, 1922, 1923, 1926, 1927 and 1928 and 3 World Series victories 1923, 1927 and 1928. Second baseman in playing days with Reds and Cardinals, 1904–1916. (Elected 1964)

MONFORD IRVIN (Monte) — Negro Leagues 1937–1948. New York N.L. Chicago N.L. 1949–1956. Regarded as one of negro leagues' best hitters. Star slugger of Newark Eagles won 1946 negro league batting title. Led N.L. in runs batted in and paced "Miracle" Giants in hitting in 1951 drive to pennant. Batted .458 and stole home in 1951 World Series. (Elected 1973)

HUGHIE JENNINGS — Of Baltimore's famous old Orioles, he was one of the game's mighty mites. A star shortstop, he was a constant threat at the plate. Once hit .397. Piloted Detroit to three championships. (Elected 1945)

BYRON BANCROFT JOHNSON — Organizer of the American League and its president from its organization in 1900 until his resignation because of ill health in 1927. A great executive. (Elected 1937)

WALTER PERRY JOHNSON — Washington 1907–1927. Conceded to be fastest ball pitcher in history of game. Won 414 games with losing team behind him many years. Holder of strikeout and shutout records. (Elected 1936)

WILLIAM JULIUS JOHNSON (Judy) — Negro Leagues 1923–1937. Considered best third baseman of his day in negro leagues. Outstanding as fielder and excellent clutch hitter who batted over .300 most of career. Helped Hilldale team win three flags in row 1923–24–25. Also played for 1935 champion Pittsburgh Crawfords. (Elected 1975)

TIMOTHY J. KEEFE — 1880–1893. Right-hander who won 346 games for Troy, Mets, Giants and Phils in only 14 seasons. His record streak of 19 straight triumphs paced Giants to flag in 1888. One of first pitchers to use a change of pace delivery. (Elected 1964)

Walter Johnson

Mickey Mantle

WILLIE KEELER – "Hit 'em where they ain't!" Baseball's greatest place hitter, best bunter. Big league career 1892–1910 with N.Y. Giants, Baltimore Orioles, Brooklyn Superbas, N.Y. Highlanders. National League batting champion 1897–1898. (Elected 1939)

JOSEPH JAMES KELLEY – 1891–1908. Standout hitter and left fielder of champion 1894–95–96 Baltimore Orioles and 1899–1900 Brooklyn Superbas. Batted over .300 for eleven consecutive years with high of .391 in 1894. Equaled record with 9 hits in 9 at-bats in doubleheader. Also played for Boston, Pittsburgh and Cincinnati of N.L. and Baltimore of A.L. Managed Cincinnati 1902 to 1905 and Boston N.L. in 1908. (Elected 1971)

GEORGE LANGE KELLY (Highpockets) – New York, Pittsburgh, Cincinnati, Chicago, Brooklyn N.L. 1915–1930 and 1932. Established major league record by hitting seven home runs in six consecutive games in 1924. Rapped homers in three successive innings in 1923. Drove in more than 100 runs four consecutive years 1921–24. Set league records for chances accepted 1862 and putouts 1759 by first baseman in 1920. Also led in chances accepted 1921–22–23. (Elected 1973)

MIKE J. KELLY (King) – Colorful player and audacious base-runner. In 1887 for Boston he hit .394 and stole 84 bases. His sale for $10,000 was one of the biggest deals of baseball's early history. (Elected 1945)

RALPH McPHERRAN KINER – Pittsburgh, Chicago N.L. Cleveland A.L. 1946–1955. Hit 369 home runs and averaged better than 100 runs batted in per season in ten-year career. Only player to lead his league or share lead in homers seven years in a row 1946–1952. Twice had more than 50 in season. Set N.L. mark of 101 four-baggers in two successive years with 54 in 1949 and 47 in 1950. Led N.L. in slugging Pct. three times. (Elected 1975)

WILLIAM J. KLEM – Umpire National League 1905–1951. Known as "The Old Arbitrator." Umpired in 18 World Series. Credited with introducing arm signals indicating strikes and fair or foul balls. Famous quote: "Baseball is more than a game to me. It's a religion." Retired as active umpire in 1940. Named chief of N.L. staff in 1941. (Elected 1953)

SANFORD KOUFAX (Sandy) – Brooklyn N.L. 1955–1957. Los Angeles N.L. 1958–1966. Set all-time records with 4 no-hitters in 4 years, capped by 1965 perfect game and by capturing earned-run title five seasons in a row 1962–1966. Won 25 or more games three times. Had 11 shutouts in 1963. Strikeout leader four times, with record 382 in 1965. Fanned 18 in a game twice. Most valuable player 1963. Cy Young Award winner 1963–65–66. (Elected 1972)

NAPOLEON LAJOIE (Larry) – Philadelphia N.L. 1896–1900. Philadelphia A.L. 1901. Cleveland A.L. 1902–1914. Philadelphia A.L. 1915–1916. Great hitter and most graceful and effective second baseman of his era. Managed Cleveland 4 years. League batting champion 1901–1903–1904. (Elected 1937)

KENESAW MOUNTAIN LANDIS – Baseball's first commissioner. Elected 1920 – died in office 1944. His integrity and leadership established baseball in the respect, esteem and affection of the American people. (Elected 1944)

ROBERT GRANVILLE LEMON – Cleveland A.L. 1941–1942, 1946–1958. Gained coveted 20-victory class seven times in nine-year span. Became only sixth pitcher in 20th century to post 20 or more wins in seven seasons. Had 207–128 record for career. Paced A.L. or tied for lead in victories three times, shutouts once, innings pitched four seasons and complete games five years. Hurled no-hitter in 1948. (Elected 1976)

WALTER FENNER LEONARD (Buck)—Negro Leagues 1933–1950. First baseman of Homestead Grays when team won Negro National League pennant nine years in a row 1937–1945. Teamed with Josh Gibson to form most feared batting twosome in negro baseball from 1937 to 1946. Ranked among negro home run leaders. Won Negro National League batting title with .391 average in 1948. (Elected 1972)

FREDERICK CHARLES LINDSTROM—New York, Pittsburgh, Chicago, Brooklyn N.L. 1924–1936. Compiled lifetime .311 batting mark including seven seasons of .300 or better. One of only three players to amass 230 or more hits a year twice. As youngest player—age 18—in World Series history, he tied record with four hits in game in 1924. Equaled major league record by collecting nine hits in 1928 doubleheader. (Elected 1976)

CONNIE MACK

THEODORE AMAR LYONS—Chicago A.L. 1923–1946. Entire active pitching career of 21 seasons with Chicago A.L. Won 260 games, lost 230. Tied for League's most victories 1925 and 1927. Best earned run average, 2.10 in 1942 when he started and finished all 20 games. Pitched no-hit game Aug. 21, 1926 against Boston. Pitched 21-inning game May 24, 1929. (Elected 1955)

CONNIE MACK—A star catcher but famed more as manager of the Philadelphia Athletics since 1901. Winner of 9 pennants and 5 World Championships. Received the Bok award in Philadelphia for 1929. (Elected 1937)

MICKEY CHARLES MANTLE—New York A.L. 1951–1968. Hit 536 home runs. Won league homer title and slugging crown four times. Made 2415 hits. Batted .300 or over in each of ten years with top of .365 in 1957. Topped A.L. in walks five years and in runs scored six seasons. Voted most valuable player 1956–57–62. Named on 20 A.L. All-Star teams. Set World Series records for homers 18; runs 42; runs batted in 40; total bases 123; and bases on balls 43. (Elected 1974)

CHRISTY MATHEWSON

HENRY EMMET MANUSH—1923–1939. Slugging outfielder for 6 major league clubs. Batting champion of A.L. at .378 with 1926 Tigers. Lifetime average of .330 in 2009 major league games. Had 2524 hits. (Elected 1964)

WALTER J. V. MARANVILLE (Rabbit)—Boston, Pittsburgh, Chicago, Brooklyn and St. Louis N.L. 1912–1935. Played more games, 2153, at shortstop than any other National League player. At bat total 10078, surpassed by only one National Leaguer, Honus Wagner. Made 2605 hits in 23 seasons. Member of 1914 Boston Braves "Miracle Team" that won pennant, then World Series from Athletics in 4 games. (Elected 1954)

RICHARD WILLIAM MARQUARD (Rube)—New York, Brooklyn, Cincinnati, Boston N.L. 1908–1925. Three-time 20-game winner with Giant champions of 1911–12–13. Tied all-time record with 19 victories in a row while winning 26 and losing 11 in 1912. Led N.L. in winning percentage and strikeouts in 1911. Tied for most victories in 1912. Hurled no-hit game against Dodgers in 1915. (Elected 1971)

CHRISTY MATHEWSON—New York N.L. 1900–1916. Cincinnati N.L. 1916. Born Factoryville, Pa., August 12, 1880. Greatest of all the great pitchers in the 20th century's first quarter. Pitched 3 shutouts in 1905 World Series. First pitcher of the century ever to win 30 games in 3 successive years. Won 37 games in 1908. "Matty was master of them all." (Elected 1936)

JOSEPH VINCENT McCARTHY—Chicago N.L. 1926–1930. New York A.L 1931–1946. Boston A.L. 1948–1950. Outstanding manager who never played in major leagues. The major league teams managed by him during 24 years never finished out of first division. Won pennants Chicago N.L. 1929, New York A.L. 1932–36–37–38–39–41–42–43. Won seven World Championships with New York Yankees, four of them consecutively 1936–37–38–39. (Elected 1957)

JOHN J. McGRAW

STANLEY FRANK MUSIAL

THOMAS F. McCARTHY—One of Boston's "Heavenly Twins" under manager Frank Selee. Outstanding base runner who stole 109 bases for the Browns in 1888. Pioneer in trapping fly balls in the outfield. Holds N.L. record for assists in outfield, 53 with Boston in 1893. Played 1268 games in major leagues. (Elected 1946)

JOSEPH JEROME McGINNITY (Iron Man)—Distinguished as the pitcher who hurled two games on one day the most times. Did this on five occasions. Won both games three times. Played with Baltimore, Brooklyn and New York teams in N.L. and Baltimore in A.L. Gained more than 200 victories during career. Recorded 20 or more victories seven times. In two successive seasons won at least 30 games. (Elected 1946)

JOHN J. McGRAW—Star third baseman of the great Baltimore Orioles, National League champions in the 1890s. For 30 years manager of the New York Giants starting in 1902. Under his leadership the Giants won ten pennants and three World Championships. (Elected 1937)

WILLIAM BOYD McKECHNIE—Manager of Pittsburgh N.L. 1922–1926. St. Louis N.L. 1928–1929. Boston N.L. 1930–1937. Cincinnati N.L. 1938–1946. Only N.L. manager to win pennants with three different clubs—Pittsburgh 1925; St. Louis 1928; Cincinnati 1939, 1940. Won World Series 1925 and 1940. Named No. 1 major league manager 1937 and 1940. Active in baseball as manager, coach, player 1906 to 1953. (Elected 1962)

JOSEPH MICHAEL MEDWICK (Ducky Wucky)—St. Louis N.L. 1932–1940, 1947, 1948. Brooklyn N.L. 1940–1943, 1946. New York N.L. 1943–1945. Boston N.L. 1945. Led N.L. in batting in 1937 with .374 average, batted .353 in 1935, .351 in 1936, .332 in 1939. Lifetime total 2471 hits, batting average .324. Named to All-Star teams 1935–36–37–38–39. Most valuable player N.L. 1937. Led N.L. in runs batted in and two base hits 1936–37–38. Batted .300 or more 15 times. (Elected 1968)

STANLEY FRANK MUSIAL (The Man)—St. Louis Cardinals 1941–1963. Holds many National League records, among them: games played 3026; at bat 10972 times; 3630 hits; most runs scored 1949; most runs batted in 1951; total bases 6134. Led N.L. in total bases 6 years. Slugging percentage 6 years. Most valuable player 1943–46–48. Played in 24 All-Star games. Lifetime batting average .331. (Elected 1969)

CHARLES A. NICHOLS (Kid)—Right-handed pitcher who won 30 or more games for seven consecutive years, 1891–1897, and won at least 20 games for ten consecutive seasons, 1890–1899 with Boston N.L. Also pitched for St. Louis and Philadelphia N.L. One of few pitchers to win more than 300 games, his major league record being 360 victories, 202 defeats. (Elected 1949)

JAMES H. O'ROURKE—"Orator Jim" played ball until he was past fifty, including twenty-one major league seasons. An outfielder and catcher for the

Boston Red Stockings of 1873, he later wore the uniforms of the championship Providence team of 1879, Buffalo, New York and Washington. (Elected 1945)

MELVIN T. OTT (Mel) — New York N.L. 1926–1948. One of few players to jump from a high school team into majors. Played outfield and third base and managed club from December 1941 through July 1948. Hit 511 home runs, N.L. record when he retired. Also led in most runs scored, most runs batted in, total bases, bases on balls and extra bases on long hits. Had a .304 lifetime batting average. Played in eleven All-Star games and in three World Series. (Elected 1951)

LEROY ROBERT PAIGE (Satchel) — Negro Leagues 1926–1947. Cleveland A.L. 1948–1949. St. Louis A.L. 1951–1953. Kansas City A.L. 1965. Paige was one of the greatest stars to play in the negro baseball leagues. Thrilled millions of people and won hundreds of games. Struck out 21 major leaguers in an exhibition game. Helped pitch Cleveland Indians to the 1948 pennant in his first big league year at age 42. His pitching was a legend among major league hitters. (Elected 1971)

HERBERT J. PENNOCK (Herb) — Outstanding left-handed pitcher in the A.L. and executive of Philadelphia N.L. club. Among rare few who made jump from prep school to majors. Saw 22 years of service with Philadelphia, Boston and New York teams in A.L. Recorded 240 victories, 161 defeats. Never lost a World Series game, winning five. In 1927 pitched 7⅓ innings without allowing hit in third game of series. (Elected 1948)

EDWARD S. PLANK (Gettysburg Eddie) — One of greatest left-handed pitchers of major leagues. Never pitched for a minor league team, going from Gettysburg College to the Philadelphia A.L. team, with which he served from 1901 through 1914. Member of St. Louis F.L. in 1915 and St. Louis A.L. in 1916–17. One of few pitchers to win more than 300 games in big leagues. In eight of 17 seasons won 20 or more games. (Elected 1946)

EDWARD S. PLANK

CHARLIE RADBOURNE (Old Hoss) — Providence, Boston and Cincinnati National League 1881 to 1891. Greatest of all 19th century pitchers. Winning 1884 pennant for Providence, Radbourne pitched last 27 games of season, won 26. Won 3 straight in World Series. (Elected 1939)

EDGAR CHARLES RICE (Sam) — Washington A.L. 1915–1933. Cleveland A.L. 1934. At bat 600 or more times eight different seasons. Had 200 or more hits in each of six seasons. Batted .322 for 20-year career and had 2987 hits. Set A.L. record with 182 singles in 1925. Led A.L. in number of hits 216 in 1924 and 1926. Led A.L. in putouts for outfielders with 454 in 1920 and 385 in 1922. (Elected 1963)

WESLEY BRANCH RICKEY — St. Louis A.L. 1905, 1906, 1914. New York A.L. 1907. Founder of farm system which he developed for St. Louis Cardinals and Brooklyn Dodgers. Copied by all other major league teams. Served as executive for Browns, Cardinals, Dodgers and Pirates. Brought Jackie Robinson to Brooklyn in 1947. (Elected 1967)

EPPA RIXEY — Philadelphia N.L. 1912–1920. Cincinnati N.L. 1921–1933. Won 266, lost 251, pct. .515, E.R.A. 3.15. Set record for most victories by left-handed pitcher. Led league in victories with 25 in 1922. Gave only 1082 base on balls in 4494 innings. (Elected 1963)

ROBIN EVAN ROBERTS — Philadelphia N.L. Baltimore A.L. Houston N.L. Chicago N.L. 1948–1966. Won 286 games though usually pitching for second-division teams. Gained 20 or more victories six years in a row 1950–1955, and topped league or tied for lead in victories four successive seasons. Led N.L. five consecutive years in innings pitched 1951–1955 and complete games 1952–1956. Led in shutouts and strikeouts twice each. (Elected 1976)

JACK ROOSEVELT ROBINSON – Brooklyn N.L. 1947–1956. Leading N.L. batter in 1949. Holds fielding mark for second baseman playing in 150 or more games with .992. Led N.L. in stolen bases in 1947 and 1949. Most valuable player in 1949. Lifetime batting average .311. Joint record holder for most double plays by second baseman, 137 in 1951. Led second basemen in double plays 1949–50–51–52. (Elected 1962)

WILBERT ROBINSON (Uncle Robbie) – Star catcher for the famous Baltimore Orioles on pennant clubs of 1894, 1895 and 1896, he later won fame as manager of the Brooklyn Dodgers from 1914 through 1931. Set a record of 7 hits in 7 times at bat in single game. (Elected 1945)

EDD J. ROUSH – Chicago A.L. 1913. New York N.L. 1916, 1927–1930. Cincinnati N.L. 1916–1926, 1931. Leading N.L. batter in 1917 and 1919. Batted .352 in 1921, .352 in 1922, .351 in 1923, .348 in 1924. Batted over .300 thirteen seasons. Lifetime batting average of .323. Most outfield putouts, 410 in 1920. F.L. 1914–1915. (Elected 1962)

CHARLES HERBERT RUFFING (Red) – Boston A.L. 1924–1930. New York A.L. 1930–1946. Chicago A.L. 1947. Winner of 273 games. Won 20 or more games in each of four consecutive seasons. Led in complete games 1928. Tied in shutouts 1938–39. Won 7 out of 9 World Series decisions. Selected for All-Star teams 1937–38–39. (Elected 1967)

GEORGE HERMAN RUTH (Babe) – Boston, New York A.L. Boston N.L. 1915–1935. Greatest drawing card in history of baseball. Holder of many home run and other batting records. Gathered 714 home runs in addition to fifteen in World Series. (Elected 1936)

RAYMOND WILLIAM SCHALK – Chicago A.L. 1912–1928. New York N.L. 1929. Holder of major league record for most years leading catcher in fielding, eight years; most putouts, nine years; most assists in one major league, 1810; most chances accepted, 8965. Caught four no-hit games including perfect game in 1922. (Elected 1955)

ALOYSIUS HARRY SIMMONS – Played with seven major league clubs 1924–1944. Star with Philadelphia A.L. Batted .308 to .392 from 1924 to 1934. Leading batter .381 in 1930, .390 in 1931. Most hits by A.L. right-handed batter with 2831. Led league runs batted in, runs scored, hits and total bases several seasons. Hit 3 home runs July 15, 1932. Lifetime batting average .334. (Elected 1953)

GEORGE HAROLD SISLER – St. Louis, Washington A.L. Boston N.L. 1915–1930. Holds two American League records, making 257 hits in 1920 and batting .41979 in 1922. Retired with major league average of .341. Credited with being one of best two fielding first basemen in history of game. (Elected 1939)

WARREN EDWARD SPAHN – Boston, Milwaukee, New York, San Francisco N.L. 1942–1965. Became fifth biggest winner in majors' history with 363 victories. Most victories for a left-hander. Won 20 or more games 13 seasons, six in a row. Set all-time records for years leading league in victories 8 and complete games 9. Also N.L. career highs with 665 games started; 5264 innings; 2853 strikeouts. Pitched no-hitter in 1960, another in 1961. (Elected 1973)

ALBERT GOODWILL SPALDING – Organizational genius of baseball's pioneer days. Star pitcher of Forest City club in late 1860s, 4-year champion Bostons 1871–1875 and manager-pitcher of champion Chicagos in National League's first year. Chicago president for ten years. Organizer of baseball's first round-the-world tour in 1888. (Elected 1939)

TRISTRAM E. SPEAKER (Tris) – Boston A.L. 1909–1915. Cleveland A.L. 1916–1926. Washington A.L. 1927. Philadelphia A.L. 1928. Greatest

Babe Ruth

centerfielder of his day. Lifetime major league batting average of .344. Manager in 1920 when Cleveland won its first pennant and World Championship. (Elected 1937)

CHARLES DILLON STENGEL (Casey) — Managed New York Yankees 1949–1960. Won 10 pennants and 7 World Series with New York Yankees. Only manager to win 5 consecutive World Series 1949–1953. Played outfield 1912–1925 with Brooklyn, Pittsburgh, Philadelphia, New York and Boston N.L. teams. Managed Brooklyn 1934–1936, Boston Braves 1938–1943, New York Mets 1962–1965. (Elected 1966)

CHARLES DILLON STENGEL

WILLIAM HAROLD TERRY — New York N.L. 1923–1941. Batted .401 and tied N.L. record for base hits with 254 in 1930. Made 200 or more hits in six seasons. Retired with lifetime batting average of .341, a modern N.L. record for left-handed batters. Most valuable player in 1930. Succeeded John McGraw as manager in 1932 and won pennants in 1933–36–37. (Elected 1954)

SAMUEL LUTHER THOMPSON — Detroit, Philadelphia N.L. 1885–1898. Detroit A.L. 1906. One of the foremost sluggers of his day. Lifetime batting average .336. Batted better than .400 twice. Great clutch hitter. Collected 200 or more hits in a season three times. Topped N.L. in home runs and runs batted in twice. (Elected 1974)

JOSEPH B. TINKER — Famous as a member of one of baseball's greatest double play combinations — from Tinker to Evers to Chance. A big leaguer from 1902 through 1916 with the Chicago Cubs and Cincinnati Reds and the Chicago Feds. Manager Cincinnati 1913 and Chicago N.L. 1916. Shortstop on Cubs team that won pennants in 1906, 1907, 1908 and 1910. (Elected 1946)

HAROLD J. TRAYNOR (Pie) — Rated among the great third basemen of all time, he became a regular with the Pittsburgh N.L. team in 1922 and continued as a player until conclusion of 1937 season. Managed the Pirates from June 1934 through September 1939. Holds several fielding records and compiled a lifetime batting mark of .320. One of few players ever to make 200 or more hits during a season, collecting 208 in 1923. (Elected 1948)

ARTHUR CHARLES VANCE (Dazzy) — Brooklyn N.L. 1922–1932, 1935. Pittsburgh N.L. New York A.L. St. Louis N.L. Cincinnati N.L. First pitcher in National League to lead in strikeouts for 7 straight years, 1922 to 1928. Led league with 28 victories in 1924; 22 in 1925. Won 15 straight in 1924. Pitched no-hit game against Phillies in 1925. Most valuable player N.L. in 1924. (Elected 1955)

GEORGE EDWARD WADDELL (Rube) — Colorful left-handed pitcher who was in both leagues, but who gained fame as a member of the Philadelphia A.L. team. Won more than 20 games in first four seasons with that club and compiled more than 200 victories during major league career. Was noted for his strikeout achievements. (Elected 1946)

JOHN P. WAGNER (Honus) — Louisville N.L. 1897–1899. Pittsburgh N.L. 1900–1917. The greatest shortstop in baseball history. Born in Carnegie, Pennsylvania, February 24, 1874. Known to fame as "Honus," "Hans" and "The Flying Dutchman." Retired in 1917, having scored more runs, made more hits and stolen more bases than any other player in the history of his league. (Elected 1936)

RODERICK J. WALLACE — Cleveland, St. Louis, Cincinnati N.L. St. Louis A.L. 1894–1918. One of the longest careers in major leagues. Over 60 years as pitcher, third baseman, shortstop, manager, umpire and scout. Active as player for 25 years. Set A.L. record for chances in one game at shortstop, 17, June 10, 1902. Recognized as one of the greatest shortstops. Pitched for Cleveland in 1896 Temple Cup Series. (Elected 1953)

Honus Wagner

EDWARD ARTHUR WALSH (Big Ed) — Outstanding right-handed pitcher of Chicago A.L. from 1904 through 1916. Won 40 games in 1908 and won two games in the 1906 World Series. Twice pitched and won two games in one day, allowing only one run in doubleheader against Boston on September 29, 1908. Finished big league pitching career with Boston N.L. in 1917. (Elected 1946)

LLOYD JAMES WANER (Little Poison) — Pittsburgh, Boston, Cincinnati, Philadelphia, Brooklyn N.L. 1927–1945. Made 223 hits in 1927, first year with Pittsburgh, including 198 singles, a modern major league record. Led N.L. in most singles 1927–28–29–31. Life total 2459 hits. Batting average .316. With brother Paul, "Big Poison," starred in Pittsburgh outfield 1927–1940. (Elected 1967)

PAUL GLEE WANER (Big Poison) — Pittsburgh, Brooklyn, Boston N.L. New York A.L. 1926–1945. Left-handed hitting outfielder batted .300 or better 14 times in National League. One of seven players ever to compile 3000 or more hits. Set modern N.L. record by collecting 200 or more hits eight seasons. Most valuable player in 1927 and four times selected for All-Star game. (Elected 1952)

JOHN MONTGOMERY WARD — 1878–1894. Pitching pioneer who won 158, lost 102 games in seven years. Pitched perfect game for Providence of N.L. in 1880. Turned to shortstop and made 2151 hits. Managed New York and Brooklyn in N.L. President of Boston N.L. 1911–1912. Played important part in establishing modern organized baseball. (Elected 1964)

GEORGE MARTIN WEISS — Master builder of championship teams. Was club executive in minors and majors from 1919 to 1966. Developed best minor league chain in game as New York Yankee farm manager 1932–1947. General manager of the Yankees from 1947 to 1960 which won 10 pennants and 7 World Series during this period. President of the New York Mets 1961–1966. (Elected 1971)

MICHAEL FRANCIS WELCH (Smiling Mickey) — Troy N.L. 1880–1882. New York N.L. 1883–1892. Credited with more than 300 victories during 13 seasons in majors. Won 17 games in a row in 1885 while compiling 44–11 record for league-leading .800 winning percentage. Topped 30-victory total in four years. (Elected 1973)

ZACHARIAH DAVIS WHEAT (Zack) — Brooklyn N.L. 1909–1926. Philadelphia A.L. 1927. Brooklyn outfielder for 18 years. Holds Brooklyn records for — games played 2318, at bat 8859, hits 2804, singles 2038, doubles 464, triples 171, total bases 4003, extra base hits 766. Batted .375 (1923) .375 (1924) .359 (1925), league batting leader .335 (1918). Lifetime batting average .317 with 2884 hits. Played 2406 games. (Elected 1959)

THEODORE SAMUEL WILLIAMS (Ted) — Boston Red Sox A.L. 1939–1960. Batted .406 in 1941. Led A.L. in batting 6 times; slugging percentage 9 times; total bases 6 times; runs scored 6 times; bases on balls 8 times. Total hits 2654 included 521 home runs. Lifetime batting average .344; lifetime slugging average .634. Most valuable A.L. player 1946 and 1949. Played in 18 All-Star games, named Player of the Decade 1951–1960. (Elected 1966)

GEORGE WRIGHT — Star of baseball's first professional team, the Cincinnati Red Stockings of 1869. Great shortstop and captain of champion Bostons in National League's pioneer years. (Elected 1937)

HARRY WRIGHT — Manager and centerfielder of famous Cincinnati Red Stockings, undefeated in 69 games in 1869–1870. First manager to win four straight pennants with Boston National Association 1872–73–74–75. Brother of George Wright also in Hall of Fame. Sponsored first baseball tour

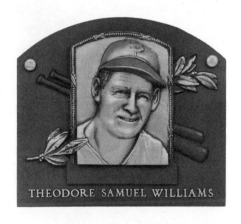

THEODORE SAMUEL WILLIAMS

The trophies in the Ty Cobb display at the Hall of Fame.

to England in 1876. Introduced knicker uniforms. Hit 7 home runs in game at Newport, Kentucky in 1867. (Elected 1953)

EARLY WYNN (Gus) — Washington, Cleveland, Chicago A.L. 1939–1963. Winner of 300 major league games. Set record by pitching 23 years in majors. Gained 20 or more victories five times and led A.L. in earned-run average in 1950. Leader in innings pitched three seasons in strikeouts twice. Tied for most victories with 23 in 1954 and led league with 22 wins at age 39 in 1959 to earn Cy Young Award. (Elected 1972)

DENTON T. YOUNG (Cy) — Cleveland N.L. 1890–1898. St. Louis N.L. 1899–1900. Boston A.L. 1901–1908. Cleveland A.L. 1909–1911. Boston N.L. 1911. Only pitcher in first hundred years of baseball to win 500 games. Among his 511 victories were 3 no-hit shutouts. Pitched perfect game May 5, 1904, no opposing batsman reaching first base. (Elected 1937)

ROSS MIDDLEBROOK YOUNGS (Pep) — New York N.L. 1917–1926. Star right fielder of champion Giants of 1921–22–23–24 when he batted .327, .331, .336 and .356. Compiled lifetime average of .322, topping .300 in nine of ten years. Twice made 200 or more hits in a season. Led league in doubles in 1919 and runs scored in 1923. Led N.L. outfielders in assists twice and tied once. (Elected 1972)

1977 Inductee to the Hall of Fame

ERNEST BANKS (Ernie) — Chicago N.L. 1953–1971. Premier shortstop and first baseman who hit 512 home runs in a nineteen-year career. Excelled in the field as well as at bat. Over seventeen years he averaged 29 home runs and 91 RBI's. One of eight players to be voted into the Hall of Fame in first year of eligibility other than the charter members. Voted N.L. most valuable player in 1958–59.

THE NAISMITH MEMORIAL BASKETBALL HALL OF FAME

Springfield, Massachusetts

By Steven Jay Levine

This statue of Dr. James Naismith, inventor of basketball, greets visitors at the entrance of the Basketball Hall of Fame.

The Naismith Memorial Basketball Hall of Fame is more than a museum containing old basketball shoes and worn out uniforms. Since opening its doors to the public in 1968, the Hall of Fame in Springfield, Massachusetts has become one of the premier tourist attractions in the United States.

April 1976 marked the arrival of the 300,000th visitor to the Hall of Fame. People from all corners of the globe have visited "Basketball's Museum and Shrine". Visitors representing every state in the Union and 25 foreign nations have visited the Basketball Hall of Fame.

The Basketball Hall of Fame is unique among all the other Halls of Fame. The "hoop shrine" recognizes competition on all levels, professional, college, high school, amateur, and international. It is dedicated to the only major sport founded in the United States.

Springfield was selected as the site for the Hall of Fame due to the fact that the game was invented there. Dr. James Naismith, for whom the Hall of Fame is named, invented the game while serving as a physical education instructor at the International Y.M.C.A. Training School, now Springfield College.

Not too long after basketball took on international proportions, the National Association of Basketball Coaches began a movement to honor the greats of the game. Many hardships and long years of planning took place before the Hall of Fame actually opened its doors to the public. The NABC which had funded the cost of sending Dr. Naismith to the 1936 Olympic Games in Berlin (where basketball was played for the first time as an official Olympic sport) also became the major influence and spearhead for the project.

The Hall of Fame is a private non-profit institution supported by its admission charges, souvenir sales, and contributions from such sources as coaches, officials, high schools, colleges, corporations and other friends of the game of basketball.

The Hall of Fame is actively involved in the Springfield community. From its sponsorship of local basketball to its support of the community's civic endeavors, the Hall of Fame plays an active role in the Springfield scene. The Hall of Fame offers basketball fans in New England the opportunity to see exciting basketball competition on a first-hand basis. The National Basketball Association Hall of Fame Exhibition Game played annually during the fall brings the finest professional players in the game to the Springfield Civic Center. The collegians are also represented in the Annual Basketball Hall of Fame Tip-Off Tournament which features some of the best collegiate talent in the country and kicks off the basketball season in November.

The most memorable aspect of the Hall of Fame is the Honors Court. It is here that the game's immortals are enshrined in a striking display of cathedral-like stained glass windows. Each electee is pictured on an individual stained glass panel that extends nearly ten feet from the floor to the ceiling. The soft lighting in the Honors Court creates a truly majestic sight.

The most important event of the year is the annual Enshrinement Day held in late April. The new electees join the ranks of basketball's immortals in an impressive ceremony held at the Hall of Fame on "Basketball's Greatest Day".

Electees are chosen from four categories-player, coach, referee, and contributor. A player may be elected five years after his last competition, a referee, five years after his officiating retirement, a coach, after he has coached for a minimum of twenty-five years, and a contributor, any time after consistently noteworthy contributions.

In 1959 the first electees were enshrined in the Honors Court. This first induction saw fourteen individuals and two teams being honored. Since that time eighty-four individuals and two teams have taken their place among basketball's immortals. As of 1976 there are ninety-eight individuals and four teams enshrined at the Basketball Hall of Fame.

There is much more to see at the Hall of Fame than one might suspect. The Hickox Library is considered by many to be the largest and most complete collection of basketball reference materials. The basketball stamp exhibit, which features stamps from various countries which have honored the game, will undoubtedly be of interest to philatelists.

There are displays which trace the development of the ball and uniform from the early days of the game through the present; an exhibit featuring rare and historical newspaper cartoons of famous players and teams; as well as the uniforms worn by such greats as Russell, Chamberlain, Cousy, West, Baylor, Mikan, Robertson, and Abdul-Jabbar.

This is only a small sampling of what the Hall of Fame has to offer. There are photographs, plaques, trophies, various audio-visual exhibits, and even a banner given by the Russian National Team to the Wichita Vickers after a game played in December 1959 in Lawrence, Kansas. The Hall of Fame also offers free basketball movies shown hourly in the Converse Movie Room. Those visitors having an interest in art will appreciate

Lee Williams, executive director of the Naismith Memorial Basketball Hall of Fame and noted sculptor Laszlo Ispanky admire an original basketball sculpture created especially for the hall.

— All photographs in this chapter, courtesy Naismith Memorial Basketball Hall of Fame

(Above) This building at Winchester Square, Springfield, was occupied by the School for Christian Workers and the Armory Hill Y.M.C.A. where basketball was first played in December, 1891.

(Right) The Game and equipment used in 1892, as illustrated in lecture material of Amos Alonzo Stagg.

(Below) Gymnasium where basketball was first played. Dr. Naismith hung a peach basket from each end of the area below the overhead track.

One of the many original paintings in the Basketball Hall of Fame, this painting depicts "Hank" Luisetti of Stanford University shooting his one-handed shot that revolutionized the game of basketball.

the many original paintings and sculptures found throughout the Hall of Fame.

Another major point of interest is the Main Museum. Upon entering the Main Museum area, the visitor finds an exact replica of the original gymnasium at the Armory Y.M.C.A., where the game was first played. The open oval area above the main floor represents the indoor track over the court to which Dr. Naismith attached the first peach basket. Sections of the floor on which the first game was played as well as Naismith's original thirteen rules are displayed. Other exhibits located in the Main Museum trace the history of the game in chronological order through uniforms, equipment, and photographs. A display dealing with the development of the basket, backboard and rim may also be seen.

A trip to the Basketball Hall of Fame is a must for the entire family. The Hall of Fame located on the Springfield College campus is open daily except Thanksgiving, Christmas, and New Year's Day. Admission is $1.50 for adults, $1.00 for students over 15, .50 for students under 15, and children under 6 admitted free. Special group rates for parties of ten or more are available.

ELECTEES

1959

FORREST C. ALLEN (Contributor 1959) — Founded National Association of Basketball Coaches. Immortal Kansas coach won 771 games and 31 championships in 39-year career. Helped organize first NCAA Tournament. Instrumental in making basketball an Olympic sport. 1885–1974

DR. H. CLIFFORD CARLSON (Coach 1959) — Invented "figure 8" offense. Led University of Pittsburgh to National Championships in 1928 and 1930. 1894–1964

DR. LUTHER H. GULICK (Contributor 1959) — Asked Naismith to create an indoor game which was to become basketball. Organized New York City Public School League, the Playground Association and assisted in the formation of the Boy Scouts and Camp Fire Girls. Chairman AAU Basketball Committee. 1865–1918

EDWARD J. HICKOX (Contributor 1959) — First Executive Secretary of Hall of Fame. NABC President (1944–1946), member Rules Committee for 18 years and historian for 20 years. Coached basketball at Springfield for 16 years. 1878–1966

CHARLES D. HYATT (College Player 1959) — A high school All-American at Uniontown, Pennsylvania High School. All-American at Pitt (1928–1930) who led his team to National Titles in 1928 and 1930. AAU All-American for nine seasons. 1908

MATTHEW P. KENNEDY (Referee 1959) — High school, college, and pro referee from 1928 to 1946. Supervisor of officials in the NBA (1946–1950). Toured with Globetrotters (1950–1957). Noted for colorful mannerisms on the court. 1908–1957

ANGELO "HANK" LUISETTI (College Player 1959) — Led Stanford to three Pacific Coast Titles (1936, 1937, 1938). All-American in junior and senior years. Revolutionized game with one-handed shooting. First player to score 50 points in a regular game. 1916–

DR. WALTER E. MEANWELL (Coach 1959) — Successful coach at Wisconsin and Missouri (290–101) winning two titles at Missouri and four outright as well as four co-Big Ten Titles. Member Rules Committee, charter member NABC. Developed valve for laceless basketball and "criss-cross" offense. 1884–1953

GEORGE L. MIKAN (College Player 1959) — Three-time All-American (1944, 1945, 1946) at DePaul. "Player of the Year" 1944–45 and 1945–46. Voted top "Player of the Half Century" by the Associated Press. Led Minneapolis Lakers to five titles. First Commissioner of American Basketball Association. Elected to NBA Silver Anniversary team in 1971, representing the greatest players in the League's first 25 years. 1924–

RALPH MORGAN (Contributor 1959) — Founded forerunner of National Basketball Rules Committee serving as a member for 26 years and organizer of the Eastern Collegiate Basketball League (now Ivy League) in 1910. 1884–1965

DR. JAMES NAISMITH (Contributor 1959) — Invented game of basketball in 1891 while serving as an instructor at the School for Christian Workers (now Springfield College) in Springfield, Massachusetts. 1861–1939

HAROLD G. OLSEN (Contributor 1959) — All-Conference player at Wisconsin. Won five titles at Ohio State (1922–1946). Instrumental in founding

George Mikan, who starred at DePaul University and as a professional with the Minneapolis Lakers.

of NCAA Tournament. President of NABC (1933) and NCAA Rules Committee. Instrumental in adoption of 10-second rule. Member 1948 Olympic Basketball Committee. Coached professional Chicago Stags 1946–1949. 1895–1953

JOHN J. SCHOMMER (College Player 1959) — An All-Time All-American selection and the first man to win twelve letters at the University of Chicago. Four-time All-American led Chicago to National Title in 1908. 1884–1960

AMOS ALONZO STAGG (Contributor 1959) — Helped Naismith in the early development of basketball while both were students and instructors at the School for Christian Workers. Played in first public basketball game on March 11, 1892. Introduced game at University of Chicago, organized Big Ten Conference, and conducted National High School Tournament which played a large part in standardizing the rules. Member of Football Hall of Fame. 1862–1965

OSWALD TOWER (Contributor 1959) — Member of Rules Committee for 49 years, and was editor of the Basketball Guide and official rules interpreter from 1915 until 1959. 1883–1968

JOHN R. WOODEN (Player 1959, Coach 1972) — Three-time All-American at Purdue 1930, 1931, 1932, "Player of the Year" 1932. Member Helms All-Time All-American Team (1943) and Grantland Rice All-Time Team (1953). Won 10 NCAA Titles at UCLA while being named "Coach of the Year" six times. 1910–

1960

ERNEST A. BLOOD (Coach 1960) — At Potsdam, New York, his teams were undefeated by high school opposition in nine years. At Passaic (New Jersey) High School his record was 200-1 with 159 straight wins. Posted record of 421–128 in 25 years at St. Benedict's Prep in N.J. Won a total of 12 N.J. State Titles. 1872–1955

VICTOR A. HANSON (College Player 1960) — Basketball All American at Syracuse in 1925, 1926, 1927. "Player of the Year" in 1927. Selected to All-Time All-American Team by Grantland Rice. Played pro basketball with Cleveland Rosenblums and baseball with New York Yankees. 1903–

GEORGE T. HEPBRON (Referee 1960) — First basketball official in the New York area. Helped with the first guidebook on how to play the game. Member of AAU Rules Committee (1896–1915) and member and secretary of the Joint Rules Committee (1915–1936). Responsible for the first rules questionnaire which attempted to codify the game. Worked to bring organization to the game. 1863–1946.

FRANK W. KEANEY (Coach 1960) — Noted basketball coach at Rhode Island changed the game's slow-break pattern of offense to the fast-break, high-scoring "Point a Minute" brand seen today. Took Rhode Island to the NIT four times. 1886–1947

WARD L. LAMBERT (Coach 1960) — Head coach at Purdue (1916–1946). Led his teams to eleven Big Ten Titles and a 371–152 record. Coached John Wooden. Pioneer of the fast-break offense. Nation's outstanding coach in 1945. 1888–1958

EDWARD C. MACAULEY (College Player 1960) — Youngest man ever elected to Hall of Fame. Named to every All-American team and Associated Press "Player of the Year" in 1949 at St. Louis University. Led St. Louis to NIT Championship in 1948 and to the Sugar Bowl Title. Played professionally with the St. Louis Hawks and Boston Celtics. Played in eight NBA All-Star Games and named All-NBA from 1950–1954. 1928–

BRANCH McCRACKEN (College Player 1960) — Three-times All-Big Ten at Indiana Named to every All-American team in senior year. As coach at Indiana, his teams won four conference titles and the National Title in 1940 and 1953. "Coach of the Year" in 1953. Coach at Indiana for 27 years (1938–1965). 1908–1970

CHARLES C. MURPHY (College Player 1960) — One of the first great "Big Men" in the game. Great offensive player at Purdue under Ward Lambert. He and Johnny Wooden led team to undefeated season and conference title in 1930. All-American in 1929 and 1930 also member of All-Time All-American team. 1907 –

HENRY V. PORTER (Contributor 1960) — Helped organize National Basketball Committee of the U.S. and Canada. First high school representative on the National Rules Committee. Pioneered development of the "molded" ball, the fan-shaped backboard, and the 29 1/2-inch ball. Helped to codify the rules of basketball, and began nationwide system of rules analysis. Noted author of basketball books. 1891–1975

1961

BERNHARD BORGMANN (Pro Player 1961) — A member of the Original Celtics. Played 2500 professional games. At 5'8", Benny was an aggressive offensive performer who was high scorer in every league in which he competed — American, National, Metropolitan, Eastern, New York State and Western Massachusetts. The All-Time All-Pro retired in 1942 and enjoyed a successful 7-year pro coaching career and then 6 good years coaching at the college level. 1899 –

FORREST S. DE BERNARDI (AAU Player 1961) — AAU All-American in 1921, 1922, and 1923. Led Hillyards to AAU Titles in 1926 and 1927. In eleven AAU Tournaments he was named All-Tournament seven times and All-American in three positions. Selected All-Time All-American in 1938. 1899–1970.

GEORGE H. HOYT (Referee 1961) — Introduced principles of officiating to referees and coaches in New England. Organized first Officials Board in Eastern Massachusetts. Associated with Eastern Massachusetts High School Tournament for 34 years, both as a regular official and later as Honorary Chief Official. Known as "Mister Basketball" in New England. 1883–1962

GEORGE E. KEOGAN (Coach 1961) — Became coach at Notre Dame in 1923. Twenty-year record of 327–96. Created "shifting man-to-man" defense. 1890–1943

ROBERT A. KURLAND (College Player 1961) — Led Oklahoma A & M to successive NCAA Titles in 1945 and 1946. Member 1948 and 1952 U.S. Olympic Teams. Elected to every All-American team and selected by Grantland Rice to the All-Time All-American Team. Selected All-League and All-AAU for six years with Phillips Oilers AAU team. 1924 –

JOHN J. O'BRIEN (Contributor 1961) — Three-sport athlete in high school. Player and referee in YMCA and professional leagues from 1908–1930. His real forte was administration. Helped organize the Interstate Pro League and the Metropolitan Basketball League. President of the American Basketball League for 25 years. 1888–1967

ANDY PHILLIP (College Player 1961) — At the University of Illinois, he became the leader of the famed "Whiz Kids" and set Big Ten scoring records (1941–1943) as Illinois won two Conference Titles. The two-time All American set many Conference records. After a 3-year stint with the U.S. Marines, he returned to Illinois in 1946 and achieved his second All-American ranking. 1922 –

ERNEST C. QUIGLEY (Referee 1961) — Known as one of basketball's most colorful and respected coaches. Became interested in basketball under the tutelege of Dr. James Naismith at the University of Kansas. AAU basketball official. Also National League umpire (baseball) working five World Series. 1880–1968

JOHN S. ROOSMA (College Player 1961) — Played on legendary Passaic Wonder Team under Ernest Blood. Outstanding athlete of the Class of 1926 at the U.S. Military Academy. Led Army to 73–13 record while scoring 44% of team's points. Coached and played for many military teams, both in the United States and overseas. 1900–

LEONARD D. SACHS (Coach 1961) — At Loyala of Chicago, he created the 2-2-1 zone defense which gave new interest to "Big Man" basketball. Noted for defensive strategy. Coached teams to 32 straight victories (1927–1929) and 20 straight wins (1939) before losing to undefeated LIU in the finals of the National Invitation Tournament. 1897–1942

ARTHUR A. SCHABINGER (Contributor 1961) — In twenty years as a coach, he had an 80% win record. Promoted intersectional scheduling of games and was a co-founder of the National Association of Basketball Coaches. NABC President 1932. Directed first Olympic Basketball Tourney in 1936. Helped develop the molded ball and founded the Official Sports Film Service as an aid to uniform rules interpretation. 1889–1972

CHRISTIAN STEINMETZ (College Player 1961) — "Father of Wisconsin Basketball". Organized first team at Wisconsin. Scoring records stood for almost fifty years until 1954. First player to score 1000 points in his college career. 1882–1963

DAVID TOBEY (Referee 1961) — Played with early New York Knickerbockers and the Philadelphia SPHAS. Pro official in New York from 1918 to 1925 and Eastern intercollegiate official from 1926 until 1946. Wrote *Basketball Officiating,* the sport's first volume on the subject. 1898–

ARTHUR L. TRESTER (Contributor 1961) — Became secretary of the struggling Indiana High School Athletic Association in 1913 and increased membership to over 800 schools. Became Commissioner of the IHSAA in 1922. IHSAA became the model for other high school associations in many states. Enabled Indiana's system of basketball tournaments to be universally recognized and accepted as a model of efficiency. 1878–1944

EDWARD A. WACHTER (Pro Player 1961) — Career included over 1,800 games and over 20 years of coaching. Carried basketball to areas where the sport was bidding for recognition. Played on Troy (N.Y.) YMCA Team and led Schenectady Company E Team to the World's Title in 1905. Named greatest center in basketball in 1922 and All-Time Center in 1928. Played on more championship teams than any other member of his generation. 1883–1966.

DAVID H. WALSH (Referee 1961) — Served as Associate Director of the Collegiate Officials Bureau from 1941–1956, and as Secretary-Treasurer of the International Association of Approved Basketball Officials from 1948–1956. Helped to establish uniformity in basketball rules and in improving the quality of the game's officiating. Distinguished 45-year career as teacher, coach and official in high school, college and professional basketball. 1889–1975

1962

JACK McCRACKEN (A.A.U. Player 1962) — "Jumpin Jack" was All-American at Northwest Missouri State in 1931 and 1932. Consistently named to A.A.U. All-America teams from 1932–1942. Recognized as one of the nation's greatest all-round players of this time. 1911–1958.

The pro jersey as seen in the Stokes room of the Naismith Memorial Basketball Hall of Fame. Stokes was an outstanding high school and college player whose promising professional career was cut short when he was stricken with traumatic encephalopathy. The Stokes room is dedicated to his memory.

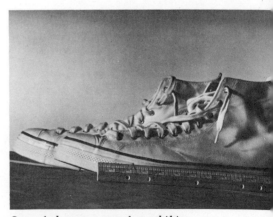

One of the most popular exhibits at the Basketball Hall of Fame is the pair of size 20 basketball shoes worn by Bob Lanier of the NBA's Detroit Pistons.

FRANK MORGENWECK (Contributor 1962)—"Pop" wielded much influence among players, coaches and owners. Spent 32 years managing, financing and promoting early professional games. His greatest contribution to basketball was his efforts in raising the standards of the game and the players. 1875–1941

HARLAN O. PAGE (College Player 1962)—At the University of Chicago, "Pat" was named 'Player of the Year' in 1910. His shooting and defense spurred Chicago teams to Western Conference Titles in 1907, 1909 (an undefeated season), and 1910, to the A.A.U. Title in 1907 and to the National Title in 1908. 1887–1965

BARNEY SEDRAN (Pro Player 1962)—Only 5'4", Barney was the leading scorer at C.C.N.Y. for three years. Enjoyed a brilliant 15-year professional career during which he played for all the major Eastern teams. 1891–1969

LYNN W. ST. JOHN (Contributor 1962)—Outstanding coach at Ohio State University in 1912 then Director of Athletics at O.S.U. from 1915–1947. Member of the NCAA Rules Committee for 25 years, was Chairman for 18 of those years. He was instrumental in the formation of the National Basketball Committee of the U.S. and Canada, and served as Chairman from 1933–1937. 1876–1950

JOHN A. THOMPSON (College Player 1962)—His outstanding career at Montana State included his selection to All-Rocky Mountain Conference teams (1927, captain in 1928, 1929 and 1930) and the honor of being named 'Player of the Year' by the Helms Foundation in 1929. 1906–

1963

ROBERT F. GRUENIG (A.A.U. Player 1963)—An A.A.U. immortal, the 6'8", 220-pound center was outstanding from 1933–1948. Named A.A.U. All-American ten times. He was recognized as the nation's greatest player in 1943 as recipient of the Los Angeles Sports Award Medallion. 1913–1958

WILLIAM A. REID (Contributor 1963)—During his 36 years as Director of Athletics at Colgate University, he coached ten basketball teams to an enviable 151–56 record. He served as President of the E.C.A.C. 1944–1945, and as Vice-President of the NCAA from 1942–1946. 1893–1955

1964

JOHN W. BUNN (Contributor 1964)—First athlete at Kansas University to earn 10 varsity letters. Distinguished 25-year college coaching career at Stanford University, Springfield College and Colorado State University (Greeley) which included 321 victories. The author of numerous books on basketball, Bunn was editor of BASKETBALL GUIDE and official Rules Interpreter from 1959–1967. Chairman of the Hall of Fame Committee of the N.A.B.C. (1949–1961) and became the first Executive Director of the Basketball Federation in 1965. 1898–

HAROLD E. FOSTER (College Player 1964)—Three-year star at the University of Wisconsin (1928–1930). Wisconsin was Western Conference Champion in 1929 and "Bud" was named to several All-Conference and All-Western teams in 1929 and 1930. Named All-American in 1930. Coached Wisconsin for 25 years, winning Big Ten Titles in 1935, 1941 and 1947 and the NCAA Championship in 1941. 1906–

NAT HOLMAN (Pro Player 1964)—A member of the Original Celtics for 8 years. Led that Celtics team with great shooting, team play, exceptional ball-handling and passing—a fabulous era in which the Celtics never lost a series. He gave up professional play in 1933 for what was to become a great 41-year coaching career at C.C.N.Y. His team won both the N.I.T. and NCAA Titles in 1950. 1896–

EDWARD S. IRISH (Contributor 1964) – In 1934, he became Basketball Director of Madison Square Garden and introduced the college doubleheader. As a result of his innovations, he was credited with making basketball a major sport; and when "Ned" began intersectional play, the game became truly national. He also contributed to the standardization of rules and coaching, and encouraged the building of larger facilities at the Garden. In 1946, he helped organize the N.B.A. and founded the New York Knickerbockers. 1905–

R. WILLIAM JONES (Contributor 1964) – Graduated from Springfield College in 1928 and continued his education at colleges abroad. At the same time, he began spreading basketball all over the world by introducing it first in Switzerland (1929). Three years later, he co-founded the International Amateur Basketball Federation (F.I.B.A.) serving as the organization's Secretary-General. The F.I.B.A. controls all international competition, and Mr. Jones still heads this group. 1906–

KENNETH D. LOEFFLER (Coach 1964) – While coaching at Geneva College, Yale, LaSalle College and Texas A&M, his teams won 310 games. At LaSalle, he won the 1952 N.I.T. Title and the 1954 NCAA Title. His St. Louis Bombers pro team won the N.B.A. Division Title in 1948. 1902–1974

JOHN D. RUSSELL (Pro Player 1964) – Acclaimed as the top defensive player of his era, "Honey" played in every major pro league in his 28-year career. He also coached the Chicago franchise. Led Seton Hall to 294 wins. As a player-coach for 20 years, Honey was chosen All-League four years in a row. He has the added distinction of being the first coach of the N.B.A. Boston Celtics (1947). 1903–1973

Three of the greatest coaches in the history of college basketball are pictured together here. They are (left to right) "Hank" Iba who compiled 14 Missouri Valley Titles, two NCAA Titles, and one Big Eight Title while at Oklahoma State and was twice named "Coach of the Year." He was selected 3 times to coach the U.S. Olympic Team and led them to victory in 1964 and 1968. John Wooden, the coach of the UCLA Bruins whose teams won ten of twelve NCAA Basketball Championships. He is the only man to be elected to the Basketball Hall of Fame as both a player and a coach. Adolph Rupp who has recorded more victories than any other college coach. While at the University of Kentucky his teams won 24 Southeast Conference Titles, four NCAA Titles and one NIT Title. He has been voted "Coach of the Year" four times and is Chairman of the Honors Committee and a Lifetime Trustee of the Hall of Fame.

1965

WALTER A. BROWN (Contributor 1965) — 1926 began serving an apprenticeship to his father, the General Manager of the Boston Arena. He succeeded his father in 1937 and became President of the Boston Garden Arena Corporation. During his 27-year reign, he made Boston the sports center of New England. He founded the National Basketball Association in 1946 and organized the Boston Celtics. 1905 – 1964

PAUL D. HINKLE (Contributor 1965) — At the University of Chicago, "Tony" was All-Conference two years, captain two years and All-American in 1920. At Butler University, he began by coaching three sports, and then became Athletic Director and eventually Dean of Indiana coaches. He led the Butler basketball team to over 500 wins in 39 seasons and a National Title in 1929. In 1942, his Great Lakes team won the National Service Title. 1899 –

HOWARD A. HOBSON (Coach 1965) — In his three-sport coaching career, "Hobby" accumulated 725 wins in 1,100 games. His 28 years as a coach began at Southern Oregon University, followed by the University of Oregon and Yale. Having conducted several basketball clinics in the U.S. and abroad, he served on the U.S. Olympic Committee (Basketball) for 12 years. 1903 –

WILLIAM G. MOKRAY (Contributor 1965) — Publicity man for the University of Rhode Island for 13 years. Then scout and Promotion Director for the Boston Celtics. Basketball Director of the Boston Garden for 21 years. Since 1946, he compiled statistics for Converse Yearbook and wrote about the game's history for the Encyclopaedia Britannica (1957), founded the N.B.A. Guide (1959) and edited the award-winning Basketball Encyclopedia (1963). 1907 – 1974

1966

EVERETT S. DEAN (Coach 1966) — As a senior at Indiana University, he was voted All-Conference and All-American. Later he returned to coach at Indiana and led his teams to 163 wins in 15 years. In 1938, he joined Stanford University and four years later they won the NCAA Crown. Everett coached for 34 years. 1898 –

JOE LAPCHICK (Pro Player 1966) — He played pro ball from 1917 – 1936 during which time he was considered to be the best center in the game. Another of the great Original Celtics. Recognized as one of America's great coaches in 20 years at St. John's University and 9 seasons with the N.B.A.'s New York Knickerbockers. 1900 – 1970

1967

CLAIR F. BEE (Contributor 1967) — A successful college and pro coach for 29 years. Clair originated basketball's three-second rule and the one-three-one zone defense and he assisted in the development of the N.B.A.'s 24-second rule. Author of a number of technical books on basketball. 1900 –

HOWARD G. CANN (Coach 1967) — Talented as a player in three sports. He coached basketball at N.Y.U. from 1922 – 1958 compiling a 409 – 232 record. 1895 –

AMORY T. GILL (Coach 1967) — He led Oregon State to 599 victories in 36 years, including 5 Pacific Coast Titles and 8 Far West Classic Titles. 1901 – 1966

ALVIN F. JULIAN (Coach 1967) — "Doggie" led Albright, Muhlenberg, Holy Cross, Dartmouth and the Boston Celtics to 381 wins collectively. His 1947 Holy Cross team won the NCAA Championship 1901 – 1967

The famed Honors Court of the Naismith Memorial Basketball Hall of Fame. It is here that the greats of the game are enshrined on stained glass panels that extend from the floor to the ceiling of the Honors Court.

1968

ARNOLD J. AUERBACH (Coach 1968) — After three years coaching at the high school level, he joined the newly-formed N.B.A. in 1946 and led the Washington Caps and Tri-Cities to 143 wins collectively. In 1950, "Red" took over the Boston Celtics and led them to 9 Division Championships and 8 consecutive World Titles. Only Pro coach to win more than 1,000 games. Named Coach of the N.B.A. Silver Anniversary Team. 1917 –

HENRY G. DEHNERT (Player 1968) — Member of the immortal Original Celtics. He originated the pivot play. With 1,900 wins behind him as a player, "Dutch" became a successful coach leading Detroit to two World Titles and Sheboygan to two Western Titles. 1898 –

HENRY P. IBA (Coach 1968) — After an incredible high school coaching record and one year at the University of Colorado, "Hank" became coach at Oklahoma State University in 1934. His teams won a total of 800 games,

63

highlighted by 14 Missouri Valley Titles, two NCAA Titles resulting in 'Coach of the Year' Awards and the 1965 Big Eight Championship. Twice led the U.S. Olympic team to victory—1964 & 1968. 1904 –

ADOLPH F. RUPP (Coach 1968) – The winningest college coach with 800 victories, including 24 Southeast Conference Titles, 4 NCAA Titles and an N.I.T. Title in 1946—all at the University of Kentucky. He trained 24 All-Americans, 7 Olympic team players and 26 professional players. 1901 –

CHARLES H. TAYLOR (Contributor 1968) – All-State twice in basketball in high school. Played 11 years of professional basketball. His successful pro career was marked by such diverse achievements as creating the first basketball clinic (1922), producing the first Converse Yearbook of Basketball (1922), designing the basketball shoe named after him (1931), and coaching the World War II Air Force Team. 1901 – 1969

1969

BERNARD L. CARNEVALE (Coach 1969) – His coaching career began with Cranford High School, whose team accumulated 51 wins in two years. In 1946, he began coaching the U.S. Naval Academy team, leading them to 257 victories in 20 years, in addition to two Southern Conference Titles and the 1946 Eastern NCAA Title. 1915 –

ROBERT E. DAVIES (Player 1969) – Enjoyed a brilliant college career at Seton Hall where he was captain for two years, Most Valuable Player for three years and All-American for two years, leading his team to 43 straight wins. Tremendous 10-year pro career with the Rochester Royals during which he was voted All-League for 7 years and was credited with leading the Royals to 3 World Titles. Leading assist man for 6 years, he originated the behind-the-back dribble. 1920 –

1970

ROBERT J. COUSY (Player 1970) – In 1946 selected All-New York City in high school basketball. At Holy Cross College as Team Captain he was Most Valuable Player and All-American for 2 years. As a Pro with the Boston

Celtics, he was instrumental in their winning 5 consecutive N.B.A. Titles (1959–1963). "Mr. Basketball" earned the reputation as one of basketball's most spectacular players starring in 13 All-Star games, making All-N.B.A. first team for 10 years and setting many records. 1928–

ROBERT L. PETTIT (Player 1970)—Voted All-State and All-American as a high school player in 1950. At Louisiana State University he was All-Southeastern Conference and Most Valuable Player for three years, All-American for two years and Consensus All-American in 1954. As a pro with the St. Louis team for 11 years, Bob was named All-League every year which included the honors of 'Rookie of the Year' in 1955 and 'M.V.P.' in 1956 and 1959. 1932–

ABRAHAM M. SAPERSTEIN (Contributor 1970)—"Abe" founded the famed touring comedy team called the Harlem Globetrotters. During his forty years with the team, the Globetrotters were internationally acclaimed, having performed before 55 million fans in 87 countries. With his coaching the team won the 1940 World Pro Title and the International Cup in 1943 and 1944, in addition to starring in two full-length motion pictures. 1902–1966

1971

EDGAR A. DIDDLE (Coach 1971)—As basketball coach at Western Kentucky University for 42 years, Ed was the first collegiate coach to guide the same team in 1,000 games. With his innovative direction, Ed's teams won or shared the Conference Title 32 times and participated in three NCAA and eight N.I.T. Tournaments. 1895–1970

ROBERT L. DOUGLAS (Contributor 1971)—Bob assembled the best black players who excelled in performance and organized the Renaissance Five. Largely a road club, the Rens won 2,318 games in 22 years. In 1933, the team won 88 consecutive games and 128 in 1934. The Rens also under Bob won the 1939 World Pro Title. 1884–

PAUL ENDACOTT (Player 1971)—Enjoyed a storied career at the University of Kansas where he was an All-Conference selection in 1921, 1922 and 1923. He led the Jayhawks to the mythical National Title in 1923, the first team ever to go undefeated in conference games. Voted National Player of the Year in 1923. In 1951, he was named to the National All-Time College Team. 1902–

MAX FRIEDMAN (Player 1971)—Acknowledged as one of the great defensive stars of his time, he played with every professional league in the East. He concluded a spectacular career with the Cleveland Rosenblums as captain and coach. Though only 5'8", "Marty" was instrumental in many team championships. 1889–

EDWARD GOTTLIEB (Contributor 1971)—He organized a South Philadelphia Hebrew Association team in 1918. Playing from 75-80 games a year, the SPHAS peaked in the 1925–26 season, defeating the Original Celtics and the Rens in a special series. The SPHAS went on to eleven championships—dominating the Eastern and American Leagues. Then "Gotty" used his organizational skills to help in establishing the B.A.A. in 1946, which later became the N.B.A. and his Philadelphia Warriors team went on to win the first B.A.A. Title in 1946. 1898–

W.R. CLIFFORD WELLS (Contributor 1971)—Coached high school basketball in Indiana for 29 years, totaling 617 victories including more than 50 Tournament Titles. From 1934 to 1964 he directed the Indiana Coaching School, in addition to conducting more than 100 clinics worldwide. Basketball coach at Tulane University for 18 years, 1945–1963. Cliff has written more than 50 articles about basketball. Member of the Rules Committee from

1952–1956. He held every office in the N.A.B.C. and was also at one time Director of the Basketball Hall of Fame. 1896–

1972

JOHN BECKMAN (Player 1972)—Had a remarkable 27-year career as a pro player. He left his greatest mark on basketball history as captain of the Celtics in 1922. Known as "The Babe Ruth of Basketball", he was credited with leading his team to its greatest pro heights and for being the main reason for the election of the Celtics as a team to the Hall of Fame. Perhaps basketball's greatest box office attraction in the 20 s and 30 s. 1895–1968

BRUCE DRAKE (Coach 1972)—Basketball coach at the University of Oklahoma for 17 years, during which time his clubs won 200 games including 6 Big Six and Big Seven Titles. He created the 'Drake Shuffle' offense and actively supported legislation concerning goaltending. Chairman of the National Rules Committee for four years, N.A.B.C. President in 1951 and coached three All-American and five Olympic teams. 1905–

ARTHUR C. LONBORG (Coach 1972)—"Dutch" as a college coach, led his teams to 323 wins from 1922–1950; McPherson College (23), Washburn University (63), Northwestern (237). His 1925 Washburn team won the National A.A.U. Title, marking the last time a college team did so. N.A.B.C. President in 1935. 1899–

ELMER H. RIPLEY (Contributor 1972)—During his 17-year professional career, Elmer was considered 'one of the ten best pros' while playing with several championship teams, including the Original Celtics in 1923. He enjoyed a successful 26-year coaching career at schools such as Columbia, Yale, Notre Dame, Georgetown and West Point, totaling 298 wins in the process. Coached the Harlem Globetrotters for 3 years, prepared the Israel Olympic team in 1956 and the Canadian Olympic team in 1960. 1891–

ADOLPH SCHAYES (Player 1972)—At New York University he was All-Metropolitan for three years and All-American once. He had a brilliant 15-year pro career with the N.B.A.'s Syracuse Nationals. An N.B.A. All-Star twelve times, he was named to the N.B.A. Silver Anniversary Team. As a coach he was named N.B.A. Coach of the year in 1966 when his Philadelphia team won the N.B.A. Title. 1928–

1973

HARRY A. FISHER (Contributor 1973)—Team leader and scoring star at Columbia University from 1902–1905, during which that school won two titles and enjoyed two undefeated seasons. In 1905, he was appointed to the original committee which rewrote the collegiate basketball rules. Columbia hired him as its first full-time basketball coach in 1906, where he led his teams to a remarkable 101–39 record and three titles. 1882–1967

MAURICE PODOLOFF (Contributor 1973)—With his legal and administrative background (undergraduate and law degree at Yale), he was asked to assume the leadership of the Basketball Association of America in 1946. Through his diplomacy and personal integrity, he led the growing B.A.A. into a merger to form the National Basketball Association in 1949. He guided the N.B.A. through its early uncertain years and secured the first TV contract in 1954, which led to national recognition for the N.B.A. 1890–

ERNEST J. SCHMIDT (Player 1973)—Led his Winfield, Kansas High School team to three state championships and was thus named All-State three times. At Kansas State College, he continued a championship parade by leading his team to 47 straight wins and four Conference Titles from 1930–1933. All-Conference selection for four years and scoring leader for three years. All-American in 1932. 1911–

1974

JOSEPH R. BRENNAN (Player 1974) — "Poison Joe" went directly from high school to a brilliant 17-year professional career. He joined the famous Brooklyn Visitations in 1919 and led them to basketball prominence. As the League scoring leader, Brennan led the Visitation Triangles to the "Met" League Championship and the unofficial World's Championship in 1931. 1900 –

EMIL S. LISTON (Contributor 1974) — His distinguished coaching career began while an undergraduate at Baker University when he led Baldwin High School to the Kansas State Title in 1912. After coaching success at Fort Scott, Kansas, Kemper Military, Michigan College and Wesleyan College Emil returned to Baker University where he stayed as head coach for 25 years. Organized the Kansas Coaches Association. He originated the idea of a National Small College Tournament and organized the NAIB in 1937. Then 8 teams the NAIB has grown to become today's 500 member NAIA. 1890 – 1949

WILLIAM F. RUSSELL (Player 1974) — "Big Bill" was College-Player-of-the-Year in 1956 leading the University of San Francisco to 55 straight victories. He was a key to the U.S. win in the 1956 Olympic Games. Russell joined the N.B.A. Boston Celtics in 1956 and revolutionized the game with defensive wizardry and an outstanding team concept that brought the Celtics 8 straight N.B.A. Titles and a total of 11 in 13 seasons. All-Star 11 times, M.V.P. 5 times and as player-coach later with Boston led his club to titles in 1968 and 1969. Voted to the N.B.A. Silver Anniversary Team. 1934 –

ROBERT P. VANDIVIER (Player 1974) — One of the greatest players in the history of Indiana basketball. Led his high school team to three State Championships and was thus named All-State three times. From 1922 – 1926 at Franklin College, his team had its greatest success and in 1925 he was named All-Midwest. 1903 –

1975

THOMAS J. GOLA (Player 1975) — Scored 2,461 for LaSalle University in Philadelphia as one of the state's All-Time great stars in history. The second four-year College All-American ever, Tom was recognized as one of basketball's most versatile players. Enjoyed an outstanding 10-year N.B.A. career. All-N.B.A. in 1958. 1933 –

The 1975 electees to the Basketball Hall of Fame gather in the Honors Court on Enshrinement Day. (Pictured left to right) Harry Litwack, former coach at Temple University, Bill Sharman, Boston Celtic great, Edward "Moose" Krause, a three-time All-American at Notre Dame in the 1930's and the first of the agile rebounding pivot men, and Tom Gola, a four-time All-American at LaSalle in the 1950's who went on to star in the NBA.

EDWARD W. KRAUSE (Player 1975) — All-City three sport star in high school. All-American for three years in basketball at Notre Dame University. "Moose" was considered the first agile, rebounding pivot man. He established all-time college scoring records for one game, one season and three seasons. Widely acclaimed star on Midwest and New England Pro teams. Coached basketball at Notre Dame from 1946–1951 and became Athletic Director at that school in 1949, a position he still holds. 1913–

HARRY LITWACK (Coach 1975) — High school All-Star for two years, team captain at Temple University for two years and for 7 years with the Pro Philadelphia Sphas in the Eastern and American Leagues. Amassed a record of 181–32 as Frosh coach at Temple before taking over the varsity club and establishing an incredible record of 373 wins and 13 post-season tournaments in 21 years. It is written that Harry did more with less than any coach in basketball history. 1907–

WILLIAM W. SHARMAN (Player 1975) — Scoring star and captain three years in high school. At the University of Southern California, Bill was M.V.P. in the Conference two years as well as All-American two years. Great 11-year pro career. All-N.B.A. with Celtics for 7 years. Considered one of the greatest shooting guards ever, was selected to the N.B.A. Silver Anniversary Team in 1971. After retiring as a player, Bill became an outstanding pro coach, winning titles in the ABL, A.B.A. and the N.B.A. 1926–

1976 ENSHRINEES

ELGIN BAYLOR, (Player 1976) — A high school All American 1954 and college All American at Seattle 1958. For ten consecutive years he was first team NBA All Star 1959–1970. He was NBA All Star and NBA rookie of the year 1959. Also, NBA All Star MVP in 1959. Selected on NBA 25th Anniversary All Star team 1972.

CHARLES T. COOPER, (Player 1976) — Brilliant center for the New York Wrens, 1929–1940. Led his team to 303 victories including 88 straight 1932–33. Member of the "World's Pro Championship team" in 1939. Captain of the Washington Bears when they won the "World's Pro Championship" in 1943. He was called the greatest basketball center of his era.

LAUREN "LADDIE" GALE, (Player 1976) — High school All State 1935. Pacific coast first team all conference 1938–39. Leading scorer Pacific coast northern division 1938, 1939. All American 1939. The 6'5" star forward led the University of Oregon to the first NCAA championship 1939. One of the greatest, from the Pacific northwest. Elected to the Oregon Sports Hall of Fame 1964.

WILLIAM C. JOHNSON, (Player 1976) — All City, All State, All American Central High School, Oklahoma City, 1929. All Big Six Conference 1932–1933, Conference MVP and All American in 1933 at University of Kansas. Second Team AAU. All American 1934. Selected as all-time great in Oklahoma 1975.

FRANK J. McGUIRE, (Coach 1976) — He is the only coach to win over 100 games at 3 major colleges, St Johns, North Carolina and South Carolina. The only coach to have two colleges in the NCAA final, St. Johns, 1952, North Carolina, 1957 when they won the NCAA Championship undefeated 32–0. He led teams to 8 NCAA and 5 NIT tournaments. Won 49 and lost 31 with Philadelphia Warriors in 1962. He was selected Coach of the Year 1952, 1957, 1970.

AMERICAN BOWLING CONGRESS HALL OF FAME

Greendale, Wisconsin

By Ray Nelson

Memories, sweet memories. The great years, the great moments. Memories and great moments unfold each year into one special evening in bowlers' lives. Certainly all members of the American Bowling Congress Hall of Fame can attest to that, the special night they were inducted into the Hall. And the special nights when their friends and peers were inducted can't help but bring what has been back into presence of mind.

Fortunately, not only Hall members enjoy their special nights. The thousands of bowlers and spectators who have attended the Hall of Fame ceremonies at the ABC tournament installation can sit back and recollect the memories of what they might have witnessed, or perhaps even been a part.

For many years, those great nights were limited to memories. Now the Hall is more than memories . . . it is a reality.

One highlight of the July, 1973 dedication ceremonies at Bowling Headquarters in Milwaukee was the formal opening of both the ABC and Women's International Bowling Congress Halls of Fame.

Now, bowling, the world's largest participation sport has a hallowed shrine honoring the elite.

You are invited now to take a word picture stroll through the Hall. As you enter through massive, intricately carved doors, there is an amazing sense of silence that seems to settle over all comers, young and old. It seems somehow an innate, sacred sense has been instilled in the surroundings.

However, that feeling does not detract from the pleasures of walking past the plaques representing the game's greats, it only enhances the stroll.

Each bronze tablet is the work of a skilled sculptor. As with all artistic interpretations there might be disagreement with a favorite's likeness.

Slyvia Wene Martin

—All photographs in this chapter, courtesy American Bowling Congress Hall of Fame

"Why, that doesn't even look like Marty Cassio. I knew him well," might be one comment. And the next day someone else might say, "Boy that looks just like the Cassio I knew."

All are tastefully done. Each contains a capsule resume of the career highlights of each member.

The latest inductees occupy a special place of honor during the first year, then are moved to join their friends and fellow stars.

Huge, glass enclosed kiosks contain medals, trophies, action pictures, newspaper clippings and other memorabilia associated with Hall members.

The American Bowling Congress Hall of Fame was founded in 1941 and only baseball (1936), Helms (1936) and golf (1940) have been honoring their greats longer.

Eleven men entered the Hall in the first induction ceremonies held in 1941. Now the list has grown to 77.

A national vote is conducted annually, with 75 per cent of the ballots cast by veteran writers, broadcasters, Hall members and ABC officials necessary for election.

Besides the annual induction ceremonies, held on ABC tournament lanes, Hall of Famers are remembered too with a traveling display put on view each year at the tournament building.

At the ceremonies Hall members are garbed in dark blue blazers on which the Hall crest is worn.

Judy Soutar

Beverly Ortner

Mildred White

Doris Coburn

WIBC HALL OF FAME
Stars of Yesteryear

Olga Gloor

Merle Matthews

PHILENA BOHLEN (Los Angeles, California) — Member of WIBC Board of Directors for eight years, four as fifth vice president. Instrumental in organizing Los Angeles and California WBAs. Best known as originator and designer of the WIBC flag. In 1930, took her team on cross-country exhibition, bowling 37 matches in 49 days against best women's teams in 16 states. (Inducted 1955)

CATHERINE BURLING (Cincinnati, Ohio) — Won 1934 WIBC team championship. Earned 11 state all events crowns, many singles titles, 16 city all events championships. Averaged above 190 for over 10 years from 1936 to 1946, highest 198. Rolled five 700s, highest 736. Bowling instructor and active in bowling center activities. (Inducted 1958)

EMILY CHAPMAN (Long Island, New York) — Won 1926 WIBC team championship, many local awards and titles. Organized leagues and instructed in New York City, Chicago and Poughkeepsie from 1917 until 1950s. Helped organize New York State WBA, served on its board. At age 71, she and partner won city doubles title. (Inducted 1957)

CATHERINE FELLMETH (Lake Geneva, Wisconsin) — Won 1942 WIBC team title, 1946 all events championship. Member of teams that dominated women's state, local and league events in 1940s. In 1946, became first woman named by Brunswick Corp. to its staff of champions, spent next eight years touring U.S. and Canada giving exhibitions and instructing bowlers. (Inducted 1970)

DEANE FRITZ (Toledo, Ohio) — Won WIBC team championships in 1919 and 1923, all events title in 1923. Earned 21 local and state association championship medals. Held three-game record (678) for Toledo women for years. Served on Toledo WBA board. Bowled in 45 WIBC Championship Tournaments through 1969. (Inducted 1966)

OLGA GLOOR (Vista, California) — In 1959 she won the prestigious World's Invitational tournament. That same year she helped organize the Professional Women's Bowling Association later winning two PWBA titles. Olga also earned seven state titles, four in Illinois and three in California, plus 10 Chicago and five Vista area local association championships. Twice she was named "Queen of Chicago Bowlers" and her Chicago WBA all events total of 1902 in 1963 is still the local record. Her career highs are a 290 game, a 717 three-game series, a 924 four-game series and a 195 season league average. More than a decade after her "retirement" Olga became a member of the U.S. team in the 6th American Zone Championships of the Federation Internationale des Quilleurs (FIQ) in Caracas, Venezuela.

There, in November, 1974 — at 54 years of age — she won the women's all events title and was a member of the winning five-woman team. She also won a spot on the U.S. team at the 8th FIQ World Bowling Championships. (Inducted 1976)

GOLDIE GREENWALD (Cleveland, Ohio) — Member of WIBC Board of Directors from 1921 to 1924, including one year as first vice president. Bowled in men's league in 1918 and averaged 191, rolled 732 series that year, then women's high. Bowled in many exhibitions and matches with men and rolled 300 game in exhibition in 1920. Had won more than 50 medals at time of her death in 1926 at age of 35. (Inducted 1953)

GRAYCE HATCH (Cleveland, Ohio) — Was member of WIBC Board of Directors for three years, including one as executive secretary. Won WIBC all events championships in 1925, 1927. Earned 90 medals during 50-year career, including 14 state, 11 area and 26 city championships. Was Cleveland WBA president, first vice president and treasurer. Toured with Star Baking team, was member of American bowling team that went to Germany during the 1936 Olympic Games. Member of local hall of fame. (Inducted 1953)

STELLA HARTRICK (Detroit, Michigan) — Won 1942 WIBC doubles championship. Earned special award for high series 620, of 1941 WIBC Championship Tournament. Member of seven state championship teams, won two state singles and two all events titles and many local championships. Member of local hall of fame. At age of 74 bowled 578 three-game series. (Inducted 1972)

MADALENE HOCHSTADTER (Chicago, Illinois) — Captained team that won 1927 WIBC championship. Managed several major Chicago-area tournaments originated by husband. Was treasurer of the Illinois WBA and director of the Windy City WBA. Bowled in 46 WIBC Championship Tournaments, including 38 consecutive years from 1930 until her death in 1970. (Inducted 1967)

EMMA JAEGER (Toledo, Ohio)—Won nine WIBC championships, all events in 1918, 1921, 1928, 1929; team in 1919, 1923; singles in 1921, 1922, 1923. In 35-year span also won nine state, 37 local and three other tournament championships, amassing 125 trophies and medals. At age of 73 still bowled in two leagues, averaging 140–150. (Inducted 1953)

MERLE MATTHEWS (Huntington Beach, California)—A three-time WIBC champion, first gained national attention when she won the 1948 doubles title. She captained the powerhouse Linbrook Bowl team of Los Angeles that won back-to-back team titles in 1962 and '63, only the second team to do so, Linbrook's 1962 score of 3061 still is the WIBC tournament record. In 1958 Miss Matthews staged a down to the wire duel with perennial winner Marion Ladewig to capture the BPAA All-Star Tournament (now the U.S. Women's Open).

Miss Matthews has won eight California WBA titles and 18 Los Angeles WBA crowns. She claimed the California all events title in 1951, doubles in 1954, singles and all events in 1958 and was a member of four state champion teams. Her 18 Los Angeles titles include three all events, three singles, one doubles, and 11 team championships.

Miss Matthews helped organize both the PWBA, of which she was the second president, and the Western Women Bowlers, a tournament association for high-average performers. She has recorded eight 700-plus series, topped by a 745, and a four-game 926. Her best single game and average are 290 and 191, respectively. (Inducted 1974)

FLORETTA McCUTCHEON (Pasadena, California)—Most widely known woman bowler of pre-1940s because of bowling tours, exhibitions and instruction clinics throughout the U.S. During 10 years of exhibition bowling, averaged 201-plus, had 10 perfect games, bowled more than 100 700-plus three-game series, five 800-plus series. Taught estimated 250,000 women and children to bowl. Averaged 206 in WIBC league in 1938–39, a record that stood until 1952–53. Wrote bowling booklets, organized leagues. Was Windy City (Ill.) WBA director. (Inducted 1956)

DOROTHY MILLER (Chicago, Illinois)—Won 10 WIBC championships—more than any other woman—team in 1928, 1931, 1933, 1935, 1940, 1948; doubles, 1929, 1934, 1940; all events, 1938. Also won 13 state titles, 20 local championships. Earned 93 first place medals in tournaments during 30-year career. Named "Quarter Century Club Bowler of the Year" in 1961. (Inducted 1954)

JOSEPHINE MRAZ (Cleveland, Ohio)—Member of WIBC Board of Directors seven years, three as director, three as treasurer and one as second vice president. Helped organize National 600 Bowling Club, was charter member of WIBC Pioneer Club. Was active in organizing women's bowling associations in Ohio and Pennsylvania for 45 years. Served as Cleveland WBA secretary for 45 years. Had 179 high average and won many bowling awards. Member of local hall of fame. (Inducted 1959)

CONNIE POWERS (Highland, Michigan)—Won WIBC doubles championship in 1939, member of 1957 and 1959 WIBC championship teams. Bowled in 35 consecutive WIBC Championship Tournaments. Had women's high average of 195 in 1946–47 season. Bowled 987 in four games across eight lanes in 1951 All-Star, record for men and women that stood 10 years. Won one team, one doubles, three all events state titles, many Detroit championships. Member of local hall of fame. (Inducted 1973)

LEONA ROBINSON (Phoenix, Arizona)—Won 1929 WIBC team championship. Earned 50 medals, pins and trophies in 35-year bowling career. Won many state and local titles in Kansas City, Mo., and California. Had highest averages in Kansas City for 15 years. Once bowled 33 consecutive error-free games in leagues and tournaments. Organized many leagues, wrote bowling columns for Kansas City newspapers during 1930s. (Inducted 1969)

ANITA RUMP (Fort Wayne, Indiana)—Won two WIBC singles championships, 1928 and 1930. Won first local title in 1926, doubles with her mother. Also earned nine state all events titles, was a member of 15 state championship teams, won five state doubles and one singles crown. Was a bowling instructor and active in AJBC organizing. Charter member of Les Dames de 700 Club. (Inducted 1962)

ADDIE RUSCHMEYER (White Plains, New York)—Began bowling in early 1900s, won first bowling trophy in 1911 and bowled for more than 60 years. Charter member of Greater New York City WBA. Traveled with Uncle Joe Thum's bowling team to Europe in 1933 and earned "women's international championship." Had highest average of 183 in 1933. Competed against men bowlers in exhibitions. (Inducted 1961)

ESTHER RYAN (Milwaukee, Wisconsin)—Won three WIBC championships, all events in 1934, team titles in 1939 and 1947. Her team won nine state and 13 local titles and its members earned 178 individual championships, 48 of them won by her. Served as Milwaukee WBA secretary for 33 years. (Inducted 1963)

MYRTLE SCHULTE (St. Louis, Missouri)—Won WIBC singles and all events championships in 1931 and team title in 1932. Her 1931 singles score of 650 and 1742 all events were records at the time. Won first city title in first season of bowling, 1924, earned many additional championships, including state doubles. Organized city's first evening league for women. Served as St. Louis WBA president and sergeant-at-arms. (Inducted 1965)

VIOLET SIMON (San Antonio, Texas) — Won 1935 WIBC doubles championship. Averaged 202 in league in 1934–35. Won two doubles, one singles and one all events titles in state tournament city singles and all events. Introduced tenpins in San Antonio, helped organize associations throughout state and area. Instrumental in organizing Texas WBA. Had 26 consecutive series over 600, including a 706 and 713. (Inducted 1960)

TESS SMALL (Wisconsin Rapids, Wisconsin) — Won WIBC all events, team and doubles championships in 1940, team title in 1942. Her 663 team contribution was best series of 1942 tournament. Won seven state team and two doubles titles in Illinois and several local championships in Chicago. Also a noted bowling instructress. (Inducted 1971)

GRACE SMITH (Albuquerque, New Mexico) — Won three WIBC team titles, including first team to win consecutive championships (1924–1925), and two doubles crowns. Was a spectator at WIBC organization meeting, November 29, 1916, then joined first women's league in Chicago in 1917. Had high average among Chicago women for five seasons, won five city team titles and one state team championship. Was Illinois WBA secretary for 18 years and local association secretary for seven years. Instructed, organized leagues and promoted junior bowling from 1925 to 1947. (Inducted 1968)

LOUISE STOCKDALE (Buena Park, California) — Won WIBC doubles championship in 1922, her first national tournament, and all events in 1937. Her all events performance included a 278 game and nine games without an error. Bowled in first Detroit women's league. Won many Detroit and Michigan championships. Named to Detroit hall of fame. (Inducted 1953)

ELVIRA TOEPFER (E. Detroit, Michigan) — She was a member of two WIBC team champions, in 1957 and 1959. Elvira finished second in the 1958 World's Invitational tournament. With teammate Anita Cantaline, she won the 1956 Women's National Doubles Championships of the Bowling Proprietors' Association of America, and the same pair were second in 1959. She also won 12 state titles, including four individual match game championships. In Detroit WBA all events Elvira earned 15 titles. She was a member of the "All-City Team" five times and was named "Queen of Detroit Bowlers" eight times. During the 1950s and '60s she traveled extensively giving exhibitions and conducting clinics. Elvira was active on the pro tour and finished fifth in a PWBA

event as recently as 1970. Her career highs are a 289, a 752 three-game series and a 205 league average. (Inducted 1976)

SALLY TWYFORD (Nashville, Indiana) — Won six WIBC championships, singles in 1933, 1940; all events in 1930, 1933, 1941; team in 1930. Bowling career spanned 36 years during which she also won 12 state and nine local titles. Was famous exhibition bowler, organized leagues, gave instructions. Starred in bowling film for Columbia Pictures in 1943. (Inducted 1964)

CECELIA WINANDY (Chicago, Illinois) — From 1928 through 1958, Cecelia won 43 championships in every tournament she could get to. Her first national title came in 1949 when she won the WIBC all events with 1840 for her nine games. In 1958, she was a member of the Allgauer Restaurant team of Chicago that took first place with 2972. She won the Chicago Women's Bowling Association tournament's singles title in 1933, the first of seven local championships she would win through 1954.

In Illinois WBA competition, Cecelia scored 13 victories between 1940 and 1955, five team, three doubles, two singles and three all events titles. She won consecutive all events championships in 1940, '41 and '42. In 1940, she had nearly a clean sweep, with team, singles and all events wins. (Inducted 1975)

MARIE WARMBIER (Chicago, Illinois) — Won seven WIBC championships, singles in 1935, doubles in 1930, all events in 1932 and 1935, team in 1928, 1931 and 1933. Her 1935 all events score of 1911 was a WIBC record that stood until 1959. Traveled 16,000 miles in 1935 and 1936 giving exhibitions, challenging top men bowlers. Had an exhibition average in the 190–200 range, rolled a 300 game and had several 700 three-game series. Had been bowling only 10 years at time of her death in 1937. (Inducted 1953)

Cecelia Winandy

Connie Powers

Meritorious Service

WINIFRED BERGER (Sonoma, California) — Began bowling in 1928, and, during the next 47 years, she eventually held every league office. For 13 consecutive years Mrs. Berger was president or treasurer of the San Francisco WBA, and she held every office in the California WBA except treasurer. As a bowler, Win — as she prefers to be called — won seven local championships and a state doubles title. Win became the first living bowler inducted in the California WBA Hall of Fame in 1965. She was elected to the San Francisco WBA Hall of Fame in 1966. Selection as a WIBC member emeritus came in 1970. (Inducted 1976)

MARGARET HIGLEY (San Jose, California) — Member of WIBC Board of Directors for 22 years, as director from 1945 to 1955, as sergeant-at-arms from 1955 to 1967. Was Omaha, Neb., WBA president, vice president and secretary and Nebraska WBA president. Was secretary-treasurer of National Women Bowling Writers Association from 1956 to 1967. WIBC member emeritus. First person named to Omaha Hall of Fame. Served as director of San Jose WBA and active in AJBC organizations. (Inducted 1969)

NORA KAY (Toledo, Ohio) — Member of WIBC Board of Directors, 1932 to 1955, including sergeant-at-arms the last 22 years. WIBC member emeritus. Served as president, vice president and director of Wisconsin WBA. Was association and league organizer in cities in New York, Wisconsin and Ohio, held local association offices in nearly every city. On runner-up team in 1923 WIBC Championship Tournament, won many state and local titles. (Inducted 1964)

JEANNETTE KNEPPRATH (Milwaukee, Wisconsin) — Was WIBC president for 36 years from 1924 to 1960, third to serve in that capacity. During tenure, membership grew from 2,885 in 29 cities to more than 1½ million in over 2,100 cities. First woman to receive BBIA "Industry Service Award" in 1961. Served one year as WIBC vice president. Wisconsin WBA secretary from 1924 to 1970. Bowled in 44 WIBC Championship Tournaments from 1919 to 1966. WIBC life member. (Inducted 1963)

IOLIA LASHER (Albany, New York) — Member of WIBC Board of Directors for 29 years, 1934 to 1963, serving as second vice president, third vice president and director. Helped organize Albany WBA and served as secretary-treasurer. President of the New York State WBA 1932 to 1958. Named to state hall of fame. WIBC member emeritus. (Inducted 1967)

BERTHA McBRIDE (St. Paul, Minnesota) — Member of the WIBC Board of Directors for 19

Jeannette Knepprath   *Bertha McBride*

years, from 1948 to 1967, including six years as third vice president. Held one or more association or league offices for 36 consecutive years. Named WIBC member emeritus. Served as president of Minnesota WBA five years, secretary 12 years. Was St. Paul WBA president five years and president of Minnesota Bowling Council one year. Named to local hall of fame. (Inducted 1968)

EMMA PHALER (Columbus, Ohio) — WIBC executive secretary for 38 years, from 1927 to 1965, the sixth to serve in that capacity. During tenure, WIBC membership grew from 5,357 members in 27 cities to nearly 2.7 million in over 2,700 local associations. Initiated WIBC Hall of Fame. Implemented construction of first headquarters building in Columbus, Ohio, 1958. Served as Columbus WBA secretary in 1926–27. WIBC life member. (Inducted 1965)

GERTRUDE RISHLING (Omaha, Nebraska) — Served on WIBC Board of Directors for 17 years, from 1954 through 1971. WIBC member emeritus. Represented WIBC on National Bowling Council for 1½ years. Made contributions on WIBC insurance matters. Was president of Omaha WBA, first vice president of Nebraska WBA, organized 600 club in Omaha and served on Omaha JBA board. Was president of every league she bowled in for 42 years. Member local hall of fame. Won several state and local titles. (Inducted 1972)

BERDIE SPECK (St. Louis, Missouri) — Member of the WIBC Board of Directors for 34 years, last 30 as first vice president. St. Louis WBA secretary for 40 years and state president for 11 years. WIBC member emeritus. Active in bowling promotion and association organizing. Bowled in 41 consecutive WIBC Championship Tournaments, attended 43 consecutive WIBC Annual Meetings. (Inducted 1966)

PEARL SWITZER (South Bend, Indiana) — Served on WIBC Board of Directors for 32 consecutive years, 1934–1966. WIBC member emeritus.

Bowled in 34 consecutive WIBC Championship Tournaments, 1933 to 1969. Was association president in Racine, Wis., one year; president of South Bend-Mishawaka WBA for 11 years and secretary 23 years; was state association president and secretary. Active in AJBC work. Member of local, state halls of fame. (Inducted 1973)

GEORGIA E. VEATCH (Morton Grove, Illinois) — WIBC first vice president since 1962, she retired after 26 years on the board. During that time she chaired several committees, including the WIBC building committee that helped plan the new Bowling Headquarters in Milwaukee, Wis.

A journalist, Miss Veatch has been a prolific writer on bowling. She edited *The Woman Bowler* magazine, WIBC's official publication, from 1947 to 1959. From 1947 to 1963 she edited *Prep Pin Patter*, then the official publication of the American Junior Bowling Congress. She originated and edited the *Windy City Rangefinder*, official publication of the Windy City Women's Bowling Association. She is a charter member of the National Women Bowling Writers Association. A former Chicago school teacher, Miss Veatch also holds a degree in physical education and a master's in psychology and education.

Miss Veatch is a former Windy City WBA president of 26 years and was president or secretary of the Chicago Bowling Council for 20 years. She originated the Professional Women Bowlers Association in 1959 and was PWBA executive director for nine years. (Inducted 1974)

MILDRED WHITE (Rockford, Illinois) — Mrs. Mildred White is the personification of the phrase "service to the game." She was a member of the WIBC Board of Directors from 1944 through 1972, having been appointed a director in 1944 and being elected to that position two years later. In 1948, she was elected fifth vice president, and in 1960, she was elected second vice president, an office she held until her retirement in July, 1972. She was named a WIBC member emeritus in 1972.

During her board service, Mrs. White was a member of every committee except finance and budget, including the legislative committee for 18 years. She was chairman of three committees over the years. Mrs. White has been chairman of the Illinois Junior Bowling Association for 28 years, organized the Rockford JBA and was its first president. (Inducted 1975)

ANN WOOD (Cincinnati, Ohio) — Member of WIBC Board of Directors for 23 years, from 1945 to 1968, including fourth vice president, 1950–1968. Developed format for WIBC Queens Tournament and served as its manager through 1968. Served Ohio WBA from 1943 through 1960s, including second vice president. Member of Cincinnati WBA board since 1930, including secretary from 1938 to present. WIBC member emeritus. (Inducted 1970)

Superior Performance

DORIS COBURN (Buffalo, New York) — She turned professional in 1963. In 1975 she won the richest women's tournament. In 1974 she bowled the second-highest three-game ever by a woman (813). She captained the teams that won the 1970 and '72 WIBC championships, with the 1970 winning total, 3034, ranking as second best ever in WIBC tournament annals. Doris has competed in 60 consecutive PWBA tournaments, finishing in the top 10 in 41 of them and winning three pro titles. (Inducted 1976)

HELEN DUVAL (Berkeley, California) — Won 1969 WIBC team and all events championships, latter with 1927 for nine games. Has won many state and local association tournaments. Had 210 league average in 1970–71. Noted bowling instructress, clinician. Served as director and second vice president of California WBA, director of Alameda County WBA. Active in AJBC organizations. (Inducted 1970)

SHIRLEY GARMS (Island Lake, Illinois) — Captained WIBC championship teams in 1955 and 1965, won doubles title in 1964. Was runner-up in 1964 Queens Tournament. Won BPAA All-Star Tournament in 1962. "Woman Bowler of Year" in 1961 and 1962. Named "Queen of Chicago Bowlers" five times, "Bowler of the Decade" in Chicago in 1970. Has more than 70 state, area and local tournament wins. (Inducted 1971)

JOAN HOLM (Chicago, Illinois) — At 41 the hall's second youngest inductee, became the first Chicago woman to average over 200 when she finished the 1965–66 league season with 207 to lead the nation's women. She also recorded her 300 game that season. Miss Holm was a member of the team that won the 1966 WIBC title, the Gossard Girls, and also of teams that won the BPAA tournament in 1960, '61 and '66.

She captained the U.S. women to two team titles in the 1971 World Bowling Championships of the Federation Internationale des Quilleurs (FIQ) in Milwaukee and also bowled for the U.S. team in the FIQ American Zone Tournament in Bogota, Colombia.

She has scored nine three-game series of 700-plus, the highest 734. Her best four-gamer, 992, set a women's record in 1960–61 and currently is tied for

Shirley Garms   *Joan Holm*

Marion Ladewig

Mildred Martorella

fourth. Miss Holm has won 10 Illinois WBA titles and eight Chicago WBA crowns. Her 1920 all events total in the 1964 state tournament still is the Illinois record. (Inducted 1974)

MARION LADEWIG (Grand Rapids, Michigan) —Won two WIBC all events championships (1950 and 1955), one team title (1950) and one doubles crown (1955). Named "Woman Bowler of the Year" nine times. Won eight BPAA All-Stars and four World's Invitational including both in 1963. Runner-up in 1962 WIBC Queens Tournament. Had league average of 204 in 1952–53. Named Michigan's "Woman Athlete of All Time" and member of Michigan's Athletic Hall of Fame, only bowler and first woman. Only woman in Grand Rapids Sports Hall of Fame. (Inducted 1964)

SYLVIA WENE MARTIN (Philadelphia, Pennsylvania) —Won WIBC doubles championship in 1959. Only woman to bowl three 300 games, two in tournaments. Won BPAA All-Star in 1955 and 1960. "Woman Bowler of the Year" in 1955 and 1960. Named Philadelphia's "Outstanding Athlete" in 1963 and Pennsylvania's "Sportswoman of the Year" in 1961. Had 206 league averages in 1952–53 and 1953–54. Won many state and local championships. (Inducted 1966)

MILDRED MARTORELLA (Rochester, New York) —Had a lot to celebrate as she observed her 28th birthday on January 11. In less than 10 years, her bowling career had progressed from her first junior championship to national Hall of Fame status, the youngest woman ever to be selected. That distinction previously belonged to Beverly Ortner of Tucson, Arix., who was 33 when named to the WIBC Hall of Fame in 1972.

Millie's almost endless list of bowling accomplishments in little less than a decade made her a natural for eventual enshrinement in WIBC's honor group. No doubt her selection was accelerated by physical problems that have kept her from competitive bowling for nearly two years and make her re-

turn to league and tournament play a question mark. Her patented hook ball resulted in a 148 average in her first league competition in 1962 at the age of 15, a mixed American Junior Bowling Congress league. At 16, she was up to a 174 average to lead the Northpark, Junior Girls League. The following year she was averaging 182 and won the New York State Junior Girls Championship.

She stepped into the adult bowling world at the age of 18, joining a WIBC league during the 1964–65 season, where she averaged 193, and joining the Professional Women Bowlers Association. During 1965–66—her first full season as an adult bowler—Millie maintained a 203 average in the North Parkettes Singles Classic League, destined to be the spot of her WIBC record averages.

WIBC's grueling Queens Tournament soon took on the look of a "Millie benefit" as the young lefthander earned victories in the 1970 and 1971 events and finished second in 1969. She holds the event's high average record (216 for 28 games in 1970), is tied for second in that category (215 in 1967, with Maureen Harris of Madison, Wis.), and is the leading Queens money winner ($9,275). She was the first to win more than one Queens title and the first to record back-to-back victories. Along the way, Millie also won five other WIBC titles—team in 1970 and 1972, doubles in 1971 and 1973 and all events in 1972. (Inducted 1975)

BEVERLY ORTNER (Tucson, Arizona)—Bowled first WIBC sanctioned 800 three-game series by a woman, 267–264–287/818 and first four-game series over 1000 mark, 1005. Averaged 206 during 1967–68, 205 in two leagues during 1968–69. Has 300 game and 22 other three-game series above 700 mark. Member of 1969 WIBC team champions. Won many state and local titles in Sioux City and Iowa. Member of state hall of fame. (Inducted 1972)

JUDY SOUTAR (Kansas City, Missouri)—At 31, Mrs. Soutar is the second youngest ever named to the WIBC Hall of Fame. Judy first learned to bowl when she was four years old, and she went on to become a teenage wonder. She launched her pro career at 16, and, when only 18, she finished second in the 1962 World's Invitational. Months later she won her first national title. In 1963 Judy was recipient of the Alberta E. Crowe Star of Tomorrow Award. After finishing second 13 times during the next nine years, Judy finally won her first PWBA title in 1972. She added two more pro wins and was named in 1973 "Woman Bowler of the Year," an honor she repeated in 1975. Judy teamed with Gloria Bouvia to win the 1969 and 1970 WIBC doubles titles, the 1969 victory coming on a record 1315 total. She won three WIBC titles in 1974—all events, team and Queens Tournament. (Inducted 1976)

ABC HALL OF FAME

Buddy Bomar   *Ray Bluth*

FRANK BENKOVIC (Milwaukee, Wisconsin)—He was the first to win successive doubles championships in the ABC tournament. His 2259 pins in the Gold Coast tournament in Chicago in 1932 is the nine game tournament all events record.

In team match between Heils and Hermann Undertakers in 1938, Benkovic averaged 232 for 18 games, the best three-game series being 812 on games of 245–278–289. During World War II, Benkovic traveled tens of thousands of miles giving bowling exhibitions in more than 250 camps.

JAMES BLOUIN (Blue Island, Illinois)—He made his mark on the lanes, in the days when match game challenge matches were the determining factor for the stamp of greatness. Blouin was possessed of steely nerves and a strong, slow curve ball he seemed to push rather than roll. For many years he took on all comers both in the Chicago area and around the nation.

RAYMOND ALBERT BLUTH (St. Louis, Missouri)—Rolled the first 300 game in ABC Masters finals play in 1962. His 806 for the first three games of that set is a Masters record.

Bluth was a member of the St. Louis Budweiser team formed in 1954. He rolled 267, 267, 300 in the Buds' record three game 3858 total. He had bowled with the Jockey Coopers in Chicago and earlier had been a member of the Ziern Antiques of St. Louis, the great young club whose lineup included Don Carter, Pat Patterson and Tom Hennessey.

JOSEPH BODIS (Cleveland, Ohio)—He was the first man to head the ABC tournament 10-year average listings, starting with a 205–20 figure in 1934. The following year he upped that to 205–76, a record that stood for 11 tournaments until another Hall of Famer, Junie McMahon, registered 206–69.

HERBERT BOOTH BOMAR (Chicago, Illinois)—Has been one of bowling's most articulate and prominent instructors. For a number of years while on the Brunswick promotion staff he conducted clinics around the nation on the latest teaching methods. Since becoming a securities salesman he has retired from professional and league bowling.

ALBERT R. BRANDT (Lockport, New York)—Gained his greatest fame on Oct. 25, 1939 when he rolled the alltime record ABC sanctioned league series of 886. This came on games of 297, 289 and 300 in a Lockport league. Although best known for the 886, Brandt has proven an outstanding bowler over the years. In the 1946–47 All-Star tournament, he battled Andy Varipapa to the wire only to lose the title in the final of the 100 games.

FRED BUJACK (Detroit, Michigan)—Won more ABC championships (8) than any other bowler until fellow Hall of Famer Bill Lillard tied his mark. He and three other deceased Hall of Fame members, Therm Gibson, Lou Sielaff and George Young, were the nucleus of the great E & B team formed in 1944. It won three ABC tournament Regular team titles and four team all events titles (two of each as Pfeiffer Beer) between 1949 and 1955, constantly battling the great Stroh's teams for the supremacy of Detroit and the nation.

WILLIAM BUNETTA (Fresno, California)—In addition to topflight individual performances for two decades, gained great respect as one of the game's finest instructors. Many young professionals came to Bunetta for advice in the early stages of their career.

NELSON BURTON, SR. (St. Louis, Missouri)—Spent most of his early years in Dallas, moving to St. Louis in 1938. In addition to his brilliant ABC tournament career, he was considered one of the top head and head match game stars in the 1930s and 1940s. A fearless competitor, Burton was particularly noted for risking his own money in these matches instead of depending on sponsors.

Bill Bunetta

LOUIS CAMPI (Dumont, New Jersey)—Won the first PBA tournament, the Empire open in Albany, New York in 1959. He and fellow Hall of Famer Lindy Faragalli were stars of the fabled Faber Cement Block team that was the highest scoring team in the East in the 1950s and early 60s.

ADOLPH DOMIANUS CARLSON (Chicago, Illinois)—In 1928 he defeated Charley Daw for the match game championship, defended successfully against Walter (Skang) Mercurio of Cleveland and then lost in 1929 to Joe Scribner of Detroit. Carlson at age 61 led the Chicago Masters Traveling league with a 201 average in 1957–58.

DONALD JAMES CARTER (Miami, Florida)—The first star to score a "grand slam" of bowling's match game titles. He won the All-Star, World's Invitational, PBA National championship and the 1961 ABC Masters.

Carter started as a youth with the veteran Hermann Undertakers of St. Louis, then he went to the Ziern Antiques whose lineup included Ray Bluth, Pat Patterson and Tom Hennessey. After two years with the Pfeiffers of Detroit, he returned to St. Louis when the Budweiser team was reorganized in 1954. He bowled 266, 253, 235 in Buds' record 3858 series in 1958. In 1970, Carter was voted the greatest bowler in history in a poll of veteran writers by Bowling magazine.

MARTIN CASSIO (Rahway, New Jersey)—One of the first to bowl a 300 game in national match game play, at a time when that type of competition did not qualify for ABC sanction. He did it against the Stroh's of Detroit in 1944. He finished fifth in the first All-Star tournament in 1941 and in 1946 led the ABC tournament 10-year averages with 203. That same year he starred in AMF's first bowling film, Ten Pin Magic.

JOHN CRIMMINS (Detroit, Michigan)—In the 1937 National Elks tournament he shared in all four

titles—team, doubles, singles, all events— with a 2156 count in all events that still is the record. In 1957 at the age of 62, Crimmins briefly led the ABC singles with 705. He won the first All-Star in 1941.

CHARLEY DAW (Milwaukee, Wisconsin)—Had a rocking chair motion, dropping the ball into his backswing without pushing it away from his chest as he went into his delivery. He was the first to roll two 700 series in ABC tournaments. In 1936 was on team that bowled special matches during Olympics.

EDWARD P. DAY (Milwaukee, Wisconsin)—Made his name as a member of the champion Heil Products team in Milwaukee, then bowled more than a decade with top Chicago teams. One of his last associations was with the Falstaff team captained by fellow Hall of Famer Buddy Bomar. Day went into virtual retirement in the late 1950s, then won the Championship Bowling tournament filmed in Toledo in 1959 as a national TV series. He seldom bowled again.

EBBER DARNELL EASTER (Winston-Salem, North Carolina)—The Sarge, who came to national attention during World War II while stationed at Truax Field in Madison, Wisconsin, once turned down reenlistment as a first sergeant to bowl, in 1938, in his first ABC tournament. Then he went back into service as a private. Easter developed his own ball grip, featuring an offset finger hole, that still is used. He became the ABC tournament's oldest champion in 1950. He actually first bowled in 1896 but made no serious attempt at major competition until the early 1940s.

JOSEPH LAWRENCE FALCARO (New York, New York)—One of bowling's most controversial but highly publicized figures. He gained early fame throughout the country in his early years as a trick bowler, and in the east especially gave many benefit bowling exhibitions under the sponsorship of the Coca Cola company, His greatest accomplishment was winning the national match game championship from Joe Scribner in 1929. He later defended the title against Scribner but forfeited it in 1933.

ALFRED JOSEPH FARAGALLI (Wayne, New Jersey)—Starred with leading teams, particularly the high scoring Faber Cement Blocks. A teammate and often a doubles partner was Lou Campi, a fellow Hall of Famer. Another was Tony Sparando, a Hall member. Hit television jackpot on June 18, 1957, when he rolled 300 game worth $10,000 on film series at Chicago. Had 835 in same series and total earnings of $17,100.

BASIL FAZIO (Delton, Michigan)—In fall of 1955 won seven straight live television matches in Chicago. Had 802 in Detroit, first live 800 ever televised. At the age of 60, he was undefeated for six

Adolph Carlson

Ned Day

Edward Kawolics

matches in the ABC Masters before losing the title when Pete Tountas, 29, came out of the losers bracket to win both matches in the double elimination finals.

RUSSELL HERMAN GERSONDE (Milwaukee, Wisconsin)—Won 12 doubles titles in major tournaments, seven with Barkow, four with Frank Benkovic and one with Ernie Imse. His five Wisconsin state all events titles is an all time record. Gersonde started bowling in 1924.

THERMAN GIBSON (Detroit, Michigan)—Won $75,000 for rolling six straight strikes on the Jackpot Bowling show on Jan. 2, 1961. He won seven ABC championships as a member of the fabled E & B Pfeiffer lineups that included George Young, Fred Bujack and Lou Sielaff, the captain, all deceased, and Chuck O'Donnell, Don Carter and Bill Bunetta. All seven are in the Hall of Fame.

RICHARD LEE HOOVER (Akron, Ohio)—On Feb. 10, 1946, Hoover rolled the highest series, 847, ever compiled in league play by a teenager. The total was tied in 1969 by Wayne Chester, San Francisco. Hoover also is the youngest to win the All-Star tournament; he won the 1950–51 event the day after his 21st birthday.

JOSEPH GEORGE JOSEPH (Lansing, Michigan)—Noted for one of the smoothest deliveries in the bowling game, was an outstanding semipro football player and softball pitcher in his younger days. He hurled 50 no-hit softball games.

FRANK CLEMENCE KARTHEISER (Chicago, Illinois)—Considered one of the nation's top head to head competitors. He defeated another Hall of Fame star, Billy Knox of Philadelphia, by 68 pins in a 60 game match, although he was trailing by 141 with only seven games remaining. Coming from behind to win matches was a trait of this steady performer. He was losing to Eddie Krems after 30 games of a 40 game match by 104 pins but came on to win by 46 with a great finishing spurt. In 1926 he rolled a 233 average for 40 games to beat another Chicago star of the era, Louis Levine.

EDWARD KAWOLICS (Chicago, Illinois)—As a professional, Kawolics was ineligible to compete in the 5th world tournament of Federation Internationale des Quilleurs in Mexico City in November, 1963. He was, however, named coach of both the men's and women's teams, the first ever to represent the United States and ABC in world competition.

WILLIAM KNOX (Philadelphia, Pennsylvania)—In 1913 in Toledo, Ohio, Knox rolled the first 300 game in ABC tournament history. 10 years later he won the ABC all events title with 2019, the first total above 2000 and the record until 1933. His average for 22 ABCs was 191.

Therman Gibson

JOHN KOSTER (East Nyack, New York)—The first to win four ABC tournament titles, a record unmatched until Joe Wilman won his fourth in 1954. Bill Lillard tied them in 1956, then broke the deadlock in 1962.

EDWARD HENRY KREMS (Chicago, Illinois)—Possibly the best all around bowler in Chicago in the 1920s, starring in team, doubles and individual competition. He was the second bowler to roll three 700s on ABC tournament lanes, and from 1926 through 1935 had a 200 ABC average.

JOSEPH FRANK KRISTOF (Columbus, Ohio)—Another Buddy Bomar recruit, joining Buddy in 1946 from his native Toledo to perform on such great Chicago teams as the Kathryns, Tavern Pales and Pabst Beers. Known as one of the game's great stylists, Joe later moved to Columbus to open his own pro shop.

PAUL ALBERT KRUMSKE (Prospect Heights, Illinois)—Captained numerous great Chicago teams, among them King Louie and Meister Brau. He has developed many young stars. Krumske was secretary of the Chicago Classic league for many years and won its average title several times.

Krumske was voted Chicago's bowler of the half century in a 1951 Chicago Bowler newspaper poll. Krumske won the national match game title in 1944 from Ned Day, but lost the title a month later in the All-Star tournament.

HERBERT W. LANGE (Watertown, Wisconsin)—Rose to early stardom as an undergraduate at the University of Wisconsin. He was the first to roll all 200 games (nine) in one ABC tournament, doing it in 1922 and repeating in 1934. He also was the first to have five all events totals above 1900. His 214.2 average for three consecutive ABCs stood for 27 years.

WILLIAM TERRELL LILLARD (Houston, Texas)—After winning his first two ABC tournament titles in 1955 with the famed Detroit Pfeiffers, Lillard made bowling history on March 24–25, 1956. He became the first man to win four titles in one ABC tournament bowling with the team and team all events champion Falstaffs, pairing with Stan Gifford for the doubles crown and capturing the individual all events title as well. He gained his seventh title in 1962, then tied Hall of Famer Fred Bujack for the most lifetime tournament championships when he notched his eighth in 1971.

MORTIMER JOEL LINDSEY (Stamford, Connecticut)—At the age of 64 he finished fourth in the Bowlers Journal tournament and until age slowed him up a few years later he entered many events where most of the competitors were less than half his age.

EDWARD ANTHONY LUBANSKI (Detroit, Michigan)—In 1959, Lubanski became the second man to win four ABC titles in one tournament. For many years, Lubanski was "the last" of the top stars still using a two-finger ball.

ENRICO MARINO (Los Angeles, California)—Oldtime movie comedian Harold Lloyd and Ned Day, also in the Hall of Fame, operated the Llo-Da-Mar bowling center in Santa Monica for many years.

JOHN O. MARTINO (Syracuse, New York)—Made his mark in three levels of the game. He was an outstanding bowler, holding a 190 average after 41 ABC tournaments. In 1929 he won the all events title in an international tournament held in Stockholm, Sweden. He was also active in administrative positions serving as ABC president (1947–48) and also president of the New York state and Syracuse associations. He also wrote a bowling column for Syracuse newspapers and served as the first president of the Bowling Writers Association of America.

JAMES McMAHON, JR. (River Edge, New Jersey)—One of the great ABC tournament bowlers of all time. Starting with his first tournament, in 1937, he rolled four straight 1800s, missed by 21 pins in 1941 with a 1779 and then had seven more 1800s.

He bowled with leading New York area teams until 1945, when he moved to Chicago. There he bowled with Monarch and Meister Brau teams until moving to Fair Lawn, New Jersey shortly before winning the 1951–52 All-Star tournament. McMahon held the ABC 10 year average record, 207–1 for 90 games through the 1951 season.

WALTER MERCURIO (Cleveland, Ohio)—Most crucial moment in bowling occurred more than 40 years ago. In 1926 he and Bodis were paired against the great Adolph Carlson and young star Paul Krumske in a doubles match. Both Bodis and Mercurio struck out in the 10th frame of the final game to win the match by nine pins.

STEVE JOSEPH NAGY (Cleveland, Ohio)—Bowled in his first ABC tournament in 1939, as a Booster division entrant. 13 years later he and Johnny Klares collaborated for the alltime ABC doubles record, 1453, and Nagy just missed the all events record with a 2065 total.

He rolled a 299 game in the 1952 ABC Masters. His 300 game in 1954 was the first ever rolled on a bowling film series. He won the 1955–56 All-Star after tying for the 16th spot in the fianls and defeating Graz Castellano, New York, in a historic rolloff that started at 2 a.m.

JOSEPH JOHN NORRIS (San Diego, California)—Become well known through his bowling feats with the Chene-Trombley team of Detroit, started on the road to super stardom when he organized the Stroh's Beer team in 1933. Under his captaincy the Stroh's won the 1934 ABC championship and later held the national match game championship between 1942 and 1945.

The Stroh's were the first team to wear white uniforms, carry white bowling ball bags and make extensive exhibition tours. They competed in the 1936 Olympics in Berlin, Germany, won numerous national and sectional titles and generally set the pace for nationally sponsored teams. Norris often has been called the best leadoff bowler in history.

CHARLES O'DONNELL (St. Louis, Missouri)—A member of the Budweiser lineup of Pat Patterson, Don Carter, Bill Lillard, Dick Weber, Ray Bluth and Tom Hennessey, all of whom are in the Hall or on the ballot for election. O'Donnell's 236–6 average for 84 games in the All-Star doubles league in 1961–62 in St. Louis is the record in two-man competition.

Joe Norris

CLAUDE PATTERSON, JR. (St. Louis, Missouri) — A member of the Ziern Antiques, a great St. Louis team that included Tom Hennessey, Ray Bluth and Don Carter at the beginning of their careers. Pat was a member of the Budweiser club when it was organized and succeeded Whitey Harris as captain. He remained as captain of the group when it later became the Don Carter Gloves team and helped the club to the 1962 Classic team title.

CONRAD ANTHONY SCHWOEGLER (Madison, Wisconsin) — Became a bowling sensation when he won the 1942 All-Star at age 24. He repeated as champion in 1948. He was considered one of the great stylists for a big man, 6-3 and 225 pounds, at the height of his career.

LOUIS A. SIELAFF (Detroit, Michigan) — Captained the Pfeiffer Beer team, only three-time ABC team and four-time team all events champions, since its organization as E&B in 1944. In May, 1958, Sielaff turned over the Pfeiffer captaincy to Eddie Lubanski, but remained as seventh man in the lineup.

WILLIAM SIXTY, SR. (Milwaukee, Wisconsin) — Wrote for the Milwaukee Journal sports staff from 1914 to 1974. He is noted nationally for both golf and bowling writing, plus being highly proficient at both sports. He has won several state golf and match bowling championships. Sixty pioneered in writing nationally syndicated bowling lessons. In 1956 he won a first prize in Bowling magazine's annual writers contest and also was honored with a watch by the Bowling Writers Association of America for meritorious service.

He has captained several outstanding Milwaukee teams and was captain of the match game champion Heil Products team. In open play, Sixty set the Wisconsin record in 1938 with 300–300–278–878. He won the Wisconsin match championship in 1931, 1932, 1937 and 1944.

JAMES SMITH (Buffalo, New York) — Principally an exhibition bowler. In 1910 he began a nationwide tour that lasted through 1915, rested several months, then continued the exhibition schedule from late 1916 until 1924. He met all comers during the tours and was said to have averaged 205 per game against every imaginable lane condition and pin weight. He bowled from the corner and never attempted to develop a "pretty" curve or hook ball delivery.

TONY SPARANDO (Rego Park, New York) — Impaired vision has failed to keep Sparando from becoming one of the East's alltime great stars. Tony is one of the few remaining top stars who "pin" bowl rather than spot bowl. Among famous Eastern teams he bowled with were Bowlers Journal and Faber Cement Block. Teammates on the Fabers included Hall of Famers Lou Campi and Lindy Faragalli.

Billy Sixty   *Andy Varipapa*

BARNEY SPINELLA (Miama, Florida) — Quite famous in the hardwood duckpin circles and once held the world's record average for five games — 145. He was a three-time ABC tournament champion, taking the all events title in 1922 and 1927 and sharing the doubles with brother Chris in 1922. In addition, he was one of the most feared match game bowlers, beating such greats as Andy Varipapa and Walter (Skang) Mercurio in head and head battles.

HARRY HARVEY STEERS (Chicago, Illinois) — On April 18, 1955, Steers was presented with a diamond lapel pin for being the first man to bowl in 50 ABC tournaments. Steers missed the first ABC tournament, in 1901, but was a scoremarker for it. The next year he participated, and won the doubles event. He missed again in 1903, then bowled in every one starting with 1904.

Steers won the first Petersen Classic, held in Chicago in 1921. He created several longevity records, including having never missed a game for 34 years in the Chicago Randolph league, which went out of operation in 1946. He bowled in every Chicago city and Illinois state bowling association tournament until he moved to Phoenix in 1958.

OTTO STEIN, JR. (St. Louis, Missouri) — Compiled an outstanding record in St. Louis where few challenged his supremacy as a match game bowler in the 1920s and 30s. One of the first to roll three 1900 all events totals in the ABC tournament.

FRANK THOMA (Chicago, Illinois) — One of four Thoma brothers who earned a combined five ABC tournament championships during a nine-year period. Winner of several Illinois state titles.

ANDREW VARIPAPA (Hempstead, New York) — Developed trick shot bowling to its peak and through that ability was starred in the first bowling film short, Strikes and Spares, in 1934. He has made more such films than any bowler. Also, he has been a leading instructor and exhibition bowler, one of the first to make countrywide tours.

Varipapa's bowling ability often has been overshadowed by his trick shooting, but his achievements on the lanes have been almost legendary. At the age of 55 he won the 1946–47 All-Star tournament and the following year became the first bowler to repeat as All-Star champion.

Walter Ward

Dick Weber

Billy Welu

In 1959 he "broke" the Phillies Jackpot on national television to win $6000 as he collected nine strikes in a row. At the age of 78 Varipapa developed painful wrist and arm problems that prevented his bowling right-handed. He took to bowling left-handed and 18 months later was averaging 180.

WALTER G. WARD (Scottsdale, Arizona)— Kept a scrapbook record of every game he has bowled since 1929. During World War II he gave exhibitions at 263 service bases. During his career Ward has rolled an amazing 317 series of 700 or more pins.

RICHARD ANTHONY WEBER (St. Louis, Missouri)—A struggling postal clerk in Indianapolis, then a bowling lanes employee, when the St. Louis Budweisers signed him in 1955, their second year. He was an immediate success as the anchorman of the famous lineup whose leadoff was Don Carter. Other were Ray Bluth, Pat Patterson, Tom Hennessey and captain Whitey Harris. He bowled 258, 258, 259 in Buds' record 3858 series in 1958.

He is the leading tournament money winner of all time, his total exceeding $500,000 for 20 years of top-flight play. He has won more Professional Bowlers association titles—24—than anyone and has served as PBA president for a two-year term.

Weber is noted for his ability to "adjust" or correct his delivery at the foul line. He and Don Carter have had a neck and neck battle for "alltime greatest" honors. Carter got the edge, 18 votes to 12, in a poll of veteran bowling writers by Bowling maga-

zine in 1970. In 1970, he became the youngest ever elected to the ABC Hall of Fame.

WILLIAM JOSEPH WELU (Houston, Texas)— After serving a short stint with the St. Louis Budweisers, became captain of the St. Louis Falstaffs and led them to national honors in ABC and BPAA team action. Welu also was a great individual performer, scoring back to back victories in the 1964 and 1965 ABC Masters and winning the All-Star in 1959. At 6-4½ and 230 pounds, Welu was living proof that big men can be big stars in bowling.

JOSEPH WILMAN (Chicago, Illinois)—The second man to win four ABC tournament championships. He also was the first with two 2000s in the tournament. Wilman was one of the game's leading instructors and analysts. He was an excellent radio and television commentator on bowling. He was noted for his ability to "play" lanes and was famous for his ready grin and rapid gum chewing.

In the 1955–56 All-Star, he missed winning his second title when he drew the 1–2–10 washout in the final frame and missed the spare. Wilman was voted the BBIA Industry Service Award in 1959. He was a member of the Brunswick promotion staff and a Past President of Hall of Fame board from 1962–66.

PHIL WOLF (Chicago, Illinois)—Came to Chicago in 1899, where he soon gained a reputation as a rough and ready competitor who gave no quarter in a match. He won his third ABC title at the age of 58.

GEORGE YOUNG (Detroit, Michigan)—A member of the three time ABC champion Pfeiffer Beer team until illness forced him to curtail his bowling in early 1959. He had one of the most glittering ABC tournament records; besides his titles, he held an unparalleled string of nine consecutive all events totals above 1800 and between 1942 and 1958 (with three years out for World War II when there was no tournament) his only total below 1800 was 1778 in 1949. His 202 lifetime average was the highest in history for 20 or more tournaments.

GILBERT ZUNKER (Milwaukee, Wisconsin)—A fine team bowler who helped make the Heil Products, with other Hall of Fame members Marino, Daw, Day and Sixty, a feared club in the middle 1930s. Zunker died at the age of 39 after suffering a cold for a brief time. He had a colorful, jaunty air.

Meritorious Service

HAROLD ALLEN (Detroit, Michigan)—Became the youngest bowler ever to win an ABC championship when at the age of 18 he combined with his brother, Ray, for the doubles title in 1918. He also won another "eagle" when he bowled with the champion Krakow Furniture team of Detroit in 1937. Allen competed in 46 ABC tournaments, 45 of them consecutively averaging 188. Illness sidelined him in 1964.

FRANK K. BAKER (Milwaukee, Wisconsin)—ABC's uncanny ability to pick the right man at the right time to take over the helm as secretary was certainly exemplified by the selection of Frank K. Baker to become only its fourth top leader in 1951. Baker had served as a member of the board of directors and also held leadership positions in the Salt Lake association. He also had been a successful executive in the newspaper and radio fields, and that background was to serve him in good stead with the Congress.

Never content with the status quo, Baker, however, had one creed about the game he loved, "Is it good for the game?" and steadfastly followed that tenet until his retirement in 1972. Baker has remained active in his role of secretary emeritus, principally working with the NBC promotion committee and on the international scene.

ELMER H. BAUMGARTEN (Milwaukee, Wisconsin)—Served as ABC secretary from 1933 to 1951, directing the Congress through turbulent times and on into the beginning of the boom. He was elected as an ABC director in 1925 and third vice president in 1930. He was named acting ABC secretary in 1932 due to the illness of A. L. Langtry. Baumgarten was elected to the secretary position a year later, and moved from his Chicago home to Milwaukee.

While serving as secretary he was known as a tower of strength for the game through the Depression years and World War II. He was a rugged individualist who believed in action and complete authority. His rigid demands for honesty, fair play and strict adherence to rule and regulations stamped him "Mr. ABC" in the eyes of Congress members.

ROBERT F. BENSINGER (Chicago, Illinois)—Served as chairman of the board of the Brunswick corporation from 1950 until his retirement in 1963. He originally joined the firm in 1918 when it was known as the Brunswick-Balke-Collender Co. His great-grandfather helped form the company in 1845 and "R.F." was fourth in the line of Bensingers to serve as company president.

Bensinger's support of bowling went far beyond the role of manufacturing firm executive. Under his guidance the company built up a large staff of star players for exhibition work and personal appearances. Many Hall of Famers were under Brunswick contract at one time or another, among them Frank Benkovic, Buddy Bomar, Ned Day, Buzz Fazio, Therm Gibson, Steve Nagy, Joe Norris, Andy Varipapa, Joe Wilman and Joe Joseph.

The company also was a leader in billiards with Willie Hoppe, Charley Petersen and Willie Mosconi among those under contract. When Bensinger first joined the corporation he was employed as a lumber wagon driver. He became vice president in 1925 and president in 1931 before becoming board chairman.

LeROY CHASE (Peoria, Illinois)—Devoted his life to bowling, writing about the game for 40 years

Joe Wilman

Frank Baker

as a member of the Peoria Journal-Star sports staff and serving in such executive capacities as president of the Illinois Bowling association and the Bowling Writers Association of America. He was one of the first recipients of a BWAA writing award. He was third vice president of ABC at the time of his death. He was elected to the board of directors in 1959 and became a vice president in 1965.

Chase bowled in 32 ABC tournaments and had eight sanctioned 700 series. He was among the first to be inducted into the Illinois Bowling association's Hall of Fame.

CHARLES O. COLLIER (Chicago, Illinois) — A familiar and colorful personality at ABC tournament installations from 1912 to 1951 when he supervised the construction and maintenance of the tournament lanes for Brunswick. One of the top stars of his day, Collier rolled in 39 ABC tournaments and compiled a 186 lifetime average. For more than three decades he captained the famous Brunswick Mineralite team which included fellow Hall of Famer Harry Steers.

WILLIAM DOEHRMAN (Fort Wayne, Indiana) — Bowled in 64 ABC tournaments, a participation record unprecedented in the sports world. He is one of only two bowlers to participate in more than 60 ABCs. Doehrman broke the record of 57 appearances, held by fellow Hall member Harry Steers, at the 1968 tournament in Cincinnati. He has improved on that string of consecutive appearances each year.

Those appearances have been anything but token. In 1922 he captained the Fort Wayne Lincoln Life team to the ABC championship. He has bowled more games (573) and knocked down more pins (104,090) than any other bowler in the history of the ABC tournament. His average is a remarkable 181. Doehrman is the only bowler to exceed 100,000 pins. He has been a member of three Indiana state championship teams as well as the coholder of a state doubles title. He once rolled a 749 series.

JACK HAGERTY (Toledo, Ohio) — Spent nearly 60 years as a Toledo bowling proprietor and played a prominent role in obtaining and helping stage five ABC tournaments in that city between 1913 and 1926. He was a charter member and president of the Bowling Proprietors Association of America, and also presided over the Ohio State B.A. He was a prime organizer of the Central States tournament, once the most important of all regional events. He served as an ABC director in 1912–13 when he operated a four lane establishment in Tiffin, Ohio.

CORNELIUS (CONE) HERMANN (St. Louis, Missouri) — Elected to the Greater St. Louis bowling association Hall of Fame in 1964 and received the Bowling Writers Association of America Rip Van Winkle award in 1957 shortly before his death.

PETER HOWLEY (Chicago, Illinois) — The only man to bowl in the first 46 ABC tournaments (1901–1949), averaging 178, finally retiring because of illness. Howley bowled in Chicago's better leagues from the 1920s onward and was a president of the city's proprietor organization. He was general manager of several bowling and billiard establishments in the Windy city. He rolled a perfect game in 1900 at the age of 18.

ABRAHAM L. LANGTRY (Milwaukee, Wisconsin) — Served for 25 years as secretary of the ABC. Upon taking office in 1907 as the Congress' second administrative leader he moved ABC headquarters from Dayton, Ohio to Milwaukee. He administered Congress business through the first stages of growth and widespread public respect.

It often has been written that Langtry ran the Congress out of a rolltop desk in the early days when he was co-owner of the Langtry-McBride bowling establishment. It was his vision and determination during a period when ABC needed an uncompromising leader that helped build its sturdy foundation on which the game rests.

SAM LEVINE (Cleveland, Ohio) — A wearer of many hats. He founded the Cleveland Kegler bowling newspaper in 1937 and continues as its editor and publisher. He has helped raise thousands of dollars for charity with innovations that included a bowlers' picnic and sending children to summer camp through bowlers rolling 300 games. He broadcasted bowling for two decades, handled many live television programs and announced syndicated match game shows.

When fellow Hall of Famer Steve Nagy became seriously ill in 1965 Levine developed a trust fund that helped ease the payment of many bills. The fund still helps Nagy's widow, Helen, and their daughter. In 1961 Levine established the Flowers for the Living award to honor persons still alive who have been good for bowling. He has been president of the Bowling Writers Association of America and has won first place in the Editorial division of BOWLING's annual writing competition three times. He is secretary of the Cleveland and Ohio Bowling Proprietors associations.

DAVID LUBY (Chicago, Illinois) — Founded the Bowlers Journal in 1913. He was a traveling shoe salesman who scurried back to Chicago each week to bowl in the famed Randolph league. Out of this interest grew plans for the weekly newspaper, which later became a national monthly publication under the leadership of his late son, Mort Sr., who is also in the Hall. His grandson, Mort Jr., is the present editor and publisher.

Luby was widely respected for his impartiality and judgment. He often was called on to arbitrate disputes. In 1919 he was elected an executive committeeman of the ABC, a position equivalent to today's director. Luby served in that capacity until his death. He was succeeded by Elmer Baumgarten, who later became president and subsequently the third secretary of the ABC.

MORT LUBY, SR. (Chicago, Illinois) — First suggested the formation of a bowling Hall of Fame in 1937, an idea that was realized in 1941. He served as publisher of the National Bowlers Journal from 1925 until his death in 1956, having taken over the publication upon the death of his father, Hall of Famer Dave Luby. The Lubys are the only father-son Hall combination.

Luby was a founding father of the Bowling Writers Association of America and was on hand when such diverse organizations as the Bowling Proprietors Association of America and the Billiard and Bowling Institute held their inaugural meetings. He named the first All-America team in 1937, campaigned for the establishment of an all-star singles tournament and founded the Bowlers Journal championships.

It was the creation of that tournament in 1947 that triggered the greatest crisis of his career. Upon finding that his own tournament director had attempted to falsify the standings, Luby exposed the attempted fraud in his own magazine as well as stories in the national news wires. The BWAA presented him a Certificate of Merit for "risking without fear, his personal and business reputation in his exposé . . ." The oganization's Distinguished Service award is named for him.

HOWARD McCULLOUGH (Chicago, Illinois) — President of the organization that operated the 1932 ABC tournament in Detroit and was credited with a last minute ticket sales campaign that saved the tournament from a Depression era failure. He was noted for his work with charity promotions, notably as chairman of the March of Dimes sports committee in the 1950s. He was instrumental in founding the Detroit Bowling Council, one of the first citywide bowling councils of its kind.

McCullough served as an executive in the Brunswick corporation for 24 years before his retirement. He directed its national sales staff after moving to the firm's Chicago headquarters.

LOUIS P. PETERSEN (Chicago, Illinois) — A scoring system and a bowling tournament have etched Petersen's name indelibly in the upper strata of bowling contributors. He started his famous Petersen Classic in 1921, won by fellow Hall member Harry Steers, and that event now attracts more than 20,000 entrants. Petersen also originated the point system bearing his name. It awards a point for each 50 pins, a point for each game won and is used in several match game tournaments.

He also was instrumental in forming the All-Star tournament with the Chicago Tribune in 1941 and was a founder of the Bowling Proprietors Association of America in 1932.

MILTON RAYMER (Chicago, Illinois) — Founded the American Junior Bowling Congress. As a teacher at Tilden Tech high school in Chicago, Raymer created a four-team high school bowling league that grew to citywide proportions and eventually evolved into the, American High School Bowling Congress. In 1946 the American Junior Bowling Congress was founded with Raymer as its executive secretary. He held the post for 15 years.

From a membership of 8,767 in 1946 he led the growth to 410,000 boys and girls of high school age and under. The program, now sponsored by the American Bowling Congress and Women's International Bowling Congress, has more than 750,000 members.

DENNIS J. SWEENEY (St. Louis, Missouri) — A charter member of the Bowling Proprietors Association of America, he pioneered the scheduling of two leagues nightly in an establishment. At one time he published his own Sunday newspaper besides covering bowling for the five St. Louis dailies in existence at the time. He was elected to the St. Louis Bowling Hall of Fame and also received the Bowling Writers Association of America Rip Van Winkle award in recognition of his contributions to the game.

SAM WEINSTEIN (Chicago, Illinois) — Known as the "Tenpin Tattler," a title he has held through 40 years of bowling broadcasting on Chicago radio and television stations. He has been producer and announcer of several televised bowling shows and his movie of a gag bowling routine with comedian Jerry Lewis and fellow Hall member Paul Krumske raised thousands of dollars for muscular dystrophy research. Weinstein's shows helped make Krumske famous as the "Bowling Professor."

In 1939 Weinstein established the first retail bowling pro shop. He has three outlets today and also handles billiard and golf supplies. He received the Mort Luby Distinguished Service award in 1964. The honor is given to distinguished service to the sport of bowling. His benevolence to others is widespread.

VERN ELI WHITNEY (Milwaukee, Wisconsin) — Founded the ABC Hall of Fame in 1941, a year after he had joined the Congress staff as its first public relations manager. He had taken that position as a kind of stopgap during a local newspaper strike, hoping to get back soon to his first love of newspapering.

He accomplished the giant task of putting all lifetime ABC tournament participation records on file cards during the lean bowling days of World War II and his collection of Oddities and Statistics became a byword of the ABC Yearbook.

THE HALL OF FAME OF BOXING

New York City, New York

Photos and biographies are by courtesy of Nat Loubet and Ring Magazine.

The Hall of Fame of Boxing is located in New York City in the offices of *Ring Magazine* just a block from Madison Square Garden. There are three categories of boxers in the Hall of Fame selections.

The Pioneers consist of boxers active many years ago, going back into the nineteenth century. The Old Timers are boxers active 35 or more years ago, and the Moderns are boxers active in the last 35 years, but retired for at least two years. The first two categories are selected by a Board of Directors made up of twenty boxing experts. To qualify for

Georges Carpentier

James J. Corbett

Jack Dempsey

the Hall of Fame a boxer must receive 75% of all the votes cast. Selections are made annually.

The Moderns elections to the elite membership in the Hall of Fame are made on a worldwide basis and again must receive at least 75% of the votes cast. The selections are made by radio and television sportscasters, newspaper sports writers, and other qualified boxing experts.

There are 128 Hall of Fame members. In the Pioneers group there are 31 members, in the Old Timers there are 57, and in the Moderns there are 40 members. The most recent selections made in 1974 were Dick Tiger and Gene Fullmer in the Moderns category. There were two Old Timers elected, Frank Klaus and George (K. O.) Chaney, and in the Pioneers category Dick Curtis, an English lightweight who was undefeated for eight years beginning in 1820, was honored by the Board.

Some representative biographies of outstanding Hall of Fame boxers follow. The *Ring Magazine* publishes material that gives detailed biographies of boxers in the Hall of Fame.

The Immortal 128

(Inaugurated 1954)

Pioneer Group—Elected by Directors

1954 James Figg	1954 John Morrissey	1961 Tom Spring	1970 Professor Mike Donovan
1954 Jack Broughton	1954 Jem Mace	1962 Ned Price	1971 Nobby Clark
1954 Tom Cribb	1955 William (Bendigo)	1963 Jem Ward	1972 Tom Chandler
1954 Tom Hyer	Thompson	1964 Sam Collyer	1973 Paddy Ryan
1954 Daniel Mendoza	1956 Bill Richmond	1965 Jake Kilrain	1974 Dick Curtis
1954 Tom Sayers	1957 Peter Jackson	1966 James (Deaf) Burke	
1954 Gentleman John Jackson	1958 Tom Molineaux	1967 Barney (Young) Aaron	
1954 John C. Heenan	1959 John Gully	1968 Jacob Hyer	
1954 Arthur Chambers	1960 Don Donnelly	1969 Joe Goss	

Elected by Old-Timers Committee

1954 John L. Sullivan	1956 Jem Driscoll	1960 Freddie Welsh	1968 Philadelphia Jack O'Brien
1954 Jack McAuliffe	1957 Kid McCoy	1960 Johnny Kilbane	1969 Leo Houck
1954 Young Griffo	1957 Charley Mitchell	1960 Tommy Burns	1969 Jeff Smith
1954 Nonpareil Jack Dempsey	1957 Battling Nelson	1961 Jack Root	1970 Kid Williams
1954 James J. Corbett	1957 Packey McFarland	1961 Pancho Villa	1970 Harry Wills
1954 Bob Fitzsimmons	1957 Les Darcy	1962 Willie Ritchie	1971 Paul Berlenbach
1954 Joe Gans	1958 Ad Wolgast	1963 Tom Gibbons	1971 Tiger Flowers
1954 Jack Johnson	1958 Mike Gibbons	1964 Georges Carpentier	1972 Billy Papke
1954 Stanley Ketchel	1958 Tommy Ryan	1964 Ted (Kid) Lewis	1972 Fidel LaBarba
1954 James J. Jeffries	1959 Tom Sharkey	1965 Johnny Coulon	1973 Jack Delaney
1955 Terry McGovern	1959 Jack Dillon	1965 Young Corbett II	1973 Frankie Genaro
1955 Joe Walcott	1959 George Kid Lavigne	(Billy Rothwell)	1974 George K.O. Chaney
1955 Abe Attell	1959 Jimmy Wilde	1965 Owen Moran	1974 Frank Klaus
1955 Sam Langford	1959 Pete Herman	1966 Battling Levinsky	
1956 George Dixon	1960 Joe Choynski	1967 Joe Jeannette	

Elected by Modern Writers and Broadcasters

1954 Jack Dempsey	1957 Johnny Dundee	1965 Billy Conn	1972 Maxie Rosenbloom
1954 Joe Louis	1958 Tony Zale	1966 Archie Moore	1972 Fritzie Zivic
1954 Henry Armstrong	1959 Kid Chocolate	1966 Kid Gavilan	1972 Beau Jack
1955 Benny Leonard	1959 Rocky Marciano	1967 Ray Robinson	1973 Gus Lesnevich
1955 Gene Tunney	1960 Jack Britton	1968 Max Baer	1973 Sammy Angott
1955 Harry Greb	1961 Lew Tendler	1969 Carmen Basilio	1974 Dick Tiger
1955 Mickey Walker	1962 Billy Petrolle	1969 Jersey Joe Walcott	1974 Gene Fullmer
1956 Tony Canzoneri	1962 Marcel Cerdan	1970 Max Schmeling	
1956 Jimmy McLarnin	1963 Willie Pep	1970 Ezzard Charles	
1956 Barney Ross	1964 Lou Ambers	1971 Rocky Graziano	
1956 Tommy Loughran	1964 Jim Braddock	1971 Sandy Saddler	

Joe Gans

James Jeffries

Biographies of some of the celebrated boxers in the Hall of Fame

GEORGES CARPENTIER was born January 12, 1894, at Lens, France. Weight, 175. Height 5 feet, 11½ inches. Managed by Francois Deschamps. Carpentier, known as "The Orchid Man," started his professional career in 1907 and retired in 1927. In 1912 he lost on a foul in 19 rounds to Frank Klaus in a bout advertised as for the middleweight title. In his first American fight he defeated Battling Levinsky on October 12, 1920 in Jersey City, N.J., on a four round knockout to win the light heavyweight title.

In his next start, at Boyle's Thirty Acres, Jersey City, N.J., for the heavyweight title, he was stopped in four rounds by Jack Dempsey in the first "Million Dollar" gate. Carpentier lost his light heavyweight title to Battling Siki by a knockout in the sixth round, on September 24, 1922, at Paris, France. The "Orchid Man" served in the French Army in World War I, as a Lieutenant in the Aviation Corps. He fought in every division from flyweight through heavyweight. He had a total of 106 fights and scored 51 knockouts. In 1964 he was elected to the Boxing Hall of Fame.

JAMES J. CORBETT known as "Gentleman Jim." Born, September 1, 1866, San Francisco California. Participated in the first of the "big gloves" contests when he won the heavyweight crown from John L. Sullivan at New Orleans, La. in 1892. He kayoed the Boston Strong Boy in the 21st round. Purse of $25,000 and a stake of $20,000. Managed by William A. Brady.

Corbett, who rose from a bank teller to a world champion, was a father of a new school of boxing, science instead of pure brawn. Lost title to Bob Fitzsimmons in 1897, 14 rounds at Carson City, Nevada, on a solar plexus blow. Fought James J. Jeffries twice, losing the first time at Coney Island, May 11, 1900 by a knockout in 23 rounds and again in San Francisco, August 14, 1903 by a knockout in ten rounds. Was the most successful of all boxer-thespians. He starred in "Gentleman Jack," "The Cadet" and "Cashel Bryon's Profession." Appeared in many plays.

JACK DEMPSEY known as the "Manassa Mauler." Born, June 24, 1895, Manassa, Colo. He won the title from Jess Willard, July 4, 1919, at Toledo, Ohio, when he provided the fireworks for the celebration by knocking out Willard in 3 rounds.

On September 23, 1926 he lost the heavyweight crown to Gene Tunney at Philadelphia in a rainstorm. He failed to regain the title from Tunney in 10 rounds the following year at Chicago, precipitating the famous "Long Count" controversy. He later became a referee, promoter and proprietor of the Jack Dempsey Restaurant in New York City. Elected to Boxing Hall of Fame in 1954. For complete story of his life see Nat Fleischer's book, "Jack Dempsey, the Idol of Fistiana."

JOE GANS was born in Baltimore, Md., November 25, 1874. Height, 5 feet, 6¼ inches. Weight, 133 pounds. Known as the Old Master. Exceedingly clever. Began boxing career in 1891. Managed by Al Herford. Started business career in fish market. Participated in 156 battles and won 54 by knockouts. Gans was defeated eight times, on points by Dal Hawkins in 1906, and Bobby Dobbs in 1897, by two kockouts at hands of Elbows McFadden and Terry McGovern in 1899 and 1900, respectively. He was also beaten by Frank Erne when he stopped because of an injury at end of 12 rounds in 1900. He lost to Sam Langford in 1903 and was stopped by Battling Nelson twice in 1908. Won lightweight title from Frank Erne at Fort Erie by one round knockout in 1902. Jimmy Britt claimed crown after Gans put on weight, then Gans fought Britt for title and regained it at San Francisco, October 31, 1904, on a foul in 5 rounds.

At Goldfield, Nevada, on September 3, 1906, Gans won from Battling Nelson on a foul in 42 rounds to retain the title but in a return bout at Colma,

California, July 4, 1908, Gans was knocked out by Nelson in the 17th round to lose the championship. Gans died on August 10, 1910 at Baltimore, Maryland from tuberculosis. Elected to Boxing Hall of Fame in 1954.

HARRY GREB was born in Pittsburgh, Pa., June 7, 1894, of Irish-German parents. Greb started his boxing career as a middleweight and fought as a light heavyweight also. He held the world middleweight and American light heavyweight crowns. He won the former from Johnny Wilson and the latter from Gene Tunney. Managed by George Engel and Red Mason.

He engaged in many thrilling encounters. His most vicious was with Mickey Walker which he won in 15 rounds. When he fought Gunboat Smith, a heavyweight, he was only a middleweight yet stopped the Gunner in one round. He fought Tunney five times, Gene winning twice, losing once and the other two were no decision contests. He was an indefatigable worker, a windmill in action. He feared no one. He tried hard to get Jack Dempsey to meet him but without success. He died from an eye operation on October 22, 1926. Was elected to the Boxing Hall of Fame in 1955.

JAMES JACKSON JEFFRIES known as the Boilermaker and the California Grizzly. Born April 15, 1875 at Carroll, Ohio. Started fighting in 1896. Won the heavyweight title from Bob Fitzsimmons on June 9, 1899 by a knockout in the 11th round. This was only his 13th professional fight.

Retired undefeated in 1905 but made a comeback when urged to do so and was knocked out by Jack Johnson at Reno, Nevada, July 4, 1910, in the 15th round. Managed by William A. Brady. His greatest fight was with Tom Sharkey at Coney Island, a 25 round victory fought on November 3, 1899. Another great battle was that with Corbett at Coney Island, May 11, 1900, in which he stopped Corbett in the 23rd round. Jeffries after his retirement, lived on his farm at Burbank, Calif., where for a time he promoted amateur fights. He died there after a long illness on March 3, 1953. Elected to Boxing Hall of Fame in 1954.

BENNY LEONARD was born in New York City on April 7, 1896. He received his schooling in New York public and high schools. He started boxing when a kid. He learned his fisticuffs in street battles. Leonard made his debut as a professional at 15 at the Fairmont A. C. under Billy Gibson, later his manager and also pilot of Gene Tunney. Benny took the name of Leonard after an announcer, unable to pronounce Leinert, called him by that name. He fought the greatest lightweights and welterweights of his period and was recognized as one of the greatest scientific fighters and most talkative boxer of modern times. He often has been ranked with Joe Gans and Young Griffo as most scientific. He could jab and feint his way out of trouble, and if that wouldn't suffice, he would talk his way out of a jam.

Leonard was knocked out on four occasions during his entire career of 22 years. When he first started, he was kayoed by Mickey Finnegan in two rounds. Later he was stopped by Frankie Fleming and Joe Shugrue as a lightweight and by Jimmy McLarnin when Benny was trying a comeback as a welterweight. Leonard scored many knockouts. He was a master on offense as well as defense. With Jack Johnson, he was recognized as one of the greatest feinters in ring history. He fought two ten round no decision bouts with Freddie Welsh, the lightweight king before stopping the champion in the ninth round in New York to win the world crown in 1917. He held the championship until 1925 when he retired undefeated. He made an unsuccessful comeback in 1931. His last fight was in 1932 when he was knocked out by Jimmy McLarnin.

Leonard was one of the leading New York ring officials. He collapsed and died in the St. Nicholas Arena ring, April 18, 1947, while refereeing a bout. He served in two World Wars. Leonard held the lightweight crown 7 years. He was one of two lightweight champions to retire undefeated. The complete story of his life appears in "Leonard the Magnificent" by Nat Fleischer. He was elected to the Boxing Hall of Fame in 1955.

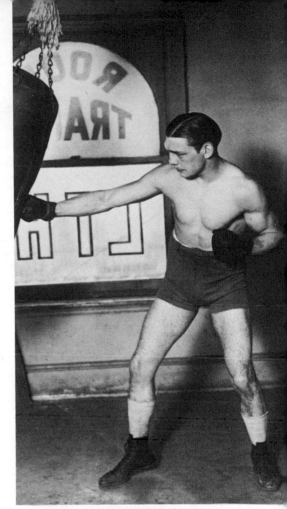

Harry Greb

Benny Leonard

89

Joe Louis

"Sugar Ray" Robinson

Rocky Marciano

JOE LOUIS was born in Lexington Alabama, May 13, 1914: Christened Joseph Louis Barrow. He comes from hardy Cherokee Indian, Negro and White stock. Height 6 feet 1¾ inches and weight 201 pounds. Started his boxing career as an amateur. Won light heavyweight championship in National tournament in 1934. Was Golden Gloves title holder. Began pro career under the management of Julian Black and John Roxborough. On July 4, 1934 at Chicago he started his professional career by knocking out Jack Kracken in one round. Scored 43 knockouts, won seven decisions and lost four bouts in a total of 54 contests as a simon pure. Dropped decisions to Johnny Miler, Max Marek, Clinton Bridges and Stanley Evans. Beat Evans in a return bout. Was runner-up to Marek in light heavyweight class, National AAU chanpionships in Boston, 1933. Won National AAU light heavyweight title in St. Louis, April, 1934.

One of the most powerful hitters in the history of boxing and is favorably compared with such stars as Jack Dempsey and Jim Jeffries and more recently with Joe Fraser and Ali. In his first year as a professional he scored 10 knockouts in a dozen fights. He won the world heavyweight title at Chicago, Illinois, June 22, 1937, by knocking out James J. Braddock in 8 rounds. Set world record for successful defenses of heavyweight title, with 25. Lost only once as a pro prior to retirement in 1949, Max Schmeling stopping him in 12th round, in non-title bout. Later, when champion, knocked out Schmeling in 2:04 of opening round. Received total of $20,757 during first two years of fighting and grossed more than $4,400,000 in regular matches, exhibitions and radio and television in 13 years. Was first Negro heavyweight champion since Jack Johnson won the crown in 1908. Largest gate was with Bill Conn in their second fight, $1,925,505, in which the ringside seats sold for $100.

Made comeback on September 27, 1950 and lost in 15 rounds at Yankee Stadium to Ezzard Charles. His final comeback fight was with Rocky Marciano on October 26, 1951, in which Rocky scored a kayo in 8 rounds. Fought such men as Primo Carnera, King Levinsky, Paolino Uzcudun, Schmeling, Jack Sharkey, Bob Pastor, Braddock, Conn, Lou Nova and Jersey Joe Walcott. Was a sergeant in the U.S. Army in World War II, traveling throughout the world entertaining troops. Louis was elected to Boxing Hall of Fame in 1954.

ROCKY MARCIANO was born in Brockton, Mass., on September 1, 1924. height 5 feet, 11 inches. weight 184 pounds. Managed by Al Weill. An all-around athlete, he played football and baseball in high school, and was given a tryout as a catcher with the Chicago Cubs farm team at Fayetteville, N.C. During the war he served overseas with an amphibious unit. A heavyweight with the Fort Lewis (Wash.) boxing team, he went to the National Junior A. A. U. tournament in Portland, Ore., in 1945 where he knocked out four opponents in two nights but broke his hand.

Marciano, who was undefeated, was one of the hardest hitters in the game. He scored 5 knockouts in 9 fights. Among his knockout victims were Rex Layne, Freddie Beshore, Joe Louis, Lee Savold and Harry Matthews. He won the world heavyweight title on September 23, 1952, by a knockout over Jersey Joe Walcott in 13 rounds at Philadelphia, Pa., then repeated in one round in Chicago, in first title defense and stopped Roland La Starza in 11, in his second bout. In 1954 Marciano twice successfully defended his title against Ezzard Charles, winning in 15 rounds and stopping Charles in 8. Died Aug. 31, 1969 in an airplane accident.

RAY ROBINSON was born in Detroit, Michigan, May 3, 1920. Height, 5 feet 11 inches. Weight, 147–156 pounds. Managed by George Gainford. Started boxing career as an amateur. Scored 69 knockouts in 85 bouts, forty of the knockouts in the first round. Won the Golden Gloves featherweight title in 1939 and lightweight crown in 1940 in New York and in Inter-city competition. As an amateur fought under the name of Walker Smith. Began boxing career at Salem Crescent AC of Harlem in New York. Turned professional in 1940 and went on to win forty straight before losing his first ring battle to Jake La Motta on February 5, 1943, his second bout with Jake. Fought light-weights, welters and middleweights.

Gained welterweight title after Marty Servo abdicated his throne. By consent of N.B.A. and N.Y. Commission, a Robinson-Tommy Bell match was arranged to decide Servo's successor, and Ray won in 15 rounds. Defeated La Motta in five out of six bouts. He fought the cream of welters and middleweights. Rated one of the greatest ringmen of all time. Clever and terrific puncher. Won middleweight crown on Feb. 14, 1951. at Chicago, Ill., stopping La Motta in 13 rounds. Then gave up welterweight honors. Lost middleweight title to Randy Turpin at London, England, July 10, 1951, on 15 round decision. Regained it September 12, 1951, at Polo Grounds, New York, stopping Turpin in 10 rounds. Fight grossed $767,626.17, largest in history for non-heavyweight fight. As middleweight champion he tried to annex the world light heavyweight title and fought Joey Maxim for the crown at the Yankee Stadium on June 25, 1952 and was stopped in the 14th round when Ray collapsed from the heat. Retired as undefeated middleweight champion on December 18, 1952. Toured with a theatrical group in U.S. and Europe in 1954 and announced his return to the ring on October 29 but did no boxing during the year.

Robinson returned to the ring in 1955 and though losing to Ralph (Tiger) Jones, fought his way to a title shot, mainly with a victory over leading middleweight contender Rocky Castellani. On December 9, he knocked out Bobo Olson in Chicago in the second round. Then he halted Olson in four rounds on May 18, 1956, at Los Angeles, Cal., in defense of title. In 1957 he lost the title to Gene Fullmer on January 2 on a decision and regained it on May 2, winning crown for fourth time, by knocking out Fullmer in five rounds. Robinson then lost the title to Carmen Basilio on a split fifteen rounds decision on September 23, at Yankee Stadium, New York and on March 25, 1958 in Chicago, Ray regained the title, outpointing Basilio in 15 rounds, by a split decision. Due to his failure to defend his title against Basilio in 1958, the N.B.A. vacated his throne.

MAX SCHMELING was born in Klein-Luckaw, Germany, September 28, 1905, and was christened Maximilian Schmeling. His height was 6 feet, 1 inch

Max Schmeling

and he scaled 195 pounds. He was managed by Arthur Bulow in Germany and Joe Jacobs in America. Schmeling won the middleweight and light heavyweight championship of Germany as an amateur prior to turning professional in 1924. Max fought 36 professional fights, losing one to Jack Taylor, an American, before he gained his first championship by beating Max Diekmann for the light heavyweight crown of Germany. In 1928 he was stopped by Gypsy Daniels in one round.

Schmeling came to America in 1928. He knocked out Joe Monte in his first start in the fifth round and the following year won from Joe Sekyra in 10, Uzcudun in 15 and knocked out Pietro Corri in one and Johnny Risko in nine. He won the world heavyweight title on a foul from Jack Sharkey in final of elimination tournament at Yankee Stadium in 1930 and lost it to Sharkey in Garden Bowl in 1932 in 15 rounds. On June 19, 1936, Schmeling knocked out Joe Louis in the 12th round at New York City, thereby placing himself in line for a title bout. He subsequently was knocked out in a return match, this time for the heavyweight championship, by Joe Louis in 2:04 of the first round on June 22, 1928.

During his career he faced opponents such as Paolino Uzcudun, Jack Sharkey, Max Baer, Joe Louis, Johnny Risko, Mickey Walker, Young Stribling and Steve Hanras. He served as a paratrooper with the German Army in World War II. After the war, he became a referee in Germany and the owner of a mink farm and a soft drink business. Was Ring's Fighter of Year in 1930.

John L. Sullivan

Gene Tunney

JOHN L. SULLIVAN (1878–1892), American heavyweight champion who won the title in 1882 by knocking out Paddy Ryan, and engaged in the last bare knuckle championship fight knocking out Jack Kilrain, 75 rounds, at Richburg, Miss., in 1889. He lost his title to Jim Corbett in 1892. He popularized boxing in the United States.

GENE TUNNEY was born in New York, N.Y., May 25, 1898, of Irish parentage. Height, 6 feet, ½ inch Weight, 192 pounds. After attending parochial schools, as a youth he worked in a steamship office. Tunney fought around the small clubs of New York until World War I. He enlisted in the Marines and in France, he won a regimental boxing championship in the A.E.F. He won the vacant American light-heavyweight title in a bout with Battling Levinsky. January 13, 1922, in Madison Square Garden, and lost the title to Harry Greb on May 23, 1922. He was badly whipped in that fight. Tunnery regained the crown from Greb on February 23, 1923.

Gene's knockout of Tommy Gibbons in 12 rounds on June 5, 1925, cleared the path of challengers and brought Tunney into the spotlight for a shot at Dempsey's heavyweight title. He won the heavyweight title in a ten-round decision at Sesquicentennial Stadium, September 23, 1926 and successfully defended the crown against Dempsey at Soldier's Field, Chicago, on September 22, 1927, in the "Battle of the Long Count." Tunney fought only once more before retiring as undefeated world heavyweight champion, knocking out Tom Heeney at Yankee Stadium, July 26, 1928, in 11 rounds. Tunney collected the largest sum up to that time for one fight, $990,445 for the second bout with Dempsey. He also figured in a fight that lost the greatest amount in history, that with Heeney. Tex Rickard dropped $152,000 on the show. Tunney received $525,000 as a guarantee for that bout. He lost only once in his entire career and that was to Harry Greb, the middleweight tiger.

After his retirement he became an executive of many concerns, among them the Denham Tire Co., the Stamford Construction Co., and the Morris Plan. He was elected to Boxing Hall of Fame in 1955 and was the Ring Fighter of the Year in 1928.

AD WOLGAST was born on February 8, 1888 at Cadillac, Michigan, Ad was of German-American stock. Weight 133 pounds. Height 5 feet 4½ inches. Tom Jones was his manager. Wolgast, like Battling Nelson, was a ring terror, a fighting demon of the tear-in style. He started his career in 1906 at the age of 18 and had a picturesque career. Wolgast fought several twenty round fights before he gained national recognition.

On February 22, 1910, Wolgast won the world lightweight title when he knocked out Nelson in the fortieth round of a grueling battle, one of the toughest ever fought in the division. Two years later, on November 28, 1912, Wolgast was deposed by Willie Ritchie who won on a foul at Daly City, California, in the sixteenth round. Wolgast made a fortune during his ring career but after retirement he lost everything.

In 1908 he fought Abe Attell in a ten round no-decision bout and from then on went down the line meeting all comers. Among others, he tackled Frankie Picato. Matty Baldwin, George Memsic, Tommy O'Toole, Battling Nelson, Tommy Murphy, Lew Powell, and Charley White. There wasn't a fighter of note in his class whom he didn't tackle. In 1920 Wolgast became ill and was sent to a sanitorium. He died on April 14, 1955.

Ad Wolgast

CITIZENS SAVINGS ATHLETIC FOUNDATION

Los Angeles, California
by W. R. Bill Schroeder

Citizens Savings Athletic Foundation, formerly Helms Athletic Foundation (1936 - 1970), was instituted on October 15, 1936. The Athletic Foundation is now in its fortieth year of continuous operation.

The Athletic Foundation was created for the purpose of serving wholesome sports in many ways. For eleven years the Athletic Foundation occupied headquarters in downtown Los Angeles.

Since 1936, an extensive awards program has been carried on, at all levels — junior, high school, amateur and professional.

Helms Hall was erected in 1948, a charming two-story building, with adjoining covered patio. At this time, the Athletic Foundation established its Halls of Fame, originally for College Football, College Basketball, Track and Field, Swimming and Diving, Tennis, Golf, Boxing and Automobile Racing. This was long before most Halls of Fame, encompassing such sports, were developed.

As the years passed, the Athletic Foundation was encouraged to create additional Halls of Fame, now having grown to twenty-nine in number — Athletic Trainers, Automobile Racing, Badminton, Amateur, Collegiate and Professional Basketball, Women's Basketball, Boxing, Collegiate Athletic Directors, Collegiate Sports Information Directors, Fencing, Collegiate and Professional Football, Golf, Gymnastics, Handball, Noteworthy Contributors to Sports, Racquetball, Rowing, Soaring, Swimming and Diving, Synchronized Swimming, Tennis, Track and Field, Turners, Volleyball, Weightlifting, Winter Sports, and Amateur Wrestling.

All who are chosen for Hall of Fame recognition become recipients of Citizens Savings Athletic Foundation awards.

Also in 1948, the Athletic Foundation created its outstanding museum. Lodged in it, now Citizens Savings Hall, 9800 South Sepulveda

—All photographs in this chapter, courtesy Citizens Savings Athletic Foundation

Boulevard, Los Angeles, California 90045 — just across Sepulveda Boulevard from Los Angeles International Airport — are thousands of awards which have been entrusted by distinguished athletes, coaches and sportsmen. In addition, a countless number of uniforms worn by renowned athletes of the past and present are displayed — as are hundreds of photographs. A wealth of sports memorabilia is displayed in the museum.

The Citizens Savings Athletic Foundation's most important awards are granted to those who are cited for World Trophy honors. Six awards are granted annually to the world's most outstanding amateur athletes, either man or woman, in the six areas — Africa, Asia, Australasia, Europe and North and South America. Selections are dated back to 1896, the year in which the first of the Modern Olympic Games were staged at Athens, Greece. The names of all of those cited, since 1896, are engraved upon the huge World Trophy, which reposes in Citizens Savings Hall.

The Athletic Foundation's sports library is considered to be the finest and most complete in existence. It covers all sports, and includes a remarkable Olympic Games collection. The library consists of thousands of volumes, research files, publications, photographs and sports films.

College Basketball All-America Teams are chosen annually by the Athletic Foundation, dating back to 1905. College Basketball National Championship Teams selections date back to 1901. National Championship College Football Teams are also chosen annually, with selections dating back to 1883, as are Player of the Year selections.

For the California area, the Athletic Foundation annually grants Ath-

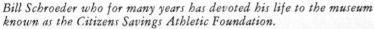

Bill Schroeder who for many years has devoted his life to the museum known as the Citizens Savings Athletic Foundation.

lete of the Year awards—dating back to 1890 in Northern California, and 1900 in Southern California. Athlete of the Month awards are granted, dating back to 1936 in Southern California, and 1937 in Northern California.

The High Schools award program, first developed in 1937, honoring athletes in both Northern California and Southern California, is most extensive. Awards are granted for all sports, for both boys and girls, and are presented at special ceremonies.

The Olympic Games display, lodged in Citizens Savings Hall, is one of the finest in the world. In the very large collection are Olympic Games memorabilia, uniforms, photographs, and a great number of medallions entrusted by those who won them.

World Trophy, Halls of Fame, Athlete of the Year and Athlete of the Month selections are made by the Citizens Savings Hall Board, composed of Jim Cour, United Press-International; Bud Furillo, Radio KIIS; Chuck Garrity, Los Angeles Times; Fred Hessler, Radio KMPC; Allan Malamud, Los Angeles Herald-Examiner; Allin Slate, Radio KNX; Jack Stevenson, Associated Press; Gil Stratton, Radio KNX; W. R. Bill Schroeder, and Elwood A. Teague, chairman.

High Schools awards are acted upon by an All-Southern California and All-Northern California Board of Athletics.

Northern California Athlete of the Year, and Athlete of the Month awards are acted on by a Citizens Savings Board composed of William Conlin, Sacramento Union; Louis Duino, San Jose Mercury-News; Eric Prewitt, Associated Press; Joe Sargus, United Press-International; Marco Smolich, Sacramento Bee; Bob Valli, Oakland Tribune; and Roger Williams, San Francisco Examiner.

With all of its many activities—maintenance of the museum and library and film service, sports research, executive assignments, awards selections and awards programs, and involvement in civic affairs of sports, the Athletic Foundation's supervisory staff is extremely small . . . W. R. Bill Schroeder, Managing Director, 1936 — 1976; Braven Dyer, Jr., Assistant Director, 1950 — 1976; Patricia Donnelly, Executive Secretary, 1973 — 1976; and Sally Gutierrez, Librarian, 1970 — 1976.

The Athletic Foundation's sports museum and sports library are open to the public without charge. Hours are: Monday through Friday, 9 a.m. to 5 p.m., and Saturday, 9 a.m. to 3 p.m. Annual visitation at the sports museum is approximately 40,000. It is estimated that more than 1,150,000 persons have visited the sports museum since 1948, including athletes, coaches and sports dignitaries from all over the world.

It is estimated that more than 150,000 awards have been granted by the Athletic Foundation since 1936.

Citizens Savings Athletic Foundation, formerly Helms Athletic Foundation, observed its fortieth anniversary on October 15, 1976.

The Athletic Foundation's original benefactor was the late Paul H. Helms, and the Helms family, 1936 — 1970. Citizens Savings and Loan Association of California has been the benefactor since 1970.

The National Bowling Hall of Fame and Museum is located in the first floor wing of Bowling Headquarters in Greendale, Wisconsin.

Interior view of the Bowling Hall of Fame showing the display of the enshrined bowlers and their accomplishments.

The Fresh Water Fishing Hall of Fame at Hayward, Wisconsin, which will be enlarged.

The proposed expanded Fishing Hall of Fame will be in the shape of a muskie with large displays of record fish, casting pools, and other features.

(on following page)
The Professional Football Hall of Fame, Canton, Ohio, is an impressive building with many exciting displays of historic memorabilia and a 250 seat theater that features films of famous games.

The Jim Thorpe statue and the curving ramp to the exhibition areas greet the visitor on his arrival and give a hint of the excitement to come.

Every one of the 28 NFL teams has its own individual exhibition in the unique Professional Football Today display.

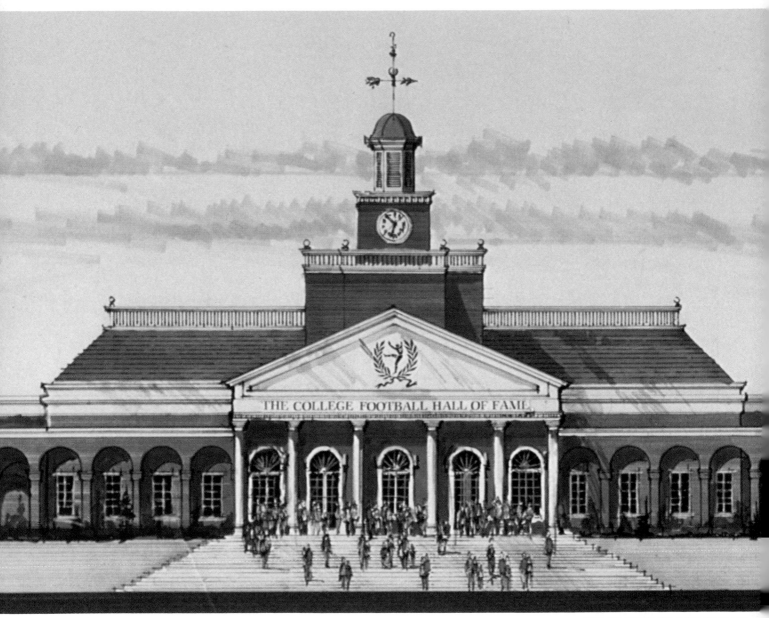

The College Football Hall of Fame will occupy this new building shown in the rendering of the architects. It will be a part of the King's Island Family Entertainment Complex which is on interstate 71, south of Columbus, Ohio about 70 miles and north of Cincinnati about 25 miles.

CITIZENS SAVINGS ATHLETIC FOUNDATION
HALLS OF FAME

These lists omit coaches, noteworthy contributors, athletic directors, public relation directors and others that are included in the CSA Foundation listing.

The autographed baseball collection.

AUTOMOBILE RACING

Drivers:

TONY BETTENHAUSEN
JIMMY BRYAN
BOB BURMAN
EARL COOPER
BILL CUMMINGS
RALPH DE PALMA
PETER DE PAOLO

DAN GURNEY
SAM HANKS
HARRY HARTZ
EDDIE HEARNE
TED HORN
PARNELLI JONES
REX MAYS
LOUIS MEYER
TOMMY MILTON

RALPH MULFORD
JIMMY MURPHY
BARNEY OLDFIELD
JOHNNY PARSONS
JIM RATHMAN
MAURI ROSE
WILBUR SHAW
BILL VUKOVICH
ROGER WARD

BADMINTON
Players - Amateur:

Men:

JOSEPH C. ALSTON
DAVID G. FREEMAN
CHESTER GOSS
WALTER KRAMER
HAMILTON B. LAW
CARL WICKHAM
 LOVEDAY
A. MARTEN MENDEZ

JOHN RICHARD
 MITCHELL
DR. DONALD CLARK
 PAUP
JAMES R. POOLE
DONALD RICHARDSON
T. WYNN ROGERS
T. M. ROYCE
RICHARD O. YEAGER

Women:

LOIS ALSTON
BERTHA BARKHUFF
 CUNNINGHAM
HELEN GIBSON
JUDY DEVLIN
 HASHMAN
EVELYN BOLDRICK
 HOWARD

ETHEL MARSHALL
BEATRICE MASSMAN
LOMA MOULTON SMITH
HELEN NOBLE TIBBETTS
MARGARET VARNER
THELMA KINGSBURY
 WELCOME
JANET WRIGHT
ZOE SMITH YEAGER

BASEBALL
Major League

Players:

GROVER CLEVELAND
 ALEXANDER
ADRIAN 'CAP' ANSON
LUCIUS APPLING
EARL AVERILL
FRANK BAKER
DAVID BANCROFT
JACOB BECKLEY
JAMES BELL
CHARLES ALBERT
 'CHIEF' BENDER
LAWRENCE BERRA
JAMES BOTTOMLEY
LOUIS BOUDREAU
ROGER BRESNAHAN
DENNIS BROUTHERS
MORECAL 'MINER' BROWN
JESSE 'CRAB' BURKETT
ROY CAMPANELLA
MAX CAREY
FRANK 'HUSK' CHANCE
JOHN 'JACK' CHESBRO
FRED CLARKE
JOHN CLARKSON
ROBERTO CLEMENTE
TYRUS COBB
GORDON COCHRANE
EDWARD COLLINS

JAMES COLLINS
EARLE COMBS
CHARLES COMISKEY
STANLEY COVELESKI
SAMUEL CRAWFORD
JOSEPH CRONIN
WILLIAM 'CANDY' CUMMINGS
HAZEN 'KIKI' CUYLER
JAY HANNA 'DIZZY' DEAN
EDWARD DELEHANTY
WILLIAM DICKEY
JOSEPH DI MAGGIO
HUGH DUFFY
JOHN EVERS
WILLIAM EWING
URBAN 'RED' FABER
ROBERT W.A. FELLER
ELMER FLICK
EDWARD 'WHITEY' FORD
JAMES FOXX
FRANK FRISCH
JAMES 'PUD' GALVIN
H. LOUIS GEHRIG
CHARLES GEHRINGER
JOSH GIBSON
VERNON GOMEZ
LEON 'GOOSE' GOSLIN
HENRY GREENBERG
CLARK C. GRIFFITH
BURLEIGH GRIMES

ROBERT 'LEFTY' GROVE
CHARLES HAFEY
JESSE HAINES
WILLIAM HAMILTON
STANLEY 'BUCKY' HARRIS
CHARLES HARTNETT
HARRY HEILMANN
WILLIAM 'BILLY' HERMAN
HARRY HOOPER
ROGERS HORNSBY
WAITE HOYT
CARL HUBBELL
MONTE IRVIN
WALTER PERRY JOHNSON
WILLIAM 'JUDY' JOHNSON
TIMOTHY KEEFE
WILLIAM KEELER
JOSEPH KELLEY
GEORGE KELLY
MICHAEL KELLY
RALPH KINER
SANFORD KOUFAX
NAPOLEON LAJOIE
WALTER LEONARD
THEODORE LYONS
MICKEY MANTLE
HENRY MANUSH
WALTER MARANVILLE
RICHARD 'RUBE' MARQUARD
CHRISTOPHER MATHEWSON

THOMAS MC CARTHY
JOSEPH 'IRON MAN'
  MC GINNITY
JOHN MC GRAW
JOSEPH MEDWICK
STANLEY MUSIAL
CHARLES 'KID' NICHOLS
JAMES O'ROURKE
MELVIN OTT
SATCHEL PAIGE
HERBERT PENNOCK
EDWARD PLANK
CHARLES RADBOURN
EDGAR 'SAM' RICE
EPPA RIXEY

WILBERT ROBINSON
JACKIE ROBINSON
EDD ROUSH
CHARLES 'RED' RUFFING
GEORGE 'BABE' RUTH
RAYMOND SCHALK
ALOYSIUS SIMMONS
GEORGE SISLER
WARREN SPAHN
TRISTRAM SPEAKER
WILLIAM TERRY
SAMUEL THOMPSON
JOSEPH TINKER
HAROLD 'PIE' TRAYNOR
ARTHUR 'DAZZY' VANCE

GEORGE 'RUBE' WADDELL
JOHN 'HONUS' WAGNER
RODERICK WALLACE
EDWARD WALSH
LLOYD WANER
PAUL WANER
JOHN MONTGOMERY WARD
MICKEY WELCH
ZACHARIAH 'ZACH' WHEAT
THEODORE WILLIAMS
EARLY WYNN
DENTON 'CY' YOUNG
ROSS YOUNGS

BASKETBALL

Amateur - Men: There are some coaches included in this list.

Players and Coaches:

SAM BALTER
DON BARKSDALE
GALE BISHOP
VINCE BORYLA
RICHARD BOUSHKA
OMAR BROWNING
BART CARLTON
GORDON CARPENTER
JACK COLVIN
TEE CONNELLEY
CHARLES DARLING
FORREST
  DE BERNARDI
BERRY DUNHAM

HAL FISCHER
HERMAN FISCHER
JOE FORTENBERRY
ROBERT GRUENIG
BURDETTE HALDORSON
HAROLD HEWITT
VICTOR HOLT
CHARLES HYATT
ROBERT KURLAND
LESTER LANE
GRADY LEWIS
FRANK LUBIN
ANGELO LUISETTI
WILLIAM MARTIN
FRANK MC CABE

JOHN P. MC CAFFREY
JACK MC CRACKEN
JAMES MC NATT
MELVIN MILLER
WILLIAM H. MILLER
MARTIN NASH
LESTER O'GARA
TOM PICKELL
JAMES POLLARD
FRED PRALLE
GEORGE REEVES
BILL REIGEL
JESSE RENICK
GEORGE RODY
ROBERT SANDERS

JERRY SHIPP
MILTON SINGER
DICK SMITH
GEORGE STARBUCK
GARY THOMPSON
RONALD TOMSIC
GERALD TUCKER
DICK WELLS
WILLIAM WHEATLEY
GEORGE WILLIAMS
HOWARD WILLIAMS
WARREN WOMBLE
GEORGE YARDLEY

Amateur - Women

Players:

CAROLE PHILLIPS
  ASPEDON
ALLINE BANKS
LEOTA BARHAM
LORETTA BLANN

ALBERTA LEE COX
JOAN CRAWFORD
MILDRED DIDRIKSON
SANDRA FIETE
LURLYNE GREER
MARY WINSLOW
  HOFFAY

RITA HORKY
CORRINE JAAX
EVELYN JORDAN
MARY MARSHALL
LOMETA ODOM
DORIS ROGERS
MARGARET SEXTON

BARBARA SIPES
LUCILLE THURMAN
HAZEL WALKER
KATHERINE WASHINGT
NERA WHITE
ALBERTA WILLIAMS

College Players:

TUSTEN ACKERMAN, Kansas
LEW ALCINDOR, UCLA
ELGIN BAYLOR, Seattle
WESLEY BENNETT, Westminster, Pa.
LOUIS BERGER, Maryland
CHARLES BLACK, Kansas
ROBERT BOOZER, Kansas State
WILLIAM BRADLEY, Princeton

GUS BROBERG, Dartmouth
ARTHUR BROWNING, Missouri
HERBERT BUNKER, Missouri
BART CARLTON, Ada, Oklahoma
RICHARD CARMICHAEL,
  North Carolina
CHARLES CARNEY, Illinois
LEWIS CASTLE, Syracuse
WILT CHAMBERLAIN, Kansas
WILLIAM CHANDLER, Wisconsin
DAVID CHARTERS, Purdue
JOHN COBB, North Carolina
ROBERT COUSY, Holy Cross
FORREST DE BERNARDI,
  Westminster, Mo.
DAVE DE BUSSCHERE, Detroit
TERRY DISCHINGER, Purdue
GEORGE DIXON, California
WALTER DUKES, Seton Hall
LE ROY EDWARDS, Kentucky
PAUL ENDACOTT, Kansas
WAYNE ESTES, Utah State

RAYMOND EVANS, Kansas
ARNOLD FERRIN, Utah
HARRY FISHER, Columbia
DARRELL FLOYD, Furman
GEORGE GARDNER, Southwestern
GEORGE GLAMACK, North Carol.
THOMAS GOLA, La Salle
EMANUEL GOLDBLATT, Pennsyl
GAIL GOODRICH, UCLA
RICHARD GROAT, Duke
LEE GUTTERO, Southern Californi
CYRIL HAAS, Princeton
CLIFF HAGAN, Kentucky
DALE HALL, U.S. Military Academy
VICTOR HANSON, Syracuse
ELVIN HAYES, Houston
JULIAN HAYWARD, Wesleyan
WALTER HAZZARD, UCLA
DICK HEMRIC, Wake Forest
DON HENNON, Pittsburgh
BILL HENRY, Rice
FRED HETZEL, Davidson

National championship UCLA game balls.

ARTHUR HEYMAN, Duke
PAUL HINKLE, U. of Chicago
ERNEST HOUGHTON, Union
MARCUS HURLEY, Columbia
CHARLES HYATT, Pittsburgh
DARRELL IMHOFF, California
GEORGE IRELAND, Notre Dame
CHARLES KEINATH, Pennsylvania
THEODORE KIENDL, Columbia
GILMORE KINNEY, Yale
EDWARD KRAUSO, Notre Dame
ROBERT KURLAND,
    Oklahoma State
BOB LANIER, St. Bonaventure
ANTHONY LAVELLI, Yale
GEORGE LEVIS, Wisconsin
JOHN LOBSIGER, Missouri
ARTHUR LOEB, Princeton
CLYDE LOVELLETTE, Kansas
JAMES LOVELY, Creighton
JERRY LUCAS, Ohio Sate
ANGELO LUISETTI, Stanford
ED MACAULEY, St. Louis
PETE MARAVICH, Louisiana State
ROBERT MATTICK,
    Oklahoma State
DAN MC NICHOL, Pennsylvania
GEORGE MIKAN, De Paul
BOBBY MOERS, Texas
STANLEY MODZELEWSKI-
    STUTZ, R.I.

JOHN MOIR, Notre Dame
MAX MORRIS, Northwestern
RICK MOUNT, Purdue
CALVIN MURPHY, Niagara
CHARLES MURPHY, Purdue
CHARLES NASH, Kentucky
WILLIAM NASH, Columbia
PAUL NOWAK, Notre Dame
JOHN O'BRIEN, Columbia
JOHN O'BRIEN, Seattle
ARNOLD OSS, Minnesota
HARLAN 'PAT' PAGE, Chicago
HUBERT PECK, Pennsylvania
ROBERT PETTIT, Louisiana State
ANDREW PHILLIP, Illinois
FRED PRALLE, Kansas
SAM RANZINO, North Carolina State
JOSEPH REIFF, Northwestern
JESSE RENICK, Oklahoma State
RICHARD RICKETTS, Duquesne
OSCAR ROBERTSON, Cincinnati
GUY RODGERS, Temple
ELWOOD ROMNEY, Brigham Young
JOHN ROOSMA,
    U.S. Military Academy
LEONARD ROSENBLUTH,
    No. Carolina
CRAIG RUBY, Missouri
JOHN RUDOMETKIN, So. California
BILL RUSSELL, San Francisco
CAZZIE RUSSELL, Michigan

JOHN RYAN, Columbia
FORREST SALE, Kentucky
JOSEPH SCHAAF, Pennsylvania
DONALD SCHLUNDT, Indiana
JOHN SCHOMMER, Chicago
ALPHONSE SCHUMAKER, Dayton
CAREY SPICER, Kentucky
GERALD SPOHN, Washburn
DAVID STALLWORTH, Wichita
CHRISTIAN STEINMETZ, Wisconsin
GEORGE SWEENEY, Pennsylvania
HELMER SWENHOLT, Wisconsin
SID TANENBAUM, New York
JOHN 'CAT' THOMPSON, Montana State
GERALD TUCKER, Oklahoma
WESTLEY UNSELD, Louisville,
CHESTER WALKER, Bradley
BILL WALTON, UCLA
FRANK WARD, Montana State
JERRY WEST, West Virginia
SIDNEY WICKS, UCLA
GEORGE WILLIAMS, Missouri
LES WITTE, Wyoming
JOHN WOODEN, Purdue
RAY WOODS, Illinois
JEWELL YOUNG, Purdue
ROBERT ZAWOLUK, St. John's

Major League:

Players:

PAUL ARIZIN
ELGIN BAYLOR
CARL BRAUN
WILT CHAMBERLAIN
ROBERT COUSY
WAYNE EMBRY
LARRY FOUST
JOE GRABOWSKI

HAL GREER
RICHIE GUERIN
CLIFF HAGAN
TOM HEINSOHN
BAILEY HOWELL
SAM JONES
JOHN KERR
CLYDE LOVELLETTE
ED MACAULEY
SLATER MARTIN

GEORGE MIKAN
VERN MIKKELSEN
WILLIE NAULLS
BOB PETTIT
ANDREW PHILLIP
JAMES POLLARD
FRANK RAMSEY
ARNOLD RISEN
BILL RUSSELL
ADOLPH SCHAYES

BILL SHARMAN
JACK TWYMAN
GEORGE YARDLEY
LENNY WILKENS
MAX ZASLOFSKY

BOXING

Pugilists - Professional:

LOU AMBERS
HENRY ARMSTRONG
ABE ATTELL
PAUL BERLENBACH
JACK BRITTON
TONY CANZONERI
'KID' CHOCOLATE
BILLY CONN
JAMES J. CORBETT
JOHNNY COULON
JACK DELANEY
JACK DEMPSEY
JACK DILLON
'DIXIE' KID
GEORGE DIXON
JOHNNY DUNDEE
JACKIE FIELDS
BOB FITZSIMMONS
JOE GANS

FRANKIE GENARO
MIKE GIBBONS
TOMMY GIBBONS
HARRY GREB
PETE HERMAN
'ACE' HUDKINS
JAMES J. JEFFRIES
JACK JOHNSON
LOUIS 'KID' KAPLAN
STANLEY KETCHEL
JOHNNY KILBANE
FRANK KLAUS
FIDEL LA BARBA
SAM LANGFORD
GEORGE 'KID' LAVIGNE
BENNY LEONARD
TED 'KID' LEWIS
BATTLING LEVINSKY
TOMMY LOUGHRAN

JOE LOUIS
JOE LYNCH
KID MC COY
TERRY MC GOVERN
JIMMY MC LARNIN
ROCKY MARCIANO
ARCHIE MOORE
DAVEY MOORE
BATTLING NELSON
PHILADELPHIA
    JACK O'BRIEN
MANUEL ORTIZ
BILLY PAPKE
WILLIE PEP
WILLIE RITCHIE
RAY ROBINSON
MAXIE ROSENBLOOM
BARNEY ROSS
JACK ROOT

TOMMY RYAN
SANDY SADDLER
TOM SHARKEY
MYSTERIOUS BILLY SMITH
JOHN L. SULLIVAN
BUD TAYLOR
LEW TENDLER
GENE TUNNEY
PANCHO VILLA
JOE WALCOTT
MICKEY WALKER
'KID' WILLIAMS
MIDGET WOLGAST

FENCING
Amateur:

Men:

ALBERT AXELROD
NORMAN C. ARMITAGE
GEORGE C. CALNAN
HUGO CASTELLO
JULIO M. CASTELLO
LAJOS S. CSISZAR
JOSE R. de CAPRILES
MIGUEL A. de CAPRILES
IRVING DE KOFF
ANDRE DELADRIER

CLOVIS F.J. DELADRIER
MICHAEL DE CICCO
RALPH B. FAULKNER
MAXWELL GARRET
RALPH M. GOLDSTEIN
ROBERT GRASSON
SHERMAN HALL
GRAEME M. HAMMOND
ALVAR HERMANSON
JOHN R. HUFFMAN
TRACY JAECKEL
JOSEPH L. LEVIS

EDWARD F. LUCIA
JAMES MONTAGUE
JAMES MURRAY
LEO G. NUNES
W. SCOTT O'CONNOR
J. BROOKS B. PARKER
J. SANFORD SALTUS
GEORGIO L. SANTELLI
CHARLES R. SCHMITTER
STANLEY S. SIEJA

Women:

HARRIET KING
HELENA MAYER
MAXINE MITCHELL
JANICE LEE YORK
  ROMARY
MARIA CERRA TISHMAN
MARION LLOYD VINCE

FOOTBALL
College:

Players:

FRANK ALBERT (Stanford)
CHARLES ALDRICH (Texas Christian)
JOSEPH ALEXANDER (Syracuse)
ALAN AMECHE (Wisconsin)
STANLEY BARNES (California)
BERT BASTON (Minnesota)
SAMUEL BAUGH (Texas Christian)
GARY BEBAN (UCLA)
HUBERT BECHTOL (Texas)
ANGELO BERTELLI (Notre Dame)
JOHN BERWANGER (Chicago)
FELIX BLANCHARD (Army)
LYNN BOMAR (Vanderbilt)
JAMES BRADSHAW (Nevada)
CHARLES BRICKLEY (Harvard)
JOHN H. BROWN (Navy)
JOHN MACK BROWN (Alabama)
BUDDY BURRIS (Oklahoma)
DICK BUTKUS (Illinois)
CHRISTIAN CAGLE (Army)
DAVID CAMPBELL (Harvard)
BILLY CANNON (Louisiana St.)
FRANK CARIDEO (Notre Dame)
HUNTER CARPENTER (Va. Tech)
WALKER CARPENTER (Geo. Tech)
CHARLES CARROLL (Washington)
HOWARD CASSADY (Ohio State)
GUY CHAMBERLAIN (Nebraska)
PAUL CHRISTMAN (Missouri)
EARL CLARK (Colorado State)
JOSH CODY (Vanderbilt)
WILLIAM CORBUS (Stanford)
GEO. CONNOR (H. Cross, N. Dame)
HECTOR COWAN (Princeton)
EDWIN COY (Yale)
GERALD DALRYMPLE (Tulane)
CHARLES DALY (Harvard, Army)
TOM DAVIES (Pittsburgh)
ERNIE DAVIS (Syracuse)
GLENN DAVIS (Army)
PAUL DES JARDIEN (Chicago)
JOHN DE WITT (Princeton)
GLENN DOBBS (Tulsa)
NICK DRAHOS (Cornell)
MORLEY DRURY (So. California)
WILLIAM DUDLEY (Virginia)
MARSHALL DUFFIELD (So. Calif.)

WALTER ECKERSALL (Chicago)
GLEN EDWARDS (Washington St.)
BEATTIE FEATHERS (Tennessee)
ROBERT FENIMORE
  (Oklahoma State)
JOHN FERRARO (So. California)
WESLEY FESLER (Ohio State)
WILLIAM FINCHER (Georgia Tech)
HAMILTON FISH (Harvard)
CLINTON FRANK (Yale)
RAYMOND FRANKOWSKI
  (Washington)
ROD FRANZ (California)
BENJAMIN FRIEDMAN (Michigan)
EDGAR GARBISCH (Army)
MICHAEL GARRETT (So. California)
GEORGE GIPP (Notre Dame)
MARSHALL GOLDBERG (Pittsburgh)
OTTO GRAHAM (Northwestern)
HAROLD GRANGE (Illinois)
ROBERT GRAYSON (Stanford)
HUNTINGTON HARDWICK
  (Harvard)
T. TRUXTON HARE (Pennsylvania)
CHARLES HARLEY (Ohio State)
TOM HARMON (Michigan)
HOWARD HARPSTER
  (Carnegie Tech)
EDWARD HART (Princeton)
LEON HART (Notre Dame)
HOMER HAZEL (Rutgers)
WILLIAM HEFFELFINGER (Yale)
MELVIN HEIN (Washington State)
TED HENDRICKS (Miami, Florida)
WILBUR HENRY (Wash. & Jefferson)
WILLIAM HESTON (Michigan)
HERMAN HICKMAN (Tennessee)
FRANK HINKEY (Yale)
JAMES HITCHCOCK (Auburn)
JAMES HOGAN (Yale)
JEROME HOLLAND (Cornell)
WILLIAM HOLLENBACH
  (Pennsylvania)
EDWIN HORRELL (California)
LESLIE HORVATH (Ohio State)
MILLARD HOWELL (Alabama)
DONALD HUTSON (Alabama)
HERBERT JOESTING (Minnesota)

CALVIN JONES (Iowa)
CHARLES JUSTICE (North Carolina)
MORTON KAER (So. California)
KENNETH KAVANAUGH
  (Louisiana St.)
EDGAR KAW (Cornell)
RICHARD KAZMAIER (Princeton)
JOHN KIMBROUGH (Texas A & M)
FRANK KINARD (Mississippi)
NILE KINNICK (Iowa)
HARRY KIPKE (Michigan)
RON KRAMER (Michigan)
JOHN LATTNER (Notre Dame)
ELMER LAYDEN (Notre Dame)
LANGDON LEA (Princeton)
JAMES LEECH (Virginia Military)
DARRELL LESTER (Texas Christian)
GORDON LOCKE (Iowa)
SID LUCKMAN (Columbia)
JOHN LUJACK (Notre Dame)
WILLIAM MC COLL (Stanford)
BANKS MC FADDEN (Clemson)
LEWIS MC FADIN (Texas)
ALVIN MC MILLIN (Centre)
FRANK MC PHEE (Princeton)
ROBERT MC WHORTER (Georgia)
EDWARD MAHAN (Harvard)
LE ROY MERCER (Pennsylvania)
LOUIS MICHAELS (Kentucky)
WAYNE MILLNER (Notre Dame)
DONN MOOMAW (UCLA)
HAROLD MULLER (California)
CLARENCE MUNN (Minnesota)
BRONKO NAGURSKI (Minnesota)
ERNEST NEVERS (Stanford)
MARSHALL NEWELL (Harvard)
LEO NOMELLINI (Minnesota)
ANDREW OBERLANDER (Dartmo
DAVID O'BRIEN (Texas Christian)
PAT O'DEA (Wisconsin)
ELMER OLIPHANT (Purdue, Army
BENJAMIN OOSTERBAAN (Mich
VITO PARILLI (Kentucky)
CLARENCE PARKER (Duke)
JAMES PARKER (Ohio State)
ROBERT PECK (Pittsburgh)
STANLEY PENNOCK (Harvard)
GEORGE PFANN (Cornell)

The Heisman Trophy corner.

ERNY PINCKERT (So. California)
FREDERICK POLLARD (Brown)
BARNEY POOLE (Mississippi, Army)
DUANE PURVIS (Purdue)
RICK REDMOND (Washington)
ROBERT REINHARD (California)
ROBERT REYNOLDS (Stanford)
LESLIE RICHTER (California)
GEORGE SAVITSKY (Pennsylvania)
GALE SAYERS (Kansas)
ADOLPH SCHULZ (Michigan)
FRANK SCHWAB (Lafayette)
PAUL SCHWEGLER (Washington)
GAIUS SHAVER (So. California)
THOMAS SHEVLIN (Yale)
O. J. SIMPSON (So. California)
FRED SINGTON (Alabama)
FRANK SINKWICH (Georgia)
EMIL SITKO (Notre Dame)
FRED SLATER (Iowa)
BRUCE SMITH (Minnesota)
ERNEST SMITH (So. California)
HARRY SMITH (So. Calfornia)

NEIL SNOW (Michigan)
MORTIMER SPRAGUE (Army)
DON STEPHENSON (Georgia Tech)
KENNETH STRONG (New York)
EVERETT STRUPPER
  (Georgia Tech)
HARRY STUHLDREHER
  (Notre Dame)
GEORGE TALIAFERRO (Indiana)
JAMES THORPE (Carlisle)
BENJAMIN TICKNOR (Harvard)
GAYNELL TINSLEY (Louisiana State)
CHARLES TRIPPI (Georgia)
J. EDWARD TRYON (Colgate)
DOAK WALKER (So. Methodist)
KENNETH WASHINGTON (UCLA)
JIM WEATHERALL (Oklahoma)
GEORGE WEBSTER (Michigan State)
HAROLD WEEKES (Columbia)
ED WEIR (Nebraska)
D. BELFORD WEST (Colgate)
BYRON WHITE (Colorado)
DONALD WHITMIRE (Alabama, Navy)

EDWIN WIDSETH (Minnesota)
RICHARD WILDUNG (Minnesota)
GEORGE WILSON (Washington)
ALBERT WISTERT (Michigan)
ALVIN WISTERT (Michigan)
ALEXANDER WOJCIECHOWICZ (Fordham)
RON YARY (Southern California)

Major League

Players:

BEN AGAJANIAN
FRANK ALBERT
LANCE ALWORTH
JON ARNETT
DOUGLAS ATKINS
BRUNO BRADUCCI
CLIFFORD BATTLES
SAMUEL BAUGH
CHARLES BEDNARIK
JAMES BENTON
RAYMOND BERRY
JOHN BLOOD
  (MC NALLY)
RAYMOND BRAY
GENE BRITO
JAMES BROWN
ANTHONY CANADEO
GINO CAPPELLETTI
EARL CLARK
CHARLES CONERLY
JAMES CONZELMAN
ARTHUR DONOVAN
JOHN DRISCOLL
WILLIAM DUDLEY

GLEN EDWARDS
THOMAS FEARS
RAY FLAHERTY
DANIEL FORTMANN
FRANK GIFFORD
OTTO GRAHAM
HAROLD GRANGE
FORREST GREGG
LOUIS GROZA
MELVIN HEIN
WILBUR HENRY
ARNOLD HERBER
WILLIAM HEWITT
CLARKE HINKLE
ELROY HIRSCH
ROBERT HUBBARD
ARTHUR HUNTER
DONALD HUTSON
WALTER KEISLING
FRANK KILROY
ROBERT LAYNE
EDDIE LE BARON
ALPHONSE LEEMANS
SID LUCKMAN
ROY LYMAN
JACK MANDERS

GINO MARCHETTI
JAMES MARTIN
OLLIE MATSON
GEORGE MC AFEE
HUGH MC ELHENNY
MARLIN MC KEEVER
EDWARD MEADOR
DICK MODZELEWSKI
MARION MOTLEY
GEORGE MUSSO
BRONKO NAGURSKI
AL NESSER
ERNEST NEVERS
RAY NITSCHKE
LEO NOMELLINI
DON PAUL
JOE PERRY
PETER PIHOS
RAYMOND RENFRO
LESLIE RICHTER
JAMES RINGO
ANDY ROBUSTELLI
KYLE ROTE
TOBIN ROTE
ROBERT ST. CLAIR
JOSEPH SCHMIDT

VICTOR SEARS
EDWARD SPRINKLE
BRYAN BART STARR
ERNEST STAUTNER
KENNETH STRONG
JOSEPH STYDAHAR
JAMES THORPE
YELVERTON TITTLE
GEORGE TRAFTON
CHARLES TRIPPI
EMLEN TUNNELL
CLYDE TURNER
JOHN UNITAS
NORMAN VAN BROCKLIN
STEVE VAN BUREN
DOAK WALKER
ROBERT WATERFIELD
ALEX WEBSTER
FRED WILLIAMS
LAWRENCE WILSON
ALEX WOJCIECHOWICZ
CLAUDE 'BUDDY' YOUNG
PAUL YOUNGER

GOLF
Amateur

Men:

BILLY BURKE
H. CHANDLER EGAN
CHARLES EVANS, JR.
JOHNNY FARRELL
ROBERT A. GARDNER
VICTOR GHEZZI
ROBERT T. JONES
W. LAWSON LITTLE, JR.
FRANCIS OUIMET

HENRY PICKARD
JOHNNY REVOLTA
FRANK STRANAHAN
JESS W. SWEETSER
JEROME TRAVERS
WALTER TRAVIS
WILLIE TURNESA
HARVIE WARD
MARVIN WARD

Women:

DOROTHY CAMPBELL
GLENNA VARE COLLETT
MARGARET CURTIS
JO ANNE GUNDERSON
BEATRIX HOYT
BETTY JAMESON
ALEXA STIRLING
VIRGINIA VAN WIE

Professional

Men:

WILLIE ANDERSON
TOMMY ARMOUR
JERRY BARBER
JAMES M. BARNES
JULIUS BOROS
JACK BURKE, JR.
HARRY COOPER
JAMES DEMARET
LEO DIEGEL

OLIN DUTRA
DOUG FORD
RALPH GULDAHL
WALTER HAGEN
BEN HOGAN
JOCK HUTCHISON
W. LAWSON LITTLE, JR.
LLOYD MANGRUM
JOHN MC DERMOTT
CARY MIDDLECOFF
BYRON NELSON

PAUL RUNYAN
GENE SARAZEN
DENNY SHUTE
ALEX SMITH
HORTON SMITH
MAC DONALD SMITH
SAM SNEAD
CRAIG WOOD
LEW WORSHAM

Women:

PATTY BERG
BETTY JAMESON
BETSY RAWLS
LOUISE SUGGS
MILDRED DIDRIKSON
    ZAHARIAS

GYMNASTS

The World Trophy and an 1880's racing bicycle, two of the free-standing exhibits.

Men:

RAYMOND BASS
DALLAS BIXLER
FRANK CUMISKEY
WILLIAM DENTON
JOSEPH
    GIALLOMBARDO*
GEORGE GULACK
FRANK HAUBOLD
ALFRED JOCHIM

PAUL KREMPEL
FRANK KRIZ
JOHN MAIS
FREDERICK MEYER
CHESTER PHILLIPS*
ARTHUR PITT
CURTIS ROTTMAN
GEORGE WHEELER
HERMAN WITZIG
ROLAND WOLFE

Women:

MARIAN TWINING
    BARONE
META NEUMANN ELSTE
CLARA SCHROTH
    LOMADY

HANDBALL

Players:

SAM ATCHESON
AL BANUET
ROBERT BRADY

FRANK COYLE
VICTOR HERSHOWITZ
JIM JACOBS
MAYNARD LASWELL
GUS LEWIS

OSCAR OBERT
JOSEPH PLATAK
GEORGE QUAM
KENNETH SCHNEIDER
ANGELO TRULIO

RACQUETBALL

Athletes:

CHARLES BRUMFIELD   DR. BUD MUEHLEISEN

ROWING

Pioneer Oarsmen:
ELLIS WARD
GILBERT WARD
W. HENRY WARD
JOSHA WARD

Coxswains:
DONALD F. BLESSING
CLIFFORD GOES
DONALD GRANT
CORNELIUS S. SEABRING

Crew — Oarsmen:
RAYMOND ANDRESEN
JOHN COLLYER
HORACE E. DAVENPORT
WAYNE FRYE
HOWARD T. KINGSBURY JR.
CHARLES LUEDER
ARTHUR J. OSMAN
RUDOLPH RAUCH
HOWARD W. ROBBINS
R. H. SANFORD

FRANK B. SHAKESPEARE
FRED SPUHN
ALEXANDER STRONG
FRANK STRONG
RICHARD WAILES

Single Sculls:
JOSEPH W. BURK
FRANK B. GREER
JOHN B. KELLY, SR.
JOHN B. KELLY, JR.
DONALD M. SPERO
EDWARD H. TEN EYCK

Strokes:
DARCY CURWEN
PETER D. DONLON
D. T. EDDY
ELWOOD FOOTE
JOHN GARDINER
THEODORE GARHART
FRANCIS L. HIGGINSON
CLYDE KING

JOHN LEH
EDWARD N. PACKARD
EDWARD G. STEVENS
R. W. 'SI' WEED

Single-Double Sculls:
KENNETH F. BURNS

Double Sculls:
BERNARD P. COSTELLO, JR.
PAUL V. COSTELLO
JAMES T. FIFER
JAMES GARDINER
W. E. GILMORE
DUVALL HECHT
CHARLES MC ILVAINE
JOHN B. KELLY, SR.
JOHN MULCAHY
KENNETH MYERS
EDWARD H. TEN EYCK
WILLIAM M. VARLEY

*Also cited as coach

8-OAR CREWS

Vesper Boat Club—1900
Olympic Games Champions:
ROSCOE C. LOCKWOOD
EDWARD MARSH
EDWIN HEDLEY
WILLIAM CARR
JOHN F. GEIGER
JAMES B. JUVENAL
HARRY G. DE BAECKE
JOHN O. EXLEY
LOUIS C. ABEL, Coxswain

Harvard University—1914:
LEVERETT SALTONSTALL
JAMES TALCOTT, JR.
HENRY H. MEYER
HENRY S. MIDDENDORF
J. WILLIAM MIDDENDORF
DAVID P. MORGAN
LOUIS CURTIS
CHARLES C. LUND
HENRY L. F. KREGER, Coxswain
JAMES WRAY, Coach

U.S. Naval Academy—1920
Olympic Games Champions:
VIRGIL V. JACOMINI
EDWIN D. GRAVES
WILLIAM C. JORDAN
EDWARD P. MOORE
ALDEN R. SANBORN
DONALD H. JOHNSON
VINCENT J. GALLAGHER
CLYDE W. KING
SHERMAN R. CLARK, Coxswain
RICHARD A. GLENDON, Coach

Yale University—1924
Olympic Games Champions:
LEONARD G. CARPENTER
FREDERICK SHEFFIELD
ALFRED M. WILSON
JAMES S. ROCKEFELLER
J. LESTER MILLER
HOWARD T. KINGSBURY, JR.
BENJAMIN M. SPOCK
ALFRED D. LINDLEY
LAURENCE R. STODDARD,
  Coxswain
EDWIN O. LEADER, Coach

University of California—1928
Olympic Games Champions:
MARVIN STALDER
JOHN BRINCK
FRANCIS FREDERICK
WILLIAM G. THOMPSON
WILLIAM DALLY
JAMES WORKMAN
HUBERT CALDWELL
PETER D. DONLON
DONALD F. BLESSING, Coxswain
CARROLL F. EBRIGHT, Coach

Columbia University—1929:
HENRY G. WALTER, JR.
JOHN F. MURPHY
SAMUEL R. WALKER
WILLIAM B. SANFORD
ARTHUR DOUGLAS
WILLIAM H. BLESSE
HORACE E. DAVENPORT
ALISTAIR MAC BAIN
ROBERT B. BERMAN, Coxswain
RICHARD J. GLENDON, Coach

University of California—1932
Olympic Games Champions:
WINSLOW HALL
HAROLD TOWER
CHARLES CHANDLER
BURTON JASTRAM
DAVID DUNLAP
DUNCAN GREGG
JAMES BLAIR
EDWIN SALISBURY
NORRIS GRAHAM, Coxswain
CARROLL F. EBRIGHT, Coach

University of Washington—1936
Olympic Games Champions:
HERBERT R. MORRIS
CHARLES W. DAY
GORDON B. ADAM
JOHN G. WHITE
JAMES B. MC MILLIN
GEORGE E. HUNT, JR.
JOSEPH HARRY RANTZ
DONALD B. HUME
ROBERT G. MOCH, Coxswain
ALVIN M. ULBRICKSON, Coach
A. DELOS SCHOCH,
member of regular-season crew

University of California—1948
Olympic Games Champions:
JACK STACK
JUSTUS SMITH
DAVID BROWN
LLOYD BUTLER
GEORGE AHLGREN
JAMES HARDY
DAVID TURNER
IAN TURNER
RALPH PURCHASE, Coxswain
CARROLL F. EBRIGHT, Coach

U.S. Naval Academy—1952
Olympic Games Champions:
FRANK B. SHAKESPEARE
WILLIAM B. FIELDS
JAMES R. DUNBAR
RICHARD F. MURPHY
ROBERT M. DETWEILER
HENRY A. PROCTOR
WAYNE T. FRYE
EDWARD G. STEVENS, JR.
CHARLES D. MANRIG, Coxswain
RUSSELL S. CALLOW, Coach

U.S. Naval Academy—1953:
FRANK B. SHAKESPEARE
WILLIAM B. FIELDS
JAMES R. DUNBAR
RICHARD F. MURPHY
ROBERT M. DETWEILER
HENRY A. PROCTOR
WAYNE T. FRYE
EDWARD G. STEVENS, JR.
ROBERT JONES, Coxswain
RUSSELL S. CALLOW, Coach

Yale University—1956
Olympic Games Champions:
THOMAS CHARLTON, JR.
DAVID WIGHT
JOHN COOKE
DONALD BEER
CHARLES GRIMES
CALDWELL ESSELSTYN
RICHARD WAILES
ROBERT MOREY
WILLIAM R. BECKLEAN, Coxswain
JAMES A. RATHSCHMIDT, Coach

Cornell University—1957:
JOHN VAN HORN
BOB STALEY
DAVE DAVIS
TODD SIMPSON
WILLIAM SCHUMACHER
CLAYTON CHAPMAN
GEORGE FORD
PHIL GRAVINK
CARL SCHWARTZ, Coxswain
R. HARRISON SANFORD, Coach

Vesper Boat Club—1964
Olympic Games Champions:
JOSEPH AMLONG
HUGH FOLEY
STANLEY CWIKLINSKI
THOMAS AMLONG
EMORY CLARK
BOYCE BUDD
WILLIAM KNECHT
WILLIAM STOWE
ROBERT ZIMONYI, Coxswain
ALLEN P. ROSENBERG, Coach

4-OAR CREWS

Columbia College — 1878:
EDWIN E. SAGE
CYRUS EDSON
H. C. RIDABOCK
J. T. GOODWIN

Lake Washington R. C. — 1960
Olympic Games Champions:
ARTHUR D. AYRAULT
THEODORE A. NASH
RICHARD D. WAILES
JOHN A. SAYRE

Pennsylvania Barge — 1928
Olympic Games (2nd):
ERNEST H. BAYER
WILLIAM G. MILLER
GEORGE A. HEALIS
CHARLES G. KARLE

PAIR-OAR CREWS

Stanford Crew Association
Olympic Games Champions:
EDWARD P. FERRY
CONN FINDLAY
KENT MITCHELL, Coxswain

Potomac Boat Club — 1968
Olympic Games (2nd):
ANTHONY P. JOHNSON
LAWRENCE A. HOUGH

Harvard University — 1947
8-Oar Crew:
FRANCIS CUNNINGHAM, JR.
PAUL W. KNAPLUND
FRANK R. STRONG
JUSTIN E. GALE
ROBERT G. STONE, JR.
RICHARD S. EMMETT, JR.
CLARENCE S. CLARK
MICHAEL J. SCULLY
ALBERT C. PETITE, Coxswain
THOMAS D. BOLLES, Coach

University of Washington — 1948
Olympic Games Champions
4-Oar Crew:
WARREN D. WESTLUND
ROBERT D. MARTIN
ROBERT I. WILL
GORDON S. GIOVANELLI
ALLEN J. MORGAN, Coxswain

SWIMMING

Men:

GEORGE BREEN
MICHAEL BURTON
RICHARD CLEVELAND
CLARENCE CRABBE
CHARLES DANIELS
JEFFREY FARRELL
PETER FICK
RALPH FLANAGAN
ALAN FORD
L. B. GOODWIN
H. JAMISON HANDY
HARRY HEBNER
CHESTER JASTREMSKI
DUKE KAHANAMOKU
ADOLPH KEIFER
GEORGE KOJAC
FORD KONNO
LUDY LANGER
MICHAEL MC DERMOTT
PERRY MC GILLIVRAY
FRANK MC KINNEY
JAMES MC LANE
JACK MEDICA

KEO NAKAMA
YOSHI OYOKAWA
WALLY RIS
CARL ROBIE
MURRAY ROSE
NORMAN ROSS
RICHARD ROTH
ROY SAARI
CARROLL SCHAEFFER
CLARK SCHOLES
DON SCHOLLANDER
BILL SMITH
WALTER SPENCE
MARK SPITZ
ALLEN STACK
MICHAEL TROY
JOSEPH VERDEUR
W. L. WALLEN
JOHN WEISSMULLER
WILLIAM WOOLSEY
WILLIAM YORZYK

Divers — Men:

DAVID BROWNING
EARL CLARK
ROBERT CLOTWORTHY
RICHARD DEGENER
PETER DESJARDINS
GEORGE GAIDZIK
BRUCE HARLAN
SAMMY LEE
CLARENCE PINKSTON
AL PATNIK
MICHAEL RILEY
KENNETH SITZBERGER
HAROLD SMITH
GARY TOBIAN
ROBERT WEBSTER
ALBERT WHITE
BERNARD WRIGHTSON

Women:

CATHERINE BALL
SYBIL BAUER
ETHELDA BLEIBTREY
CARIN CONE
ANN CURTIS
DONNA DE VARONA
GERTRUDE EDERLE
CATHY FERGUSON
CAROLYN GREEN
BRENDA HELSER
ELEANOR HOLM
LENORE KIGHT
CLAUDIA KOLB

HELENE MADISON
SHELLEY MANN
NANCY MERKI
DEBORAH MEYER
MARTHA NORELIUS
KATHERINE RAWLS
SYLVIA RUUSKA
CHRIS VON SALTZA
HELEN WAINWRIGHT
SHARON STOUDER
SUZANNE ZIMMERMAN
LILLIAN WATSON

Divers — Women:

LESLIE BUSH
GEORGIA COLEMAN
VICTORIA DRAVES
MARJORIE GESTRING
SUE GOSSICK
JUNE STOVER IRWIN
MICKI KING
PATRICIA MC CORMICK
ELSIE HANNEMAN MC EVOY
HELEN MEANY
PAULA JEAN MYERS POPE
HELEN CRLENKOVICH MORGAN
ZOE ANN OLSEN
THELMA PAYNE SANBORN
ELIZABETH BECKER PINKSTON
DOROTHY POYNTON
KATHERINE RAWLS
AILEEN RIGGIN
ANN ROSS

TENNIS
Amateur—Men:

Players:

WILMER ALLISON	JACK KRAMER	VINCENT RICHARDS	HOLCOMBE WARD
J. DONALD BUDGE	WILLIAM LARNED	ROBERT L. RIGGS	MALCOLM WHITMAN
OLIVER A. CAMPBELL	GEORGE M. LOTT	FRED 'TED' SCHROEDER	R. NORRIS WILLIAMS
DWIGHT DAVIS	GENE MAKO	RICHARD SEARS	ROBERT WRENN
RICHARD GONZALES	CHARLES MC KINLEY	E. VICTOR SEIXAS	
WILLIAM JOHNSTON	MAURICE MC LOUGHLIN	WILLIAM T. TILDEN	
	R. LINDLEY MURRAY	TONY TRABERT	
	FRANK A. PARKER	H. ELLSWORTH VINES	

Women:

Players:

JULIETTE ATKINSON	SARAH PALFREY COOKE	DARLENE HARD	ELISABETH MOORE
PAULINE BETZ	MARGARET OSBORNE duPONT	DORIS HART	ELIZABETH RYAN
LOUIS BROUGH	SHIRLEY FRY	HELEN JACOBS	HAZEL HOTCHKISS WIGHTMAN
MARY K. BROWNE	ALTHEA GIBSON	BILLIE JEAN KING	
MAY SUTTON BUNDY	NANCY RICHEY GUNTER	MOLLA B. MALLORY	
MAUREEN CONNOLLY		ALICE MARBLE	
		HELEN WILLS MOODY	

TRACK AND FIELD
Men:

PLATT ADAMS	HARRISON DILLARD	JAMES LIGHTBODY	ALMA RICHARDS
DAN AHEARN	GILBERT DODDS	DALLAS LONG	ROBERT RICHARDS
DAVID ALBRITTON	JAMES DONAHUE	PETER MC ARDLE	RALPH ROSE
HORACE ASHENFELTER	HENRY DREYER	JOSEPH MC CLUSKEY	PATRICK RYAN
RICHARD ATTLESEY	CHARLES DUMAS	PATRICK MC DONALD	JAMES RYUN
ROBERT BACKUS	BEN EASTMAN	MATT MC GRATH	JACKSON SHOLZ
RAYMOND BARBUTI	BARNEY EWELL	LESLIE MAC MITCHELL	ROBERT SEAGREN
LEE BARNES	RAY EWRY	ROBERT MATHIAS	MELVIN SHEPPARD
ROBERT BEAMON	J. J. FLANAGAN	RANDY MATSON	MARTIN SHERIDAN
GREGORY BELL	M. W. FORD	RALPH METCALFE	JAY SILVESTER
AL BLOZIS	EDWARD GORDON	EARLE MEADOWS	ARNOLD SOWELL
WILLIAM BONTHRON	LOUIS GREGORY	'TED' MEREDITH	CURTIS STONE
JOHN BORICAN	FORTUNE GORDIEN	BILLY MILLS	LESTER STEERS
RALPH BOSTON	ALEX GRANT	CHARLES MOORE, JR.	ANDREW STANFIELD
DONALD BRAGG	G. R. GRAY	GLENN MORRIS	F. MORGAN TAYLOR
HERMAN BRIX	ARCHIE HAHN	BOBBY MORROW	JOHN THOMAS
T. E. BURKE	EDWARD HAMM	LORIN MURCHISON	WILBUR THOMPSON
LEE CALHOUN	GLEN HARDIN	LON MYERS	EDDIE TOLAN
MILTON CAMPBELL	BOB HAYES	J. S. MITCHELL	WILLIAM TOOMEY
KENNETH CARPENTER	FRANKLIN HELD	RONALD MORRIS	JACK TORRANCE
SABIN CARR	GEORGE HORINE	WILLIAM NIEDER	FORREST TOWNS
ROY COCHRAN	CLARENCE HOUSER	PARRY O'BRIEN	CORNELIUS WARMERDAM
THOMAS CONNEFF	DE HART HUBBARD	AL OERTER	BERNARD WEFERS
HAROLD CONNOLLY	CORNELIUS JOHNSON	GEORGE W. ORTON	MALVIN WHITFIELD
TOM COURTNEY	RAFER JOHNSON	HAROLD OSBORN	FRED WILT
RALPH CRAIG	HAYES JONES	JESSE OWENS	FRED WOLCOTT
GLENN CUNNINGHAM	JOHN PAUL JONES	CHARLES PADDOCK	JOHN WOODRUFF
WILLIE DAVENPORT	JOHN A. KELLEY	MELVIN PATTON	FRANK WYKOFF
GLENN DAVIS	JOHN J. KELLY	EULACE PEACOCK	C. K. YANG
HAROLD DAVIS	ABEL KIVIAT	MYER PRINSTEIN	
JACK DAVIS	ALVIN KRAENZLEIN	JOIE RAY	
RON DELANY	MICHAEL LARRABEE	GEORGE RHODEN	
CLARENCE DE MAR	DONALD LASH	J. GREGORY RICE	

Women:

EARLENE BROWN	EVELYNE HALL	WILMA RUDOLPH
ALICE COACHMAN	FRANCES KAZUBSKI	JEAN SHILEY
OLGA CONNOLLY	MABEL LANDRY	HELEN STEPHENS
LILLIAN COPELAND	MARJORIE LARNEY	WYOMIA TYUS
MILDRED DIDRIKSON	MILDRED MC DANIEL	STELLA WALSH
DOROTHY DODSON	EDITH MC GUIRE	WILLYE WHITE
MAE FAGGS	BETTY ROBINSON	

Walking:

JOHN DENI
HARRY HINKEL
HENRY LASKAU
WILLIAM MIHALO
WILLIAM PLANT
RONALD ZINN

VOLLEYBALL
Amateur

Men:

SPARTICO ANZUINI
HOLLY BROCK
WILBUR CALDWELL
ROLF ENGEN
A. H. MASSOPUST
JAMES MONTAGUE
CARL OWENS
MICHAEL O'HARA
WILLIAM OLSSOM

SIDNEY NACHLAS
PEDRO VELASCO
JAMES WARD
SAMUEL M. WARD
JOHN WEIBLE
HAROLD WENDT
JAMES WORTHAM

Women:

CAROLYN GREGORY CONRAD
JEAN K. GAERTNER
LOIS ELLEN HARAUGHTY
ZOANN NEFF MC FARLAND
LOU SARA CLARK MC WILLIAMS
LINDA MURPHY
NANCY OWEN
JANE WARD

WEIGHTLIFTING

PAUL ANDERSON
DICK BACHTELL
DAVID BERGER
ISAAC BERGER
DAN CANTORE
JOHN DAVIS
JOE DI PIETRO
CLYDE B. EMERICH
JAMES GEORGE
PETER GEORGE

JOHN C. GRIMEK
GARY GUBNER
WALTER IMAHARA
EMERICH ISHIKAWA
MICHAEL KARCHUT
RUSSELL KNIPP
TOMMY KONO
BILL MARCH
JOE MARCH
DAVID MAYOR

JOE MILLS
MICHAEL MUNGIOLI
KEN PATERA
JOSEPH PULER
LOU RIECKE
HAROLD SAKATA
NORBERT SCHEMANSKY
DAVID SHEPPARD
FRANK SPELLMAN
STANLEY STANCZYK

STEPHEN STANKO
ANTHONY TERLAZZO
JOHN TERPAK
JOHN TERRY
CHARLES VINCI

WINTER SPORTS
Amateur

Men:

RICHARD BUTTON
Figure Skating
RICHARD DURRANCE
Skiing
ALF ENGEN
Skiing
KENNETH HENRY
Speed Skating
IRVING JAFFEE
Speed Skating
DAVID W. JENKINS
Figure Skating

HAYES ALAN JENKINS
Figure Skating
CHARLES JEWTRAW
Speed Skating
RICHARD TERRY
  MC DERMOTT
JOHN A. SHEA
Speed Skating
'BUDDY' WALLACE
  WERNER
Skiing

Women:

TENLEY ALBRIGHT
Figure Skating
BARBARA COCHRAN
Skiing
ELIZABETH DU BOIS
Speed Skating
PEGGY FLEMING
Figure Skating
GRETCHEN FRASER
Skiing
CAROL HEISS
Figure Skating

ANNE HENNING
Speed Skating
DIANNE HOLUM
Speed Skating
KIT KLEIN
Speed Skating
ANDREA MEAD LAWRENCE
Skiing
JEAN SAUBERT
Skiing
PENNY PITOU ZIMMERMAN
Skiing

WRESTLING
Amateur:

CHARLES ACKERLY
DAVID ARNDT
RICHARD W. BAUGHMAN
PETE BLAIR
NED BLASS
DOUGLAS BLUBAUGH
GLENN BRAND
CONRAD CALDWELL
RICHARD DIABATISTA
GEORGE S. DOLE
ROSS FLOOD
DAN GABLE
VERN GAGNE
ANTHONY GIZONI
LARRY HAYES
STANLEY HENSON, JR.
ROBERT HESS

DON HODGE
DICK HUTTON
BURL JENNINGS
MERLE JENNINGS
ALAN D. KELLEY
WILLIAM KERSLAKE
WILLIAM H. KOLL
LOWELL LANGE
GEORGE LAYMAN
FRANK LEWIS
HARDIE LEWIS
VERNON LOGAN
LAWRENCE MANTOOTH
WAYNE MARTIN
TERENCE MC CANN
EARL MC CREADY
CHARLES MC DANIEL

JOE MC DANIEL
GEORGE M. MEHNERT
PETER MEHRINGER
ALLIE MORRISON
NORVARD NALAN
WILLIAM J. NELSON
GENE NICKS
M. A. 'DOC' NORTHRUP
EDWIN PEERY
HUGH PEERY
BEN PETERSON
ARNOLD PLAZA
ROBIN REED
JACK RILEY
JOSEPH SAPORA
JOE SCARPELLO
ELLIOTT SIMONS

VIRGIL SMITH
WILLIAM SMITH
JOHN SPELLMAN
HARRY STEELE
RALPH TEAGUE
JACK VAN BEBBER
RUSSELL VIS
WILLIAM WEICK
WAYNE WELLS
ALFRED WHITEHURST
SHELBY WILSON
HENRY WITTENBERG
KEITH YOUNG

THE U.S.F.S.A. MUSEUM AND HALL OF FAME

Boston, Massachusetts

Located in the Sears Crescent Building at City Hall Plaza in Boston is a treasury of figure skating memorabilia: The United States Figure Skating Association Museum and Hall of Fame. The distinctive features and memorable moments of the sport of figure skating are highlighted in this showcase of rare and interesting items from around the world.

A prominent part of the Museum's collections are its trophies and medals, which offer a retrospective look at competitive figure skating. Among the names connected with them are those of some of the most outstanding figure skating champions. The variety of design and configuration spans time and continents. They come from this and other eras and from many countries.

There is a complete set of the commemorative medals of the Olympic Winter Games, gathered through the efforts of Mr. Benjamin T. Wright, who is largely responsible for the establishment and growth of the Museum. There is a collection of badges from three-time Olympic champion Gillia Grafström of Sweden, donated by his widow, Mrs. Cecile Grafström. These, along with the medals and trophies and an array of skating pins from many countries, are exhibited in display cases in the Museum proper. The walls of the room will also feature awards and pictures of those installed annually in the U.S.F.S.A. Figure Skating Hall of Fame and a Presidents' Corner with pictures and biographical information about those who have held the office in the U.S.F.S.A.

Also among the wall displays are works of art that depict skating scenes. The long-time affinity between artists and skaters is reflected in the Museum's paintings, prints and porcelains.

There is an exhibit depicting the evolution of the figure skate with many models of skates which added functional changes leading to the present blade and boot combination. A written explanation details how and where the various changes came about.

The handsome and spacious room which houses the Museum exhibits is separated by a reception area from the smaller well-appointed library.

A view of the interior of the Hall of Fame showing some of the display cases.

—All photographs in this chapter, courtesy United States Figure Skating Association Museum and Hall of Fame

The Sears Crescent Building on City Hall Plaza in Boston where the Hall of Fame is located.

It contains many of the known books written about figure skating, some of them rare and valuable and some that have been restored. Decades of skating achievement are chronicled in pamphlets and periodicals in both English and foreign languages and in two complete bound sets of "Skating" magazine, all of which are fascinating to peruse.

There are also rule books and publications from the U.S.F.S.A. and other skating associations from around the world, as well as programs and protocols of United States and international competitions. All library and museum materials are catalogued, including original manuscripts and correspondence among skating greats such as Sonja Henie, Maribel Vinson Owen, Captain T. D. Richardson, Ulrich Salchow and others.

The complete works of Captain T. D. Richardson, donated by his widow, Mrs. Mildred (Allingham) Richardson of London, gives a unique insight into the world of international figure skating over a 50-year span, including the first World Championship to be held in England in 1898. In addition to his books and profuse correspondence, we have the fruits of Capt. Richardson's work as international correspondent on winter sports for several London-based periodicals and newspapers. His fabulous picture collection, now mounted in albums, includes early photos of Sonja Henie, Karl Schäfer, Gillis Grafström, Cecilia Colledge, Megan Taylor, as well as many other world champions.

Visitors will enjoy the many scrapbooks and photo albums that tell the day-by-day story of the sport and its best-known participants. These have been preserved so that future generations may be brought back to those moments with a distinct feeling for the attitudes and atmosphere of the time. There has been started a collection of postal and greeting cards depicting skaters and skating scenes. Many of these are quite unusual and interesting. Some of them are copies of works of art. The film collection, too, lends itself to this recapturing. Viewers may arrange to see 16mm sound films of National and World Championships featuring some of the great performances of Hall-of-Famers and others.

A collection of materials has been formed pertinent to the air disaster that struck the 1961 U.S. World Team. The members of that team were among those who lost their lives in a plane crash in Brussels, Belgium. They were on their way to the World Figure Skating Championships in Prague, Czechoslovakia. The collection includes news clippings, photographs, and telegrams, some of which express condolences in beautiful poetry.

The U.S.F.S.A. Memorial Fund, of which the Museum is a part, was established in 1961 as a living memorial to the members of that team. The Memorial Fund is recognized by the Internal Revenue Service as a charitable organization. Thus, donations to the Museum of either cash or items of historical or fine arts value are deductible for income tax purposes to the extent permitted by the Internal Revenue Code.

Memorabilia to be donated should be offered by letter to:

Chairman, U.S.F.S.A. Museum Committee
Sears Crescent — Suite 500
City Hall Plaza
Boston, Massachusetts 02108

The letter should describe the proposed item and all the pertinent facts known about it and should specify any terms that are to apply such as donation or loan. Upon acceptance by the Committee, the item should then be sent to the Museum.

The Museum moved to its present location in 1975 from The Skating Club of Boston at which a satellite collection is still maintained. The need for more spacious and accessible quarters is met very well in the U.S.F.S.A. suite at the Sears Crescent. This distinctive red brick building, built in 1841, has been restored in a manner that is at once compatible with modern office needs and representative of the charming architectural style of its era. The suite is shared by the Central Office of the U.S.F.S.A. and "Skating" magazine. The public is welcome to visit during regular office hours, Monday through Friday 8:30 a.m. to 4:30 p.m.

The Museum is easily reached by public transportation. The Government Center station of the MBTA's Green Line and Blue Line has its entrance just outside the doors. Visitors to Boston may exit from the Central Artery at Haymarket Square and locate a parking garage within walking distance. Located at the heart of the historic Freedom Trail, the Museum should be included in the itinerary of the history buff and sports enthusiast alike.

* * *

The major highlight of the relatively short existence of the USFSA Museum and Hall of Fame to date occurred last May in Washington, D.C. on the occasion of the Annual Meeting of the Association, when the first inductees into the Hall of Fame were announced.

INDUCTEES

CATEGORY A

Amateur competitive record or noteworthy contributions in style or technique

TENLEY E. ALBRIGHT SONJA HENIE
SHERWIN C. BADGER DAVID W. JENKINS
THERESA WELD BLANCHARD HAYES ALAN JENKINS
IRVING BROKAW ANDREE JOLY & PIERRE BRUNET
RICHARD T. BUTTON AXEL PAULSEN
PEGGY GALE FLEMING ULRICH SALCHOW
GILLIS GRAFSTROM KARL SCHAFER
CAROL E. HEISS MARIBEL Y. VINSON

CATEGORY B

Noteworthy contribution in an amateur nonskating capacity

THERESA WELD BLANCHARD A. WINSOR WELD
CAPT. T.D. RICHARDSON, O.B.E. REGINALD J. WILKIE
ULRICH SALCHOW

CATEGORY C

Noteworthy contribution as a professional

PIERRE BRUNET HOWARD NICHOLSON
JACQUES GERSCHWILER EDI SCHOLDAN
JACKSON HAINES EDDIE SHIPSTAD & OSCAR JOHNSON
SONJA HENIE MONTGOMERY S. WILSON
GUSTAVE LUSSI

THE NATIONAL FRESH WATER FISHING HALL OF FAME

Hayward, Wisconsin

In the pleasant woodland of northwest Wisconsin noted as "muskie" country, an attractive and ambitious new Hall of Fame has become a reality. The original idea was spawned in 1960. Ten years later five persons formed a non-profit organization and developed a concept which today is the basis of a total project. Dedicated to education, good sportsmanship and charitable purposes, the organization has begun plans for expansion through contributions from anglers, sportsmen's clubs, manufacturers of fishing tackle and related equipment such as motors and boats.

The present Hall of Fame is a single two-story building with a variety of exhibits that interest fisherman because they show the development of tackle, motors, and lures as fishing has changed through the years. Fishing is a sport for everyone and it's enjoyed by more people throughout the world than any other recreational pastime. It is enjoyed equally by women and men and by girls and boys. People in every economic stratum enjoy fishing and like to think about it and talk about it.

The expanded project when completed will have a set of buildings including a library-theater plus a Hall of Fame building in the shape of a giant muskie breaking water from a sparkling reflection pool. This huge fish will rise high and measure up to 160 feet from tail to mouth.

State and World record fish will be displayed and there will be certain enshrined fishermen selected on the basis of their contributions to and achievements in the sport of freshwater fishing. The mouth of the big fish will be an observation deck.

There will be exhibits consisting of live fish in aquariums showing the fish in their natural habitats. There will be casting pools, demonstration areas, open air shelters, and instruction in fly-tying and casting.

THE NATIONAL COLLEGIATE FOOTBALL HALL OF FAME

Near Cincinnati, Ohio

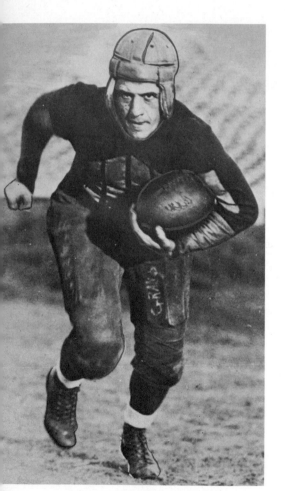

Harold "Red" Grange

Walter Camp . . . Amos Alonzo Stagg . . . Knute Rockne . . . Pop Warner . . . Tom Harmon . . . Red Grange . . . George Gipp . . .

These gallant heroes and their cheering crowds of the glory years of college football have been joined by a new group of already legendary figures . . . names like Bear Bryant . . . Joe Namath . . . Woody Hayes . . . Gale Sayers . . . Darrell Royal . . . O. J. Simpson and Ara Parseghian.

Regardless of the generation they are all there in pictures, action scenes, memorabilia and movies at the National Collegiate Football Hall of Fame located at the Kings Island Family Entertainment Complex 20 miles north of Cincinnati, Ohio. The Hall of Fame is scheduled to open in April 1978.

The names of college football's greatest players, coaches and teams, many of them already enshrined in the Hall of Fame by its sponsor, the National Football Foundation, a non-profit educational organization, are presented in a new and unique format. An immediate impression of the stature of college football and its importance for Americans, young and old, is established by the bright colorful displays of the interior. The MacArthur Bowl, awarded annually to the nation's best major college football team, and impressive displays of Hall of Fame and Gold Medal honorees reflect the rewards of successful competitive effort. Fine art, murals and rare pictures also add a rare quality to the enshrinement area.

The learning process has just started. If one has a specific interest, the Information Center can answer the most detailed question without delay.

Pagentry Mixed with Education

Everywhere one looks in this 40,000 square foot building the pageantry, power and the spectacle that perpetuates college football comes to life . . . like lifesize figures of football's greatest figures speaking and reliving some of the most memorable moments of their careers.

THE MacARTHUR BOWL

The MacArthur Bowl is awarded annually by the National Football Foundation to the outstanding college football team of the season. In the years since it was first offered for competition in 1959, the Bowl has become perhaps the most celebrated and most keenly sought-after football trophy in competition. Certainly it is the most striking.

The Bowl was the gift of an anonymous donor in the name of the late General of the Army, Douglas MacArthur. General MacArthur served for several years as chairman of the Foundation's National Advisory Board, and the Bowl was designed by Tiffany & Co. from suggestions made by the General himself. The Bowl measures 25 by 18 inches on its base and stands ten inches tall. It represents a huge stadium with rows of seats carved in relief. Minature goal posts stand on a field of etched yard lines. The entrance arches on the stadium exterior are used for engraving the names of winning teams and there

is room for 100 of these. As a result, the Bowl can remain in competition for all but a few years of football's second century.

Almost 400 ounces of silver went into the Bowl, which took eight months to fashion.

Winners in previous years have been: Syracuse University, 1959; University of Minnesota, 1960; University of Alabama, 1961; University of Southern California, 1962; University of Texas, 1963; University of Notre Dame, 1964; Michigan State, 1965; Michigan State and the University of Notre Dame, 1966; University of Southern California, 1967; Ohio State University, 1968; University of Texas, 1969; Ohio State University and University of Texas, 1970; University of Nebraska, 1971; University of Southern California, 1972; University of Notre Dame, 1973; University of Southern California, 1974; University of Oklahoma, 1975; University of Pittsburgh, 1976.

Some may first want to visit a live stage show in a 250-seat theatre that will give, for the first time anywhere, a history of American college football in song and music.

Others may wish to stop in one of the several mini-theatres and take in an intimate locker room talk . . . or watch as Gold Medal honoree Dwight David Eisenhower talks football . . . or listen as someone like Mrs. Ann Hayes, wife of the Ohio State coach, discusses her thoughts on the game and Woody himself.

The Evolution of the Game.
The first collegiate football game,
Princeton vs. Rutgers, 1869.
—From a painting
by Herb Mott

Some will turn to another one of the multi-faceted theatres and watch educational films that deal with great tackles impossible pass receptions and spectacular runs in slow motion . . . like Roy Reigel's wrong way run in the 1929 Rose Bowl . . . or how the proper technique, football equipment and uniforms evolved to the present. You can even watch in full length some of the memorable games . . . like Notre Dame's 7 − 0 victory over Bud Wilkinson's Oklahoma Sooners in 1957 . . . or the 10 − 10 tie between Notre Dame and Michigan State or the famous

upsets like the Illinois upset of the Michigan team in 1939 . . . and the Irish's 1913 victory over Army, 35 − 13 as Gus Dorais opened the eyes of the Eastern teams to the possibilities of the forward pass.

Walking through this large area one has reminders of other Hall of Fame honorees and may wish to take an historical look at Heisman: The Man and the Trophy.

There is also a chance to get a close look at men such as Amos Alonzo Stagg, known as the Grand Old Man of the Game . . . an athlete and

115

coach who is also enshrined in the Basketball Hall of Fame, . . . Pop Warner and the 8 through 16-year old youngsters that play football in organized youth leagues . . . and the great bands and their outstanding half-time shows which will be shown on special video tape screens showing the evolution of these halftime pageants. There is an in-depth display on how equipment and good conditioning protects players from injuries.

A Computer Information Center

One of the unique special features of this museum is a complete computer information center that will answer any question one might have about records, players, coaches and teams. A nearby electronic game room tests the viewers' ability to call controversial plays from football's history or test ones' personal strategy against decision made by great coaches in tense moments. They call this Monday morning quarterbacking.

The entire visit will probably be highlighted by a long, educational walk through football's time tunnel, a display depicting particular football eras. The excitement of great games and players is recaptured in a fascinating treatment that spans from the first game in 1869 between Rutgers and Princeton to the present, characterized by television, million dollar budgets and complex and sophisticated plays.

Many of the social and economic trends that affected football and major events in the history of the United States that changed the course of the game . . . like Teddy Roosevelt's tense warning in 1906 to watch the 'violence,' will be part of the time tunnel.

This display also takes a look at football, small college style . . . or the early 1960's when emphasis was switched to more wide open play and the 'in' thing was to have the wing T, slot T, flanker T, split T as part of the offense . . . One can spend time reading some of Grantland Rice's most famous stories.

For those who wish to get deeper into the history of college football a fine library and archives, with a resident research historian, is located in the Hall of Fame. It is the type of room where dad can relive his playing days . . . or a son can slip in and confirm all of those stories about father being a four-year letterman . . . for the graduate student or professional writer, the library is the perfect place to find the information to write a research paper or story about college football.

There is a rathskeller which has continual music of college fight songs and a malt shop with an outdoor patio that overlooks the football field. A complete merchandise and book center is also available where you can browse.

A Relaxed Atmosphere

The Hall of Fame has created an environment which emphasizes the National Football Foundation's goals of informing young Americans about the principles of football, honoring the great players and coaches who helped develop the game. They wish to entertain the visitor in a

Bronko Nagurski

pleasant relaxed atmosphere while stepping into the legends of past generations.

This site in mid-America, located within 600 miles of 60 per cent of the total population of the United States, is owned by the Taft Broadcasting Company, an original group broadcasting company that in recent years has expanded into other phases of entertainment and leisure time activities.

Kings Island, opened in 1972, is a complete family vacation center. The 1600 acre entertainment complex includes a theme park with six special areas. Europe comes to life on International Street; the world's fastest roller coaster highlights Coney Island; a monorail train takes one through Lion Country Safari; Scooby Doo is host in the Happy Land of Hanna Barbera; the sky ride passes an Eiffel Tower that is one-third the size of the original in Paris, and finally, a taste of frontier life is created in a western style town. Throughout the park there are numerous rides and a wide variety of live entertainment ranging from a Broadway-style show in a 1400 seat theatre to a country music group and a roaming clown band.

Ernie Nevers

The Jack Nicklaus Golf Center, designed by Nicklaus himself, is a complete golf facility with two 18-hole courses and restaurant. The plan calls for an annual visit there by leading golfers when the PGA Tour holds the Ohio Kings Island Open in September.

The Swiss chalet charm of the 300-room Kings Island Inn, is a part of the facility which has indoor-outdoor swimming and tennis courts. There is also a 300-site Kings Island campground.

The College Football Hall of Fame is located at the main entrance to Kings Island just off I — 71, 20 miles north of Cincinnati. The charm of the college campus is quickly evident in the red brick Georgian Colonial building, and in the surrounding grounds that bring out the rustic beauty of the wooded hills.

Seminars and clinics with leading football authorities are offered throughout the year. High school and college coaches and youth group leaders can schedule use of the library, classrooms and theatre inside and a well groomed, regulation-size football field is available outside to conduct their own clinic.

The National Football Foundation annually honors high school scholar-athletes through the local chapters and sponsors a graduate fellowship program for collegiate players who have excelled in the classroom as well as on the field. At the present time there are 82 chapters nationally and over 180 member colleges.

Former coaches and players are inducted in the Hall of Fame each December in New York City and at the same time the Foundation presents its three highest honors, the MacArthur Bowl, the Distinguished American Award and the Gold Medal to national leaders. Five former presidents of the United States have been recipients of the Gold Medal and over 350 players and 75 coaches have been inducted into the Hall of Fame.

117

THE GOLD MEDAL

The Gold Medal Award represents the highest individual honor which the National Football Foundation and Hall of Fame can bestow. The recipient shall have contributed in a significant manner to college football and his career shall embody the highest ideals for which the game of football stands.

GOLD MEDAL QUALIFICATIONS

1. The recipient must have been closely associated with college football as a player (varsity or scrub) as Justice Byron White, President Kennedy, President Eisenhower, President Nixon, Governor Reagan, President Ford; or a manager as President Hoover, General MacArthur; coach as Amos Alonzo Stagg, Tom Hamilton and Red Blaik; or business, political or educational leader of national influence as Roger Blough, Chairman of the Board of U.S. Steel Corp., Don Lourie, Undersecretary of State, Chairman of the Board of Pan-American Airways, Frederick L. Hovde, President of Purdue University, Gerald Zornow, Chairman of the Board of Eastman-Kodak, and Chester J. LaRoche, Chairman of the Board of Young and Rubicam or an inter-national film star like John Wayne, all of whom played as undergraduates.

2. He must be an American Citizen, most of whose business life has been spent in the United States.

3. He must have achieved success in an industrial, business, financial, educational, professional, or related career.

4. He must have an unblemished reputation for honesty and integrity in both his business and public life.

5. He must have "contributed notably in public service to the welfare of his country and fellow citizens," whether as a private citizen or as a Government official, or both.

6. He must have shown a capacity for dedicated institutional commitment to the problems of our competitive economy versus a centrally dictated society and a concern for the human spirit as well as the mind. We would place the quality of living alongside of high accomplishment or mere competence.

7. At the time of his selection he may be an elected or appointed Federal or State Government official, or a member of Congress of any State Legislative body. But he shall not be selected because of political power or glamour, and he shall not be preferred or turned down because of affiliation with any political party.

8. He must have carried into his professional life the basic values taught in amateur sport.

1976 Inductees

Twelve new members were inducted into the College Football Hall of Fame in December, 1976. They were Eddie Cameron, Washington and Lee back, John David Crow, Texas A & M back, Vick Janowicz, Ohio State back, Tom Fears, UCLA and Santa Clara end and back, Darold Jenkins, Missouri center, Vic Markov, Washington tackle, Ollie Matson, San Francisco back, Creighton Miller, Notre Dame back, Jackie Parker, Mississippi State back, Bill Swiacki, Columbia and Holy Cross end, Dexter Very, Penn State end and Coach George Munger of Pennsylvania.

The College Football Hall of Fame is open everyday of the year except major holidays. Hours vary according to the season. There is an admission charge and also a reduced price ticket for admission to both the Hall of Fame and Kings Island. Special discounts are available for school and tour groups. Note that the opening is scheduled for April 1978.

MEMBERS OF THE
NATIONAL FOOTBALL HALL OF FAME

PLAYERS *(Year indicated in final season)*

Alabama
1925 John Mack Brown*
1925 Allison Hubert
1930 Frederick W. Sington
1932 John Lewis Cain
1934 Donald Hutson
1935 Millard F. "Dixie" Howell*

Amherst
1906 John (Jack) Houghton Hubbard

Arkansas
1929 Wear K. Schoonover
1949 Clyde Scott

Army (Harvard)
1902 Charles D. Daly*

Army (Purdue)
1917 Elmer Oliphant*

Army
1902 Paul B. Bunker*
1915 Alexander (Babe) Weyand
1916 John J. McEwan*
1923 Harry Wilson (Penn State)
1924 Edgar W. Garbisch
1929 Christian K. Cagle*
1929 Mortimer 'Bud' Sprague (Texas)*
1946 Felix (Doc) Blanchard
1946 Glenn Davis

Auburn
1932 James Hitchcock*
1936 Walter Gilbert

Baylor
1931 Barton Koch*

Boston
1940 Charles O'Rourke

Boston University
1952 Harry Agganis*

Brown
1911 William E. Sprackling
1916 Frederick D. (Fritz) Pollard

Bucknell
1932 Clark Hinkle

California
1921 Stanley N. Barnes
1922 Dan McMillan (Southern Cal.)*
1922 Harold (Brick) Muller*
1925 Edwin (Babe) Horrell
1937 Robert Herwig*

Carlisle
1904 James Johnson*
1908 Albert Exendine*
1912 James Thorpe*

Carnegie Tech
1928 Howard Harpster

Centenary (Geneva)
1926 Robert C. (Cal) Hubbard

Centre
1921 Alvin (Bo) McMillin*

Chicago (Bucknell)
1894 Andrew R. E. Wyant*

Chicago
1899 Clarence Herschberger*
1906 Walter H. Eckersall*
1908 Walter P. Steffen*
1914 Paul R. Desjardien*
1935 John J. Berwanger

Indicates deceased

Clemson
1939 James Banks McFadden

Colgate
1914 Ellery Huntington
1915 Earl Abell*
1919 D. Belford West*
1925 J. Edward Tryon

Colorado College
1929 Earl (Dutch) Clark

Colorado University
1937 Byron R. White

Columbia
1902 Harold H. Weekes*
1903 William Warner*
1933 Cliff Montgomery
1938 Sid Luckman

Cornell
1896 Clinton Wyckoff*
1903 William Morley*
1915 Charles Barrett*
1915 John E. O'Hearn
1915 Murray Shelton
1922 Edgar L. Kaw
1923 George Pfann
1938 Jerome (Brud) Holland

Dartmouth
1915 Clarence W. Spears*
1916 Ed Healey
1925 Andrew J. Oberlander*
1928 Myles Joseph Lane
1931 William H. Morton

Duke
1933 Fred Crawford*
1936 Clarence (Ace) Parker
1938 Dan Winfield Hill
1938 Eric Tipton
1939 George Anderson McAfee

Fordham
1936 Alexander Wojiechowicz

Georgia
1913 Robert McWhorter*
1942 Frank Sinkwich
1946 Charles Trippi

Georgia Tech
1917 George E. Strupper*
1919 Joseph Guyon*
1920 Bill Fincher
1920 A. R. (Bucks) Flowers
1928 Henry R. (Peter) Pund

Harvard
1893 Marshall Newell*
1895 Charles Brewer*
1900 William Reid
1901 David C. Campbell*
1909 Hamilton Fish
1911 Robert Fisher*
1913 Percy Landgon Wendell*
1914 H. R. (Tack) Hardwick*
1914 Stanley B. Pennock*
1915 Edward W. Mahan*
1919 Edward L. Casey*
1930 Benjamin H. Ticknor
1941 Endicott Peabody

Hobart (Toledo)
1929 Merle Gulick

Holy Cross
1938 William Osmanski

Illinois
1915 Bart Macomber*
1921 Charles (Chuck) Carney
1925 Harold E. (Red) Grange
1946 Alex Agase
1946 Claude (Buddy) Young

Indiana
1903 Zora Clevenger*
1946 Pete Pihos

Iowa
1921 Aubrey Devine
1921 F.F. (Duke) Slater*
1922 Gordon C. Locke*
1939 Nile Kinnick*

Iowa State
1939 Edward (Ed) John Bock

Kansas
1930 James Bausch
1947 Ray Evans

Lafayette
1897 Charles Rinehart*
1922 Frank John (Dutch) Schwab*

Lehigh (Wesleyan)
1912 Vincent Joseph (Pat) Pazzetti*

Louisiana State
1910 G. E. (Doc) Fenton*
1935 Dr. Abe Mickal
1936 Gaynell Tinsley
1939 Ken Kavanaugh

Michigan
1901 Neil Worthington Snow*
1904 William M. Heston*
1908 Adolf (Germany) Schulz*
1911 Albert Benbrook*
1914 John Maulbetsch*
1923 Harry Kipke*
1926 Benjamin Friedman
1927 Benjamin G. Oosterbaan
1933 Francis M. "Whitey" Wistert
1940 Thomas D. Harmon
1942 Albert A. Wistert
1943 Elroy Hirsch (Wisconsin)

Michigan State
1938 John Pingel

Minnesota
1903 Edward L. Rogers*
1907 Robert Marshall*
1910 John Francis McGovern*
1916 Bert Baston
1927 Herbert Joestring*
1929 Bronko Nagurski
1934 J. L. (Pug) Lund
1936 Edwin Widseth
1941 Bruce Smith*
1942 Richard Wildung

Mississippi
1937 Frank (Bruiser) Kinard
1947 George (Barney) Poole
    (North Carolina, Army)
1948 Charles (Chuck) Conerly

Mississippi College
1921 Edwin (Goat) Hale

(continued)

Missouri
1920 Ed Travis (Tarkio)
1940 Paul Christman*
1943 Robert Steuber

Montana
1927 William Kelly*

Navy
1906 Jonas H. Ingram*
1912 John Patrick Dalton*
1913 John H. (Babe) Brown, Jr.*
1926 Thomas J. Hamilton
1927 Frank 'Wick' Henry Wickhorst*
1934 Fred Borries, Jr.
1934 Slade Cutter

Navy (Alabama)
1944 Donald Whitmire

Nebraska
1915 Guy B. Chamberlin
1921 Clarence Swanson*
1925 Ed Weir
1933 George H. Sauer

New York University
1928 Kenneth Strong

University of North Carolina
1949 Charles (Choo Choo) Justice

Northwestern
1917 John (Paddy) Driscoll*
(Great Lakes Naval Station)
1943 Otto Graham

Notre Dame
1913 Ray Eichenlaub*
1904 Louis (Red) Salmon*
1920 George Gipp*
1921 Heartly (Hunk) Anderson
1924 James Crowley
1924 Elmer F. Layden*
1924 Edgar (Rip) Miller
1924 Harry Stuhldreher*
1924 Adam Walsh
1925 Don C. Miller
1929 Jack Cannon*
1930 Frank Carideo
1931 Marchmont Schwartz
1943 Angelo Bertelli
1947 George Connor
1947 John Lujack
1949 Leon Hart

Ohio State
1919 Charles W. (Chick) Harley*
1920 Gaylord Stinchcomb*
1930 Wesley E. Fesler
1945 Les Horvath
1945 William Willis
1956 James Parker

Oklahoma
1913 Claude Reeds*
1915 Forest Geyer*
1952 Billy Vessels

Oklahoma State
1947 Robert Fenimore

Oregon
1913 John W. Beckett
1930 John Kitzmiller
1948 Norman VanBrocklin

Pennsylvania
1895 Winchester D. Osgood*
(Cornell)
1896 George H. Brooke*
(Swarthmore)
1896 Charles Gelbert*
1896 Charles (Buck) Wharton*
1897 John H. Minds*
1900 T. Truxton Hare*
1905 Vincent Stevenson*

1906 Robert Torrey*
1908 William M. Hollenback*
1909 Hunter Scarlett*
1912 Leroy E. Mercer*
1949 Charles (Chuck) Bednarik

Penn State
1912 J. L. (Pete) Mauthe*
1913 Eugene (Shorty) Miller*
1922 William Glen Killinger

Pittsburgh
1907 Joseph Thompson (Geneva)*
1913 Huber Wagner
1916 Robert Peck*
1918 George McLaren*
1920 Herb Stein
1922 Tom Davies*
1938 Marshall Goldberg

Princeton
1884 Alexander Moffat*
1890 Hector W. Cowan*
1890 Knowlton L. Ames*
1893 Phillip King*
1895 Langdon Lea*
1895 Arthur Wheeler*
1895 Gary Cochran*
1900 William Edwards*
1900 A. R. T. (Doc) Hillebrand*
1900 Arthur Poe*
1903 John R. DeWitt*
1907 James B. McCormick*
1911 Edward J. Hart*
1914 Harold Ballin*
1921 James Stanton Keck*
1921 Donold Lourie
1935 John A. C. Weller*
1951 Richard Kazmaier

Purdue
1937 Cecil F. (Cece) Isbell

Rice
1946 Weldon Gaston Humble
1949 James (Froggy) Williams

Rutgers
1924 Homer H. Hazel*

University of the South
1904 Henry Disbrow Phillips*
1910 Frank Alexander Juhan*

St. Mary's
1927 Larry Bettencourt

Santa Clara
1937 Nello Falaschi

Sewanee
1899 Henry Seibels*

Southern California
1926 Morton Kaer
1927 Morley Drury
1931 Ernie Pinckert
1933 Aaron Rosenberg
1933 Ernest "Ernie" Frederick Smith
1939 Harry Smith
1947 John Ferraro

Southern Methodist
1928 Gerald Mann
1935 Robert Wilson
1949 Ewell (Doak) Walker
1950 Kyle Rote

Stanford
1925 Ernest A. Nevers
1933 William Corbus
1935 Robert H. Grayson
1935 Robert (Bones) Hamilton
1935 Robert Odell (Horse) Reynolds
1941 Frank Albert
1951 William F. McColl

Swarthmore
1906 Robert (Tiny) Maxwell*
(Chicago)

Syracuse
1920 Joseph Alexander*
1926 Victor Hanson

Tennessee
1909 Nathan W. Dougherty
1930 Robert Lee (Bobby) Dodd
1931 Herman Michael Hickman*
1931 Eugene T. McEver
1933 William Beattie Feathers
1938 Bowden Wyatt*
1940 Robert Lee Suffridge*
1940 George Cafego

Texas
1942 Malcolm Kutner
1947 Bobby Layne

Texas A & M
1907 Joe Utay
1927 Joel Hunt
1937 Joseph Routt*
1940 John C. Kimbrough

Texas Christian
1928 Raymond (Rags) Matthews
1936 Samuel Baugh
1938 Charles (Ki) Aldrich
1938 Robert David O'Brien

Tulane
1931 Gerald Dalrymple*
1934 Claude Simons*

UCLA
1939 Kenneth Washington*
1952 Donn Moomaw

Vanderbilt
1904 John J. Tigert*
1920 Josh Cody*
1924 Lynn Bomar*
1927 William D. Spears
1937 Carl Hinkle

Virginia
1941 William M. Dudley

Virginia Military Institute
1920 James Leech*

Virginia Polytechnic Institute
1905 C. Hunter Carpenter*

Washington
1925 George Wilson*
1928 Charles Carroll
1931 Paul "Schweg" Schwegler

Washington & Jefferson
1919 Wilbur F. (Fats) Henry*

Washington & Lee
1916 Harry Killinger (Cy) You
Washington State
1930 Melvin J. Hein

Wesleyan University
1905 Henderson 'Dutch' Van Sur
1912 C. Everett Bacon

West Virginia
1919 Ira E. Rodgers*
1935 Joseph L. Stydahar

West Virginia Wesleyan
1931 Clifford F. Battles

Williams
1920 Ben Lee Boynton*

Wisconsin
1899 Patrick J. O'Dea*
1912 Robert (Butts) Butler*
1942 David N. Schreiner*

Yale
- 1889 William (Pa) Corbin*
- 1889 Amos Alonzo Stagg*
- 1891 W. W. (Pudge) Heffelfinger*
- 1891 Thomas L. (Bum) McClung*
- 1894 Frank A. Hinkey*
- 1895 William Hickok*
- 1896 Samuel B. Thorne*

- 1900 Gordon F. Brown*
- 1904 James J. Hogan*
- 1905 Thomas L. Shevlin*
- 1909 Edward H. (Ted) Coy*
- 1910 John Reed Kilpatrick
- 1911 Arthur Howe*
- 1913 Douglas (Bo) Bomeisler*
- 1913 Henry H. Ketcham

- 1921 Malcolm Aldrich
- 1923 William N. Mallory*
- 1923 Marvin (Mal) Stevens (Washburn)
- 1931 Albert (Albie) Booth*
- 1937 Clinton E. Frank
- 1937 Lawrence (Larry) Kelley

COACHES *(Including Colleges Coached and Date of Election)*

*Alexander, William A., Georgia Tech., 1951

*Anderson, Dr. Edward, Holy Cross, Iowa, 1971

Armstrong, Ike, Utah, 1957

Bell, Madison (Matty), Haskell Institute, Carroll College, Texas Christian, Texas A & M, Southern Methodist, 1955

*Bezdek, Hugo, Arkansas, Oregon, Penn State, 1954

Bible, Dana X., Louisiana State U., Texas A & M, Nebraska, Mississippi College, Texas, 1951

Biermann, Bernard W., Mississippi A & M, Tulane, Minnesota, 1955

Blaik, Earl (Red) Henry, Wisconsin (Asst.), Dartmouth, Army, 1965

*Caldwell, Charles W. Jr., Williams, Princeton, 1961

*Camp, Walter, Yale, Stanford, 1951

*Cavanaugh, Frank W., Holy Cross, Dartmouth, Boston College, Fordham, 1954

Crisler, Herbert O. (Fritz) Minnesota, Princeton, Michigan, 1954

*Dobie, Gilmore, Washington, Navy, Cornell, Boston College, 1951

*Donohue, Michael J. Auburn, Louisiana State, 1951

*Dorais, Charles E. (Gus), Detroit, 1954

Engle, Charles (Rip), Penn State, Brown, 1973

Faurot, Donald B., Missouri, Kirksville, 1961

Godfrey, Ernest, Ohio State, Wittenberg, 1972

*Hall, Edward K., Illinois, 1951

*Harlow, Richard C., Penn State, Colgate, Western Maryland, Harvard, 1954

*Harper, Jesse C., Notre Dame, 1971

*Haughton, Percy P., Cornell, Harvard, Columbia, 1951

*Heisman, John W., Oberlin, Akron, Auburn, Clemson, Georgia Tech, Pennsylvania, Wash. & Jefferson, Rice, 1954

*Higgins, Robert A., W. Va. Wesleyan, Washington (St. Louis), Penn State, 1954

*Ingram, William, William and Mary, Indiana, U.S. Naval Academy, California, 1973

Jennings, Morley, Ouachita, Baylor, 1973

*Jones, Howard H., Syracuse, Yale, Ohio State, Iowa, Duke, Southern California, 1951

Jones, L. McC. (Biff), Army, Louisiana State, Oklahoma, Nebraska, 1954

*Jones, Thomas A. D. (Tad), Syracuse, Yale, 1958

*Kerr, Andrew, Stanford, Washington & Jefferson, Colgate, 1951

*Leahy, Frank William, Boston College, University of Notre Dame, 1970

*Little, George E. Miami (Ohio), Wisconsin, Cincinnati, 1955

Little, Lou, Georgetown, Columbia, 1960

*Edward (Slip) Madigan, St. Mary's, 1974

McCracken, Herbert, Allegheny, Lafayette, 1973

*McGugin, Daniel, Vanderbilt, 1951

*McLaughry, DeOrmond (Tuss), Westminster, Amherst, Brown, Dartmouth, 1962

Meyer, L. R. (Dutch), Texas Christian, 1956

*Moore, Bernie H., Louisiana State, 1954

Morrison, Ray, Southern Methodist, Vanderbilt, Temple, Austin, 1954

*Munn, Clarence (Biggie), Albright, Syracuse, Michigan State, 1959

Bill Murray, Children's Home, Delaware, Duke, 1974

*Ed (Hooks) Mylin, Lafayette, Bucknell, 1974

*Neale, Earle (Greasy), Muskingum, West Virginia, Wesleyan, Marietta, Washington & Jefferson, University of Virginia, West Virginia University, Yale, 1967

*Neyland, Robert R., Tennessee, 1956

Neely, Jess, Southwestern, Clemson and Rice, 1971

*Norton, Homer, Centenary, Texas A & M., 1971

*O'Neill, Frank J. (Buck), Colgate, Syracuse, Columbia, 1951

*Owen, Bennie, Oklahoma, 1951

*Phelan, James, Missouri, Purdue, Washington, St. Mary's, 1973

*Robinson, E. N., Nebraska, Brown, 1955

*Rockne, Knute K., Notre Dame, 1951

*Romney, E. L. (Dick), Utah State, 1954

*Roper, William W., Princeton, Missouri, 1951

*Sanford, George Foster, Columbia, Rutgers, 1971

*Schmidt, Francis A. T., Tulsa, Arkansas, Texas Christian, Ohio State, 1971

*Shaughnessy, Clark D., Tulane, Loyola (N.O.), Chicago, Stanford, Maryland, Pittsburgh, 1968

Shaw, Lawrence (Buck), North Carolina State, Nevada, Santa Clara, California, Air Force, 1972

*Smith, Andrew L., Pennsylvania, Purdue, California, 1951

*Snavely, Carl, Bucknell, Cornell, North Carolina, Washington University, 1965

*Stagg, Amos Alonzo, Springfield, Chicago, College of Pacific, 1951

*Sutherland, John B. (Jock) Lafayette, Pittsburgh, 1951

*Thomas, Frank W., Chattanooga, Alabama, 1951

Wade, W. Wallace, Alabama, Duke, 1955

Waldorf, Lynn (Pappy), Syracuse, Oklahoma City U., Kansas, Oklahoma A & M, Kansas State, Northwestern, California, 1966

*Warner, Glenn S. (Pop), Georgia, Cornell, Carlisle, Pittsburgh, Stanford, Temple, 1951

*Wieman, E. E. (Tad), Michigan, Princeton, 1956

*Wilce, John W., Ohio State, 1954

*Williams, Henry L., Minnesota, 1951

Wilkinson, Charles (Bud), Oklahoma, 1969

*Woodruff, George W., Lehigh, Pennsylvania, 1963

*Yost, Fielding H., Michigan, 1951

*Zuppke, Robert, Illinois, 1951

---

*Deceased

121

THE PRO FOOTBALL HALL OF FAME

Canton, Ohio

The Pro Football Hall of Fame is located in Canton, Ohio, in the northwest corner of the city, just off Interstate Highway 77. Highway exits for both northbound and southbound traffic are clearly marked on the freeway. Literally hundreds of other signs on lesser roads in the Canton and Stark County area guide the visitor directly to the Hall of Fame site. Canton is located approximately 40 minutes south of the Ohio turnpike and about one hour north of Interstate 70, another major east-west artery. I-77 connects directly to both of these major routes. Canton is also located on U.S. Highways 30 and 62.

Canton lies approximately 53 miles south of Cleveland, 100 miles west of Pittsburgh, 120 miles northeast of Columbus and around 225 miles from such centers as Detroit, Cincinnati and Buffalo.

Why Canton for the Hall of Fame Site?

The Pro Football Hall of Fame is located in Canton, Ohio, for three primary reasons: (1) the American Professional Football Association, the direct forerunner of the National Football League, was founded in Canton on September 17, 1920. (2) The Canton Bulldogs were an early-day pro football power, even before the days of the NFL. They were also a two-time champion of the NFL in 1922 and 1923. The great Jim Thorpe, the first big-name athlete to play pro football, played his first pro football with the Bulldogs, starting in 1915. (3) Canton citizens early in the 1960s launched a determined and well-organized campaign to earn the site designation for their city.

Historical Background

The Pro Football Hall of Fame concept, as far as Canton was concerned, first was placed before the public by the Canton Repository on December 6, 1959. That newspaper challenged its readers with the headline: "PRO FOOTBALL NEEDS A HALL OF FAME AND LOGICAL SITE IS HERE!"

Canton civic groups quickly took up the challenge and, by January 25, 1961, William E. Umstattd of The Timken Company was in a position,

—All photographs in this chapter, courtesy Pro Football Hall of Fame

as the selected representative of his city, to make a formal bid to the National Football League for acceptance of Canton as the site for a pro football hall of fame. Three months later, Canton was granted this official site approval.

Wooded parkland was donated from the city and a civic fund-raising campaign had, by February 8, 1962, acquired pledges totalling $378,026. Ground-breaking for the original construction was held on August 11, 1962, and on September 7, 1963, the building was first opened to the public.

The original two-building complex, containing 19,000 square feet of interior space, was almost doubled in size when a $620,000 expansion project was completed in May, 1971. The expanded three-building complex now contains 34,000 square feet of interior space.

Dick McCann, long-time general manager of the Washington Redskins, was named the Hall's first director on April 4, 1962. Mr. McCann died in November, 1967, and in April, 1968, Dick Gallagher, a long-time pro football coach, scout and general manager, was named the new director. He served until his retirement on December 31, 1975. To date, a successor has not been named.

Operation of the Hall of Fame

The Pro Football Hall of Fame operates as an independent, non-profit organization. Its 14-member Board of Directors includes nine members from Canton and/or Stark County. Other directors include Lamar Hunt of the Kansas City Chiefs, K. S. (Bud) Adams Jr. of the Houston Oilers, Art Rooney of the Pittsburgh Steelers and George Halas of the Chicago Bears. The 14th director is NFL Commissioner Pete Rozelle.

In its day-to-day operation, the Pro Football Hall of Fame works very closely with all facets of the pro football family—the Commissioner's office, the 28 NFL clubs, NFL Films and NFL Properties. The cooperative

George Halas, veteran coach and a founder of the National Football League, with two of his players.

efforts of all of these organizations have contributed greatly to the overall success of the Pro Football Hall of Fame. In turn, the Hall strives to serve as the best possible historical showplace and repository for the sport of pro football.

The Component Parts

Of a most obvious nature, the Pro Football Hall of Fame serves as a hallowed honoring spot for the greats of the pro football world and two large galleries are devoted to the display of the niches of the enshrinees of the Hall.

The Hall also represents its sport in a great many other colorful and entertaining ways. Included in the three-building complex are (1) three large exhibition areas where the history of pro football from the very beginnings in 1892 right up to the present day is detailed in memento, picture and story form, (2) a 250-seat movie theater where a football action movie is shown without additional charge every hour, (3) a rapidly-growing research library and (4) a bustling and popular gift and souvenir shop.

A seven-foot bronze statue of Jim Thorpe greets each visitor as he enters the Hall. The visitor then ascends a gently-sloped ramp to the original Exhibition Rotunda. The emphasis is heavy on unusual mementoes in this area and the displays are arranged in rough chronological order from the first pro football game in 1892 to the present day.

The Enshrinee Mementoes Room, located in a second building, honors each enshrinee in picture or memento form. A third large exhibition room, the Leagues and Champions Room, graphically outlines the histories of all major leagues of professional football. Also featured in this brightly-hued room are display stories of the Super Bowl, and Pro Bowl and the Evolution of Football Equipment.

Throughout the major exhibition areas, electronic devices encourage each fan to participate actively in history as he tours the Hall. Rearview movie projectors, taped voice recordings, question-and-answer boards and selective slide machines all play a part in telling the total story of pro football.

Displays are constantly being updated and remodelled. The Professional Football Today display, created in 1969 and updated every year, is the oldest major display in the Hall and all other major displays have been created new or remodelled since 1971.

Pertinent Basic Data

The Pro Football Hall of Fame is open every day of the year except for Christmas. From Memorial Day through Labor Day, it is open daily from 9 a.m. to 8 p.m. The hours for the remainder of the year are 9 a.m. to 5 p.m. daily. Admission is $2.00 for adults, 50 cents for children under 14. There is a family rate (parents and all dependent children) of $4.50. Substantial reductions are offered for groups. Information on group rates and other matter may be obtained by phoning (216) 456-8207 or by writing to the Pro Football Hall of Fame.

The Method of Selection of Enshrinees

Election of new members to the Pro Football Hall of Fame is solely the responsibility of the 27-member Board of Selectors, a committee largely made up of sports writers. Each pro football city has one representative with two from New York City, because of its two teams. The 27th member is the highest officer of the Pro Football Writers Association who is not already a member.

The selection committee meets each year on the day before the Super Bowl to elect a new class of enshrinees. To be elected, a nominee must obtain approximately 80 percent of the vote of those selectors in attendance. Present rules call for the election of between three and six new enshrinees each year. Any fan may nominate any pro football contributor or player simply by writing to the Pro Football Hall of Fame. The only limitation is that a player must have been retired at least five years and a coach must be retired. Other contributors (owners, administrative personnel, etc.) may be nominated and elected while they are still active.

The Enshrinement of New Members . . . Football's Greatest Weekend

The highlight of every year at the Pro Football Hall of Fame is the annual Football's Greatest Weekend celebration which is usually scheduled in late July or early August. A huge civic festival precedes the two major events of the celebration: (1) the enshrinement of new members to the Pro Football Hall of Fame and (2) the annual AFC-NFC Hall of Fame pre-season football game.

Except for the staging of the enshrinement and the game, which is handled by the Hall's staff and a select committee of volunteers, the festival is organized and conducted by the Greater Canton Chamber of Commerce with numerous volunteer citizens' committees serving as integral parts of the overall organization.

Typical attendance during a Festival weekend will show up to 1000 at the Mayor's Breakfast, several hundred at the Women's Fashion Show, 1500 at the Civic Banquet, from 150,000 to 200,000 at the parade, from 8,000 to 10,000 at the enshrinement and a capacity 19,500 at the game. In addition, up to 5,000 out-of-town visitors will have visited the Pro Football Hall of Fame for the first time. AND . . . other millions will have seen the highlights of the enshrinement and the entire game on the far-flung ABC-TV sports network. ABC-TV has featured this activity on its Wide World of Sports series since 1971 and is contracted to continue this coverage at least through 1978.

The Annual AFC-NFC Hall of Fame Game

The annual Hall of Fame game is played at Fawcett Stadium, a Canton city high school stadium which seats approximately 19,000 and which is located directly across the street from the Pro Football Hall of Fame.

Vince Lombardi, Green Bay Packer coach, being carried from Miami Orange Bowl by Jerry Kramer following victory in Super Bowl #2, January 14, 1968.

127

The first game of the series was played in 1962, a year before the Hall was opened. Except for 1966, there has been a Hall of Fame game in Canton every year since.

The AFC-NFC series began in 1971 and, in a period through 1983, all 26 teams of the National Football League will appear in the game. As new teams are added to the league, it is anticipated that they will take their place in the rotation. Every game will be an inter-conference affair and exact opponents have been scheduled through 1983.

So that the press corps covering the annual Hall of Fame game would have satisfactory working conditions, the Hall in 1974 constructed a $90,000 press box. The two-deck facility contains working space for 73 writers on the lower level. The upper level contains a large television broadcast booth, three radio broadcast booths and three VIP booths. This fully-carpeted and modern facility is topped off by an electrically equipped and spacious photo deck on the roof.

Attendance at the Pro Football Hall of Fame

Almost two millions fans have visited the Pro Football Hall of Fame since its opening in September, 1963. The attendance pace, slow at first, quickened dramatically in the early 1970s. Daily checks of the guest register show that, in a year's time, visitors come from every state in the United States and up to 60 to 70 foreign nations. Year-by-year attendance is as follows:

1963 — 22,195	1967 — 52,989	1972 — 247,203
(four months)	1968 — 58,833	1973 — 330,029
1964 — 63,036	1969 — 80,881	1974 — 261,567
1965 — 60,026	1970 — 122,738	1975 — 235,404
1966 — 56,468	1971 — 220,881	

Sammy Baugh

Raymond Berry

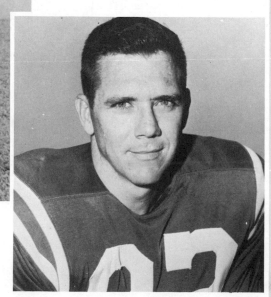

Chuck Bednarik

*The sculpture of Bobby Jones and accompanying sun dial at the entrance of
the World Golf Hall of Fame at Pinehurst, North Carolina, honoring
the great gentleman and champion who did so much to popularize the game
in the 1920's. The bronze statue of the Pinehurst Golf Boy was located
on the putting green of the Pinehurst Hotel and Country Club until
moved to the Hall of Fame.*

One of the very interesting displays of golf clubs in the World of Golf Hall of Fame showing the evolution of the game through its long history.

A replica of a golf club maker's shop as it appeared years ago when every professional had to qualify as a mechanic of some ability able to make and repair clubs as well as having expertise in the game.

(on following page)
The World Golf Hall of Fame as seen from the edge of the fourth green of the famous Number Two Course at Pinehurst, North Carolina. The very impressive building houses many exciting reminders of past players and tournaments that make up a part of the history of this internationally popular game.

FROM A WATERCOLOR PAINTING BY KAY SMITH

The United States Hockey Hall of Fame, Eveleth, Minnesota, is a modern new structure housing many interesting displays giving the history and growth of American hockey including high school and college players and teams as well as Americans who have succeeded in professional hockey.

(on preceding page)
The Pimlico Race Course in Baltimore, Maryland, operated by the Maryland Jockey Club where the second jewel of the Triple Crown is contended each year in the Preakness Stakes. The National Jockeys' Hall of Fame is in the Preakness Room on the third floor of the clubhouse.

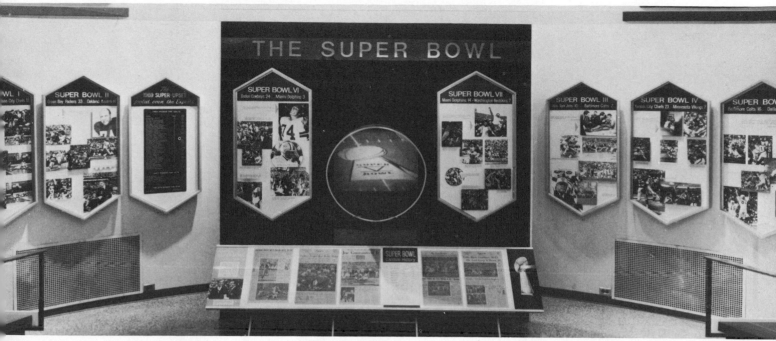

A display devoted to the super bowls, including the plays and the players, recalls many past thrills and heroes.

THE ROSTER OF ENSHRINEES

Alphabetical listing of the 88 members of the Professional Football Hall of Fame. Listing includes enshrinee's name, college if any, year of enshrinement. His primary contribution is listed first, followed by listing of all other known contributions to pro football.

*Deceased member. #Player-coach.

CLIFF BATTLES, West Virginia Wesleyan (1968) – Halfback and Quarterback, 6-1, 201 – 1932 Boston Braves, 1933 – 36 Boston Redskins, 1937 Washington Redskins (six playing seasons). ALSO: Head Coach, 1946 – 47 Brooklyn Dodgers (AAFC).

SAMMY BAUGH, Texas Christian (1963 charter) – Quarterback, 6-2, 180 – 1937 – 52 Washington Redskins (16 playing seasons). ALSO: Head Coach, 1960 – 61 New York Titans (AFL), 1964 Houston Oilers (AFL); Assistant Coach, 1965 Houston Oilers (AFL), 1966 Detroit Lions.

CHUCK BEDNARIK, Pennsylvania (1967) – Center and Linebacker 6-3, 230 – 1949 – 62 Philadelphia Eagles (14 playing seasons).

*BERT BELL, Pennsylvania (1963 charter) – Commissioner, 1946 – 59 National Football League; Founder, Philadelphia Eagles, 1933 (Bought Frankford franchise and moved it to Philadelphia). ALSO: Head Coach, 1936 – 40 Philadelphia Eagles, 1941 Pittsburgh Steelers; Club President. 1933 – 40 Philadelphia Eagles, 1941 – 46 Pittsburgh Steelers.

RAYMOND BERRY, Southern Methodist (1973) – End, 6-2, 187 – 1955 – 67 Baltimore Colts (13 playing seasons). ALSO: Assistant coach, 1968 – 69 Dallas Cowboys. 1973 – 75 Detroit Lions. Cleveland Browns, starting in 1976.

*CHARLES W. BIDWILL, Loyola of Chicago (1967) – Owner and President, 1933 – 47 Chicago Cardinals.

JIM BROWN, Syracuse (1971) – Fullback, 6-2, 228 – 1957 – 65 Cleveland Browns (nine playing seasons).

PAUL E. BROWN, Miami of Ohio (1967) — Head Coach and General Manager, 1946–49 Cleveland Browns (AAFC), 1950–62 Cleveland Browns (NFL). ALSO: Head Coach and General Manager, 1968–69 Cincinnati Bengals (AFL), 1970–75 Cincinnati Bengals (NFL). General Manager, Cincinnati Bengals, starting in 1976.

ROOSEVELT BROWN, Morgan State (1975) — Offensive Tackle, 6-3, 225 — 1953–65 New York Giants (13 playing seasons). ALSO: Assistant Coach, 1966–70 New York Giants.

TONY CANADEO, Gonzaga (1974) — Halfback, 5-11, 195 — 1941–44, 1946–52 Green Bay Packers (11 playing seasons).

*JOE CARR (1963 charter) — President, 1921–39 National Football League, ALSO: Co-organizer, American Professional Football Association (Forerunner of NFL) 1920: Founder, Columbus Panhandles, 1904.

*GUY CHAMBERLIN, Nebraska (1965) — End, 6-2, 210 — 1919 Canton Bulldogs (preNFL), 1920 Decatur Staleys, 1921 Chicago Staleys, 1922–23, Canton Bulldogs, 1924 Cleveland Bulldogs, 1925–26 Frankford Yellowjackets, 1927 Chicago Cardinals (nine playing seasons). Head Coach, 1922–23 Canton Bulldogs #, 1924 Cleveland Bulldogs #, 1925–26 Frankford Yellowjackets #, 1928 Chicago Cardinals.

JACK CHRISTIANSEN, Colorado State U. (1970) — Defensive Back, 6-1, 185 — 1951–58 Detroit Lions (eight playing seasons). ALSO: Head Coach, 1963–67 San Francisco 49ers. Assistant Coach, 1959–63 San Francisco 49ers.

EARL (DUTCH) CLARK, Colorado College (1963 charter) — Quarterback, 6-0, 185 — 1931–32 Portsmouth Spartans, 1934–38 Detroit Lions (seven playing seasons). ALSO: Head Coach, 1937–38 Detroit Lions #, 1939–42 Cleveland Rams.

GEORGE CONNOR, Holy Cross and Notre Dame (1975) — Offensive Tackle, Defensive Tackle, Linebacker, 6-3, 240 — 1948–55 Chicago Bears (eight playing seasons).

*JIMMY CONZELMAN, Washington of St. Louis (1964) — Quarterback, 6-0, 180 — 1920 Decatur Staleys, 1921–22 Rock Island Independents, 1923–24 Milwaukee Badgers, 1925–26 Detroit Panthers, 1927–29 Providence Steamrollers (10 playing seasons). Head Coach, 1922 Rock Island Independents #, 1923–24 Milwaukee Badgers #, 1925–26 Detroit Panthers #, 1927–29 Providence Steamrollers #, 1930 Providence Steamrollers, 1940–42, 1946–48 Chicago Cardinals. Owner, 1925–26 Detroit Panthers.

ART DONOVAN, Boston College (1968) — Defensive Tackle, 6-3, 265 — 1950 Baltimore Colts, 1951 New York Yanks, 1952 Dallas Texans, 1953–61 Baltimore Colts (12 playing seasons).

*JOHN (PADDY) DRISCOLL, Northwestern (1965) — Quarterback, 5-11, 160 — 1919 Hammond Pros (pre-NFL), 1920 Decatur Staleys, 1920–25 Chicago Cardinals, 1926–29 Chicago Bears (11 playing seasons). ALSO: Head Coach, 1921–22 Chicago Cardinals #, 1956–57 Chicago Bears. Assistant Coach, 1941–55, 1958–62 Chicago Bears; Director of Research and Planning, 1963–68 Chicago Bears.

BILL DUDLEY, Virginia (1966) — Halfback, 5-10, 176 — 1942, 1945–46 Pittsburgh Steelers, 1947–49 Detroit Lions, 1950–51, 1953 Washington Redskins (nine playing seasons). ALSO: Assistant Coach, 1953 Washington Redskins #.

*ALBERT GLEN (TURK) EDWARDS, Washington State (1969) — Tackle, 6-2 1/2, 260 — 1932 Boston Braves, 1933–36 Boston Redskins, 1937–40

Roosevelt Brown

Washington Redskins (nine playing seasons). ALSO: Head Coach, 1946–48 Washington Redskins. Assistant Coach, 1941–45 Washington Redskins.

TOM FEARS, Santa Clara and UCLA (1970)—End, 6-2, 215—1948–56 Los Angeles Rams (nine playing seasons). ALSO: Head Coach, 1967–70 New Orleans Saints. Assistant Coach, 1959, 1962–65 Green Bay Packers, 1960–61 Los Angeles Rams, 1966 Atlanta Falcons, 1971–72 Philadelphia Eagles.

RAY FLAHERTY, Gonzaga (1976)—Head Coach, 1936 Boston Redskins, 1937–42 Washington Redskins, 1946–48 New York Yankees (AAFC), 1949 Chicago Hornets (AAFC). ALSO: End, 6-0, 195—1926 Los Angeles Wildcats (AAFC), 1927–28 New York Yankees (NFL), 1929 1931–35 New York Giants. (nine playing seasons). Assistant Coach, 1933–35 New York Giants #.

*LEONARD (LEN) FORD, Morgan State and Michigan (1976)—Defensive End, 6-5, 260—1948–49 Los Angeles Dons (AAFC) (Offensive End), 1950–57 Cleveland Browns, 1958 Green Bay Packers (11 playing seasons)

DANIEL J. FORTMANN, M.D., Colgate (1965)—Guard, 6-0, 210— 1936–43 Chicago Bears (eight playing seasons).

BILL GEORGE, Wake Forest (1974)—Linebacker, 6-2, 230—1952–65 Chicago Bears, 1966 Los Angeles Rams (15 playing seasons). ALSO: Assistant coach, 1972–73 Chicago Bears.

OTTO GRAHAM, Northwestern (1965)—Quarterback, 6-1, 195— 1946–49 Cleveland Browns (AAFC), 1950–55 Cleveland Browns (NFL) (10 playing seasons). ALSO: Head Coach, 1966–68 Washington Redskins.

HAROLD (RED) GRANGE, Illinois (1963 charter)—Halfback, 6-0, 185— 1925 Chicago Bears, 1926 New York Yankees (AFL), 1927 New York Yankees (NFL), 1929–34 Chicago Bears (nine playing seasons). ALSO: Assistant Coach, 1935–39 Chicago Bears.

LOU GROZA, Ohio State (1974)—Offensive Tackle, Placekicker, 6-3, 250—1946–49 Cleveland Browns (AAFC), 1950–59, 1961–67 Cleveland Browns (NFL) (21 playing seasons). ALSO: Assistant coach, 1968–69 Cleveland Browns.

Lou Groza

The history of the growth of professional football, the merger of the leagues and the expansion shows the dynamic nature of the game.

Evolution ...OF THE UNIFORM

The uniform in football as in every other sport and activity has undergone many changes through the years. The startling evolution of the football uniform is dramatically displayed at the Hall of Fame.

*JOE GUYON, Carlisle and Georgia Tech (1966)—Halfback, 6-1, 180— 1919 Canton Bulldogs (pre-NFL), 1920 Canton Bulldogs, 1921 Cleveland Indians, 1922–23 Oorang Indians, 1924 Rock Island Independents, 1924–25 Kansas City Cowboys, 1927 New York Giants (eight playing seasons).

GEORGE HALAS, Illinois (1963 charter)—Founder, Decatur Staleys, 1920. President, 1922–76 Chicago Bears. Head Coach, 1920 Decatur Staleys #, 1921 Chicago Staleys #, 1922–29 Chicago Bears #, 1933–42, 1946–55, 1958–67 Chicago Bears. Co-organizer, American Professional Football Association (forerunner of NFL), 1920. ALSO: End, 6-1, 180—1919 Hammond Pros (pre-NFL), 1920 Decatur Staleys, 1921 Chicago Staleys, 1922–29 Chicago Bears (11 playing seasons).

ED HEALEY, Dartmouth (1964)—Tackle, 6-3, 220—1920–22 Rock Island Independents, 1922–27 Chicago Bears (eight playing seasons).

MEL HEIN, Washington State (1963 charter)—Center, 6-2, 225—1931–45 New York Giants (15 playing seasons). ALSO: Head Coach, 1947 Los Angeles Dons (AAFC): Assistant Coach, 1947–48 Los Angeles Dons (AAFC), 1949 New York Yanks (AAFC), 1950 Los Angeles Rams; Supervisor of Officials, 1966–73 American Football League/Conference.

*WILBUR (PETE) HENRY, Washington and Jefferson (1963 charter)— Tackle, 6-0, 250—1920–23 1925–26 Canton Bulldogs, 1927 New York Giants, 1927–28 Pottsville Maroons, (eight playing seasons). ALSO: Co-coach, 1925–26 Canton Bulldogs #; Head Coach, 1928 Pottsville Maroons #.

*ARNIE HERBER, Regis College (1966)—Quarterback, 6-0, 200— 1930–40 Green Bay Packers, 1944–45 New York Giants (13 playing seasons).

*BILL HEWITT, Michigan (1971)—End, 5-11, 191—1932–36 Chicago Bears, 1937–39 Philadelphia Eagles, 1943 Phil-Pitt (nine playing seasons).

CLARKE HINKLE, Bucknell (1964)—Fullback, 5-11, 201,—1932–41 Green Bay Packers (10 playing seasons).

ELROY HIRSCH, Wisconsin and Michigan (1968)—Halfback and End, 6-2, 190—1946–48 Chicago Rockets (AAFC), 1949–57 Los Angeles Rams (12 playing seasons). ALSO: Assistant to President, 1960–68 Los Angeles Rams.

ROBERT (CAL) HUBBARD, Centenary and Geneva (1963 charter)—Tackle, 6-5, 250—1927–28 New York Giants, 1929–33, 1935 Green Bay Packers, 1936 New York Giants, 1936 Pittsburgh Pirates (nine playing seasons).

LAMAR HUNT, Southern Methodist (1972)—Founder, American Football League, 1959. Owner, 1960–62 Dallas Texans (AFL), 1963–76 Kansas City Chiefs.

DON HUTSON, Alabama (1963 charter)—End, 6-1, 180—1935–45 Green Bay Packers (11 playing seasons). ALSO: Assistant Coach, 1944–45 Green Bay Packers #, 1946–49 Green Bay Packers.

*WALT KIESLING, St. Thomas of Minnesota (1966)—Guard, 6-2, 245—1926–27 Duluth Eskimos, 1928 Pottsville Maroons, 1929–33 Chicago Cardinals, 1934 Chicago Bears, 1935–36 Green Bay Packers, 1937–38 Pittsburgh Pirates (13 playing seasons). Head Coach, 1939–42, 1954–56 Pittsburgh Steelers. Co-Coach, 1943 Phil-Pitt, 1944 Card-Pitt. ALSO: Assistant Coach, 1937–38 Pittsburgh Pirates #, 1939, 1941 Pittsburgh Steelers, 1945, 1948 Green Bay Packers, 1949–54 Pittsburgh Steelers Advisory Coach, 1957–61 Pittsburgh Steelers.

FRANK (BRUISER) KINARD, Mississippi (1971)—Tackle, 6-1, 210—1938–44 Brooklyn Dodgers, 1946–47 New York Yankees (AAFC) (nine playing seasons).

*EARL (CURLY) LAMBEAU, Notre Dame (1963 charter)—Founder, Green Bay Packers, 1919. Head Coach and General Manager, 1921–49 Green Bay Packers (# in 1921–29). Head Coach, 1950–51 Chicago Cardinals, 1952–53 Washington Redskins. ALSO: Halfback, 6-0, 195—1919–20 Green Bay Packers (pre-NFL), 1921–29 Green Bay Packers (11 playing seasons).

RICHARD (NIGHT TRAIN) LANE, Scottsbluff, Nebr., Junior College (1974)—Defensive Back, 6-2, 210—1952–53 Los Angeles Rams, 1954–59 Chicago Cardinals, 1960–65 Detroit Lions (14 playing seasons). ALSO: Special Staff Assistant, 1966–71 Detroit Lions.

DANTE LAVELLI, Ohio State (1975)—End, 6-0, 199—1946–49 Cleveland Browns (AAFC), 1950–56 Cleveland Browns (NFL) (11 playing seasons).

BOBBY LAYNE, Texas (1967)—Quarterback, 6-2, 190—1948 Chicago Bears, 1949 New York Bulldogs, 1950–58 Detroit Lions, 1958–62 Pittsburgh Steelers (15 playing seasons). ALSO: Assistant Coach, 1964–65 Pittsburgh Steelers.

*VINCE LOMBARDI, Fordham (1971)—Head Coach, 1959–67 Green Bay Packers; 1969 Washington Redskins. ALSO: Assistant Coach, 1954–58 New York Giants; General Manager, 1959–68 Green Bay Packers; General Manager, 1969–70 Washington Redskins.

SID LUCKMAN, Columbia (1965)—Quarterback, 6-0, 195—1939–50 Chicago Bears (12 playing seasons). ALSO: Assistant Coach, 1954, 1956–70 Chicago Bears; Vice President 1952–58 Chicago Bears.

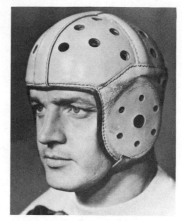

Clarke Hinkle

Richard (Night Train) Lane

133

*WILLIAM ROY (LINK) LYMAN, Nebraska (1964)—Tackle, 6-2, 252—1922–23 Canton Bulldogs, 1924 Cleveland Bulldogs, 1925 Canton Bulldogs, 1925 Frankford Yellowjackets, 1926–28, 1930–31, 1933–34 Chicago Bears (11 playing seasons).

*TIM MARA, (1963 charter)—Founder, New York Giants, 1925; President, 1925–59 New York Giants.

GINO MARCHETTI, San Francisco (1972)—Defensive End, 6-4, 245—1952 Dallas Texans (NFL), 1953–64, 1966 Baltimore Colts. (14 playing seasons).

*GEORGE PRESTON MARSHALL, Randolph-Macon (1963 charter)—Founder, Boston Braves, 1932 (name changed to Redskins in 1933 and moved to Washington in 1937). President of club, 1932–65. President-emeritus, Washington Redskins, 1966–69.

OLLIE MATSON, San Francisco (1972)—Halfback, 6-2, 220—1952, 1954–58 Chicago Cardinals, 1959–62 Los Angeles Rams, 1963 Detroit Lions, 1964–66 Philadelphia Eagles. (14 playing seasons).

GEORGE McAFEE, Duke (1966)—Halfback, 6-0, 177—1940–41, 1945–50 Chicago Bears (eight playing seasons). ALSO: Game official, 1959–65 National Football League.

HUGH McELHENNY, Washington (1970)—Halfback, 6-1, 193—1952–60 San Francisco 49ers, 1961–62 Minnesota Vikings, 1963 New York Giants, 1964 Detroit Lions (13 playing seasons).

JOHN (BLOOD) McNALLY, St. John's of Minnesota (1963 charter) Halfback, 6-0, 185—1925–26 Milwaukee Badgers, 1926–27 Duluth Eskimos, 1928 Pottsville Maroons, 1929–33 Green Bay Packers, 1934 Pittsburgh Pirates, 1935–36 Green Bay Packers, 1937–38 Pittsburgh Pirates, 1939 Pittsburgh Steelers (15 playing seasons). ALSO: Head Coach, 1937–38 Pittsburgh Pirates #, 1939 Pittsburgh Steelers #, Assistant Coach, 1936 Green Bay Packers #.

AUGUST (MIKE) MICHALSKE, Penn State (1964)—Guard, 6-0, 209—1926 New York Yankees (AFL), 1927–28 New York Yankees (NFL), 1929–35, 1937 Green Bay Packers (11 playing seasons). ALSO: Assistant Coach, 1937 Green Bay Packers #. 1948–49 Baltimore Colts (AAFC).

WAYNE MILLNER, Notre Dame (1968)—End, 6-0, 191—1936 Boston Redskins, 1937–41, 1945 Washington Redskins (seven playing seasons). ALSO: Head Coach, 1951 Philadelphia Eagles; Assistant Coach, 1945 Washington Redskins #. 1946–48 Washington Redskins, 1949 Chicago Hornets (AAFC), 1950 Baltimore Colts (NFL), 1951 Philadalphia Eagles, 1954–55 Washington Redskins.

LEONARD (LENNY) MOORE, Penn State (1975)—Flanker-Running Back, 6-1, 198—1956–67 Baltimore Colts (12 playing seasons).

MARION MOTLEY, South Carolina State and Nevada (1968)—Fullback, 6-1, 238—1946–49 Cleveland Browns (AAFC), 1950–53 Cleveland Browns (NFL), 1955 Pittsburgh Steelers (nine playing seasons).

BRONKO NAGURSKI, Minnesota (1963 charter)—Fullback, 6-2, 225—1930–37, 1943 Chicago Bears (nine playing seasons).

*EARLE (GREASY) NEALE, West Virginia Wesleyan (1969)—Head Coach, 1941–50 Philadelphia Eagles. ALSO: End, 6-1, 170—1915, 1917 Canton Bulldogs (pre-NFL).

*ERNIE NEVERS, Stanford (1963 charter)—Fullback, 6-1, 205—1926–27 Duluth Eskimos, 1929–31 Chicago Cardinals (five playing seasons). ALSO:

Ollie Matson

Gino Marchetti

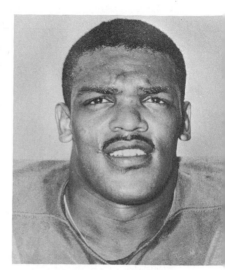

Lenny Moore

Jim Parker

Hugh McElhenny

Head Coach, 1926–27 Duluth Eskimos #, 1929–31 Chicago Cardinals #, 1939 Chicago Cardinals.

LEO NOMELLINI, Minnesota (1969)—Defensive Tackle, 6-3, 264—1950–63 San Francisco 49ers. (14 playing seasons).

*STEVE OWEN, Phillips U. (1966)—Head Coach, 1931–53 New York Giants (# in 1931, 1933). Tackle, 6-2, 235—1924–25 Kansas City Cowboys, 1926–31, 1933 New York Giants (nine playing seasons). ALSO: Assistant Coach, 1956–57 Philadelphia Eagles.

CLARENCE (ACE) PARKER, Duke (1972)—Quarterback, 5-11, 168—1937–41 Brooklyn Dodgers, 1945 Boston Yanks, 1946 New York Yankees (AAFC). (seven playing seasons.)

JIM PARKER, Ohio State (1973)—Guard, Tackle, 6-3, 273—1957–67 Baltimore Colts (11 playing seasons).

FLETCHER (JOE) PERRY, Compton Junior College (1969)—Fullback, 6-0, 200—1948–49 San Francisco 49ers (AAFC), 1950–60, 1963 San Francisco 49ers (NFL), 1961–62 Baltimore Colts. (16 playing seasons). ALSO: Assistant Coach, 1968–72 San Francisco 49ers.

Andy Robustelli

Jim Taylor

PETE PIHOS, Indiana (1970)—End, 6-1, 210—1947–55 Philadelphia Eagles (nine playing seasons).

*HUGH (SHORTY) RAY, Illinois (1966)—Technical Advisor and Supervisor of Officials, 1938–52 National Football League.

*DAN REEVES, Georgetown (1967)—Owner, 1941–45 Cleveland Rams, 1946–71 Los Angeles Rams (served as president and general manager periodically during this tenure).

ANDY ROBUSTELLI, Arnold College (1971)—Defensive End, 6-0, 230—1951–55 Los Angeles Rams, 1956–64 New York Giants (14 playing seasons). ALSO: Assistant Coach, 1962–64 New York Giants #. Director of Operations, New York Giants, starting in 1974.

ART ROONEY, Georgetown and Duquesne (1964)—Founder, Pittsburgh Pirates, 1933. President, 1933–38 Pittsburgh Pirates, 1939–40, 1946–75 Pittsburgh Steelers, Vice President, 1941–46 Pittsburgh Steelers.

JOE SCHMIDT, Pittsburgh (1973)—Linebacker, 6-0, 222—1953–65 Detroit Lions (13 playing seasons). ALSO: Head Coach, 1967–72 Detroit Lions.

ERNIE STAUTNER, Boston College (1969)—Defensive Tackle, 6-2, 235—1950–63 Pittsburgh Steelers (14 playing seasons). ALSO: Assistant Coach, 1963 Pittsburgh Steelers #, 1964 Pittsburgh Steelers, 1965 Washington Redskins, 1966–76 Dallas Cowboys.

KEN STRONG, New York University (1967)—Halfback, 5-11, 210—1929–32 Staten Island Stapletons, 1933–35 New York Giants, 1936–37 New York Yanks (AFL), 1939, 1944–47 New York Giants (14 playing seasons). ALSO: Assistant Coach, 1940, 1962–65 New York Giants.

JOE STYDAHAR, West Virginia (1967)—Tackle, 6-4, 230—1936–42, 1945–46 Chicago Bears (nine playing seasons). ALSO: Head Coach, 1950–52 Los Angeles Rams, 1953–54 Chicago Cardinals; Assistant Coach, 1947–49 Los Angeles Rams, 1963–64 Chicago Bears.

JIM TAYLOR, Louisiana State (1976)—Fullback, 6-0, 216—1958–66 Green Bay Packers, 1967 New Orleans Saints (10 playing seasons)

*JIM THORPE, Carlisle (1963 charter)—Halfback, 6-1, 190—1915–17, 1919 Canton Bulldogs (pre-NFL), 1920 Canton Bulldogs, 1921 Cleveland Indians, 1922–23 Oorang Indians, 1923 Toledo Maroons, 1924 Rock Island Independents, 1925 New York Giants, 1926 Canton Bulldogs, 1928 Chicago Cardinals (12 playing seasons). ALSO: President, 1920 American Professional Football Association. Head Coach, 1915–17, 1919–20 Canton Bulldogs #, 1922–23 Oorang Indians #.

Y. A. TITTLE, Louisiana State (1971)—Quarterback, 6-0, 200—1948–49 Baltimore Colts (AAFC), 1950 Baltimore Colts (NFL), 1951–60 San Francisco 49ers, 1961–64 New York Giants (17 playing seasons). ALSO: Assistant Coach, 1965–69 San Francisco 49ers, Assistant Coach, 1970–73 New York Giants.

*GEORGE TRAFTON, Notre Dame (1964)—Center, 6-2, 235—1920 Decatur Staleys, 1921 Chicago Staleys, 1922–32 Chicago Bears (13 playing seasons). ALSO: Assistant Coach, 1944 Green Bay Packers, 1945 Cleveland Rams, 1946–49 Los Angeles Rams.

CHARLEY TRIPPI, Georgia (1968)—Halfback and Quarterback, 6-0, 185—1947–55 Chicago Cardinals (nine playing seasons). ALSO: Assistant Coach, 1956–57 Chicago Cardinals, 1963–65 St. Louis Cardinals.

*EMLEN TUNNELL, Toledo and Iowa (1967)—Defensive Back, 6-1, 200—1948–58 New York Giants, 1959–61 Green Bay Packers (14 playing seasons). ALSO: Assistant Coach, 1963–73 New York Giants.

CLYDE (BULLDOG) TURNER, Hardin-Simmons (1966)—Center, 6-2, 235—1940–52 Chicago Bears (13 playing seasons). ALSO: Head Coach, 1962 New York Titans (AFL); Assistant Coach, 1952 Chicago Bears #, 1954–56 Chicago Bears.

NORM VAN BROCKLIN, Oregon (1971)—Quarterback, 6-1, 190—1949–57 Los Angeles Rams. 1958–60 Philadelphia Eagles (12 playing seasons). ALSO: Head Coach, 1961–66 Minnesota Vikings; Head Coach, 1968–73 Atlanta Falcons.

STEVE VAN BUREN, Louisiana State (1965)—Halfback, 6-1, 200—1944–51 Philadelphia Eagles (eight playing seasons). ALSO: Personnel Director, 1954–55 Philadelphia Eagles. Assistant Coach, 1956 Philadelphia Eagles.

BOB WATERFIELD, U.C.L.A. (1965)—Quarterback, 6-2, 200—1945 Cleveland Rams, 1946–52 Los Angeles Rams (eight playing seasons). ALSO: Head Coach, 1960–62 Los Angeles Rams; Assistant Coach, 1958 Los Angeles Rams.

ALEX WOJCIECHOWICZ, Fordham (1968)—Center and Linebacker, 6-0, 235—1938–46 Detroit Lions, 1946–50 Philadelphia Eagles (13 playing seasons).

Y. A. Tittle

1976 ENSHRINEES

FRANK GIFFORD, Southern California (1977)—Halfback, joined the New York Giants in 1952 as the Giants first draft choice. He became pro football's first successful halfback option threat. He played in both offensive and defensive backfields. After playing nine seasons he retired for a season then returned to play three more seasons.

FORREST GREGG, Southern Methodist (1977)—Guard and tackle with the Green Bay Packers. Credited for much of the success of their vaunted sweep. Played one year for Dallas Cowboys and returned to the Packers in 1971. Coach of the Year for Cleveland Browns 1976.

GALE SAYERS, University of Kansas (1977)—Halfback. Selected as Chicago Bears first draft choice—1965. Established a league record of 22 touchdowns as a rookie including 6 in one game to tie another record. He was all Pro for five straight years, rushing for 4956 yards and catching 112 passes for 1307 yards. He scored 56 touchdowns.

BART STARR, University of Alabama (1977)—Quarterback. He was 17th draft choice of the Green Bay Packers in 1956. Under Vince Lombardi in the 1960's he emerged as an outstanding field general. Played for sixteen seasons and was named MVP in the first two Super Bowls.

BILL WILLIS, Ohio State University, Guard (1977). He spent eight years with the Cleveland Browns in the All America conference beginning in 1946 on a team that won either the league or division championship each year that he was with the team. Considered the fastest middle guard of his day.

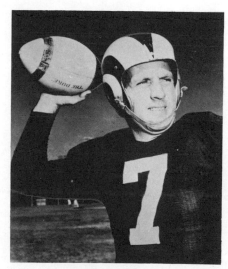

Bob Waterfield

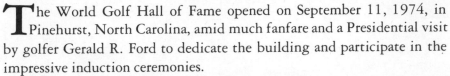

THE WORLD GOLF HALL OF FAME

Pinehurst, North Carolina

Harry Vardon

The World Golf Hall of Fame opened on September 11, 1974, in Pinehurst, North Carolina, amid much fanfare and a Presidential visit by golfer Gerald R. Ford to dedicate the building and participate in the impressive induction ceremonies.

Historic Pinehurst, long recognized as one of America's premier golf resorts, has added new dimensions to entertainment in recent years to give further credence to its claim as one of the most complete recreational facilities in the world.

Golf has been Pinehurst's principal attraction since the early 1900s when the North and South Amateur Championship began being played. In recent years other new recreational pursuits have been added, including both golf courses and tennis courts.

The Hall of Fame sits in majestic splendor among the towering pine trees overlooking the Pinehurst Country Club's famous Number Two Course and has some thirty thousand square feet of exhibit and display space tastefully arranged with exhibits that range from the origin of the golf tee to the club makers' shop of another era.

One unique feature of the main exhibit building is the world's finest collection of golfing artifacts and memorabilia, including the collection of Laurie Auchterlonie, honorary professional at the revered Royal and Ancient Golf Club in St. Andrews, Scotland. There is also a Golf History Wall, a 90-foot display depicting the evolution of the game over the past 500 years. The wall gives solid credence, in a fascinating visual manner, to the claim that golf was being played in Scotland before Columbus discovered America.

Behind the exhibit hall is the actual shrine itself which displays the plaques of the great champions and personalities who are inducted into the Hall of Fame each year. This section is an island completely surrounded by water and shimmering fountains which frame the striking high-columned structure which borders the fourth green and fifth tee of the famed Pinehurst Country Club's Number Two Course, long heralded as one of the best of the older courses in the world. It was designed by the late Donald Ross, a transplanted Scottish professional who designed some 600 courses throughout the United States.

A Place to Preserve the Lore of the Game

Golf, as all other sports, has many champions of the past and present whose deeds deserve to be permanently etched into history through recognition in one permanent museum. The game is one that has great affectionate appeal to its followers and players, and the events of the past are recalled with pleasure and dismay through the historic tournaments in which championships were won or lost as a part of the "rub of the green."

The shot that won or lost a match or tournament frequently is recalled twenty or thirty years after the event. The surge of a bright new star battling an established veteran through the last nine holes is the sort of story that appeals to every golfer. The legendary figures who have risen to the peaks of many championships in themselves are a part of the very character of this great game where victory or defeat is a matter of nerves and inches.

To enshrine in the Hall of Fame those whose accomplishments have through the years thrilled thousands of followers throughout the world is a fitting tribute to those men and women who in the years of competition have contributed to the game through the excellence of their performance and their general demeanor in the sport. Bobby Jones the individual was every bit as great as Robert T. Jones winner of the Grand Slam.

Golf is a social game that attracts varying degrees of intensity in application and performance. Whether a player or a spectator, the personal or vicarious thrill in executing a great shot or seeing one appeals almost equally to the enthusiastic golfer.

This Hall of Fame and museum in such an appropriate setting will please the golfer whether he is club champion or a twenty-six handicapper. It will hold interest for the TV viewer who has never held a club or missed a one-foot putt. It is just a very wonderful shrine and museum.

Members of the Hall of Fame

The accomplishments of the thirteen first inductees into the World Golf Hall of Fame attest to their combined excellence over a period of many years. As a group they won 97 major championships, including 23 British Opens, 22 United States Opens, 20 PGA's, 18 Masters, 12 United States Amateurs and 2 British Amateurs.

There were eight more enshrined in 1975, six players of the era preceding 1930 and two whose contributions to the game are acknowledged on the basis of their service. These latter two are Joseph C. Dey and Fred Corcoran.

The so-called pre-modern selections of players whose main accomplishments occurred before 1930 were made by a special committee of the Golf Writers Association of America and the President of the World Golf Hall of Fame. They each had to receive at least 75% of the votes cast. These six won a combined total of 26 national championships.

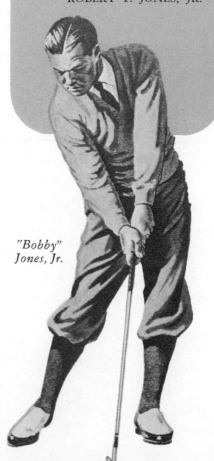

Golf has been called "The Most Human of Games" and a "Reflection of Life". One reason we enjoy it and that it challenges us is it enables us to run the entire gamut of human emotions not only in a brief space of time, but likewise without measurable damage to ourselves or to others.

The game as played on the golf course represents only a modest part of the pleasure, enjoyment and satisfaction that comes to a person because he is a golfer.

One of the very important attractions of golf is that it provides a wide and varied assortment of topics for conversation.

The lore of the game, the story of its development and of the stirring deeds of the great players of the past must always command the respectful attention of those who play golf at all regularly.

ROBERT T. JONES, JR.

"Bobby" Jones, Jr.

1974 SELECTIONS

PATRICIA J. "PATTY" BERG — Charter member of Ladies PGA, supplemented a great tournament record by conducting thousands of instructional clinics around world. Winner of more than 80 events, including U.S. Amateur (1938), U.S. Open (1946) and seven Titleholders championships. Voted outstanding woman athlete of the year in 1938, 1943, and 1955.

WALTER C. HAGEN — Winner of 11 major championships — five PGA (1921, 1924, 1925, 1926, 1927), four British Open (1922, 1924, 1928, 1929), two U.S. Open titles (1914, 1919). Played on seven Ryder Cup teams, "The Haig" was a colorful, flamboyant personality and golf's first great showman. Toured the world in 1937–1938, becoming an international emissary for the game.

WILLIAM BENJAMIN HOGAN — One of golf's all-time great shotmakers and strategists. Winner of nine major championships, three in 1953. He won PGA (1946, 1948); U.S. Open (1948, 1950, 1951, 1953); Masters (1951, 1953); and British Open (1953) in only appearance there. Possessed great dedication and discipline, and was a master at charting plan of execution in playing major championships.

ROBERT TYRE JONES, JR. — Winner of 13 major championships, including the "Grand Slam" in 1930 — the U.S. Open and Amateur, the British Open and Amateur. Won U.S. Open (1923, 1926, 1929, 1930), U.S. Amateur (1924, 1925, 1927, 1928, 1930), British Amateur (1930). Runner-up in four U.S. Opens and two U.S. Amateurs. Walker Cup Member five times. Honorary member Royal and Ancient Golf Club of St. Andrews. Retired at age 28. Truly one of golf's legendary figures, deserving of his place in history.

JOHN BYRON NELSON — Astounded the golfing world in 1945 by scoring 11 consecutive victories. Winner of five major championships — U.S. Open (1939), PGA (1940, 1945), Masters (1937, 1942). Known for being an excellent player of long irons and pin-point driving. A classic stylist who set the low-scoring record average of 68.33 in 1945 while winning 18 of 30 tournaments.

"Patty" Berg

Ben Hogan

Byron Nelson

Gary Player

Jack Nicklaus

Walter Hagen

Francis Ouimet

Arnold Palmer

Gene Sarazen

Sam Snead

JACK W. NICKLAUS — First player to win more than $2,000,000 in prize money and one of the most feared competitors the game has ever known. Winner of most major championships (14) at age 33. Won U.S. Amateur (1959, 1961), U.S. Open (1962, 1967, 1972), Masters (1963, 1965, 1966, 1972), PGA (1963, 1971, 1973), British Open (1966, 1970). Attained a level of perfection that made him automatic favorite to win any event he entered.

FRANCIS D. OUIMET — In 1913, as a 20-year-old unknown amateur, he beat Harry Vardon and Ted Ray in playoff for U.S. Open scoring 72 to Vardon's 77 and Ray's 78. Won the U.S. Amateur (1914, 1931). Member of America's Walker Cup team from 1922 to 1949. Elected captain of Royal & Ancient Golf Club of St. Andrews, Scotland, in 1951; first American ever accorded this honor.

ARNOLD D. PALMER — Emanator of magnetic charm that dramatized the game throughout the world. His unrelenting boldness led him to many championships and endeared him to his fans who became the cadre of "Arnie's Army." In seven years, he won four Masters championships (1958, 1960, 1962, 1964). Won U.S. Amateur (1954), U.S. Open (1960), British Open (1961, 1962). First professional golfer to exceed $1,000,000 in prize money winnings.

GARY PLAYER — One of the most dedicated and determined players in the history of golf. Has won all four major events — U.S. Open (1965), British Open (1959, 1968), PGA (1962, 1972), Masters (1961, 1974). Holder of numerous U.S. Tour titles, he has also won more major events throughout the world than any player in the game, including the Brazilian Open, Australian Dunlop International, Australian Masters, Piccadilly Match Play (five times), Canada Cup (1965), World Series, and Australian PGA.

GENE SARAZEN — First golfer to win each of the four modern Grand Slam championships when famous double-eagle led way to 1935 Masters playoff victory. Won 67 matches in PGA championships including titles in 1922, 1923, 1933 during long career. Won U.S. Open (1922, 1932), British Open (1932). Six times on Ryder Cup team. Twice winner PGA Seniors (1954, 1958). Scored hole in one in 1973 British Open at age 71.

SAMUEL JACKSON SNEAD — Durable possessor of classic swing through long championship career. Winner of three Masters (1949, 1952, 1954), three PGA (1942, 1949, 1951), one British Open (1946). Four times runner-up U.S. Open, only major title unwon. Once scored 59 in competition. Named to Ryder Cup team eight times, twice captain. PGA Senior champion six times. Known as The Slammer due to long accurate drives.

Willie Anderson

Thomas Morris, Jr.

John Taylor

Glenda Vare

"Chick" Evans

"Babe" Zaharius

HARRY VARDON — One of Britain's famed triumvirate which included James Braid and John H. Taylor, Winner of British Open six times (1896, 1898, 1899, 1903, 1911, 1914). Won U.S. Open (1900). A master of great grace and gentlemanly demeanor. Popularized overlapping grip which bears his name. Represented England 18 times in 12 years in international competition. Renowned for his play of full wood shots.

MILDRED "BABE" ZAHARIAS — Generally regarded as the greatest female athlete in history. A master of all sports, set three world records in 1932 Olympics. Won U.S. Amateur (1946), British Amateur (1947), first American to do so. Captured three U.S. Open crowns (1948, 1950, 1954), the latter by a record 12 strokes.

1975 SELECTIONS

WILLIE ANDERSON — Emigrated to the United States and dominated U.S. golf at the turn of the century. Won the U.S. Open in 1901, 1903, 1904 and 1905 and was in the top five in eleven Opens. He is the only golfer ever to have won three consecutive Open titles, and was the first to win it four times. He also won the Western Open four times — 1902, 1904, 1908 and 1909.

CHARLES "CHICK" EVANS — One of golf's truly great competitors, Evans won the U.S. Open and the U.S. Amateur in 1916 and won the Amateur again in 1920. His score of 286 in the Open held for twenty years. His competitive career in the U.S. Amateur covered more than fifty years. He won eight Western Amateur Championships and was on five Walker Cup teams. Established the Evans Scholars Foundation, a caddie scholarship fund administered by the Western Golf Association.

THOMAS MORRIS, JR. — Won his first victory in the British Open in 1868 at age 18. He subsequently won that title three more times — 1869, 1870 and 1872. His winning total of 149 in 1870 held for 30 years. As a result of winning three Opens in succession, he was given permanent possession of the Championship Belt. One of the early greats of the game whose career was cut short by his untimely death at the age of 25.

JOHN H. TAYLOR—Was part of Britain's great triumvirate with Harry Vardon and James Braid. Winner of five British Opens—1894, 1895, 1900, 1909 and 1913. He won the French Open twice, one German Open, the British PGA twice and represented England ten times in international play. Helped organize the association that was the forerunner of the British PGA.

GLENDA COLLETT VARE—Considered one of the greatest women golfers in the history of the game, Mrs. Vare won the U.S. Women's Amateur six times—1922, 1925, 1928, 1929, 1930 and 1935, the Canadian Women's Amateur twice and the French Amateur twice. She also won the North and South Women's Championship in 1922, 1923, 1924, 1927, 1929, and 1930. She was on the Curtis Cup team four times and was captain in 1948 and non-playing captain in 1950. The Vare Trophy, given for the lowest stroke average on the LPGA tour, is named in her honor.

JOYCE WETHERED—Entered only eleven championships during her career—six British and five English—and won nine of them. She won the British Women's Championship four times—1922, 1924, 1925 and 1929 and was runner-up and semi-finalist the other two times she played. In her prime she was thought to be the equal of all but half a dozen men golfers in the British Isles.

FOR DISTINGUISHED SERVICE

FRED CORCORAN—Vice President and Tournament Director of the International Golf Association; Tournament Director of the LPGA, 1948–1960, and the PGA, 1936–1947, manager of two Ryder Cup teams; co-founder of LPGA and PGA Hall of Fame and Golf Writers Association of America; winner of the Richardson Award and the Walter Hagen Award; pioneer manager of athletes and has devoted a lifetime of exemplary service to the game.

JOSEPH C. DEY, JR.—A dedicated and tireless administrator who worked unceasingly and faithfully for the betterment of the game. Served as Executive Director of the USGA for 35 years and Commissioner of the Tournament Players Division of the PGA of America five years.

Joyce Wethered

Fred Corcoran

Joseph Dey, Jr.

Fern Nature

THE GREYHOUND HALL OF FAME

Abilene, Kansas

The Greyhound Hall of Fame—racing's monumental tribute to the swiftest of canine breeds, the Greyhound. Constructed in a choice tourist location in Abilene, Kans., the Hall of Fame is located in the very heart of America's Greyhound country. Directly across the street from the Hall of Fame is the Eisenhower Center, a complex that attracts more than a million visitors each year and a tremendous asset in bringing visitors to the Hall of Fame.

Plans were first made in 1963 to construct a Greyhound Hall of Fame that would honor the history of the Greyhound breed and pay tribute to those greyhounds and people who have enhanced the image of both the breed and sport. Through the efforts of the member tracks of the American Greyhound Track Operators Association and the membership of the National Greyhound Association, the Greyhound Hall of Fame's doors were opened to the public in April of 1973.

Throughout the Hall of Fame are memoirs, artifacts and pictorial displays about the greyhound—even in the lounge area where visitors are first greeted upon entering the Hall of Fame. Also in the lobby is a souvenir counter, where visitors may purchase jewelry, postcards and other items related to the greyhound or the Hall of Fame. Adjacent to the lobby is the Hall of Fame theatre, where visitors are shown to a 15-minute movie about greyhound racing.

Modern, elegant design combines with soft lighting to create just the proper atmosphere inside the museum area. Visitors to the Hall of Fame are continually commenting on the beauty and craft of the displays.

The first section of the museum area is dedicated to the history of the greyhound, tracing the breed back to its very origins. This section deals also with its role in ancient Greek and Roman civilizations, following the greyhound through the Middle Ages. Art and culture involving the greyhound are also subjects here, along with the historical Bulldog Cross of the 18th Century, carried out by the eccentric Lord Orford of England.

The historical displays switch to the Modern Greyhound, dealing with his important role in this country. Historical data and photos from some

—All photographs in this chapter, courtesy Greyhound Hall of Fame.

(Above) Indoor racing
at Atlantic City, 1930.

(Right) Kansas racing
in late 1880.

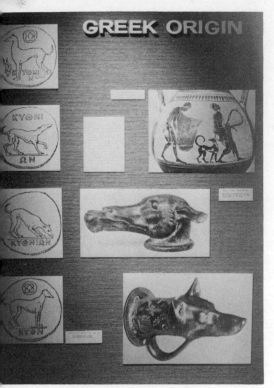

GREEK ORIGIN

*A display showing the origin
of the Greyhound.*

*Owen P. Smith invented the
mechanical lure in 1919.*

of the earliest coursing meets are on exhibit, including the first organized coursing meet in the country, at Cheyenne Bottoms near Great Bend, Kans. The unusual story of the great heavyweight wrestling champ, John Pesek, and his instrumental role in greyhound history is also displayed in the American history section. Then came O. P. Smith and the beginning of track racing. Photos of such early-day tracks as Hialeah, Atlantic City, N.J., and St. Petersburg Kennel Club are among the exhibits.

Beyond the historical section visitors enter the richness of the Hall of Fame itself, a Hall where the immortals of greyhound racing are enshrined. Down this aisle are the life stories of each Hall of Fame Greyhound, along with a plaque, picture and the official pedigree of each greyhound — beginning with the first three greyhounds enshrined: Merrill Blair's Flashy Sir, Gene Randle's Real Huntsman and Bud Carroll's Rural Rube. Joining the original three have been the other greats of racing — Traffic Officer, Lucky Pilot, the winningest greyhound in history Indy Ann, coursing greats Gangster and Golden Sahara, My Laddie, Lucky Roll, Fern Nature, Upsidedown, Kitty Dunn, the courageous Beach Comber, Sunny Concern, Never Roll, Mixed Harmony, Rocker Mac, and the latest induction, Orville Moses' Feldcrest. Also inducted in the Hall of Fame have been the first president of the National Greyhound Association, Dennis Callaghan, and the father of track racing, O. P. Smith.

The greyhound nations of the world are also honored in the museum. Last Fall Australia's Chief Havoc and Ireland's Mutton Cutlet were named as the first entrants in the International Section of the Hall of Fame.

Next on display is a history of pari-mutuel wagering, dealing with the principles of pari-mutuel and the complex equipment needed to operate a pari-mutuel facility. Another subject unfamiliar to the general public — the photo finish camera, is given mention, and on exhibit is one of the first photo finish cameras ever used at a greyhound track.

Considered the major highlight of the museum is the Hall of Fame's greyhound race-track model. With the push of a button, visitors are treated to a re-enactment of the exciting events that take place during each and every race at the track. Slides, shown on four screens above the track, are synchronized with the commentary to capture those electrifying moments just before and during a race.

The National Greyhound Association and the sport of coursing are the next subjects of exhibit. A recent addition to this section is that Jack-A-Lure display, the artificial-lure training device offered as an alternative to jackrabbits in the training process of greyhound pups. The NGA's extensive identification program, including the tattooing of all racing greyhounds, illustrates the manner in which the greyhound racing industry polices itself.

Throughout the Hall of Fame are numerous exhibits portraying behind-the-scene aspects of greyhound racing. Included are the grooming and training of greyhounds, along with the functions of a greyhound breeding farm.

The final section of the Hall of Fame is the display section of the American race tracks. Each participating track has provided its own display, with such features as the location of the track, photos of the track facilities, recognition to winners of major stake races offered at a particular track. Some also include local-color photos exclusive to the track's geographic locale.

Open throughout the year, the Hall of Fame can be a memorable experience for any visitor—especially those who already have an interest in the exciting sport of Greyhound Racing. The Greyhound Hall of Fame directors and staff wish to extend to you a special invitation to soon visit the Greyhound Hall of Fame in Abilene, Kans.

Interior view of the Greyhound Hall of Fame.

Rural Rube

Real Huntsman

Flashy Sir

Traffic Officer

HALL OF FAME
Listed in order of enshrinement

RURAL RUBE—enshrined in 1963, one of the first three immortals to be inducted into the Hall. Whelped in 1938 from a My Laddie-Lady Gangdrew breeding, Rural Rube became known as the "Man O'War" of greyhound racing. Owned by R. B. Carroll, he won 51 races in only 80 starts. A native Kansan, Rube displayed human-like qualities both on and off the track.

FLASHY SIR—out of Lucky Sir-Flashy Harmony, was also inducted in 1963 at the first Hall of Fame ceremonies. Of 1943 vintage, Flashy Sir became known as "Mr. Greyhound" around racing circles. Merrill Blair purchased him for $800, and Flashy Sir went on to win $50,000 in one year alone. At one time, he had 18 consecutive victories and was aptly tagged as the "Seabiscuit" of the Sport of Queens. His career record was 60–10–4 in 80 starts.

REAL HUNTSMAN—another of the first greyhounds to be enshrined into the Hall in 1963. Real Huntsman was whelped in 1948 out of Medora by Never Roll. Owned by Gene Randle, he earned $62,493.55 during his fabulous career. He holds the all-time consecutive win record of 27, which has yet to be seriously challenged. Real Huntsman competed in nine two-dog match races—and he won them all.

TRAFFIC OFFICER—Art Wilson's champion out of Meadows-Vixen. Whelped in 1925, Traffic Officer is still considered by many to be the best all-around greyhound in American history. After winning the coursing Futurity in 1926, he was sold to George Oswald for $3,300. Enshrined in 1964, Traffic Officer is most noted for his production of great runners.

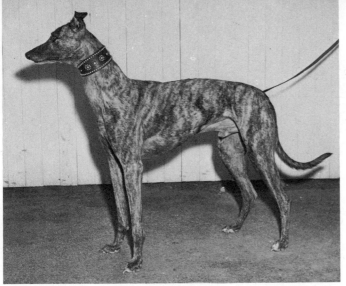

Lucky Pilot

Gangster, Imp.

LUCKY PILOT—a 1944 son of Never Roll-Dixie By. The Ray Holmes-owned speedster had an amazing career record of 61–13–7 in 92 starts. At one time he held four world records. Such a sure favorite among crowds, Lucky Pilot was limited in starts to prevent minus pools. At the time of his death, he was the leading sire in America.

Indy Ann

INDY ANN—the first female to be enshrined. Indy Ann, whelped in 1953 out of Pageant-Praying Darkie, is the winningest greyhound in racing history with 137 career triumphs. Owned by Ed Willard, she still owns the record of 61 wins for a calendar year (1956). Truly the "Caliente Queen," Indy Ann later whelped four litters of pups that were also outstanding at the South-of-the Border oval.

GANGSTER, IMP—wrestling champ John Pesek brought this greyhound to America because of his great coursing potential. Whelped in 1930 out of Non Pareil-Dusty Louise, Gangster was enshrined in the Hall of Fame in 1964, and was the first greyhound to be inducted for his accomplishments on the coursing field. He won three straight National Derby Cups and one Waterloo Cup.

MY LADDIE—son of Kitty Darling. My Laddie already had his father Traffic Officer and his son Rural Rube enshrined when he was inducted into the Hall of Fame in 1965. Whenever greyhound bloodlines are mentioned, F. W. Jones' My Laddie is a common topic of discussion. Many breeders feel his equal as a sire will never be seen.

LUCKY ROLL—son of Just Andrew, Imp.-Mustard Roll. Lucky Roll was enshrined in 1965. Whelped in 1931, the J. A. Austin-owned star was the first greyhound to win 60 races during the pari-mutuel era of the sport. His greatest donation to the sport was as a sire, and most of today's American runners can trace their ancestry back to Lucky Roll.

Lucky Roll

My Laddie

Upsidedown, Imp.

Golden Sahara

GOLDEN SAHARA—the second Hall of Famer enshrined on the basis of his coursing record. Whelped in 1929 out of Jovial Judge-Jeletz, Golden Sahara won the Derby Cup in 1931 and the Waterloo Cup in 1931 and 1932. Golden Sahara's owner was one of the pioneers of racing, Arch DeGeer. As a sire, Golden Sahara produced other great coursers such as Sonny Sahara, Sahara Son and Rhu.

FERN NATURE—a younger sister to Rural Rube, also owned by R. B. Carroll. Many who saw this 1939-whelped greyhound run insisted she was the greatest female racer of all time. Enshrined in 1965, Fern Nature won three straight Flagler Derbies and one Biscayne Derby, and was victorious in the Flagler Futurity and a pair of Miami inaugurals. *(Pictured on page 144)*

UPSIDEDOWN, IMP.—Vernie Mikels' coursing standout. Upsidedown was the son of Mutton Cutlet-Wealthy Widow and won the 1934 Waterloo Cup. His most noteworthy contribution to the sport was as a sire. In the '30s, his pups dominated coursing fields and held their own at the tracks. Upsidedown was enshrined into the Hall in 1966.

KITTY DUNN—a product of Flint Rock, Imp.-Lee's Lady, Imp. Ralphy McMinimy's Kitty Dunn divided the Fall Sapling in 1929, and at West Flagler she took on all challengers. One writer said: "There have been just four great dogs who caught the popular fancy completely, and Kitty Dunn was one of them." Kitty Dunn was whelped in 1928 and was inducted into the Hall of Fame in 1966.

BEACH COMBER—Paul Sutherland's star out of More Taxes-Soapy Hands. Beach Comber, whelped in 1945, was called "King of the Greyhounds." Crowds loved him for his famous "victory roll" after every track truimph. His nickname was "Shorty," which described his short-legged features, but what he lacked in appearance, he made up for in heart and intelligence. Enshrined in 1966, Beach Comber had a career record of 99−51−18 in 218 starts.

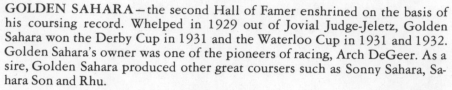

Beach Comber

Kitty Dunn

Never Roll

Sunny Concern

SUNNY CONCERN—Frank Lawman's "Queen of Greyhounds." Sunny Concern, whelped in 1923, was out of Unconcern, Imp.-Sunkist. Art Wilson said she was the best greyhound that ever coursed in a futurity year. Sunny Concern ran only fast enough to win on the track. She was enshrined into the Hall of Fame in 1967.

NEVER ROLL—1939 son of Lucky Roll-Never Fail. Owned by H. A. Alderson, Never Roll won the Wonderland Derby and chalked up four consecutive world records in 1942. Noted both as a breaker and a finisher, Never Roll followed his sire and his two sons, Lucky Pilot and Real Huntsman, into the Hall of Fame in 1968.

MIXED HARMONY—out of Larry of Waterhall, Imp.-Thrilling Sport. J. R. Hodges' star, whelped in 1944, was a great performer at Raynham, Caliente and in Florida. At the age of five, he was still winning stake and match races. His career as a sire was even more successful and he was the national sire champ in 1954 and 1955. Mixed Harmony's pups won more than 7,000 races, and he was enshrined into the Hall of Fame in 1970.

ROCKER MAC, IMP.—whelped in March of 1951, owned by R. H. Stevenson. Rocker Mac, the son of Chief Havoc-Mystery Rocca, was selected strictly on his sire merits. For seven years, he was America's top-rated sire, and his sons and daughters won more than 22,000 races. No other greyhound has approached these feats as a sire.

Rocker Mac, Imp.

Mixed Harmony

151

THE UNITED STATES HOCKEY HALL OF FAME

Eveleth, Minnesota

Located on Highway 53, the north-south highway that is the main route between Duluth and the Iron Range cities of Virginia, Hibbing and Eveleth, this Hall of Fame was dedicated on June 21, 1973. It began originally as a community project under the guidance of D. Kelly Campbell, a mining executive, who initiated a campaign to establish a United States Hockey Hall of Fame.

The amateur Hockey Association of the United States endorsed the idea. The United States Steel Corporation donated the land for the building. An exhibition game for the purpose of fund raising was played by the Minnesota North Stars and the St. Louis Blues. There were fund raising drives in the local communities. The Economic Development Administration made a grant of $666,400 to the City of Eveleth for the construction of the facility. The National Hockey League contributed $100,000. Through this united cooperation between individuals, corporations and government the Hall of Fame became a reality.

It is indeed a museum to be proud of in every respect. It is pleasing and practical in architectural design and contains a great variety of displays of past and present hockey players, equipment, and history of the game.

The building was designed by Tom Beers of Design and Planning Associates of Indianapolis, Indiana, who also did some of the design work at the Professional Football Hall of Fame in Canton, Ohio.

The first floor features the Great Hall containing twenty-five enshrinement pylons of the charter enshrinees, a general display area, theater souvenir shop, cloak room, rest rooms, director's office and service rooms. There is a mezzanine floor with a library, lounge and receiving room. On the second floor there is a major display area devoted to high school, college, amateur, international and professional hockey.

The displays devoted to the origins of hockey and to general information about player personnel, hockey equipment, skate displays and early teams that figured in the development of American Hockey are attractively arranged.

—All photographs in this chapter, courtesy United States Hockey Hall of Fame

The question arises as to why this $1,000,000 museum should be located in Eveleth which is about sixty miles north of Duluth instead of one of the larger cities that have had a long history of association with hockey. The answer is that this city of 6,000 population has sent eleven players into the National Hockey League, plus many players who have played college and amateur hockey. Eveleth has won the Minnesota state hockey tournament five times in thirteen appearances. It is often referred to as the "amateur hockey capital of the U.S.A."

The theater on the main floor seats niney-one viewers at the thirty-minute hockey movies that are shown four times daily.

There were twenty-five original enshrinees and there are now thirty-nine members of the Hall of Fame. Of this total there are twenty-six players, six coaches, six administrators and one referee. There are more people associated with amateur hockey in this museum than with the professional ranks and in this respect it is rather unusual for a sport that has been dominated by the professional leagues in the minds of the public.

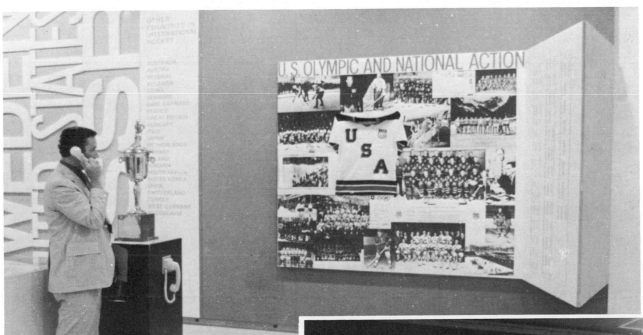

A visitor listens to an audio dealing with the United States' participation in international hockey while viewing a display on the same subject.

The slide show which runs eight minutes with musical accompaniment is the USHF's most popular exhibit. The show traces the history of the game in the United States since the 1890's.

Hobart A. H. (Hobey) Baker

Francis Charles Brimsek

Clarence J. (Taffy) Abel

HONOR ROLL

CLARENCE J. (TAFFY) ABEL (Defenseman) New York Rangers, Chicago Blackhawks 1926–1934—knew his finest moments while wearing the uniform of the New York Rangers and the Chicago Blackhawks in an era when the National Hockey League was scrambling from an offbeat collection of muscular mavericks to a solid organization. Abel's fabulous climb from Sault Ste. Marie ranks to the National Hockey League stamped him as a legend in hockey. He left an indelible imprint in pro and amateur circles as a player, coach and manager. Taffy Abel was a name beloved by hockey followers across the continent in the era of the 60-minute men: He played his first game in Sault Ste. Marie, Mich., 1918. 1900–1964

HOBART A. H. (HOBEY) BAKER (Forward) Princeton University 1911–1914—"Like his contemporaries Jim Thorp, Ty Cobb, and Jack Johnson, Hobey Baker was a fabulous athlete; like them, he had a great physique, fantastic reflexes, instant coordination of hand and eye, iron discipline, blazing courage. But to these rare abilities he added another dimension all his own . . . to the public during his career at Princeton and St. Nick's he was the college athlete supreme: the gentleman sportsman, the amateur in the pure sense playing the game "pour le sport," who never fouled, despised publicity, and professional offers." So wrote John Davies in his biography, "The Legend of Hobey Baker." 1892–1918

FRANCIS CHARKES BRIMSEK (Goaltender) Boston Burins 1938–1943, Chicago Blackhawks 1945–1950—His star flashed on the National Hockey League scene with an initial brilliance few rookies have ever matched. Coming up from Providence in the fall of 1938 he replaced the (Tiny) Thompson in the Boston Bruin's net and proceeded to blank the opposition in six of his first eight games. This performance immediately gained Brimsek the nickname, "Mr. Zero." He went on that season to win the Calder Trophy as the outstanding rookie and the Vezina Trophy as the league's leading goalie. The Bruins proceeded to capture the Stanley Cup that season as well as in 1940–41. 1915–

GEORGE V. BROWN (Administrator 1910–1937) Boston Athletic Club, Boston Arena, Boston Gardens—In 1910 the Boston Arena was built and with it the Boston Athletic Association (BAA) hockey team. George Brown was the driving force behind this team which played top amateur clubs in the Eastern United States as well as leading Canadian and college teams. When the Arena burned down in 1918 Brown formed the corporation which constructed the new Arena. He then managed both the new building as well as continuing the BAA team. This club formed the basis of the 1924 United States Olympic Team with seven of the ten players BAA members. The United States finished second losing only to Canada 6-1 in the finals. 1880–1937

WALTER A. BROWN (Administrator) Boston Gardens, Boston Bruins, International Ice Hockey Federation 1933–1964—Following in the footsteps of his father George Brown, also an enshrinee of the United States Hockey Hall of Fame, Walter Brown made great and significant contributions to American hockey, particularly in the area of the international game. 1905–1964

WILLIAM L. (BILL) CHADWICK (Referee) National Hockey League—rose from the relatively unlikely hockey background of New York City to become one of the premier referees to officiate in the National Hockey League. When he laid his whistle aside after the 1954–55 season he was the senior official in the NHL, the only American to ever achieve that position. Chadwick was a protege and long time friend of United States Hockey Hall of Fame enshrinee Tom Lockhart, President of the Amateur Hockey Association of the United States from 1937 to 1972. He played his early hockey with the Stock Exchange team in the New York Metropolitan League. 1915–

RAYMOND C. CHAISSON (Forward) Boston College—centered one of the all time great lines in the history of college hockey along with Al Dumond and John Pryor. His coach and fellow United States Hockey Hall of Fame enshrinee, the legendary John "Snooks" Kelley described Chaisson as one of his very finest hockey players during thirty-six years of college coaching. 1918–

JOHN P. CHASE (Forward) Harvard University 1924–1928—began his formal hockey career at Milton Academy playing on the 1922–23 team. Transferring to Exeter Academy the following year he played there one year before matriculating at Harvard in the fall of 1924. At Harvard, Chase's strength and skill as a hockey player soared. He played as a regular at center ice as a freshman and as a first line center on the varsity for three years. He was selected as team captain his senior year. Chase also excelled at baseball at Harvard and as an amateur player in later years. 1906–

TONY CONROY (Forward) St. Paul Athletic Club, St. Paul Saints 1915–1920—"A graceful, rather slightly built young man, dashing madly across the frozen Hippodrome surface of an evening, his skates cutting their way along the ice, his stick skillfully guiding a puck through a maze of enemy sticks, skates, and bodies has become something of a spectacle in St. Paul bearing repetition. . . ." So wrote a St. Paul hockey writer of Anthony (Tony) Conroy. 1895–

CARL S. (CULLY) DAHLSTROM (Forward) Chicago Blackhawks 1937–1945—played high school hockey at Minneapolis and then went on to play for the Minneapolis Millers in the American Hockey Association. The American Hockey Association was a strong minor professional league of that time and sent many promising players into the National Hockey League. It was there that he caught the eye of Major Fred McLaughlin of the Chicago Blackhawks who was always on the lookout for promising American talent. Dahlstrom didn't let McLaughlin down as he won the Calder Trophy as the National Hockey League's rookie of the year in 1937–38. Dahlstrom was one of three American players, enshrinees Karakas and Brimsek were the others, to win the Calder Trophy between 1935–36 and 1938–39. In the semi-final playoffs against the New York Americans he scored the winning goal in a 1–0 overtime victory in the second game. In the finals against Toronto he scored the key first goal in the 4–1 victory which brought the Stanley Cup to the Windy City. 1913–

VICTOR DES JARDINS (Forward) Chicago Blackhawks, New York Rangers, Minor professional teams—Sault Ste. Marie's second member of the United States Hockey Hall of Fame. Taffy Abel was initially selected in 1973, Vic Des Jardins played a key role in the early days of Eveleth hockey when the town was represented in the United States Amateur Hockey Association

Victor Des Jardins

155

(USAHA). At that time there was no professional hockey in the United States and the USAHA represented the highest level of the game in the nation. An early writer said of him: "Des Jardins of Eveleth, while one of the very smallest centers (5'9", 160 lbs.) in the game, is one of the very smartest and is very capable on offense and defense." 1900 –

DOUGLAS EVERETT (Forward) Dartmouth College – was, along with his fellow United States Hockey Hall of Fame enshrinee Myles Lane, one of the great players to come out of Dartmouth during the 1920's. He played his first hockey for Colby Academy in 1921 – 22 and served as captain of that team. Later he amazed fans with his stick handling ability, speed, and hard shot as a member of Dartmouth teams from 1922 – 1926. Everett was All-College in his sophomore and junior years at Dartmouth, as selected by the Boston Transcript, and was named by the New York Herald Tribune to one of the earliest All-American Teams. 1905 –

JOHN B. GARRISON (Forward-Defenseman) Harvard University 1928 – 1932 – attended the local Country Day School in West Newton and as a school boy there had the unparrelled record of playing six years on the varsity! He then went on to Harvard where he was a regular on the Freshman Team and then a varsity regular for three seasons at center ice. Garrison was adept at any forward position as well as on defense. 1909 –

JOHN L. (DOC) GIBSON (Administrator) International Hockey League 1903 – 1907 – a graduate of the Detroit Medical School, was a fine player in Canada and was prevailed upon by the late Merv Youngs, then a cub reporter and later editor of the Houghton Mining Gazette, to join the Portage Lake (Houghton-Hancock) organization. Gibson was a native of Berlin, Ontario, now Kitchener. 1954

FRANCIS F. X. (MOOSE) GOHEEN (Defenseman) St. Paul Athletic Club 1915 – 1917, St. Paul Saints 1920 – 1932 – learned his hockey on the outdoor ranks of White Bear Lake and nearby St. Paul. He was not only a great hockey player but also an outstanding football and baseball performer as well. In the fall of 1915 Goheen joined the St. Paul Athletic Club, one of the strongest American amateur teams of its time. Goheen, along with such other greats as Tony Conroy, Cy Weindenborner and Ed Fitzgerald, helped capture the McNaughton Trophy in 1916 – 17. This trophy, now in the hands of the Western Collegiate Hockey Association, was then symbolic of American amateur hockey supremacy. St. Paul won the cup again the following year as well as the Art Ross Cup from Lacime, Quebec in Montreal. Goheen then joined the U.S. Army for World War I service. 1894 –

MALCOM K. GORDON (Coach) St. Paul's School 1888 – 1917 – In 1882 he arrived as a "new kid" at the St. Paul's School in Concord, New Hampshire. He not only was an only child and knew no one else in the school, he was a Southerner, dropped down in the heyday of reconstruction into a nest of hostile Yankees. In one of those odd incongruities of life, this Southerner was to play a major role in shaping what is regarded as an essentially Northern game – our great sport of hockey. The game had been earlier introduced at St. Paul's from Canada, but Malcom Gordon is regarded as the individual who helped formalize the game by putting down on paper what is regarded as the first set of rules in the United States. This occurred in 1885 and in 1888 he was made hockey coach. Play at St. Paul's was strickly intramural, but in 1896 Gordon took the first St. Paul's team to New York to play at the old St. Nicholas Rink. 1868 – 1964

AUSTIE HARDING (Forward) Harvard University 1935 – 1939 – followed quickly at Harvard on the heels of his fellow Noble and Greenough graduate Fred Moseley and soon established his own niche as an all time Crimson ice great. Harding also played four varsity years at prep school and then captained the Harvard freshmen. Then began three outstanding varsity years during

Douglas Everett

Austie Harding

Frank "Goose" Goheen

Stewart Iglehart

which he led the squad in scoring each year with 30, 25, and 30 point efforts respectively. The Boston born skater's abilities were recognized early in his college career when hockey writer Irving Burwell wrote in March, 1937: "Harvard's forward line-against Yale will have Harding, without question the best American college hockey player of today at center. 1917 –

VICTOR HEYLIGER (Coach) University of Michigan, University of Illinois, United States Air Force Academy — with his ever present cigar clenched between his teeth, came out of the East to forge an outstanding coaching record at his alma mater, Michigan, as well as at the University of Illinois and the United States Air Force Academy. The stocky, black haired coach played high school hockey at Concord and prep school hockey at the Lawrence Academy in Groton, Connecticut. Entering Michigan in 1934, he starred in 1935 – 36 – 37, earning All-American honors at forward. He scored 116 goals a school record at the time which was later broken by one of his players, Gordon McMillan. 1915 –

STEWART IGLEHART (Defenseman) Yale University, Crescent Athletic Club, New York Rovers 1929 – 1936 — occupies a unique position in American sports being the only man to have represented the United States internationally in two sports: hockey on the 1933 World Championship Team and polo in the 1936 International Match. He has been one of only a handful of men in polo to earn a ten goal rating. But as he says himself: "I have played many sports, some better than others, but hockey was always number one. I felt it gave me wings, an extra dimension and when I dream dreams of past accomplishments, let me dream in hockey." 1910 –

EDWARD J. JEREMIAH (Coach) Dartmouth College 1937–1943 and 1945–1967—entered Dartmouth in 1926 after high school at Somerville, Massachusetts and prep school at Hebron Academy in Maine. He won nine letters at Somerville, three each in football, hockey, and baseball were earned at Hebron.

After picking up two football, three hockey, and two baseball letters at Dartmouth, Jeremiah entered the professional hockey ranks as a member of the New Haven hockey team of the Canadian-American League, and then split the next season between the New York Americans and the Boston Bruins of the National Hockey League. He split the 1932–33 season between the Boston Cubs and the New Haven team, again in the Canadian-American League. His last year of playing was the 1934–35 season with Cleveland of the International League. 1905–1967

VIRGIL JOHNSON (Defenseman) Chicago Blackhawks, Minor professional teams—came out of Minneapolis South High School where he participated in both hockey and football to play sixteen years of professional hockey. Johnson was small in stature at 5'8 1-2" and 160 lbs. (He quarterbacked his high school football team at 120 lbs.), but nonetheless was a master stick checker and backwards skater who could take the puck away from anyone. Fellow United States Hockey Hall of Fame enshrinee John Mariucci, who remember him well, recalls: "He was a magician with his stick. He was like a terrier after a rat when he moved in and stole the puck. He could do it against the best stick handlers." 1912–

MICHAEL G. KARAKAS (Goaltender) Chicago Blackhawks 1935–1940, Montreal Canadians 1944–1946—though born in Aurora was reared in Eveleth, and was the first of a number of players coached by enshrinee Cliff Thompson to go on to stardom in the National Hockey League.

Karakas had his first hockey training on the ice in a lot near the Spruce Mine at Eveleth, where he and other sons of Oliver Iron Mining Company (now United States Steel, donators of the site of the United States Hockey Hall of Fame) fought out their hockey battles. He played hockey on the Eveleth High School Team for three years, and later, while attending Eveleth Junior College, he joined the Rangers, and amateur club which won the state championship in 1931. Karakas's work attracted the attention of a scout for the Chicago Shamrocks, American Hockey Association, who sent him to that club. He was used as a back-up goalie that year and a regular the next. He received the American Hockey Association's cup as the most valuable goalie in the league. 1911–

JOHN (SNOOKS) KELLEY (Coach) Boston College—At 7:45 a.m. on Friday, January 13, 1933 forty-five students from Boston College assembled at

Michael G. Karakas

Myles J. Lane

the Boston Arena for the first practice session of a revitalized BC hockey team under the watchful eye of John Kelley, their volunteer coach who had graduated three years before. Fifteen days later, under the young teacher from Cambridge, the team defeated Northeastern 8–6 on Arena ice to begin a legend. "Snooks" had been a star player for Cambridge Latin and Dean Academy before enrolling at Boston College. He played for the 1928–29 Eagles and was the squad's top player, graduating in 1930 after the stock market had wiped out hockey as a varsity sport. 1907–

MYLES LANE (Defenseman) Dartmouth College 1924–1928—ranks as one of Dartmouth College's greatest athletes of all time. From 1925 until his graduation in 1928, Lane earned three letters in hockey and football respectively and another in baseball. He was captain of the 1927–28 hockey team leading them to a 6–4 record. Lane gained national prominence by becoming the first American collegian to successfully enter the ranks of professional hockey joining the New York Rangers in 1928. While at Dartmouth he established records for the most goals in one game by a defenseman, 5, most goals in a season by a defenseman, 20, and most career goals by a defenseman, 50, 1903–

JOE LINDER (Forward-Defenseman) Portage Lake Hockey Club, Hancoack Hockey Club, Shamrock Hockey Club, Duluth Curling Club, Duluth Hockey Club 1904–1920—was described by contemporaries and those who have made a study of the game as the "first great American born hockey player." A powerful rawboned, virtually irresistible skater, playmaker and team leader, Linder was involved in the American hockey scene as an amateur and professional player from 1904–1920. From then until his death in 1948, he remained on the scene as a coach, manager and sponsor of the game in the Superior–Duluth area of Minnesota. 1886–1948

THOMAS F. LOCKHART (Administrator) Amateur Hockey Association of the United States 1937–1972—His name has been synonomous with amateur hockey in the United States since the early 1930's when he took over the organization and promotion of the game in New York City. Long interested and active as a cyclist, boxer and track competitor, he organized the Eastern Amateur Hockey League in 1933 and in the fall of 1937 founded the Amateur Hockey Association of the United States (AHAUS) 1892–

SAM L. LOPRESTI (Goaltender) Chicago Blackhawks 1940–1942—born in Elcor but raised in Eveleth, is one of two American hockey players to have his name written into the National Hockey League record book. On page 93 you'll find the category: "Most shots, One Team, One Game" followed by: 83 Boston Bruins, March 4, 1941 at Boston. Boston defeated Chicago 3 2. Chicago goaltender was Sam LoPresti". On that night in Boston with fellow Evelethian and Hall of Famer Frank Brimsek in the opposing nets LoPresti turned aside 27 saves in the first period, 31 in the second, and 22 in the last. After the game the late Johnny Crawford, a Bruins forward, summed it up best when asked if LoPresti was really good or just lucky: "He was good all right if he hadn't been good he wouldn't be alive now." 1917–

JOHN P. MARIUCCI (Defenseman) Chicago Blackhawks 1940–1942, 1945–1948—His name is indelibly etched into the history of American hockey as well as that of his native Minnesota. He has, in the words of an old but appropriate cliche become a legend in his own time. Mariucci was another Cliff Thompson coached player who went on to bigger and better things. After high school he went on to the University of Minnesota starring on the undefeated team of 1939–40. While at the U he was also an outstanding football player. Turning pro in the fall of 1940 Mariucci played briefly for Providence of the American League before joining the Hawks for the balance of the season. In Chicago he became a fixture manning the Blackhawks defense until the end of the 1948 season and eventually becoming team captain in the process. 1916–

John P Mariucci

159

Edwin N. (Doc) Romnes

WILLIAM C. MOE (Defenseman) New York Rangers—like his fellow enshrinee Vic Heyliger, was one of those relatively unique hockey people who shared the hockey heritage of both the East and West. Born in Danvers, Massachusetts, Moe grew up in Minneapolis where he was attracted to the ice game. After playing in local amateur leagues and then with the amateur Eastern League Baltimore Orioles, he hooked on with the professional American Hockey League Philadelphia Rockets, later moving on to the Hershey Bears of the same league. He gained laurels as the most-valuable player in the American League for the 1943–44 season and attracted the notice of Lester Patrick of the Rangers, who gave up four players to obtain his services. 1916–

FRED MOSELEY (Forward) Harvard University 1932–1936—His fellow United States Hockey Hall of Fame enshrinee John Chase has perhaps best summed up Fred Moseley, the hockey player: "Throughout his hockey career he was a tremendous team player . . . a tireless, powerful skater, a great backchecker, and a leader on and off the ice." 1913–

GEORGE OWEN, JR. (Defenseman) Boston Bruins 1928–1933—Shortly after his birth George Owen's parents moved to the Boston area and young George grew up and learned his hockey there. He attended Newton High School and went on to Harvard in the fall of 1919. He captained the Freshman team and then served two terms as varsity captain, a relatively rare feat at Harvard. As a college hockey player he was equally at home on defense or at center. Owen also played football and baseball for the Crimson, serving as captain of the latter during his senior year. 1901 –

WINTHROP H. (DING) PALMER (Forward) Yale University 1926–1930—is the all-time leading goal scorer in the history of Yale University hockey, notching 87 goals from 1928–30. He also picked up nine assists and ranks No. 4 on the all-time Yale point list with 96. It is freely admitted that assists were not recorded with the same detail as they are now. Palmer played on varsity squads that lost just six games in three years. In 1927–28, the Elis were 13-4-0, but improved that to 15-1-1 in 1928–29. The 1929–30 team called the "greatest amateur hockey team in history" by E. S. Bronson, was 17-1-1. The teams Palmer played on posted an aggregate record of 45-6-2 during his three years. 1906–1970

CLIFFORD JOSEPH (FIDO) PURPUR (Forward) Chicago Blackhawks, Detroit Red Wings, St. Louis Eagles, Minor professional teams—When he stepped on the ice with the St. Louis Eagles in 1934 he became up to this point in time (1974) North Dakota's only native son to play in the National Hockey League. With hockey developing at a fast pace no doubt more of the Sioux state's sons will be seen in major league rinks. Purpur made the NHL when he was twenty and when the Eagles folded after 1934–35 season he signed with the American Hockey Association St. Louis Flyers. He stayed with the Flyers until 1942 when he returned to the NHL with the Chicago Blackhawks. In St. Louis Purpur was idolized by the fans because of his gutsy play, great speed, and small stature, but also because he always took time out to talk to the fans and sign autographs for the youngsters. 1914–

Frank J. (Coddy) Winters

EDWIN N. (DOC) ROMNES (Forward) Chicago Blackhawks, Toronto Maple Leafs, New York Americans 1930–1940—broke into the National Hockey League at a time when there were but two American born players in the league. Fortunately for him the Chicago Blackhawks team which he joined got off to a bad start and Romnes got a chance at center and played regularly thereafter. Romnes played a high school hockey in White Bear Lake and St. Paul, as well as a year at St. Thomas College, before joining the professional St. Paul Saints in 1927. It was after three years with the Saints that he made the jump to the big time. Romnes played in the Stanley Cup finals on four different occasions: 1930–31, 1933–34, 1937–38, all with Chicago, and 1938–39 with the Toronto Maple Leafs. He was a winner in 1933–34 with fellow enshrinee Taffy Abel and in 1937–38 with enshrinees Cully Dahlstrom and Mike Karakas. 1907 –

CLIFFORD R. THOMPSON (Coach) Eveleth High School 1926–1958 – coached Eveleth High School from 1920 to his retirement in 1958. During that time his teams won 534 games while losing only 26 and tieing 9. The highlight of Thompson's career came during the years 1948–51 when his teams won 78 straight victories including four straight Minnesota state championships. Eveleth won the state title a total of five times under Thompson's leadership. Simultaneous to his high school coaching Thompson also handled the Eveleth Junior College team compiling a career record of 171 games won and 28 lost. 1893 –

WILLIAM THAYER TUTT (Administrator) International Ice Hockey Federation 1959–1973 – of Colorado Springs, Colorado is president of the El Pomar Foundation and the Broadmoor Hotel, Inc. and its related companies. It has been while serving in these capacities that Tutt has exercised his administrative abilities in hockey. 1902 –

ALFRED (RALPH) WINSOR (Coach) Harvard University 1902–1917 – dominating figure of the first twenty years of Harvard hockey was without question Ralph Winsor, Class of 1902. The early period of Harvard hockey might well be called the "Winsor Era." He played in 1901 and captained the 1902 team. Then he coached with outstanding success from 1902 to 1917, during which time Harvard had 124 wins and 29 defeats. The teams of 1903, 1904, 1905, 1906, 1909 and 1919, when he was assistant coach, were undefeated. Over these years he complied a 23 win 5 loss record against arch rival Yale. As might be expected Winsor developed many stars. Foremost among them was S. Trafford Hicks, Class of 1910, and captain of the 1910 team. Another was Morgan B. Phillips, Class of 1915, who tallied nine goals in games against the Eli. 1881 –

FRANK J. (CODDY) WINTERS (Forward-Defenseman) Cleveland Crescents, Clevelands, Cleveland Athletic Club – 1925 – started out as an ice polo player in his home town of Duluth. As ice polo gave way to hockey, Winters took up the game, being placed at rover where his great speed could be utilized to the best advantage. Winters played with the Duluth Northern Hardware team through the 1908 season during which the Duluth team played a series of games with a Cleveland All-Star team at the new Elysium Rink there. 1884–1944

LYLE Z. WRIGHT (Administrator) Minneapolis Arena 1924–1963 – was identified with organized hockey from the first moment it existed in Minneapolis and remained identified with it, in one capacity or another, until his death. Wright served in the Canadian artillery in World War I and moved to Minneapolis in 1919. After four years of playing hockey himself he brought the famed Ching Johnson from Eveleth to Minneapolis to play for the Minneapolis Millers. He managed the Millers, then playing in the American Hockey Association from 1928 until 1931 when he moved to Chicago to become business manager of the Blackhawks. He returned to Minneapolis in the early 1930's and remained there for the remainder of his life serving in varying capacities with the Minneapolis Arena eventually attaining the office of president. 1898–1963

Two ways of spurting

Position for lifting the puck

Facing off

Checking

THE NATIONAL MUSEUM OF RACING

Saratoga Springs, New York

By Robert F. Kelley

It would be extremely difficult to establish an exact date for the start of the National Museum of Racing. It was conceived in the thinking and in the resulting conversation of people with long backgrounds in the sport; as it neared birth it found imaginative help from the townspeople of Saratoga, and when it came into being it was embraced by all of racing. From its earliest beginnings, it was national in thinking and today stands as the shrine for Thoroughbred traditions that stretch back into colonial times in America.

"The purpose for which this corporation is formed," reads a part of the constitution of the National Museum of Racing, Inc., "is to establish a museum for the collection, preservation and exhibition of books; documents and other printed or written material; statuary, paintings, films, memorials and any and all other kinds of articles associated with the origin, history and development of horse racing and the breeding of the Thorough-bred horse."

It was in 1950 that the constitution was adopted and the Museum came officially into being. There were about ten years of planning and semiofficial existence before this. F Skiddy von Stade, last president of the Saratoga Association, George D. Widener, Walter M. Jeffords, Bayard Tuckerman, Jr., Howell E. Jackson, C. V. Whitney and John Hay Whitney, were leaders among the people of racing. Always strong in his enthusiasm was also Carleton F. Burke, the California racing figure who spent so many of the Augusts of his life at Saratoga.

It is altogether fitting that the inaugural catalogue of the Museum should be dated 1963, for that is the Centennial year of Saratoga, the oldest active racing center in the country. Thus it was logical that the Museum be located in Saratoga Springs.

Intelligent and real help in the establishment came from the people of the community. Early workers were John Sexton, of the school faculty, later High School principal; Fred Eaton, journalist and now managing

—All photographs in this chapter, courtesy National Museum of Racing, Inc.

editor of *The Saratogian*; Kenneth K. Burke, then head of the Chamber of Commerce, and Dennis A. Mansfield. All of it was spearheaded in Saratoga by Addison Mallery, then mayor of the city. The Mayor, with the help of Francis Dorsey, City Attorney, secured, in 1951, the first home for the Museum, a part of the old Canfield Casino, owned by the City of Saratoga. Here, in that year, Mayor Mallery, von Stade and C. V. Whitney, the first president of the Museum, officiated at ceremonies which opened the first exhibit.

It was under the inspired and determined leadership of Walter Jeffords, during his presidency, that the Museum attained its real status. Its building, designed by the architect, A. L. Noel, was constructed; its collections added to, and carefully designed, and the culmination of Mr. Jeffords' great efforts came with the dedication of the building by Governor Averell Harriman in 1955. During all this period, the difficult financing of the growing project was ably assisted by Saratoga banker, Andrew Douglas, long its treasurer.

The Museum's superb collection of equine art and sculpture and its varied collection of old and new memorabilia has come by gift and loan from individuals, The Jockey Club, racing associations and Universities and from fourteen states, North, South, East and West.

The Hall of Fame of Horse Racing in the Walter M. Jeffords Memorial Wing.

The cataloging of this collection is further evidence people in all phases of the sport are interested to the extent of helping the Museum in any way they can. It is the work of Dr. Joseph C. O'Dea. Dr. O'Dea, educated here at Notre Dame and Cornell and post graduate work at Erlangen in Germany, is a distinguished practitioner and research man in Veterinary medicine who served with the Supreme Allied Command in Europe during the war, then returned to his home at Avon, New York where he breeds Thoroughbreds and Standardbreds. At various times he has served as consultant to the U.S. Equestrian team, but this work started through his interest in equine art.

Originally he planned to catalogue a portion of the Museum collection as a result of his interest in Henry Stull, whose work is well represented in the collection. Once started, he carried on to do the entire collection, donating the manuscript to the Museum.

HALL OF FAME OF THOROUGHBRED TRAINERS

Harvey Bedwell   *Fred Burlew*

HARVEY GUY BEDWELL, born in 1876 in Roseboro, Oregon, was the leading trainer for six consecutive years 1912–1917. He had a keen eye for horseflesh as indicated by the deal he made for Commander J.K.L. Ross when he bought Sir Barton, the first Triple Crown winner (1919) for $10,000.

PRESTON M. BURCH, born in 1884 in Augusta, Georgia, was a breeder, owner, general manager, farm manager, stable agent and bloodstock adviser during a long career in racing. He was the second of three generations of horsemen. He recommended that John Sanford buy George Smith and his advice was proven correct when the colt won the 1916 Kentucky Derby. His greatest success was with Mrs. Sloane's Brookemeade Stable where he developed Atlanta, Bold, Capeador, Closed Door, Dart By, Flower Bowl, Grandharva, Going Away, Grand Canyon, More Sun, Picador, Sailor Sunny Dale and Tritium. He always contended that George Smith was the greatest horse.

WILLIAM P. BURCH, a native of Cherow, South Carolina, was the father of Preston Burch and one of the foremost trainers in the days following the Civil War. His last horse of note was My Own, winner of the Maryland Handicap and the Saratoga Cup in 1926. He died in Saratoga at the age of 80.

FRED BURLEW, born in 1871, spent 45 years in racing—37 as a trainer during which career he saddled 977 winners and won 124 stake races with 75 horses. In 1905 he was given the responsibility of training Beldame, a four year old mare owned by August Belmont. Beldame won the Surburban Handicap over males and finished her career with 17 victories in 31 races earning $102,570 in an era of small purses. She was out of the money just four times. He bought a sore legged colt named Morvich from Max Hirsch for $7,5000 in 1920. He later sold him to Benjamin Block, but he continued to train the horse. Morvich was undefeated in 1921 as a two year old winning 11 races. In 1922, his first start was the Kentucky Derby in which he was the favorite of the racing fans and he won much to the surprise of other trainers who felt that he was just a sprinter who could not go the distance. "I knew my horse, they didn't," remarked Burlew.

J. DALLETT "DOLLY" BYERS was a three time national steeplechase riding champion. He once rode five straight winners at the Manly Steeplechase in Far Hills, Maryland and on another occasion rode four consecutive winners at Temple Gwathmey Steeplechase. After his career in riding he turned to training and had some successes particularly with Tea Maker, winner of four stake races in 1952 at the age of 9. Byers passed away in December 1966 at his home in Aiken, South Carolina.

FRANK CHILDS, on his eightieth birthday in 1967, said, "If there is a better way of life I've yet to hear of it," referring to his long career in racing. He had one Kentucky Derby winner, Tomy Lee, who survived a foul claim after beating Sword Dancer by a nose in 1959. He induced Fred Turner, Jr. to enter Weldy in the Del Mar Futurity which he won netting the owner $62,300.

WILLIAM DUKE trained horses in France where he developed Prestige for William K. Vanderbilt. He also trained the Aga Khan's stable. In 1925, he returned to the United States, as trainer for Gifford A. Cochran, who had purchased two colts, Coventry and Flying Ebony. Coventry won the Preakness which then preceded the Kentucky Derby. The day before the Derby, Cochran learned that Earl Sande was available and instructed Duke to start Flying Ebony in the Derby with Sande up. Cochran refused to go home that night because he feared that his friends would persuade him to withdraw the colt. The 1925 Derby was the first to be broadcast on radio. On a sloppy track, Sande took Flying Ebony to the front early in the race and stayed there for a length and half victory.

LOUIS FEUSTEL was the trainer of the Champion of Champions, Man O' War, winner of 20 races in 21 starts for the Riddle Farm. The single loss was to Upset in the Sanford Memorial at Saratoga. He beat Upset on four other occasions. He won both the Preakness and the Belmont, but was not entered in the Kentucky Derby. In fact he never was raced in Kentucky. He earned $186,089 for the eleven wins in 1920 making Feustel, the leading trainer of that year. Man O' War set records in the Withers, Belmont, Dwyer, Lawrence Realization and the Jockey Club stakes carrying from 115 to 138 pounds. He carried 130 or more pounds in nine races.

SUNNY JIM FITZSIMMONS'S career as a trainer spanned seven decades in which he saddled 2,266 winners including 148 stakes races, winning a total of more than $13,000,000. He was most closely associated with the Woodword and Phipps families. His good nature and sunny disposition made him a beloved figure amongst horsemen and fans alike. Many of his wins were in the big classic races including two Triple Crown winners, Gallant Fox and Omaha. He trained Bold Ruler, winner of the Preakness and Sire of Secretariat and Nashua, winner of the Preakness and the Belmont. He trained Nashua for the match race against Swaps at Washington Park in Chicago in the summer of 1955 in which Nashua won by six lengths.

JOHN GAVER was a Princeton graduate (1924) who found the conventional jobs in teaching or business too dull and found employment as an assistant trainer for the Harry Payne Whitney stable. When John Hay Whitney and his sister needed someone to manage their extensive racing interests, they turned to Gaver. He was the leading trainer in 1942 and 1951 and developed many champions including Tom Fool, Shut Out, Devil Diver, Third Degree, Capot, Tangled, Amphitheatre, The Rhymer, Guillotine, One Hitter, Hall of Fame, Straight Face, Cohoes, Outing Class, Stage Door Johnny, and Malicious.

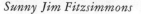

Sunny Jim Fitzsimmons   *John M. Gaver*

THOMAS JEFFERSON HEALEY started training horses in the latter years of the nineteenth century working primarily for two owners, Richard T. Wilson and Walter J. Salmon. He won the Preakness five times and a number of other important stakes races. In 1931, he took over some of the C.V. Whitney stable and developed Top Flight winner of five of the top filly and mare stakes. He was also the trainer of Equipoise as a five year old.

SAM HILDRETH trained five horses that won in excess of $100,000—Zev, Mad Hatter, Grey Lag, Mad Play and King James. He was the leading money winning trainer for nine seasons and for three consecutive seasons—1909, 1910, and 1911, was America's leading owner. He won the Belmont more

Max Hirsch

Thomas Hitchcock Sr.

Hirsch Jacobs

Ben Jones

often than any trainer in history except James Rowe including back to back victories in 1916 and 1917, with horses owned by August Belmont.

MAX HIRSCH, born in 1880, in Fredericksburg, Texas and lived until 1969 spending 68 years in thoroughbred racing. In 1968, his final year of racing his horses won $914,356. He started at the age of 14 as a jockey, but became too heavy so he took up training. His greatest successes were for the King Ranch for whom he trained three Kentucky Derby winners, Bold Venture — 1936, Assault, son of Bold Venture — 1946, and Middleground, also a son of Bold Venture in 1950. He won the Triple Crown with Assault and the Preakness with Bold Venture. He won the Belmont with Vito, 1928, Middleground, 1950, and High Gun, 1954.

THOMAS HITCHCOCK was originally a well known polo player being ranked at 7 goals or better from 1891 through 1920 and in three of those years he was rated at 10 goals. He captained America's first International Polo Team. He shifted his attention to steeplechasing and won the American Grand National in 1906 with Good and Plenty and again in 1938 with Annibal. He introduced fox hunting to Aiken, South Carolina in the early 1900's. He died in 1941 at the age of 80. His son, Thomas Jr., who was the greatest polo player in American polo history was killed in a plane crash in England in 1944 during World War II.

MOLLIE HUGHES was born near Amsterdam, New York, 28 miles from Saratoga, his favorite track. He began his long career in 1893 on the Hurricana Farm owned by General Stephen Sanford. At the age of 26, he was named head trainer in 1913 by John Sanford, the General's son. He won the 1916 Kentucky Derby with Geroge Smith. In 1918, George Smith carrying 130 pounds beat Exterminator at 120 pounds and Omar Khayam at 115 pounds both younger Derby winners in the 1-1/2 miles Bowie Handicap. He was a great steeplechase trainer as well, winning the Grand National at Belmont six times.

JOHN J. HYLAND in the early 1890's told his foreman J. Simon Healy to sell Hastings a colt he didn't like. Healy instead hid the colt and brought him out later to beat every colt in the barn. Hyland told Healy to assign his best rider to Hastings who went on to win the 1894 Belmont, but more important than that he became the grandsire of Man O'War. Hyland trained winners on both sides of the Atlantic winning the Belmont, also with Henry of Navarre and Masterman, 1902. He won more than $50,000 in purses in Germany. He was a close friend of President U.S. Grant. He was known a sharp judge of his apprentices. One of those who learned under him and became a noted horseman was Louis Feustel, trainer of Man O' War.

HIRSCH JACOBS started his racing by training racing pigeons in Brooklyn but soon switched to thoroughbreds. Beginning in 1933 and for the next twelve years he was the leading American trainer in 11 out of 12 years without having a single significant horse in his stable. His big break came in 1943 when he came up with Stymie who was running the third race of his life finishing seventh against a field of maidens in a claiming race for $1500 when Jacobs claimed him. He raced Stymie 57 times in the next two seasons winning seven races. Due to the reduction of racing in World War II in 1944 Stymie raced just 19 times winning nine races totalling nearly a quarter million dollars. When he was retired at 8, Stymie had raced 131 times winning 35 races and was the world's leading money winner with $918,485. With the money Stymie earned, Jacobs and his partner bought a farm in Maryland which he named Stymie Manor. Between 1946 and 1960, Jacob's horses won 3,513 races earning $18,311,412.

BEN JONES was born in 1883 in Parnell, Missouri, the son of a bank president who let it be known at an early date that he was going to seek a more active life than the bank career appeared to offer. After knocking around west-

One of the charming displays of valuable paintings of thoroughbreds in the Hall of Fame.

ern fairs he found a home as trainer for Herbert M. Woolf, owner of Woolford Farm. In 1938, he won the Kentucky Derby with Lawrin. In 1939, he became the trainer for Warren Wright of Calumet Farm. During the next years, the Calumet stable led the nation in earnings eleven times and in 1947 won $1,402,436. He saddled six Kentucky Derby winners, five of whom were ridden by Eddie Arcaro. He trained Triple Crown Winner, Whirlaway, in 1941, and assisted his son in training Citation in 1948. The magic names of Pensive, Twilight Tear, Armed, Coaltown, Fervent, Faultless, Ponder Pot O' Luck, Bewitch and Wistful along with Whirlaway and Citation were trained by Ben Jones.

H.A. "JIMMY" JONES was the son of Ben Jones. He trained eight of the top champions of the Calumet stable dynasty. He saddled three Kentucky Derby Winners: Citation, 1948, Iron Liege, 1957, and Tim Tam, 1958. He trained the winners of 30 races of $100,000 or more. Some of the top horses that he trained were A Glitter, Armed, Barbizon, Bewitch and Two Lee.

ANDREW JACKSON JOYNER was born in North Carolina in 1860 and was discovered while working as a postal clerk by William P. Burch. He moved north and picked up experience at tracks in the Baltimore area. In 1905 he was hired by Ben Ali Haggin and Sydney Paget. He trained Cairngorm to win the Preakness in 1905 and another 184 winners earning $528.316, Whiskbroom II was one of his greatest horses, winner of the 1913 Suburban Handicap at a mile and a quarter in two minutes flat carrying 139 pounds.

J. HOWARD LEWIS was noted as an excellent judge of horses and a top trainer of and rider of steeplechasers. He was born and grew up in the Philadelphia vicinity where he attended Swarthmore College with, amongst others, Samuel D. Riddle. He trained horses for Joseph P. Widener and won the Manly Memorial eight times, The Temple Gwathmey five times and the Grand National five times.

HENRY McDANIEL was trainer for the stable of Willis Sharpe Kilmer who was intent on winning the Kentucky Derby. His Sun Briar was the winter favorite in 1918 but when he did not respond to training Kilmer suggested that McDaniel buy a gelding to train with him. He found a big raw-boned gelding named Exterminator for whom he gave $9,000 plus two fillies. After the purchase they learned that Exterminator was eligible for the Derby so they entered him, and he won by a length and went on to win a total of fifty races during an eight year career. McDaniel trained for a total of 62 years working for a number of owners. He won the Belmont stakes in 1933 with Joseph E. Wideners Hurryoff. He died January 24, 1948 in Coral Gables, Florida.

BILL MOLTER, like Max Hirsch, was born in Fredericksburg, Texas. He began as a jockey for Preston Burch but became a trainer when he outgrew the jockey weight limits. In the 1946-55 years his horses won 1392 races and earned over seven million dollars. One year he won 184 races to beat Jacobs record of 177. He came up with one of the best colts in history, Round Table. He was foaled the same day as Bold Ruler and the same year as Gallant Man. With Round Table, he won a gross championship and the season's money record with $600,258. Although he finished third in the Kentucky Derby in 1957, Round Table won eleven straight races setting track records and beating older horses. In 1958, he was Horse of the Year. When he retired at 5, Round Table had won 43 of 66 starts and earned $1,749,869 the all time leading money winner. At the time of his death from a heart attack in 1960, Molter's horses had won 2,158 races totalling $11,983,035.

BERT MULHOLLAND trained for George D. Widener for thirty-five years. He was the winner of more than 800 races earning more than $6,500,000. Some of his greatest horses were Battlefield and Jaipur along with Jamestown, High Fleet, Stefanita, Platter, Evening Out, Rare Treat, Crewman, Bold Hour and Ring Twice. He was stricken with a heart attack at the age of 83 and died in 1968.

JOHN NERUD was born February 9, 1913 on a a cattle ranch in Nebraska. He rode in rodeos and match races in his teens and became a licensed trainer at 18. He traveled the country working the tracks and was jockey agent for Ted Atkinson, prior to World War II. He trained for Herbert M. Woolf after the war and became famous with Switch On, a gelding that earned $122,000. In 1957 he trained Gallant Man for Ralph Lowe and lost the Kentucky Derby by a nose, but won the Belmont Stakes when Gallant Man beat Bold Ruler. His greatest horse was Dr. Fager named for a Boston surgeon who had saved his life after he suffered a severe head injury. Dr. Fager won 18 of 22 starts earning $1,002,642 and set the world record of 1.32-1/2 for the mile at Arlington Park under 134 pounds in 1968 when he was Horse of the Year, grass champion, and champion sprinter.

JOHN W. ROGERS made his reputation by training Artful to a victory over Sysonby in the Futurity at Sheepshead Bay in 1904. Sysonby had won his first four races and was an odds-on favorite to win easily, but lost to Artful by five lengths and then never lost another race. Rogers won the Belmont with Tanya for H.P. Whitney in 1905 and repeated in 1906 for the same owner with Burgomaster.

JAMES ROWE SR. born in 1857 in Fredericksburg, Virginia began riding when he was ten years old and was national riding champion at the age of fif-

John Nerud

teen. He rode Joe Daniels and Springbok to consecutive victories in the Belmont Stakes. As a trainer he won the Belmont with George Kinney and Panique for the Dwyer Brothers. He had six Belmont winners for James R. Keene: Commando, Delhi, Peter Pan, Colin, Sweep, and Prince Eugene. He won the Kentucky Derby with Hindoo and the Preakness with Broomspun. He had a wide and varied career and died at the age of 72 in 1929. He said that as an epitaph he wanted only three words, "He trained Colin." That great horse won fifteen races out of fifteen starts.

D. MICHAEL SMITHWICK along with his brother Alfred was part of one of the greatest steeplechase teams ever produced in America. Paddy rode the horses trained by Mikey. The greatest horse and money winner, trained by Smithwick, was Mrs. Ogden Phipps's Neji, who set an all-time steeplechasing earnings record of $270,000. In thirteen out of fourteen years Mikey was the nation's leading steeplechase trainer from 1957 through 1970.

ALFRED PATRICK "PADDY" SMITHWICK was the steeplechase rider who successfully rode the horses trained by his brother, Mikey. He rode two national champions Neji 1955, 1957 and 1958 and Bon Nouvel, 1958. As a rider he was noted for his balance on a jumper and his ability to ride a bad performer. He died in 1973 after a long bout with cancer.

Alfred P. Smithwick

HERBERT J. THOMPSON trained horses for Col. E.R. Bradley and within a span of 20 years trained four Kentucky Derby winners, Behave Yourself—1921, Bubbling Over—1926, Burgoo King—1932, and Broker's Tip—1933, the only maiden ever to win the Derby.

MARION H. VAN BERG from Columbus, Nebraska started at county-fair tracks and then at Detroit, Chicago and Omaha. He led all owners in his number of victories in 1952, 1955, 1956 and from 1960 through 1970. He won 4,697 races and earned $13,936,965.

R.W. WALDEN was a well known trainer in the nineteenth century. He saddled seven Preakness winners, a record that still stands. Beginning with Duke of Magenta in 1878, Walden won five successive Preaknesses for George Lorillard. He also won the Belmont four times.

CHARLIE WHITTINGHAM from San Diego, California has been a trainer and owner as well as stablehand and aspiring jockey since 1930. He succeeded in training winners of big races and thus earned the reputation of sending horses to the post that were always dangerous. He beat Swaps with Porterhouse, Nashua with Mr. Gus, Bold Ruler with Nashville and Ridan with Black Sheep. Horses that he trained earned over a million dollars five years in a row from 1970 through 1974.

William C. Winfrey

WILLIAM C. WINFREY has been a trainer since 1932. In 1949, he went to work for Alfred G. Vanderbilt and stayed there until 1958. From 1963 until 1965 he was with the Phipps stable. In 1964 he was the leading money-winning trainer with such champions as Queen Empress and Bold Lad and won more than one million dollars.

THE HALL OF FAME OF THOROUGHBREDS

AMERICAN ECLIPSE

Year	Age	Starts	1st	2nd	3rd	Earnings
1816	2	0	0	0	0	......
1817	3	0	0	0	0	......
1818	4	1	1	0	0	$ 300
1819	5	2	2	0	0	1,000
1820	6	0	0	0	0	......
1821	7	1	1	0	0	500
1822	8	3	3	0	0	3,200
1823	9	1	1	0	0	20,000
Totals		8	8	0	0	$ 25,000

ARMED

Year	Age	Starts	1st	2nd	3rd	Earnings
1943	2	0	0	0	0	......
1944	3	7	3	1	0	$ 4,850
1945	4(SW)	15	10	4	0	91,600
1946	5(SW)	18	11	4	2	288,725
1947	6(SW)	17	11	4	1	376,325
1948	7	6	1	1	2	12,200
1949	8	12	3	3	5	36,250
1950	9	6	2	3	0	7,525
Totals		81	41	20	10	$817,475

ARTFUL

Year	Age	Starts	1st	2nd	3rd	Earnings
1904	2(SW)	5	3	2	0	$ 57,805
1905	3(SW)	3	3	0	0	23,320
Totals		8	6	2	0	$ 81,125

ASSAULT

Year	Age	Starts	1st	2nd	3rd	Earnings
1945	2(SW)	9	2	2	1	$ 17,250
1946	3(SW)	15	8	2	3	424,195
1947	4(SW)	7	5	1	1	181,925
1948	5	2	1	0	0	3,250
1949	6(SW)	6	1	1	1	45,900
1950	7	3	1	0	1	2,950
Totals		42	18	6	7	$675,470

BATTLESHIP

Year	Age	Starts	1st	2nd	3rd	Earnings
(Steeplechasing in U. S.)						
1932	5	0	0	0	0	......
1933	6(SW)	4	3	0	0	$ 2,150
1934	7(SW)	6	4	1	0	8,600
		10	7	1	0	$ 10,750
(Steeplechasing in England)						
1935	8	0	0	0	0	......
1936	9	5	1	1	0	$ 808
1937	10	13	5	2	0	4,553
1938	11(SW)	5	1	0	1	37,150
		23	7	3	1	$ 42,511
Totals		55	24	6	4	$ 71,641

BELDAME

Year	Age	Starts	1st	2nd	3rd	Earnings
1903	2(SW)	7	3	1	1	$ 21,185
1904	3(SW)	14	12	1	1	54,100
1905	4(SW)	10	2	4	2	26,850
Totals		31	17	6	4	$102,135

BEN BRUSH

Year	Age	Starts	1st	2nd	3rd	Earnings
1895	2(SW)	16	13	1	1	$ 21,398
1896	3(SW)	8	4	1	1	26,755
1897	4(SW)	16	7	3	3	17,055
Totals		40	24	5	5	$ 65,208

BLUE LARKSPUR

Year	Age	Starts	1st	2nd	3rd	Earnings
1928	2(SW)	7	4	1	1	$ 66,970
1929	3(SW)	6	4	1	0	153,450
1930	4(SW)	3	2	1	0	51,650
Totals		16	10	3	1	$272,070

BOLD RULER

Year	Age	Starts	1st	2nd	3rd	Earnings
1956	2(SW)	10	7	1	0	$139,050
1957	3(SW)	16	11	2	2	415,160
1958	4(SW)	7	5	1	0	209,994
Totals		33	23	4	2	$764,204

BOSTON

Year	Age	Starts	1st	2nd	3rd	Earnings
1836	3	3	2	0	0	$ 700
1837	4	4	4	0	0	2,000
1838	5	11	11	0	0	8,900
1839	6	9	8	1	0	19,300
1840	7	7	7	0	0	14,700
1841	8	5	4	0	0	2,900
1842	9	5	3	1	1	2,400
1843	10	1	1	0	0	800
Totals		45	40	2	1	$ 51,700

BROOMSTICK

Year	Age	Starts	1st	2nd	3rd	Earnings
1903	2(SW)	9	3	4	0	$ 25,400
1904	3(SW)	15	6	4	3	37,970
1905	4	15	5	3	2	11,360
Totals		39	14	11	5	$ 74,730

BUCKPASSER

Year	Age	Starts	1st	2nd	3rd	Earnings
1965	2(SW)	11	9	1	0	$568,096
1966	3(SW)	14	13	1	0	669,078
1967	4(SW)	6	3	2	1	224,840
Totals		31	25	4	1	$1,462,014

BUSHER

Year	Age	Starts	1st	2nd	3rd	Earnings
1944	2(SW)	7	5	1	0	$ 60,300
1945	3(SW)	13	10	2	1	273,735
1946	4	0	0	0	0	......
1947	5	1	0	0	0	......
Totals		21	15	3	1	$334,035

BUSHRANGER

Year	Age	Starts	1st	2nd	3rd	Earnings
1932	2	5	0	1	1	$ 250
1933	3	0	0	0	0	......
1934	4	7	4	1	0	3,050
1935	5(SW)	4	3	1	0	5,730
1936	6(SW)	5	4	0	0	11,605
Totals		21	11	3	1	$ 20,635

CICADA

Year	Age	Starts	1st	2nd	3rd	Earnings
1961	2(SW)	16	11	2	3	$384,676
1962	3(SW)	17	8	4	2	298,167
1963	4(SW)	8	4	2	1	100,481
1964	5	1	0	0	0	350
Totals		42	23	8	6	$783,674

CITATION

Year	Age	Starts	1st	2nd	3rd	Earnings
1947	2(SW)	9	8	1	0	$ 155,680
1948	3(SW)	20	19	1	0	709,470
1949	4	0	0	0	0	......
1950	5(SW)	9	2	7	0	73,480
1951	6(SW)	7	3	1	2	147,130
Totals		45	32	10	2	$1,085,760

COLIN

Year	Age	Starts	1st	2nd	3rd	Earnings
1907	2(SW)	12	12	0	0	$129,205
1908	3(SW)	3	3	0	0	48,905
Total		15	15	0	0	$178,110

COMMANDO

Year	Age	Starts	1st	2nd	3rd	Earnings
1900	2(SW)	6	5	1	0	$ 41,084
1901	3(SW)	3	2	1	0	17,112
Totals		9	7	2	0	$ 58,196

COUNT FLEET

Year	Age	Starts	1st	2nd	3rd	Earnings
1942	2(SW)	15	10	4	1	$ 76,245
1943	3(SW)	6	6	0	0	174,055
Totals		21	16	4	1	$250,300

DAMASCUS

Year	Age	Starts	1st	2nd	3rd	Earnings
1966	2(SW)	4	3	1	0	$ 25,865
1967	3(SW)	16	12	3	1	817,941
1968	4(SW)	12	6	3	2	332,975
	Totals	32	21	7	3	$1,176,781

DARK MIRAGE

Year	Age	Starts	1st	2nd	3rd	Earnings
1967	2	15	2	3	2	$ 19,906
1968	3(SW)	10	9	0	0	322,433
1969	4(SW)	2	1	0	0	20,450
	Totals	27	12	3	2	$362,789

DISCOVERY

Year	Age	Starts	1st	2nd	3rd	Earnings
1933	2	14	2	3	5	$ 8,397
1934	3(SW)	16	8	3	3	49,555
1935	4(SW)	19	11	2	2	102,545
1936	5(SW)	14	6	2	0	34,790
	Total	63	27	10	10	$195,287

DOMINO

Year	Age	Starts	1st	2nd	3rd	Earnings
1893	2(SW)	9	9	0	0	$170,790
1894	3(SW)	8	6	0	1	19,150
1895	4(SW)	8	4	2	0	3,610
	Totals	25	19	2	1	$193,550

DR. FAGER

Year	Age	Starts	1st	2nd	3rd	Earnings
1966	2(SW)	5	4	1	0	$112,338
1967	3(SW)	9	7	0	1	484,194
1968	4(SW)	8	7	1	0	406,110
	Totals	22	18	2	1	$1,002,642

ELKRIDGE

Year	Age	Starts	1st	2nd	3rd	Earnings
1940	2	0	0	0	0	......
1941	3	1	1	0	0	$ 1,000
1942	4(SW)	20	7	5	1	28,130
1943	5(SW)	18	2	2	2	8,455
1944	6(SW)	8	4	0	1	17,235
1945	7(SW)	15	3	2	3	27,575
1946	8(SW)	9	3	2	1	35,285
1947	9(SW)	9	2	1	0	19,275
1948	10(SW)	15	3	2	3	31,225
1949	11(SW)	11	3	1	0	26,950
1950	12(SW)	7	3	2	1	29,925
1951	13	10	0	1	3	5,625
	Totals	123	31	18	15	$230,680

EQUIPOISE

Year	Age	Starts	1st	2nd	3rd	Earnings
1930	2(SW)	16	8	5	1	$156,835
1931	3	3	1	0	0	3,000
1932	4(SW)	14	10	2	1	107,375
1933	5(SW)	9	7	1	1	55,760
1934	6(SW)	6	3	1	1	15,490
1935	7	3	0	1	0 ·	150
	Totals	51	29	10	4	$338,610

EXTERMINATOR

Year	Age	Starts	1st	2nd	3rd	Earnings
1917	2	4	2	0	0	$ 1,350
1918	3(SW)	15	7	4	3	36,147
1919	4(SW)	21	9	6	3	26,402
1920	5(SW)	17	10	3	2	52,805
1921	6(SW)	16	8	2	5	56,827
1922	7(SW)	17	10	1	1	71,075
1923	8(SW)	3	1	1	2	4,250
1924	9	7	3	0	2	4,140
	Totals	100	50	17	17	$252,996

FAIR PLAY

Year	Age	Starts	1st	2nd	3rd	Earnings
1907	2(SW)	10	3	3	2	$ 16,735
1908	3(SW)	16	7	8	1	70,215
1909	4(Eng)	6	0	0	0	......
	Totals	32	10	11	3	$ 86,950

GALLANT FOX

Year	Age	Starts	1st	2nd	3rd	Earnings
1929	2(SW)	7	2	2	2	$ 19,890
1930	3(SW)	10	9	1	0	308,275
	Totals	17	11	3	2	$328,165

GALLORETTE

Year	Age	Starts	1st	2nd	3rd	Earnings
1944	2	8	3	3	2	$ 7,950
1945	3(SW)	13	5	2	1	94,300
1946	4(SW)	18	6	5	2	159,160
1947	5(SW)	18	3	6	5	90,275
1948	6(SW)	15	4	4	3	93,850
	Totals	72	21	20	13	$445,535

GOOD AND PLENTY

Year	Age	Starts	1st	2nd	3rd	Earnings
1902	2	0	0	0	0	......
1903	3	0	0	0	0	......
1904	4(SW)	10	8	1	1	$ 17,140
1905	5(SW)	2	2	0	0	11,570
1906	6(SW)	4	3	0	0	14,455
1907	7	5	1	3	0	2,650
	Totals	21	14	4	1	$ 45,815

GREY LAG

Year	Age	Starts	1st	2nd	3rd	Earnings
1920	2(SW)	13	4	5	2	$ 17,202
1921	3(SW)	13	9	2	1	62,596
1922	4(SW)	6	5	1	0	26,937
1923	5(SW)	5	4	1	0	26,990
1924	6	0	0	0	0	......
1925	7	0	0	0	0	......
1926	8	0	0	0	0	......
1927	9	2	2	0	0	1,400
1928	10	4	1	0	2	1,550
1929	11	0	0	0	0	......
1930	12	0	0	0	0	......
1931	13	4	0	0	1	40
	Totals	47	25	9	6	$136,715

HANOVER

Year	Age	Starts	1st	2nd	3rd	Earnings
1886	2(SW)	3	3	0	0	$ 14,335
1887	3(SW)	27	20	5	1	87,632
1888	4	3	0	3	0	1,450
1889	5(SW)	17	9	6	1	15,470
	Totals	50	32	14	2	$118,887

HINDOO

Year	Age	Starts	1st	2nd	3rd	Earnings
1880	2(SW)	9	7	1	1	$ 9,800
1881	3(SW)	20	18	1	1	49,100
1882	4(SW)	6	5	1	0	12,975
	Totals	35	30	3	2	$ 71,875

IMP

Year	Age	Starts	1st	2nd	3rd	Earnings
1896	2	11	3	4	2	$ 1,310
1897	3	50	14	10	9	4,934
1898	4(SW)	35	21	6	3	12,340
1899	5(SW)	31	13	3	5	30,735
1900	6(SW)	31	8	10	9	18,185
1901	7	13	3	2	1	2,565
	Totals	171	62	35	29	$ 70,069

JAY TRUMP

Year	Age		Starts	1st	2nd	3rd	Earnings
1959	2		4	0	0	0	......
1960	3		4	0	1	0	$ 220
1961	4		0	0	0	0	......
1962	5		2	2	0	0	650
1963	6		2	1	1	0	trophy
1964	7		3	3	0	0	trophy
1964	(Eng)	7	3	2	0	0	1,840
1965	(Eng,Fr.)	8	5	2	0	1	61,715
1966	9		3	2	1	0	trophy
	Totals	15	26	12	3	1	$64,425

JOLLY ROGER

Year	Age	Starts	1st	2nd	3rd	Earnings
1924	2	7	1	0	0	$ 850
1925	3(SW)	4	2	1	0	3,880
1926	4(SW)	11	4	1	3	13,110
1927	5(SW)	8	6	2	0	63,075
1928	6(SW)	7	3	2	2	45,950
1929	7	4	0	1	3	4,050
1930	8(SW)	8	2	2	1	12,325
Totals		49	18	9	9	$143,240

KELSO

Year	Age	Starts	1st	2nd	3rd	Earnings
1959	2	3	1	2	0	$ 3,380
1960	3(SW)	9	8	0	0	293,310
1961	4(SW)	9	7	1	0	425,565
1962	5(SW)	12	6	4	0	289,685
1963	6(SW)	12	9	2	0	569,762
1964	7(SW)	11	5	3	0	311,660
1965	8(SW)	6	3	0	2	84,034
1966	9	1	0	0	0	500
Totals		63	39	12	2	$1,977,896

KINGSTON

Year	Age	Starts	1st	2nd	3rd	Earnings
1886	2(SW)	6	2	4	0	$ 11,350
1887	3(SW)	18	13	2	2	17,850
1888	4(SW)	14	10	3	1	17,045
1889	5(SW)	15	14	1	0	22,520
1890	6(SW)	10	9	1	0	16,890
1891	7(SW)	21	15	5	1	26,815
1892	8(SW)	20	13	6	1	17,390
1893	9	25	9	8	5	7,660
1894	10	9	4	3	2	2,675
Totals		138	89	33	12	$140,195

LEXINGTON

Year	Age	Starts	1st	2nd	3rd	Earnings
1852	2	0	0	0	0	......
1853	3	5	4	1	0	$ 30,600
1854	4	2	2	0	0	26,000
Totals		7	6	1	0	$ 56,600

LONGFELLOW

Year	Age	Starts	1st	2nd	3rd	Earnings
1869	2	0	0	0	0	......
1870	3(SW)	5	4	0	0	$ 3,100
1871	4(SW)	6	5	1	0	4,450
1872	5(SW)	5	4	1	0	3,650
Totals		16	13	2	0	$ 11,200

LUKE BLACKBURN

Year	Age	Starts	1st	2nd	3rd	Earnings
1879	2(SW)	13	2	6	1	$ 1,985
1880	3(SW)	24	22	0	1	46,975
1881	4	2	1	0	0	500
Totals		39	25	6	2	$ 49,460

MAN O' WAR

Year	Age	Starts	1st	2nd	3rd	Earnings
1919	2(SW)	10	9	1	0	$ 83,325
1920	3(SW)	11	11	0	0	166,140
Totals		21	20	1	0	$249,465

MISS WOODFORD

Year	Age	Starts	1st	2nd	3rd	Earnings
1882	2(SW)	8	5	1	2	$ 6,600
1883	3(SW)	12	10	1	0	51,230
1884	4(SW)	9	9	0	0	21,070
1885	5(SW)	12	7	4	0	19,370
1886	6(SW)	7	6	1	0	20,000
Totals		48	37	7	2	$118,270

NASHUA

Year	Age	Starts	1st	2nd	3rd	Earnings
1954	2(SW)	8	6	2	0	$192,865
1955	3(SW)	12	10	1	1	752,550
1956	4(SW)	10	6	1	0	343,150
Totals		30	22	4	1	$1,288,565

NATIVE DANCER

Year	Age	Starts	1st	2nd	3rd	Earnings
1952	2(SW)	9	9	0	0	$230,495
1953	3(SW)	10	9	1	0	513,425
1954	4(SW)	3	3	0	0	41,320
Totals		22	21	1	0	$785,240

NEJI

Year	Age	Starts	1st	2nd	3rd	Earnings
1952	2	0	0	0	0	......
1953	3	2	0	0	0	$ 200
1954	4(SW)	18	5	5	3	41,005
1955	5(SW)	8	5	1	2	92,630
1956	6(SW)	6	2	3	1	26,820
1957	7(SW)	4	3	0	0	75,975
1958	8(SW)	5	2	1	2	34,246
1959	(Eng) 9	3	0	0	1	141
1960	10	3	0	1	0	3,010
Totals		49	17	11	9	$274,047

OLD ROSEBUD

Year	Age	Starts	1st	2nd	3rd	Earnings
1913	2(SW)	14	12	2	0	$ 19,057
1914	3(SW)	3	2	0	0	9,575
1915	4	..	..	..	..	......
1916	5					
1917	6(SW)	21	15	1	3	31,720
1918	7	..	..	..	..	......
1919	8	30	9	7	5	12,182
1920	9	8	1	2	0	1,295
1921	10	2	1	0	0	700
1922	11	2	0	1	0	200
Totals		80	40	13	8	$ 74,729

OMAHA

Year	Age	Starts	1st	2nd	3rd	Earnings
1934	2	9	1	4	0	$ 3,850
1935	3(SW)	9	6	1	2	142,255
1936	(Eng) 4(SW)	4	2	2	0	8,650
Totals		22	9	7	2	$154,755

PAN ZARETA

Year	Age	Starts	1st	2nd	3rd	Earnings
1912	2(SW)	19	13	3	2	$ 3,512
1913	3(SW)	33	15	8	3	8,895
1914	4	28	13	9	2	7,085
1915	5(SW)	26	15	6	4	7,540
1916	6	11	7	1	3	3,085
1917	7	34	13	4	7	8,965
Totals		151	76	31	21	$39,082

PETER PAN

Year	Age	Starts	1st	2nd	3rd	Earnings
1906	2(SW)	8	4	1	1	$ 29,660
1907	3(SW)	9	6	2	0	85,790
Totals		17	10	3	1	$115,450

REGRET

Year	Age	Starts	1st	2nd	3rd	Earnings
1914	2(SW)	3	3	0	0	$ 17,390
1915	3(SW)	2	2	0	0	12,500
1916	4	2	1	0	0	560
1917	5(SW)	4	3	1	0	4,643
Totals		11	9	1	0	$ 35,093

ROSEBEN

Year	Age	Starts	1st	2nd	3rd	Earnings
1903	2	1	0	0	0	......
1904	3	9	3	2	1	$ 2,405
1905	4(SW)	29	19	5	2	22,085
1906	5(SW)	22	11	5	3	27,870
1907	6(SW)	14	7	4	2	13,995
1908	7	26	9	5	4	6,340
1909	8	10	3	4	0	2,415
Totals		111	52	25	12	$ 75,110

ROUND TABLE

Year	Age	Starts	1st	2nd	3rd	Earnings
1956	2(SW)	10	5	1	0	$ 73,326
1957	3(SW)	22	15	1	3	600,383
1958	4(SW)	20	14	4	0	662,780
1959	5(SW)	14	9	2	2	413,380
Totals		66	43	8	5	$1,749,869

SALVATOR

Year	Age	Starts	1st	2nd	3rd	Earnings
1888	2(SW)	6	4	1	0	$ 17,590
1889	3(SW)	8	7	0	1	70,450
1890	4(SW)	5	5	0	0	25,200
Totals		19	16	1	1	$113,240

The colorful display of jockey's silks in the Hall of Fame.

SARAZEN

Year	Age	Starts	1st	2nd	3rd	Earnings
1923	2(SW)	10	10	0	0	$ 37,880
1924	3(SW)	12	8	1	1	95,640
1925	4(SW)	10	5	0	1	48,160
1926	5(SW)	14	4	1	1	42,970
1927	6	4	0	0	1	100
1928	7	5	0	0	2	250
	Totals	55	27	2	6	$225,000

SEABISCUIT

Year	Age	Starts	1st	2nd	3rd	Earnings
1935	2(SW)	35	5	7	5	$ 12,510
1936	3(SW)	23	9	1	5	28,995
1937	4(SW)	15	11	2	1	168,580
1938	5(SW)	11	6	4	1	130,395
1939	6	1	0	1	0	400
1940	7(SW)	4	2	0	1	96,850
	Totals	89	33	15	13	$437,730

SECRETARIAT

Year	Age	Starts	1st	2nd	3rd	Earnings
1972	2(SW)	9	7	1	0	$ 456,404
1973	3(SW)	12	9	2	1	860,404
	Totals	21	16	3	1	$1,316,808

SIR ARCHY

Year	Age	Starts	1st	2nd	3rd	Earnings
1807	2	0	0	0	0	......
1808	3	2	0	0	0	......
1809	4	5	4	1	0	......
	Totals	7	4	1	0	......

SIR BARTON

Year	Age	Starts	1st	2nd	3rd	Earnings
1918	2	6	0	1	0	$ 4,113
1919	3(SW)	13	8	3	2	88,250
1920	4(SW)	12	5	2	3	24,494
	Totals	31	13	6	5	$116,857

SWAPS

Year	Age	Starts	1st	2nd	3rd	Earnings
1954	2(SW)	6	3	0	2	$ 20,950
1955	3(SW)	9	8	1	0	418,550
1956	4(SW)	10	8	1	0	409,400
	Totals	25	19	2	2	$848,900

SYSONBY

Year	Age	Starts	1st	2nd	3rd	Earnings
1904	2(SW)	6	5	0	1	$ 40,058
1905	3(SW)	9	9	0	0	144,380
	Totals	15	14	0	1	$184,438

TOM FOOL

Year	Age	Starts	1st	2nd	3rd	Earnings
1951	2(SW)	7	5	2	0	$155,960
1952	3(SW)	13	6	5	1	157,850
1953	4(SW)	10	10	0	0	256,355
	Totals	30	21	7	1	$570,165

TOP FLIGHT

Year	Age	Starts	1st	2nd	3rd	Earnings
1931	2(SW)	7	7	0	0	$219,000
1932	3(SW)	9	5	0	0	56,900
	Totals	16	12	0	0	$275,900

TWENTY GRAND

Year	Age	Starts	1st	2nd	3rd	Earnings
1930	2(SW)	8	4	2	1	$ 41,380
1931	3(SW)	10	8	1	1	218,545
1932	4	2	1	1	0	915
1933	5	0	0	0	0	......
1934	6	0	0	0	0	......
1935	7	3	1	0	1	950
1935	7(Eng)	2	0	0	0	......
	Totals	25	14	4	3	$261,790

TWILIGHT TEAR

Year	Age	Starts	1st	2nd	3rd	Earnings
1943	2(SW)	6	4	1	1	$ 34,610
1944	3(SW)	17	14	1	1	167,555
1945	4	1	0	0	0	......
	Totals	24	18	2	2	$202,165

WAR ADMIRAL

Year	Age	Starts	1st	2nd	3rd	Earnings
1936	2(SW)	6	3	2	1	$ 14,800
1937	3(SW)	8	8	0	0	166,500
1938	4(SW)	11	9	1	0	90,840
1939	5	1	1	0	0	1,100
	Totals	26	21	3	1	$273,240

WHIRLAWAY

Year	Age	Starts	1st	2nd	3rd	Earnings
1940	2(SW)	16	7	2	4	$ 77,275
1941	3(SW)	20	13	5	2	272,386
1942	4(SW)	22	12	8	2	211,250
1943	5	2	0	0	1	250
	Totals	60	32	15	9	$561,161

JOCKEYS IN THE NATIONAL MUSEUM OF RACING HALL OF FAME

Frank David Adams rode his first race at the age of 14 at Agua Caliente. He was known as Dooley and was a top steeplechase jockey, beginning in 1946 with 28 winners. In 1947 he rode 23 winners, and 20 winners in 1948. From 1949 through 1955 he was the leading steeplechase jockey. He won the Saratoga Steeplechase Handicap and the Beverwyck Steeplechase Handicap four times.

Johnny Adams belongs to the exclusive 3,000 winners club of the jockey profession. In fact he won 3,270 races. His total winnings in purses came to $9,743,109. He rode for the Hasty House Farm, winning the Preakness in 1954 on Hasty Road. He rode the same horse to victory in the Derby trial, but finished second to Determine in the Derby.

Eddie Arcaro was one of the glamour jockeys of all time. He won the Kentucky Derby five times and the Preakness and Belmont Stakes six times each. At the time of his retirement his mounts had won $30,039,543, first among jockey winnings. He won 4,779 races including 549 stakes races. He won the Kentucky Derby on Lawrin, 1938, Whirlaway, 1941, Hoop, Jr., 1945, Citation, 1948 and Hill Gail, 1952. He says that Citation was the best horse he ever rode.

Ted Atkinson, a Toronto, Canada native achieved much of his fame riding for the Greentree Stable. He rode the great Tom Fool to a perfect record of 10 victories in 10 starts in 1953 as a four year old. He won the Brooklyn, Metropolitan, and Suburban Handicaps during that great season. He was leading rider in 1944 and 1946. He won 3,795 races in his career and his mounts earned $17,449,360.

Carroll K. Bassett was a polo player, fox hunter and steeplechase rider. He rode Battleship, son of Man O' War, in all of his American races. In 1938 Battleship became the first American-bred and owned horse to win The Grand National at Aintree. Bassett was also a distinguished sculptor whose statue of Man O' War stands over the grave of that great horse.

George H. (Pete) Bostwick was noted as a steeplechase and flat racer as well as a fox hunter, polo player and trainer. He won the Corinthian twice, the Temple Gwathmey, the Harbor Hill, and the Meadow Brook three years in a row. He owned his own stable and trained his horses, including Cottesmore, who won the Meadow Brook, North American, Beverwyck, Grand National and Temple Gwathmey.

Sam Boulmetis rode for 19 years during which time he won 2,783 races and total purses of $15,425,935. He rode for Sam Riddle for many years and was also associated with the Greentree Stable. He rode Tosmah, one of the great mares, to many victories. He also rode such stakes winners as Vertex, Errard King and Helioscope.

Steve Brooks rode for 33 years, rolling up the impressive total of 4,447 wins and earning for the owners $18,214,947. He rode some of the great horses of the era including Round Table, Citation, Ponder, Princequillo, Wistful, Stymie and Armed. He rode Citation in his last race before retirement in the Hollywood Gold Cup in 1951, and won with the $100.000 purse making the great Triple Crown winner the first of thoroughbred racing's million dollar winners.

Frank Coltiletti, from the Bronx of New York City, rode after World War I in the decade of the '20s and the early '30s. He won many stake races, including the Travers, Preakness, Chesapeake, Dixie Handicap, Hopeful, Futurity. He rode for many of the top stables and was noted for getting the most out of the horse.

Eddie Arcaro

Sam Boulmetis

Robert H. Crawford was a steeplechase rider in a 10 year career that ended in 1928. He rode the great Jolly Roger who won $143,240 in The Brook Steeplechase, and he rode The Brook (for whom the race was named) to victories in 1918 in the Beverwyck, Glendale and Shillelah. He won the Grand National twice.

Buddy Ensor rode from 1915 into the 1940's, but personal problems prevented him from riding from 1922 through 1931. He was noted for being able to handle bad actors. He rode for Harry Payne Whitney, Walter M. Jeffords, R.T. Wilson, Rancocas and Tom Healey. Early in his career in 1919, he rode 33 winners in 11 days.

Buddy Ensor

Laverne Fator, from Idaho, was third in the national standings in 1919, his first year of riding. In 1925 and 1926, he was leading money-winning jockey, winning 143 races of 511 mounts in 1926. He rode back to back winners in the Belmont Futurity in 1925 and 1926 on Pompey and Scapa Flow.

Mack Garner was one of the most popular jockeys in the golden era of the 1920's and into the '30's. He rode 1,346 winners, earning $2,419,647 in an age of small purses. He beat Zev, with Earl Sande up, on In Memoriam in the Latonia Derby, and rode the same horse against Zev and Sande in a match race that was given to Zev by a nose in a disputed decision. He won the Belmont twice on Blue Larkspur in 1929 and on Hurry Off in 1933. He won the Kentucky Derby in 1934 on Cavalcade. He died suddenly of a heart attack after riding four horses at River Downs on October 28, 1936.

Edward R. (Snapper) Garrison was famous for putting the expression "garrison finish" into the language. His driving finishes to a close victory were his trade mark. He started out at the age of 12 shoeing horses and then became a stable hand under "Father Bill" Daly, a tough trainer of that era. His chance to ride occurred when he was 14 and one of the regular jockeys was unavailable. For the next 15 years his was the biggest name amongst the riders. He won over $2,000,000 and nearly 700 races. He won the Belmont once, the Withers and Tremont three times and the Suburban twice.

Edward R. Garrison

Henry Griffin was taken from an orphanage on Staten Island along with his younger brother in 1890 at the age of 14 as indentured servants. James Shields, who took the boys, owned a stable, and within a few days Griffin had ridden five winners. After three years he was earning over $20,000 a year and was one of the leading jockeys. In 1895 he won the Belmont Futurity making it back to back since he won in 1894 on Butterflies. That same day in 1895 he rode five winners, tying a record. He also won the Withers, Manhattan and Suburban Stakes during his career.

Eric Guerin won nearly 2700 races and over $17,000,000 in purses. He rode Native Dancer to victory in nine starts as a two year old and was in the irons the next year when Dark Star beat him when he was up on Native Dancer. He went on to ride Native Dancer to the three year old championship despite the Derby loss. That same year he rode Porterhouse to six straight wins and the two year old championship. He won the Belmont on High Gun for back-to-back victories in that big race.

Eric Guerin   *William Hartack*

William John Hartack was the first rider to win $3,000,000 in one year, 1957. He has ridden five Kentucky Derby winners, tying Eddie Arcaro. In the decade of the 1950's he rode 43 stake victories one year. He is the fifth jockey in history to win more than 4000 races and his $25,878,063 in purses is fourth in the money winning list.

Albert Johnson won a number of big races including two each Kentucky Derbies, Belmont Stakes, and the Black Eyed Susan at Pimlico. In 1922 he was the leading jockey, earning $345,054. He won the 1926 Kentucky Derby on Bubbling Over, having won the 1922 Derby on Morvich. He won the Belmont in 1925 on American Flag and repeated in 1926 on Crusader, both by Man O' War.

The upset king of the jockeys was **Willie Knapp** who rode to a number of stakes victories on horses that were not given a chance to win. In 1917 he rode a 9 year old named Borrow to win the Brooklyn Handicap, beating Regret, the only filly to win the Kentucky Derby, Old Rosebud, the 1914 Kentucky Derby winner, and Omar Khayyam, the 1917 Derby winner. In 1918 he rode Exterminator at 30−1 odds to win the Kentucky Derby by a length. In the 1919 Sanford Stakes he rode Upset at Saratoga to victory over Man O War.

Clarence Kummer rode Man O War in nine of his victories but, due to a fractured collar bone, was not riding the day of the defeat by Upset. He rode Vito to victory in the Belmont Stakes and Coventry to win the Preakness, the only first place finish by the horse. His career was cut short by his premature death in 1930

Known as "The Flying Dutchman," **Charlie Kurtsinger** rode many of the leading horses to victory in the '20's and '30's. He was the leading money winning jockey in 1931 and 1937 and was the fourth rider in history to win the Triple Crown. He rode War Admiral to his Triple Crown victories in 1937 and won the Kentucky Derby in 1931 on Twenty Grand. He also rode Captain Hal, Menow, Dark Secret, and won the Preakness in 1933 on Head Play. He died in Louisville, the scene of many of his victories, from complications of pneumonia at the age of 39.

Three of the best known names in the thoroughbred world are Triple Crown, Sir Barton and Man O War. Jockey **John Loftus** was closely associated with all three. In 1919 Loftus rode Sir Barton to a five-length victory on a heavy track in the Kentucky Derby. Sir Barton with Loftus up went on to become the first Triple Crown winner. Loftus rode Man O War ten times, winning in all but the one defeat by Upset. He won nine stakes victories on Man O War, including Keene Memorial, Youthful, Hudson, Tremont, United States Hotel, Grand Union, Hopeful and Futurity. He also rode the great horse in his match race win over Sir Barton.

During a career of more than forty years, **Johnny Longden** rode 32,406 mounts resulting in total purse earnings of $24,665,800 while compiling a winning record of 19 percent. He rode 6,032 winners to become the premier winning jockey until supplanted by Bill Shoemaker. He was winner of the Triple Crown on Count Fleet in 1943. He has also been a successful trainer, saddling Majestic Prince to victories in the Kentucky Derby and the Preakness and a second in the Belmont in 1961.

Danny Maher was an American jockey who had most of his successes in England around the turn of the century. He rode three Epsom Derby winners—Cicero, Rock Sand and Spearmint. After a brief career on the New York tracks he went to England in 1900 and ultimately became a naturalized English citizen and married an English actress. In England he rode 1421 winners out of 5,624 mounts before his death at the age of 35 of consumption (tuberculosis).

In 1932 the leading American jockey was **Linus McAtee**. He started riding in 1914 and in the ensuing years he had ridden to the top of his profession. When his contract with Harry Payne Whitney was expired in 1932 McAtee left the racetrack. He had managed his money well enough to retire to the golf links and take it easy. He rode Whiskery to victory in the 1927 Kentucky Derby and Clyde Van Dusen, son of Man O War, to victory in 1929. He also rode many other great stakes winners, including Twenty Grand, Exterminator, Jamestown, and the fillies, Bateau and Mother Goose.

Conn McCreary was the hero of the impossible dream. His greatest successes were in the '40's during which time he rode many winners at the New York tracks. His career had been in a decline in 1951 when miraculously he suddenly had his greatest victory. He was considered washed up as a top jockey but the owner overruled his trainer to hire McCreary to ride Count Turf in

John Loftus

John Longden

Conn McCreary   *James McLaughlin*   *Isaac Murphy*

the Kentucky Derby. The horse was lightly regarded and was lumped together with other horses in the mutuel field where the winner paid $31.20. Alone he most likely would have been 100–1. There were twenty horses in the race. Under these unusual circumstances Count Turf won by four lengths. McCreary also won the Derby in 1944 on Pensive and he won the Preakness on Pensive and Blue Man in 1952.

One of the top steeplechase riders in the '20's and '30's was **Rigan McKinney**. He rode Green Cheese, Rioter, Chenango, Beacon Hill, Annibal, Ammagansett, and Ossabaw. He led in both races won and purses earned in 1933, '36 and '38. In 1931 he won the Grand National on Green Cheese in record time. He was also noted in the show ring, as a polo player, and as a breeder and trainer.

During the 1880's **Jimmy McLaughlin** had a sensational start in a riding career in which he won 67 stakes races. He won the Belmont Stakes six times and won the Kentucky Derby on Hindoo in 1881 and the Preakness on Tecumseh in 1885.

In early 1900's a young man from New York's east side named Goldstein attracted the attention of Sunny Jim Fitzsimmon. The two of them went to California in 1904 where Goldstein, under the name of **Walter Miller**, served his apprenticeship. They returned to New York where Miller was very popular and won important races including the Brooklyn Handicap, Dwyer, Alabama, Preakness, Toboggan, Belmont Futurity, Saratoga Cup and the Travers.

Isaac Murphy, who rode before the twentieth century, still holds the lifetime record for winning averages for jockeys—628 victories in 1412 races, a 44 percent winning record. He was a black, the son of James Burns, a freeman. He adopted the surname of his grandfather Green Murphy. He rode his first winner in Lexington, Kentuckey in 1876. His advise to another jockey was, "Just be honest and you'll have no trouble and plenty of money." In the late 1960's his grave was moved from a negro cemetery to a site near Man O War's statue, also in the bluegrass country of Lexington.

Ralph Neves is the only jockey ever to have been pronounced dead on the public address system, be removed to the hospital to be transferred to the morgue and return to the track to ride the next day. This occurred on May 8, 1936 at Bay Meadows when a horse named Flanakins tripped, sending his jockey, Ralph Neves, crashing headlong into the rail, caromed back onto the track where he was trampled by four horses. The track doctor and two physicians from the crowd found Neves was not breathing and had no pulse. The track announcer sadly entoned "We regret to inform you, the jockey is dead. Please stand in silent prayer." Neves was taken to the hospital and placed in the cold storage room. After about ten minutes he came to and managed to get out of the room and hail a cab back to the track wearing only the white sheet they had used to cover him. He was back in the saddle the next day and went on to win the meet's riding title from such great jockeys as Johnny Longden, Jackie Westrope and Johnny Adams. In his career he won 536 races and 31 major stake races at Santa Anita and altogether he won 173 stakes and almost $14,000,000 in purses.

Joseph A. Notter led the 1908 jockeys' money list with $464,322, a total that stood as a record until 1923. He rode Regret when she became the only filly ever to win the Kentucky Derby. He rode Maskette and Thunderer to wins in the 1908 and 1915 Belmont Futurity and trained Kerry Patch to win the 1932 renewal of this race. He rode Colin, Peter Pan, Sweep and Pennant, and was in the saddle when Whisk Broom II won the Handicap Triple Crown in 1913 including the mile and a quarter Suburban Handicap run in 2:00 minutes.

A colorful Irish rider of the early twentieth century was **Winnie O'Connor** from the Red Hook section of Brooklyn. He was an accomplished boxer and bicycle rider as well as a jockey who rode in Europe as well as the United States. He was successful at flat racing and later in steeplechase riding. In 1901 he was America's leading rider with 253 winners, 221 seconds and 192 thirds out of 1047 mounts.

George M. Odom was first a successful jockey and later a noted trainer. From 1899 through 1904 he compiled an impressive record as a jockey. He is the only person to have won the Belmont as both jockey and trainer. As a trainer he saddled Tintagel to win the 1935 futurity. He trained Busher for Louis B. Mayer.

Part of the reputation enjoyed by **Frank O'Neill** as one of the top jockeys in the early years of the twentieth century was earned as the rider of Beldame, one of the most famous fillies in thoroughbred history. In 1904 he won the Alabama, Carter, Gazelle and Saratoga Cup on the great Beldame. O'Neill also won the Metropolitan on Roseben, the Brooklyn, Adirondack, Great American, Aqueduct, Astoria, Juvenile, Lawrence Realization, Matron, National Stallion, Saranac, Spinaway, Swift and Travers. He closed his career in Europe where he won many important stakes.

Gilbert Patrick or (**Gilpatrick**) as he is listed in some of the record books is considered by racing historians to be the outstanding jockey of the nineteenth century. He rode Boston to 40 victories in 45 starts. He lost a match race to the mare, Fashion, who carried 111 pounds to 126 for Boston, when races were run in heats. He rode Charmer to an unbeaten string of victories. He rode Lexington, son of Boston, in a four mile race against time in 7:19 ¾ breaking the record of 7:26. Gilpatrick was the Johnny Longden of the nineteenth century.

Sam Purdy gained immortality in one match race between the North and the South. The race was held at the Union Course in New York in May 1823 between American Eclipse of the North and a horse named Henry representing the South. The race was run in heats and Henry won the first heat. The northern backers were dissatisfied with the riding of William Crafts, their jockey. Sam Purdy (then retired from riding at the age of 38) came dressed in the colors of the North under a long coat, and he stepped forward offering his services in the next heat. He removed his coat, and to the roar of the crowd, accepted the mount, winning the next two heats and salvaging the honor of northern horsemen.

John Reiff was one of the smallest jockeys of all time, but he had some big wins. He won the Epsom Derby in England in 1907 on Orby. He led the French jockeys in 1902, the year that he won the French Derby on Retz. Although he was born in Middletown, Missouri, he and his brother Lester were mainly known on European tracks.

On the list of glamour jockeys of the roaring twenties the name of **Earle Sande** must be at the very top. True there were Garner, Workman, Fator, and

Kummer and others, but Damon Runyon immortalized Sande with his poem beginning "Say, have they turned the pages, back to the past once more." Sande was a Triple Crown winner on Gallant Fox and did leave an impressive record. He won three Kentucky Derbies, one Preakness and five Belmont Stakes. He was national riding champion in 1921, '23 and '27. He won the Kentucky Derby on Zev at 10 to 1 in 1923 and on Flying Ebony in 1925 and neither horse won another stake.

Earl Sande

"**Carrol Shilling** was the best rider I ever saw." That was the estimate of Cal Shilling by knowledgeable horsemen. "He was a master-mechanic astride a horse, with natural riding instincts that his boyhood on the Texas cattle ranches had brought out to the utmost." He was denied a license for rough riding in 1912 and spent most of his time as exercise boy, stable foreman, and trainer. He eventually soured on the world and took to drinking, and he ended up in 1950 dead under a horse van.

William L. Shoemaker is a living legend. He won his third mount March 20, 1949 at Golden Gate Fields. The next year, he tied for races won and in 1951 he was leading money winner. In 1953 he won a record 485 races and in 1956 he became the first jockey to win over $2,000,000 in purses in one year. He has passed the 7100 mark in wins. The stakes he has won and the horses he has ridden are a large part of the racing history of this generation.

William Lee Shoemaker

From rags to riches and back to rags, tells it all in describing the sensational jockey career of **Tod Sloan**. Horse racing fans of the turn of the century rated Sloan as the greatest jockey of his time. He was orphaned at five years of age in Kokomo, Indiana and ran away from Kokomo at age 17 with a carnival balloonist who soon was killed in an accident. Sloan went to Chicago to join two older brothers who were jockeys. He started to ride and was good enough to attract the attention of James R. Keene and William C. Whitney, both noted turfman. In 1897 Sloan rode 137 winners in 369 mounts for a percentage of 37.1 and then followed up in 1898 with 166 winners in 362 mounts for a remarkable winning percentage of 45.1 He is credited with creating the present riding style with short stirrup leathers crouched over the withers, first called monkey-on-a-stick. At the peak of his career Tod went to England where he became very famous even changing his name to J. Todhunter Sloan. There he became one of the world's big spenders squandering a million dollars in two years on wardrobes, secretaries, valets and high living. His riding career soon faded and he went into vaudeville and minor movies and died in California in 1933 obscure and penniless.

Tod Sloan

Jimmy Stout became famous for falling off a horse. It was not just any horse, however. He fell off Granville at the start of the 1935 Kentucky Derby while riding for Sunny Jim Fitzsimmons. To his credit Mr. Fitz never said a word about it, although he must have been keenly disappointed. His confidence in Stout apparently was unshaken because Jimmy rode Granville to a nose victory over Bold Venture in the Preakness, and to a big win in the Belmont Stakes, the first of three in his riding career. He rode Johnstown to a 10 length victory in the 1939 Derby. In 1944 Stout achieved an unique kind of racing immortality by figuring in the first triple dead heat win in a stake race aboard Bouseet in the Carter Handicap at Aqueduct. The others at the wire were Wait A Bit and Brownie. Stout won a number of important stakes including the Jockey Gold Cup with Count Arthur in 1936 and Fenelon in 1940. He won the Travers on Fenelon and the Brooklyn Handicap in 1940 on Isolater and repeated on Fenelon in 1941. He always claimed that Granville over-all was the best horse he ever rode.

Another of the colorful jockeys that typified the popular concept of these little men who handled the big horses for the big purses for that era was **Fred Taral**. He commanded top money from his patrons Walcott and Campbell and later from James R. Keene. As an inseparable companion of another bon vivant, John L. Sullivan the heavyweight champion, he needed the big earnings to keep pace with their life style. Together they were known as Big and Little Casino. Taral on the track had another nickname, "Dutch Demon." He was a driving rider who used the whip so effectively that his mounts did not want to see him. He rode the famous Domino to a number of victories, but they had to hood the great stallion to get Taral safely mounted. Taral won the handicap triple crown in 1894. He won the Preakness that same year on Assignee and 1895 he won the Preakness and Belmont on Belmar. He won most of the major stakes of the time and went to Europe where he rode successfully.

Bayard Tuckerman Jr. was known as the dean of New England racing. He was one of the leading steeplechase riders in the world and later, the first president of Suffolk Downs and a foremost breeder of thoroughbreds. He competed as an amateur against professional riders and competed in the American Grand National at Belmont. He owned a number of top horses including Steel Viking, Lavender Hill, Orco and The Crack.

One of the favorite jockeys of the gay nineties was **Nash Turner** who gained fame because of his victories on a mare named Imp, the darling of the track crowd. Every time Imp won a race band played *My Coal Black Lady*, a popular tune of that period. During her career Imp started 171 races winning 62. Turner rode her in a number of these victories as well as the first Debutante Stakes in 1895, two Great Americans, two Saratoga Specials, the Alabama, the Clark Handicap, the Flash, the Jerome, the Matron, the National Stallion, the Swift and the Withers.

One of the favorite riders for the Whitney stable in the '20's and '30's was **Raymond (Sonny) Workman.** He rode the most spectacular race of the decade on Equipoise in the 1930 Futurity. He was turned sideways at the post and Equipoise lost all four shoes in the mud, but he managed to win by a half length. He rode Top Flight the best of her sex as a 2 year old and also as a 3 year old. He also rode Questionaire, Wiskery, Victorian, Flying Heels and Menow. He won 1169 races, 870 seconds, and 785 thirds to total purses of $2,862,667.

George Woolf

George Woolf known as the "Iceman" for his coolness in the saddle, was another of the real glamour jockeys of the '30's and '40's. He won the Belmont Futurity on Occupation in 1942, on Occupy in '43 and Pavot in '44. In the same years he swept the American Derby at Chicago's Washington Park on Alsab, Askmenow and By Jimmy. He rode Seabiscuit to victory over War Admiral in the 1938 match race at Pimlico. He rode Seabiscuit to a nose win over Ligaroti in a winner take all match at Del Mar. He won all the major United States stakes races except the Kentucky Derby. On January 3, 1946 he was aboard Please Me at Santa Anita when the horse stumbled throwing Woolf into the inner rail. He struck his temple and never regained consciousness, dying the next morning. He had ridden 3,784 mounts to 721 victories earning $2,856,125 in purses. In memory turf writers annually present the George Woolf Memorial Award to a jockey who in their opinion has been a credit to his profession. The award is a replica of the Woolf statue in the paddock gardens at Santa Anita.

THE
NATIONAL JOCKEYS
HALL OF FAME

Pimlico Race Course,
Baltimore, Maryland

The National Jockeys Hall of Fame is permanently quartered at the Pimlico Race Course, Baltimore, Maryland. It was founded in 1955 at this historic track dating back to 1870, the second oldest thoroughbred track in America next to Saratoga founded in 1864.

The Hall of Fame actually is in the third floor of the clubhouse dining facilities which feature portraits of the jockeys each painted by artist Henry Cooper. It happens that all but two of the jockeys selected for this Hall of Fame are also in the National Museum of Racing Hall of Fame in Saratoga Springs, New York. The two exceptions are Jackie Westrope, and Laffit Pincay, Jr.

The National Jockeys Hall of Fame follows:

	Year of Enshrinement		Year of Enshrinement		Year of Enshrinement
Eddie Arcaro	1955	Sonny Workman	1957	Linus (Pony) McAtee	1961
Earl Sande	1955	Laverne Fator	1958	Joe Notter	1961
George Woolf	1955	Snapper Garrison	1958	Steve Brooks	1962
John Longden	1956	James McLaughlin	1958	Bill Hartack	1963
Isaac Murphy	1956	Mack Garner	1959	Johnny Adams	1964
Tod Sloan	1956	Carroll Shilling	1959	Jackie Westrope	1965
Ted Atkinson	1957	Willie Shoemaker	1959	Laffit Pincay Jr.	1975
Walter Miller	1957	Johnny Loftus	1960		

Biographies of the jockeys appear in the preceeding chapter devoted to the National Museum of Racing with the exception of Jackie Westrope and Laffit Pincay, Jr. — Photographs courtesy of National Museum of Racing, Inc.

John Adams	*Ted Atkinson*	*Mack Garner*	*Raymond Workman*

LACROSSE
HALL OF FAME MUSEUM

Baltimore, Maryland

(Below) Lt. Col. Thomas Truxtun, captain of the 1937 Army team that climaxed a remarkable season by beating Navy, All-American for three consecutive years, called the greatest lacrosse player of his day. He was killed in action near Baguio, Luzon, Philippine Islands June 6, 1945 and posthumously decorated with the Bronze Star and the Silver Star.

The Lacrosse Foundation, Inc. was incorporated in 1959 as a non-profit organization dedicated to the promotion and development of the sport of lacrosse. The Lacrosse Hall of Fame Museum, located in the Newton H. White, Jr. Athletic Center on the Johns Hopkins University campus in Baltimore, Maryland, was dedicated in 1966.

There have been 118 lacrosse greats inducted into the Hall of Fame since its inception in 1959. Anywhere from three to seven individuals are chosen each year for this honor. The selection process consists of three steps. First, a poll of sportswriters and other knowledgeable people is taken. This poll is used as a guide by a nominating committee which makes a recommendation to the Board of Directors as to whom they feel are the most qualified of those being considered. It is the responsibility of the Board of Directors to elect the honorees from this list of qualified candidates submitted by the committee.

The Lacrosse Foundation provides a variety of services to the public designed to promote the sport. It operates a film rental service, publishes the *Lacrosse Newsletter,* acts as a clearing house of information, distributes the Official NCAA Lacrosse Guide, maintains historical and current records in every phase of the game, and administrates a regional representative program. It is the aim of these services to further accelerate the rate of growth of the sport.

Mike O'Neill of Johns Hopkins dives attempting to score, but Dan Mackesey, #30 of Cornell makes the save in 1976 game won by Cornell, 15 to 8. —Photo by Jeff Wagner

The Shamrock Lacrosse Club, champions of the world (1871). —Photo courtesy Public Archives of Canada

HALL OF FAME INDUCTEES

	ELECTED		ELECTED
Laurie D. Cox, Harvard	1957	**Thomas S. Strobhar**, Johns Hopkins	1959
Charles E. Marsters, Harvard	1957	**Reginald Truitt, (Dr.)**, Maryland	1959
Cyrus C. Miller, New York U.	1957	**William C. Wylie**, Maryland	1959
William C. Schmeisser, Johns Hopkins	1957	**J. Sarsfeld Kennedy**, Crescent A.C.	1960
Roy Taylor, Cornell	1957	**Irving B. Lydecker**, Syracuse	1960
Carlton P. Collins, Cornell	1958	**C. Gardner Mallonee**, Johns Hopkins	1960
R.T. Abercrombie M.D., Johns Hopkins	1958	**Leon A. Miller**, Carlisle	1960
Albert A. Brisotti, New York U.	1958	**John H. Paige**, Colgate	1960
Andrew Kirkpatrick, Jr., St. John's	1958	**Herbert T. Scott**, Jarvis Coll. Inst.	1960
Norris Barnard, Swarthmore	1959	**Edward M. Stuart**, Johns Hopkins	1960
Cyril Brower, Hobart	1959	**F. Morris Touchstone**, Geo. Williams	1960
William A. Davis, Crescent A.C.	1959	**Avery F. Blake**, Swarthmore	1961
Waldemar H. Fries, Cornell	1959	**Frederic A. Fitch**, Syracuse	1961
William Hudgins, Johns Hopkins	1959	**William Harkness**, Ottawa	1961
John Knipp, Johns Hopkins	1959	**William Maddren**, Johns Hopkins	1961
Victor Starzenski, Stevens Tech.	1959	**William H. Moore, III**, Johns Hopkins	1961

—Unless indicated otherwise, photographs in this chapter, courtesy Lacrosse Hall of Fame Museum.

U.S. Naval Academy team, 1930. —Photo courtesy Pickering Studio, Annapolis, Md.

	ELECTED		ELECTED
Conrad Sutherland, Princeton	1961	Edwin E. Powell, Maryland	1964
Fred C. Billings, Navy	1962	Roy D. Simmons, Syracuse	1964
Henry C. Ford, Swarthmore	1962	Joseph H. Deckman, Maryland	1965
Harland W. Meistrell, Princeton	1962	Henry S. Frank, Johns Hopkins	1965
William Kelso Morrill, Johns Hopkins	1962	Albert B. Heagy, Maryland	1965
Walter Oster Norris, St. John's	1962	Joseph J. Julien, Rutgers	1965
Victor K. D. Ross, Syracuse	1962	Philip Lamb, Swarthmore	1965
D.C. Turnbull, Jr., Johns Hopkins	1962	Glenn N. Thiel, Syracuse	1965
Fred C. Alexander, Harvard	1963	John I. Turnbull, Johns Hopkins	1965
Thomas N. Biddison, Sr., Johns Hopkins	1963	Milton S. Erlanger, Johns Hopkins	1966
John E. Faber (Dr.), Maryland	1963	William Wilbur Evans, Maryland	1966
Carl Hartdegen, Lehigh	1963	Royce N. Flippin, Navy	1966
Robert B. Pool, St. John's	1963	Avery H. Gould, Dartmouth	1966
Jason G. Stranahan, Union	1963	Donaldson N. Kelly, Johns Hopkins	1966
Ferris Thomsen, St. John's	1963	Edwin L. Lotz (Dr.), St. John's	1966
Harry E. Wilson (Col.), Army	1963	Malcolm A. MacIntyre, Yale	1966
H. Fenimore Baker, Jr., Swarthmore	1964	John W. Boucher, St. John's	1967
Frank G. Breyer, Johns Hopkins	1964	Lorne Randolf Guild, Johns Hopkins	1967
Walter T. Collins (Col.), Yale	1964	Russell S. Hawkins, Sr., New York U.	1967
Francis L. Kraus, Hobart	1964	Victor J. Jenkins, Syracuse	1967
Miller Moore, U. of Pa.	1964	Fred Cecil Linkous, Maryland	1967
Claxton J. O'Connor, St. John's	1964	Sifford Pearre, Johns Hopkins	1967

	ELECTED
Albert W. Twitchell, Rutgers	1967
Gaylord R. Auer	1968
Morris D. Gilmore, Navy	1968
James D. Iglehart, Balto. A.C.	1968
Philip Lee Lotz, St. John's	1968
Gordon Scott Pugh (DDS), Maryland	1968
Winthrop A. Smith, Yale	1968
A. Gordon Armstrong, Johns Hopkins	1969
Charles F. Ellinger, Maryland	1969
Caleb R. Kelly, Jr., Johns Hopkins	1969
John F. Kelly, Jr., Maryland	1969
F. Gibbs LaMotte, Mt. Wash. Club	1969
William F. Logan, Johns Hopkins	1969
Frederick A. Wyatt, Union	1969
Ivan M. Marty, Maryland	1970
Fritz R. Stude, Johns Hopkins	1970
Thomas Truxtun, Army	1970
Carlton J. Ferris, Hobart	1971
Frederic M. Hewitt, Maryland	1971
Howard Myers, Jr., Virginia	1971
Arthur F. Spring, U. S. Naval Acad.	1971
Church Yearly, Johns Hopkins	1971
William H. Dobbin, Hobart	1972
George A. Latimer, Rutgers	1972
William N. Ritch, Syracuse	1972
Norwood S. Sotheron, Maryland	1972
John C. Tolson, Johns Hopkins	1972
Harry G. Beggs, Yale	1973
Tyler Campbell, Princeton	1973
Willis P. Bilderback, Rutgers	1973
John D. Lang, Johns Hopkins	1973
Everett W. Smith, Jr., St. John's	1973
John F. Christhilf, Maryland	1974
John C. Donohue, St. John's	1974
B. H. Kaestner, Jr., Johns Hopkins	1974
Charles G. McAnally, U. of Pa.	1974
Louis A. Robbins, Syracuse	1974
James F. Adams, Johns Hopkins	1975
Lloyd M. Bunting, Johns Hopkins	1975
J. H. Lee Chambers, Jr., Navy	1975
J. V. Hartinger, Army	1975
William U. Hooper, Jr., Virginia	1975

Action in 1932 showing Hall of Famer Russell S. Hawkins, center in white helmet, trying for a goal while playing for the Crescent A.C. against the Philadelphia Lacrosse Club.

Action around the goal in the 1976 NCAA Championship game between Cornell and Maryland at Brown University, won by Cornell, 16 to 13 in overtime.

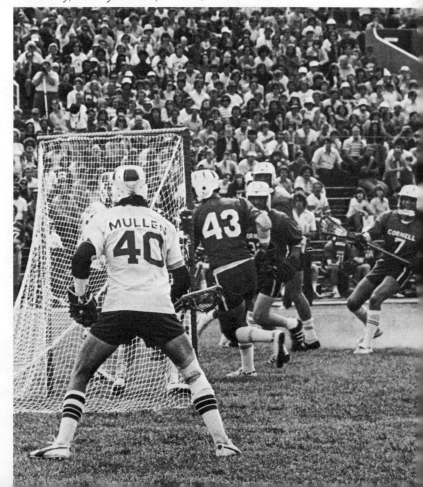

THE NATIONAL SKI HALL OF FAME

Ishpeming, Michigan

By Dave Guilford

The United States Ski Association owns and operates the National Ski Hall of Fame and Ski Museum. This fire-resistant building was built in 1953 and dedicated in February, 1954, on the occasion of the Golden Jubilee of the National Ski Association founded at Ishpeming. On May 29th, 1962, the National Convention changed the name from National Ski Association of America to the United States Ski Association.

The idea of such a building to recognize the great people in American skiing and to house the National Trophies, old skis, equipment, photographic records, publications and files was suggested by Mr. Harold A. Grinden, National Historian at the NSA Convention in Milwaukee in 1941. In 1944, NSA President Roger Langley, Arthur Barth and John Hostvedt joined Mr. Grinden at the 40th Anniversary Banquet in Ish-

One of the display areas in the Hall of Fame.

peming and recommended that such a building be built at the birthplace of the National Ski Association as a "Shrine of Skiing."

The Hall of Fame is located in Ishpeming because the National Ski Association was originally formed here in 1904 by a group from Ishpeming headed by Carl Tellefsen. The building consists of two floors with the first floor mainly the museum and the second the Hall of Fame section.

There are many Ski Trophies, the latest addition being the Jeff Wright Memorial Trophy. There are also many skis of various types. One in particular is the pair worn by Torger Tokle when he broke the record on Pine Mountain in 1941 with a jump of 289 feet.

In the Hall of Fame section are the pictures of all of the Honored Members placed neatly on the outside walls. Currently there are 186 Honored Members. There are many displays, including one on the Bietila family, the Founders' Display by the Ishpeming Ski Club, and the Olympic display consisting of only Olympic materials. There is a library containing books, magazines and information on famous persons in skiing.

On one rack you'll see a 10 foot birch travelling ski that has the feel of another era. The tip of the ski comes almost to a point, then broadens out into an ornate second point about the size and shape of an arrowhead. An elaborate floral pin-stripe pattern is cut into the top of the ski. And the bindings are a pair of leather straps with a piece of hide nailed to the ski to give the boot some grip.

The racks of skis are only part of the display of mementos, but for skiers they are perhaps the most intriguing area. The skis vary greatly — some of the skinny touring skis are modern in design while others are little more than boards. One "travelling ski" is 4-1/2 inches wide; another Lapland-style ski is less than three inches wide and looks perfectly snow-worthy.

There's a pair of all-white skis, camouflaged for use by ski troops in Italy in World War II. A pair of big Finnish travelling skis used by woodcutters in the Upper Peninsula forests 90 years ago. A pair of handmade skis that apparently served as a showroom model for a local craftsman — penciled on the binding area is the message, "I make skis for you $15." An imposing, 12-foot-long pair that was used by California gold miners in the 1880s in the Sierra Nevadas.

Then there's the pair of hickory "yoompin'" skis that made ski history, back in 1909, when Oscar Gunderson rode them to a world jumping record of 138 feet at Chippewa Falls, Wis. On a nearby wall is a display of clippings from newspapers of the day, including a dispute over the record.

Another cross-country ski, made in Norway more than a century ago, has an elk skin foot pad. Near it is a similar ski whose maker seems to have anticipated current fishscale bottoms of some X-C skis by covering the bottom with hide. At least, if you run your hand along the hide, the bristly hairs seem like they might flop back and forth like the fishscale bottoms are supposed to.

Suicide Ski Hill,
scene of annual competition.

—Unless indicated otherwise,
all photographs in this chapter
courtesy Ski Hall of Fame Archives

187

Art Devlin stretches out.

Andrea Mead Lawrence
—Photo by Nancy Graham

A display of the equipment used by the Ski Patrol.

And in one corner of the room is the granddaddy of them all—a replica of an ancient Arctic ski and pole found in a Swedish marsh. Its estimated age is 4,000 years, which once more sets the mind to boggling. Man has been sliding on snow for 40 centuries in one form or another.

Looking at the pole, which resembles nothing so much as a canoe paddle, you might wonder how he did it. Other old-time poles also look pretty impractical compared to today's equipment. Some are bamboo, some are much heavier wood. By far the most unwieldy-looking are the Lapland-style poles—thick as broomsticks and a foot or two longer.

History in the ski hall isn't confined to the racks of skis. You might talk to the attendants, volunteers from the Ishpeming senior citizens group.

Perhaps because it isn't a mountain town, skiing hasn't become a million-dollar tourist industry in Ishpeming. There are no ski bars or chalet communities, although there are plenty of places for downhill or cross-country skiing across the Upper Peninsula. And there's plenty of snow.

Organized skiing in the area dates back to the founding of the Ishpeming Ski Club, the nation's third oldest, in 1901. Penned in the neat, flowing script of the turn of the century, the club bylaws are on display at the Hall of Fame. They tell us:

"The name of this club shall be the Ishpeming Ski Club, the object of which shall be to promote the Ski-sport by frequent outings and annual tournaments such as long distance races and hill contests . . .

"Men of all nationalities and good character are eligible to membership by application . . .

"The dues shall be Three Dollars ($3.00) for each fiscal year . . ."

Displays on Olympic competition, the U.S. Ski Patrol, trophies complete with miniature gold-plated skiers wearing the shirt and ties that were the uniform of past tournaments, ski literature and the Hall of Fame proper round out the ski hall.

The Hall of Fame is a display of photographs and career data of athletes and ski-sport builders who have contributed to the sport's growth in North America. Those selected to the hall are chosen by an 11-member committe of the USSA. If you have any suggestions, you can contact the committee by writing to ski hall curator Ray Leverton, Box 191, Ishpeming, Mich., 49849.

HONORED MEMBERSHIP

1956

ARTHUR J. (RED) BARTH — President of the NSA in 1949; first American Olympic ski jumping judge in Europe.

AKSEL HOLTER — Secretary of the NSA 1904–09; editor of the American Ski Annual and jumping competitor.

EDWARD F. TAYLOR — Second Director of the National Ski Patrol System and alpine competitor.

CARL TELLEFSEN — First President of the National Ski Association of America, this Norway-born sports leader was a jumping competitor during early-day tourneys in Northern Michigan beginning in 1887.

1957

FRED HARRIS — NSA Treasurer 1929–31; built first ski jump at Hanover, N.H., for the Dartmouth Outing Club.

FRED H. McNEIL — Newspaper man and winter sports enthusiast who became first president of the Pacific Northwest Ski Association in 1930.

1958

CHARLES M. (MINNIE) DOLE — Founder of the National Ski Patrol System and leader in organization of the ski troops during World War Two.

RICHARD DURRANCE — America's top alpine racer of the 1930's, Olympian of 1936; four-event competitor representing Dartmouth Outing Club.

HAROLD GRINDEN — Lifetime Historian of the NSA and USSA; a founder of the National Ski Hall of Fame; NSA president 1928 and 1929.

ROGER LANGLEY — NSA President, 1936–1948; executive secretary 1948–1954; editor of the American Ski Annual.

ANDREA MEAD LAWRENCE — Double Gold Medal winner of the 1952 Winter Olympics, giant slalom and slalom.

HANNES SCHNEIDER — The "father of modern ski teaching," organized an early-day ski school in Austria, developed the Arlberg technique, then came to America.

MARTHINIUS STRAND — Founder and first president of the Intermountain Ski Association 1938 to 1944; jumping official.

GORDON WREN — Olympic jumper and four-event competitor; first American to leap over 300 feet.

1959

ALEXANDER BRIGHT — Alpine racer and Olympian of 1936.

DR. RAYMOND S. ELMER — NSA president 1930-31; pioneer New England ski leader.

ALF ENGEN — National ski jumping champion of 1940, established American distance records three times; four-way ski great.

ROBERT (BARNEY) McLEAN — Captain of the 1948 Olympic Team; jumper and racer.

CHARLES N. PROCTOR — The Dartmouth Outing Club's four-way ski great and an Olympian of 1928.

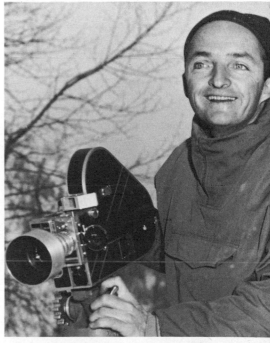

Richard Durrance
—Photo by Margaret Durrance

189

Torger Tokle in Duluth, 1941

TORGER TOKLE—National ski jumping champion of 1941 and hill distance breaker who came to America from Norway when a young man. He was killed in action in 1945 while serving with the 10th Mountain Troops in Italy.

1960

GRETCHEN FRASER—First American to win Olympic medals—Gold in the Slalom and Silver in the Alpine Combined.

1961	1962
No Honors Voted	No Nominations

1963

ARTHUR DEVLIN—National Jumping Champion of 1946, Olympian of 1948, 1952 and 1956; four-way ski great.

LARS HAUGEN—Seven times national ski jumping champion, 1912, 1920, 1923 and 1926; Olympian of 1924 and 1928.

CASPER OIMOEN—National jumping champion of 1934; Olympian of 1936.

MAGNUS SATRE—Four times national cross-country champion, 1928, 1929, 1930 and 1933, and Olympian of 1928. The "iron man."

1964

ROY MIKKELSEN—U.S. Olympic ski jumper of 1932 and 1936, Mikkelsen was national jumping champion of 1933 and 1935 and also rated among the nation's top downhill and slalom competitors from 1933 to 1942. He served in the Mountain Troops and Ranger Invaders during World War Two.

ROLF MONSEN—Three times a U. S. Olympian, 1928, 1932 and 1936, Monsen's North American competitive career began as a member of the Montreal Ski Club during the 1922 Canadian nationals and he won the cross-country and nordic combined. The following year he swept the jumping, cross-country and combined at Montreal. Later Monsen removed to Lake Placid, New York, and became a citizen of the U.S.

WENDELL T. ROBIE—First president of the California Ski Association, now the Far West, and organizer of the Auburn Ski Club, Robie provided the leadership which resulted in the Sierra Nevada being opened to winter travel in 1931.

WALLACE (BUDDY) WERNER—Among the great four-event skiers of America, Buddy was a ski jumping product of famed Howelsen Hill, but he decided to concentrate on the alpine phase of competition upon entering the senior ranks. The Great Rocky Mountain skier thrice was an Olympian—competing in the 1956 games in Italy, kept out of Squaw Valley in 1960 because of an injury, and going back in 1964 to Austria. Following the events near Innsbruck, Buddy lost his life in a Swiss avalanche on April 2, 1964.

1965

WALTER BIETILA—One of the "flying Bietilas" and Olympic jumper of 1936 and 1948; now jumping official.

BURTON H. BOYUM—Former curator of the National Ski Hall of Fame in Ishpeming, Michigan, and ski-sport administrator.

DR. AMOS R. LITTLE, JR.—Manager of Olympic teams and competition official.

EUGENE PETERSEN—Secretary of the National Ski Association during the years of 1918, 1919, 1920 and 1921, this outstanding ski official and histo-

"Bud" Werner

Walter Bietila

rian now resides in Siljan, Norway. A one-time resident of Fox River Grove, Illinois, he is a member of the Norge Ski Club of Chicago and served that organization twice as president, upwards of 15 years as secretary, as well as being historian and author of the club's 25th and 50th anniversary reviews.

1966

ASARIO AUTIO — First national cross-country champion; won in 1907 at Ashland, Wisconsin.

ERLING HEISTAD — Organizer of interscholastic competition in New England; developer of ski talent going on to intercollegiate and Olympic teams.

DAVID LAWRENCE — First national men's giant slalom champion; won in 1949 at Slide Mountain, Nevada.

LAWRENCE MAURIN — Ski jumper and international official; first American style judge at Obersdorf, Germany.

JOHN McCRILLIS — Pioneer ski leader in New England and the Pacific Northwest who later co-authored the first American book on skiing, "Modern Ski Technique," and produced the first American ski instructional movies.

GRACE CARTER LINDLEY McKNIGHT — First women's national slalom champion; won in 1938 at Stowe, Vermont.

CHARLES A. PROCTOR — Dartmouth College professor who in association with Sir Arnold Lunn helped introduce slalom competition to North America.

HANNES SCHROLL — First national men's slalom champion; won in 1935 near Seattle, Washington.

LOWELL THOMAS — Radio commentator and author who as an enthusiastic skier helped promote the sport.

CONRAD THOMPSON — First national ski jumping champion; won in 1904 at Ishpeming.

MARIAN (MARGARET) McKEAN WIGGLESWORTH — First women's national downhill champion; won in 1938 at Stowe, Vermont.

HENRY S. WOOD — First national downhill champion; won in 1933 at Warren.

KATY RUDOLPH WYATT — First women's national giant slalom champion; won in 1949 at Slide Mountain, Nevada.

Katy Rudolph Wyatt

1967

ED BLOOD — Olympian of 1932 and 1936; intercollegiate ski coach and association official.

HENRY HALL — First American ski jumper to establish world distance marks; 203 feet in 1917 at Steamboat Springs, Colorado and 225 feet in 1921 at Revelstoke, British Columbia, Canada. National champion in 1916.

HJALMAR HVAM — Winner of three gold medals during the 1932 nationals at Olympic Hill near Tahoe City, California, Class B jumping, the cross-country and nordic combined.

JILL KINMONT — Former national women's slalom champion who was paralyzed ever since her neck was broken in a racing accident in 1955.

TONI MATT — Former national downhill champion of 1939 and 1941, and national combined winner of 1941; member 1950 FIS team.

DAVE McCOY — Coach and developer of feminine ski racers; supporter of junior ski teams; veteran of 30 years ski racing and winner of numerous championships; developer of the Mammoth Mountain ski area.

RAGNAR OMTVEDT — Three-time national jumping champion, 1913, 1914 and 1917, whose competitive career ended with a broken leg while representing the United States in the first Olympic Winter Games in 1924.

OTTO SCHNIEBS — Former coach at Dartmouth College and St. Lawrence University, who developed ski talents of many Olympians and sloganized the skiing as "More than just a sport, a way of life."

HANS (PEPPI) TEICHNER — Developer of recreational ski programs in lower Michigan; one time alpine competitor and veteran of the U.S. Mountain Troops.

1968

JULIUS BLEGEN — National cross-country champion of 1911 and 1912; Olympic team coach of 1932; NSA treasurer 1937 to 1942.

HELEN BENDELARI BOUGHTON-LEIGH McALPIN — American born skier who began her racing career as a British subject and as a member of the British FIS teams of 1932, 1933 and 1934, but subsequently returned home to captain the first U.S. international women's ski team in the FIS and the 1936 Olympics.

CLARITA HEATH BRIGHT — Former California who was a member of the first women's U.S. Olympic team in 1936; also contributed to skiing through efforts in instruction.

JOHN P. CARLETON — The leading intercollegiate skier from 1918 to 1925 (Dartmouth College and Oxford University); international nordic and alpine competitor; Olympian of 1924.

HENRY PERCY DOUGLAS — Founder and first president of the Canadian Amateur Ski Association (1921), this native of Tarrytown, N.Y. played a leading role in skisport's development years throughout Eastern North America. He learned to ski in 1893 while a student at Cornell University and upon moving to Canada he became a member of the Montreal Ski Club organized in 1904. Douglas authored a book of memoirs, "My Skiing Years."

JOHN ELVRUM — Ski jumper who set the American distance record at 240 feet at Big Pines, California, and then stayed on to establish a ski school for children and eventually developed the Snow Valley Ski Area.

ALF HALVORSON — Nordic competitor and official who played major roles in establishing the United States Eastern Amateur Ski Association and the Canadian Amateur Ski Association.

SELDEN J. HANNAH — North American ski great with championships won in nordic and alpine competitions of the NSA, Canadian Amateur Ski Association, Intercollegiate Ski Union and USSA during a continuing 50-year ski career.

SIR ARNOLD LUNN — Drafter of the world's first downhill—slalom competition rules, organizer of the first FIS alpine world championships in 1931 at Murren, Switzerland; set the first modern-day slalom course in 1922; founder of Kandahar Ski Club and events so named around the world; instrumental in getting the first U.S. women's ski team established in Europe. Perhaps more than any other individual, Sir Arnold stands as a giant in the early development of alpine skiing.

GEORGE KOTLAREK — Winner of six national ski jumping championships: Boys' title in 1927, Class C in 1928, Class A in 1936 and Veterans in 1948, 1950 and 1954. Named to 1944 All-American Ski Team.

LeMoine Batson

The Lacrosse Hall of Fame, located on the campus of Johns Hopkins University, Baltimore, Maryland, is located in the right wing of this impressive memorial which also serves as an athletic center for a variety of athletics at Johns Hopkins.

(on following page)
The National Museum of Racing in Saratoga Springs, New York is a superb structure with priceless collections of paintings, sculpture, and memorabilia that have come from individuals to provide a distinctive museum in which the visitor can devote hours in pleasant viewing.

Triple Crown Winner Secretariat.
This chestnut colt is the superhorse of the era and
as such is featured in this book of super performers.
His stakes record follows: As a two year old
he won the Sanford, Hopeful, the Futurity,
Laurel Futurity and the Garden State.
As a three year old he won the Bay Shore, the
Gotham, the Kentucky Derby, the Preakness Stakes,
the Belmont Stakes, the Arlington Invitational,
the Marlboro Cup, the Man O' War and the
Canadian International Championship. He was
Horse of the Year as both a two year old and
three year old. He won $1,316,808. He made
21 starts, won 16 races and broke five track records.
including . . . Gotham: 1 mile at Aqueduct in 1:35
          Kentucky Derby: 1¼ miles in 1:59
          Belmont Stakes: 1½ miles in 2:24
          Marlboro Cup: 1⅛ miles in 1:45 and
          Man O' War: 1½ miles at Belmont 2:24

COURTESY OF CLAIBORNE FARM   FROM WATERCOLOR SKETCHES AND A PAINTING BY KAY SMITH

The Skiing Hall of Fame, Ishpeming, Michigan, honors the competitors who through the years have pioneered in bringing about the great popularity of skiing as well as the more recent competitors in this international sport.

Interior view of the Skiing Hall of Fame showing an area of the interesting displays that attract many devotees of this rapidly growing sport.

*The National Hall of Fame and Amateur Softball Association Headquarters
in Oklahoma City, Oklahoma.*

The Wrestling Hall of Fame, Stillwater, Oklahoma, on the campus of Oklahoma State University was formally dedicated in September 1976.

OLE R. MANGSETH—Top flight ski jumper in pioneering days of the NSA, this Hall of Famer served the NSA as treasurer from 1925 to 1928 and was active as a jumping coach until his death in 1952.

ROLAND PALMEDO—For more than half a century a contributor to affairs of the NSA and USSA at all levels; organizer of ski teacher certification; international competition official; founder of the Amateur Ski Club of New York.

ERNEST O. PEDERSON—The University of New Hampshire's four-way ski great who won the American-Canadian all-round championships of 1927, 1928 and 1930. Lengthy military career included Rifle Company Commander of 87th Mountain Infantry and then Executive Officer of the Mountain Warfare Training Center at Camp Hale in Colorado.

John Bower

1969

LeMOINE BATSON—The widely-heralded competitive career of this American-born ski jumper included membership on two United States Olympic teams, the first Winter Games of 1924 in France and the third Winter Games in 1932 at Lake Placid, New York. His top-flight ski jumping began in 1917 and continued more than 20 years. He was president of the Central Division in 1939 and 1940 during which slalom and downhill clubs were incorporated into membership.

JOHN BOWER—America's four-way ski great who in 1968 won the Holmenkollen cross-country and, placing well in ski jumping, captured the Holmenkollen Combined Championship which is generally conceded to be the world's most coveted nordic honor. Now coaching at Middlebury College.

DR. HAROLD C. BRADLEY—Grand old man of American skiing and retired chemistry professor from the University of Wisconsin, "Doc" Bradley helped pioneer skiing in Wisconsin, Idaho, Colorado and California, with seven sons to help him do it. He served as secretary of the Central Ski Association, was among organizers of the Wisconsin Hoffers' Club and was among organizers of alpine competitions at Sun Valley in cooperation with resort founder W. Averell Harriman. Famous as a skiing mountaineer, Doc Bradley recently voiced regret that he had to give up the sport five years ago.

NANCY GREENE—This outstanding Canadian skier from Ottawa, Ontario, climaxed a lengthy racing career in 1968 with Olympic Gold Medal and World Cup Championships. Rated the greatest woman competitor to date in North American ski history, Miss Greene's championships include five gold medal awards of the United States Ski Association. In 1966 she won 17 major races in the United States and Canada, including the Dominion Championships, the U.S. Nationals and the Roch Cup.

Nancy Greene

W. AVERELL HARRIMAN—Founder of Idaho's Sun Valley as the nation's first ski resort planned from the ground up. Ambassador Harriman's skisport building contributions have not been forgotten by the younger generation. He founded the Harriman Cup ski racing tourney which in its heyday gained the highest international reputation of any similar event in the country, and he provided unqualified backing to competitive skiing at the intercollegiate, senior divisional and junior western levels.

HARRY WADE HICKS—An organizer of the 1932 Winter Olympic Games at Lake Placid, Hicks also served as president of the United States

Eastern Amateur Ski Association. He was a cross-country ski enthusiast and an authoritative writer on winter sports topics, particularly the organization of community effort which led to the development of numerous snow sports programs throughout the United States and Canada.

JOHN HOSTVEDT — Nordic and alpine competitions official at the divisional, national and international levels, Hostvedt was a co-founder of the National Ski Hall of Fame in Ishpeming, Michigan, and long active in affairs of the Central Ski Association.

CARL HOWELSEN — This Norwegian-born ski jumping champion fathered competition and recreational skiing in Colorado, where he won the National Ski Jumping Championships in 1921 while a member of the Steamboat Springs Winter Sports Club. Before reaching Colorado in 1910, Howelsen was among the founders of Chicago's Norge Ski Club, while in 1903 back in Norway he had won the Holmenkollen cross-country and the combined championship of what is considered the world championship of Nordic competition. He died in Norway.

ALICE DAMROSCH WOLFE KAIER — Mrs. Kaier was a New Yorker extremely active for many years in international skiing circles. She assembled the National Ski Association's first women's ski team for the 1935 FIS World Championships and the 1936 Winter Olympics. She represented the NSA at FIS Congresses of 1938, 1949, 1951 and 1953. Her ski activity continued through the 1960 Winter Olympics in Squaw Valley, indelibly marking her as the initial promoter of International skiing competition for women of the United States.

COL. GEORGE EMERSON LEACH — Mayor of Minneapolis when it was known as the "Ski Capital of America," Col. Leach was manager of the National Ski Association's first Olympic Ski Team in 1924 and during the Winter Games near Chamonix, France, represented the United States during the ski congress which resulted in founding of the Federation of International Skiing.

HARRY LIEN — Norway-born ski jumper who emerged from the United States Army following World War One to become a crowd-pleasing rider representing Chicago's Norge Ski Club, Lien's competitive career spanned both the professional and amateur eras of the National Ski Association of America. He represented the United States during the 1924 Winter Olympics and, through membership in the Sons of Norway, continues to actively support the programs of the United States Ski Association.

ERNIE McCULLOCH — Major competitive seasons of this outstanding Canadian skier were 1950 through 1953 following which he was polled "Skier of the Half Century" by a board of sports writers. First for the Sun Valley Ski Club and then for the Mont Tremblant Ski Club, McCulloch's record was phenomenal and he was dubbed the "Grand Slam Champion" in the world press after winning the National Giant Slalom, the North American Championships, the National Downhill and the Harriman Cup, all in 1950. He has coached national ski team members of Canada and the United States and is chief examiner of the Canadian Ski Instructors' Alliance.

FRED PABST — Former University of Wisconsin ski jumping great who became an alpine expert while studying the business investment possibilities of recreational skisport, Pabst during the early 1930's financed the creation of the skisport area conglomerate in Eastern Canada, New England and Wisconsin. His activity since 1941 has centered at the Big Bromley Ski Area near Manchester, Vermont.

JACK REDDISH — Boy wonder skier of the early-day alpine era, Reddish's spectacular 14-year competitive career included winning the national downhill in 1948, the national slalom in 1948, 1950 and 1952, three national combined championships, the Bradley Plate four-way championship in 1947, the Harriman Cup of 1949, and many other events of national import. His seventh place in the Olympic slalom of 1948 was outstanding, while his win of the Kandahar the same winter was almost incredible.

HERMAN (JACK RABBIT) SMITH-JOHANNSEN—A legend in his lifetime, Jack Rabbit was Norway-born in 1875 and reached Canada via Cleveland, Ohio, where he met his late wife, Alice Robinson, carrying with him cross-country skills and nordic enthusiasm. Trained in the Norwegian army and armed with a degree in Civil Engineering, Jack Rabbit had a hand in cutting North America's most famous ski touring trail, the Maple Leaf in the Laurentians; others also in Vermont. His trophies won include triumph at 60 years of age over much younger competitors and at 93 years of age he was still going strong.

SIEGFRIED STEINWALL—Swedish-born ski jumper whose career includes honors won under two flags and upon two continents, Steinwall was rated the nation's top amateur soon after reaching the United States 50 years ago at a time when professionals were the top riders of the National Ski Association. He served as ski coach at Dartmouth College in 1927-28, is the founder and lifetime member of the Swedish Ski Club of New York City, and, along with 14 other Americans of foreign birth, was honored on the "Wall of Fame of Sports" during the New York World's Fair of 1939–40.

GEORGE H. WATSON—Known as the "Mayor of Alta," an office to which he had himself specially elected, Watson deeded the surface rights to his vast mining claims to the Federal Government for winter sports development. He believed Alta had a "higher purpose than that of a ghost town" and he had learned to ski because he "jolly well had to" during pioneering silver mining days.

BETTY WOOLSEY—Member of the first United States Women's Ski Team for the 1935 FIS World Championships and the first Olympic Team of 1936, this great competitor won the National Downhill and National Combined of 1939. Her competitive career included races won all over North America. She was top American of the 1936 Olympics, seventh in slalom and 14th in downhill. Former editor of Ski Illustrated, Miss Woolsey for many years was a contributor to American Ski Annuals.

THE WURTELE TWINS, RHONA and RHODA—With lengthy and renowned ski racing careers on both sides of the border while representing clubs of both the Canadian Amateur Ski Association and the National Ski Association of America, the Wurtele twins won numerous championships of both associations and also have contributed to skisport in other ways for North America. Rhoda won the NSA Downhill in 1947 and the North American Downhill in 1949, while Rhona captured the NSA Slalom in 1946, the NSA Giant Slalom in 1952 and the NSA Combined Championships of 1946 and 1947.

1970

PAUL BIETILA—Paul Bietila rode skis for the last ime on February 5 1939, a practice jump the morning of the National Championship Tournament in St. Paul, Minnesota. He crashed into an iron restraining post at the edge of the runway, and for three long weeks after the accident he fought hard to live. Paul died February 25th. A student at University of Wisconsin, Paul was rated the best ski jumper in America at the time of his death. He was 19 years of age.

FRED BRUUN—Co-founder and first president of the Central Ski Judges' Association, Fred Bruun enabled the National Ski Association of America to get its judges approved and accepted for service in the big international tournaments of Europe.

Displays honoring two of the members of the Hall of Fame inducted in 1970. (Above) John Clair, Jr. and (Below) John Thompson.

Birger Rudd

Art Tokle looking at the Olympic ski jump at Squaw Valley

JOHN J. CLAIR, JR. — Eastern Amateur Ski Association official whose ski-sport career exemplified what an amateur skier could do for the advancement of skiing at the divisional, national and international levels. Founder of the Long Island Ski Club and member of the National Ski Patrol System.

GODFREY DEWEY — With a skisport career dating back to 1904 in Lake Placid, New York, Dewey spearheaded the effort to bring the Third Winter Olympic Games to Northern New York State and to the United States for the first time in 1932.

WILLIAM T. ELDRED — Editor and publisher whose magazines enriched the lives of thousands of skiers. In 1938 he started Empire State Ski News and, following mergers with Western Skiing, Ski Illustrated and Ski Sheet, emerged as the guiding genius of the national magazine named SKI.

THOR C. GROSWOLD, SR. — A long record of active participation in skiing world affairs made Thor Groswold a classic example of a sport builder at the divisional, national and international levels. Born in Konigsberg, Norway, Groswold skied competitively in his home land before coming to America in 1923 to establish himself in Colorado and become a leading light in the Denver Rocky Mountain Ski Club. A top competitor in both nordic and alpine phases, he moved out to become a world-famed ski official and also became a ski manufacturer of note.

OLE. HEGGE — Norwegian ski great who won a silver medal in cross-country during the 1928 Olympics and, following his arrival in America in 1929, again represented Norway during the 1932 Olympics at Lake Placid, New York, before becoming an American citizen. Member of Salisbury Outing Club and winner of almost 50 tourneys as a nordic and combined competitor.

CORTLANDT T. HILL — Pioneer member and former president of the California Ski Association, now known as the Far West Ski Association. Corty Hill's skisport career enhanced the Olympic Movement, materially aided the Federation of International Skiing and helped expansion of the National Ski Association of America into the United States Ski Association.

JANETTE BURR JOHNSON — National Downhill Champion of 1948 and 1950; North American Downhill Champion of 1950; Olympian of 1952 and winner of numerous European races; winner of bronze medal for giant slalom during 1954 FIS World Championships.

L. B. (BARNEY) Mac NAB — MacNab was the first president of the Mount Hood Ski Patrol, organized for the winter of 1937 – 38. The Mount Hood patrol was a prototype for the National Ski Patrol System, which sought MacNab's services as an advisor. Barney wore Badge No. 17 in the NSPS.

RICHARD MOVITZ — National Slalom Champion of 1946, Movitz helped spearhead the ski-youth movement following World War Two. He also was an Olympian of 1948, an FIS competitor of 1950, and an international ski official.

GEORGE A. NEWETT — Influential editor and publisher of The Ishpeming Iron Ore who, along with nine Norway-born skiers, was a founder of the National Ski Association of America on February 21, 1904, in Ishpeming. Long recognized as "the man who Americanized the skisport".

THE RUDD BROTHERS, BIRGER and SIGMUND — both won ski jumping chamionships of the National Ski Association of America--Birger in 1938 and Sigmund in 1937. Both also have been world championship jumpers and world distance record holders on several occasions. Birger during the 1936 Olympic Winter Games in Germany accomplished a feat which possibly may never again be equalled--winning both the Downhill Ski Race and the Special Ski Jumping.

LLOYD SEVERUD — Five times National Veterans' Ski Jumping Champion, lifelong student of ski jumping who has served as coach of both the United States and Canadian ski jumping teams.

SNOW-SHOE THOMPSON — John Albret Thompson, sometimes spelled Thomson, was the skiing pioneer who tracked the Sierra Nevada to carry mail between California and Western Utah Territory, later to become Nevada, for 20 years beginning in 1856. He skied on groove-less but cambered implements known in those times as "Norwegian snow-shoes," and he actually wrote quasi-scientific articles defining ski contests and ski techniques that are remarkably similar to today's slalom, downhill and recreational skiing formats. He died at 49 years of age in 1876 at his Diamond Valley Ranch and was buried not far distant at Genoa in Nevada.

ARTHUR TOKLE — National Ski Jumping Champion of 1951 and 1953, Olympian of 1952, winner of dozens of tourneys during his competitive career, and coach of U. S. ski jumping teams 1960 through 1968.

PAULA KANN VALAR — National Downhill Champion of 1946; powerhouse of the U. S. Olympic Team in 1948; FIS World Championship competitor of 1950; winner of two Kate Smith International Team Trophy downhill races; certified ski teacher examiner of the United States Eastern Amateur Ski Association.

JOHN WICTORIN — Founder and president of the Swedish Ski Club of New York City, John Wictorin's ski interests spanned the North American continent. He was a championship contending cross-country competitor, winner of the New York State title in 1927. Best known as "Mr. Swix" he became a ski waxing expert, seemingly always present to serve as a tourney official and advise competitors.

1971

REIDAR ANDERSEN — Winner of 18 tournaments, including the United States and Canadian ski jumping championships, during a 1939 tour of North America, Anderson also was a Norwegian Olympian during the 1932 Winter Games at Lake Placid, New York. He contributed greatly to the growth of skisport in North America.

WARREN CHIVERS — Eldest member of the famous Chivers family of Hanover, New Hampshire, Warren (Winger) Chivers in the mid-1930s at Dartmouth College launched an intercollegiate skiing career that probably has not been equalled since by his diversified performance in ski jumping, cross-country, downhill and slalom and the combined venues of nordic and alpine scoring. He also won the National Cross-Country in 1937, was an Olympian of 1936 and represented the U. S. during the 1937 Pan American championships in Chile.

SVERRE ENGEN — During a 40-year ski career he was outstanding as a jumping competitor, instructor, writer, resort operator, avalanche control expert and producer of ski movies. Sverre also was a top alpine ski racer, with his high-stature support of skisport documented as a sports builder-ski athlete.

SIGI ENGL — This Austrian-born one-time European downhill and slalom ski great has headed the Sun Valley Ski School since 1952. Coming to America in 1936, Sigi won the Harriman Cup Downhill in 1940 and the National Open Slalom of 1941 at Yosemite National Park. Veteran of the 10th Mountain Division during World War Two. Rated among the nation's top ski executives.

NATHANIEL GOODRICH — Early-day skier who became editor of the American Ski Annuals and Eastern Ski Annuals during the 1930s. As librari-

Sverre Engen, Ogden, Utah on February 16, 1930, first winter in America.

an of Dartmouth College he had a discriminating taste for literature and this was reflected in the outstanding quality of the annuals he edited. Too, he was extolled as a ski pioneer whose association with Roland Palmedo, Sir Arnold Lunn and Prof. Charles A. Proctor "was instrumental in introducing alpine competition to America."

JAMES GRIFFITH — Jimmy died Dec. 6, 1951 from injuries sustained four days earlier when at Alta for Olympic team training. He crashed head-on into a tree. He was on leave from the U. S. Air Force at the time. Jimmy began his ski career in 1941 at Sun Valley, becoming a member of the U. S. FIS team in 1950 when he finished as the top American. He also held the National Downhill Championship in 1950. He was 22.

JAMES R. HENDRICKSON — An outstanding ski jumper who gave his life for the sport. He sustained fatal injuries during the Norge Tournament at Fox River Grove, Illinois on January 18, 1948. A one-time National Class B Champion, his greatest fame came in 1936 when selected for the U. S. Olympic Team. He had won Central Division and West Coast titles in 1935 and 1936. A veteran of the U. S. Army with service in Europe during World War Two.

SALLY NEIDLINGER HUDSON — Olympic and FIS ski team member, Sally's ski career began during the 1940s. Her lengthy ski racing record includes winning the National Open Alpine Combined Championship in 1953. Member of the Squaw Valley Ski Club and active within the Far West Ski Association.

CHICK IGAYA — Waiver of the 40-year age requirement for ski athlete nominees was voted by the Ski Hall committee as a gesture of international amity ahead of the 1972 Olympic Winter Games in Sapporo, Japan. A member of the Dartmouth Outing Club and an Olympian representing Japan in the 1952, 1956 and 1960 Winter Games, Igaya's North American record includes six NCAA championships and five gold medals of the National Ski Association.

RON MacKENZIE — A leading figure in the development of both recreational and competitive skiing as a teacher, coach, planner, builder, organizer and promoter. He was a charter member of the New York State Winter Sports Council and a key figure in a 20-year battle to secure a major ski development on state-owned lands in the Adirondacks. Member of the National Ski Patrol System, coach-manager of the U. S. Nordic Team at the FIS World Championships. Active for many years in the Olympic movement.

NELS NELSEN — The late Nels Nelsen, (1894–1943) established the world distance ski jumping record at 240 feet during a tourney in 1925 at Revelstoke. He taught skiing in Canada and played an active role in affairs of both the National Ski Association of America and the Canadian Amateur Ski Association for many years.

GUTTORM PAULSEN — A noted ski jumper, one of the nation's top ski jumping judges, and for many years affiliated with the Norge Ski Club. A native of Norway, Paulsen was a veteran of Holmenkollen competition before coming to America. He won the National Class B championship in 1929 and then moved into a Class A career of distinction. Retiring from competition he continued to contribute to skisport for many years, serving as a judge during the 1952 Winter Olympics in Norway. He also served as secretary to the Central Division.

PAUL JOSEPH PERRAULT — In the greatest individual performance in the history of North American ski jumping, Jumping Joe Perrault, in less than two hours on the afternoon of February 26, 1949, on giant Pine Mountain slide in Iron Mountain, Michigan, defeated two World champions and broke the North American distance record twice. He defeated Petter Hugsted of

Norway, the current Olympic champion and Matti Pietikainen, who the following year won the FIS World Championship for Finland. He was an Olympian in 1952 and, as a resident of Ishpeming, is among the volunteers contributing greatly to the historical display program of the National Ski Hall of Fame.

OTTAR SATRE — Member of an illustrious pioneer ski family, Ottar was a versatile competitor in cross-country, jumping and nordic combined during the period from 1930 to 1942. A transplanted Norwegian, his American ski career included the national cross-country title of 1935, runner up in both combined and national championships the same year, and capturing numerous divisional and regional championships in Class A and B. He was a member of the 1936 U. S. Olympic Team.

ALBERT E. SIGAL — A former president of the United States Ski Association (1954 and 1955), Sigal served skisport in many capacities. He was instrumental in assisting the securing of manpower for Ski Mountain Troops during World War Two; he was the liaison between the National Ski Patrol System and the Fourth Air Force Search and Rescue Missions in the mountains along the Pacific Coast during World War Two. He served organized amateur skiing in many capacities for more than 27 years, including services to the Olympic movement during the Winter Games of 1948 and 1960. A Blegen Award winner in 1953, and Ski Patrolman of the Year for 1943-1944.

1972

THE BAKKE BROTHERS, MAGNUS and HERMOD — Magnus was active in skisport for 39 years as a coach of ski jumping and cross-country teams and as a certified judge for national and international events, including the 1960 Olympic Winter Games. They were instrumental in the building and promotion of the internationally famous 90-meter ski jumping hill of the Leavenworth Winter Sports Club. Hermod once an outstanding ski jumper, was hill captain or tournament chairman for the Leavenworth tournaments from 1932 to 1969. Begun in Norway, Hermod's ski jumping career spanned more than 45 years; at 60 years of age he still jumped the 90-meter hill at Leavenworth.

Nancy Reynolds Cooke

NANCY REYNOLDS COOKE — National Women's Closed and Open Slalom Champion of 1940, National Women's Closed Downhill and Alpine Combined Champion of 1941, holder of an enviable competitive record throughout North America; named for the 1940 Winter Olympics cancelled because of World War Two; also member of the U. S. Team at the FIS World Championships of 1938; a fund raiser for the U. S. Ski Team and active with her husband, J. Negley Cooke, in affairs of the USSA and the U. S. Ski Educational Foundation.

DONALD FRASER — World-famed early-day American downhill and slalom competitor and holder of a distinguished competitive record within the National Ski Association, the United States Ski Association, the Federation of International Skiing and the Olympic movement. Twice winner of the Silver Skis on Mt. Ranier, Washington; the 1938 Pan American Slalom Champion, and Olympian of 1936. Husband of Gretchen Kunigh Fraser, America's first Olympic gold medal skier and herself an Honored Member of the Ski Hall of Fame.

FRED ISELIN — Swiss-born Fred Iselin introduced thousands of Americans to skisport. He came to America in 1939 in the wake of a downhill ski racing career of formidable proportions. North America's most famous alpine events knew him too — the Far West Kandahar, the Harriman Cups, the FIS Internationals of 1939 in California, the Silver Skis at Mt. Ranier in Washington and many others. Then came ski teaching, first at Sun Valley, then as co-director of the Aspen Ski School and Buttermilk Mountain Ski School and then as co-director of the Aspen Ski School and Buttermilk Mountain Ski School and then his own ski school at Aspen Highlands. Born in 1914, Iselin's life was snuffed out at age 57 by a ski-injury embolism.

SIGRID STROMSTAD LAMING — Mrs. Laming became the FIRST WOMAN champion of the National Ski Association when in 1932 women for the initial time was permitted to enter the National Ski Championships held at Lake Tahoe in California. She won the cross-country race, the only women's event contested, thus winning the first Gold Medal of the NSA and USSA. She also was an excellent ski jumper, with a known leap of 32 meters. Native of Norway and member of the famous Stromstad family, she had two brothers and two sisters who were top-ranking Olympic and FIS competitors in nordic and alpine.

EARLE BE LITTLE — Little's volunteer contributions to skisport and his active participation for more than 30 years marked him among the top sports builders in North America. His influence extended into Western Canada, the Western States and eventually was felt world wide. Highlight of his career came in Squaw Valley, California, where in 1959 he served as Director of Competition for the North American Ski Jumping Championships and in 1960 as Secretary of Competition for the Olympic Winter Games.

JOHN E. P. MORGAN — John Morgan's long career as a skisport builder on all levels covered nearly 40 years. The USSA, the NSPS, the 10th Mountain Division and innumerable ski area developments, both large and small, benefitted from his warm dedication to the skisport. Morgan was employed by Averell Harriman to work on the development of what today is known as Sun Valley Ski Resort in Idaho. There is a Morgan Ridge on Sun Valley maps in his honor. He helped design and construct the first chair lift in the world for Sun Valley, and they secured the 1937 alpine national tourney for the new resort.

Dorothy Hoyt Nebel

DOROTHY HOYT NEBEL — FIS skier of 1938, Olympian of 1940, PNSA Slalom Champion of 1939, USEASA Alpine Champion of 1940 and 1941; winner of numerous Class A competitions, including the Arnold Lunn Trophy, the Silver Skis at Mt. Rainier; numbered among America's earliest Class A rated internationalists; ski racing coach, ski teacher and lifelong skisport builder.

WILLIS S. OLSON — This outstanding ski jumper's career began as a teenager with record shattering performances and carried through to every class championship of the USSA — Class C, Class B, Class A and Veterans' Class. Member of two Olympic teams (1952 and 1956) and two FIS teams (1950 and 1954); undefeated University of Denver intercollegiate ski great and three times NCAA champion. Best known as Billy "The Kid" Olson.

ERLING STROM — Erling Strom came to America in 1919, first herding cattle as a cowboy in Arizona. He had served in the King's Guard and was a ski expert renowned for coaching the Crown Prince, later King Olav. Erling reached Colorado during 1926 to win his first ski tourney in America. He captured many other events, including many divisional titles before moving on to Lake Placid, New York, where he established a ski school and taught skisport for 11 years. In 1932 Erling was a member of the first skiing party ever to scale Mt. McKinley, North America's highest mountain. Later he operated ski schools at Stowe, Vermont and Banff, Alberta, Canada.

Birger Torrissen

BIRGER TORRISSEN — This Norway-born American's continuing ski career for 40 years has materially aided the growth of skisport divisionally, nationally and internationally. A strong nordic event competitor, Birger was an Olympian of 1936. His championships won included the Eastern Amateur's nordic combined of 1934. He was attached to the 10th Mountain Division as a ski instructor, has coached many junior champions.

1973

HANNAH LOCKE CARTER — Member of four American Women's Ski Teams, 1936 through 1939, and named to the 1940 Olympic Ski Team; an international competitor who helped pave the way for increased skisport participation by American women.

HOWARD CHIVERS — National Nordic Combined Champion of 1942, Canadian National Cross-Country Champion of 1937; named for the 1940 Winter Olympics and FIS Championships cancelled because of World War Two.

COREY ENGEN — Nordic National Champion in 1952; National Veterans' Alpine Combined Champion of 1959, 1962 and 1969; winner of more than 200 awards in Alpine and Nordic events and was Captain of the 1948 U. S. Olympic Nordic Team.

LUGGI FOEGER — International competitor and ski teacher turned American ski area manager and developer; long involved in affairs of the United States and Canadian Ski Associations; veteran of the 10th Mountain Division during World War Two.

SVERRE FREDHEIM — Top American (11th place) in the 1936 Winter Olympics ski jumping event; named to the 1940 Olympic Ski Team and as an Olympic competitor in 1948 at the age of 41 years placed 12th at St. Moritz; an active competitor until 60, he won numerous divisional championships in all classes.

CARL HOLMSTROM — Top ranking national ski jumper and winner of numerous tournaments while representing the Duluth Ski Club and the Bear Mountain (New York) Winter Sports Association; member of the 1932 and 1936 Olympic ski teams. He gave 50 years to skisport--25 as a judging official.

ARTHUR KNUDSEN — Ski team pin salesman and volunteer fund raiser extraordinary; a ski jumping competitor turned association official; president of the Racine Ski Club on 22 occasions; Director Emeritus of Central Division; awarded lifetime meberships by many ski clubs; served the USSA during the 1960 Winter Olympics and the FIS World Ski Jumping Championships.

GEORGE MACOMBER — Olympian of 1948 and 1952, FIS team member in 1950; National Alpine Combined Champion of 1949, National Veterans' Champion in 1962; former president of the Eastern Amateur Ski Association and long active in ski affairs at the national and international levels.

MALCOLM McLANE — Long-time USSA officer, Blegen Awardee of 1959 for service to Skisport and Olympic Planning; captain of the Dartmouth Ski Team of 1949; Rhodes Scholar and international intercollegiate competitor.

J. STANLEY MULLIN — Able and articulate spokesman for organized skisport, a champion of the principal of amateurism and national leader against removing the Ski Hall of Fame from Ishpeming.

HARALD SORENSEN — Named to two All-American ski teams, captured numerous divisional crowns and twice runner-up in national ski jumping tournaments, his skiing career spread over six decades; winner in 1971 of the Russell Wilder Memorial for focusing the interest of America's youth on the sport of skiing.

1974

RICHARD BUEK — was an athlete and twice a national Downhill champion. He managed a 12th in the Olympic Downhill despite a fall. Nominated by Slide Mt. Rose Ski Team with biographical material by Bill Berry.

*There are several racks
to show the changes in skiing.*

FRANK ELKINS — A ski sport builder who wrote and promoted skiing first in the New York Times and then in the Long Island Press all his adult working life. The author of two ski books. Nominated by Lowell Thomas, Jr., with biographical material from Historian Bill Berry and Editor J. William Berry of the Long Island Press.

E. O. "BUCK" ERICKSON — is a newspaperman's newspaperman. He influenced his colleagues to take up reporting the excitement of our sport. For 38 years he reported the ski news. He was responsible for bringing foreign competitors to this country's tournaments. He is nominated by the Iron Mountain Kingsford Winter Sports Association with biographical material by them.

JAMES E. FLAA — is a ski sport builder who devoted his life to the expansion of Junior competition programs. He is a 50-year veteran who unselfishly gave of himself so others could excel. Nominated by the Ishpeming Ski Club with biographical material by W. H. Treloar.

Coy Hill

COY HILL — is an athlete and ski sport builder. He was the National Class 'A' Champion Jumper in 1952 with a 203 foot hill record at Salisbury, Connecticut, and a number of years second and third. In 1964 and 1970 he was the National Veterans Champion. In 1952, as a guest of the Austrian Ski Association, he took part in Ski Flying at Seefeld, Austria and Obersdorf, Germany. In this country he has been instrumental in building a number of our big hills and has been an inspiration to many young jumpers. Nominated by his Ishpeming Ski Club with biographical material from Dr. Don Hurst.

FELIX C. KOZIOL — is a ski sport builder. In his 42 years with the U.S. Forest Service he developed many ski areas in the Teton National Forest. In 1934 he recognized the need for avalanche control which prompted him to scientifically research the problem. He is a co-author of the Alta Avalanche Studies and many other publications. He is also a Blegen Award recipient. He has found time to officiate at competitions and serve as secretary to the Intermountain Ski Association. His nomination is by the skiers of Alta, Utah, with biographical material from Sverre Engen.

DR. HANS KRAUS — is a ski sport builder. A medic to many ski greats and professional advisor to two presidents. Bill Kidd lauds Dr. Kraus as one who caused his World championship after a serious injury. He is also an author of ski publications. Nominated by J. N. Cooke and Lowell Thomas, Jr. with biographical material by the late Fred Elkins.

ALLISON MERRILL — is an athlete and a ski sport builder. As an athlete he was an FIS Nordic Combined Team member in the 1950s. He was National Team coach from 1954 to 1973. Nominated by the Nordic Committee and Nordic Program Director Jim Balfanz.

STRAND MIKKELSEN — is an athlete who won the national Jumping title in 1929. He set a hill record at the Greenfield Olympic Trials with a broken ski and again the Tecker Hill record fell after he jumped 257 feet. He is nominated by his biographer Enzo Serafini and friends.

SONDRE NORHEIM — is renowned as the father of modern day skiing. In the 1850s he revolutionized skiing with his invention of bindings which held the boot down securely to the ski. Also the first to design a ski with bottom and side camber. He also invented the Telemark Turn which initiated the slalom. Biographical material by Jacob Vaage, Director of the Norwegian Ski Museum and Edward Milligan of the North Dakota Historical Society.

WILLY SCHAEFFLER — is an athlete and ski-sport builder. As a junior he was Austria's four-way champion. Migrating to the United States after World War II he became Denver University's coach which won 12 National NCAA championships. He was Head Coach for our National Alpine Team from

1970 to 1973. He is a Blegen Award Recipient. Nominated by the Board of Directors of USSA, with biographical material by Chairman Lynn Johnson.

1975

RALPH G. BIETILA — The continuing 42-year ski jumping career of this two-time Olympian, FIS competitor, 1941 National Junior Champion, 1963 National Veteran Class Champion and skisport building in the Nordic venues has been and continues to be an inspiration to youth within the framework of the USSA. Ralph Bietila's flights from the nation's large-size ski trajectories reflect sportsmanship and courage. Nominee of the Ishpeming Ski Club, the biographical sketch for this "Flying Bietila" was written by Sports Writer Craig Remsburg, The Mining Journal, Marquette, Michigan.

JIMMY ELLINGSON — A skisport builder whose career as founder of the Flying Eagle Ski Club provided the coaching and competitive inspiration which sent many boys (a few girls, too) on to divisional, national and international fame. For 41 years the Flying Eagles have commanded respect in ski jumping circles, seven maturing into national senior champions and moving outward to Olympic and FIS competition. Proposed by Eau Claire ski leaders, including two Honored Ski Hall Members, Billy Olson and Snoball Severud, with biographical by Sports Editor Ron Buckli of the Leader-Telegram.

A. ANDREW HAUK — More than just a skier for 50 years, Andy Hauk has established a career of involvement — from ski club member to Olympic Games organizer, including, along the way, numerous voluntary roles in organized skisport, area development advocate, racing competitor, author, speaker, participant in ski area development and much more. Proposed by Far West Ski News Editor Russ Tiffany and Ski Writer Burt Sims, Los Angeles Examiner; the Southern Skis Ski Club and Honored Ski Hall Members Hannah Locke Carter, J. Stanley Mullin and John Elvrum. Biographical by Editor Tiffany.

SVEN JOHANSON — A list of cross-country ski races won by Sven Johanson would look like a roster of such events held in Scandinavia and North America during the past four decades. It includes the Swedish, New York, New Hampshire, Maine, Vermont, Northwest, John Craig Memorial, Donner Trail Memorial, plus the 1955 North American and the 1957 National Championships. Sven was a member of the USA's FIS Team in 1958 and the Olympic Team in 1960. He was Coach of the U.S. Army's Biathlon Training Center in Alaska and accompanied the Biathlon Team to several World Championships. He's also an all-around athlete, having won championships in many sports. Nominated by Alaska Division officials Bill McClure, Judy Moerlein, Lowell Thomas, Jr., and Major Jack Ferguson, with biographical material compiled by the latter.

STEVE.P. KNOWLTON — There is a nonpareil quality to the skisport career of Steve Knowlton. He is a ski racing champion, a promoter of skisport and, in general, has contributed 36 years to its development. A standout competitor at Holderness School and University of New Hampshire, Steve served with the 10th Mountain Division during World War Two, following which he won national and divisional alpine championships, represented the U.S. in the 1946 Olympics and 1950 FIS World Championships, and then moved on to promoting ski area development in Colorado. Proposed by Colorado ski leaders, with nominating petition by Ski Hall Honored Member Gordon Wren and the biographical by USSA Director Art Masbruch.

S. JOSEPH QUINNEY — An early-day president of the Utah Ski Club, Joe Quinney organized, conducted, officiated and judged at the many national and regional jumping contests at Ecker Hill. From this famous Ecker Hill came many of the greatest American Olympians, both Nordic and Alpine, as Utah skisport moved to Alta and other area developments. Perhaps Joe Quinney's

Felix Koziol

greatest contribution was his role in making skiing possible at Alta for millions of persons and then remaining at the helm of the operation which has always been regarded as one of the finest ski areas in the world. Nominated by a group of Intermountain Division members, including President Robert Oliver, Utah Governor Calvin Rampton, Ski Hall of Famers Alf Engen and Felix Koziol, with biographical by Editor Will Pickett of Alta Powder News.

ROBERT REID—Among the first American-born athletes to puncture the myth of eternal Scandinavian supremacy in Nordic ski competition, Bob Reid won the 1924 National Cross-Country Championship, the 1927 Canadian National Championship, many divisional cross-country events, including the 100-mile Portland, Maine; and Berlin event in 1926. Reid capped his career at 34 years of age by competing in the 1932 Winter Olympic Games. Nominated by the oldest ski club in America, the Nansen Ski Club of Berlin, Reid's biographical was written by Enzo Serafini, former editor of Eastern Skier and member of the Ski Hall Committee.

DR. MERRITT HENRY STILES—A former president of the USSA, Dr. Stiles has been heavily involved in organized skiing locally, regionally, nationally and internationally since 1958. Under his leadership the National Ski Association became known as the United States Ski Association, with its competitive programs reaching their present stature. Dr. Stiles was recipient of the 1965 Blegen Award. He continues to ski better than ever. Proposed by Miss Gloria Chadwick of Big Sky of Montana, with biographical by Ski Writer Bill Keil of the Historical Committee.

HANS STRAND—This Norwegian-American's skisport career, first as an athlete and then as a builder, stands out brightly. For 50 years Hans has been active in the competitive and ski administration roles of the Central and Eastern Divisions, with particular emphasis on the standout ski jumping programs at New York's Bear Mountain State Park. His trophy room is filled with awards, photos and other memorabilia attached to some of the nation's most famous ski trajectories. And he also can count the many ski jumpers who through his coaching, qualified for Olympic and FIS competition. Nominated by the Ramapo Ski Club, with biographical by J. H. (Red) Carruthers of the Historical Committee.

RALPH J. TOWNSEND—Coach of skiing at Williams College, the emphasis is that he be designated as both a ski athlete and skisport builder. His ski career includes national championships won, preceded by an interscholastic and intercollegiate competitive career, and followed by an active skisport building role in the Eastern Ski Association, the Eastern Intercollegiate Ski Association and the USSA and the Olympic movement. He has been an integral part of skiing in the United States for the last 35 years. Nominated by the Intercollegiate Ski Association, with biographical by Enzo Serafini of the Historical Committee.

1976

WILLIAM BANKS (BILL) BERRY—Skisport writer and historian to the USSA and Auburn Ski Club of California. Berry's continuing newspaper career extends back more than 50 years and has included skisport and general news assignments throughout the United States and Canada. A native of Potsdam, N.Y., his newspaper career began on The Ottawa (Canada) Journal and extends to feature editor of Far West Ski News.

EDMUND COUCH, JR.—Internationally-recognized ski jumping hill designer, Couch's career began as a junior through-the-ranks competitor through to long service as chairman of the USSA's ski hill engineering committee.

BYRON NISHKIAN—An up-through-the-ranks skisport administrator, Nishkian first served as president of the Yosemite Winter Club, then as director and president of the Far West Ski Association, member of the Organizing

Susan Corrock Zoberski

Committee for the 1960 Olympic Winter Games in Squaw Valley, president of the USSA and climaxed his career by organizing the 1975 Federation of International Skiing Congress in San Francisco.

KATHY KREINER—Started skiing at age three, racing at age seven. Named to World Cup team October 1971 at age 14 and competed in 1972 Olympics. With Betsy Clifford, only World Cup event winner on team (GS gold medal Pfronten, West Germany, January 1974). Has placed third two times. Also enjoys water-skiing, tennis and motor bikes. Current Canadian downhill and slalom champion.

SIGURD OVERBYE—Member of the 1924 United States Olympic Ski Team, Overbye was a noted Nordic Combined competitor, strongest at cross-country and winner of national championships in 1916, 1923 and 1926. With his election, the Ski Hall of Fame membership includes all members of the 1924 Olympic Ski Team.

ROGER PEABODY—Involved in many "firsts" of skisport, Roger Peabody's contributions ranged from top-flight alpine competition and contention for Olympic team selection through area management, long service as Executive Vice-President of the Eastern Ski Association and now as an elected member of the Eastern's Board.

HARRY G. POLLARD—National Director of the National Ski Patrol System since 1968, Harry Pollard has a skisport career dating back to 1932. A Nordic competitor during school days at the Middlesex School in Concord, Mass., he has served the USSA in numerous capacities but is best known for constant striving to make the sport better in all ways, especially in the area of safety.

JAKOB VAAGE—Considered the world's foremost ski historian, Vaage has contributed many little-known facts to enrich the historical program of the United States Ski Association. He serves as curator to the Norwegian Ski Museum at Holmenkollen and has visited the United States on three occasions to research skisport history in North America.

Special Listing of Olympic Medal Winners

BARBARA ANN COCHRAN—who won the slalom at Sapporo, Japan, in 1972.

ANNE HEGGTVEIT (HAMILTON)—who won the slalom at Squaw Valley in 1960.

JIMMY HEUGA—bronze medalist, behind Kidd, in the slalom at Innsbruck in 1964.

BILLY KIDD—silver medalist in the slalom at Innsbruck, also in 1964.

PENNY PITOU (ZIMMERMAN)—silver medalist in both the downhill and the giant slalom at Squaw Valley in 1960.

JEAN SAUBERT—silver medalist in the giant slalom and bronze medalist in the Slalom at Innsbruck in 1964.

BETSY SNITE (RILEY)—silver medalist in the slalom, also at Squaw Valley.

LUCILE WHEELER (VAUGHN)—winner of the bronze medal in downhill at Cortina, Italy, in 1956.

SUSAN CORROCK ZOBERSKI—bronze medalist in the downhill at Sapporo.

Barbara Cochran

Jimmy Heuga

Billy Kidd

SAN DIEGO'S HALL OF CHAMPIONS

San Diego, California

When your home area year after year develops such spectacular athletes as Maureen Connolly Brinker, Archie Moore, Gene Littler, Ted Williams, Billy Casper, Mickey Wright, Don Larsen and Bob Gutowski, sooner or later the idea of a San Diego Hall of Champions becomes inevitable.

Hence, it is not surprising that the Breitbard Athletic Foundation, conceived to honor hometown sports stars, got the idea first and did something about it.

To begin with, the Foundation was able to convince city and county officials that here was an idea worthy of their backing and that here was an idea which, when given life, would be a real attraction to both home folks and visitors.

As a result, the Hall of Champions became a reality in the House of Charm in Balboa Park, the remodeling being done with money allocated by the City Council and the Board of Supervisors, and by money from civic-minded individuals and firms.

The Hall itself is a thing of beauty. It has nine major displays of trophies, equipment and clothing from our greatest athletes, it has many large and small photos of historic moments in the lives of these modern-day gladiators, and it has the San Diego Hall of Fame, especially honoring this most select corps.

There are few metropolitan areas that have been the home of so many truly magnificent combatants of the sports arena.

Where else would you find the likes of the nonpareil Archie Moore, holder of the light-heavyweight crown at the advanced age of 42 (give or take a few years); where else would you find such greatness as that which flamed from the mercurial racket of "Little Mo" Connolly, beaten only by injury; and where else but in San Diego would you find a batsman like the mighty Ted Williams, the last .400 hitter in either major league, and certainly one of baseball's all-time greats?

The Hall will permanently enshrine these superstars of our town, and it is there that visitors do vicariously find the same thrill experienced by those who witnessed firsthand their matchless exploits.

—All photographs in this chapter, courtesy San Diego Hall of Champions

Florence (Flo) Chadwick enters the water to begin her historic English Channel swim. Flo ranks as the greatest long-distance woman swimmer in history Her long-remembered triumph of the English Channel came on August 18, 1950 when she crossed from France to Dover, England in 13 hours and 20 minutes. It was faster by one hour and 19 minutes than the record set 24 years earlier by the storied Gertrude Ederle. A 54 x 40 enlargement of this picture is on display in the Hall.

And, of course, as the years roll by, new heroes of the gridiron, track, court, ring and diamond will rise to put their name on the same level as those whose names are already legend.

The Hall then is not only a "sports museum," but a living monument to the American way of life as exemplified by our sweat-shirted heroes. And, in San Diego, we have had so many.

The Hall was opened January 10, 1961 with a large civic ceremony in adjacent Alcazar Gardens attended by top-ranking dignitaries, many members of the Hall of Fame and hundreds of interested sports fans. By late 1967, nearly 700,000 persons had visited the Hall including Music Man's Meredith Willson, Batsman Ted Williams, Sportswriter Joe Williams, the Sporting New's Taylor Spink and many other noted figures visiting San Diego.

HOW HALL OF FAME SELECTIONS ARE MADE

All members are elected by the Board of Governors of the Breitbard Athletic Foundation. Before their election, however, a Hall of Fame committee goes over lists of 50 or more possible choices, and after research and discussion nominates five candidates (each year) for the Board to vote upon. The Board is expected to elect at least one "old-timer" — a candidate from the 1900–1935 era—and at least one from the modern era, since 1935. Not more than three may be elected in a single year. The Committee and the Board are scrupulously thorough in their research and their deliberation before they vote.

HALL OF CHAMPIONS

Jim Londos, all-time greatest professional wrestler, world champion for 14 years, 1930-1944, and 1946.

Dr. William McColl, all-American end Stanford University, 1950, 1951; great pro star, Chicago Bears, 1952-59.

LANCE ALWORTH – All-time American Football League wide receiver, holder of AFL and San Diego Charger all-time receiving records. *(Inducted 1972)*

STAN BARNES – University of California 1920 "Wonder Team," National Football Hall of Fame. *(Inducted 1970)*

RAY "IKE" BOONE – Major league infielder 13 years, twice member of American League All-Star game. *(Inducted 1973)*

MAUREEN CONNOLLY BRINKER – The "Little Mo" who won three world titles at Wimbledon. *(Elected 1956)*

EARLE BRUCKER – Great catcher and coach of Philadelphia Athletics. *(Elected 1960)*

LEO CALLAND – USC captain, unpaid coach and "Player of Game" 1923 Rose Bowl game. *(Inducted 1974)*

BILL CASPER, JR. – 1959 and 1966 U.S. Open Golf champion, San Diego's first. *(Elected 1962)*

FLORENCE CHADWICK – English Channel record holder. *(Elected 1961)*

ROBERT ELLIOTT – Most valuable player in National League in 1947 driving in 113 runs for Boston. *(Elected 1966)*

DR. DAVE FREEMAN – Unquestionably the greatest badminton player of all time. *(Elected 1958)*

EDWIN V. GODDARD – All American at Washington State College in 1934 and 1935 . . . great all-around player. *(Elected 1963)*

ROBERT GUTOWSKI – World record holder pole vault, 15 feet, 8¼ inches, April 27, 1957. *(Elected 1964)*

REAR ADMIRAL THOMAS J. HAMILTON – U.S. Naval Academy All-American halfback in 1926. Coach of West Coast Navy team which won three All-Service football championships from 1931

through 1933; later coached and was athletic director of Naval Academy. *(Inducted 1976)*

BUD HELD – World record holder, javelin, 268 feet, 2½ inches, May 20, 1953. *(Inducted 1968)*

EVELYN BOLDRICK HOWARD – 1940 and 1942 U.S. national singles badminton champion and Uber Cup Committee member. *(Inducted 1975)*

DON LARSEN – The only man to pitch a perfect World Series game . . . Oct. 8, 1956. *(Elected 1963)*

GENE LITTLER – 1953 U.S. Amateur and 1961 U.S. Open Golf champion. *(Elected 1962)*

JIM LONDOS – All-time greatest professional wrestler, world champion for 14 years, 1930–1944, and 1946. *(Elected 1966)*

OLIN CORT MAJORS – Captain Univ. of California "Wonder Team" of 1920, one of Cal's all-time great athletes. *(Elected 1966)*

DR. WILLIAM McCOLL – All American End, Stanford University, 1950, 1951; great pro star, Chicago Bears, 1952–59. *(Elected 1964)*

BILL MILLER – 1932 Olympic Games pole vault champion. *(Elected 1957)*

BILL MILLS – 1964 Olympic 10,000-meter champion. *(Inducted 1970)*

RON MIX – 1960 through 1968, and 1968 AFL-NFL All-Pro team. *(Inducted 1975)*

ARCHIE MOORE – World's light-heavyweight boxing champion. *(Elected 1956)*

DR. "BRICK" MULLER – All-Time All-American end of California's "Wonder Team" era. *(Elected 1953)*

FLORENCE CHAMBERS NEWKIRK – 1924 Olympic bronze swimming medal; 1951, 1953, 1955 English Channel swimmer. *(Inducted 1971)*

LOWELL NORTH – 1968 Olympic Star Class sailing champion. *(Inducted 1969)*

"MILKY" PHELPS – San Diego State's greatest cager, and a "Little All-American". *(Elected 1955)*

CLARENCE PINKSTON – San Diego's first Olympic champion – in 1920. *(Elected 1962)*

REUBEN "RUBE" POWELL – National archery champion, 1951, '52, '53, '56, member of National Archery Hall of Fame. *(Inducted 1974)*

LEE RAMAGE – Met the very best light heavyweight and heavyweights of his day for professional record of 72–12–1. *(Inducted 1972)*

PAUL RUNYAN – Two-time PGA and PGA World's Seniors champion, member Golf's Hall of Fame. *(Elected 1965)*

RUSS SAUNDERS – All-time Trojan halfback of the late '20s. *(Elected 1960)*

AMBY SCHINDLER – USC All-American quarterback 1937, "Player of Game" 1940 Rose Bowl and 1940 College All-Star game. *(Inducted 1973)*

BOB SKINNER – 13 years in National League. Played in two World Series, helping Pittsburgh beat New York Yankees in 1960 and St. Louis beat the Yankees in 1964. Was on NL All-Star teams in 1958, '60 and '62. *(Inducted 1976)*

HAROLD "DUTCH" SMITH – 1932 Olympic high-diving champion. *(Inducted 1969)*

ALBERT BRYAN SPROTT – "Pesky" Sprott, Univ. of California 1920 "Wonder Team" star and great track man. *(Elected 1963)*

WILLIE STEELE – 1948 Olympic Games broadjump champion. *(Elected 1958)*

KAREN HANTZE SUSMAN – 17 U.S. national tennis titles, 1962 Wimbledon women's singles champion. *(Inducted 1971)*

"COTTON" WARBURTON – Mercurial All-American USC quarterback of "Thundering Herd" days. *(Elected 1959)*

TED WILLIAMS – All-time great major league batter. *(Elected 1954)*

"MICKEY" WRIGHT – Six national titles make her all-time greatest woman golfer. *(Elected 1961)*

Ted Williams, the splendid splinter, hits one of his 521 home runs off Mike Garcia, August 31, 1953. One of the all-time greatest sluggers of baseball displays the classic swing familiar to major league fans and players. Williams is the third-ranking home run hitter of all-time with 521, hit .344 for 16 full seasons in the major leagues (all with the Boston Red Sox), won the American League batting title six times, is the last man to hit .400 (.406 in 1941), was named Most Valuable Player in the AL in 1946 and 1949. In 1960, his final year, Williams, then 42, hit .316 and was named Player of the Decade by Taylor Spink in the Sporting News.

SOFTBALL
HALL OF FAME

Oklahoma City, Oklahoma

By Hugh Scott and Dave Hill

T he history of sports has been marked by the occasional appearance of an athlete who seems to have been touched by a magical hand, whose extraordinary skills are embellished by an intangible spark of greatness, an athlete who seems destined to leave an indelible stamp on his or her chosen avocation. Such are the men and women enshrined in the Softball Hall of Fame.

Greatness assumes many shapes and forms, like subtle colors blending into a deep blue hue, but in any form greatness separates the legends from the mere mortals in the arena of sport. Proficiency and skill can be honed by practice and dedication but the really outstanding athletes, the Hall of Famers, come to the arena with greatness already programmed into their personalities.

The purpose of the Softball Hall of Fame is to honor and give recognition to those men and women who have played so brilliantly and competed so well during their careers and while doing so have contributed to the development and growth of the sport.

The birth of the Softball Hall of Fame took place in Mesa, Arizona during the ASA Commissioner's Council Meeting in January 1957. Preliminary work to set out procedures and regulations was done by a special committee headed by Smith Barrier, then softball commissioner from North Carolina.

The original and permanent Hall of Fame Committee included Charles McCord, chairman, members Ford Hoffman, Charles Walker, Bruce Campbell, Miss Lou Hamilton, Nick Barack, Pierce Gahan, Joe Barber, Miss Jimmie Mims, James Lewis and B. E. Martin, ex officio.

During the meeting in Mesa the proposed rules and procedures as prepared by Barrier's committee were adopted that included limiting the number of admissions the first year to five men and two women, no more than seven to be admitted in 1958 and no more than five in the years 1959 and 1960. After that a maximum of three would be eligible each year.

A display of modern softball bats in the Hall of Fame.

An interior view of some of the displays including various balls and a modern uniform.

However, during the Mesa meeting it was decided that special distinction should be given the first year and that honors would go to only four nominees out of fifteen candidates which included eleven men and four women who had been proposed. The four nominees chosen to be the first ever Hall of Famers of amateur softball were elected in the following order; Harold "Shifty" Gears of Rochester, New York, Sam "Sambo" Elliott of Decatur, Georgia, Amy Peralta Shelton of Tempe, Arizona, and Marie Wadlow of Peoria, Illinois.

The maximum of three candidates making the Hall of Fame each year stood up until 1972 when the Hall of Fame Committee recommended to the Commissioner's Council that the maximum number be increased to five and that beginning in 1973 12-inch slow pitch players be considered for admission. Up to 1972 only fast pitch players were considered and eligible for Hall of Fame recognition.

One of the very first requisites for consideration as a nominee is that a player must have been retired from active competition at least three years. The length of playing time at a national level is also an important consideration; however there is no minimum playing time required.

After a candidate is nominated he or she must still pass the close inspection and scrutiny of the Hall of Fame Committee. To be elected to the Hall of Fame a nominee must receive at least three-fourths vote of the committee members present and voting. No candidate may be elected with less than five committee members present. After going through that, the respective candidates must then pass the final clearance of approval by the one hundred plus Commissioner's Council.

In order to be nominated a player must have his or her candidacy submitted by the ASA commissioner from the area where the candidate resides or played during his or her career.

—All photographs in this chapter, courtesy Amateur Softball Hall of Fame

HALL OF FAMERS

The date shown at the end of each biography indicates the year of enshrinement.

JOHN BAKER (Westport, Connecticut) pitcher — Started playing softball while in grade school at the age of 11 and before he hung it up he had competed in top competition for 26 years. He retired after the 1953 season.

He appeared in four National Tournaments and established a 6 – 2 mark. His pitching accounted for some 780 victories and he lost only 120 games. He registered 58 no-hitters and struck out more than 10,000 batters during his career. 1961

VIRGINIA BUSICK (Fresno, California) pitcher — Started playing softball in 1937, took four years out during World War II, with her pitching efforts spanning 17 years.

The first time she played "Big League" softball came when she joined the Fresno Rockets in 1946. She stayed with them until 1951 and came back in 1957. Her pitches were blazing fast, and were timed at 103 miles an hour. 1971

ESTELLE CAITO (Phoenix, Arizona) second base — Retired from softball in 1965 after a 25-year career. She played in nine National Tournaments and was a star for the Orange Lionettes when they won three National Championships in 1955, 1956 and 1962. 1973

TOM CASTLE (Rochester, N.Y.) first base — He had a spectacular .340 batting average in his career in softball.

In 1936, when Castle joined Kodak, they won the National Championship and four years later repeated the same feat, the only team in the Eastern part of the nation to accomplish that mark. 1964

JIM CHAMBERS (Oshkosh, Wisconsin) pitcher — In one National Tournament game in 1946 he struck out 43 men and fanned 117 during the tourney. In his career, he struck out 4,380 batters and counted 209 no-hitters.

He hurled the Chicago Match Corp. team to two runner-up spots in National Tournaments. 1966

JEANNE CONTEL (Fresno, California) third base — Joined the Fresno Rockets in 1951 and for the next 14 years, she played in 11 National Tournaments.

She was honored with an All-American selection in 1953, 1955, 1957 and 1963. 1969

BEN CRAIN (Omaha, Nebraska) pitcher — Every sport has an "Iron Man" of one sort or another and Ben Crain could very well be considered in that area.

To show how strong he was, he pitched close to 1,000 games in his career, with an 85 per cent won-lost record. He was powerful at the plate as well, stroking an average of 20 round trippers a year, boosting over 300 out of the park in the plate appearances that wound up with a shining .375 batting average. 1961

JERRY CURTIS (Clearwater, Florida) outfielder — Started pitching in 1949 in City League Softball with Gulf Lumber. He joined the Clearwater Bombers in 1951 and was a regular infielder until 1960. He moved to the outfield until 1964 and managed the Bombers in 1966 and 1967. He played for the Bombers when they won seven of their nine championships. 1972

FRANK DE LUCA (Stratford, Connecticut) pitcher & infielder — Honored for his outstanding play in the Industrial Slow Pitch ranks. DeLuca actually started his career in fast pitch in 1945 and continued until 1958. At that time, he switched to Industrial Slow Pitch and his career really began to soar.

To support his credentials as a pitcher, DeLuca compiled a pitching record of 737 wins and just 121 losses. And to prove that pitchers can also swing a bat, his lifetime batting average was .484. 1974

MARGARET DOBSON (Portland, Oregon) third base — To be the leading hitter in a National Tournament is an accomplishment in itself, and when you stroke a .615 that's even better. That's what Margaret Dobson did when she was playing with the Erv Lind Florists in 1950.

She played in nine National Tournaments and was always one of the top fielders on the scene. 1964

SAM ELLIOTT (Decatur, Georgia) pitcher — His first taste of softball competition was in 1934 at the age of 22; he went on to play for 21 seasons appearing during that time in seven regionals and six National Tournaments. During his 21 years of competition Elliott pitched a total of 1,133 games, won 1,046 and lost only 87.

Winning the state championship his first year out put him and his teammates in the then "world" championship being held in Chicago. It didn't take long for Elliott or his teammates to realize they were in fast company; they lost their first game and were out of the tournament. 1957

ROBERT FORBES (Clearwater, Florida) outfielder — The youngest player ever to don the uniform of the Bombers. In fact he was the youngest in the history of the famous organization . . . just 14 years old.

His best National Tournament, the third of his career, came in 1956 when the Bombers captured their third title and he was named to the All Tournament honors for the third time. 1966

HAROLD GEARS (Rochester, New York) pitcher — Began as a sandlotter back in 1922, moving up quickly from playground competition to city league play. In 1928 he drew attention by winning 45 games in a row. His ability to find the plate and his uncanny analysis of opposing batsmen contributed to his meteoric success. 1957

He started playing at the age of 14, and it goes without saying that his record in national championship play is impressive. (20 wins, 6 losses, 15 shutouts, 242 strikeouts, 3 no-hitters), but save your breath for his lifetime exploits. The amazing recapitulation shows 866 victories and 115 defeats. Of the 981 games in which he has played, 373 have been shutouts and 61 of them no-hitters. En route he fanned exactly 13,244 batters. 1957

WARREN GERBER (Cleveland, Ohio) pitcher — Fireball Gerber's softball career started at the age of 13; a schoolboy whiz, his career spanned 17 years of top notch competition during which time he recorded over 500 wins including some 50 no-hitters. 1960

Margaret Dobson

Sam "Sambo" Elliott

Ambidextrous pitcher Harold "Shifty" Gears

BETTY EVANS GRAYSON (Portland, Oregon) pitcher—Her softball ability was spotted at an early age when she was a mainstay on a boys' team in Glencoe Grade School. At 13, she played city league ball and was good enough with her hitting and fielding to be named to the city all-star team.

During her career she racked up 465 wins against only 99 losses. She pitched in five National Championships with the Lind Florists. In 1945 she pitched 115 consecutive scoreless innings. Fifty-one no-hitters were registered by Grayson during her career, three were perfect games. 1959

Carolyn Thome Hart

PAT HARRISON (Stratford, Connecticut) outfielder—Played for eleven years with the South Hill Queens of Vancouver, British Columbia; the Erv Lind Florists of Portland, Oregon and the Raybestos Brakettes of Stratford, Connecticut.

Harrison compiled a lifetime batting average of .303 before retiring in 1972. She participated in eleven National Tournaments and was named to the All-American team in 1966, 1968 and 1970 and picked for the second team in 1963. 1976

CAROLYN THOME HART (Pekin, Illinois) outfielder—She led Pekin in hitting three years and was runner-up four other times. She was named All American four times. 1966

LEROY HESS (Aurora, Illinois) catcher—It is often said that the best place for a player to see the whole action of a softball game is behind the plate. That was the spot that Leroy Hess had as he managed and played with the Stephens-Adamson Sealmasters for 17 years.

Hess played in four National Tournaments and was his team's manager in the 1958 trip to the big event. 1968

JOHN HUNTER (Clearwater, Florida) pitcher—If you had to find another nickname besides "Big John" for John Hunter you might call him "Mr. MVP." The powerful pitcher of the Bombers won that laurel so many times in National Tournaments, that his trophy case sparkled with the rewards.

His lifetime chart shows 275 wins and 19 losses and his strike out average was just under 2 per inning. Hunter never lost in state or regional competition. 1963

Hugh "Lefty" Johnston

HUGH JOHNSTON (Orlando, Florida) first base—A big, powerful Irishman, who played most of his softball years with the Zollner Pistons, Johnston was a craftsman at first base as well as powerful with the bat.

The big, left-handed first baseman was born in Belfast, Ireland in 1916 and didn't really get down to serious softball until he was 22 years old. 1961

CHARLES JUSTICE (Detroit, Michigan) pitcher—Few persons in the history of softball can touch the record that Charlie Justice has achieved. His overall pitching record was 873 wins and 92 losses. Although his hitting figures are missing in part, he would be classified as a man "with a big stick."

Charlie Justice is truly a great man . . . a great pitcher, a great hitter, a great teacher. And probably one of the greatest softball ambassadors of all time. 1974

BERNIE KAMPSCHMIDT (Ft. Wayne, Indiana) catcher—Considered by most the greatest catcher in softball, Kampschmidt not only was strong defensively but was a standout clutch hitter.

He played in more than 2,500 games. During his career with the Pistons, which spanned 15 years, the team played 1,442 games, winning 1,253 of them. In 1942 the Pistons were 99–2. 1959

KATHRYN "SIS" KING (Shelton, Connecticut) catcher & outfielder—In three years with the Brakettes, she had an overall .322 batting average. One of the all-time sluggers of the game, King never batted under .300 with Phoenix in the Pacific Coast Women's League. In five of the six National Tournaments

One of the electronic displays in the museum.

she played in, King was voted to the first All-American team . . . 1959, 1962, 1963, 1964 and 1965.

The Connecticut resident represented the United States in the 1st World Softball Championship in 1965 at Melbourne, Australia. In 1967, she represented the U.S. at the Pan American Games in Winnipeg, Canada. 1975

CLYDE KIRKENDALL (Findlay, Ohio) pitcher — Passed away in 1957. His career spanned 25 years of top competition that included competing in eleven national tournaments. He was a member of five national champion teams.

He still holds several national records including pitching the longest number of innings in a game — 33; he struck out 67 during that game. He pitched 167 no-hit games during his career including eight no-hitters in national tournament play. In the first 10 games he pitched in national tourney play he gave up just one run. His lifetime won-lost record was 1,144 wins and 52 losses. 1959

NINA KORGAN (New Orleans, Louisiana) pitcher — In 1935 she started on a pitching career that would, over a period of fourteen years, record pitching feats that won six National Championships. 1960

RONALD KRONEWITTER (Mishawaka, Indiana) pitcher — There are a number of softball players in the sport today who have never heard of the 14 inch softball, but Hall of Famer Kronewitter played his first three years with this size ball as a pitcher.

In a three-year span he won 55 games and lost only seven playing with the East End Pirates two years and the Doc Gross Specials one year. The next three years, with the standard 12-inch ball, he compiled 53 wins including 10 no-hitters, as opposed to five setbacks. 1967

MARJORIE LAW (Tempe, Arizona) pitcher, outfielder, infielder — Played for the Phoenix Ramblers for 18 years and helped her team win three ASA National Championships. She was the only player to have been selected to the All-American team at three different positions. 1975

AL LINDE (Midland, Michigan) pitcher-outfielder — Better known for his pitching prowess than for his hitting, Linde, during his twenty-year career in top competition, holds the distinction of having been named to the All-American team as both a pitcher and outfielder.

Linde, who has posted more than 200 no-hit games during his career, pitched a total of 240 innings in 1946 and struck out 438 batters. 1958

Amy Peralta May

Kay Rich

B. E. MARTIN (Newark, N.J.) ASA Executive Secretary-Treasurer — Dedication was one of the key elements in the personality of Martin. In his years of activities, he helped get many projects off the ground. He was one of the founders of the Amateur Softball Association and helped guide it through some of the early days of existence. 1963

AMY PERALTA MAY (Tempe, Arizona) pitcher — Played with the Ramblers of Phoenix, Arizona from 1938 through 1951. An all-sports star at Tempe High School, May's first season with the Ramblers was as an outfielder and bench warmer.

May pitched more than 500 games during her career, 300 of them shut-outs and 50 no-hitters. When she was not pitching for the Ramblers she played the outfield and was considered one of the best hitters in softball. She batted cleanup for the Ramblers for ten years. 1957

GLORIA MAY (Fresno, California) first base — In 10 of 15 National Tournaments, she played errorless ball. She handled more than 400 chances in National Tournament play and made only four errors. She is high on the list as one of the all-time defensive first basemen. 1973

CLARENCE MILLER (Memphis, Tennessee) pitcher — Born in 1923, started his softball career in 1940 which saw him garner All-American recognition on three different occasions, 1948, 1952 and 1954. He retired after the '55 season. 1960

JAMES RAMAGE (Fort Wayne, Indiana) shortstop — One of organized softball's greatest shortstops, Jim Ramage's career got off to an early start when, as a youngster of 18, he played in his very first year of major competition with Nick Carr Boosters, who went on to win the National Championship in 1939.

Ramage compiled a lifetime batting mark of .293 in softball's toughest competition. He led the old National Softball League in home runs in 1948 and 1951. During his career he was named to a number of All-American and All-Star teams. 1960

DONALD RARDIN (Lexington, Kentucky) pitcher & infielder — The only man in ASA history to play on championship teams in both the Open Slow and Industrial Slow Pitch divisions. In fact, he was a member of five National Championship teams.

His years in industrial play were as a pitcher but Rardin was an infielder in Open competition. He compiled a lifetime batting average of .606 and had a lifetime pitching record of 234 wins and 39 defeats. Rardin played in over 2400 organized softball games. 1975

MYRON REINHARDT (Alexandria, Kentucky) outfielder — Retired from active play in 1968. Selected as the first Slow Pitch player to the Hall of Fame in 1973, he played for South Ward Boosters of Newport, Ky. in 1948, '49, and '50. The Boosters, a fast pitch team, won three straight Kentucky titles and placed fifth in the 1949 National Fast Pitch Tournament at Little Rock, Arkansas.

Reinhardt switched to slow pitch in 1950 and proceeded to make All American five times, played in 11 of the first 13 slow pitch National Tournaments and played on five National Championship teams. 1973

KAY RICH (Fresno, California) outfielder-infielder — One of the finest gal softball players to don spikes and a glove is Kay Rich, who played her top flight softball on the Pacific Coast.

Over nine years in the Pacific Coast Women's Softball League, one of the strongest in the country, she had a lifetime .312 batting average. This was built on 375 hits in 1,201 trips to the plate. 1963

DON ROPP (Aurora, Illinois) third base — During his last 13 years with Sealmaster he compiled a .325 lifetime batting mark while continually facing one of the most rugged softball schedules in the country. He holds team records for a single season in doubles (25), triples (11), and walks (44) and is runner-up in single season marks in hits, runs, home runs and RBI's and stolen bases.

In 912 games, Don connected for 864 base hits, including 131 home runs. He received 377 walks in his career while striking out only 274 times, one of only two regulars on the club ever to walk more than strike out. He batted in the cleanup position throughout his last 14 years and was team captain during the last eleven. 1972

RUTH SEARS (Santa Ana, California) first base — Her career in softball started in 1936 with the Green Cat Cafe in the Santa Ana City league. She was one of the original members of the famed Orange Lionettes starring with the Lionettes from 1937 until her retirement in 1955.

Born in Canada, she boasted a lifetime batting average in major competition of .425. She batted .585 with Orange in her first season and led the team in hitting every year with the exception of two. 1960

Ruth Sears

ALBERTA KOHLS SIMS (Alexandria, Kentucky) outfielder — Played left field for the Dana Gardens team of Cincinnati, Ohio for eleven straight years.

Sims was selected to the All-American team in 1961, 1962, 1963 and 1964 and in 1964 was named the Most Valuable Player. She led the Dana Gardens team to three straight National ASA Championships, 1962–1964. 1976

BOBBY SPELL (Lake Charles, Louisiana) pitcher — Established many records but his record of having given up only one earned run in the first $159\frac{2}{3}$ innings of national tournament competition may never be equaled. In national tournament competition, Bobby Spell pitched $205\frac{1}{2}$ innings, gave up only eight earned runs, a liftime earned run average in national tournament play of .272, struck out 258 batters and compiled an 18–9 record. Spell retired as an active player in 1970. 1976

BOB SPRENTALL (Clearwater, Florida) outfielder — He was so good in the outfield that he was named to the All-American team four times and helped the Bombers win five of their eight National Championships.

He was named to that select All-American crew in 1955, 1956, 1957 and 1960. 1968

JOHN SPRING (Aurora, Illinois) pitcher — From 1963 through July of 1966, he pitched for the Sealmasters of Aurora, Ill., where he won 76 and lost 5 and was a member of their 1965 National Championship team.

Here is how his record book looks: he played on five National Championship teams (Briggs 1952–53, Raybestos Cardinals 1955–58, Aurora 1965); in 1952, pitched Briggs to World Industrial Championship; in 1955, pitched Ft. Monmouth, N. J., to All Army Championship; averaged five no-hitters per season over the 17 years; 17 consecutive National Tournaments; National Tournament Record; Won 41, Lost 12; National All-American Team, 1952, '53, '54, '55, '56, '58, '62, '63; National All-American 2nd team, 1959, '61; ASA Clinics, 1956, 1962 in Europe; ASA Clinic, 1961, Far East; Lifetime pitching record — won 483, lost 62. 1970

ROY STEPHENSON (Muttontown, N.Y.) pitcher — During his career, he played in four State Tournaments, compiling a record of 15 victories and two losses. On the Regional Tourney level, he took part in 15 of these affairs, stacking up a total of 40 victories and three defeats. 1965

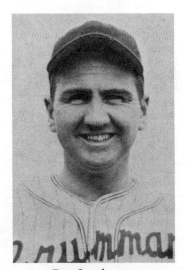

Roy Stephenson

MICKEY STRATTON (Stratford, Connecticut) catcher — During her 10 years of play with the Raybestos Brakettes, Mickey helped the Stratford, Conn. girls to four National Championships and was named to the National All-Star team five times. 1969

BERTHA TICKEY (Stratford, Connecticut) pitcher — In 23 years of pitching Bertha won 757 and lost 88. She has hurled 162 no-hit, no-run games. She was named 18 times to the National All-Star Team and eight times was chosen the Most Valuable Player of the Tournament. 1972

An alcove in the Hall of Fame showing photo portraits of members and an account of their achievements.

RICHARD TOMLINSON (Clearwater, Florida) shortstop — After moving from Montreal to Clearwater in 1959, Rickey Tomlinson became one of the all-time great players for the Clearwater Bombers.

In ten years with the Bombers, he led the club in hitting seven times. He was the first Bomber player to achieve 100 hits in a season, and had a .345 career batting average with the Bombers. During the years he was with the team, he batted .384 in 1967 for a career high. 1973

M. MARIE WADLOW (Peoria, Illinois) pitcher — Started her softball career with the Tabernacle Baptist Church of St. Louis in 1929 and completed her outstanding softball activity in 1950 with the famous Caterpillar Dieselettes. 1957

PAT WALKER (Orlando, Florida) outfielder — Named to the All-American team in 1966 and 1968 and was picked for the second team in 1961. In sixteen years of competition, she compiled a lifetime batting average of .314. Walker did do a limited amount of pitching and compiled a 47–24 record with an ERA of 1.92. 1976

BILL WEST (Ft. Wayne, Indiana) pitcher — How would you like to say that you pitched and won 32 games in a row in major competition? That is only one of the outstanding marks of Bill West, who played the biggest part of his softball career with the Zollner Pistons.

During his 10 years with the Pistons, West was considered the No. 1 pitcher. He combined two basic essentials . . . blazing speed and remarkable control. In 1946 and '47 his record was 60–6 against the best in the U.S. and Canada. 1968

NOLAN WHITLOCK (Rossville, Georgia) shortstop — There is no doubt in the minds of most people who have followed the game of softball over the years that Nolan Whitlock could be called "Mr. Shortstop" of the sport. 1967

RAY WICKERSHAM (Palatine, Illinois) outfielder — For 11 straight years he batted in the third position, which many managers consider the spot for the best sticker on the team. His power at the plate was well known and he compiled a batting average of .290 in his career, and was above the .300 mark in his last four seasons.

M. Marie Wadlow

In 617 games with the Sealmasters, he compiled 527 hits, including 67 home runs, and drove in 159 runs. He collected 181 walks while striking out only 173 times, one of only two Sealmasters who had more walks than strike-outs. 1971

DOT WILKINSON (Phoenix, Arizona) catcher—Considered the greatest woman softball catcher of all time, she did it the hard way, using a five-fingered glove, rather than the normal catcher's mitt. She played softball for over a quarter of a century and was named 19 times to the All-American team. 1970

FRANKIE WILLIAMS (Detroit, Michigan) second base—In 1964, he became the first player in the Atlantic Seaboard Major Softball League to ever hit over .400 when he posted a .423 average. In seven of the 10 years with the Cardinals, he was the Team's batting champion: 1957, .404; 1960, .330; 1961, .375; 1962, .369; 1973, .370; 1964, .430; 1965, .412.
He holds four of the All-Time Cardinal Individual Season Records: Most Runs Scored, 77; Most Hits, 103; Hitting Streak, 23; and three .400 seasons. 1970

BILLY WOJIE (New Haven, Connecticut) third base—During his playing career, he played with Columbus Auto Body Bears, New Haven Raybestos Cardinals and Stratford. In his seven years with the Cardinals, he hit .286. He won the batting title in 1955 and '56 with .312 and .290 averages. He was All New England six years and played in eight National Tournaments. 1967

JOHN ZEIGLER (Miami, Florida) outfielder—Between 1947 and 1965 Zeigler was one of the most amazing players to compete in ASA competition. He performed in 10 National Tournaments and was selected to the All-American team in 1952 and he led his Miami American Industrial Sales team to the finals. And, again, in 1960 as his key hits were primarily responsible for the Bombers winning the championship. Zeigler competed in National Tournaments in 1949, '50, '51, '52, '53, '55, '57, '58, '60 and '61. 1971

Nolan Whitlock

HALL OF HONOR • MANNER OF SELECTION

*The ASA has established a Hall of Honor. An individual may be selected for the Hall of Honor in any one of five categories. One is for **Umpires** who have umpired for at least fifteen years and have worked in at least five ASA National Tournaments; **Managers** who have been in their position for at least fifteen years and have managed teams in at least five ASA National Tournaments; **Sponsors** who have been active for at least ten years and have had at least four of their teams qualify for ASA National Tournaments; **ASA Commissioners** who have held their position for at least fifteen years. The final category is **Meritorious Service** and includes any combination of the four previous categories. This category can also be used to honor an organizer or financial contributor to softball.*

A total of sixteen individuals were named to the Hall of Honor in 1976.

COMMISSIONERS	UMPIRES	SPONSORS
Nick Barack	George Dickstein	William S. Simpson
Columbus, OH	Forest Hills, NY	Bridgeport, CT
Fred Hoffman	Bernard Iassogna	Charles Hurd
St. Joseph, MO	Bridgeport, CT	Aurora, IL
Elinar Nelson	Art Solz	Fred Zollner
Minneapolis, MN	Minneapolis, MN	Ft. Wayne, IN
W. W. Kethan	Ray Ernst	William J. Pharr
Houston, TX	Cincinnati, OH	McAdenville, NC

MERITORIOUS SERVICE	MANAGERS
Leo Fischer	Commie Currens
Chicago, IL	Cincinnati, OH
Raymond Johnson	Bill Fenton
Nashville, TN	Seattle, WA

THE INTERNATIONAL SWIMMING HALL OF FAME

Fort Lauderdale, Florida

By Buck Dawson and Richard Mullins

Astronaut Dave Scott (left) and Fred Schmidt at Hall of Fame ceremonies.

The most beautifully situated of all the Halls of Fame is the International Swimming Hall of Fame, located on a palm-lined peninsula one block from the ocean, extending into the Intracoastal Waterway, just north of the Bahia Mar Yacht Basin in Fort Lauderdale, Forida.

The Swimming Hall of Fame became "International" during the 1968 Olympics when representatives of the 97 nations programming competitive swimming, diving, water polo and synchronized swimming made it the first International Hall of Fame. The new museum building was dedicated that same year by Dr. Harold Henning, President of FINA, christening the new building with a ceramic crock of water from the Mexico City Olympic pool.

The Swimming Hall of Fame differs from other halls in that it is not only the shrine, museum and library for international swimming, but the complex has an Olympic-sized pool which hosts more national and international swimming, diving competitions than anywhere else in the world.

Could Mark Spitz have beaten Johnny Weissmuller in a swimming race? Is Klaus Dibiasi a greater diver than Pete Desjardins? How would John Naber fare against Adolph Kiefer? Is it true that today's women swimmers are faster than the men of the 1920s? What have humans learned from fish? Who are the Olympic medalists in swimming over the past half century?

These are just a few of the typical questions put to guides at the International Swimming Hall of Fame by some of the 40,000 visitors who tour the swim shrine each year. Almost always they get an informed answer because this complex, situated on a dramatic waterfront site in Fort Lauderdale, Florida, is the world mecca for aquatics.

Introducing the "Swimathon"

The Hall of Fame was built by a grant by the City of Fort Lauderdale and an auditorium wing donated by John E. duPont. As is the pattern with most of the halls of fame, the first years of financing depended on a few dedicated men and never quite made it; but a scheme called "Swimathon" was devised in 1973, which allows thousands of children to donate a penny a length they swim to support the Hall of Fame. Since this plan was introduced, the Hall of Fame and its programs, including exhibits, upkeep and administration, have been solvent and virtually supported by thousands of swimmers everywhere.

Tours are 10:00 4:00 every day. The museum is open 365 days a year with exhibits that range from the world's largest sports stamp collection to the world's smallest trophy. There are 12-ft. high murals of the great moments in the sport, and most of the sculpture that is significant and interesting to swimmers. For those who want action, a small admission charge gets a swim in the same pool that so many champions have trained in, including Johnny Weissmuller.

Induction Ceremonies

The Induction Ceremonies for the new Honorees takes place each April and exhibits cover the medals and records of 169 Honorees from Johnny Weissmuller to Mark Spitz. There is a Hawaiian waterfall in the entranceway where Arthur Godfrey eulogizes Duke Kahanamoku, who, like Johnny, is lifelike in wax. Other exhibits include Mark Spitz, Esther

President Gerald Ford being presented with plaque by Executive Director Buck Dawson.

Standing see-through cases and various displays.

Williams, Buster Crabbe, Don Schollander, Adolph Kiefer, Eleanor Holm and Capt. Matthew Webb, the man who first swam the English Channel in 1875.

Olympic medals from ancient Greece to the present are shown under glass with the highlights of each Games and the autographed swimsuits worn by the recent gold medal swimmers.

Beautiful and unusual trophies are displayed in standing see-through cases around the carpeted center shrine area where people can sit and look around them at the FINA Prize Eminence, the sports sculpture of Princeton's Prof. Joe Brown, and many many others dating from a swimming fresco dated 850 B.C. from the Palace of the Nimrods and a diving figure in bronze dated 480 B.C. found in Southern Italy. In the Swimming Hall of Fame, you can also see how to do it in murals, movies and in a modern library complete with books dating from 1600, one by Benjamin Franklin.

The Hall is proud of the fact that Astronaut Dave Scott was a competitive swimmer at Michigan and West Point; and that Olympic gold medalist Fred Schmidt was the frogman who first got to, and opened, the capsule on the last three moon drops — the longest dives on record from the moon to the middle of the Pacific Ocean. Both Scott and Schmidt have visited the Hall, and the street around the complex was renamed "Hall of Fame Drive" in a ceremony that included the astronaut and Buster Crabbe, who as "Flash Gordon" joked that he was the first to the moon.

Julius Caesar, Lord Byron, Winston Churchill, Franklin Roosevelt, John Quincy Adams, Charlemagne, Chairman Mao and former President Gerald Ford are among those people who found swimming an important part of their life.

The Hall even compares fish and the Olympic swimmers who swam like fish in an exhibit of stingrays and turtles and porpoises, with Spitz and others doing something very like the fish are doing. The story of swimmer Ernest Hemingway and "The Old Man and the Sea" is shown complete with the great marlin, with stand-in "Stubby" Kruger doing the aquatic scenes for Spencer Tracy. With all the huge trophies, there is also the world's smallest, says Believe It or Not Ripley. It's a gold thimble mounted on a gold collar button and it belonged to the late R. Max Ritter, Olympic swimmer and later the International President of FINA who actually wore the collar button.

Many Unique Features

How does this Hall of Fame pack 2800 years of swimming into one museum? Through a series of mushrooms labeled to cover the interesting aspects of swimming, diving and water polo from Egyptian hieroglyphics to the latest strokes, and lists of the names and pictures of milestone events of most everyone in between.

A visit to this Hall of Fame must include a tour of the grounds which includes a 3600-tile wrap-around ceramic mural of King Neptune's court on which the City Commission insisted the artist, Linzee Prescott, put clothes on the mermaids! There is an Honoree Walkway around the outside of the auditorium wing where kids can compare their hand and footprints with the many Honorees who have signed the cement blocks. There are pictures etched in metal on the pillars where you can walk through swimming's past and see a tree planted each year in honor of a different swimming country. Inside the auditorium are heroic figures representing all phases of aquatics.

Most of the murals in the building are done by William Linzee Prescott, who your tour guide will proudly tell you is the only living Bicentennial exhibit. Prescott's ancestor was Col. William Prescott who said "Don't fire until you see the whites of their eyes" from Bunker Hill while Linzee was Captain of the British Frigate firing on Boston! Two generations later, the daughter of Captain Linzee married William Prescott, the great historian who wrote "Conquest of Mexico." Prescott is the only direct descendent and has done models, portraits, posters and murals throughout the Hall which comes off as a nautical art museum. Prescott has also been in "Believe It or Not" and sometimes the guests wonder if the whole museum doesn't need Ripley to verify the fantastic stories that go with every person honored.

Let's Take a Tour

Adjacent to the turnstiles and souvenir counter is a display featuring Ernest Hemingway's *Old Man and the Sea*, complete with mounted marlin, photos of the author with Spencer Tracy and memorabilia of Stubby Kruger, the famous clown diver who doubled for the actor in the movie. Across the entranceway aisle is a display case containing many of Weissmuller's medals and trophies, a precious, irreplaceable collection.

Among the eye-catching displays are wall-sized enlargements of synchronized swimmers (the largest pin-ups in town), Spitz, Mike Troy, Murray Rose, Mike Finneran, Micki King, Jesse Owens and other sports figures. Still seated, you can view the immense world map on the south wall that shows that three-fourths of the world is covered by water. The map also has models of each Olympic stadium since 1896, while an adjoining display has medals from the Ancient Greece Games to the present day.

The "boat theatre" on the east wall is used for receptions and also boasts a color slide series as well as cartoons depicting swimming through a humorist's eyes, along with manniquins modeling early swimwear. The theatre's name? "Ye Olde Swimming Hole of Fame."

. . . and On the Second Level

Going up the stairs you find charts and statistics indicating how swimming times have improved over the years, as well as photo sections devoted to marathon swimming and English Channel swimming. The vast north wall is given over to one of the nation's largest caricature murals illustrating Florida's sunny Gold Coast, peopled by some 500 recognizable aquatic faces. If you can't identify them all from memory, there is a

The National Collegiate and Scholastic swim trophy by Joe Brown.

223

numbered index to check. The opposite wall is an Underseascape from The Glass House in Tuxedo, N.Y., this one featuring our finny friends. It is here, naturally, where you'll find a display honoring Jacques Cousteau, the amphibian.

Take a look out the side door at the replica of a ship's bridge, in memory of Francis McDermott and the Navy V-5 World War II program. Visiting school children have been known to ring the great bell, making the bridge-tender on the real Las Olas bridge look high and low to find out where the boat is that's signaling to pass!

The east mural here is alive. It's an all-glass wall that overlooks the pool and diving well where you can have a balcony seat to watch the athletes perform almost under you. Incidentally, between the view and the pool is the six-ton reinforced concrete statue "Swimmer" by Don Seiler who carved a mustache on the head to make it resemble a certain swimmer who won seven gold medals at the Munich Olympics. More than once, this gigantic statue has held up to 50 kids who like the King Kong type of playing.

Most of the second level belongs to the Honorees, for here are their personal alcoves, with photos, drawings, clippings, medals, trophies and memorabilia, proving why they were chosen to be part of this elite company. They represent nearly every swimming nation and aquatic sport. Not only swimmers, divers and coaches, but also Outstanding Contributors, without whom the sport of swimming simply could not function.

Headquarters for the American Swim Coaches Association

The International Swimming Hall of Fame is also headquarters for the American Swim Coaches Association and the College Coaches Swim Forum. It is the largest distributor of how-to-do-it swim books from water safety and kiddie swimming to the latest dives and strokes. A delightful staff of girls, who must have been chosen at least partly for their looks, will help answer your questions. The Hall has a mascot that is a spitz dog. Guess what his name is?

The first Honorees (aquatic greats chosen by some 2000 coaches, athletes and officials) were inducted in 1965 at colorful ceremonies attended by more than 4000, including celebrities from virtually every sport. This stellar group was headed by such immortals as Johnny Weissmuller (now Honorary Chairman), Duke Kahanamoku, Buster Crabbe, Don Schollander and 20 others. Since then, some 150 more have joined them so that by 1977 there will be a total of 175 enshrined here — which is not very many when you realize that there are literally hundreds of millions of swimmers throughout the world.

The Pool

Before we visit the Honoree Alcoves in the Museum, let's take a quick tour of the pool complex. Unquestionably, more "name" swimmers have worked in this pool than any other in the world, from Weissmuller to Naber, from deVarona to Babashoff. The 3000-seat bleachers provide

A mural in the International Swimming Hall of Fame auditorium.

excellent viewing of the many events held in the pool every year: East-West College Meet, AIAW, YMCA and YWCA Nationals (some 2000 competitors), the cream of the divers from a dozen nations for the annual International Meet, Masters Swimming and Diving, National Synchronized Swimming, Pan Am Games Trials, to mention only a few. (Last spring the diving meet starred Klaus Dibiasi, Jenni Chandler, Greg Louganis and Nemsenov, among others).

When not in use by the "heavies," the pool is home for the Fort Lauderdale Swim Team, coached by Jack Nelson, mentor for the 1976 Olympic Women's Swim Team. And when FLST leaves, the public plunges in, for it is a municipal pool, owned and operated by the City of Fort Lauderdale.

"The World of the Olympics" in the International Swimming Hall of Fame.

The first date given following the name and country is the date of enshrinement.

GRETA ANDERSEN (Denmark) 1969 – Channel swimmer, marathon champion, 100 M Gold Medal 1948 Olympics.

MILLER ANDERSON (USA) 1967 – Won 16 major diving titles, overcoming crippling war injury.

DAVE ARMBRUSTER (USA) 1966 – 40 years coach and writer. Developed butterfly stroke.

BILL BACHRACH (USA) 1966 – Coached Johnny Weissmuller, 2 Olympic teams, IAC to every AAU championship in 1924.

CATIE BALL (USA) 1976 – 1967 – 1968 "World Breaststroker of the Year." Catie Ball is rated the USA's top all-time breaststroker.

WALTER BATHE (Germany) 1970 – 1912 Double Olympic breaststroke Gold Medal winner.

CARL BAUER (USA) 1967 – Father of Age-Group Swimming.

SYBIL BAUER (USA) 1967 – First woman to break an existing men's world record. Olympic backstroke winner – 1924.

SIR FRANK BEAUREPAIRE (Australia) 1967 – Swam from 1903 to 1928, won 6 Olympic medals and 14 world records.

ETHELDA BLEIBTREY (USA) 1967 – First U.S. Women's Olympic champion, 3 gold medals – 1920.

ARNE BORG (Sweden) 1966 – 1928 Olympic champion. 1500 meter world record 11 years.

ERNST BRANDSTEN (Sweden-USA) 1966 – Olympic competitor, Sweden; and 4 times U.S. Olympic diving coach.

GRETA BRANDSTEN (Sweden) 1973 – First woman Olympic tower diving champion.

MA BRAUN (Holland) 1967 – Great Dutch coach; developed daughter and several other Olympic champions.

STAN BRAUNINGER (USA) 1972 – Coached 6 National champion teams plus Hall of Famers Wally Laufer, Adolph Kiefer, Miller Anderson.

GEORGE BREEN (USA) 1975 – Won 22 U. S. Nationals. Two Olympic teams.

DAVID "SKIPPY" BROWNING (USA) 1975 – 1952 Olympic springboard diving champion.

MIKE BURTON (USA) 1977 – 3 Olympic Golds.

FREDY CADY (USA) 1969 – Great Olympic Diving Coach and USC Swim Coach.

TEDFORD CANN (USA) 1967 – World record holder and U.S. champion. Won Congressional Medal of Honor, WWI.

JOAQUIN CAPILLA (Mexico) 1976 – 1956 Olympic gold medal in 10m platform diving. Bronze in 3m springboard diving. 1952 Olympic silver 10m platform diving. 1948 Olympic bronze 10m platform diving. Three-time U.S. National AAU Champion. Four-time Pan-American Champion.

FORBES CARLILE (Australia) 1976 – Australia's first modern pentathlon Olympic competitor (1952) and youngest Olympic coach (1948)

THE SIX CHAMPION CAVILLS (Australia) 1970 – Swimming's most colorful family.

FLORENCE CHADWICK (USA) 1970 – English Channel Record Holder.

ANDREW "BOY" CHARLTON (Australia) 1972 – Won 400M in 1924 Olympics. Also in 1928 & 1932 Games.

SHERM CHAVOOR (USA) 1977 – 32 years including head coach of the 1972 Women's Olympic team.

EARL CLARK (USA) 1972 – Only U.S. grand-slam diver, 1941.

STEVE CLARK (USA) 1966 – 3 Olympic gold medals (1964), 11 U.S. national titles.

JACK CODY (USA) 1970 – Famed Multnomah Coach.

GEORGIA COLEMAN (USA) 1966 – 1932 Olympic springboard champion. First woman to do the men's list.

GEORGE CORSAN, SR. (Canada) 1971 – 1st mass class swim teacher, developed Y Swimming (Author, builder, innovator).

JAMES E. COUNSILMAN (USA) 1976 – U.S. Olympic coach 1964 & 1976. 15 consecutive Big Ten Crowns (1961 – 76). President, ASCA and Founding President of the ISHOF.

JACQUES YVES COUSTEAU (France) 1967 – The world's premier oceanographer.

BUSTER CRABBE (USA) 1965 – 1932 Olympic champion, multi-World Record and Aquacades star.

LORRAINE CRAPP (Australia) 1972 – Twice set 4 world records in one race. 1956 Olympic gold.

CAPT. BERT CUMMINS (Great Britain) 1974 – Longest service as great swimming journalist.

ANN CURTIS (USA) 1966 – 1948, 400-meter Olympic champion, multi-U.S. championships.

PETER DALAND (USA) 1977 – For many years the coach of USC swimming teams.

C. M. "CHARLIE" DANIELS (USA) 1965 – First great American swimmer, 4 gold medals in 3 Olympics, 1904 – 06 – 08.

RAY DAUGHTERS (USA) 1971 – Coached WAC Swimmers to 30 W.R., 301 American records, 64 National Champions. Twice U.S. Olympic Coach.

Dawn Fraser (right), winner of three consecutive Olympic gold medals in the 100-meter free style, with Sharon Stouder, who captured three gold and one silver medal in the 1964 Olympics in Tokyo. —Associated Press Wirephoto

DICK DEGENER (USA) 1971 — 1936 Olympic Springboard Diving Champ. Won 15 straight Nationals.

PETE DESJARDINS (USA) 1966 — Double Olympic diving winner, 1928. Many time national champion.

DONNA DE VARONA (USA) 1969 — Greatest swimmer of early 60's.

OLGA DORFNER (USA) 1970 — First U.S. women's world record, 1916.

VICKIE DRAVES (USA) 1969 — 1948 Double Olympic Diving Champion.

FANNY DURACK (Australia) 1967 — First women's Olympic champion — 1912.

GERTRUDE EDERLE (USA) 1965 — First woman to swim English Channel. Also Olympic swimmer and national champion.

CHARLOTTE EPSTEIN (USA) 1974 — W.S.A. organizer. Pioneer force in U.S. women's swimming.

JEFF FARRELL (USA) 1968 — Appendectomy five days before 1960 Olympic Trials. Made the team, won 3 gold medals.

HAROLD FERN (Great Britain) 1974 — Long-time A.S.A. and FINA secretary.

JENNIE FLETCHER (England) 1971 — 1st great woman swimmer. Undefeated W.R. 1905 – 1911. Olympic Gold Medal 1912.

ALAN FORD (USA) 1966 — First to break 50 second for 100-yard F.S.

BENJAMIN FRANKLIN (USA) 1968 — America's first famous swimmer and coach.

DAWN FRASER (Australia) 1965 — Gold medal, 3 Olympics. First woman to go under 1 minute for 100 meter FS and win 3 Olympics, 1956 – 60 – 64.

ELLEN FULLARD-LEO (USA) 1974 — 75 years as the Grand Dame of Hawaiian swimming.

HIRONOSHIN FURUHASHI (Japan) 1967 — His world record performances symbolized Japanese return to greatness after WWII.

CLAIRE GALLIGAN (USA) 1970 — First AAU National Champion.

MARJORIE GESTRING (USA) 1976 — 1936 Olympic gold medal in 3m springboard diving. 8 U.S. National AAU Championships (6 springboard and 2 tower).

BUDD GOODWIN (USA) 1971 — 19 U.S. championships 1901 – 1915 Olympic and Congressional Gold Medals.

SHANE GOULD (Australia) 1977 — 3 golds, a silver and a bronze in the 1972 Olympics.

BEULAH GUNDLING (USA) 1965 — Premier Aquatic Artist and 5 U.S. (solo) synchronized swimming titles.

DEZSO GYARMATI (Hungary) 1976 — 1952 – 56 – 64 Olympic gold medals. 1948 Olympic silver medal.

GEORGE HAINES (USA) 1977 — 26 years a coach, who gained his greatest renown at Santa Clara Swim Club.

ALFRED HAJOS (Hungary) 1966 — First Olympic swimming champion — 1896.

ZOLTEN DE HALMAY (Hungary) 1968 — 10 medals in five Olympics — 1896 – 1908.

L. DE B. HANDLEY (USA) 1967 — First U.S. women's Olympic coach, swimming journalist, early champion.

An aerial view of the International Swimming Hall of Fame showing the pool and the building.

JAM HANDY (USA) 1965—1904–1924 Olympic teams. Pioneer in science of swimming technique.

BRUCE HARLAN (USA) 1973—1948 springboard Olympic diving champion and later great Michigan coach.

KAREN HARUP (Denmark) 1975—1948 Olympic backstroke champion. Placed in 4 events.

HARRY HEBNER (USA) 1968—1912 Olympic backstroke champion, 35 U.S. National championships.

JON HENDRICKS (Australia) 1973—1956 double Olympic sprint champion.

WILLIAM HENRY (Great Britain) 1974—Great English swimmer who founded Royal Life Saving Society.

CHARLES HICKCOX (USA) 1976—1968 Olympic gold medals in 200m I.M., 400m I.M. and silver medal in the 100m backstroke. 2 Pan-American gold medals, 8 World records, 9 National AAU and 7 NCAA Championships.

JOHN HIGGINS (USA) 1971—1st W. R. Butterfly breaststroke. Won 11 U.S. National Championships, coach and official.

GEORGE HODGSON (Canada) 1968—Retired undefeated after double win in 1912 Olympics.

ELEANOR HOLM (USA) 1966—All 3 backstroke and I.M. World Records. Olympic champion 1932.

MARTON HOMONNAY (Hungary) 1971—Three times Olympic water polo gold medal.

DICK HOUGH (USA) 1970—Late 30's breast-stroke king.

STEVE HUNYADFI (Hungary, Italy, USA) 1969 5-time Olympic Coach.

RAGNHILD HVEGER (Denmark) 1966—Great wartime champion, 19 world F.S. records, some for 15 years.

ALEX JANY (France) 1977—Medalist in the 1948 & 1952 Olympics.

JOHN JARVIS (England) 1968—Triple gold medal winner—1900 Olympics.

CHET JASTREMSKI (USA) 1977—15 world records.

DUKE KAHANAMOKU (USA) 1965—4 Olympics, 4 gold medals. World surfing, swimming ambassador.

BETH KAUFMAN (USA) 1967—First U.S. Age-Group Swimming national chairman for 10 years.

WARREN KEALOHA (USA) 1968—First double Olympic backstroke winner—1920–1924.

ANNETTE KELLERMAN (Australia) 1974—World record holder & movie star who was swimming's greatest saleswoman.

EDWARD T. KENNEDY (USA) 1966—Olympic manager, 45 years coach guiding force of Swim Forum.

ADOLPH KIEFER (USA) 1965—Didn't lose a backstroke race in 8 years, including 1936 Olympics.

BARNEY KIERAN (Australia) 1969—Pre-record book champion of champions.

COR KINT (Holland) 1971—1939 World backstroke records lasted 21 years.

BOB KIPHUTH (USA) 1965—1932, 1936, 1948 U.S. Olympic coach. Won 200 consecutive dual meets at Yale.

KUSUO KITAMURA (Japan) 1965—At 14, youngest man to win Olympic gold medal—1932.

GEORGE KOJAC (USA) 1968—1928 Olympic backstroke champion, freestyle medalist.

ADA KOK (Holland) 1976—1968 Olympic gold medal in 200m butterfly. 1964 silver medal in 100m butterfly and 400m medley relay. 10 World Records. 3 European Championships. "European Swimmer of the Year" in 1963, 1965 and 1967.

CLAUDIA KOLB (USA) 1975—5-year Queen of I.M. 1968 double gold. 29 Nationals.

FORD KONNO (USA) 1972—Double gold star of 1952 Olympics who always beat the best.

JOH AND ILSA KONRADS (Australia) 1971—8 World Records in one week, 37 in two years 1958–1960.

INGRID KRAMER (DDR) 1975—3 golds, 1 silver—Rome & Tokyo Olympic diving.

ETHEL LACKIE (USA) 1969—1924 Olympic Champion 100 M.

FREDDY LANE (Australia) 1969—First man to break a minute.

WALTER LAUFER (USA) 1973—Scored more points than any other team in 1926 U.S. Nationals. On 2 Olympic teams.

SAMMY LEE (USA) 1968—Double platform diving winner—1948–1952 Olympics.

COMMODORE LONGFELLOW (USA) 1965—Founded Red Cross Water Safety and Learn-to-Swim programs.

FRED LUEHRING (USA) 1974—First Editor of NCAA Guide. Pioneer coach and contributor.

HELENE MADISON (USA) 1966—1932 double Olympic champion, held all 17 freestyle world records.

MARIO MAJONI (Italy) 1972—Olympic gold medal water polo player & later national coach.

MATT MANN II (Great Britain-USA) 1965—1952 Olympic coach, 13 NCAA team titles at Michigan.

SHELLY MANN (USA) 1966—1956 Olympic Champion. World Record Holder Fly and I.M.

JOHN MARSHALL (Australia) 1973—3 post-war Olympic teams. First middle distance world record holder to swim hard all the way.

CHARLES McCAFFREE, JR. (USA) 1976—He has been—at one time or another during 45 years—a coach, editor, manager, chairman, organizer, president or honoree for achievement and service of almost everything in American swimming.

HENDRIKA MASTENBROEK (Holland) 1968—3 gold, 1 silver medal, 1936 Olympics.

PAT McCORMICK (USA) 1965—Only diver to win 4 Olympic gold medals 1952–56.

TURK McDERMOTT (USA) 1969—Nine straight breast-stroke crowns.

Adolph Kiefer's honoree display case.

Don Schollander, first swimmer to win 4 gold medals in one Olympics.— Newspaper Division, Field Enterprises, Inc.

FRANK McKINNEY (USA) 1975—First great modern backstroker. 1956 and 1960 Olympic Champion.

JIMMY McLANE (USA) 1970—Triple Olympic Gold Medal winner 1948–52.

HELEN MEANY (USA) 1971—17 U.S. National AAU Diving Titles. 1928 Olympic Champion.

JACK MEDICA (USA) 1966—1936 Olympic champion. First to win 3 titles in 3 straight NCAA meets.

DEBBIE MEYER (USA) 1977—3 Olympic golds.

PAMELA MORRIS (USA) 1965—The first triple winner (solo, duet, team) in synchronized swimming.

KEO NAKAMA (USA) 1975—First great modern Hawaiian swimmer.

JIM NEMETH (Hungary) 1969—All-time top water polo goal scorer.

AL NEUSCHAEFER (USA) 1967—First great American high school coach, Trenton, New Jersey.

MARTHA NORELIUS (USA) 1967—First woman double Olympic winner in 400 meter freestyle—1924–28.

THE NOVAK SISTERS (Hungary) 1973—Long careers highlighted by 1952 Olympic gold medals.

WALLY O'CONNOR (USA) 1966—No. 1 U.S. water poloist at 4 Olympics. Also national champion swimmer.

WILLY DEN OUDEN (Holland) 1970—First girl to break a minute in 100 yd. freestyle.

YOSHI OYAKAWA (USA) 1973—1952 Olympic champion. Last great straight-arm backstroker.

HENRI PADOU (France) 1970—All time water polo great.

AL PATNIK (USA) 1969—17 U.S. National Diving titles.

MIKE PEPPE (USA) 1966—1948–52 Olympic diving coach, coached Ohio State to 33 major titles in 33 years.

BETTY BECKER PINKSTON (USA) 1967—First woman double Olympic diving winner—1924–28.

CLARENCE PINKSTON (USA) 1966—Olympic champion (1920) and coach of champions.

DOROTHY POYNTON (USA) 1968—First to win two successive Olympic tower diving crowns—1932–1936.

ERICH RADEMACHER (Germany) 1972—1920's Breaststroke King. 25 German National Championships. 2 Olympic Water Polo teams.

EMIL RAUSCH (Germany) 1968—1904 double Olympic winner, last to win with sidestroke.

KATHERINE RAWLS (USA) 1965—Most U.S. titles for a woman in swimming and diving, medley World Record 1930's.

AILEEN RIGGIN (USA) 1967—First woman springboard diving champion—1920.

MICKEY RILEY (Galitzen) (USA) 1977—4 medals in the 1928 & 1932 Olympics.

WALLY RIS (USA) 1966—1948 double Olympic champion. 5 straight National AAU 100 titles.

R. MAX RITTER (Germany-USA) 1965—1908–1912 Olympic teams, a FINA Founder and President.

CARL ROBIE (USA) 1976—1968 Olympic gold medal in 200m butterfly. 1964 Olympic medal in 200m butterfly. 4 World Records, six-time U.S. National AAU Outdoor Long Course champion in 200m butterfly (1961–62–63–64–65–68), 1965 500m freestyle, 1965–66 Indoor Short Course in 200m butterfly, 1967 NCAA 200 fly, 1965 400 I.M. NCAA champion.

TOM ROBINSON (USA) 1974—Coached National champion swimmers and team at Northwestern University.

MURRAY ROSE (Australia) 1965—4 gold medals, 1956–60 Olympics, Multi-Australia and U.S. national champion.

NORMAN ROSS (USA) 1967—13 world records, 18 U.S. Nationals, 3 Olympic gold medals—1920.

SYLVIA RUUSKA (USA) 1976—1956 Olympic bronze medal in 400m freestyle (at age 13, youngest medal winner).

ROY SAARI (USA) 1976—The first swimmer to break 17 minutes in the 1500m freestyle (16:58.7) at the U.S. Olympic Trials, September 2, 1964, in New York.

SOICHI SAKAMOTO (USA) 1966—Hawaiian coach who developed most world champions, 1938–1956.

CHARLIE SAVA (USA) 1970—Coached ten straight U.S. women's team titles.

E. CARROLL SCHAEFFER (USA) 1968—First great college swimmer (Pennsylvania), 37 American, 5 world records.

DON SCHOLLANDER (USA) 1965—First swimmer to win 4 gold medals in one Olympics—1964.

CHARLES E. SILVIA (USA) 1976—Recipient of Collegiate & Scholastic Swimming Trophy and Honoree in Helms (Citizens Savings) Hall of Fame. Author of "Life Saving & Water Safety Today" (9th printing; 200,000 copies).

BILL SMITH (USA) 1966—1948 double Olympic winner. Multi-world record Freestyler.

SPENCE BROTHERS WALTER, WALLACE & LEONARD (Great Britain) 1967—Set U.S. and world marks individually and as medley relay.

MARK SPITZ (USA) 1977—7 gold medals and world records in the 1972 Olympics, named "World Swimmer of the Year" in 1967, 1971 & 1972, 2 gold medals, a silver & bronze in 1968 Olympics.

JAN STENDER (Holland) 1973—Many Olympic and world record holders plus team champions at Hilversum-Robbens.

GALINA PROZUMENSCHIKOVA STEPANOVA (Soviet Union) 1977—Won 5 medals in 3 Olympics.

SHARON STOUDER (USA) 1972—3 golds, 1 silver at 1964 Tokyo Olympics.

EVA SZEKELY (Hungary) 1976—1952 Olympic gold medal in 200m breaststroke. 1956 Olympic silver medal in 200m breaststroke. Fourth in 1948 Olympic 200m breaststroke. 10 World Records, 5 Olympic Records, 101 Hungarian National Records, 68 Hungarian National Championships.

HENRY TAYLOR (Great Britain) 1969—Triple Olympic Gold medal winner 1906-08.

DAVID THEILE (Australia) 1968—Double Olympic backstroke winner—1956-1960.

MIKE TROY (USA) 1971—1960 Double Olympic Gold Medal multi butterfly and free style world records.

JOHN TRUDGEN (Great Britain) 1974—Englishman who invented the stroke bearing his name.

YOSHIYUKI TSURUTA (Japan) 1968—Only Olympic backstroker to repeat—1932-36.

NELL VAN VLIET (Holland) 1973—1948 Olympic champion who held all breaststroke records.

JOE VERDEUR (USA) 1966—1948 Olympic champion, 12 times world butterfly—breaststroke record breaker.

CHRIS VON SALTZA (USA) 1966—1960 Olympic champion, first great age-group swimmer.

HELEN WAINWRIGHT (USA) 1972—Medaled in 2 Olympics plus 17 U.S. National Championships in swimming and diving.

MATTHEW WEBB (Great Britain) 1965—First man to swim English Channel, 1875.

BOB WEBSTER (USA) 1970—1960-64 Olympic double diving winner.

JOHNNY WEISSMULLER (USA) 1965—5 Olympic gold medals, 51 national championships. Swimmer of the Half Century.

AL WHITE (USA) 1965—First Olympic double diving winner—1924.

ALIC WICKAM (Solomon Islands) 1974—Brought the crawl stroke to the western world.

Chris Von Saltza, after smashing the Olympic record in the 100-meter free style at age 16. —UPI Telephoto

ESTHER WILLIAMS (USA) 1966—1939 National champion. Aquacades and movie swim star.

MINA WYLIE (Australia) 1975—1912 Olympic champion. Won Australian Championships 20 years in a row.

BILL YORZYK (USA) 1971—First Olympic butterfly Champion 1956 U.S. National Champion and highpoint winner.

ALBERTO ZORRILLA (Argentina) 1976—1928 Olympic gold medal in 400m freestyle. Argentine and South American champion and record holder in freestyle and backstroke, 1929 to 1932.

Mark Spitz, winner of seven gold medals in the 1972 Olympic games. —Associated Press Wirephoto

THE INTERNATIONAL TENNIS HALL OF FAME AND TENNIS MUSEUM

Newport, Rhode Island

OBJECTIVES

The National Lawn Tennis Hall of Fame and Tennis Museum was founded in 1954 as a non-profit, tax-exempt organization to function as the officially accredited agency of tennis in illuminating its past glories, honoring those distinguished in making its history, and promoting its welfare. (In 1976 Hall of Fame President James H. Van Alen announced that the name had been changed to International Tennis Hall of Fame and Tennis Museum).

In the selection of those to be inscribed in history through enshrinement in the Hall of Fame, the highest standards of sportsmanship, no less than transcendent playing skill, are a consideration. The preservation of these standards, a prized tradition of tennis contributing so much to its worth in the development of the character of youth, is of primary concern to the directors of the National Lawn Tennis Hall of Fame and Tennis Museum in their dedication to the advancement of the game's welfare.

The attractiveness and character of the Newport Casino structure that houses the Hall of Fame, and whose permanence as its home has been made secure in the space of a few years, are a source of pride. There the game was cradled, with the holding of the first National Championship in 1881, and no sport has a more fitting or noble shrine.

But the Hall of Fame is something more than a lovely physical property. It is an inspiration for the young, setting them a goal that can be attained only through the sacrifice, perseverance, and strength of character that won a place for those already enshrined there. Sport still has its ideals. None are loftier than those represented by the Tennis Hall of Fame.

Allison Danzig

The History of the Introduction of Tennis to the United States

When Mary Outerbridge arrived in New York on the steamship from Bermuda in February of 1874, bringing with her a book of rules, rac-

An aerial view of the Newport Casino complex which includes—championship lawn tennis courts, a souvenir shop, a very pleasant restaurant and cocktail lounge, along with the International Tennis Hall of Fame and the Van Alen Auditorium.
—Photo by John Hopf

quets, balls, and a net for a new game called "Lawn Tennis," she could have had no idea she was setting the stage in the United States of America for a sport which it is now estimated has about 30,000,000 participants, as well as millions more spectators. At that time the customs agents held up the equipment because they had never seen anything like it before, but within a few days she was allowed to pay duty and claim it.

This set was used during the summer of 1874 at the Staten Island Cricket and Baseball Club, and is considered to be the first set laid out in a more or less public place. At about the same time a set of "Sphairistike," as it was then officially named, was brought from old England to New England and was set up in the summer of 1875 at Mr. William Appleton's place at Nahant, Massachusetts. Another set was installed at the estate of Mr. William Watts Sherman of Newport, Rhode Island, and within the next two or three years there were several lawn tennis courts in use in Newport.

The origin of the game we know as "lawn tennis" is generally credited to Major Walter Clopton Wingfield, who claimed to have invented and first played this game at Nantclwyd, Wales, in 1873, and for which he was granted an English patent in July 1874. He had adapted the ancient game of "tennis" (now called "court tennis"), then as now played on indoor courts, so that it could be played outdoors on grass courts of his unique "hourglass" design. To do this he drew up a set of rules which included attributes of several other games, such as badminton and racquets.

Lawn tennis has been the chief attraction of the Newport Casino since it was built in 1880. Commissioned by James Gordon Bennett, publisher of the "New York Herald" and summer resident of Newport, the Casino was designed by the noted architectural firm of McKim, Mead and White, and is considered an outstanding example of the "shingle period." The main building on Bellevue Avenue contains stores on the ground floor, and the second story houses the various rooms of what was originally an aristocratic and exclusive gentlemen's club. To the rear are several acres of land on which the grass tennis courts were laid out. Stanford White designed a beautiful little ballroom-theatre which was built at the

One of the displays showing the international flavor of the Hall of Fame honoring the great French stars of the '20s and '30s and some of the great stars that followed them on the international scene.

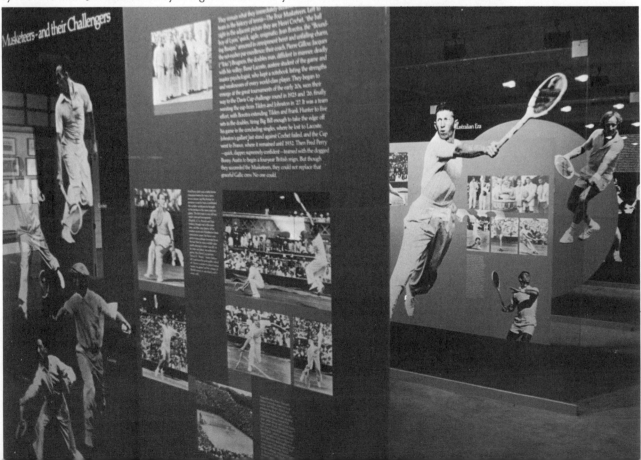

back of the property, linked by an ornate two-story porch with a building which then enclosed a "court tennis" court. In spite of damage by fire and hurricane, these buildings are all still in use, as are the grass courts.

Tournaments

The first so-called "national" tennis tournament was held at the Staten Island Cricket and Baseball Club beginning September 1, 1880, but it was found that the players from other tennis clubs had been using different types of balls, different heights of the net, etc. It was such differences in the equipment and rules that led to the founding of the United States (National) Lawn Tennis Association in New York on May 21, 1881. Thirty-three clubs were represented, and within a short time the first official championship was awarded to the Newport Casino for August 31 to September 3 of that year.

No reason was given for the choice of the Casino, but Henry W. Slocum, Jr., who was the second United States champion, stated: "No better place than the Newport Casino could have been selected. The grounds were picturesque and the courts well kept. The accommodations for the players were good, and Newport being then, as now, a very fashionable resort, the most beautiful women of the country graced the tournament with their presence."

Newport was, indeed, the logical choice. Most of the players at that time were in "Society" or considered acceptable, a great many of them being college students. And in 1881 Newport was a pre-eminent social resort.

It is well known that Richard Dudley Sears of Boston won the first men's singles championship and then continued to win it for seven successive years, retiring undefeated. Prior to 1890 the men's doubles championships were also played at Newport, subsequently being held for many years at the Longwood Cricket Club near Boston.

Until the U.S.L.T.A. decided to move the National Men's Singles Championships to the West Side Tennis Club courts in Forest Hills, New York, in 1915, they were held at the Newport Casino—a period of 34 years. Thus the Newport Casino can justifiably be considered the "cradle" of lawn tennis in the U.S.A.

The transfer of the national championships from Newport to Forest Hills was the result of a long controversy. The tournaments had been attracting more and more spectators, and the seating arrangements were inadequate for the crowds who appeared. Newport, being on an island, was inaccessible for out-of-towners, and it was also short of restaurants and hotels. The West Side Tennis Club, which originated on the west side of New York City, had moved to Forest Hills, and their clubhouse courts could then accommodate 15,000 spectators. Early in 1915, after a long-deferred battle of votes and proxies at the U.S.L.T.A., the West Side Tennis Club was chosen as the new site of the "Nationals."

That year the long series of Newport Invitation Tournaments began. There were men's singles and doubles events, and invitations were eagerly sought by the best domestic and foreign players, since this tournament was considered a real "tune-up" for the Nationals, scheduled later in August. There was usually a sprinkling of local tennis talent who would boast of taking a game or two from the stars in the first round, before being eliminated. The players were always well entertained, with parties being given almost every evening in Newport's palatial mansions, Bailey's Beach, the Clambake Club, etc. The lavish hospitality was appreciated, and the Newport Casino grass tennis courts were considered by many of the competitors as "the best in the world." The amateur tournaments continued through 1967. At that time "open" tournaments were sanctioned, and the pros took over. Some tournaments were omitted during World Wars I and II, but the list of Newport amateur singles winners includes Tilden, Johnston, Vines, Riggs, Budge, Talbert, Gonzales, Richardson, McKinley and Ralston of the United States, as well as Australians Rosewall, Anderson, and Laver.

From 1965 through 1970 a Men's Professional Tournament was held, using the Van Alen Scoring System. Almost all of those competing had previously played at the Casino as amateurs. These tournaments were moderately successful, but the interest in women players had been growing, and from 1971 through 1974 the Virginia Slims Grasscourts Championships took the place of the previously all-male tournaments. The young lady players took Newport by storm; long lines formed on Bellevue Avenue waiting for tickets; there was standing room only. Unfortunately, the format of the women's professional circuit has changed so that Newport has been eliminated. Now the Tennis Hall of Fame Tournament is host again to the amateurs. In 1974 the National Men's Amateur Grasscourts Championships were held on the Casino courts, and in 1975 the Men's and Women's Championships took place there in July.

How the Tennis Hall of Fame Began

In 1952 Mr. James H. Van Alen, whose family had been summer residents of Newport for several generations, and who had played tennis at the Casino since childhood, originated the idea of the National Tennis Hall of Fame. He was then serving as President of the Casino, and after preliminary discussions with various tennis officials and prominent former players, he received a sanction from the United States Lawn Tennis Association for its establishment at the Newport Casino in 1954. A meeting was held in New York, and the National Lawn Tennis Hall of Fame and Tennis Museum, Inc., was formally organized as a nonprofit corporation. William J. Clothier, National Singles Champion in 1906, was elected President by the Board of Directors. Other officers were: James H. Van Alen, Vice-President, and Archbold van Beuren, Secretary-Treasurer. Henry Heffernan of Newport was named Executive Director to assist Mr. Clothier, and he later served as Secretary-Treasurer for many years.

An appeal was made through tennis organizations and interested individuals for the donation of tennis memorabilia for display in the new

Part of the horseshoe piazza of the historic casino structure in which the Hall of Fame is situated.

—Photo by Bob Moulton

Honoring some of the Australian stars who dominated the game for so many years.

museum, as well as financial support. Mr. Clothier personally devoted himself to soliciting items for exhibit; as a former National Champion who had played in tournaments all over the United States and abroad for many years, he was well known in the tennis community and was able to acquire a sizable collection of photographs, important silver trophies, antique tennis racquets, etc., which he and Mr. Heffernan set up in the four rooms of the Casino building which comprised the office and museum. A young lady was hired to take care of the clerical and secretarial work as well as to be a receptionist for the museum. For the first few years Mr. Clothier paid a large part of the expenses out of his own pocket, although others of the Board of Directors gave some financial assistance. Dedica-

237

The Davis Cup emblematic symbol of the International team championship.

tion festivities were held on July 9, 1955, with many distinguished guests in attendance, and the Hall of Fame stayed open for the remainder of the lawn tennis season, which ends on October 31.

Since the Directors were from various parts of the country, most of the meetings were held in New York. One of the first questions to be answered was "Who shall be elected as enshrinees in the Hall of Fame, and how shall they be elected?" The consensus was that those United States players who had been outstanding champions should be of first importance, and that there should also be a category covering persons who had made significant contributions to the game of tennis in other ways. Character and sportsmanship were cardinal considerations. It was decided to begin with the very early players, and in 1955 a group of seven men were elected as "enshrinees," including Richard Dudley Sears, the first national champion, and James Dwight, known as the "Father of Tennis in the U.S.A." The induction ceremonies were held on the center court of the Casino on Saturday of Tennis Week, August 19. These ceremonies have continued to be held each year, usually on Saturday, the day of the semifinal matches of the important annual tournament.

The Museum Grows

Among the first items acquired for display, those of primary importance were: "The Sears Bowl," a handsome sterling silver punch bowl, the first national championship trophy, won by Richard Dudley Sears of Boston; a bronze statue of Pierre Etchebaster, a court tennis champion for 28 years; a model of the Philadelphia court tennis court; and photographs of the first Davis Cup Team of 1900 and the first Davis Cup Team to go abroad in 1905. In 1956 the widow of "Little Bill" Johnston presented the museum with a collection of his important medals and trophies, and in 1957 Maurice McLoughlin donated his imposing silver national championship cup. After the death of Molla Bjurstedt Mallory the museum was given her scrapbooks, photographs, medals, one of her tennis racquets, tennis books, a bronze bust, and a beautiful silver trophy. Numerous interesting old racquets have been donated, as well as one of the first molds on which tennis racquets were fashioned in the United States. Many of the inductees have given photographs and trophies. One wall has a collection of tennis cartoons, donated by the artists. A large number of items relating to the Davis Cup matches have been put together as the result of gifts of memorabilia from former United States captains and other interested persons, and a "Davis Cup Room". Several fine tennis paintings and drawings have been given, and there are many original illustrations from old magazines such as "Harper's" and "Leslie's."

A small but excellent reference library has accumulated, containing many books on tennis now out of print. Two fine collections of old tennis books and "annuals" have been presented "in memoriam," and many single volumes have been donated or purchased. There are also files of old tennis magazines and U.S.L.T.A. Yearbooks.

MEMBERS OF THE TENNIS HALL OF FAME

The first members to be enshrined were Richard Sears, the first U.S. singles champion, Joseph Clark, James Dwight, Malcolm Whitman, Henry Slocum, Bob Wrenn and Oliver Campbell. All of these men played tennis and were champions before the turn of the century. The official list of the Hall of Fame members arranged alphabetically with an indication of National Championship as singles (S) or doubles (D) player and number of times is listed below. The foreign players were not named until 1975.

AMERICANS

Women:

Mrs. Pauline Betz Addie, 1939–46 (10-S, 9-D)
Mrs. Ellen Hansell Allerdice 1887 (1-S)
Juliette Atkinson, 1894–1902 (3-S, 10-D)
Mrs. Maude Bargar-Wallach, 1908–16 (1-S)
Mrs. Maureen Connolly Brinker, 1950–54 (5-S, 1-D)
Mary K. Browne, 1912–25 (4-S, 10-D)
Mrs. May Sutton Bundy, 1904–28 (2-S, 1-D)
Mable Cahill, 1891–93 (2-S, 2-D)
Mrs. Louise Brough Clapp, 1941–57 (1-S, 17-D)
Mrs. Sarah Palfrey Fabyan Cooke Danzig, 1928–45 (4-S, 19-D)
Mrs. Althea Gibson Darben, 1952–58 (3-S, 2-D)
Mrs. Margaret Osborne duPont, 1938–60 (3-S, 23-D)
Darlene Hard, 1955–69 (4-S, 12-D)
Doris Hart, 1942–55 (4-S, 16-D)
Mrs. Shirley Fry Irvin, 1944–56 (1-S, 5-D)
Helen Jacobs, 1927–41 (4-S, 4-D)
Mrs. Molla Bjurstedt Mallory, 1915–28 (15-S, 9-D)
Alice Marble, 1932–40 (5-S, 8-D)
Elisabeth Moore, 1891–1909 (4-S, 6-D)
Mrs. Helen Wills Moody Roark, 1922–38 (7-S, 6-D)
Ellen Roosevelt, 1890 (1-S, 1-D)
Elizabeth Ryan, 1914–34 (1-S, 3-D)
Eleonora Sears, 1911–17 (5-D)
Bertha Townsend, 1888–89 (2-S)
Marie Wagner, 1908–22 (6-S, 4-D)
Mrs. Hazel Hotchkiss Wightman, 1909–43 (6-S, 28-D)

Men:

Fred Alexander, 1901–18 (1-S, 12-D)
Wilmer Allison, 1927–35 (2-S, 5-D)
Karl Behr, 1906–15 (0)
Don Budge, 1934–38 (4-S, 10-D)
Oliver Campbell, 1888–92 (3-S, 5-D)
Malcolm Chace, 1892–95 (3-S, 4-D)
Joseph Clark, 1883–89 (1-S, 2-D)
William Clothier, 1901–14 (2-S)
Dwight Davis, 1898–1901 (1-S, 4-D)

John Doeg, 1927–31 (1-S, 2-D)
Dr. James Dwight, 1882–88 (5-D)
Bob Falkenburg, 1943–48 (1-S, 3-D)
Chuck Garland, 1917–20 (1-S, 3-D)
Pancho Gonzalez, 1948–70 (13-S, 6-D)
Bitsy Grant, 1930–41 (3-S, 1-D)
Clarence Griffin, 1913–24 (1-S, 4-D)
Harold Hackett, 1906–12 (9-D)
Fred Hovey, 1890–96 (3-S, 3-D)
Frank Hunter, 1922–30 (2-S, 4D)
Joe Hunt, 1936–43 (2-S, 2-D)
Bill Johnston, 1913–27 (3-S, 5-D)
Jack Kramer, 1939–47 (4-S, 9-D)
Bill Larned, 1892–1911 (8-S)
Art Larsen, 1949–56 (5-S, 4-D)
George Lott, 1924–34 (1-S, 13-D)
Gene Mako, 1933–39 (1-S, 8-D)
Maurice McLoughlin, 1909–15 (2-S, 3-D)
Don McNeill, 1937–50 (5-S, 6-D)
Gardnar Mulloy, 1939–57 (7-D)
R. L. Murray, 1914–18 (3-S)
Frank Parker, 1933–49 (8-S, 3-D)
Theodore Pell, 1905–15 (3-S, 5-D)
Vinnie Richards, 1918–26 (7-S, 20-D)
Bobby Riggs, 1936–41 (9-S, 7-D)
Dick Savitt, 1950–60 (3-S)
Ted Schroeder, 1940–51 (5-S, 9-D)
Dick Sears, 1881–87 (7-S, 6-D)
Vic Seixas, 1942–66 (3-S, 10-D)
Frank Shields, 1928–45 (0)
Henry Slocum, Jr., 1886–90 (2-S, 1-D)
Bill Talbert, 1941–54 (2-S, 19-D)
Bill Tilden, 1913–29 (16-S, 18-D)
Tony Trabert, 1951–55 (8-S, 7-D)
John Van Ryn, 1927–37 (4-D)
Ellsworth Vines, 1930–32 (4-S, 3-D)
Holcombe Ward, 1899–1906 (2-S, 7-D)
Watson Washburn, 1913–22 (2-D)
Malcolm Whitman, 1896–1902 (4-S, 2-D)
Dick Williams, 1912–26 (6-S, 5-D)
Sidney Wood, 1930–45 (0)
Bob Wrenn, 1891–97 (4-S, 3-D)
Beals Wright, 1899–1910 (1-S, 3-D)

NON-AMERICANS

Fred Perry, Britain
Jean Borotra, France
Henri Cochet, France
René Lacoste, France
Jacques Brugnon, France

NON-PLAYERS

George Adee, Administrator
Perry Jones, Administrator
Julian Myrick, Administrator
Jimmy Van Alen, Innovator
Arthur Nielsen, Builder

Alistair Martin, Administrator
Larry Baker, Administrator
Allison Danzig, Journalist

THE NATIONAL TRACK AND FIELD HALL OF FAME OF THE UNITED STATES OF AMERICA

Charleston / Huntington, West Virginia

The National Track and Field Hall of Fame broke ground for its new facilities between Charleston and Huntington, West Virginia, November 27, 1976, thus culminating several years of preparation for this exciting day of dedication to a future important shrine for track and field athletes.

On August 30, 1974, this organization held its first induction of stars into the Hall of Fame, honoring twenty-six on that occasion.

A new group of inductees was selected on June 13 and 14, 1975, including ten athletes who collectively have won 120 national titles in their careers and a total of fifteen gold medals in the Olympic Games. There were also three coaches inducted in the 1975 group.

On June 12, 1976, the third group of athletes and important contributors to the progress of track and field was selected including two sprinters, three middle distance men, one distance man, two women and an all around track man, coach, and author.

The new facilities are on fifty acres of land with an option on an additional adjacent fifty acres. The site is situated on interstate 64 midway between Charleston and Huntington, West Virginia. The funding of the complex began with an appropriation of $902,500 by the West Virginia legislature and $1,205,000 by a federal grant from the Economic Development Administration. Other funds to complete the project will come from private and public sources. It is anticipated that from ten to twelve million dollars will be required to complete the complex.

The building program is conceived to be undertaken in two phases.

1. Construction of the shrine building which will include three acres, the museum, the library and archives, and the auditorium.
2. Construction of an indoor-outdoor 400-meter track completely under a removable roof and a permanent cross country course with dormitories for athletes and coaches.

—All photographs in this chapter, courtesy The National Track and Field Hall of Fame of the United States of America

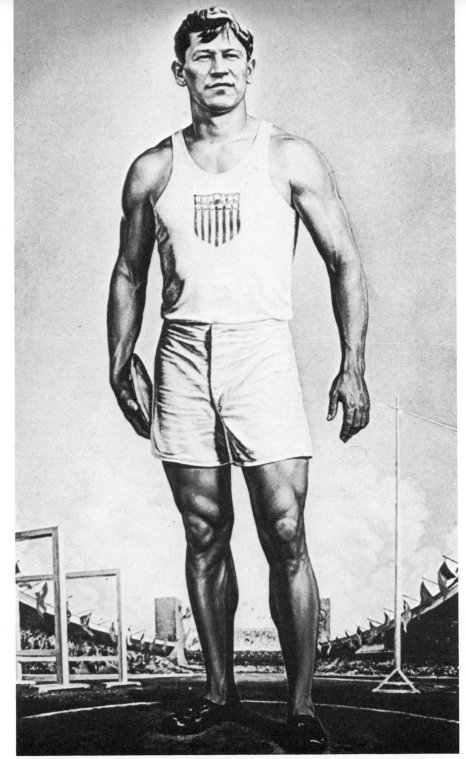

The greatest athlete in American history may have been this Sac-Fox Indian who ex-celled in football, baseball, and track. He was the only athlete in history to win both the pentathlon and decathlon in the Olympic Games. Jim Thorpe in modern terms under present conditions would have been a national hero.

Events planned for the future include summer youth camps, programs for the handicapped, national and international track meets, coaches' seminars, a training site for future Olympic teams, and research studies on health and physical fitness.

Biographies of the track and field inductees into the Hall of Fame by the year of their induction follow.

The architect's rendering of the appearance of the National Track and Field Hall of Fame, Charleston, West Virginia.

HALL OF FAME

CHARTER MEMBERS

RALPH H. BOSTON, born May 9, 1939 in Laurel, Mississippi, a graduate of Tennessee State, was Olympic champion in 1960, runner up in 1964 and bronze medalist in 1968. He broke Jesse Owens' 25-year-old world mark in the long jump of 26'–11¼'' in 1960 and was the first 27-footer.

LEE Q. CALHOUN, 1956–60 Olympic champion 110 hurdles, only man to repeat in this event. Equaled world record in 1960, was not broken until 1973. Graduate of North Carolina Central University. Born February 23, 1933 in Laurel, Mississippi.

GLENN CUNNINGHAM, born in Atlanta, Kansas, in 1909 was the premier miler of the 1930s. He broke world mile record in 1934 and world 800 meter record in 1936. Member of two Olympic teams. Attended Kansas University, NCAA and AAU champion.

"Hal" Davis

GLENN DAVIS, born September 12,1934 in Wellsburg, West Virginia and now resides in Barberton, Ohio, where he grew up and is now the high school track coach. He was two-time, 1956 and 1960 Olympic 400-meter hurdles champion and a two-time world record holder, his best time being 49.2 seconds. He also was a member of the winning 1600 meters relay team in 1960 at Rome. Graduate of Ohio State University. He won three national AAU intermediate hurdles titles and in 1958 set a world record in winning the NCAA 440-yard.

HAROLD "HAL" DAVIS equaled world 100-meter record in 1941 —lost only one important race in career and was never defeated in 220. American sprint champion 1940–43 but World War II ruined his Olympic game chances. Graduate of University of California. Born January 5, 1921 in Salinas, California.

MILDRED "BABE" (DIDRIKSON) ZAHARIAS, born June 26, 1914 in Beaumont, Texas. Died 1956. In the 1932 Olympic games where she was restricted to three events she won the 80 meter hurdles, the javelin throw and placed second on a disputed judges decision in the high jump. Also gained renown in basketball and golf, and recently was voted into the Golf Hall of Fame.

HARRISON DILLARD, born July 8, 1923 in Cleveland, Ohio where he still resides and is identified with youth activities work as well as a regular newspaper columnist. Though best known as a hurdler, Dillard won the Olympic 100-meter title in 1948 and four years later won the gold medal in his specialty. He was a member of the winning USA sprint relay team in both 1948 and 1952. In 1946 and 1947 he was both NCAA and National AAU high hurdles champion, representing Baldwin-Wallace College, and was supreme in the hurdles for almost a decade.

RAY C. EWRY, born 1873 in Lafayette, Indiana, was supreme in all the standing jumps. Sweeping every standing jump (total of 8) in the 1900, 1904 and 1908 Olympics. He won more gold medals than any other Olympic track and field athlete.

RAFER L. JOHNSON, 1960 Olympic champion in decathlon. Broke world record in 1955, regained it in 1960. Graduate of UCLA. Born August 18, 1935 in Hillsboro, Texas.

ALVIN C. KRAENZLEIN, born December 12, 1876 and died January 6, 1928. The only track man to win four individual gold medals in the Olympic games, capturing the 60 meters, the high and low hurdles and the long jump in 1900. A former University of Wisconsin, University of Pennsylvania and New York Athletic Club athlete, he held the world records in the 120-yard high hurdles and long jump and also won seven national AAU championships in four events.

ROBERT B. MATHIAS, 1948–1952 Olympic champion in decathlon. Only man to repeat in this all-around test, won first title as Tulare (California) high school boy, second as Stanford University senior in 1950 then twice in 1952. Presently United States Congressman from California. Born November 17, 1930 in Tulare, California.

LAWRENCE "LON" MYERS, born in 1858 in Richmond, Virginia. Won 15 U.S. titles in four events (100 to 880 yards) in a six-year span from 1879 to 1884, running for the Manhattan (N.Y.) Athletic Club in the pioneer days before the AAU was organized. His championship, 440-yard record of 49²/₅ seconds was not surpassed for fifteen years.

PARRY O'BRIEN, 1952–56 Olympic champion in shot put. First 60-footer. Graduate of University of Southern California. Born January 28, 1932 in Santa Monica, California.

ALFRED A. "AL" OERTER was unprecedented four consecutive— 1956–60–64–68 Olympic championships in discus. First 200-footer, broke world record on four occasions in 1962–63–64. Graduate of University of Kansas. Born September 19, 1936 in Astoria, New York.

HAROLD M. OSBORN, born in Butler, Illinois on April 13, 1899—is the only Olympic decathlon champion who also won an individual title (high jump), a feat he accomplished in 1924 Olympic games. Representing University of Illinois and Illinois Athletic Club he won 18 national AAU indoor and outdoor titles.

Parry O'Brien

"Al" Oerter

JESSE OWENS won four gold medals in 1936 Olympic games. Won 100, 200 meters, long jump and ran first leg on 400-meter relay team. Broke three world records and equaled a fourth on a single day—May 25, 1935 in the Big Ten Championships at Ann Arbor, Michigan. World record in long jump stood 25 years. Attended Ohio State University. Born September 12, 1913 in Danville, Alabama.

WILMA RUDOLPH, born June 23, 1940 in Clarksville, Tennessee where she now resides. In the 1960 Olympic games she won the 100 meters and 200 meters and anchored the winning USA sprint relay team. She won a bronze medal in the 1956 Olympic games as a member of the relay team. She won four straight national AAU sprint titles, 1959–1962 and four other national AAU indoor and outdoor titles. She is a graduate of Tennessee State.

Jesse Owens winning the 220 yard dash in 20.3 at the Big Ten meet in Ann Arbor, Michigan on a glorious May day in 1935. This was perhaps the greatest individual performance of all time for on this day Owens equaled or broke four world records in winning four events in one afternoon—the 100 and 220 yard dashes, the 220 yard low hurdles and the long jump.

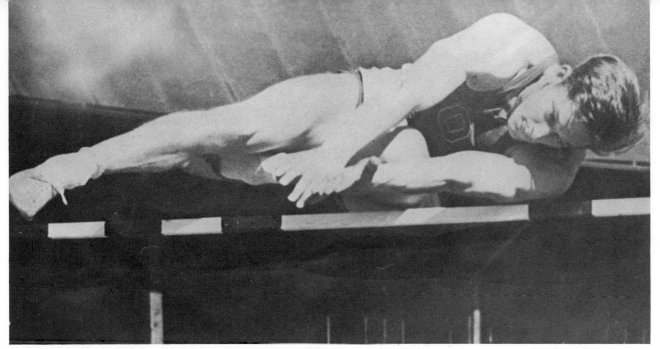

"Les" Steers

ROBERT I. "BOB" SIMPSON, born in Bosworth, Missouri. Developed the modern hurdling technique and became the premier of 1915–1917, attending the University of Missouri. Set world high hurdles record and tied low hurdles record. Coached track at University of Missouri (where he coached Charter Hall of Famer Brutus Hamilton) and Iowa State.

LESTER "LES" STEERS set world record in high jump of 6′–10⅞″ then improved it to 6′–11″ the same year. Record stood until 1953. War deprived him of opportunity to compete in Olympic games. Graduate of University of Oregon. Born June 16, 1917, in Eureka, California.

CORNELUIS "DUTCH" WARMERDAM, considered greatest pole vaulter of all time. First man to vault 15 feet, did so 43 times (outdoors and indoors) before anyone else cleared that height. Set world record 15′–7¾, which stood until 1957. Graduate of California State University in Fresno. Born June 22, 1915 in Long Beach, California.

MALVIN G. WHITFIELD, born October 11, 1924 in Bay City, Texas. Now employed by the Department of State and working with the new emerging nations of Africa. Ran the 400 and 800 meters in two Olympics and was 800 meters champion in 1948 and 1952 and a member of the winning 1600-meter relay team in 1952. He won five national AAU half-mile titles and one indoor crown. He was twice NCAA half-mile champion. He attended Ohio State.

"Dutch" Warmerdam

COACHES

DEAN B. CROMWELL, the most successful track and field coach in history. Coached University of Southern California from 1909 to 1948. Won 12 NCAA team championships and had 82 individual champions. Coached 14 world record holders, ten Olympic champions and was head coach of the 1948 Olympic team. Died in 1962 at the age of 82.

BRUTUS HAMILTON, born July 19, 1900 in Peculiar, Missouri, died in 1970. Placed second in the decathlon and fifth in the pentathlon in the 1920 Olympic games. He was a track and football standout at the University of Missouri. He was the Olympic coach in 1952. Coached at Westminster College, (Fulton, Missouri), University of Kansas and for 33 years at the University of California (Berkeley) where he was also Athletic Director and Dean of Students. Served as member and chairman of the NCAA Rules Committee. He was National Track Coach in 1965.

MICHAEL C. "MIKE" MURPHY, track and field coach in the late 19th and early 20th centuries. Organized and coached the combined New York Athletic Club and University of Pennsylvania team which won 14 individual events in 1900 Olympics and coached 1908–1912 Olympic teams. His Yale and Pennsylvania teams won a total of 15 intercollegiate AAAA team titles from 1887 to 1913 and his New York Athletic Club team won 10 national AAU team titles, 1894 to 1910. Slight of build, he was a rare personality. Died 1913, father of Sen. George L. Murphy, California, former motion picture star.

CONTRIBUTORS

AVERY BRUNDAGE, born September 28, 1887. Died 1975. Member of the 1912 U.S. Olympic team and was national all-around champion (ten events in one day) three times. He was past president of the Amateur Athletic Union, the United States Olympic Committee and headed the International Olympic Committee for 20 years until his retirement following the 1972 Olympic games. He was a graduate of the University of Chicago in Civil Engineering.

DANIEL J. FERRIS, born 1889 in Pawling, New York. Employed by the Amateur Athletic Union in 1912 as secretary to the late James E. Sullivan. Served 30 years as secretary-treasurer of the Amateur Athletic Union and now is secretary emeritus of the organization. He is a member of the executive council of the International Amateur Athletic Federation, world governing body of track and field. He has attended every Olympic game since 1912. He was an outstanding sprinter before retiring to devote himself to administrative work and sportswriting.

1975 INDUCTEES

HORACE ASHENFELTER III was born on January 23, 1923 in Collegeville, Pa. He was the 1949 NCAA two-mile-run champion as a collegian at Pennsylvania State University who later competed in the 1952 Helsinki and the 1956 Melbourne Olympic Games. Ashenfelter's victory in the 3,000-meter steeplechase with a record time of 8:45.4 in Helsinki was the biggest upset of the Games being the only USA victory in this "foreign" event. "Ash" won 9 National AAU outdoor distance titles (including 3 in the steeplechase) and five indoor AAU distance championships. Horace Ashenfelter III was honored with the Sullivan Award following his Helsinki triumph.

ALICE COACHMAN DAVIS, born November 9, 1923, in Albany, Georgia, studied at Tuskegee Institute in Alabama; however, she received her B.S. Degree from Albany State College, Albany, Georgia. Between 1939 and 1948 she won 25 AAU indoor and outdoor championships in the sprints and high jump. In the 1948 London Olympics she won the gold medal in the high jump setting an Olympic Record of 5'6⅛." She was the first American Woman to win a gold medal in track and field in the post war Olympics. She is a member of the Citizens Savings (Helms) Hall of Fame and Tuskegee Institute Athletic Hall of Fame. She has taught physical education and has coached track and field at the high school level.

JOHN J. FLANAGAN, born in the county of Limerick, Ireland in 1873, was a member of the 1900, 1904 and 1908 United States Olympic teams. He won gold medals in the hammer throw at each of the three Games, placed third in the discus throw in 1904, and set the World Record in the hammer throw in 1897, with a throw of 150 feet 8 inches at Bayonne, New Jersey. He went on to break the World Record 16 times until he achieved the distance of 184 feet 4 inches in July, 1909. John Flanagan won seven AAU hammer throw titles and six more in the 56-pound weight throw. After retiring from the police force, John returned to Ireland where he coached two-time Olympic gold medal winner, Dr. Patrick O'Callighan.

Horace Ashenfelter III, (998) of Penn State University who won the 3000 meter steeplechase in the 1948 Olympic Games in Melbourne, Australia and nine national AAU outdoor distance championships plus the coveted Sullivan trophy as America's top athlete.

Alice Davis a great all-around woman athlete from Tuskegee Institute who specialized in the sprints and high jump and set an Olympic record in the latter in winning the gold medal in 1948 at a height of 5' 6⅛".

RALPH METCALFE, born on May 29, 1910 in Atlanta, Georgia, attended Marquette University. During his three varsity years and two post-collegiate years of competition, he won more sprint titles than any other runner of that time. He annexed the National AAU 200 meters or 220 yards five straight years, 1932 through 1936; the National AAU 60 meters three years (1933, 1934 and 1936), and he anchored the Marquette 400-meter relay which won the National AAU title in 1934, 1935, and 1936. At the 1936 Berlin Olympic Games, Metcalfe finished in the 100 meters behind Jesse Owens and he won the gold medal as a member of the sprint relay team which set a World Olympic Record of 39.8.

As a congressman from the state of Illinois, he has served on many important U.S. Congressional Committees, including several concerned with amateur sports in the United States.

BOBBY JOE MORROW, born in Harlingen, Texas on October 15, 1935, was undefeated throughout his senior year in high school and continued this record as a freshman at Abilene Christian College, Texas, climaxing his freshman year by winning the National AAU title. During 1956, Morrow swept both springs in the NAIA, NCAA and final Olympic trials. In the 1956 Melbourne Olympics he won the 100 and 200 meters and anchored the World Record sprint relay. In the year following the Olympics, Bobby won doubles in the NAIA and NCAA sprints, and in 1958 he won both AAU sprint titles.

Sports Illustrated selected Morrow "1956 Sportsman of the year," the first track athlete to be so recognized. As an individual runner or member of the Abilene Christian College or USA relay teams, this great athlete set nine World Records as he won fourteen national sprint championships. Bobby Morrow was named Sullivan Award winner as the outstanding amateur athlete of 1957.

BOB RICHARDS, born on February 20, 1926 in Champaign, Illinois. He vaulted in three Olympics with a third in London in 1948 and firsts in 1952 and 1956. He is the only man to win two gold medals in the Olympic pole vault event. Bob won the AAU all-around award in 1953 and the decathlon in 1951, 1954 and 1955. He made the Olympic team in the decathlon in 1956, but an injured tendon caused him to finish 12th.

Bob Richards was the second man in history to vault 15 feet and he cleared it a total of 126 times! His best vault was 15 feet 5 inches outdoors and 15 feet 6 inches indoors. Even though he managed to tie for first only once in the NCAA, he improved enough to win nine outdoor AAU titles (including two ties), and eight indoor AAU titles (including one tie) and went on to Olympic glory.

HELEN STEPHENS, born February 3, 1918 in Fulton, Missouri, was a member of the 1936 Berlin Olympic team that won the 100-meter in 11.5, setting a World Record. She also anchored the winning 400-meter relay team to a new Olympic Record of 46.9, and she competed in the javelin throw. In 2½ years of active competition, during 1935–37, she won over 70 consecutive races and never lost to a woman.

She won 4 AAU championships in the 100 and 200-meter sprints. She served for a short time in the U.S. Women's Marine Corps during WW II and has been in the United States Government service for nearly 30 years. Helen Stephens was voted the Alumni Award of Distinction from William Woods College in Fulton, Missouri in 1965.

JAMES FRANCIS THORPE, a Sac-Fox Indian, named Wa-Tho-Huck (Bright Path) was born on May 28, 1888 in Prague, Oklahoma. He was the only athlete in history to win both the pentathlon and decathlon in the Olympics. He accomplished this feat at the 1912 Stockholm Olympics Games and placed fourth in the high jump and seventh in the long jump events. In the decathlon he won 4 of the 10 events outright, scoring 700 points more than his nearest opponent, a record point score for 12 years. In winning the 1912 Olympic pentathlon he was first in 4 of the 5 events.

(Above) Bob Richards, the only two time winner in the Olympic pole vault event, 1952 and 1956, as well as one of the top decathlon competitors of his day.

(At right) Two of the Top American athletes of their era, Helen Stephens, sprinter and javelin thrower and Jesse Owens, all-time sprinter, hurdler, and long jump champion, relax at the Berlin Olympics.

In a 1950 poll, U.S. Sports Writers and Broadcasters voted Jim Thorpe the outstanding male athlete of the first half of the 20th century.

WILLIAM A. TOOMEY, was born in Philadelphia on January 10, 1939 and he was reared in New York City and Connecticut. He graduated from the University of Colorado and received the Masters Degree from Stanford University. Bill won the National AAU pentathlon title four times in the five year period 1960 through 1964 and he became the only man to win five straight National AAU decathlon titles (1965 through 1969).

He was the Pan-American Games champion in 1967 and the Olympic gold medalist at the 1968 Mexico Games. Bill competed in 33 decathlon contests before he set a World Record in December 1969 with an all-time best of 8,417 points. Bill Toomey has served the President's Council on Physical Fitness and has recently been appointed to the President's Commission on Amateur Sports in the U.S.A.

STELLA WALSH, born on April 3, 1911 in Wierzchownia, Poland, grew up in the United States but competed for her native country in the 1932 Los Angeles and 1936 Berlin Olympics. She won first place in the 100m in the 1932 games and 2nd place in same event in 1936 games. During her athletic career she held World Records in the 60m, 100m, 200m and 220-yard dashes. During this period she also held 31 National AAU indoor and outdoor championships covering the sprints, long jump, discus and pentathlon events. Her career in track and field extended from 1930 to 1955, probably the longest of any track and field athlete, male or female.

COACHES

MILLARD E. "BILL" EASTON, graduated from Indiana University. He coached winning teams at Hammond, Indiana High School, at Drake University and at the University of Kansas. In the 8-year period 1951 to 1959, Bill's Kansas teams won cross country, indoor and outdoor NCAA titles—a string of 24 consecutive championships.

Bill Easton coached Bill Nieder, Olympic champion and world record shot putter; Al Oerter, four-time Olympic Champion and world record holder as well at 30 athletes to All-American status. Mr. Easton was the first U.S. Track Coaches Association track coach of the year in 1960. He had also served as secretary and president of the association.

EDWARD P. HURT, was born on February 12, 1900 in Brookneal, Virginia. He graduated from Howard University and later earned a Master's degree from Columbia. Dr. Hurt was awarded the Dr. of Laws (LLD) degree from Morgan State College. As a faculty member and track coach at Morgan State from 1929 through 1970 he produced eight individual NCAA Champions, 12 AAU Champions, three NCAA Relay Champions and six AAU relay championship efforts.

Eddie Hurt was named Track and Field News Coach of the year 1950 and U.S. Track Coaches Association indoor coach of the year 1970. He was a member of the 1959 Pan-Am and 1969 U.S. Olympic coaching staff.

MERITORIOUS SERVICE

EDWARD M. "TED" HAYDON created the University of Chicago Track Club, a significant development which holds great potential for amateur track and field in the United States. Chicago Track Club members include young age group athletes, varsity college, national and international class competitors. Despite the no pay, run-for-fun emphasis, many Chicago Track Club members have become American and World Record holders and Olympians.

This track club concept might very well be the future of athletics in the United States. Edward "Ted" Haydon has been and still is a true contributor to the great sport of track and field.

DOLORES A. BOECKMANN (DEE BECKMANN) is one of the pioneer women in sports in the United States—not only as an athlete (competed in 800-meter run as a member of the 1928 U.S. Olympic team) but as a coach (coach of the U.S. Women's track and field team at the 1936 Olympic Games, Berlin). She was the first woman Coach chaperone to lead a U.S. Women's squad to the Olympic games. She held all of the women's records in track and field events during the 1919–1920 era under the western AAU Association. (now Ozark AAU)

DR. J. KENNETH DOHERTY has been outstanding in four areas of track and field—author, meet promoter, coach, and athlete. He has authored four coaching textbooks, widely used in United States colleges and high schools, that have been translated into four languages—Russian, Finnish, Spanish and Japanese. He was Director of the Pennsylvania Relay Carnival, Philadelphia Inquirer Charities Meet, the first USA-USSR dual meet, Philadelphia, 1959, and of the Big Ten (Jesse Owens Greatest Day) Championships, 1935.

He was head coach at the University of Michigan, 1939–1948 (7 of a possible 18 Conference Team Championships) and at the University of Pennsylvania, 1948–1959. Doherty was National AAU Decathlon Champion in 1928 and 1929, American record-holder in 1929, and bronze medallist at the 1928 Olympic Games, Amsterdam. Born in Detroit, he attended what is now Wayne State University '27, and received a Ph.D. degree in Educational Psychology at the University of Michigan, '48.

ROBERT L. HAYES was born in Jacksonville, Florida on December 20, 1942. He won gold medals in the 1964 Olympics in the 100 meters (World Record: 10.0 secs.) and record 400 meters relay. His great anchor leg in the Tokyo Games epitomizes his sobriquet as the "World's Fastest Human." His career lasted four years at Florida A&M where in sixty-two 100 yards or 100 meters finals he lost only two, both in one week after he had been ill. Hayes' times were phenomenal: 9.1 in 1963 at St. Louis (Semi-final AAU 100 yard) and 10.0 (100 meters) for World's record in the Olympics. He ran 09.3 or faster nineteen times.

HAYES WENDELL JONES won the 1964 Olympic games 110-meter high hurdles championship. He had finished third four years earlier. Born in Starkville, Miss., he was graduated from Eastern Michigan University where he competed in track and field. One of the finest hurdlers in history he was virtually unbeatable indoors for five years. He won five National AAU outdoor titles and captured six National AAU indoor championships.

BILLY MILLS, an American Indian, born in Pine Ridge, So. Dakota, June 30, 1938. After attending Haskell American Indian Institute in Lawrence, Kansas, Mills attended the University of Kansas. He established an American and World record when he ran 27:11.6 in the 1965 AAU Championships six-mile. Mills ran the greatest race of his career and one of the most memorable of all time when he defeated what was considered the strongest field ever assembled in the 10,000 M. at the 1964 Olympic games. His winning time of 28:24.4 was an Olympic record.

CHARLES PADDOCK dominated the sprints of the 1920s and was known as the "World's Fastest Human" in his day. Paddock was the glamour boy of track athletes in the eyes of the public, who still remember his exuberant finishing style arms upraised and chest thrown forward in leap at the tape. Paddock won the Olympic 100 (10.8) in 1920, and was 5th in 1924. Paddock was second in the 200 at both the 1920 and 1924 Olympics. He held the World record in the 100 meters (10.4) and 200 meters (21.6) and was co-holder of the 100-yard record (9.6). He ran on the USA Relay team that won the Olympic gold medal. Paddock won 5 AAU sprint titles from 1921 to 1924 and

A display featuring Ken Doherty as a competitor in the Track and Field Hall of Fame before the new construction.

dominated the larger invitational meets. He ran the first 9.5 100-yard race. Paddock was born in Gainesville, Texas, August 11, 1900. He died in World War II as a Captain in the Marines.

STEVE PREFONTAINE, a native of Coos Bay, Oregon, was called by many the best ever American distance runner. Only hours before his untimely death he had electrified a Eugene, Oregon, crowd by winning the 5000 meters, the event in which he was expected to compete in the '76 Olympic Games. Pre had a sometimes stormy career, but the 5'9'', 145 pounder was known as a tremendous competitor. During his brief career he set a national record for the high school two-mile at 8:41.5. He was a four-time NCAA 3 mile champion, three-time NCAA cross country champion, and had set ten American records in events from 2000 M to 10,000 M. Prefontaine finished fourth in the 5000 M in the 1972 Olympics. He was 24 years old when he died on May 30, 1975.

JOIE RAY was America's predominant miler in the decade 1915–1925. He won 17 National AAU Championships in distances ranging from 880 yds. to six miles. He lives in Michigan. No one in history ever has won eight National AAU one-mile crowns achieved by Ray between 1915 and 1923. Also, he was the most popular indoor miler of his day, in his final year of competition equaled the world's best at Paavo Nurmi, Finland, 4:12. Ray, known as "Chesty Joie" because of his confidence on the track, was a member of the 1920, 1924, and 1928 U.S. Olympic teams. His best finish place was fifth in 1928 Olympic Games marathon at Amsterdam.

MAE FAGGS STARR, born in Bayside, New York, April 10, 1932, is a graduate of Tennessee State University, Nashville, Tennessee. She ran for the Tennessee State Tigerbelles and the New York City Police Athletic League. She was on three consecutive USA Women's Olympic Teams 1948, 1952, and 1956. Held the American record in the 100-yd. dash (10.7) and 220-yd. dash (25.1) at one time. She was Indoor AAU National Champion in the 220-yd. dash in 1949, 1952. In 1955 she was a member of the US Pan American team and ran on the winning 4 × 100 meter dash. She was a member of the winning Olympic 4 × 100 Meters Olympic team. She has been a successful teacher and worker with the young people of Cincinnati, Ohio.

FORREST "SPECK" TOWNS, born February 6, 1914 in Fitzgerald, Georgia, was the first man to run under fourteen seconds for the 110 m-120 yard hurdles. (13.7-1936 Oslo, Norway.) He was a gold medal winner at the 1936 Olympics 110 m hurdles. (Olympic record 14.1); British Empire Record 1936-14.2; National AAU Record 1936-14.2; NAAU record 1936-14.2; NCAA record 1936-14.1. He was never defeated in dual meet competition. "Speck" Towns served as assistant track coach, University of Georgia 1938 (January thru June) and Head Track Coach August 1938, May 1942, Army of the U.S. May 1942–March 1946, when he served in Africa and Europe (Bronze star medal award); Head track coach, University of Georgia 1946–1975; member Helms Hall of Fame; Bulldog Hall of Fame; Georgia Hall of Fame. Member NCAA Rules Committee 1968–71.

THE HALL OF FAME OF THE TROTTER

Goshen, New York

The Hall of Fame of the Trotter has been described as one of the most unique and best specialty museums in the country. It has a National Historic Landmark for a neighbor. It is concerned with people and horses, a special kind of horse. Their story is told in the Hall of Fame of the Trotter, a museum and Hall of Fame for the sport of harness racing, located in the heart of a village where so much harness horse history has been written—Goshen, New York.

Housed in the former Good Time Stable at 240 Main Street, the museum's back door opens out on famous Historic Track, the only sporting site in America to be designated a National Landmark. Grand Circuit

Harness racing's Hall of Fame was originally a stable constructed in 1913. The atmosphere of the stable remains although the stalls have been converted into exhibition space.

—All photographs in this chapter, courtesy Hall of Fame of the Trotters

Missing atop the Museum is the trotting horse weathervane which was stolen December 26, 1975 and later recovered in a New York Gallery.

racing is conducted the first week in July at Historic and for the past decade or so, matinee harness racing is held at the track, too — usually the last three weekends in May including Memorial Day.

When the Hall of Fame of the Trotter opened in 1951, a careful attempt was made to preserve the stable atmosphere of the building.

Stalls remain stalls although they've been changed into exhibition rooms. Hay chutes became miniature stages for statuary and trophies. The loft became a home for sulkies and wagons once pulled by famous champions, along with the original mobile starting gate developed in 1937 by Steve Phillips. Throughout the museum are reminders of a sport's great past and illustrations of its popular present. A balance of the old and the new is the result of careful exhibit planning designed to make a visitor aware of the sport's heritage as well as the color and excitement of today's racing.

Because of its growing collections with their accompanying need for more exhibit space the Hall of Fame has constructed two additions to its original stable. The first was a gallery to mount the museum's large

(Continued on page 256)

The trotting horse as a weathervane is featured in this display emphasizing his importance during Victorian times.

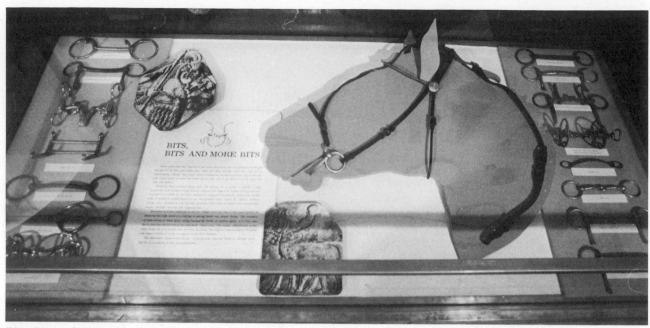

Bits, Bits and More Bits describe the many bits of iron used in guiding a horse to the Winner's Circle.

FRESH YANKEE *(Joe O'Brien, driver)*   **ALBATROSS** *(Stanley Dancer, driver)*

HARNESS
HORSE OF
1970

HARNESS
HORSE OF
1971-1972

HARNESS
HORSE OF
1973

HARNESS
HORSE OF
1974

SIR DALRAE *(James Dennis, driver)*   **DELMONICA HANOVER** *(Del Miller, driver)*

The permanent trophies of the Pacing and Trotting Filly Triple Crowns are featured in the Living Hall of Fame room.
The life-like statuettes of the Hall of Famers are shown in the background.

collection of Currier and Ives trotting prints as well as a splendid oil painting collection. A much larger wing was completed in July, 1972. Included within it was a room to honor those persons elected by members of the United States Harness Writers Association to their Living Hall of Fame. Exquisite statuettes, lifelike in appearance to the people they represent, are on view. No other Hall of Fame, anywhere, honors its own in similar manner.

A large gallery-auditorium, next to the USHWA Living Hall of Fame, presents harness racing films, as well as providing a place for lectures, concerts, exhibits. Upstairs, professionally prepared exhibits dramatically continue the story of the American trotting horse while also spotlighting the international magnitude of the sport. A history of weathervanes is shown here, neighboring displays about the world pacing champion, Steady Star, and the first North American trotting millionaire, Fresh Yankee. Children can step up and peek into a diorama of the famed Dan Patch. There is an evolution of the sulky display and a pictorial that traces the once popular pasttime of long distance trotting. Featured, too, is a portrayal of Hambletonian, the horse, and the three-year-old trotting stake named for him — an exhibit sponsored by the DuQuoin State Fair.

Dioramas, statuettes, drawings and paintings of world champion trotters and pacers and the Immortal horses that preceded them: all are found in the Hall of Fame of the Trotter whose Standardbred library is probably the most complete to be found anywhere. Modern-day sulkies, pulled by Triple Crown winners, point their shafts upward, representing such

SAVOIR (*John S. Chapman, driver*)   **KEYSTONE ORE** (*Stanley Dancer, driver*)

HARNESS HORSE OF 1975

HARNESS HORSE OF 1976

Three of the first honorees inducted into the International Swimming Hall of Fame in 1965,
(left to right) Johnny Weissmuller, Duke Kahanamoku and Buster Crabbe. These men helped
to establish competitive swimming as a popular international sport.

(on the following pages)
The International Swimming Hall of Fame, Fort Lauderdale, Florida, is
a fascinating collection of the memorabilia of the top performers in aquatics
for several generations tastefully displayed in a building that adjoins an Olympic sized
pool with diving boards and platforms for use in championship meets and events.
FROM A WATERCOLOR PAINTING BY KAY SMITH

The National Lawn Tennis Hall of Fame and Tennis Museum, is located in
the Newport Casino, Newport, Rhode Island, where championship lawn tennis
in the United States began in 1881 and has continued up to the present day
as the scene of major tournaments and matches.
FROM A WATERCOLOR PAINTING BY KAY SMITH

SPORTS HALL OF FAME

*The Hockey Hall
of Fame and
Canada's Sports
Hall of Fame,
on the grounds
of the Canadian
National Exposition,
Toronto, Ontario,
Canada are housed
in one building,
the Hockey Hall
of Fame on
the left and the
Canadian Sports
on the right.*

FROM A
WATERCOLOR PAINTING
BY KAY SMITH

The Canadian Football Hall of Fame, Hamilton, Ontario, an attractive building in central Hamilton, presents displays of the history of this popular Canadian sport including visual and sound recordings.

Next to the Hall of Fame is the half mile oval, Historic Track, whose 22 acres sits quietly among the residents of Goshen, New York.

greats as Adios Butler, Bret Hanover, Nevele Pride, Most Happy Fella, Super Bowl, Ayres, Speedy Scot and Romeo Hanover. All were contributed to the Hall as tributes to the winners of harness racing's supreme events.

The museum received its charter from the University of the State of New York as an educational institution. A young people's program brings in thousands of youngsters annually. Tours, movies, story hours and field trips are planned for them. An annual membership progam helps support the Hall of Fame and in return, included among its benefits, the museum gives out large, full-color reproductions of prints and paintings taken from its collection. The institution is open year round and is free.

HARNESS HORSE OF THE YEAR

1970 . . . FRESH YANKEE
1971 & 1972 . . . ALBATROSS
1973 . . . SIR DALRAE

1974 . . . DELMONICA HANOVER
1975 . . . SAVOIR
1976 . . . KEYSTONE ORE

THE NATIONAL WRESTLING HALL OF FAME

Stillwater, Oklahoma

Sponsored by the United States Wrestling Federation

(Pictured above)
Focal point of the National Wrestling Hall of Fame is this life-size green marble statue, spotlighted in the Hall of Founders. Sculptured in Italy in the 19th century, it is a copy of the Greek classic, The Wrestlers, by Cephisodotus. The original, more than 2,000 years old, stands in the Uffizi Gallery in Florence, whence this copy was obtained.

—All photographs in this chapter, courtesy National Wrestling Hall of Fame

The National Wrestling Hall of Fame was dedicated on Saturday, September 11, 1976 with colorful week-end activities in which fourteen men associated with the history of amateur wrestling were enshrined.

The 10,000-square-foot Georgian style building and other incidentals to the establishment of the Hall of Fame were paid for by popular subscription at a cost exceeding $500,000. The attractive structure stands on the northeast corner of the Oklahoma State University campus adjacent to the athletic complex on ground donated by the University to the United States Wrestling Federation.

The concept of a National Wrestling Hall of Fame was developed early in 1972 by Myron Roderick, then executive director of the U.S. Wrestling Federation, and Dr. Melvin D. Jones of Oklahoma City, an insurance executive and avid sports booster.

After agreeing in principle to the idea, they added Bill Aufleger, president of the Stillwater Development Co., Stillwater banker Bob McCormick and Oklahoma State University representatives Dennis Schick and Moses Frye to the core group and met with Dr. Robert B. Kamm, president of the university. Dr. Kamm pledged OSU support, including donation of the land and services, if the Hall of Fame could be landed for Stillwater.

The Oklahoma group was among 14 widespread communities bidding for the Hall of Fame at the USWF governing council meeting in April, 1972. By the late July meeting of the council, the field had narrowed to Oklahoma and Iowa, and at that meeting the Hall of Fame formally was awarded to the Oklahoma group.

A non-profit corporation, the U. S. Amateur Wrestling Hall of Fame, Inc., was formed to raise funds, construct the building and present it debt-free to the USWF for operation as a Hall of Fame. Ralph Ball, Oklahoma City architect, Veldo Brewer of Holdenville, former University of Oklahoma president Dr. George Cross and the late Oliver S. Willham, former OSU president, all were active in the corporation from its inception.

At a May, 1976, meeting in Tulsa, a new corporation was formed blending members of the former corporation and representatives of the USWF into the National Wrestling Hall of Fame, Inc. The Board of Governors of this corporation will be active in continued fund-raising for completion of the interior and operation of the Hall.

A $20,000 grant was obtained from the Oklahoma Department of Tourism and Recreation and was expended on displays and furnishings.

The National Wrestling Hall of Fame is the only such structure in the United States developed entirely for the sport of wrestling.

Displays in the museum span the history of wrestling from its earliest beginnings as a competitive sport some 5,000 years ago to the achievements of the 1976 Olympians. Dotting the spacious display cabinets are championship trophies, plaques and medals, early-day and modern Olympic and collegiate uniforms, unusual equipment and hundreds of photographs, programs, books and clippings.

Personal memorabilia of the 14 Distinguished Members spice many of the displays, such as the track and field medals of Ed Gallagher, Dr. Clapp's first rule book with his hand-written editing notes, Hugo Otopalik's 1915 championship plaque, the voucher for Billy Sheridan's first coaching paycheck — $30 for the 1911 season, the Golden Gloves won by Danny Hodge, etc.

Plaques covering the 100-foot Wall of Champions list individual winners from all areas and eras of competitive tournament wrestling.

The 14 charter members were selected from a list of 56 candidates nominated by the general public over a six-month period. The names then were submitted to a nationwide committee of 18 electors, each of whom cast a ballot for 25 candidates. Approval by 75 per cent, or 14 of the electors, was required for induction to the Hall of Fame. Nominations for the second annual election are now being accepted and forms for nomination may be obtained from the Hall of Fame office at 405 West Hall of Fame Avenue in Stillwater, Okla., 74074.

One of four large display cabinets, this is devoted to medals, trophies, photos, etc. from the 1930s. Featured are 1932 Olympic gold medal from Jack VanBebber and 1936 Olympic silver medal from Ross Flood.

Dr. Raymond Clapp

MEMBERS OF THE
WRESTLING HALL OF FAME

DR. RAYMOND CLAPP, Doctor of Medicine, was an outstanding athlete and coach, but his principal contribution to the sport of wrestling took place as he led development of early-day collegiate rules and collegiate tournaments.

Dr. Clapp became chairman of the NCAA wrestling rules committee in 1927 and served for 18 years. In many respects, it could be said that he WAS the rules committee during its formative years. Through his leadership, a distinct and progressive code of rules for college and high school competition was developed and adopted. He organized and conducted the first National Collegiate tournament in 1928. Four years earlier, Dr. Clapp had inaugurated the Missouri Valley tournament, forerunner of the present Big Eight Conference championships.

FENDLEY COLLINS, as an undefeated 175-pound wrestler under Edward C. Gallagher at Oklahoma State, won the Canadian amateur championship in 1926 and the U. S. national amateur title in 1927. After two brief years of high school coaching, he assumed the reins at Michigan State in 1930 and guided the Spartans to 158 victories, against 84 losses and 11 ties. Three times his teams were runners-up in the NCAA tournament, and his wrestlers won 28 national titles in collegiate and amateur meets.

Collins was active in all phases of wrestling. He served on national rules and officials' committees and on the United States Olympic Committee. He was coach of the U. S. team in the 1955 Pan American Games and manager of the 1964 Olympic team. Some of his most noteworthy activities concerned international competition and education of America to the differences in style and procedures. He founded the Pan American Wrestling Confederation, served as its first president, and later was named honorary president for life.

TOMMY EVANS left an indelible imprint on the sport of wrestling as a champion athlete and a champion coach. Evans wrestled for University of Oklahoma in 1951, 1952 and 1954, missing the 1953 season because of injury. He won 42 of 43 matches and scored 20 falls, an aggressive style which he carried forward into his coaching career. He was National Collegiate champion in 1952 and 1954 and both times was voted outstanding wrestler of the NCAA tournament, at that time only the second athlete to win such honors twice.

His wrestling career carried Evans around the world, to Helsinki, Finland, in 1952, and to Melbourne, Australia, in 1956, as a member of United States Olympic teams. At Melbourne, he wrestled in both freestyle and Greco-Roman competition.

EDWARD C. GALLAGHER, as a collegian, excelled in football and track. He was clocked once in 9.8 seconds while winning the 100-yard dash in the

Fendley Collins

Tommy Evans

Edward C. Gallagher

4-foot square wallboard, covered with plexiglass, displays early-day wrestling memorabilia, including (top center) photo of participants in first NCAA tournament in 1928, along with program for that meet.

Southwest Conference meet, and his 99-yard run in the Kansas State football game the same year, 1908, still stands as the OSU school record. He received his degree in electrical enginering, but chose a career coaching football and track, and teaching physical education. He remained at his alma mater for several years, then went to Baker University in Kansas.

In 1916, he returned to Oklahoma State as director of athletics. Gallagher introduced scientific wrestling to gym classes and put his first varsity team on the mat that year. He applied his engineering knowledge of leverage and stress to the development of more than 300 wrestling holds. He was the first to organize systematic practice situations, and devoted close attention to diet and training methods. In 23 years of coaching he produced 19 undefeated teams. His wrestlers won 138 dual meets, tied four and lost only five. During the 10 years prior to 1932 his teams scored 68 consecutive victories.

ART GRIFFITH — His coaching career spanned two great dynasties, first for 15 years at Central High School in Tulsa, Oklahoma, and then for 13 seasons at Oklahoma State University. His records were fabulous. His high school teams won 94 of 100 matches, 50 of them in a row, and 10 Oklahoma scholastic championships. A dozen times, his Braves were undefeated, and they won the only two national high school tournaments conducted.

Succeeding Edward C. Gallagher, he took the reins at Oklahoma State in 1941 and amassed eight NCAA championships in 13 attempts. His teams produced 78 victories against seven losses and four ties, and 10 times were undefeated. His wrestlers won 27 individual NCAA titles. When he became the Cowboys' coach, they already had won 27 consecutive dual meets. Under his leadership, that streak was extended to a record 76 before a loss in 1951. He was U.S. Olympic coach in 1948.

Art Griffith

261

Cliff Keen

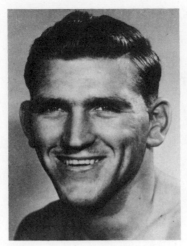

Danny Hodge

George Mehnert

Rex Peery

Dave McCuskey

Hugo Otopalik

DANNY HODGE, in the collegiate style of wrestling, had no peer, indeed no challenger. He won every one of his 46 bouts for the University of Oklahoma, 36 of them by fall, an astonishing 78 per cent. During his junior and senior years, he pinned 20 consecutive opponents. And no collegiate foe ever took him to the mat from the standing position. Three times a National Collegiate champion at 177 pounds, he twice was voted the outstanding wrestler of the NCAA tournament.

In one 10-day span in 1956, his junior year, Hodge won the NCAA title and national amateur championships in both Greco-Roman and freestyle, winning every bout in those three tournaments by fall. Twice he was an Olympic wrestler, placing fifth in 1952 at Helsinki before his college career started, and winning the silver medal in the 1956 Games at Melbourne. There, in the championship bout, he led his Bulgarian opponent by a wide margin when a controversial fall was called against him.

CLIFF KEEN – After 45 years at the University of Michigan, the longest coaching career in wrestling history, the answer was clear. He could develop champions. Cliff Keen was an undefeated wrestler under Edward C. Gallagher at Oklahoma State University and won the Missouri Valley national invitational championship. In 1924, he won the Olympic trials but was sidelined by a broken rib. His substitute ultimately lost in the Olympic finals at Paris. He also was a football and track star.

His Michigan teams twice were NCAA runners-up and they won 13 Big Ten Conference championships, placing in the top three in the conference 40 times. They won 276 dual meets against 88 losses and 11 ties. His wrestlers captured 11 National Collegiate titles and 81 conference crowns.

DAVE McCUSKEY – A 1930 graduate of the University of Northern Iowa, where he was an outstanding football halfback, baseball pitcher and track star, he immediately joined the coaching staff of the teachers' college and built a national power in the sport of wrestling.

In 21 years there, he produced 102 victories, 31 losses and seven ties. His efforts bore fruit in the form of a National Collegiate team championship in 1950 and national amateur titles in 1949, 1950 and 1951. His Panthers were NCAA runners-up for four times. In 1953, McCuskey moved to the University of Iowa and again embarked on a construction program of great wrestling teams. His Hawkeyes won 160 matches against 69 losses and seven ties and laid the groundwork for NCAA championships in the mid-1970s.

GEORGE MEHNERT was the first "superstar" of amateur wrestling and the only United States wrestler ever to win two gold medals in the Olympic Games, in 1904 at 115 pounds and in 1908 at 119 pounds. Representing the National Turnverein, a sporting club in Newark, New Jersey, Mehnert first attracted attention in 1900 for his skills in wrestling and basketball. He won the metropolitan amateur wrestling title in 1901 and his first of six national amateur championships in 1902.

Virtually unbeatable over a seven-year span through 1908, he wrestled 59 bouts in national amateur tournaments and lost only one — to fellow Olympic champion George Dole of Yale in the 1907 finals. One of Mehnert's victories during this period was by fall in seven seconds, for many years the fastest on record.

HUGO OTOPALIK was perhaps the first great collegiate wrestler to become a great wrestling coach. He was the 175-pound Western Conference champion for Nebraska, under Dr. Raymond G. Clapp, in 1915, 1916 and 1917, and also starred in the backfield of the Cornhuskers' first football powers. He held the rank of first sergeant during World War I and served with the Red Cross in the European theater during World War II.

Otopalik became director of athletics at Kearney State in Nebraska in 1918 and joined the staff at Iowa State in 1920. He had not planned to become a coach, but when Charles Mayser resigned in 1923, Otopalik agreed to "handle" the wrestling team until a replacement could be found. He continued to "handle" the team for 29 years, developing many individual national champions. His 1933 Cyclones were recognized as co-champions of the NCAA tournament with Oklahoma A&M. Over the years, his teams compiled a dual meet record of 160 victories, 66 losses and five ties and won seven team championships in the Big Eight Conference. In 1932, Otopalik coached the United States Olympic team, which won three gold medals and was acclaimed as the championship team.

REX PEERY fathered the greatest legend in the history of wrestling. So monumental were his personal achievements, and those of his family, that they tend to overshadow his outstanding coaching career and his many contributions to the development of the sport. Rex Peery was a three-time National Collegiate champion at Oklahoma State University under coach Edward C. Gallagher. For the next 29 years, he established a great coaching career, 13 years in Oklahoma high schools and 16 years at the University of Pittsburgh.

Two unforgettable milestones mark his Pittsburgh coaching tenure. In 1952, 1953 and 1954 he coached his elder son, Hugh, to National Collegiate championships. In 1955, 1956 and 1957, he coached his younger son, Ed, to those same honors. Can any family, in any sport, equal those achievements of nine national championships in nine attempts? As a wrestler, Rex Peery was undefeated in dual meets. He added the 1935 national amateur championship to his collegiate laurels. As a coach, he produced 233 victories, 58 losses and six ties. His Pittsburgh teams twice were NCAA runner-up and he developed 13 individual collegiate champions and 23 Eastern champions.

MYRON RODERICK — In his three years as a wrestler at Oklahoma State University, he won 42 of 44 matches and three National Collegiate championships, one at 137 pounds, then two more at 130 pounds. He placed fourth in the 1956 Olympic Games at Melbourne, losing a split decision to the eventual champion. But it was as coach of the Cowboys that he attained his greatest stature. And there was no interlude between his two careers. From national champion in 1956 to the new torch-bearer of the great Oklahoma State coaching tradition in 1957 was an abrupt but highly successful transition.

In 1958, when he led the Cowboys to the NCAA team title he was, at 23, the youngest coach ever to guide a national champion team in any sport. In his 13 years of coaching, he produced seven NCAA team champions. His Cowboys won 140 dual meets, lost only 10 and tied seven, once stringing 84 con-

263

Myron Roderick

Billy Sheridan

Jack VanBebber

secutive duals without a loss. His wrestlers won 20 individual NCAA championships and four gold medals in the Olympic Games. He also coached his teams to two national amateur championships, was the United States coach in the 1963 World Games and was assistant coach in the 1964 Olympics.

BILLY SHERIDAN was a wrestler of legendary stature in his native Scotland in the early years of the 20th century, but it was as coach at Lehigh University that he earned lasting renown. At the age of 19, in 1905, he won the Scottish wrestling crown at nine stone, or 126 pounds. Wrestling eight or nine times a week without ever losing a bout, he reigned as featherweight and lightweight champion of the British Isles until 1908.

In 1908, he emigrated to Ontario, Canada, but two years later moved to Philadelphia. To earn some extra money, he agreed to pose for the famous sculptor, Tait McKenzie, at the University of Pennsylvania and chanced to observe the wrestling team in action. Unable to resist involvement, he offered suggestions and was invited to serve as coach and trainer. In 1911, he was recommended to Lehigh in a similar role. Thus began his famed coaching career. It lasted 40 years, until his retirement in 1952, and produced 223 dual meet victories, only 83 losses and seven ties. In this 40-year period, he developed 59 Eastern Intercollegiate champions, five National Collegiate champions, five national amateur titlists and three Olympians. He also coached winning teams in soccer and lacrosse.

JACK VanBEBBER vanquished the nation's finest wrestlers seven times, but when he set out to conquer the world, he had to hitch-hike. At the 1932 Olympic Games in Los Angeles, as he awaited his final bout for the gold medal, VanBebber suddenly learned that the time schedule had been altered and he was due on the mat within the hour, six miles away. No transportation was provided, or available, so he set out afoot. After two miles, a passing motorist gave him a ride to the arena.

Once at the scene, however, his opponent proved no more effective than his earlier victims. And Blackjack VanBebber became champion of the world with a decision over Eino Leino of Finland, a four-time Olympian who already owned gold, silver and bronze medals. VanBebber was undefeated as a collegiate wrestler for Oklahoma State University in 1929, 1930 and 1931, winning three NCAA championships at 155 and 165 pounds. He captured national amateur titles the same three years, then moved to Los Angeles in 1932 and won another.

THE AQUATIC HALL OF FAME AND MUSEUM OF CANADA, INC.

Winnipeg, Manitoba

In 1967, Canada's Centennial year, the City of Winnipeg made a national application and was awarded the honor of sponsoring the Aquatic Hall of Fame and Museum of Canada Inc. The natatorium complex, which covers an area of more than 13 acres, is located on Poseidon Bay, Winnipeg, Manitoba, named after the Greek God of the Sea and the Protector of all waters.

Winnipeg was host to the Pan-Am Games in July, 1967 and the Pan-Am Natatorium is the jewel remaining from a most happy and successful sporting venture.

The pool is one of the largest indoor bodies in the world. It measures 50 meters × 75 feet of a minimum depth of 6' 6'' with a diving complex of two 1-meter and two 3-meter boards and a tower complex of 3, 5, 7.5 and 10 meters in addition to a beginners' pool.

In this international complex a number of national and international events have been held at which many world swimming records and every Pan-Am Games record have been broken.

The ancient history of aquatics is particularly well depicted at this excellent institution. It has on display copies of many exquisite artifacts. Artifacts and memorabilia valued in the hundreds of thousands of dollars have already been donated by interested sponsors.

The Aquatic Hall of Fame pays tribute to competitors in swimming, diving, water polo and synchronized swimming who have attained international renown or given distinguished service to these sports.

The Hall of Fame is a fine meeting place with assembly rooms, library and research center. It has the commencement of a very fine aquatic library. It has one of the finest sports stamp collections in the world.

Visitors to Winnipeg are well advised to view this magnificent facility and assured a most rewarding experience. It is open every day, 9 a.m. till 10 p.m., throughout the year. Admission is free.

*Copy of the **Bronze Statuette** of a diver, attributed to about 460 B. C., found in Perugia, Italy. The original is in the Museum of Antique Arts, Munich, Germany.*

—All photographs in this chapter, courtesy The Aquatic Hall of Fame and Museum of Canada, Inc.

Features of the Museum

- *3 Graceful Mermaids*

- *"The Sea"* — *represented by the sea-mother with her suckling children, surrounded by Tritons riding on dolphins straight out of the water into the immortal world of fantasy. The Tritons are sons and daughters of Poseidon.*
  "The Sea" is by Kai Nielsen 1882–1924 described as "The Greatest scupltor of Denmark" Bing and Grøndahl, Copenhagen Porcelain. On permanent loan to the Aquatic Hall of Fame and Museum of Canada Inc.

- *Play of the Waves* — *A work of Jean René Gaugin who was born in Paris in 1881, artist and craftsman, who worked at Bing & Grøndahl, Denmark and sculptured in a special material "roche ceramic," of fired clay, which is burnt in different color tones, Jean René Gaugin was the son of Paul Gaugin. Play of the Waves is 50cm high. It was a gift to the Aquatic Hall of Fame in 1973.*

- *The model of the celebrated* **"Cutty Sark"** *found a new berth at the Pan-Am Pool on the 22nd of November, 1969, being the hundredth anniversary of the launching of the Cutty Sark. The model is dressed with the flags of the celebration. The Cutty Sark Club has taken new headquarters in "The Suite" at the Pan-Am Pool; and the numerous ship models which the members have are on display at the Aquatic Hall of Fame.*

- *Poseidon* — *Greek God of the sea and protector of all waters with his "wand." This "wand" was adopted as the symbol of the Aquatic Hall of Fame and Museum of Canada Inc. in 1967. A pin or tie bar is presented to those who are named to the Aquatic Hall of Fame of Canada.*

- *Bas-Relief dating back to 880 B.C., taken from the Palace of Nimroud. The original relief is located in the British Museum, London. It depicts fugitives escaping from soldiers by swimming a river, one of them using a head-high over-arm crawl, and the others using underwater air skins, to escape.*

Three Graceful Mermaids

"The Sea"

The Aquatic Hall of Fame, Winnipeg, Manitoba

HALL OF FAME

GEORGE ATHANS (British Columbia), 1950 British Empire Games, Auckland gold medalist, 3 meter diving.

JACK AUBIN (Ontario), 1930 British Empire & Commonwealth Games — 200 yards breaststroke 2'.35".4.

MARY BAGGALEY (British Columbia), 1938 British Empire & Commonwealth Games — 440 yards free style relay 4'.48".3.

SANDRA BEAUPRÉ, nee Marks (Quebec), 1971 Synchronized swimming.

F. MUNROE BOURNE (Quebec), 1930 British Empire Games, Hamilton gold medalist, 100 yards free style 56'.0.

BEVERLEY BOYS (Ontario), 1969 Winnipeg International Diving Champion, 1969 United States National Champion, 1969 Leningrad International Diving Champion, 1970 British Commonwealth Games, Edinburgh, double gold medalist, 3 meter and tower diving, 1971 Swedish Cup, 3 meters champion, Swedish International Tower Champion.

GEORGE BURLEIGH (Ontario) 1930 British Empire & Commonwealth Games — 800 yards free style relay 8'.42".4; 1934 British Empire & Commonwealth Games — 100 yards free style 55".0, 800 yards free style relay 8'.40".6, 300 yards free style relay 3'.11".2.

CANADIAN RELAY TEAM Munroe Bourne, Quebec; James Thompson, Ontario; James Rose, Coach, Ontario; Bert Gibson, Ontario.

ELIZABETH CARRUTHERS (Alberta) 1971 Pan-Am Games, Cali, Columbia, gold medalist, 3 meter diving.

LEONARD S. CHASE (Quebec) 1966 British Empire & Commonwealth Games — 440 yards medley relay 4'.10".5.

LESLIE CLIFF (British Columbia) 1971 Pan Am Games, Cali, Columbia, 3 gold medals, 200 meters individual medley 2'.30".03; 400 meters individual medley 5'.13".31; Gold medal Canadian Team 400 yards medley relay 4'.35".5.

ANGELA COUGHLAN (Ontario) 1971 Pan Am Games, Cali, Columbia, Gold medal Canadian Team 400 medley relay 4'.35".5.

LT. COL. JOHN W. DAVIES, C.D. (Quebec) 1969 Distinguished Service.

PHYLLIS DEWAR (British Columbia) 1934 British Empire & Commonwealth Games, 100 yards free style 1'.03".0; 440 yards free style 5'.45".6; Team member woman's 300 yards medley relay 3'.42".0; Team member woman's 440 yards free style relay 4'.21".8; 1938 British Empire & Commonwealth Games, Team member woman's 440 yards free style relay 4'.48".3.

TOM DINSLEY (British Columbia) 1963 Pan-American Games, Sao Paulo gold medalist, 3 meter diving.

SYLVIA DOCKERILL, 1971 Pan Am Games, Cali, Columbia, Gold medal, 100 meters breaststroke 1'.18".63.

D. DOBSON, 1938 British Empire & Commonwealth Games, 440 yards free style relay 4'.48".3.

LENORA FISHER, now Gilchrist (British Columbia) 1955 Pan-Am Games, Mexico, gold medalist, 100 meters backstroke.

JENNY FLETCHER, 1907 World records England, before coming to Canada.

BENJAMIN GAZELLE (Ontario) 1934 British Empire & Commonwealth Games, 300 yards medley relay 3'.11".2.

BERT GIBSON (Ontario) 1930 British Empire & Commonwealth Games, 800 yards free style relay 8'.42".4.

J. A. "SANDY" GILCHRIST (British Columbia) 1966 British Empire & Commonwealth Games, 440 yards medley relay 4'.10".5.

DONNA MARIE GURR (British Columbia) 1971 Pan-Am Games, Cali, Columbia, 3 gold medals, 100 meters back stroke 1'.07".18; 200 meters back stroke 2'.24".73; Gold medal Canadian Team 400 yards medley relay 4'.35".5.

PHYLLIS HASLAM (Saskatchewan) 1934 British Empire & Commonwealth Games, 300 yards medley relay 3'.42".0.

GEORGE HODGSON (Quebec) 1911 won mile championship 25'.27".25, Intra-Empire championships at the Festival of the Empire, Crystal Palace, London, England. Festival was the real birth of the Empire Games. 1912 Olympic Games, gold medalist in 400 meter free style 5'24".4 and 1500 meter free style 22'00".0 — world records.

R. HOOPER, 1934 British Empire & Commonwealth Games, 800 yards free style relay 8'.42".4.

The Olympic size pool in the Aquatic Hall of Fame

JANE M. HUGHES (British Columbia) 1964 World Records, 880 yards free style, 1966 British Empire & Commonwealth Games, Jamaica, Team member woman's 440 yards free style 4'.10".8 (new world record).

FLORENCE HUMBLE (Quebec) 1934 British Empire & Commonwealth Games, 400 yards free style relay 4'.21".8.

MARGARET HUTTON (Ontario) 1934 British Empire & Commonwealth Games, 400 yards free style relay 4'.21".8.

RALPH W. HUTTON (British Columbia) 1966 British Empire & Commonwealth Games, Jamaica. gold medalist, 440 yards member Canadian medley relay team; World record holder 400 meter free style; 1967 Pan-American Games, Winnipeg, 200 meters backstroke 2'.12".55.

RONALD JACKS (British Columbia) 1966 British Empire & Commonwealth Games, 110 yards butterfly 1'.00".3.

GEORGE LARSEN (Ontario) 1934 British Empire & Commonwealth Games, 800 yards free style relay 8'.42".4.

MARION B. LAY (British Columbia) 1966 British Empire & Commonwealth Games, 110 yards free style 1'.02".3; Team member woman's 440 yards free style relay 4'.10".8 (new world record).

DOROTHY LYNN, 1938 British Empire & Commonwealth Games, 440 yards free style relay 4'.48".3.

HELEN L. KENNEDY (Ontario) 1966 British Empire & Commonwealth Games, Team member woman's 440 yards free style relay 4'.10".8 (new world record).

IRENE MacDONALD (Vancouver) 15 times Canadian Champion, 6 times United States National Champion, 1954 British Empire Games, Vancouver Bronze Medal; 1958 at Cardiff, Wales, Silver medal; 1956 Olympics, Bronze medal; 1966 Rome Bronze medal; 1957 Female Athlete of the year of the United States.

SANDRA MARKS, now Madame Beaupré, at Quebec City, 1963 Pan-American Games, bronze medal winner in synchronized swimming and numerous other national and international competitions.

JUDITH MOSS, now Mrs. Kennedy (Manitoba) 1934 British Empire Games, London, gold medalist 3 meter diving.

BILL PATRICK (Alberta) 1954 British Empire & Commonwealth Games, Vancouver. Gold medalist, tower diving.

ALFRED PHILLIPS (Ontario) 1930 British Empire Games, Hamilton double gold medalist, 3 meter and tower diving.

IRENE PIRIE (Ontario) 1934 British Empire & Commonwealth Games, 400 yards free style relay 4'.21".8.

ROBERT PIRIE (Ontario) 1934 British Empire & Commonwealth Games, 800 yards free style relay 8'.40".6; 1938 British Empire & Commonwealth Games, 110 yards free style 59".6, 400 yards free style 4'.54".6.

RICHARD W. D. POUND (Quebec) 1962 British Empire & Commonwealth Games, Perth gold medalist, 110 yards free style, (B.E.C.G. record 55.8).

W. PUDDY, 1934 British Empire & Commonwealth Games, 300 yards medley relay 3'.11".2.

NANCY ROBERTSON (Ontario) 1971 Pan-Am Games, Cali, Columbia, gold medalist, Tower diving.

PETER SALMON (British Columbia) 1950 British Empire & Commonwealth Games, 110 yards free style 1'.00".7.

MARGARET CAMERON "PEG" SELLER, nee Shearer (Quebec) 1968 Distinguished Service.

HELEN STEWART, now Hunt (British Columbia) 1955 Pan-American Games, Mexico, gold medalist, 100 meters free style.

MARY STEWART (British Columbia) 1961–62 World Record Holder, 100 meters butterfly 1'.08".8 (1961); 110 yards butterfly 1'09".0 (1961); 100 meters butterfly 1'.07".3 (1962); 110 yards

PEARL STONHAM (Quebec) 1930 British Empire Games, Hamilton, gold medalist in tower diving.

ELAINE TANNER, now Nahrgang (British Columbia) 1966 British Empire & Commonwealth Games, Jamaica. 4 gold, and 2 world records, 100 yards backstroke, 100 yards Butterfly, 220 yards Butterfly (new world record), 110 yards Butterfly, 440 yards individual medley relay, Team member woman's 440 yards free style relay (new world record), 1967 Pan-American Games, Winnipeg, 2 gold, and 2 world records, 100 meters Backstroke 1'.07".32, 200 meters Backstroke 2'.24".44.

JAMES THOMPSON (Ontario) 1930 British Empire & Commonwealth Games, 800 yards free style relay 8'.42".4.

ELIZABETH WHITTAL, now Courvette (Quebec) 1955 Pan-American Games, Mexico, 2 gold medals, 400 meters free style, 100 meters Butterfly.

JANE WRIGHT, 1971 Pan Am Games, Cali, Columbia, Gold medal Canadian Team 400 yards medley relay 4'.35".5.

THE BRITISH COLUMBIA
SPORTS HALL OF FAME

Vancouver, B.C.

Formally opened in August, 1966, by Premier W.A.C. Bennett, the British Columbia Sports Hall of Fame is housed in the B.C. Pavilion, on the grounds of the Pacific National Exhibition.

Registered as a Public Non-Profit Society, the Hall was established by a grant from the B.C. Centennial Sports Committee, under the chairmanship of Mr. L. J. Wallace. Mr. Frank Read became the founding Chairman.

Although physically located in Vancouver, the Hall belongs to all British Columbians. It is their permanent tribute to the achievements of this Province's outstanding athletes, coaches, builders and administrators, past, present and future.

Within the Hall, the history and development of each sport is traced through the display of photos, scrapbooks, artifacts, mementos and other

Harry Jerome, male athlete of B.C.'s first century

—All photographs in this chapter,
courtesy British Columbia
Sports Hall of Fame

Torchy Peden with his racing partner, brother Doug.

articles of historic significance. Among such memorabilia, the Hall houses one of the most impressive collections of Olympic, Pan-American, and Commonwealth Games medals assembled anywhere for permanent display. Members elected to the Hall of Fame are featured in their appropriate sport sections.

Also included within the Hall is the International Area, citing British Columbians who have won medals in the Olympic, Pan-American and Commonwealth Games, with their names listed on an International Honor Roll.

The displays within the Hall will expand each year with the continuing story of sport in British Columbia, and of the people who contribute to this fascinating legend.

The Trustees of the Hall are deeply grateful to the many people who have entrusted the priceless personal records of their careers to our care. *Many articles of historic value have been contributed by the general public. Such gifts are warmly welcomed.*

A debt of gratitude is owed to the many people, companies, organizations and governments at all levels, who through their kind personal interest and support have helped make the B.C. Sports Hall of Fame a meaningful part of our provincial community. It is this spirit of cooperation and generosity that has made it possible for the Hall to continue its function as a public service. A theatre and sports film library for education and research are an integral part of the Hall's facilities.

271

THE BRITISH COLUMBIA SPORTS HALL OF FAME

THEY BROUGHT US HONOUR

THE ELECTED MEMBERS

WE REMEMBER WITH PRIDE.

1966 ELECTIONS
Baker, Norm
Black, David*
Black, Kenneth
Brown, R.P. 'Bob'*
Cardinall, Eric J.H.*
Chandler, William R.*
Eccleston, Faye (Burnham)
Hepburn, Douglas
Hume, Fred J.*
Hungerford, George
Jerome, Harry
Johnston, R.N. 'Bob'*
Leonard, Stanley
McIlwaine, Mary (Stewart)
McKinnon, Archibald
McLarnin, James
McNaughton, Duncan
Patrick, Frank*
Patrick, Lester*
Peden, William John 'Torchy'
Phipps, R.G. *
Read, Frank
Richardson, John M.*
Russell, John*
Schwengers, Bernard P.*
Smith, Stanley*
Stacey, G. Nelles*
Taylor, Fred W. 'Cyclone'
Townsend, William
Turner, David
Williams, Percy
Wilson, Ruth
Wright, Dr. Jack*
1956 Olympic Fours without cox
1954 B.E.G. Eights with cox

*Deceased

1967 ELECTIONS
Andrews, George L. 'Porky'
Crookall, John*
Dickinson, William A.
Douglas, James
Gillis, Duncan*
Moore, Douglas Lorne 'Buzz'
Norman, Percy*
Osborne, Robert F.
Peden, Douglas
Spring, Clifford*
Turnbull, Alex*
Turner, Margaret (Taylor)
Woodward, Reginald P.*

1968 ELECTIONS
Athans, Dr. George
Chapman, Charles
Fletcher, Douglas
Hunt, Helen (Stewart)
Patrick Lynn
Patrick, Murray
Underhill, John E.*

1969 ELECTIONS
Alderson, Lillian (Palmer)
Chapman, Art
Humber, Bruce
Nahrgang, Elaine (Tanner)
Parnell, Bill
Raine, Nancy (Greene)

1970 ELECTIONS
Avery, Frank
Fieldgate, Norman
Hunt, Lynda (Adams)
Kulai, Dan
Mawhinney, Bill
Underhill, Eileen (George)

1971 ELECTIONS
Johnston, John
Kieran, Audrey (Griffin)
Pomfret, Jack
Robertson, E.A. Sandy
Sanford, Aubrey

1972 ELECTIONS
Davies, James A.
Hunt, Edmund Arthur 'Ted'
MacDonald, Irene
Magnussen, Karen
Samis, John C.

1973 ELECTIONS
Hutton, Ralph
McLean, Kenny
Spencer, James H.
Todd, Margaret (Sutcliffe)

1974 ELECTIONS
Clarkson, Reginald L.
Cowan, John Lawrence 'Jack'
Morris, Jim
Sweeny, 'Violet' (Pooley)*
Westling, Gunnar

1975 ELECTIONS
Bailey, Byron L.
Bell, Rita (Panasis)
Gloag, Norman G.
Lovett, Claire
Main, Lorne
Spray, Robert B.

BRITISH COLUMBIA HALL OF FAME

1966

NORMAN BAKER born in Victoria, Feb. 17, 1923. Voted Canada's outstanding basketball player of the century. Played on first Canadian championship team, the Dominoes, at age 16 and led team to two more titles. Turned pro and was standout with Vancouver Hornets and three U.S. teams, Boston, New York and Chicago.

DAVID BLACK born Troon, Scotland in 1883. The four-time Canadian pro champion spent 25 years as pro at Vancouver's Shaughnessy Golf Club. Came to Canada in 1905 as the pro at a Quebec course. Two-time B.C. open winner. A strong putter, he and Duncan Sutherland beat the great Walter Hagen and partner in an exhibition match at Point Grey in 1929. Won 1924 Washington State open.

KENNETH McKENZIE BLACK born Vancouver, July 23, 1912. The son of David Black became one of the best amateurs in Canadian golf history. Won the Canadian amateur in 1939 and was a finalist three times. On 11 Willingdon Cup teams and was B.C. amateur champ three times, Canadian Western Open and B.C. closed champ. Beat Byron Nelson and other top U.S. stars in 1936 Golden Jubilee Tournament at Vancouver, where he had a record closing round at 63 at Shaughnessy.

ROBERT P. BROWN born Scranton, Pa., July 5, 1876. The man who was to become Vancouver's "Mr. Baseball" turned pro after a brilliant career at Notre Dame University in the mid-1890's. As the fiery field leader of Spokane Indians, Bob led the club to the Pacific Coast League pennant before heading for Vancouver. Won many pennants, friends and honors in his 45 years at Vancouver.

ERIC JOHN H. CARDINALL born Halstead, Essex, England, Dec. 14, 1880. After settling in Vancouver in 1907, Cardy Cardinall compiled an outstanding tennis record. He was city singles champ from 1909–1913, and Army singles champion while serving with the 72nd Seaforth Highlanders. Also left his mark as an oustanding builder and administrator.

WILLIAM E. CHANDLER born Beautiful Plains, Man., Feb. 10, 1883. By 1906, Vancouver-raised Bill Chandler had become one of North America's greatest marathoners. Over a period of about eight years he was virtually unbeatable at distances from five to 15 miles. Four-time Pacific Coast champ. Probable highlight of the Vancouver Athletic Club runner's career was the 1913 San Francisco International Race in which he easily defeated a picked field of the 15 best marathoners on the continent.

FAYE (BURNHAM) ECCLESTON born Vancouver, June 2, 1920. Excelled in five sports and was also a member of national basketball championships Vancouver Hedlunds. She was named to 10 B.C. field hockey teams and was B.C.'s top player in 1950. Played in a world softball tournament in 1944 and managed B.C.'s female track and field team in 1949.

DOUGLAS IVAN HEPBURN born Vancouver, Sept. 16, 1926. Doug overcame the childhood handicap of a club foot to become the world's strongest man. Astounded observers by winning the world weightlifting championship in Stockholm in 1953 with a series of lifts that broke all existing records. Returned to Vancouver and a year later won a gold medal at the 1954 British Empire Games by completely dominating his division.

FREDERICK J. HUME born Sapperton, B.C., May 2, 1892. An outstanding soccer and lacrosse player in his youth, Fred Hume made a life-long contribu-

David Black, three times Canadian P.G.A. champion

273

tion to the sport in general. An astute administrator, he became mayor of both New Westminster and Vancouver. Revolutionized western field lacrosse by importing eastern stars, making New Westminster virtually the world lacrosse capital. Also active in soccer.

GEORGE HUNGERFORD born Vancouver, Jan. 2, 1944. He was the B.C. half of Canada's coxless pairs who upset favored Germany to win a rowing gold medal at the 1964 Olympics. Toronto's Roger Jackson was the other member of the UBC-Vancouver Rowing Club team. Dropped as an original member of Canada's eight-oared team, Hungerford, 20, had just recovered from a bout of mononucleosis. It was a particularly fine performance.

HARRY WINSTON JEROME born Prince Albert, Saskatchewan, Sept. 20, 1940. A product of North Vancouver High School, Harry became the top star of the U.S. NCAA Championship University of Oregon Track Team and earned recognition as one of history's greatest sprinters. Once co-holder of three world records (100 yards: 9.1; 100 meters: 10 seconds flat; and the 4 x 100 relay: 38 seconds) Jerome shared the 100 yards world mark of 9.1 for 14 years. Highlights of his career include a bronze medal in the 100 meters at the 1964 Tokyo Olympics, and gold medals in the 100 yards and 100 meters respectively at the 1966 Commonwealth and the 1967 Pan-Am Games. B.C. Male Athlete of Century.

ROBERT JOHNSTON born Charlottetown, P.E.I., in 1868. A powerful rower who pioneered a rich dynasty of oarsman, Bob Johnston dominated Pacific Northwest as an amateur and pro in the 1890's. He came to Vancouver in 1889 and soon won the Pacific Coast sculling title, twice beating the U.S. champ. In a match with world champ Jake Gaudaur, he lost by just two lengths on Burrard Inlet. Johnston later turned to coaching and produced many champions.

Stanley Leonard

STANLEY LEONARD born Vancouver February 2, 1915. His competitive golf record includes U.S. tour victories in the 1958 Greensboro Open, the 1960 Western Open, and the 1958 $100,000 Tournament of Champions. He was 8 times Canada Cup teams and twice won the Individual Championship. Played in 10 Augusta Master Tournaments, finished 5 times in the top ten, was twice 2 shots behind the winner, in 2nd and 4th place. In 1959, he was named World Golfer of the Year and received his award in New York from Bobby Jones.

WALLACE MAYERS born New Westminster, Nov. 5, 1908. An outstanding all-round athlete, Wally was best known for his basketball ability. Being a member of four Canadian championship teams. Led New Westminster Adanacs to B.C.'s first national title in 1929. Earlier starred at UBC in soccer, tennis (B.C. junior claycourts champ in 1926) and swimming (third in 1927 national finals). His brilliant career was curtailed in 1939 by the outbreak of war.

ARCHIBALD McKINNON born Govan, Scotland, in 1896. Archie, himself proficient in many sports, arrived in Victoria in 1913. In the next 50 years, helped produce many of the area's great athletes through his dedicated Victoria Y program. His record as a builder of champions is unsurpassed in Canada. Coached track and field and swimming at Olympic and British Empire Games.

JAMES McLARNIN born in Ireland, Dec. 17, 1905. This one-time Vancouver newsboy is rated one of history's most talented and colorful fighters. Jimmy, who came to Vancouver at age two, was discovered by Charles (Pop) Foster. McLarnin won the world title in 1933, knocking out Young Corbett in the first round for the welterweight crown. He became a boxing idol in the 1930's, beating all the great fighters — including Barney Ross after losing his title to Ross.

DUNCAN McNAUGHTON born in Cornwall, Ont., 1910. Won Canada's only gold medal of 1932 Olympics with upset victory in high jump event. Forced to change his jumping style on ruling by judges, Vancouver-raised McNaughton fought his way to jump-off at 6'5-5/8" and then won first place. Established himself as outstanding all-round athlete before transferring to USC from UBC.

FRANK PATRICK born Drummondville, Que., Dec. 23, 1885. One of the fine players of his day, co-starred with Lester on the Renfrew club before moving west to Nelson. Went to Victoria with Lester. When Lester stayed in Victoria, Frank built another artificial rink on Georgia Street and created the Vancouver Millionaires. With Frank as manager-captain, this team won Vancouver's only Stanley Cup in 1915 and reached the finals of two others.

LESTER PATRICK born Drummondville, Que., Dec. 31, 1883. Came west in 1907 after starring with Montreal Wanderers and Renfrew. He and brother Frank constructed world's first artificial rink in Victoria. Created Victoria Cougars of new major Pacific Coast League in 1912. A brilliant administrator and executive, the "Silver Fox", as he was affectionately known, helped rewrite the rules of hockey. Later founded the New York Ranger dynasty.

Lester Patrick

WILLIAM JOHN PEDEN born Victoria, April 16, 1906. Made his name in international athletics as his era's most exciting six-day cyclist. Nicknamed Torchy because of his flaming red hair. Teamed with brother Doug in many events. Torchy earned more than $20,000 a year from cycling, finishing a record 148 races. Competed in 1928 Olympics and dominated U.S. six-day races 1930–1935. Coached two Olympic teams. His special forte was his great strength and stamina.

ROY G. PHIPPS born Vancouver, in 1889. From 1906 to 1926 Roy was one of Canada's finest basketball players. At 17, he was captain of the championship Vancouver YMCA team. He then played for McGill University and led that team to the Canadian intercollegiate title. Later, Roy was the floor leader of the senior YMCA team in the northwest International League, a team that won six league championships.

FRANK READ born Vancouver, March 3, 1911. Frank made his first international mark as a coach when his eight-oared UBC team won a gold medal at the 1954 British Empire Games. In 1955, his crew fashioned a sensational upset over Russia before losing in the Henley Regatta final. His peak moment was at the 1956 Olympics when his four-oared crew won the gold medal and his eights won the silver. His eight-oared crew was barely beaten in the 1960 Olympic final.

JOHN MORLEY RICHARDSON born Durham, Eng., 1900. Gave more than 50 years to the betterment of soccer, beginning in 1919. Ardent supporter of young players and was made honorary president of B.C. Juvenile and Junior Association. Secretary of B.C. Football Association for 22 years and 12 years a member of the B.C. council, Canadian Socer Football Association. Left his mark as a devoted worker among the young people.

JOHN RUSSELL born Edinburgh, Scotland, in 1885. Settling in Vancouver in 1905, John dedicated more than 50 years service to soccer, as a player, builder and administrator. Playing career began in 1907 with Vancouver Athletic Club. Elected president of B.C. Football Association in 1920 and later of the Dominion Football Association.

BERNARD P. SCHWENGERS born Ainsley, England, Aug. 21, 1880. Compiled a brilliant national and international tennis record as a singles player. Considered Canada's outstanding player of his era. Bernie won the Pacific Northwest singles five consecutive years (1909–1913) and the Canadian title twice. Top singles player on two Canadian Davis Cup teams and was undefeated on the 1913 team that reached the final.

Percy Williams and coach

Stanley V. Smith

STANLEY V. SMITH born in Vancouver, June 18, 1897. From 1919, Stan Smith contributed almost 50 years to the administrative needs of B.C. amateur sport. Active in many areas but his greatest challenge was four years as general chairman of the 1954 British Empire Games in Vancouver. International officials hailed it as the most successful gathering in the event's history.

G. NELLES STACEY born May 9, 1888. Considered the veritable heart of B.C. rowing in this century. A member of Vancouver Rowing Club for 60 years. An outstanding oarsman in his day. Honorary Rowing Club president and honorary member of Pan-American Games, of British Empire Games Rowing Committee and member C.A.A.O. selection committee

MARY STEWART born Vancouver, Dec. 8, 1945. She set world swimming records for 100 metres and 100 yards butterfly. Held U.S. records for same events. Before she was 17, Mary had held every Canadian freestyle and butterfly record up to 220 yards. She won a gold medal, five silvers and two bronze in international games. Mary was voted Canada's female Athlete of the Year in both 1961 and 1962 by both the AAU of Canada and The Canadian Press.

FREDERICK W. "CYCLONE" TAYLOR born Tara, Ont., June 23, 1885. One of hockey's all-time greats. Dubbed "Cyclone" because of his blazing speed. A star at age 13, Fred played senior in Manitoba. Led Ottawa Silver Seven to the 1909 Stanley Cup. Joined Vancouver Millionaires from Renfrew Millionaires in 1911, leading the club to Vancouver's only Stanley Cup win in 1915. Scored an amazing 148 goals in 126 Vancouver games.

WILLIAM TOWNSEND born in Durham, Eng., May 6, 1909. Billy moved to Nanaimo with his family at age three and was to become an outstanding pro boxer. Won the Canadian lightweight and welterweight titles before turning pro. Began boxing in 1923 at age 14, turned pro in 1928 and had engaged in more than 300 bouts when he retired in 1934. Lost only 22 matches and fought four world champions. Some of his bouts are still remembered as ring classics.

DAVID TURNER born in Scotland, in 1903, Dave Turner was voted Canada's outstanding soccer player in the last half century. Learned the game in Edmonton, where he grew up. Dave began playing with Cumberland and St. Andrews in the high-calibre B.C. League, then moved to the U.S. and on to Toronto's Ulster United. After one year with Ulster, he joined Westminister Royals—a soccer power in the late 1920's and early 1930's.

PERCY ALFRED WILLIAMS born Vancouver, May 19, 1908. Just one year out of Vancouver's King Edward High School, Percy went to Amsterdam to become the sensation of the 1928 Olympics by winning gold medals in the 100 and the 200 meters against what was the finest field of sprinters ever assembled. He had previously tied the world 100-yards mark of 9.6, and following the Olympics clinched his domination of the world's top stars by going unbeaten in a spectacular series of indoor matches in New York, Chicago, Boston and Philadelphia. Williams' Olympic double still stands as the most brilliant solo achievement by any Canadian in international competition.

RUTH WILSON born Calgary, Alberta, April 27, 1919. Led Vancouver Hedlunds to five straight national basketball titles (1942–1946), managed Pan-American Games team in 1959 and coached Vancouver Eilers to two national titles. Played in two world softball tournaments and coached in another. Member of eight B.C. golf teams and one Canadian team. B.C. doubles and mixed doubles champion in tennis. Coached bronze medal basketball team, 1967 Pan-American Games.

DR. JOHN WRIGHT born Nelson. Voted Canada's outstanding tennis player of the first half century. He won the Canadian singles title three times and was ranked first in national ratings seven times. Jack played on every Canadian Davis Cup team from 1923–1933. Met and defeated many of the world's top ranking players. Once extended the famed Bill Tilden, then at his peak, to five sets before losing. A skilled and tenacious competitor.

UBC-VRC (Fours without cox) All B.C. born, the quartet of Don Arnold, Lorne Loomer, Walter d'Hondt and Archie McKinnon startled the rowing world with an easy victory at the 1956 Olympics. With Arnold at stroke, Loomer No. 2, d'Hondt No. 3 and McKinnon at bow, the team won by four lengths. Same team set a world record over 2,000 metres during Olympic trials. Ironically, members originally went to Melbourne as spares for Canada's eight-oared team.

UBC-VRC (Eights without cox) UBC-Vancouver Rowing Club eight-oared team achieved B.C.'s first major breakthrough in modern international rowing by winning the gold medal at the 1954 British-Empire Games. The Canadian team defeated Russia at the 1955 Henley Regatta before losing the final to the U.S. UBC team members were Glen Smith, Grand Forks; Tom Toynbee, Douglas McDonald, both of Ganges; Mike Harris, Abbotsford; Laurie West, Vancouver; Herman Kovits, Lashburn, Sask.; Ken Drummond, Flin Flon; Bob Wilson, Kamloops and cox Ray Sierpina, Richmond.

Vancouver Rowing Club — 1904

GEORGE L. ANDREWS born Victoria, Sept. 18, 1917. George (Porky) Andrews was one of Canada's outstanding basketball players for two decades. Member of two national championship teams (1935–46). Player coach of famed Victoria Dominoes, pro Vancouver Hornets and Alberni Athletics—a team he started in 1949. Named All-Coast guard and won All-American mention while at University of Oregon (1939–1942).

JOHN CROOKALL born Toronto, Feb. 6, 1899. A standout field lacrosse player with Vancouver teams from 1911–1925. Dot, as he was known, played for five Mann Cup winners, four in succession with Vancouver Athletic Club (1911–1914). Vancouver once won the Mann Cup from Toronto by 2–1 score, Crookall scoring both goals. Turned pro in 1919. Member of Canadian Lacrosse Hall of Fame.

WILLIAM A. DICKINSON born Vancouver, Sept. 22, 1918. Scored 611 goals, 330 assists in 398 games during 17-year box lacrosse career. Bill played on one Mann Cup winning team and four B.C. champions. Most valuable player in league in 1946 with Salmonbellies. Referee for five years, league commissioner for six years and coached for two years. Member of Canadian Lacrosse Hall of Fame.

JAMES DOUGLAS born New Westminster, March 12, 1919. Considered one of best box lacrosse players of his era. Jim was on two Mann Cup winning teams (1939–1943) and five league champions. Leagues most valuable player in 1939. Scored 466 goals, 182 assists in only 218 games during 11-year career with New Westminster teams. Canadian Lacrosse Hall of Fame member.

DUNCAN GILLIS born Cape Breton, N.S., in 1885. B.C.'s first international star. Moved to B.C. at age 19 and joined Vancouver police force. Beat the great Jim Thorpe and won silver medal in 16-pound hammer throw at 1912 Olympics, first medal won by a B.C. athlete in international games. Later became Canada's heavyweight wrestling champion. Set B.C. native hammer throw record that was unsurpassed until 1967. Acclaimed as "one of the world's greatest all-round athletes."

DOUGLAS LORNE MOORE born Regina, April 20, 1921. Played or coached against representative rugby teams from nine countries. Buzz of Meralomas represented Vancouver, B.C., or Canada 27 straight years, excluding a four-year Navy hitch. Captained B.C.'s 1959 Japan tour and Canadian 1962 Britain tour. First Canadian named Honorary Barbarian, most coveted award in rugby. President Vancouver Rugby Union 1954–1966, member B.C. Rugby Union 12 years.

PERCY NORMAN born New Westminster, March 14, 1904. Canada's top swimming and diving coach for 25 years. Coached Canada's 1936 Olympic team and 1954 British Empire Games. Park Board recognized the Vancouver Amateur Swimming Club mentor by naming an indoor pool after him. Majority of Vancouver area coaches producing world champions received basic training from Percy, who developed many swimmers and divers during his long career.

ROBERT F. OSBORNE born Victoria, April 10, 1913. Represented Canada in basketball at 1936 Olympics and was also an outstanding track and field athlete. Made his mark as an administrator. Coached 1948 Olympic basketball team; track and field manager 1959 and 1963 Pan-American Games teams; past AAU of Canada chairman and of B.C. Branch; Member at large, Canadian Olympic Association.

DOUGLAS PEDEN born Victoria, April 18, 1916. Starred in five sports, becoming world-ranked in basketball and cycling. Doug and Torchy Peden

Lacrosse — 1900

won 32 of 38 races as the outstanding brother team of cycling history. Doug was high scorer of Canada's 1938 Olympic basketball team, and a key member of the Vancouver pro Hornets. Advanced to class A in baseball (Albany, N.Y.) once playing for famed House of David; played three international rugby matches and won three area tennis championships.

CLIFFORD SPRING born Draper, Ont., Jan. 24, 1888. One of Canada's finest field lacrosse players (New Westminster Salmonbellies 1905-1936). Doughy, once a baker, played on five national championship teams—including B.C.'s first. Came out of retirement to play box lacrosse and once scored nine goals in one game at age 48. Member of Canadian Lacrosse Hall of Fame.

ALEX TURNBULL born Paris, Ont., Dec. 6, 1883. One of the truly great field lacrosse players. A member of the 1908 Canadian Olympic team, he received the first prize for goal scoring in those Olympics. Played for New Westminster Salmonbellies (1897-1909). On six championship teams, including the 1900 world champions. Member Canadian Lacrosse Hall of Fame.

MARGARET (TAYLOR) TURNER born Calgary, Jan. 14, 1912. Dominated Canadian badminton scene from 1935-1940. Canadian ladies singles champ in 1935, national doubles champ 1938 and 1939. Won B.C. singles title five times. Captured singles title at major U.S. tournament in 1940. Also excelled at tennis.

REGINALD PERCIVAL WOODWARD born Constantinople, Feb. 8, 1869. Founding father of B.C. Rugby Union and was active in the game for 70 years in Vancouver. Reggie played in Vancouver's first match, continuing in area and international play until 1909. Helped clear Brockton Point Oval out of Stanley Park wilderness. Coached and headed rugby union many years. Outstanding rower and cricketer. Honorary Vancouver Rowing Club member from 1916 and former president.

1968

GEORGE DEMETRIE ATHANS born Vancouver, Jan. 4, 1921. Considered Canada's all time best male diver, George's great career was peaked by his outstanding performance at the 1950 British Empire Games in Auckland, N.Z., where he won a gold and silver medal respectively in the springboard and tower events. He also received a special accolade from BEG competitors for his sportsmanship during the meet. He competed for Canada at the 1936 Berlin Olympics, and while attending the University of Washington was U.S. Pacific Coast champion from 1938-1942. He was Canadian titlist for four straight years, and after retirement helped coach protege Irene MacDonald to the U.S. open championship and a bronze medal at the 1960 Rome Olympics.

CHARLES WINSTON CHAPMEN born Victoria, April 11, 1911. Another of the fine crop of athletes out of Victoria in the '30's, Chuch starred in football, lacrosse and soccer, but was pre-eminent in basketball. As captain of the Blue Ribbons and then the Dominoes, he led these Victoria teams to an unprecedented five Canadian Championships and seven B.C. Titles. He and younger brother Art are the only two Canadians to win so many championships. A star of the Canadian team that won a silver medal at the 1936 Berlin Olympics, Chuck is rated one of Canada's all-time best in basketball.

DOUGLAS FLETCHER born Leicester, England, Nov. 18, 1892. Honoured as a builder in the sport of lacrosse, he was president of the Greater Victoria Lacrosse Association for 26 years and was made a life member of both the B.C. and National associations in 1964. He made an outstanding contribution to minor lacrosse as both referee and administrator, was awarded the Diamond Hockey Stick by the B.C. Hockey Association in 1964, and was chosen Sports Celebrity of the Year for Victoria in 1968.

Dr. George Athans — 1948

279

HELEN MONCRIEFF (STEWART) HUNT born Vancouver, Dec. 28, 1938. Preceded sister Mary as Canada's top woman swimmer of her time, beginning at age 15 by winning a silver medal in the freestyle relay at the 1954 British Empire Games in Vancouver. In 1955, won a gold medal in the freestyle at the Pan Am Games in Mexico, and added silver medals in the medley and freestyle relay events. In 1956, Helen broke the listed world record for the freestyle, a mark that was re-broken three weeks after by Australia's great Dawn Fraser. Competed for Canada at the 1956 Melbourne Olympics, won a silver medal in the freestyle at the 1959 Pan Games.

LYNN PATRICK born Victoria, February 3, 1912. Eldest son of Hall of Famer and all-time hockey great Lester Patrick, Lynn was yet another of those amazing Victoria all-round athletes of the '30's, starring in many sports, but majoring in hockey. He played with the Canadian championship Blue Ribbons basketball team, with the B.C. Reps Rugby Team, and later played pro football with the Winnipeg Blue Bombers. Called to play for Lester's New York Rangers in 1935, Lynn played eight seasons with the Broadway Blues and was named to the 1941–42 NHL All-Stars. Later coached the Boston Bruins and was Managing Director of the St. Louis Blues.

MURRAY PATRICK born Victoria, June 28, 1915. The fourth member of the Patrick family to be named to the Hall, Muzz was outstanding in basketball (with Lynn on the Victoria Dominoes), boxing, cycling, and hockey. He won the Canadian Heavyweight Amateur Boxing Championship in 1936, and went to New York to join Lynn on the New York Rangers hockey club, played four seasons, and later became coach and general manager of that team. He also had time along the way to compete in six-day bike racing in the Montreal Forum.

JOHN EDWARD UNDERHILL born Vancouver, Sept. 3, 1902. A pioneer star, and one of the greatest in Canadian badminton competition, he dominated the scene both regionally and nationally for much of his 22-year playing career. He was B.C. Singles Champion in 1927–28–29–31–35 and Canadian singles titlist in 1928–32. He won the doubles championship five times, each time with a different partner. Many of his greatest successes came while partnered with his wife, Eileen, in mixed doubles competition. With Eileen, he shared in the winning of three Canadian mixed doubles championships.

Lynn Patrick   *Murray Patrick*

1969

LILLIAN (PALMER) ALDERSON born Vancouver, June 23, 1923. At age 16, Lillian in 1929 marked herself as a track star of extra brilliance by running sprint times that bettered the winning times at the 1928 Olympics. In 1930, she set a new world mark of 5.8 in the 50-yard dash, and won three firsts in the Empire Games Trials at Hamilton. At the 1932 Los Angeles Olympics, she shared a silver medal for Canada on the 4 x 100 relay team that was just beaten by the U.S. team that set a world record in the event.

ARTHUR CHAPMAN born Victoria, October 28, 1912. Like his brother, Art was an outstanding all-round athlete who reached par excellence in the sport of basketball. He was a great play-maker with the Victoria Blue Ribbons and Dominoes dynasties that dominated Canadian basketball in the thirties and early forties and with five national titles, and was with Chuck on the silver medal winning Canadian team at the 1936 Olympics, along with another Victorian and Hall of Famer, Doug Peden. As captain of the Vancouver Hornets of the late '40's, he was one of the outstanding stars and floor leaders of the Northwest Pro League on a great team that was dominated by ex-Victoria teammates including Norm Baker, Doug Peden, Porky Andrews and Rich Nichol.

BRUCE HUMBER born Victoria, Oct. 11, 1913. Honoured as an athlete and builder, he made his first mark as an outstanding sprinter while attending Seattle's Roosevelt High School. There he set all-time City Prep marks of 9.9 and 21.8 in the 100 and 220 yards respectively. Later, at the University of Washington, he ran times of 9.6 and 20.8 that stood as school records for more than thirty years. He ran on the fourth-place 1936 Canadian Olympic relay team in Berlin. After service in the R.C.A.F., he turned to coaching and was for ten years volunteer coach at Victoria's Y, where he helped produce many outstanding runners.

ELAINE (TANNER) NAHRGANG born Vancouver, Feb. 22, 1951. Known as "Mighty Mouse", this teenage girl from West Vancouver's Hillside High met and defeated the world's best swimmers over her brief but meteoric four-year career in top international competition. Rated on her record as Canada's all-time best woman swimmer, Elaine's triumphs include an historic four gold and three silver medals at the 1966 Commonwealth Games in Jamaica; two gold and two silver medals at the 1967 Pan Am Games in Winnipeg; two silver an bronze medal at the 1968 Olympics in Mexico; national championships in the U.S. and Britain, and a triumphant tour of South Africa, where she defeated the then No. One ranked backstroke swimmer in the world, Karen Muir. Along the way, Elaine set five world records in the backstroke and was close to world record times in the medley events. Coached by Howard Firby.

Elaine Tanner — 4 gold; 3 silver medals, Commonwealth Games — 1966

WILLIAM PARNELL born Vancouver, Feb. 14, 1928. Spent his collegiate career at Washington State University, where he made the All-American Track Team as a miler. He was third in the U.S. Nationals with a then excellent time of 4:09.6, competed for Canada at the 1948 and 1952 Olympics, the 1950 and 1954 British Empire Games. In the 1950 BEG at Auckland, he won the mile gold medal over a slow grass track with a new Games record of 4.11, a time that became the meet's fore-runner of the 1954 Miracle Mile in Vancouver. Bill captained the Canadian track and field team at the Vancouver BEG.

NANCY (GREENE) RAINE born Ottawa, May 11, 1943. Raised in Rossland, B.C., Nancy matured as queen of the world's skiers in 1966–67 and 1967–68, when she won the official World Championship on the international tour circuit. Her brilliant competitive career, unmatched in the history of Canadian skiing, was climaxed by her performance at the 1968 Winter Olympics in Grenoble, where she won a gold and silver medal for Canada in the slalom events. Famed as Canada's "Tiger of the Slopes". Named Female B.C. Athlete of Century.

1970

FRANK AVERY born Austin, Manitoba, Feb. 25, 1902. He moved to Vancouver to become known as that city's "Mr. Curler" through his work in pioneering and promoting curling on the B.C. coast. Frank skipped the first B.C. rink in the Brier, in 1937, and from there on compiled an outstanding record as skip of winning rinks in almost all the important competitions. His 1942 rink lost only once in the National final, while defeating the great Ken Watson of Manitoba en route to second place in the championship.

NORMAN FIELDGATE born Regina, Sask., January 12, 1932. One of the very first players signed to a B.C. Lions contract, Norm signed with the Lions in 1953, a year before entry into the WIFU, and went to play a remarkable 14 seasons and more than 200 league and play-off games for the Vancouver team. Playing both offensive and defensive end, linebacker, and other posts in the defensive unit, he became respected as one of the toughest, smartest players in the league. For many years their co-captain, he was a key figure in the Lions' drive to the 1964 Grey Cup championship, was named Western Conference All-Star linebacker in 1959 and '60, and made the All-Canadian team in 1963.

Nancy Green at Grenoble — 1968

Winner of both Lions MVP and Most Popular Player awards, the Lions' "Iron Man" rates in terms of quality and length of service as the B.C. club's all-time outstanding Canadian player.

LYNDA (ADAMS) HUNT born Vancouver, June 4, 1920. The first outstanding woman diver to come out of B.C., Lynda's competitive career spanned 16 years, to be followed by an administrative career that earns her entry to the Hall as an athletebuilder. The peaks of her competitive career include silver medals in the tower and springboard events at the 1938 British Empire Games and a bronze medal in the springboard at the 1950 British Empire Games. She also placed 9th in the tower event at the 1936 Olympics, and was Canadian Diving Champion in 1939.

DAN KULAI born Ladysmith, B.C., Nov. 10, 1907. Elected as a builder and athlete, he moved from the competitive ranks to the forefront of the world's game officials. As a player, he was inside-forward with the New Westminster Royals that won the Canadian championship in 1927 and 1928. His play contributed heavily to the ultimate choice of the Royals as the outstanding soccer team of the first half of the 20th century. In 1961 he was selected to referee the World Cup Match between Mexico and the U.S., becoming the first Canadian appointed to World Cup play. He was the first Canadian member of FIFA, soccer's would ruling body, and refereed every top local international game from 1949–69. He was also an outstanding competitor in baseball, handball, cricket and basketball.

WILLIAM C. (BILL) MAWHINNEY born Vancouver, May 7, 1929. Emerging in 1947 to defeat Stan Leonard 1-up for the first of two Province Match titles, Mawhinney went on to win every important city, regional, B.C. and national amateur crown. His Canadian titles included two Junior championships, and, in 1950, the Senior amateur championship. He was Canadian Amateur medallist in 1949 and 1952. He was an outstanding Willingdon Cup player, and defeated most of America's top amateurs while playing international matches as a member of the Morse Cup, Hudson Cup, and America's Cup teams. Bill was semi-finalist in the 1952 U.S. Amateur, won the Seattle and the Tacoma Opens, and after turning pro in 1955 was twice low medallist in area qualifying rounds for the U.S. Open. He defeated Al Balding for the Canadian PGA Match Play title in 1957.

EILEEN (GEORGE) UNDERHILL born Moosomin, Sask., April 1, 1899. Considered British Columbia's all-time best woman badminton player, Mrs. Underhill dominated the sport from 1920 into the thirties. She won the B.C. singles title 12 times, shared in the B.C. Ladies Doubles title 11 times, and the B.C. Mixed 5 times. On the national scene, she was Canadian singles champion in 1927, shared in the Doubles championship in 1926–29–30–31 and the National Mixed Doubles in the same four years. Many of her triumphs in Mixed Doubles, including the Canadian championships, were shared with her husband, John. Long known in B.C. as the First Family of badminton, the Underhills thus became the first husband-wife team elected to the B.C. Sports Hall of Fame.

1971

JOHN JOHNSTON born Vancouver, B.C., May 19, 1925. Started winning golf titles in 1953 with the New Westminster Championship. In 1967, Johnny won the Mexican Amateur, the Penticton Open, and B.C. Open as well as being selected to the Canadian Commonwealth Team. In addition to representing B.C. on the Willingdon Cup Team 6 times, the America's Cup Team 4 times, he won every city, regional, B.C. and the Canadian amateur crown in 1959.

AUDREY (GRIFFIN) KIERAN born Burgess Hill, Sussex, England, June 16, 1902. Emerged as a school girl swimmer in 1915 and won a junior race at

Audrey (Griffin) Kieran

age 13 and B.C. championship the same year. After that, she was confined to senior competition and frequently swam in open events against men. She never lost a provincial women's championship and also won seven of the 10 Through Victoria Three-Mile Swims — against male competition.

JACK POMFRET born Vancouver, B.C., Nov. 22, 1922. Jack excelled at Swimming, Basketball, English Rugby, Canadian and American Football, Fastball, Baseball, Boxing, Hockey, and Soccer. In addition, a distinguished coaching career in Basketball and Swimming is to his credit and he has held many age group senior Canadian native and open records, and competed internationally in swimming. A member of the University of Washington Huskies was selected as a Coast "All Star". Jack has served on many national and international Associations and Committees.

Jack Pomfret   *Edmund Hunt*

SANDY ROBERTSON born Vancouver, B.C., February 23, 1923. Another outstanding all round B.C. athlete and administrator, his most outstanding achievements were recorded in basketball, baseball and squash. He started his baseball career in 1941 as a 17 year old pitcher for St. Regis. He was pitching and hitting for Arnold & Quigley during 1943 (Batting average .303), 1944 (.312), 1945 (.347). After the 1946 season he was signed by the Boston Red Sox. Also was named Vancouver's Sportsman of the Year. In 1947 he played all home games with the Vancouver Capilanos and continued until 1952. Sandy's basketball career extended from 1943 to 1953 when he was an outstanding player on UBC Thunderbird Teams, Meraloma and Cloverleafs.

AUBREY SANFORD born Nanaimo, B.C. Sept. 4, 1905. Considered by the B.C. Soccer Fraternity as one of the most outstanding player executives in the history of Canadian soccer. His career spans forty years, from 1912 through the present period. He was a star player on three Dominion Championship teams while with Westminster Royals F.C., 1928, 1930 and 1931. During 1953 and again in 1955 he successfully managed the same club to the Canadian Championship. His 14 years of work in administration ranges from service to B.C. Associations to the Presidency of the Canadian Soccer Association.

1972

JAMES A. DAVIES born London, England, January 7, 1906. Represented Canada in 1928 Olympics in Amsterdam equalling world record of that era. From 1925 to 1930, won all major Provincial Cycling events as well as a Canadian Championship in 1927 at Brantford. Since 1948, Jim has held many administrative positions including operating the China-Creek Cycle Track bringing in riders from U.S.A. and England.

EDMUND (TED) ARTHUR HUNT born Vancouver, B.C., March 15, 1933. Has competed on Rugby's McKechnie Trophy winning team, captain of the Canadian Team while touring the British Isles. In Ski Jumping, Ted was a member of 1952 Olympic Team, the 1954 F.I.S. Team and placed 8th in the 1954 Swedish National Jump. 1961 and 1964 played on the Mann Cup Championship Lacrosse Team, was B.C. Lion "Rookie of the Year" in 1957 and "Top Canadian" in 1958. At UBC, Ted was undefeated Light Heavyweight Champion for 4 years. He won the "B.C. Athlete of the Year" in 1957, "Bob Gaul Memorial Award" in 1958 and "Howie McPhee Memorial Award" in 1961.

IRENE MARGARET MACDONALD born Hamilton, Ont., Nov. 22, 1933. Considered B.C. all-time best woman springboard and Platform Diver, having competed provincially, nationally and internationally. Irene won Canadian Championships 15 times, U.S. Nationals 6 times and Mexican Championships 2 times. She won Bronze and Silver Medals in the British Commonwealth Games in 1954 and 1958 respectively and a Bronze in the 1950 Olympics.

Karen Magnussen, world skating champion — 1973

KAREN D. MAGNUSSEN born Vancouver, B.C., April 4, 1952. Karen has completed a most impressive record, starting with the Kerrisdale Juvenile Free Skating Championships in 1959 through B.C. Coast Championships, B.C. Sectionals, Canadian Jr. Championships and Canadian Sr. Championships 5 times (a Canadian record). Karen competed in two Olympic Games and 6 World Competitions, and 3 North American Competitions — being North American Champion in 1971 and World Champion in 1973. In addition, Karen was "B.C. Senior Athlete of the Year" in 1971 and 1972 and "Canadian Sport Federation Athlete of the Year" in 1972.

JOHN C. SAMIS born Swift Current, Sask., Nov. 18, 1918. As one of the outstanding Canadian Badminton players of the last half century, John competed nationally as well as internationally, winning 3 national singles titles and being 4th in the world. He was the youngest player to win the Canadian singles at 15, a record which still stands. 7 Provincial Championships as well as 7 Vancouver City Championships are also part of his remarkable record.

1973

RALPH HUTTON born Ocean Falls, B.C., March 6, 1948. Has represented Canada internationally in swimming since 1963 and has participated in three Olympics, three Pan Am, and two Commonwealth Games, winning medals in all games except 1964 and 1972 Olympics. Along with his impressive international record, Ralph holds 11 Canadian Senior Records as well as establishing a world record in 1968 at the AAU long course Championships. He was a member of the 800 Metre relay team in the '72 Olympics which placed 6th and set a new Canadian record. Ralph has been known to Canada for many years as the "Iron Man".

KENNY McLEAN born Penticton, B.C., May 17, 1939. Won the Canadian All-around Rodeo Championship, a record-breaking four times, 1967 – 68 – 69 – 72. In 1961 won the International Rookie of the Year award followed in 1962 by the World Bronc Riding Championship. Kenny won the U.S. National Final in bronc riding an unprecedented three times, 1964 – 68 – 71, a feat yet to be surpassed. A winner of the Bill Linderman Award twice and is the only Canadian and one of only two in the world to win this award. No one in Rodeo in Canada has achieved such an outstanding record. Kenny is still rated as the man to beat in Canadian Rodeo competition.

JAMES H. SPENCER born North Vancouver, February 13, 1915. Started his Soccer career at the age of 9 when he played for the Queen Mary School Seniors. Played his entire juvenile career with the North Shore Bluebirds winning all the North Shore League championships, several mainland and provincial cups. Jimmy also captained the North Vancouver School Bantam team to a high school championship, coached and managed four consecutive Vancouver All-Star teams against visiting European teams.

MARGARET (SUTCLIFFE) TODD born Montreal, May 31, 1918; in B.C. since childhood. Has been on the Golf scene in Victoria since 1938. She has been a holder of eleven Victoria and District Championship titles and the runner up ten times; ladies champion of the Victoria Golf Club nine times and winner of the B.C. Provincial Championships three times and runner up five times. She has represented Canada on four international teams, as a player and once as a non-playing captain.

1974

REGINALD L. CLARKSON born Victoria, B.C., August 19, 1925. No list of B.C. great all-around athletes would be complete without the name of Reg Clarkson. Reg participated in every team sport except Hockey at either a professional or semi-professional level. His outstanding career was cut short at the age of 26 due to an illness. He was voted Vancouver's "Athlete of the Year" in 1946. Since retiring from professional sports, Reg has built himself up an enviable reputation for community service. He, also is a respectable golfer.

JOHN LAWRENCE COWAN born Vancouver, B.C., June 6, 1927. Jackie's Soccer career started in the public school system and the church teams in Grandview and the east end district in the early '30's. He won a U.B.C. Big Block in 1945 through to 1949 and was selected to the B.C. All-star team against the British touring team, Newcastle United. In 1949 he went to Europe and played with Dundee Football Club First Division and spent five years playing Scottish Soccer with a minimum of 25 games per season. He has toured Israel, Turkey, South Africa and East Africa as part of all-star team. Captained the Vancouver Canadians to Dominion Championship and retired from Soccer at the age of 29.

JIM MORRIS born Tacoma, Washington, Dec. 15, 1911. Jimmy, a resident of B.C. since 1913, has competed in Track and Field, Baseball, Lacrosse, Hockey, Basketball, Swimming, Fastball, Soccer, Rugby, and Curling with distinction. Primarily competing in the Kootenays; Jimmy has many outstanding achievements to his record. Probably best noted for his participation in Hockey, representing the 1937–38 Allan Cup Team from Trail as well as the 1938–39 World Hockey title which was won in Switzerland as one of the Trail Smoke Eaters. Jimmy has been very much involved in the development of young athletes in the Province.

MRS. VIOLET (POOLEY) SWEENY born Victoria, B.C., December, 1886. Violet Pooley's name appears an unprecedented seven times as a winner of the Pacific Northwest Golf Association as well as an unprecedented nine times as B.C. Ladies Championship winner in the sport of Golf. Mrs. Sweeny was President of the Canadian Ladies Golf Union from 1933 to 1942 as well as an Honorary Life Member of the B.C. Executive and has given long and valuable service to B.C. Golf. She donated two trophies—one for 12 and under championship and one for junior championship in the Province.

GUNNAR WESTLING born Tradstrand, Sweden, Dec. 25, 1907. Gunnar has been a resident of British Columbia since 1929 and has been following the war. Full Bore Rifle, Small Bore Rifle, and Pistol are his specialties. He has been a member of the Canadian Bisley Aggregate in 1966. Has represented Canada six times in the N.R.A. Prize Meeting and helped Canada win the Overseas Team Match in 1971 and 1972. He won the H.M. The Queen's Prize and joined seven other Canadians who have won this prize in over 100 years.

Jim Morris   *Byron Bailey*

1975

BYRON L. BAILEY born October 12, 1930 in Omaha, Nebraska, "By" Bailey played for the Detroit Lions in 1952, the year they won the National Football league championship. However, he didn't reach his prime until he joined the B.C. Lions two years later. Bailey was one of the original team members when the Lions were formed in 1954 and the hard-charging back was to star with the club for more than 10 years. He was B.C.'s leading rusher and offensive captain for five years and twice led the Western Conference in kickoff returns. In 1957 Bailey was named to the WFC All-Star team and also won the Bobby Bourne Memorial Trophy as the Lions most popular player that same year. He was on B.C.'s 1964 Grey Cup champion team. A former director of the Lions, By Bailey also is a member of the Canadian Football Hall of Fame.

RITA (PANASIS) BELL born March 29, 1921 in Vancouver, Rita (Panasis) Bell starred for more than a decade both on the basketball court and the softball diamond. In basketball she was a member of eight Canadian championship teams from 1940 to 1954. Her basketball career began in 1938, the same year in which she was approached by Abe Sapperstein of the Harlem Globetrotters with an offer to play for his professional ladies team. Percy Page, coach of the famed Edmonton Grads, rated her as the "all star centre" in his own personal Canadian all star team.

NORMAN G. GLOAG born July 9, 1919 in Vancouver, Norm Gloag has been a driving force behind the growth of basketball in Canada during the last 25 years. He was manager of the Canadian Olympic basketball team at the Melbourne Games in 1956 and was Canadian representative in basketball for the Games in 1964, 1968, and 1972 as well. He is a past president of the Canadian Amateur Basketball Association, a member of the Pan-Am Games committee and a director of the Canadian Olympic Association.

CLAIRE LOVETT born in Regina, Saskatchewan, Claire Lovett was a natural athlete who could excell in any sport she wished. And, as it turned out, Claire wished to excell in many sports and that is exactly what she did in a career which spanned more than 30 years. She was particularly adept in racquet sports and was five times the Canadian badminton champion, held six U.S. state titles, 18 provincial titles and 20 city championships. In tennis, she won the Canadian singles title in 1966 following many provincial and regional titles. Claire was also an accomplished player in basketball, ice hockey, field hockey, track and baseball.

LORNE MAIN born July 9, 1930 in Vancouver, Lorne Main is one of the finest tennis players ever to come out of the B.C. system. Picking up his first tennis racquet at the age of nine, Main soon learned how to use it better than most of his opponents. He was already Canada's top ranked junior at just 16 years of age and took the national under 18 title three years running. He was Canada's top ranked player before he was 20 and played his first Wimbledon match in 1951, losing in the second round. In the early 1950's he played all over the world in top tournaments and in 1954 he won both the Monte Carlo and Belgian singles titles. That same year he made it to the third round at Wimbleton.

ROBERT B. SPRAY born May 22, 1913 in Lingfield, Surrey, England, Bob Spray came to British Columbia in 1947 and, from that year on, rugby had been the better for it. Spray is largely responsible for building rugby into one of Canada's dominant sports. He served as founding president of the new Canadian Rugby Union, which through his dedication and perserverance was re-activated in 1965. He was instrumental in establishing a liaison with the rugby countries of the world and as a result there is a constant flow of international matches now being played in B.C. and provincial teams make regular overseas tours as well.

Lorne Main   *Robert B. Spray*

CANADIAN FOOTBALL HALL OF FAME

Hamilton, Ontario

From an article by Bob Hanley

Canadian Pro Football's Hall of Fame is more than a monument to the mighty men of the gridiron. It is a tribute to the selfless citizens of Hamilton, Ontario, who would not be defeated. The story of the Shrine is an uphill chronicle, as bitter a battle in diplomacy and economics as any of those on the football field. It didn't happen easily and that's why it is more important to the legions of founders and helpers whose faith prevailed against every conceivable obstacle.

At the time of opening in November of 1972, the building and its contents were valued at over one million dollars, an illustration of the generous involvement of so many Hamiltonians. As the City was also preparing to host the Grey Cup game, her people experienced one of the most gratifying successes in a decade of community renaissance.

It is interesting too, that the Stelco Tower in Jackson Square—the heart of the downtown urban renewal program should be opened in the same year as the Football Hall of Fame. Hamilton had many things to boast about—harbor, industry, botanical gardens, preserved historic sites, McMaster University, Mohawk College—but in most places it was best known for steel and for football.

They held an informal meeting when the Hall was almost ready and introduced the first full-time Director, Larry Smith, a retired career pilot of the Royal Canadian Air Force, a one-time boxer, and a fellow with broad and varied sports associations. Larry had done his homework well—he knew how long and hard the way had been to achievement of the Shrine—and he likened it to the motto of the R.C.A.F., "Per Ardua ad Astra."

And it was indeed just that . . . "through Adversity to the Stars". Funds were hard to come by, well-intentioned people had in many ways obstructed some of the earlier plans, but in the end a better one was found and the realized dream a vast improvement over the original humble fantasy.

Whatever your era of sport as spectator or participant, there is something just for you in this million dollar mansion for gridiron immortals;

The statue symbolizing Canadian football at the entrance of the Canadian Football Hall of Fame.

*(Above) W. V. (Bill) Cockman directs a scene for "Welcome Visitor",
a promotional film of the Hamilton area. The camera is being adjusted by
Joe Bochsler on bilingual listen-hear helmets.*

*(At left) A mannequin in the TV switching display
in the Hall of Fame.*

something to recall, something to learn, games to be replayed, careers to
be relived.

The Shrine is a triumph in concept and execution, in the audio-visual
presentation of a century of football, in the cathedral-like central core
accommodating life-size steel molded busts of the celebrated inductees,
so carefully and painstakingly sculptured by Tony Gsellmann. The Hall
of Fame combines the best elements of a royal museum, a theatre of society's culture and a highly computerized reference library of Canada's
football heritage.

It is a chronology of distant days when helmetless men played fiercely
for fun in ragged uniforms of quilted canvas. It is a record of amateur
days when man bloodied themselves for rings and sweater coats, thereby
assuaging the compulsion to compete and the need of the acclaim of
those little, but devoted, long-ago crowds. It is also a record of the modern era when professional football became a national extravaganza and an
instrument of national cohesion.

In all that it tells in so many ways, it is timeless. You could talk forever of the exalted whose deeds are perpetuated here. There is Lionel Conacher, one of the greatest all-round athletes of them all. There is Teddy
Reeve, so tough, so noble, so full of humor; Brian Timmis, the Old Man

of the Mountain and the greatest plunger of his time; Joe Krol, who was Mr. Magic; Huck Welch with the career record for punting singles; Johnny Ferraro, perhaps the greatest import who ever came to a Hamilton football club; Normie Kwong, Johnny Bright, Jackie Parker, Sam Etcheverry and "Prince" Hal Patterson. East or West your old heroes are here, and not just the Hall of Famers, but the All-Stars and the Schenley Award winners, even the Builders, then the men behind the scenes by whose toil and invention the game survived and prospered.

You will have to see it for yourself, to feel the old presences of the athletically exalted, to experience a revival in your appreciation of football. You will see the men from long ago—Grantland Rice's time . . . "It matters not whether you win or lose, but how you play the game." And you will see the ones from later eras of skilled and refined violence, when they would take your head off to win.

And when you have seen a lot and you stand there awhile, the atmosphere will take hold of you, gently but firmly. Suddenly you'll feel it as they felt it . . . the blood, sweat and tears; the pride, the prayers, the pain . . . and the glory.

SELECTION PROCEDURE

The criteria for the two categories for election to the Hall of Fame are:

Players: The qualities of character, sportsmanship, playing ability and the player's contribution to his team or to football in general shall be considered in selecting candidates. A nominee, in this category, must be retired for at least three years.

Builders: A builder is defined as one whose service, other than as an active player, was responsible for an exceptional and unquestioned contribution to Canadian Football in general and this category would include executives, both team and League; men concerned with team operation: coaches and game officials. A nominee in this category need not be retired from the game.

PLAYERS

BYRON L. (BY) BAILEY — A native of Omaha, Nebraska, Bailey attended Washington State, was with Detroit and Green Bay briefly, then recruited for the Lions by another Hall of Famer Annis Stukus. By played eight seasons as a fullback and three more as an outstanding defensive back. Baily was the recipient of the first "night" ever thrown to honor a B.C. player. That was in 1960.

Baily ran from scrimmage 783 times for 3,643 yards and 26 touchdowns in his eight years of fullbacking, and he returned 128 kickoffs for 3,114 yards. He also caught 101 passes for another 1,161 yards. By Bailey stayed on as a citizen of Vancouver when his playing days ended, and, as might be expected from the sincere and dedicated performer he was, he is putting something back into the game as a member of the Lions Directorate.

HARRY L. BATSTONE was a great running and kicking halfback and captain of the Toronto Argonauts, Interprovincial Football champions from 1920–21. He was of medium height and only 155 pounds but a triple threat man who could run, kick and plunge over players twice his size.

He, along with Lionel Conacher, ran wild in the Sculler backfield in winning a resounding victory in the first East-West Grey Cup of 1921 over the Edmonton Eskimos. The end run play was his specialty. Batstone would draw the tacklers in, wait for the exact moment, then throw a lateral to Conacher, who would be off on a dead run to the goal line.

ORMOND BEACH-From 1934–1937, he had four spectacular years with the Sarnia Imperials leading them to four senior O.R.F.U. championships and two Grey Cup finals, winning All-League and All-Canada honors in each of his playing years.

An All-American at the University of Kansas, Beach created sensational front page news as he materially helped to hold Knute Rockne's Fighting Irish of Notre Dame to a scoreless tie and lead the Jayhawkers to their first Big Six title. Even as a lowly freshmen (1929) Orm Beach was adjudged to be an outstanding anatomical example of the "Perfect Man" by Dr. James Naismith, Professor of Physical Education and inventor of the game of basketball. Beach would use this formidable physique in the services of Sarnia's quest for the Grey Cup. The Imperials hit their stride in 1933 and the pace would not slacken until the end of the decade.

AB BOX-To hoist 60 yard punts was very typical for one of the all-time greater kickers in Canadian Football, Ab Box. Outstanding with Malvern Collegiate in 1926–27 and with Malvern Grads in 1928–29, Box was a protégé of Ted Reeve and moved with Reeve to Balmy Beach in 1930–31. The 1930

Balmy Beach team, coached by Alex Ponton, powered by the kicking of Ab Box and the superb play of Claude Harris, Alex McKenzie, Harry "Red" Foster, Jimmy Keith, Ross Trimble and Ted Reeve, took the League championship. They took the Eastern final over Hamilton 8-5 and the performance of Ab Box was particularly impressive. There was no stopping the Balmy Beach team this year as they drove by Regina 11-6 in the Grey Cup. Lew Hayman and the Toronto Argonauts called on Box from 1932–1934 to help them to a Grey Cup, then Balmy Beach again from 1935–1938.

JOSEPH M. BREEN—Player, coach, referee, he earned football honors with the University of Toronto, Parkdale Canoe Club and Toronto Argonauts before serving for six years as coach of the University of Western Ontario.

His Varsity years, broken by war service overseas with the Canadian Engineers 1915–1919, Joe Breen twice captained the Varsity team. The 1920 season was especially memorable as he led the Blues to victories over Queens and over Mike Rodden's Argonauts 16-3 in the Dominion final.

JOHN BRIGHT was an All-American at Drake University in 1951, showing enormous talents as a blocker, passer, receiver and kicker. As such, he was the first round draft choice of the Philadelphia Eagles. In 1952 and 1953 he played for Calgary, racking up the League Rushing title in his first year. At Edmonton, teaming up with Normie Kwong and Jackie Parker, he was part of the most dynamic backfield in Canadian Football in the mid-fifties, winning three consecutive Grey Cups. In 1957, Bright carried for 1,679 yards; Kwong carried for 1,050 yards—a backfield rushing record unmatched by any pair of runners in any League. In 1958 he would set a new rushing record carrying 296 times for a monumental 1,722 yards.

The Eddie James Memorial Trophy for the top rusher in the Western Conference carries his name four times; 1952, 1957, 1958, and 1959. In the latter year he was honored with the Schenley Award as the Most Outstanding Player in the Country. He was chosen a W.I.F.U. All-Star in '52, '57, '58, '59, '60, '61, and '62.

TOM CASEY—During a meteoric football career with Hamilton Wildcats (1949), and Winnipeg Blue Bombers (1950–55), Casey earned All-Star ratings, honors that included being named Winnipeg's Citizen of the Year in 1956, and nationwide recognition as one of the finest halfbacks of his time. Born in Ohio, his Canadian gridiron career began after attending Hampton Institute in Virginia, serving in the navy 1944–45, and playing professional football with the New York Yankees in the All-American Conference.

An honor student in Medicine at the University of Manitoba, Casey was a perennial all-conference back with the Blue Bombers. Nicknamed "Citation," he won the Eddie James Memorial Trophy in 1950 as the leading rusher in the Western Conference.

LIONEL P. CONACHER was acclaimed Canada's greatest all-round athlete and football player of the first fifty years of the 1900–1950 era, by Sports Editors and Sportscasters in a Canadian Press Poll. As early as 1920, playing for Dr. Jack Maynard's Torontos of the O.R.F.U., Conacher was being compared with Harry Batstone of the Argos, perhaps the best all-round back in Canada at the time. The next season he moved up with Sinc McEvenue's Argonauts and led them to an undefeated season, capped by a 23-0 Grey Cup victory over the Eskimos. Conacher personally accounted for 15 points in this game.

An all-round athlete in the mold of Jim Thorpe, Conacher excelled at football, hockey (played on two Stanley Cup teams) baseball, lacrosse, boxing. Once he boxed a few exhibition rounds with the reigning heavyweight champion Jack Dempsey. At 6'1" 185 pounds, he looked like an athlete. The first time he threw a discus, it went so far, he was immediately offered a place on Canada's 1924 Olympic team.

ERNEST COX—Acknowledged as perhaps the greatest snapback or center in Canadian Football in the late 1920s, Hamilton's Ernie Cox came off the city's sandlots, just prior to the First World War, to earn undying fame with the Hamilton Tigers. After his war service, Cox launched a career in 1919 that was to carry him through 16 seasons, one of which was spent with the Hamilton Rowing Club, and the balance with the Tigers.

A perennial league and All-Canadian All-Star selection, Cox was signally honored as the first winner of the Jeff Russel Memorial Trophy, for outstanding play in the Eastern football conference in 1928. He was a member of Tigers Grey Cup Champions in 1928, 1929 and 1932 with Timmis, Sprague and others and was a member of the Hamilton Eastern finalists against Balmy Beach in 1927 and 1930. Under coach Rodden, Cox was responsible for the introduction of the cross-field direct snap to halfbacks, two of which led to touchdowns in Grey Cup games.

ROSS BROWN CRAIG launched his career in his home town, Peterborough, Ontario, and included service with Dundas, Hamilton Rowing Club, Hamilton Alerts and Hamilton Tigers. Hulky, hard-hitting, Ross "Husky" Craig—a forerunner of Brian Timmis—was a leader on O.R.F.U. Championship teams, a Grey Cup figure with the Alerts in 1912 when Hamilton won all three (Senior, Intermediate and Junior) Championships and with the Tigers in 1913. The 1913 Cup final was particularly noteworthy for Craig would score 15 points on 3 touchdowns—a single game record that was eventually tied in 1921 by Conacher and again in 1938 by "Red"

Storey. It would be eclipsed by Jackie Parker in 1956, then by Jim Van Pelt in 1958.

CARL CRONIN—From Chicago, Cronin was the first American import brought into Winnipeg in 1932, when that club decided to take a determined shot at the Grey Cup and sell football to Winnipeg fans as a major sport. As a player he was a fine field general, a superb passer and a vicious linebacker. His dressing room eloquence would have made his old coach at Notre Dame, Knute Rockne, proud.

As playing coach, with Rebholz and Kabat, he displayed fiery leadership and molded a nondescript group of rookies into a formidable football club. His forte as a coach was his drilling in fundamentals. In 1933, Winnipeg won the Western Canadian title and in a semi-final game against Lew Hayman's Argonauts at Varsity Stadium—while defeated 13-0—they gave the Toronto team a second half scare that won the plaudits of all Eastern Canada and definitely established the West as a real threat.

WES CUTLER came out of Oakwood Collegiate Institute to attend the University of Toronto. In 1931 he played for Varsity "Orfuns," winners of the O.R.F.U. series. In 1932 he played for the championship Varsity team, then joined Lew Hayman's Argonauts in 1933, helping them to win the Grey Cup that year. He also was instrumental on the Argo Grey Cup teams of 1937 and again in 1938.

He made the Canadian Press All-Stars six times from 1933 to 1938. Cutler was a great end, perhaps one of the best in the game at that time. As a fine blocker, deadly tackler as well as an exceptional pass receiver, he was honored in 1938 with the Jeff Russel Memorial Trophy.

GEORGE DIXON, a product of Bridgeport, Connecticut, established in five full seasons and parts of two others with the Montreal Alouettes that he was one of the League's most productive and exciting ball carriers. "Let George do it," was the Alouette's theme during the early sixties.

In 1962, when the Alouettes made the eastern finals for the only time in the decade, Dixon set an eastern conference rushing record of 1,520 yards, which still stands. He scored 15 touchdowns, 11 rushing and four pass receptions, to lead the eastern conference in scoring, winning the Jeff Russel trophy as the eastern conference player who best combined outstanding ability with sportsmanship and leadership qualities. He also won the Schenley as Canada's most outstanding player, the Calvert as the most popular Alouette with fans, and was a unanimous choice as "all Canadian." In seven seasons of carrying the ball for the Alouettes he averaged 6.3 yards per carry.

ABE ELIOWITZ was the first of ten Ottawa players to win the Jeff Russel Trophy, in 1935. The former Michigan State star came to the Riders in

A corner displaying trophies and historic photos.

1933 and almost immediately caught the fancy of the fans with his left-footed punting and left-handed passing.

Eliowitz played in Ottawa until 1935, then moved to Montreal where he put in two more seasons of Canadian football before returning to his home in Detroit. Eliowitz, a fullback, and at other times a halfback, was four times an All-Star. He made it as a flying wing and as a halfback with Ottawa in 1934 and 1935, and once each in these positions with Montreal in 1936 and 1937. He was leading scorer in 1935 at Ottawa with 62 points.

E. K. "EDDIE" EMERSON—The distinction of having served one club as a player for 26 seasons (1912-1937) belongs to the "Iron Man" of football, Ottawa's Eddie Emerson.

A native of Georgia, Emerson moved to Ottawa in 1909 and began playing for the Rough Riders three years later, as a center. Moved to the flying wing position, Emerson played continuously there until his retirement, a generation later, helping the Ottawa club to win two Grey Cups. On the way through he was twice nominated for the Jeff Russel Memorial Trophy.

SAM ETCHEVERRY set all the passing records in the CFL during the 9 seasons with the Alouettes. Born in Carlsbad, New Mexico, graduated from the University of Denver and recruited by "Peahead" Walker in 1952.

In the mid-fifties, 1954-55-56, Montreal swamped all opposition except in the Grey Cup game itself against the Eskimos. Sam authored a brilliant passing game with such stalwart receivers as Hal Patterson, Red O'Quinn and Joey Pal. Tom Hugo, Tex Coulter, Jim Staton, Herbie Trawick manhandled the opposition along the line. First Alex Webster, then Pat Abruzzi kept the backfield in high gear and provided the running threat which made Etcheverry's passing the more effective. Etcheverry won the Schenley Award in 1954 and the Jeff Russel Memorial Trophy in 1954 and 1958.

291

BERNIE FALONEY – Jim Trimble said of Faloney that there may be more accomplished quarterbacks but none had more intensity to win. His winning football reputation began at Maryland University where he obtained All-American status. Graduating in 1953 he was drafted by the San Francisco 49ers to play defense. By 1954 he was in Canada sharing quarterback duties with Jackie Parker as they led Edmonton Eskimos to a Grey Cup victory over Montreal. Then it was back to the U.S. for two years of armed service where he played and captained the Bolling AFB team to two undefeated seasons. In 1957 he joined the Hamilton Tiger Cats, leading the team into six Grey Cup finals from 1957 to 1964.

In 1961 he won the Schenley as Canada's most outstanding player. He was runner-up in 1959. In 1965 he was awarded the Jeff Russel Trophy. In that year he signed with Montreal where he played for two years, finishing his career in 1967 with the B.C. Lions.

A. H. "CAP" FEAR was born in Gloucestershire, England, in 1901, and first played football after moving to Canada in 1911. He starred with the Toronto Argonauts in 1919 through 1926. Played a few games for the Winged Wheelers·in Montreal between 1926 and 1928, then starred again with the Hamilton Tigers 1928 through 1932.

JOHN FERRARO – One of the greatest imports of them all, just had to make the Canadian Football Hall of Fame. A terrific all-round athlete when Hamilton Tigers secured him after his Cornell University days in 1934. Ferraro was player-coach for one year, continued as player in 1935, and moved on to Montreal to again become a player-coach, and spent altogether 6 seasons with the Big Four and one in the Senior O.R.F.U. with the Montreal Nationals. He made All-Canadian in every one of his years in Canada. He won the Ormond Beach Trophy, was named All-League and All-Canadian on no fewer than seven occasions and captured also the Imperial Oil Trophy in 1938, as the Most Outstanding Player.

HUGH GALL – A famous University of Toronto backfielder, Gall earned undying gridiron fame with the Blues from 1908 through 1912 when he became one of the great kicking halfbacks of all time.

In the 1909 inaugural Grey Cup against Parkdale, Gall put on an outstanding punting display when he not only scored a touchdown but kicked for 8 singles, a cup record that still stands. Some say he could kick the ball 70 yards which is a prodigious accomplishment. This becomes even more fascinating since Gall could do it with either foot. When Varsity headed for the 1910 Grey Cup, again Hughie Gall was there. The game was played before 12,000 people at the Hamilton AAC Grounds and ticket scalpers were getting as much as $100.00 per ticket. Toronto would defeat the Tigers 16 – 7.

Fritz Hanson   *Jack Jacobs*

TONY GOLAB – A product of Windsor Kennedy Collegiate, a member of a great Sarnia Club (1938) and for a decade the "Golden Boy" of Canadian football with the Ottawa Rough Riders, Tony Golab earned highest honors in the Canadian game as one of its finest backfielders. The Riders went to the Grey Cup in 1939, 1940, and 1941 and on each occasion the tall, handsome, blond halfback distinguished himself. The '41 game was particularly memorable for Golab when he scampered under his own high, short kick at the Winnipeg 45-yard line and took it in for the touchdown in a losing cause, with Winnipeg squeezing by 18 – 16. He won the Jeff Russel Memorial Trophy in 1941 and was a Big Four All-Star 1939, 1940 and 1941.

In 1941, he went overseas as a fighter pilot with the R.C.A.F. Flying over Cassino, in Italy in January 1944 he was shot down suffering serious shrapnel wounds in his arms and legs. Many at home who followed his career felt they had seen the last of him on the gridiron. At war's end, he returned to the Riders, triumphantly, and played outstanding football until his retirement in 1951.

DEAN GRIFFING – A graduate of Kansas State University and for a time with the Chicago Cardinals of the National Football League, Griffing became an outstanding center, then a coach in Western Canada.

In 1936 the Regina Roughriders brought in their own slate of imports including "bad man" Griffing and won the Western Championship but owing to the rule structure of the Canadian Rugby Union governing residency of imports, several of the Regina stars were declared ineligible. The Regina club under Al Ritchie and "Piffles" Taylor decided to forfeit its challenge for the Grey Cup rather than play with half a team. Griffing was noted for his ability to get the individual and collective goat of his opponents and quite often of many of the spectators in opposition cities. A hard-hitting, rugged player, he asked no quarter and gave none.

FRITZ HANSON – Revitalized by the importation of American players, the Winnipeg Football Club became the hottest team the West had ever produced. Such players as Herb Peschel, Bob Fritz, Bert Oja, Joe Perpich, Bud Marquardt and the little blond will-o-the-wisp, Fritzie Hanson, made Winnipeg a team to be reckoned with. As early as a pre-season exhibition game in 1935, there was an ominous sign for Eastern football, when Winnipeg defeated the previous year's Grey Cup champs, Sarnia Imperials. Winnipeg would easily win the Western Conference Championship as would the Hamilton Tigers in the East, with devastating victories over Queens and Sarnia in the finals.

Heavily favored to win the Cup, coach Fred Veale was blessed with a star-studded lineup including Ferraro, Welch, Turville, Timmis, Wilson, Simpson, Wilf Paterson, Jim Smiley and so many others. On a bleak, cold winter afternoon in December, Canadian football history was made and a legend was born. This was to be Hanson's day, as the slightly built flash from North Dakota slipping, sliding and speeding in the goo ran punts back for more than 300 yards on 7 returns including a memorable 78-yard touchdown run through the entire Hamilton team, leading the Winnipegs to an 18–12 victory. Said a weary and dejected Hamilton player after the game: "Sure, Winnipeg won the Grey Cup. But they had to send a greyhound to fetch it!"

BOB ISBISTER SR. — One of Hamilton's all-time great players, Bob emerged from the Hamilton City League in 1905 to begin a long career with the famous Tigers. In 1906–7, Isbister served with Tigers in the old Ontario Union. From 1908 through 1919, as flying wing and at various places in the line, he earned fame for his all-round ability, his great defensive qualities and his sportsmanship.

RUSS JACKSON attended McMaster University and won all-conference honors in both football and basketball. An exceptional student in his graduating year, he declined nomination for a Rhodes Scholarship.

His awards are numerous: Schenley Award for Most Outstanding Player 1963, 1966, 1969; Schenley Award for Outstanding Canadian 1959, 1963, 1966, 1969; Jeff Russel Memorial Trophy 1959, 1969; Grey Cup finalist four times, winning three; Ontario's outstanding athlete, Canada's outstanding male athlete, leading passer in the East, All-Canadian All-Star at quarterback, second leading passer in CFL history.

JACK JACOBS — Coming to Winnipeg in 1950 from a football background in Oklahoma, in the Armed Service, and in the National Football League (Cleveland Rams, Washington Redskins, Green Bay Packers), Indian Jacobs would lead the Bombers to an impressive 10–4 record and win All-Canadian honors his first year. Giving Winnipeg a decade of unprecedented leadership, Jacobs rewrote Western Canada records. He completed 700 passes out of 1,330 for 11,094 yards, 104 touchdowns and kicked

57 singles. In 1952 he won the Jeff Nicklin Memorial Trophy as Most Valuable Player in the West.

The 1953 season was especially outstanding. In the Western final against Darrell Royal's Edmonton Eskimos, Indian Jack replaced Joe Zaleski at quarterback and — George Trafton notwithstanding — wiped out an 18–6 deficit with a 30–24 victory for the Bombers. Completing 14 passes for 243 yards and 3 touchdowns, Jacobs took the team to the Grey Cup. He put on another aerial circus in the Cup final, throwing 46 passes, completing 28 for 326 yards; however, the Hamilton Tiger-Cats were not to be denied this day as they carved out a 12–6 hard-fought victory.

EDDIE "DYNAMITE" JAMES — In the early days of football in Western Canada few players were able to achieve the prominence of James, who became a gridiron star with Winnipeg, the Regina Pats, Winnipeg St. Johns and the Regina Roughriders through the 1920s and early 1930s.

A great plunger, a devastating force as a sixty-minute man equally at home on defense or on offense. "Dynamite" James possessed outstanding scoring ability as a football player, but above all perhaps, possessed an ability to make and hold friendships gathered from teammates and opponents, from football fans and executives alike.

GREG KABAT was one of the early imports into Canadian football, arriving in Winnipeg from University of Wisconsin in 1933. In addition to playing in the Winnipeg backfield he acted as line coach in his first season, the original year of the Winnipeg Football Club after amalgamation.

Kabat saw duty as quarterback, guard, flying wing and fullback, when necessary. A fierce competitor, Kabat was a most loyal and wholehearted servant in the first Grey Cup victory ever scored by a Western team, in 1935, for Winnipeg. Kabat was an expert place-kicker and blocker, played in the 1938 Grey Cup final made memorable by the great work of Argos' "Red" Storey. Kabat had played the entire game with a broken toe. The collapse of the Blue Bomber defense in the second half may have been due to the fact that Coach Threlfall didn't know his field leader was injured. Kabat coached the Vancouver Grizzlies in 1941 and served in many capacities with that club during its brief life.

JOE KROL gained lasting recognition as one of Canada's greatest players in a career stretching from 1932 through 1953. From championship teams with Windsor's Kennedy Collegiate, Krol moved to the University of Western Ontario to help Coach Johnny Metras win the Intercollegiate Championship in 1939. Under Coach Brian Timmis, he helped the Hamilton Wildcats to the Canadian final in 1943.

He joined Teddy Morris with Toronto in 1945 and it was here that he would become one of the Argos' best loved stars and play in five Grey Cup

Championships before retiring. In his second game played with the Argos, the Krol-to-Copeland combination was born as Joe "King" Krol threw his partner 3 touchdown passes against Montreal. The "Gold Dust Twins" teamed up again in the Grey Cup that year where on one touchdown march Krol executed a perfect onside kick to a corner in the Winnipeg end. In 1946 Krol won both the Jeff Russel Memorial and Lou Marsh Trophies. He was selected as Canada's outstanding athlete in 1946 and again in 1947.

NORMIE KWONG—Played 14 seasons with Calgary and Edmonton. In eleven years of recorded statistics, Normie gained 9,022 yards with a 5.2 yard average, third highest in CFL history. He won the Rushing title on three occasions; five times he made the All-Star team; twice he won the Schenley Award for outstanding Canadian (1955, 1956) and was named Canada's Athlete of the Year in 1955.

As coach of the Edmonton Eskimos, Frank "Pop" Ivy instituted a twin fullback system into the offense. Paired with the incomparable Johnny Bright, Kwong and company would power their way to three successive Grey Cup victories (1954–55–56). Kwong was hard-pressed to win the Rushing title in 1955 over Gerry James of Winnipeg. In the Blue Bombers' last game, James set a new record accumulating 1,205 yards on 189 carries for the year. With one more game to play, Normie was 137 yards behind. But it would indeed be a memorable game, with Parker giving the ball 30 times to the "China Clipper" for 192 yards and, ironically, the Eddie James Memorial Trophy. It was a symbolic victory—Edmonton also defeated Winnipeg in the Western final and downed the Montreal Alouettes 34–19 before nearly 40,000 ecstatic fans in Vancouver's Empire Stadium.

SMIRLE LAWSON—Canadian football's original "Big Train," Lawson leaped into lasting prominence with the University of Toronto. Playing for Varsity in the 1909 Grey Cup final, Smirle put the clincher on Toronto Parkdale in the last seconds, running 50 yards for a try (touchdown). Along with teammates Jack Newton, Hughie Gall, Billy Foulds, Al Ritchie

and coach Harry Griffith, the University of Toronto Blues would dominate the Grey Cup final again in 1910.

FRANK R. LEADLEY—Graduate of Hamilton Central Collegiate in 1914, "Pep" Leadlay moved to Hamilton Tigers (Intermediates), Canadian champions of 1915 before his service overseas in World War One.

He, like Batstone, entered Queens with a wealth of football experience for in 1919 and 1920, he played with the Hamilton Tigers in the Interprovincial Union. From 1921 to 1925, the drop-kicking backfielder would help Queens win five Intercollegiate championships and three successive Grey Cups. One of the most memorable was the 1923 encounter with the Regina Roughriders. On the surface it might seem like a mismatch that the gentlemen of Queens University were expected to do battle with the considerably older and rougher men of Regina. The Western club was accustomed to playing tough, bare-knuckle football. It was customary for each lineman to put up a dollar in a hat, all proceeds going to the first man to draw blood from his opponent. On the last play of the game, the lineman would plant his fist in the face of the man over him. However, the gentlemen of Queens still won 54–0—a tremendous humiliation for Regina but one they would rectify in the future. The 1924 Grey Cup, won by Queens, would be the last for University football.

LES LEAR was the first Canadian developed player to go to the National Football League playing guard with the Cleveland Rams, the Los Angeles Rams (1946) and the Detroit Lions (1947). In Canadian football, he was a member of three Grey Cup winning teams: Winnipeg 1939 and '41—and Calgary '48. He played in three other Grey Cup games. Lear learned his football skills as a schoolboy in Winnipeg. He first played organized football for the Deer Lodge Juniors, coached by Fred Ritter. He was promoted to Winnipeg Blue Bombers in 1938 by coach Reg Threlfall. He was selected for All-Canadian team by MacLean's magazine 1939, '40, '41 and '42. He was selected on Lionel Conacher's All-Canadian team 1939, '41 and '42. There was no selection in 1940 because there was no east-west Grey Cup that year.

In 1948, after three years in the N. F. L., Lear joined Calgary Stampeders and led them to their first Grey Cup victory. It is significant that Calgary fans of '48 sparked the Grey Cup Festivals. He was the last coach in Canada to coach a team completing an entire season without a defeat. When the Stampeders won the 1948 Grey Cup they played a total of 15 league and playoff games without a single loss.

LEO LEWIS was born in Des Moines, Iowa, went to high school in St. Paul, Minnesota, and furthered his education at Lincoln College, in Missouri. In 11 sea-

Normie Kwong

Smirle Lawson

sons with the Blue Bombers (1955–1965), Leo Lewis needed a record book of his own. He was an All-Star six times. He ran for 48 touchdowns and he caught passes for 26. He also threw the occasional touchdown pass, as the 1958 Hamilton Tiger-Cats will recall to their dismay. He scored 450 points, and that's more than Normie Kwong, Johnny Bright, Hal Patterson and Ronnie Stewart.

FRANK S. McGILL — One of Montreal's outstanding football and sports leaders, McGill (Air-Vice Marshall, G. B.) was also one of Montreal's all-round athletes in the days before the First World War. His football career spread from Montreal High School to McGill University to the famous Montreal Amateur Athletic Association Winged Wheelers. The summit of his glamorous football career came when he captained and quarterbacked the team to the Big Four title in 1919 but was unable to compete for the Grey Cup because the Canadian Championship final was cancelled owing to the late season. When his playing career was over he served as president of the Big Four in 1927.

An all-round athlete, he participated as a swimmer and water polo player on five MAAA Championship teams.

PERCY MOLSON became outstanding in football while regarded as one of Canada's greatest all-round athletes. In a career cut short by his death in the First World War, Percy Molson starred on the gridiron for Montreal High School, McGill University and the famous red and black of the Montreal Amateur Athletic Association Winged Wheelers. Captain and star back of the Wheelers in 1903–4, Percy Molson became an exceptional kicker, had sure hands and great running ability.

JACKIE PARKER came to Edmonton in 1954 as the All-American top scorer in the Southeast Conference while playing for Mississippi State University. For the next decade and a half he would electrify crowds with his spectacular plays, scrambling ability and Houdini-like ball handling.

He starred for the Eskimos from 1954 to 1962 and during this period he played on three Grey Cup Winners; he won the Schenley Award as the nation's top player three times, the Jeff Nicklin Trophy seven times; was an All-Star for eight straight seasons and scored 750 points before he brought his career to an end.

HAL PATTERSON — The football career of this outstanding receiver over 13 seasons is truly remarkable. During this period he established records which may never be broken, filled football stadia with fans attracted solely by the presence of "Prince Hal," who like a few others, possessed that magnetic charisma of the superathlete, which fills coliseums all over the world. He was a statistician's nightmare in the way he kept rewriting the record books. He

scored 75 touchdowns, 64 on pass receptions, 3 on kick-off returns. His longest kick-off return was 105 yards and his longest gain on a pass reception was 109 yards. In 1956, Patterson set another record, still standing today, gaining 338 yards on pass receptions in a single game on September 29 against the shell-shocked Hamilton Tiger-Cats.

In the same year, "Prince Hal" was awarded the Jeff Russel Memorial Trophy and the Schenley Award, as Canada's Most Outstanding Player. Most of his career was spent with the Montreal Alouettes (1953–60) but in 1961 he went to Hamilton in a momentous trade. The Tiger-Cats had finished last the previous year with a 4–10 record, but now revitalized, would be in the Grey Cup in 1961, 1962, 1963, 1964 and again 1965, in all of which "Prince Hal" would make his presence felt.

Hal Patterson   *Norman Perry*

GORDON PERRY was captain of the 1931 Montreal team, the Montreal A.A.A. Winged Wheelers, which went through the season unbeaten and untied, to go on to win the Grey Cup by defeating Regina Roughriders, 22–0, on a frozen gridiron at Molson Stadium. Gordie was one of the few football greats to come out of Quebec City. He was a real "speed boy" who first attracted attention while playing with Doug Kerr's Westward teams. With the Wheelers, he starred on a backfield that included "Huck" Welch, Benny Haynes, Warren Stevens, Wally Whitty, Johnny Bennett, Ralph St. Germain, and coached by Clary Foran.

NORMAN PERRY — Sarnia's spectacular Norm Perry found few equals as a running halfback. He was part of a backfield with Alex Hayes and Ormond Beach which brought the Grey Cup to Sarnia in the Depression '30s. For 8 years, Perry gathered experience in Junior and Intermediate football. The next 8 years were spent with the Imperials in the Senior O.R.F.U., winning the League championship 7 times and the Grey Cup once.

A perennial All-Star, he captained the Grey Cup champions in 1934, defeating Regina 20-12. He won the most valuable player honors in the same year as he brought his brilliant career to an end.

KEN PLOEN started his professional football by completing an unusual double. He played in a Rose Bowl Game and a Grey Cup Game the same year— 1957. He starred as his Iowa University team demolished Oregon State 35–19 in the Rose Bowl, but as a rookie quarterback late that year his Winnipeg Blue Bombers were 32–7 victims of Hamilton Tiger-Cats. In his 11 playing seasons with Winnipeg, Ploen made it to six Grey Cup finals and was on the winning side in four of them. He lost that first one, then won four in a row (1958, 1959, 1961 and 1962). He quarterbacked Winnipeg in all of them except the 1958 game in which he played safety and offensive halfback.

He was the hero of the 1961 Grey Cup victory over Hamilton, which was the only one ever to go into overtime. The teams were tied 14–14 and in the overtime period Ploen ran 18 yards for the winning touchdown. He was also the winning quarterback in the 1962 game, which was the only one ever spread over two days. That was the Fog Bowl Game. Play was suspended in the fourth quarter on Saturday and resumed the following day. Kenny was selected All-Western Conference quarterback in 1957, 1959 and 1965. He was All-Canadian in 1965.

S. P. QUILTY was born near Renfrew, Ontario, February 8, 1891. A graduate of high school in Renfrew, "Silver" Quilty played football first in a high school league that included Pembroke and Arnprior. In 1907 he enrolled at Ottawa University and in his freshman year, age 16, made the senior intercollegiate team at the outside wing position. Ottawa University played that year with McGill, Queens and University of Toronto. The Ottawa team won the championship in 1907 but there were no further play-offs.

During 1908–09–10–11–12 Quilty played for Ottawa University. He was the prime ball-carrier during these years and handled the kicking duties in 1908–1909. In 1913 Quilty played with the Ottawa Rough Riders in the interprovincial union.

RUSS REBHOLZ—One of the first two imports to play football in Winnipeg, Rebholz from the University of Wisconsin was enticed into Canada to play for Winnipeg St. John's Club in 1932. With the exception of one season, he remained in Winnipeg through the 1938 season.

Serving Winnipeg clubs with distinction, Rebholz, a fine all-round backfielder, superbly versatile, was outstanding in the Winnipeg Western championship in 1933, the club's Grey Cup loss to Toronto Argonauts the following season and, in the Bombers' great win over the Hamilton Tigers in 1935 when "The Wisconsin Wrath" threw two touchdown passes to Joe Perpich and Bud Marquardt. The Cup went West for the first time.

TEDDY REEVE, as a player, toiled for the Toronto Argonauts and Toronto Balmy Beach. A rugged 6′ 200 pounds, he specialized in blocking kicks and stopping plungers as they tore through the line.

Reeve won the admiration of players and fans alike in a memorable semi-final game against the Dave Sprague—led Hamilton Tigers in 1930. Reeve played the entire game against the Tigers with a broken shoulder. In the Grey Cup against Regina "he once again astounded spectators, teammates and opponents alike." Balmy Beach was leading 10–0 at half-time. Reeve, whose shoulder was still bothersome, stayed on the bench. But then the tide seemed to be turning. With Reeve on the bench and Ab Box unable to play, Regina reduced the lead to 10–6 as the clock neared the end. At this point Reeve, with his arm taped to his shoulder, entered the game. Contemporaries say he played like a man possessed. He blocked Saul Bloomfield's kick which otherwise certainly would have produced a score. And when the game was over, his still "sore" shoulder, as he called it, was inspected and it was found that he now had a cracked collar bone.

PAUL ROWE, born in Victoria, B.C., graduated from University of Oregon and started a brilliant football career with Calgary Bronks, in 1938. After three years with the Bronks, Rowe served during the Second World War but returned to Calgary to play for a co-operative team in 1945–6–7. In 1948 Rowe led the Calgary team into the Canadian final, winning the Grey Cup in a memorable game in Toronto.

In 1948 Rowe was voted one of the greatest plunging fullbacks in Canadian Football, this being but one of many honors won during his gridiron career. Forced out by injuries, in 1950, Rowe gave the Calgary Clubs twelve years of brilliant play. After his enforced retirement he continued in the game, as coach and advisor in minor football. Selected as a member of the Western All-Stars in 1939–40–46–47, Rowe was winner of the Dave Dryburgh Memorial trophy, awarded to the leading scorer in the Western League, in 1939 and 1948.

MARTIN RUBY, a man who rarely left the field, was one of the last great two-way linemen in Canadian football. Jackie Parker rated him as the greatest two-way player he ever saw or played against.

Born in Waco, Texas, in 1922, he graduated from Texas A & M in 1942, "the most valuable player in the Southwest Intercollegiate Conference." While at Texas A & M he played in three bowl games before entering the armed services. In 1946 he started his pro career with the Brooklyn Dodgers. After three years he switched to New York Yankees. In 1951 he signed with the Saskatchewan Roughriders. With the Riders seven years, he was a conference All-Star five times, including three years when he was saluted both offensively and defensively.

JEFF RUSSEL—The Jeff Russel Memorial Trophy, awarded annually in the Interprovincial Football League (Eastern Conference Big Four), honors one

Paul Rowe   *David Sprague*

of the all-time great competitors and sportsmen of the Canadian game. Jeffrey Cameron Russel, former star of Montreal's Lucas School, Lower Canada College, Royal Military College, and Montreal Amateur Athletic Association, the famous Winged Wheelers (from 1922–1925), was killed tragically in 1926 repairing a power line in a raging storm.

DICK SHATTO—When he retired from competitive football in 1965, after 12 seasons with Toronto Argonauts, he had scored more touchdowns, caught more passes and accounted for more offensive yardage (rushing and receiving) than any player in the history of Canadian football. These were only a few of the accomplishments of a young athlete from Springfield, Ohio, who dropped out of University of Kentucky as a junior, came north to embark on a football career and stayed to become an exemplary citizen of Canada.

Dick Shatto still holds 13 Argonaut club records, his 91 touchdowns have been exceeded only by George Reed, his 13,642 rushing-receiving yardage has been topped only by Reed and he was only the third C.F.L. player ever to reach the 500-point level in scoring. He finished with 542 points. He played 159 games for Argos. Only Danny Nykoluk played more. He was selected All-Canadian in 1963 and 1964, and eight times was All-Eastern 1956–7–8–9 and 1961–2–3–4).

BENJAMIN L. SIMPSON, M. A., retired principal of Westdale Secondary School, was one of Hamilton's great educators and academics, as well as a gridiron terror in his youth.

As an outstanding kicker, he played with the Hamilton Tigers from 1904–1910 revelling in his ability to cause confusion for the opposition by repeatedly kicking into touch so there could be no runback. One of the first of a great line of kickers which would follow (Billy Mallet, Sam Manson, Huck Welch, "Peps" Leadlay, Beano Wright, Frank Turville, Bert Gibb, Bob Isbister Jr.), he would help lead the Tigers to the championship in 1908 and to the Grey Cup final in 1910.

DAVID S. SPRAGUE, a fifteen-year playing veteran in Canadian football, served most of his grid-iron career with the Hamilton Tigers and the Ottawa Rough Riders. He first played football at Delta Collegiate with Huck Welch, coached by Ben Simpson. With a lineup like that, the Dominion High School Championship naturally followed.

Joining the Hamilton Tigers in 1930, it wasn't until an exhibition game against University of British Columbia, in which Sprague ran wild for 3 touchdowns, did coach Rodden realize that he had a diamond in the rough in young Sprague. He would assist the Tigers in winning two Interprovincial and one Grey Cup Championship.

ART STEVENSON joined the Winnipeg Football Club in 1937 and also enrolled in the University of Manitoba School of Medicine. Stevenson came from Hastings, Nebraska, where his brilliance in small college football earned him many accolades such as Little All-American. Stanley Woodward, the famous New York football reporter, described him in 1937 as one of the finest all-round backs in college football.

Stevenson, an accomplished runner, passer, kicker, quarterbacked the Bombers in both the 1938 and 1939 Grey Cups. In the first he ran into a hornet in the person of "Red" Storey, a one-man wrecking crew intercepting his passes and running for three touchdowns. In the second against Ottawa, Stevenson kicked the winning point in a close 8–7 victory. This win was all the more impressive when one realizes that the game was played in Ottawa's backyard, under the unfamiliar C.R.U. rules, in a biting December snowstorm. Winnipeg had travelled across half the continent in order to play against one of the great football champions Eastern Canada had produced, and still emerge as the victors.

HUGH STIRLING—Born in St. Thomas, Ontario, in 1910, "Bummer" quickly developed into an outstanding high school football star, when he graduated to the junior final in 1928, and in winning the Dominion junior title in 1930.

Moving to Sarnia Imperials, of the senior O.R.F.U., Stirling attracted wide attention, became one of the best, if not the best triple-threat backs in the game, and he ranked with the greatest kickers in the history of Canadian football. He served with the Imperials from 1931 to 1937 inclusive, and was senior O.R.F.U. All-Star in 1932–33–34–35–36–37, rated Eastern All-Star selection in 1934–35–36 and won the O.R.F.U. Most Valuable Player Award in 1936.

BRIAN M. TIMMIS—The name alone brings a gleam of excitement to an old-timer's eye. Visions of a driving, relentless figure crashing against an opponent's line are immediately conjured up. It took a while getting there but he eventually arrived in Hamilton, where he was destined to be. Boundless energy, enthusiasm, reckless disregard for his own safety were characteristic not only of Timmis, but

"Huck" Welch   Harold Bailey

Hamilton too. Helmetless, Timmis helped the Tigers smash their way to three Grey Cups (1928, 1929, 1932).

HERB TRAWICK was one of the first imports selected when Lew Hayman and Leo Dandurand started to build the powerful Montreal Alouette team in 1946. The choice was a wise one. Trawick not only played magnificently for 12 years (1946–57) but he took up permanent residence in Montreal and became an equally outstanding citizen. His work for numerous charitable organizations is well known.

Trawick was amazingly swift for a big man, and although offensive linemen invariably work under a cloak of anonymity, Herb's speed made him extremely noticeable. He was named to the All-Eastern Conference team (or All-Big Four team as it was then known) for his first five years in Canadian football (1946–50 inclusive). Later, in 1954 and 1955, he was named to the All-Star team as a guard. In 1955, his selection to the All-Star team gave him a status unequalled in the East at the time. He was the first player to make the All-Star team seven times.

JOE TUBMAN, born in New Edinburgh (Ottawa) in 1897, starred with Ottawa Rough Riders as a native product. Football in Ottawa with the Junior City League prior to 1916 led to football and hockey with the Canadian Army during the 1st World War. He played in the Ottawa Senior City League in 1919, jumping to Ottawa's Big Four team after one game. Tubman played with the Rough Riders until 1931, a total of 13 seasons, before becoming an official of the Interprovincial and O.R.F.U. as referee and umpire.

HAWLEY "HUCK" WELCH, one of the great kicking halfbacks in Canadian football history, launched a long playing career as one of the finest schoolboy players in the Dominion. At Delta Collegiate, in Hamilton, Welch was individual league scoring champion twice in a five-year stretch, and helped to win three Canadian interscholastic championships. With Hamilton Tigers, in 1928–29, Welch aided in winning two Interprovincial titles and two Grey Cups. He entered the Grey Cup scene again in 1931 with Montreal Winged Wheelers; he won the Jeff Russel Memorial trophy in 1933, was twice selected on All-Star Big Four team and was twice named All-Canadian.

With Hamilton Tigers again in 1935–6–7, he was All-Canadian in 1935, twice Interprovincial scoring champion and twice runner-up. He boasted an all-time record of 102 single points, kicking. Coached Delta C. I. seniors and Eastwood juniors, in Hamilton, served overseas with the Royal Hamilton Light Infantry, and participated in a memorable wartime championship in England, in 1944. Welch became the first post-war president of Hamilton Tigers, in 1946.

BUILDERS

LEONARD P. BACK was born July 21, 1900. His playing career in football was restricted to two seasons, with Hamilton Tiger Juniors in 1918–19. Len Back recovered from a skull fracture suffered in 1919 to become manager of the Junior Tigers in 1920. His amiability, his success in handling players and his devotion to the game led to his appointment as team manager of the Hamilton Tiger Intermediates, from 1921 through 1926, when he was named manager of Tiger Senior Ontario Rugby Football Union squad.

From 1928 until 1940 he managed the Tiger's Interprovincial team, and when the club suspended operations for the Second World War, he joined Brian Timmis and was team manager of Hamilton Wildcats when they won the Grey Cup in 1943. He returned to the Tigers when the club resumed operations and occupied his old office as manager up to the time the Wildcats and Tigers combined.

R. HAROLD BAILEY, a native Torontonian, served football with rare distinction for almost a lifetime. As a Toronto Hockey League executive, he entered football to become secretary-treasurer of the Ontario Rugby Football Union and held this office for thirty years. He was president of the Canadian Rugby Football Union in 1941 and member of the C.R.U. rules committee from 1931 through 1950.

Prominent in the development of interscholastic football throughout all Ontario, Harold Bailey was able to bring about complete co-operation with all sections of the province.

T. L. "TOM" BROOK—When football was at a low ebb in Calgary in 1948, he went out and dug up Les Lear to coach the Stampeders and to bring in some good players. Lear did a magnificent job, recruiting outstanding stars like Woody Strode, Keith Spaith and Chuck Anderson among others.

Tom Brook guaranteed the salaries on a personal overdraft and was rewarded when the Stampeders came through with an undefeated season, climaxed with Calgary's first Grey Cup victory, 12–7 over Ottawa. The team that Brook built set a record never equalled. The Stamps had a perfect 12–0 league record in 1948 and won the first 10 games in 1949 for a winning streak of 22 games. Counting a tie and two wins in 1948 playoffs, the Calgary team went 25 games without a loss.

D. WES BROWN – From office duties with the Ottawa Club, Brown carried heavy responsibilities as director, treasurer and secretary, but served also as secretary of the Interprovincial Union, and in 1948 he became permanent secretary of the Eastern division of the Canadian Football League. Admired and respected by colleagues from coast to coast in Canada, "Wes" Brown devoted his entire life to the development of football.

ARTHUR U. CHIPMAN, joining the executive of Winnipeg Football Club in 1936, served as a chairman of various committees and also as vice-president until election to the presidency of the club in 1945. A "principle man," he put the administration to the Club on an open business-like basis, not always easy to do in an athletic enterprise. Re-elected in 1946–47 and 1948, he retired at the end of the 1948 season. In 1949 he was president of the Western Interprovincial Rugby Union and in 1952 was president of the Canadian Rugby Union.

ANDREW CURRIE, besides being a player, earned his football distinction in such endeavors as writing and rewriting the C.F.L.'s rules.

Football involvement started early in his life. At 17 he played 30 minutes for the Regina Roughriders against Hamilton in the 1928 Grey Cup. By special permission from the Canadian Rugby Union he was permitted to retain his junior eligibility, and played with the Regina Pats the following week in the Dominion Junior Championship against St. Thomas. The Pats won the championship.

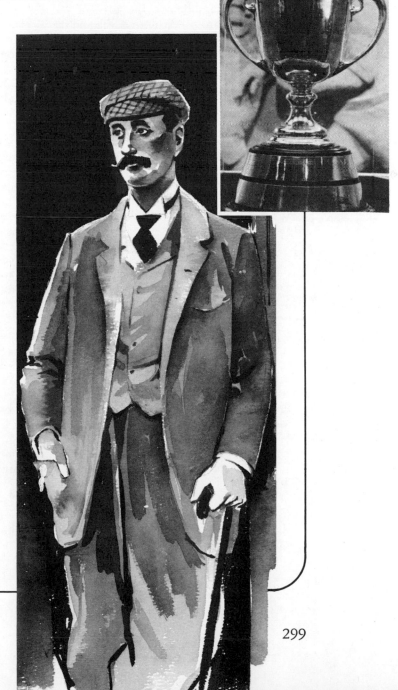

ALBERT HENRY GEORGE 4TH EARL GREY – Steeped in British traditions, a brilliant colonial administrator, Lord Grey was appointed Governor General of Canada on December 10, 1904. He was largely responsible for the outstanding success of the Quebec tercentenary celebrations in 1908. At his suggestion, the battlefield of the Plains of Abraham was preserved as a national park. Throughout his career he diligently worked for imperial unity. In 1909, he donated the Lord Earl Grey Cup as a trophy for the amateur rugby football championship of Canada. The significance of the honor would not be felt until 1921 when the West began to participate for the Dominion Championship, as it was commonly called, or the Grey Cup. Vast distances had divided the West and British Columbia, the Eastern Maritimes, Ontario and Quebec. Differences in rules made interleague play difficult. The season was frightfully short and this too complicated matters. But all these hurdles were overcome when East and West clashed on the gridiron for football supremacy. Despite the wishes of its donor, the Grey Cup was never to be a trophy for amateur team sports.

But for Lord Grey, a man who was immensely popular but had never seen a Grey Cup match, a man who like many in his era abhorred professionalism, he, inadvertently, was able to achieve a sense of national unity in a young, growing country beset with cultural and geographic problems. His $48.00 trophy carried more lasting significance than the donor could ever realize.

Albert Henry George 4th Earl Grey,
donor of the Grey Cup (inset)
symbolic of the Canadian championship.
—Sketch by Kay Smith

DR. ANDREW P. DAVIES, revered by Ottawa football, posted an eviable record of service to the game in Montreal and Ottawa. A graduate of McGill University, where he played football, he returned to his native Ottawa to become a fine outstanding and rugged player for the Rough Riders.

However, his record is highlighted more by his unselfish interest in the Ottawa Clubs and players, as player, officer of the Club and Club physician from 1915 to 1948. Dr. Davies, until his death in 1956, was regarded most highly and remained an honorary officer of the Ottawa Football Club. Following his playing career, he became an executive member of the Ottawa Club and coached the Riders in the Big Four in the late 20s.

JOHN DeGRUCHY, foremost advocate of amateur sports throughout Canada, made many significant contributions to football. Connected with football in various capacities before the turn of the century, with the old Toronto Athletic Club and the Toronto Rugby and Athletic Association, he was to become president of the Ontario Rugby Football Union through a period of twenty-five years.

President of the Canadian Rugby Union in 1925, 1930 and 1935, John DeGruchy was headed through the chairs of office again when he died, as C.R.U. vice-president, in 1940.

"SEPPI" DuMOULIN was a truly distinctive individual whether as a backfielder for the Tigers (1894–1906), or as a coach of the Hamilton Grey Cup finalists (1910) and the Winnipeg teams of 1907 and 1919. In everything, his expertise was always evident. The 1904 Tiger team was a powerhouse. Led by halfbacks like DuMoulin and Art Moore, quarterback Ballard and Wings Isbister and Lyons, they scored a staggering 349 points in 8 games and had only 47 points scored against. As Captain of the 1906 Tigers, DuMoulin led his cohorts to the Dominion Championship.

HARRY CRAWFORD GRIFFITH, coach of the first official Grey Cup Champions, University of Toronto, was a significant builder in the formative years of Canadian football.

From playing days at Ridley College and Trinity College Schools, he coached Ridley from 1899 to 1907 and from 1911 to 1949. He was coach of Toronto Varsity in 1908–9–10, winning the Canadian Championship on two occasions with solid victories over Parkdale and then Hamilton.

G. SYDNEY HALTER — The 1966 Canadian football season brought down the final curtain on the outstanding career of G. Sydney Halter, Q.C., as Commissioner of the Canadian Football League. Born in Winnipeg, April 18, 1905, Mr. Halter graduated from the Manitoba Law School as a Gold Med-

alist; was admitted to the Manitoba Bar in 1927; appointed King's Council in 1947. During the Second World War, he was Senior Judicial Officer in the R.C.A.F. with the rank of Squadron Leader.

In 1952 Mr. Halter was named a deputy commissioner of the Western Interprovincial Football Union and commissioner in 1953. In January of 1956 officials of the Big Four and the W.I.F.U. began preparations for amalgamation. The Canadian Football Council was set up with two conferences. Mr. Halter, as registrar, had the added responsibility of maintaining a common negotiation list so that Eastern and Western clubs would no longer bid against each other for the same American players. In 1957, Mr. Halter became Canada's National Football Commissioner — the first step in the formation of the present CFL structure. The CFL largely replaced the Canadian Rugby Union and took possession of the Grey Cup.

FRANK J. HANNIBAL — As vice president of the Winnipeg Rugby Football Club in 1934, and president in 1935–36, he along with Joe Ryan, Les Isard, Barry Bain, G. Sydney Halter set about rebuilding the team into a formidable contender, a process which culminated in the sensational and historic Grey Cup triumph over the Hamilton Tigers, after one short year of unceasing effort.

President of the Winnipeg Club four times, president of the Western Interprovincial Football Union, and holder of innumerable offices for a period of nearly thirty years, Frank Hannibal stood as one of the great builders of Western Canada Football.

LEW HAYMAN was an All-American in basketball and an outstanding baseball and football player at Syracuse University. He came to Canada at the invitation of an old Syracuse friend, Warren Stevens, who had just taken over as coach and sports director at University of Toronto. In his spare time he helped Buck McKenna coach Argos and when Buck took sick, Lew finished the 1932 season as the coach. In 1933 as a 25-year-old head coach, he won the Grey Cup — his first of five, he never lost a Grey Cup game. In 1933 he beat Sarnia 4 – 3 (after topping Winnipeg 13 – 0 in a semi-final game). In 1937 his Argos edged Winnipeg 4 – 3. In 1938 Red Storey ran wild for three touchdowns and Argos won 30 – 7 over Winnipeg. By 1942 Lew was in the RCAF and his Toronto Hurricanes beat Winnipeg RCAF-Bombers 8 – 5 in the final. In 1949 he coached Montreal Alouettes to a 28 – 15 win over Calgary Stampeders.

Hayman's contributions to Canadian football are many, but possibly the most important was in 1946 when he took over a staggering Montreal franchise, renamed the team Alouettes, assembled a strong, colorful aggregation and worked at getting French-Canadian sports fans interested in football. He returned to Argonauts in 1956 as General Manager, having sold his share of the Alouettes.

W. P. "BILLY" HUGHES – A McGill University graduate of 1912, the late Bill Hughes was a regular playing member of football and hockey teams that won intercollegiate championships. He started coaching while teaching at Westmount High School where he won the Montreal Intercollegiate Championship. In 1919 he coached Montreal Winged Wheelers to the Big Four Championship and in 1922 moved to Kingston to coach Queen's, which won the intercollegiate title after a playoff with Toronto Varsity.

Hughes remained with Queen's as head coach 1922–26. This was the era of the famed Tricolor Teams that won three consecutive Grey Cup championships (1922–24), won 26 league and exhibition games in succession and accumulated a record never equalled. He coached Hamilton Tigers in the 1932 and '33 seasons; Ottawa Rough Riders in 1935 and '36, winning the Big Four title in 1936.

M. I. LIEBERMAN, Q. C. was born in Toronto on June 16, 1891. He attended high school in Kingston, Ontario, and played football, hockey and baseball for his school teams.

Mr. Lieberman came west in 1912, and in 1915 played quarterback for the University of Alberta football team, earning a Block A award. In 1919 he joined the Edmonton Eskimos as a player under the famous Deacon White and continued playing until he was injured in 1921. As a result of his effort and that of Billy Foulds, the CRU president, sufficient money was raised to finance the first western challenge for the Grey Cup.

JIMMY P. McCAFFREY – When McCaffrey of the Ottawa Rough Riders took over the club as manager in 1923, he did three things: he effected an amalgamation with the old St. Brigid's Club of the Ottawa City League, of which he had been manager, he took a host of outstanding players to the Riders who were facing disbandment, and he started the Ottawa Club on the road to success.

Later McCaffrey took Ottawa to the Grey Cup Championships in 1925 and 1926. Staying on as manager, with the exception of the war years, he won the Grey Cup four times, lost out in the final on three other occasions, and talked himself out of innumerable suspensions for the alleged use of professionals (1936). In the '55 season, when things were not going very well, Coach Chan Caldwell was enjoying very little success. Ottawa lost both its preseason exhibition games and nine league games. It is reported that in their last battle with the Grey Cup bound Alouettes, the irascible Jimmy McCaffrey spiked the water bottle with alcohol. If he did, it worked – Ottawa won.

DAVE McCANN was both a quarterback and halfback for the Ottawa Rough Riders from 1907 to the war years.

Sculptured likenesses of Hall of Fame enshrinees.

Following the war, McCann coached the Ottawa Club to Dominion Championships both in 1925 over Winnipeg and again in 1926 over Toronto Varsity. As a player, one incident in particular has given him a degree of notoriety when he precipitated a riot in a 1912 game in Hamilton. Ottawa would narrowly defeat the Tigers 21–17 on a try scored by McCann. The Tigers protested vehemently that McCann had stolen the ball from Dixon of the Tigers only a split second after he caught the ball fairly and that Billy McMaster, the referee, had already blown the whistle. McMaster said, unfortunately, he blew the whistle accidently and not to signal a dead ball. Hamilton fans went berserk and assaulted McMaster with sticks and parasols.

KENNETH G. MONTGOMERY – Born in Wetaskiwin, Alberta, in 1907, he played hockey with Central Alberta champions in 1923, and was past president and executive officer of the Edmonton Athletic Club 1934–40. He was also associated with two junior hockey clubs, 1934–39, and two Memorial Cup finals. He was one of the founders and road secretary of the Edmonton Eskimo Football Club, 1938–39, and one of the founders and president of Edmonton Eskimos, 1952–53–54, winning Edmonton's first Grey Cup in 1954.

Mr. Montgomery was president of the Canadian Rugby Union in 1956, president of the Western Interprovincial Football Union in 1957, and one of the founders of the Canadian Football League.

ALVIN RITCHIE, with brief service before World War One, moved into the Regina Football Club in 1919. In addition to begin instrumental in forming the constitution for the Saskatchewan Football League, the "Silver Fox" played a leading part in sending the Regina team into 56 consecutive victories and nine Western championships.

Ritchie's Roughriders were defeated by Edmonton, the first Western team to challenge for the Grey Cup in 1921. He was manager of the Regina team defeated by Queen's University in the 1923 Cup final. Organizing the Regina Patricias in 1925, he won the Western title but lost the Canadian play-off to Montreal AAA. Losses in championship games would dog his footsteps. In 1928 he took over the senior Roughriders with Howie Milne, while coaching the Pats at the same time. The Patricias won the Junior championship that year; the Roughriders went to the Grey Cup with 17 victories on the line. The Hamilton Tigers, under Mike Rodden, however, were also undefeated and cut the Roughriders down 30–0.

JOE B. RYAN was appointed manager of the new Winnipegs in 1931. The following year he engineered the amalgamation of the Winnipeg Rugby Club and St. John's arguing that neither team was big enough or solvent enough to be a credible Grey Cup contender. He brought in Carl Cronin from Notre Dame as coach and in 1933 Winnipeg won the Western title. In 1934, with Frank Hannibal, Leo Isard, Barry Bain, G. S. Halter, Ryan helped strengthen the Winnipeg Football Club by scouting the Dakotas looking for players. The results were immediate and startling as Winnipeg won the 1935 Grey Cup. From 1931 to 1937 Ryan managed a team which won 6 Western and 3 Dominion titles.

FRANCIS "SHAG" SHAUGHNESSY played football with the University of Notre Dame, earned degrees in pharmacy and in law, coached at Clemson in South Carolina and rarely lost a game. In 1912, the Ottawa Rough Riders wanted him as their coach. McGill University offered to match the $500 Ottawa offer and double it if McGill won the Intercollegiate title. McGill did, beating Varsity 14–3 and Shaughnessy collected his $1,000.

He was a magnificent coach, canny and an opportunist. Other universities objected to the use of a professional coach as grossly unfair, but no one could argue with his results. His McGill teams were perennial champions. His players idolized him and became disciples. Billy Hughes, a "Shag" man, had outstanding teams at Queen's in the early Twenties.

ANNIS STUKUS started his football career with the Toronto Argonauts in 1935, playing fullback and punter. After three games he was switched to quarterback and led the Argos to six straight wins.

The next year he played six positions with the Argos; quarterback, end, center, fullback, tackle and flying wing. For the next two years in 1937–38 Argos won the Grey Cup. In the latter year Stukus was named an All-Canadian. He played with the Argos for the next three seasons. In 1942 he was quarterback and backfield coach with the Oakwood Indians, in 1943 with Balmy Beach and in 1944 he joined the Navy and played for H.M.C.S. York Bulldogs. As a charter member of the Toronto Indians in 1945–46 he was hoping for the eventual amalgamation of the Indians and Balmy Beach to form a second Toronto team, plans which never materialized.

N. J. "PIFFLES" TAYLOR, largely responsible for development of football in Western Canada, came up through the ranks to become president of the Regina Roughriders (1934–1936) of the Western Interprovincial Football Union (four times) and of the Canadian Rugby Union (1946).

A Westerner by way of Collingwood, Ontario, "Piffles" Taylor played his early football with Regina teams, graduated to the University of Toronto and returned to Regina after being released as a prisoner-of-war in 1918. As quarterback he helped inspire the Roughriders to win their fifth Western Championship, defeating Calgary 13–1. He quarterbacked the Regina team in 1919, the Regina Boat Club in 1922. By 1934 he was president of the club and would hold various executive positions until his death in 1946.

CLAIR J. WARNER, from South Dakota, entered Canada in 1917, moved to Regina in 1919 and entered juvenile football. From 1920 to 1924 he played junior football and joined the Regina senior club in 1925. He played eight seasons with Al Ritchie's great Roughrider teams participating in four Grey Cup finals.

After a brief spell as coach of Regina juniors, Warner graduated into executive work and became one of the bulwarks in the organization. He served on the Western Interprovincial Union executive for six years, as president in 1948, and served for five years as a member of the Canadian Rugby Union rules committee.

A. H. "BERT" WARWICK, player, coach and executive at all levels, graduated from football at St. John's College, Winnipeg, to officiating and coaching. Leading YMHA juniors, in Winnipeg, he became assistant coach of Winnipeg Blue Bombers and as head coach, led the Bombers to the Western Canada crown in 1945.

An executive with the Winnipeg Club, of which he was a life member, he rendered great service to St. Paul's College, was president of Winnipeg junior Bombers, and turned to important service with league executives.

"Shag" Shaughnessy

"Piffles" Taylor

PLAYERS/BUILDERS

WILLIAM C. FOULDS — Outstanding first as a quarterback with the University of Toronto, posting a brilliant record in 1909 and 1910, then as a coach of the Grey Cup bound Toronto Argonauts in 1911 and again in 1914, Foulds turned inevitably to the executive side of Canadian football.

As president of the Canadian Rugby Union in 1921, he received an anonymous letter suggesting that the C.R.U. look into establishing an East-West final for the Dominion Championship. The Edmonton Eskimos were the Western champs in 1921 and in order to bring them east to play for the Grey Cup, somehow the C.R.U. would have to raise the needed $4,000 for expenses. It wasn't known at the time, but it was Foulds who put up his own money to make the East-West final a reality. This was a milestone year in the history of Canadian football as the Eskimos came east with all the hoopla and spirit now traditional of the Canadian tribal rite of Grey Cup Week.

TEDDY MORRIS — A distinguished football career spanning more than three decades led Morris inevitably into the Canadian Football Hall of Fame. From Toronto playground teams, with Native Sons juniors in Winnipeg and a place in the Canadian Junior Championship final, Morris launched a spectacular career with the Toronto Argonauts in 1931. During nine years of stardom with Toronto, Morris helped win three Canadian Championships and the Jeff Russel Memorial in 1937 as the League's Outstanding Player.

Assistant coach with Argos in 1940–41, Morris coached H.M.C.S. York navy teams in 1942-3-4 winning the service championship in the latter year. He became coach of the Argonauts in 1945 and in his five-year tenure he led the Oarsmen to three Grey Cup victories. He put his heart and soul into coaching; lived and died with each play on the field.

JACK NEWTON, for more than 50 years, made great contributions to Canadian Football. From Sarnia Collegiate, through University of Toronto, Jack Newton aided Varsity to a Grey Cup Championship in 1909. A solid All-Star selection, he later coached

Teddy Morris   *Jack Newton*

the Toronto Argonauts to two Interprovincial titles and one Grey Cup victory in 1914. Moving to Sarnia Collegiate Institute as head football coach, he directed his teams to an Ontario Championship. For eight years thereafter he coached the Sarnia Intermediates to many Ontario and Canadian titles. Wherever Newton went, success on the gridiron seemed to follow.

MICHAEL J. RODDEN — From 1906, when he entered University of Ottawa, Rodden then moved to Queen's, playing football for 4 seasons (1910–1913) and was elected to four All-Star teams — at a different position each time. He won 15 letters in Tricolor sports, a record never equalled. He spent time at McGill, coached Queen's in 1916, played middle-wing for the Toronto Argonauts (1919), then coached the Argos the following year to a Grey Cup berth against "Laddie Cassels" Varsity.

Rodden won the senior O.R.F.U. title in 1921 coaching Parkdale Canoe Club, retained the championship the following year, then in 1924 with A. Buett, coached Balmy Beach to a Grey Cup position, losing 11–3 to the Batstone-Leadlay powerhouse at Queen's. Rodden's greatest clubs were developed in Hamilton. The '28 Grey Cup against Regina was especially memorable. The Roughriders had recruited 5 players from the Junior Pats including Eddie James; they were undefeated in the West and did not have a touchdown scored against them in three years. In the final Rodden's boys changed all that, beating them 30–0.

THE CANADIAN HOCKEY HALL OF FAME

Toronto, Ontario

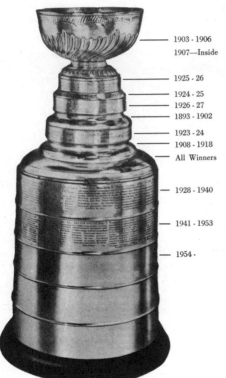

————— 1903 - 1906
1907—Inside

————— 1925 - 26
————— 1924 - 25
————— 1926 - 27
————— 1893 - 1902

————— 1923 - 24
————— 1908 - 1918
————— All Winners

————— 1928 - 1940

————— 1941 - 1953

————— 1954 -

The Stanley Cup is the oldest trophy competed for by professional athletes in North America. It was donated in 1893 by Frederick Arthur, Lord Stanley of Preston to be presented to the amateur champions of Canada. Since 1910 when the National Hockey Association took possession of the Stanley Cup, the trophy has been symbolic of professional hockey supremacy. It is exhibited in the Hockey Hall of Fame during most of the year, except when taken out for official presentation, alterations or repairs.

The Hockey Hall of Fame and Canada's Sports Hall of Fame are located in the middle of Exhibition Park, on the waterfront immediately adjacent to Ontario Place.

In one building—an unusual marriage of two Halls of Fame, one supported mainly by the National Hockey League, the other by a combination of funds from the Canadian National Exhibition and the Federal Government affords an excellent attraction. Each Hall operates as a separate entity with its own Governing Body, its own Selection Committee and its own bookkeeping. Additionally, within the building is a Souvenir Shop which is still another distinctly separate operation.

Initially, it shared space with Canada's Sports Hall of Fame which had had its embryo at Exhibition Park. They were originally opened to the public at Stanley Barracks (what is now known as the Marine Museum), moved to the Old Press Building (opposite the Queen Elizabeth Building), then in 1961 the National Hockey League underwrote construction of the present structure and was officially opened in August of that year by the then Prime Minister of Canada, the Hon. John Diefenbaker.

The two Halls shared one display area for six years, then in 1967 Metropolitan Toronto (which by this time had taken over from the City) had the east wing of the building constructed to house the Sports Hall. Each hall is dealt with separately, so as not to make it any more confusing than possible.

The Hockey Hall of Fame is a repository for records and trophies of the game of hockey as well as a place to honor properly the men—who have played highly significant rules in the development of the sport, whether as a player, official or in a builder capacity.

At the present time there are 191 Honored Members: 139 players, 44 builders and eight officials. Very basically, player candidates are selected on the basis of "playing ability, integrity, character, and their contribution to their team and the game of hockey in general". There is a three-year waiting period after retirement from what could be called 'major' hockey before a candidate can be considered—although this has been waived seven times in the past, as in such notable cases as Rocket Rich-

—All photographs in this chapter, courtesy Canadian Hockey Hall of Fame

Displays of skates, people, trophies and uniforms in the Hockey Hall of Fame.

A display of hockey sticks of various players who starred through the years.

ard, Gordie Howe and Jean Beliveau. These are elected by the Selection Committee whereas builder and official candidates are selected by the Governing Committee.

As you move into the Hockey wing of the building you will note that there are free-standing boards located throughout the display area. Builder honorees are located on a blue-backed board, officials on a green-backed board and players on a red-backed board — this is to more easily locate a specific honored member, if you wish. These boards are patterned throughout the floor area and interspersed are numerous showcases in which there is assorted memorabilia of the game.

These cases have all kinds of things of interest to the hockey fan, and probably some of interest to even the casual observer. They include such as:

. . . . . A microphone used for many years by Foster Hewitt in his broadcasts from Maple Leaf Gardens;

The evolution of the skate.

. . . . . The stick used by Bill Mosienko, and the three pucks scored when he set the record for the three-fastest goals in a game in NHL history — 21 seconds;

. . . . . A collection of significant pucks and other memorabilia related to Bobby Hull when he was the hottest thing in pro hockey during the 1960's;

. . . . . Sticks, pucks, trophies and the sweater and skates worn by Gordie Howe — Mr. Everything of the Detroit Red Wings, and the National Hockey League, and the World Hockey League.

. . . . . Collections of skates, sticks, pucks and other paraphernalia assembled in a manner to be easily seen by anyone touring the Hall.

These are just some of the highlights. The material is displayed in cases for easy viewing and while there are no formal tours as such — because of staff limitations — everything is clearly marked and the majority of people prefer to wander at will, picking out their own items of interest.

Now in addition, there are specific displays of interest — such as the Goalie Display which is built around Terry Sawchuk and incorporates such materials as the progression of masks used by Jacques Plante, from his first to present-day. Then there is the Team Canada-Soviet Display which has stimulated a great deal of favorable comment during the past years. This includes a pictorial history of the great series, a painting of Paul Henderson scoring the winning goal, two life-size forms wearing the uniforms of Paul Henderson and a composite Soviet player (the sweater was worn by the goalie, Tretiak) and the sticks of Henderson and a Soviet player.

There are also numerous materials which are, strictly speaking, non-hockey but the Curator felt that this series was more than just a hockey series — it was a cultural exchange, and he set up the display accordingly. Thus there are collections of Soviet Union materials such as a samovar, Russian dolls, and the like. And there are three good pin collections — that is the pins of sporting organizations which were exchanged between the Canadians in Moscow and the Muscovites themselves — which most people find very interesting.

Of course we cannot leave the Hockey Hall without noting that all of the National Hockey League trophies are housed here — that includes the Stanley Cup, the Hart Trophy, the Lady Byng, the Vezina, the Ross, the Norris and all of the others. This is the permanent home of all of these — unfortunately because of presentation and engraving they are usually out of the Hall during the latter part of May and all of the month of June. There are also many other trophies and awards; as well as hundreds of pictures to be seen.

It should be mentioned here that both of the Halls of Fame are FREE. That's right — FREE.

HALL OF FAME

S. G. ABEL (Sid) An All-Star at two different positions, Hart Trophy winner, captain of the Wings at 24, he established himself as one of the league's great centers on Detroit's famed Production Line between Gordie Howe and Ted Lindsay. Abel scored 189 goals in the NHL, including a personal high of 34 in the 1949–50 season and a league-leading 28 in 1948–49. Abel left Detroit in 1952 to become player-manager of Chicago Black Hawks and led that team to its first playoff berth in nine seasons.

J. J. ADAMS (Jack) was 24 when he joined Vancouver and went on to win the scoring title in the Pacific Coast League with 24 goals and 18 assists in 24 games. He later played for Toronto St. Pats and for Ottawa's Stanley Cup winners of 1926–27 with King Clancy, George Boucher, Frank Nighbor, Cy Denneny, Frank Finnigan and Alex Connell.

As coach and manager of the Wings, Adams sold hockey to Detroit, both on and off the ice. He innovated the farm system in hockey and built winning teams—12 regular season championships including a string of seven straight, and seven Stanley Cups. Only seven times in 35 years under Adams did Wings miss the playoffs. His greatest personal satisfaction came in the development of Gordie Howe, greatest scorer in NHL history.

SYLVANUS APPS (Syl) joined the Leafs in 1936 and became the first winner of the Calder Trophy, awarded at that time by National Hockey League president Frank Calder to the outstanding rookie. Apps played seven more seasons before becoming a member of the Canadian Armed Forces during World War II. In that time he played on one Stanley Cup winner, was voted All-Star center twice and to the second team three times, and won the Lady Byng Trophy in the season of 1941–42. Returning to the Leafs for the 1945–46 season, Apps continued his fine play and in the next three seasons scored 24, 25 and 26 goals to bring his career total to 201—an average of 20 per season. He also led Leafs to two more Stanley Cup triumphs, retiring after the 1947–48 season.

GEORGE E. ARMSTRONG was the son of a Scotsman and his Indian wife—a background that entitled him to claim Indian ancestry, which he has always done, proudly.

Sent to the Toronto Maple Leafs' organization by scout Bob Wilson, he was a standout junior at Stratford and with Toronto Marlboros, then played for Marlboro seniors when they won the Allan Cup in 1950. It was while at the national senior finals in Alberta that an Indian tribe officially dubbed him "Big Chief Shoot-the-puck," and he was "The Chief" ever since. It was a suitable sobriquet for the man who was to be Leafs' captain 13 of his 21 years in the National Hockey League.

IRVIN W. BAILEY (Ace)—His National Hockey League career was relatively brief, due to a disastrous incident Dec. 12, 1933, when a collision with Eddie Shore resulted in a fractured skull that terminated his playing days. But in the 7½ seasons as a starry winger with Toronto Maple Leafs, Bailey established himself as both an outstanding scorer and a super defensive star.

Bailey was the club's top scorer until Charlie Conacher hit his stride and led the NHL in both scoring and points in 1928–29. He also played on the Stanley Cup-winning team of 1932–33. When the Kid Line stole the scoring glory with the Leafs, Bailey combined with Harold (Baldy) Cotton as one of the finest penalty-killing duos in the league. Bailey's puck-ragging efficiency was renowned and it was while he was performing this specialty that his near-fatal accident occurred in Boston. After several weeks near death he came around and effected a complete recovery. Ace later coached, then joined the staff of minor officials at Maple Leaf Gardens where he was still active at the time of his induction.

D. H. BAIN (Dan) was an extraordinary athlete, often referred to as Manitoba's greatest athlete of all time.

Though born in Belleville, Ont., in 1874, he moved with his family to Winnipeg at the age of six and spent the rest of his life there. He never played professional hockey but was a member of two Stanley Cup champions, the Winnipeg Victorias of 1895–96 and 1900–01. Bain was a great leader on the ice, played center and captained the Victorias in four Stanley Cup challenge rounds. They defeated Montreal Victorias in their initial Cup triumph and Montreal Shamrocks for the second.

H. A. H. BAKER (Hobey)—The name of Hobey Baker is almost legend in United States college hockey history. He entered Princeton University in 1910, proficient not only in hockey but in football, golf, track, swimming and gymnastics. In his senior year, he captained the football team and dropkicked a 43-yard field goal to tie a game with Yale. He also captained the hockey team in his final two years. As a rover, he was a one-man team called "Baker and six other players."

After graduation in 1914, Hobey joined St. Nicholas hockey team. After a series in which his team won the Ross Cup from the Montreal Stars, a Montreal paper said: "Uncle Sam had the cheek to develop a first-class hockey player . . . who wasn't born in Montreal . . ." Baker joined the Lafayette Escadrille, a flying unit, during World War I and here too performed admirably. He survived the war but crashed while testing a new plane and was killed. Princeton's ice arena today is named after Hobey Baker and St. Paul's school competes for a sacred trophy — Hobey's stick.

M. A. BARRY (Marty) — Newsy Lalonde signed him to play for New York Americans in the spring of 1927 but he played only seven games. He went to Philadelphia Arrows, then to New Haven Eagles in 1928–29 where he won the league scoring title. He finally made the NHL to stay with Boston Bruins in the 1929–30 season and remained with them until 1935–36 when he was traded to Detroit.

It was with the Red Wings that he teamed on a line, centering Herbie Lewis and Larry Aurie, that was the scourge of the league. Wings won the Stanley Cup in 1935–36 and 1936–37, Barry won the Lady Byng Trophy and was named to the first All-Star team. Barry completed his NHL career with Montreal Canadiens in 1939–40, then returned to coaching. He died Aug. 20, 1969, of a heart attack at his home in Halifax, N.S.

JEAN A. BELIVEAU — "Le Gros Bill," as he became known because of his six-foot-three, 205-

Jean Beliveau

pound frame, scored 507 goals during his 18 full seasons in the NHL, an all-time record for a center. But he was of a character that would have made him great, won him respect anywhere, even if he had scored but half that number.

When he retired, Jean was named to an executive position with his Montreal Canadiens and designated official spokesman of the organization. This was just an acknowledgement of a capacity he had been filling for a number of years, if not by words, then by actions. He joined Canadiens as a pro in the 1953–54 season — he played five NHL games as an amateur up from Quebec Aces in two previous seasons — and from the first was a team leader, although he didn't officially become team captain until 1961. He still holds the record for most consecutive years in Stanley Cup playoffs — 16 — and he played 17 in all.

His highest single goal-scoring season was 1955–56 when he not only won the Art Ross Trophy as scoring champion with 47 goals and 41 assists but also won the Hart Trophy as the NHL's most valuable player. Three seasons later he had a 45-goal effort. In 1963–64 Jean was again voted winner of the Hart Trophy and the following season he won the Conn Smythe Trophy as most valuable player in the Stanley Cup playoffs. In his final season, 1970–71, Jean collected 16 playoff assists, another record. When he retired, the normally sport-hardened media gave him a sustained standing ovation.

CLINT BENEDICT (Benny) — Considered one of the great goaltenders of all time, he started playing hockey at the age of six and moved into senior ranks while still only 15. At the age of 34, he was forced into retirement after stopping two rifle-like shots off the stick of Howie Morenz. The first shot shattered Benedict's nose and, in a later game, the second injured his larynx.

The first Morenz shot affected Benedict's vision and prompted him to become one of the first in pro hockey to try wearing a face mask. It was tailored for him by a Boston firm but he threw it away after a 2–1 loss to Chicago. "The nosepiece protruded too far and obscured my vision on low shots," he recalled.

D. W. BENTLEY (Doug) showed such outstanding early ability that, at 16, he played senior hockey for Delisle, the Saskatchewan town where he was born Sept. 13, 1916. Bentley played junior the following two seasons, at Saskatoon and Regina, then three more as a senior at Moose Jaw, Sask. The next season, 1938, he played on a team with four other brothers at Drumheller, Alta., and in 1939 he moved up to start a 12-year stay with Chicago Black Hawks of the National Hockey League.

For several seasons he was united with brother Max and Bill Mosienko on one of the NHL's all-time great forward lines. All three scored more than

200 goals during their NHL career, Doug getting 219 and winning a scoring title in 1942–43. He was also named to the first All-Star team three times: in 1942–43, 1943–44 and 1946–47. A singular honor was bestowed on him in 1950 when a Chicago newspaper voted him the Half-Century Award as Chicago's best player up to that year.

MAX BENTLEY — At the height of his Chicago stardom, Max was the key figure in an amazing NHL trade. Toronto gave up five high-quality players for Bentley and an amateur player. With the Hawks, he had been a member of the famous Pony Line with brother Doug and Bill Mosienko, all of whom are Hockey Hall of Fame members. With Toronto, Max continued his sparkling play and was with three Stanley Cup champion teams.

Max Bentley won the Hart Trophy in 1945–46, the Lady Byng Trophy in 1942–43 and the Art Ross Trophy in 1944–45 and 1945–46. He also was voted to the first All-Star team in 1945–46. In 646 NHL games, Max scored 245 goals and had 299 assists for a total of 544 points. He also scored 18 goals in 44 playoff games.

HECTOR BLAKE (Toe) played for Hamilton Tigers, a senior team, until joining Montreal Maroons in February of 1934. Maroons won the Stanley Cup in 1934–35 but Blake sat on the bench. He started the next season with Providence but joined Canadiens in February when Maroons dealt him and Bill Miller for goalie Lorne Chabot. The rest is NHL history, Blake starring with Canadiens until retiring Jan. 10, 1948, when he broke his leg.

Blake won NHL scoring title in 1938–39, the Lady Byng Trophy in 1945–46 and for several seasons was part of one of the NHL's greatest lines, the Punch Line with Elmer Lach and Maurice (The Rocket) Richard. He scored 235 goals in 572 league games, played on two Stanley Cup winners and won the Hart Trophy in 1938–39. He returned to Canadiens as coach in 1955–56 and his teams won eight more Stanley Cups before he retired following the 1967–68 season. He was three times named to the first All-Star team and twice to the second.

R. R. BOON (Dickie) started his illustrious career with the Montreal Monarch Hockey Club in 1897 before moving up to the Montreal AAA juniors. By the 1901–02 season he was with the Montreal AAA's senior club which successfully challenged the Winnipeg Victorias for the Stanley Cup in 1902. The outstanding ability of the team won them the nickname of the "Little Men of Iron" after their 2–1 victory. In 1903, Dickie became manager of the Montreal Wanderers, a post which he held until mid-season of 1918 when the Westmount Arena burned. Boon finished his playing career with the Wanderers in 1904 and 1905 seasons, after which he became their director and coach.

EMILE BOUCHARD (Butch) made the Canadiens' team in 1941–42, and for 14 years was an outstanding defenseman in the National Hockey League. That was an era when there were many great rearguards but Bouchard was three times voted to the first All-Star team and twice more to the second team. Although he had great size and extraordinary strength, Bouchard never took advantage of his physical power to bully an opponent. He was robust but not unfair, feared but respected by his rivals. He scored 45 goals and many assists as he became a playmaking defenseman. He also played a big role in making Canadiens one of the outstanding teams of hockey history.

FRANK BOUCHER devoted more than a half-century to hockey and above all else, he was a gentleman. Considered one of the great playmakers of all time, Boucher won the Lady Byng Trophy seven times in eight seasons and he was finally given permanent possession of it. Tommy Gorman offered him $1,200 a year to play for Ottawa and he leaped at the chance. Regulars on that team were Frank Nighbor, Clint Benedict, Eddie Gerard, Cy Denneny, Punch Broadbent and brother George Boucher, all ultimately voted to the Hockey Hall of Fame, so Frank rode the bench with another fellow named King Clancy.

He played the next four years with Vancouver Maroons but when the Pacific Coast League broke up, he went to New York and wound up centering Bill and Bun Cook on one of the great lines of any era. Frank stayed with Rangers' organization from 1926 until 1944, played on two Stanley Cup winners, and was three times named to the first All-Star team and once to the second. Although retired as a player, he coached Rangers to another Stanley Cup win in 1939–40.

GEORGE BOUCHER (Buck) — An outstanding defenseman from a celebrated hockey family — that was George (Buck) Boucher who played pro for 20 years, 17 in the National Hockey League. Before turning to pro hockey, George had played three years of football with Ottawa Rough Riders and was considered a great halfback. He was born in Ottawa in 1896, and his hockey began in the Ottawa City League. He moved up to the Senators in 1915 where he played with greats like Eddie Gerard, Horace Merrill, Sprague Cleghorn, Lionel Hitchman and King Clancy. This Ottawa Senators' team won the Stanley Cup four times between 1920 and 1927.

Midway through the 1928–29 season, George was sold to Montreal Maroons and two years later he went to Chicago. An active player until 1934, he also coached Chicago, Ottawa, Boston and St. Louis.

RUSSELL BOWIE (Dubbie) — Bowie, whose style was something like that of the great Nels Stewart, collected a total of 234 goals in 80 games over a 10-year period with Montreal Victorias. A wizard with a stick, he played his entire career with this team from 1898 to 1908, when a broken collarbone brought his playing days to an end. A slim 112 pounds when he joined the Vics at age 17, he played on his first Stanley Cup championship team the same year. In the 1907 season, Bowie scored a total of 38 goals in 10 games and is one of the few players ever to score 10 goals in a single game. When Bowie retired from the game he had an average of nearly three goals per game.

F. C. BRIMSEK (Frank) — A star virtually from the day he stepped into the National Hockey League, he was also one of the few players born in the United States who rose to stardom in the sport. He replaced the great Cecil (Tiny) Thompson in Boston Bruins' nets early in the 1938–39 season and went on to win both the Vezina Trophy as the league's top goalie and the Calder Trophy as the outstanding rookie.

He was almost immediately tabbed Mr. Zero because he twice registered shutout strings of three games in a row, one lasting 231.54 minutes, the other 220.24 minutes. Brimsek played in the NHL through the 1949–50 season, the last one with Chicago Black Hawks.

H. L. BROADBENT, M. M. (Punch) — The National Hockey League record for scoring in consecutive games belongs to Broadbent, who scored one or more goals in 16 straight games during the 1921–22 season. He was an excellent rightwinger, an artist with the puck, and with his elbows. He once led the NHL in both scoring and penalties. "I had a hard time controlling those elbows of mine," he chuckled in recalling that 1921–22 season when he led the league with 32 goals.

In 1919, after distinguished World War I service, he rejoined Ottawa and stayed five seasons with their NHL club until sold to Montreal Maroons "to balance the league." He came back to Ottawa for the 1927–28 season, went to New York Americans in 1928–29, and when the stock market crashed he wired Americans' owner Bill Dwyer he was through. He quit hockey and joined the Royal Canadian Air Force. In 10 NHL seasons, Broadbent scored 118 goals. He was also on four Stanley Cup-winning teams, three at Ottawa and one with the Maroons.

WALTER BRODA (Turk) played for the International League champion Detroit Olympics in 1934–35 and shortly after was sold to Toronto Maple Leafs for then-record price of $8,000.

His pro career, all with the Leafs, spanned 16 seasons with two out for service in the Canadian armed forces during World War II. He twice won the Vezina Trophy (1940–41 and 1947–48) and shared it with Al Rollins in 1950–51 when Rollins played 39 games and Broda 31. It was in playoffs that Turk really excelled. He earned 13 shutouts in 101 playoff games, both Stanley Cup records, and established a phenomenal 2.08 goals-against record. Broda also played on five Stanley Cup winners.

WILLIAM BURCH (Billy) turned pro with Hamilton Tigers in 1923 and centered a line of the Green brothers, Redvers (Red) and Wilfred (Shorty) which carried the team to first place in the NHL in 1925. Burch was awarded the Hart Trophy that season as most valuable player to his team.

The team was transferred to New York Americans in 1926 and Burch, an excellent playmaker and stick-handler, was made captain. In 1927 he was winner of the Lady Byng Trophy but he missed much of the 1928 season because of a knee injury. Billy remained with the Americans until 1933 when he was sold to Boston, who in turn let him go to Chicago. This was his last active year as, near the end of the season, he broke a leg and decided to retire.

H. H. CAMERON (Harry) left many memories of his ability and colorful play, but probably the best-remembered was his ability to curve a shot. Cameron is believed one of the first to do this without treating his stick. Harry Cameron played on three Stanley Cup champions, all Toronto teams: the Torontos of 1914, the Arenas of 1918 and St. Patrick's in 1922.

His scoring record is outstanding when it is remembered that Cameron was a 154-pound defenseman. He almost invariably topped defense players in scoring and one year stood fourth in the league against such formidable opposition as Newsy Lalonde, Joe Malone, Frank Nighbor, Cy Denneny, Babe Dye and Punch Broadbent.

F. M. CLANCY (King) — In 1930, he was the key figure in what has since been called "the best deal in hockey." Toronto Maple Leaf manager Conn Smythe paid the then-unheard-of sum of $35,000 and two players to acquire Clancy from Ottawa. Smythe obviously saw the leadership qualities he desired in Clancy and the King repaid him by leading Leafs to their first Stanley Cup victory in 1931–32. He was twice named to each of the first and second NHL All-Star teams.

He remained an outstanding rushing defenseman until retiring early in the 1936–37 season. Clancy coached Montreal Maroons for the first half of the 1937–38 season, then became a referee. He returned to coach Leafs from 1950 to 1953, then moved up to become assistant manager.

A. V. CLAPPER (Dit) — Through his 20 seasons with Boston, Clapper played nine seasons as a right-winger and 11 as a defenseman. He was a legitimate star who was regarded as "the athlete's type of athlete." He was a big player, over six feet and 200 pounds, but he used his heft mostly to stop fights.

Dit scored his 200th goal in Toronto, in 1941, a memorable one because it gave Bruins a 1–0 victory. He was to finish with 228 goals and 246 assists,

"King" Clancy   *Bill Cook*

and a playoff record of 12 goals and 23 assists. His highest single-season scoring mark was 41 goals in the 44-game schedule of 1929–30. Clapper was to play on three Stanley Cup championship teams with Boston: 1928–29, 1938–39 and 1940–41. He was also named three times to each of the first and second NHL All-Star teams.

SPRAGUE CLEGHORN was one of the greatest but roughest defense players the game of hockey has ever known. He started out as a forward but quickly moved back to defense and played alongside Cyclone Taylor at Renfrew.

He tried to emulate Taylor's great rushing style and for five years was the darling of Wanderers' fans, once scoring five goals in one game. In 17 seasons— he missed 1918 because of a broken leg—Cleghorn scored 163 goals. He also played with two Stanley Cup championship teams, the Ottawa club of 1920 and Canadiens of 1924.

NEIL COLVILLE advanced to Philadelphia Ramblers for the 1935–36 season and the club not only won the league championship, Colville was leading scorer until about six weeks from the end of the schedule when he was sidelined by an injury. Colville moved up to Rangers in 1936 and played on the famous "bread line" for six years, during which Rangers won the Stanley Cup in 1940 and the NHL championship in 1942. Neil captained the team for six seasons and was three times named to an All-Star team.

CHARLIE CONACHER was big and strong, and with a shot that was feared by every goaltender in the National Hockey League. That was Charlie Conacher, member of a famous athletic family, who played 13 seasons in the league before retiring.

Conacher played nine seasons with Toronto before being traded to Detroit where he played one season. From 1939 until 1941, he was with New York Americans and he retired at the end of that season. During his NHL career, Conacher scored 225 goals and twice won the scoring title, in 1933–34 and 1934–35. In all, he was the league's top goal-scorer four consecutive seasons although he shared that honor with Bill Cook in 1932 and Bill Thoms in 1936. He was named three times to the first All-Star team and twice to the second.

ALEX CONNELL set a goaltending record during the 1927–28 season that has stood the test of time. He registered six consecutive shutouts and was not scored upon for 446 minutes and nine seconds, a record that still held firm 40 years later.

With Connell in goal, Ottawa won the Stanley Cup in 1926–27 and the following year he set his fabulous shutout streak. That year he allowed only 57 goals in 44 games. Alex retired in 1933 but came back for two more years in 1934 to help Montreal Maroons win the Stanley Cup. He continued to coach junior teams until 1949, spending several seasons with St. Patrick's College juniors.

WILLIAM COOK (Bill) during his 12-year stay in the National Hockey League, scored 228 goals and added another 140 assists. Cook was a member of the all-time great lines, with brother Bun Cook and play-making center Frank Boucher. He was a big, strong sharpshooter who played his entire NHL career with the New York Rangers and in that span he was on two Stanley Cup champions, 1927–28 and 1932–33.

New York Rangers entered the NHL in 1926, coinciding with the demise of the WCL and Rangers purchased both Cooks, later adding Boucher to form the great scoring unit. Bill Cook added the NHL scoring crown to his laurels in that first season, scoring 33 goals in 44 games. He tied Charlie Conacher with 34 goals to lead the league in 1931–32 and won the honors outright the following season with 28 goals. He retired from the NHL in 1937 after three times being named to the first All-Star team and once to the second.

A. E. COULTER (Art)—An athlete of exceptional physical strength and endurance, he had fierce aggressive devotion to the team principle. A defenseman, he partnered Taffy Abel as a strong unit when Chicago won the Stanley Cup in 1933–34. He made the second NHL All-Star team in 1935 but in midseason of the following year he was traded to Rangers for Earl Seibert. In retrospect, this was a deal that proved beneficial to both clubs.

A prototype of the solid defensive defenseman, Coulter succeeded Bill Cook as Rangers' captain in 1935–36 and was chosen to the second All-Star team three more times—1937–38, 1938–39, 1939–40.

W. M. COWLEY (Bill) was twice voted the Hart Trophy as the MVP to his team—1941 and 1943—and was selected four times to the first All-Star team and once to the second. His lifetime record in the NHL is 195 goals and 353 assists, plus 12 goals and 34 assists in playoffs.

Indicative of his great playmaking, he won the NHL scoring title in 1940–41 with 62 points—17 goals and 45 assists—in 46 games. In the 1943–44 season he amassed 72 points in 36 games, only to lose the scoring title when injury sidelined him for the next six weeks of the schedule.

S. R. CRAWFORD (Rusty)—A fast-skating forward with a lefthanded shot, Crawford was capable of playing at either wing or center with equal dexterity. His talent attracted Quebec Bulldogs and he joined them for the 1912–13 season, helping them win the Stanley Cup despite losing two of three games to Victoria on the latter's ice.

Crawford remained with Quebec until 1917–18 when he went to Ottawa for four games, then joined Toronto Arenas. Toronto won the Stanley Cup that year, defeating Vancouver in a five-game series. Rusty stayed another season with Toronto, went to Saskatoon in 1920, to Calgary until 1925 and joined Vancouver in 1926. He ended his career with Minneapolis in 1929.

J. P. DARRAGH (Jack) Although he was a left-handed forward, he was usually employed on right wing and once played on a great line with Nighbor and Denneny. When Broadbent moved up to right wing, Darragh shifted over to left.

One of Darragh's cleverest moves was an adroit backhand. He was also noted for clean play, clever stickhandling and ability to turn on the speed, when required. Jack Darragh was also a fine scorer; he had 24 goals in the 22-game schedule of 1919–20 and 195 in his pro career.

A. M. DAVIDSON (Scotty) shot like a meteor from junior ranks and starred as a professional until his life was snuffed out while serving in Belgium during World War I. Davidson was born in Kingston, Ont., and very early in life showed all the attributes of a great hockey player. He was a strong, powerful skater, played very cleanly, possessed an overpowering shot and was a tremendous backchecker.

CLARENCE DAY (Happy) played with University of Toronto while studying pharmacy. Charlie Querrie talked him into turning professional with Toronto St. Patrick's Dec. 13, 1924, and he was to enjoy 33 years of association with pro hockey, as a player, coach, referee and general manager.

Day became an outstanding defenseman and paired with King Clancy to form one of the great units of all time. He was captain of the first Toronto Maple Leafs team to win the Stanley Cup, in

1931–32, scoring three goals in that series. During his playing career, Day scored a total of 86 goals and assisted on another 116. He played his final season, 1937–38, with New York Americans, became a referee for two seasons, then returned to the Leafs and became a highly successful coach.

C. J. DENNENY (Cy)—His pro career began in 1914, with Toronto Shamrocks of the National Hockey Association, and he played there for two seasons before joining Ottawa Senators of the NHA in 1916. He stayed with the Senators through transition into the National Hockey League, leaving them after 1927–28 to become a player, coach and assistant manager of Boston Bruins for one season. Bruins won the Stanley Cup that season, making a total of five for Denneny in his 14-year playing career. His best individual season was 1917–18 when he scored 36 goals in 22 games. During 11 NHL seasons, Cy scored a total of 246 goals.

GORDON DRILLON played only seven seasons in the National Hockey League—six with Toronto, one with Canadiens—but in that time scored 155 goals for a seasonal average of 22.2. This was in an era when a 20-goal season was outstanding.

He was selected twice to the NHL's first All-Star team, once to the second All-Star team and also won the Lady Byng Trophy. Drillon led the league in both goals and points in 1937–38 and was a member of the 1941–42 Leafs' team that won the Stanley Cup. He broke into the Leafs' lineup in 1936–37 as a temporary replacement for the ailing Charlie Conacher. Drillon stood six-foot-two and weighed 178, and although not as aggressive as Conacher he was to prove a great asset as a goal-getter. He was sold to Montreal and played one more season, finishing his NHL career with a 50-point effort from 28 goals and 22 assists.

C. G. DRINKWATER—Although he never was a professional, Drinkwater played for four teams that won the Stanley Cup. When the Cup was first presented in 1893, he was still at McGill University, gaining fame as a hockey and football standout.

THOMAS DUNDERDALE—Elected to the Hockey Hall of Fame in 1974, he is the first Australian-born to achieve this honor. While in the PCHA, he played four years with Victoria, three with Portland, then returned for five more with Victoria.

A righthand shot, Dunderdale stood only five-foot-eight and weighed 148 pounds at the peak of his playing career. He was noted as a deft stickhandler and fast skater. When he finished playing, Dunderdale coached and managed teams in Los Angeles, Edmonton and Winnipeg.

W. R. DURNAN (Bill)—Before he reached the National Hockey League at the age of 28, he had won more glory than many people gain in a lifetime. Durnan played seven seasons with Canadiens and although his pro career was comparatively brief, he clearly established himself as one of the greatest. Bill won the Vezina Trophy six times, missing only in 1948 to Turk Broda of Toronto. He also was voted six times to the NHL's first All-Star team, played on four league championship teams and two Stanley Cup winners.

In 1948–49, he established the modern NHL record for consecutive shutouts with four, playing 309 minutes and 21 seconds of shutout hockey. He played 383 scheduled games, allowed 901 goals for an average of 2.36 goals-against, and earned 34 shutouts in NHL action.

MERVYN DUTTON (Red) played professionally with Calgary from 1921 through 1925, and when the Patricks sold the Western Canada League to Eastern interests, Dutton signed with Eddie Gerard and the Montreal Maroons.

Dutton stayed with the Maroons until 1930 when he shifted to the New York Americans. In 1936, he took over coaching and managing that club and remained with it until 1942 when the team ceased to operate. When Frank Calder, the NHL president, died in 1943, Dutton was asked to fill the post and he remained as head of the league until Clarence S. Campbell assumed the position in 1946.

CECIL H. DYE (Babe)—Although small in stature—five-foot-eight, 150 pounds—Cecil Henry Dye had a distinguished athletic career. He became a star halfback with Toronto Argonauts and was good enough in baseball to be offered $25,000 (a fabulous sum in those days) to play for Connie Mack's Philadelphia team. His official hockey career began in 1917 with Toronto Aura Lee, Ontario junior champions.

He joined Toronto St. Pats for the 1919–20 season, found it difficult to break the starting lineup, but still scored 11 goals in 21 games. In the next six seasons, using superb stickhandling and a phenomenally hard shot, he scored 163 goals in 149 games. He led the league in scoring four times, twice scored in 11 consecutive games and twice scored five goals in a game. He went on to play for Chicago in the expanded league in 1926–27 but to all intents his career ended when he broke a leg in the 1927 training camp and missed the season. He made one more try, with New York Americans in 1928–29, but scored only one goal in 41 games. That goal was No. 200, achieved in 255 games—for the highest goals-per-game record in the history of the National Hockey League.

ARTHUR F. FARRELL—His years with the Montreal Shamrocks began in 1897, when they ceased to be known as the Crystals, and ended following the 1901 playoffs against Winnipeg Victorias. During four years with the team—he missed the 1898 season—Farrell scored a total of 29 goals in 26 games, plus 13 goals in eight playoff games.

Shamrocks captured their first of two straight Stanley Cups in 1899 when they also finished in first place in the league. Farrell's best playoff came the next season when he scored 10 goals in five games. In this series he scored four goals in each of two games against Halifax Crescents.

FRANK C. FOYSTON—In 1912, he became a professional with Toronto of the National Hockey Association and he played center for that team when they won the Stanley Cup in 1913–14. By 1915–16 he was on his way to Seattle and a year later he was on another Stanley Cup winner, the first U.S.-based team to win this historic trophy. He stayed with Seattle for nine years, shifting to Victoria for two seasons and was once again on a Stanley Cup winner when the Cougars captured it in 1924–25. When Detroit purchased the team, Foyston went east and stayed in the Motor City for two years, retiring as a player after the 1927–28 season.

FRANK FREDRICKSON signed with Lester Patrick's Victoria Aristocrats (later changed to Cougars) and remained with that team until the WCL sold out to eastern interests. Cougars defeated Montreal Canadiens to win the 1925 Stanley Cup playoff but lost the next year's final to Montreal Maroons. His career took him to Detroit for half a season, then to Boston, and in the 1928–29 season to Pittsburgh. He was both coach and manager, as well as playing center for Pittsburgh in the next season when a leg injury virtually ended his playing days.

W. A. GADSBY (Bill) spent 20 seasons in the National Hockey League and proved himself a defenseman of outstanding ability.

Gadsby graduated from Edmonton junior hockey, signed to play pro with Chicago Black Hawks and

Two great goalies, Bill Durnan (left) and Turk Broda.

was sent to Kansas City for seasoning. He was cut for 12 stitches in his first game, portending the future; he was to take almost 600 stitches before hanging up his skates as a player. He moved up to the Hawks early in the 1946–47 season and remained with them through 18 games of the 1954–55 season when he was traded to New York. Another trade took him to Detroit for the 1961–62 season and he played his last five seasons with the Wings.

C. R. GARDINER (Chuck) — Born in Edinburgh, Scotland, he became one of the few born in the United Kingdom to play in the National Hockey League.

In a seven-year career with the Hawks, he played in 315 games, allowed only 673 goals for an average of 2.13 goals-against, and registered 42 shutouts. He also played in 21 Stanley Cup contests, scoring five shutouts and giving up only 35 goals for a phenomenal 1.66 goals-against average. Gardiner won the Vezina Trophy twice, in 1931–32 and 1933–34, was selected to the first All-Star team on three occasions and to the second All-Star team once.

H. M. GARDINER (Herb) — The true hockey potential of Herb Gardiner will never be known. He didn't arrive in the National Hockey League until he was 35 but he quickly established himself by winning the Hart Trophy as the most valuable player to his team, Montreal Canadiens. He stayed with Canadiens until, during the 1929 season, he was loaned to Chicago where he acted as manager. Montreal recalled him for the playoffs but later sold him to Boston, which in turn, sold him to Philadelphia Arrows of the Canadian-American League where he became manager and coach. He stayed in Philadelphia until 1949, later coaching the Ramblers and Falcons.

J. H. GARDNER (Jimmy) enjoyed more than a decade as an outstanding player and was associated with two great teams, as a member of the Montreal Hockey Club's "Little Men of Iron," and with Montreal Wanderers. Those "Little Men of Iron" won the Stanley Cup in 1901–02 after a stubborn stand against Winnipeg and Wanderers won the Cup in 1909–10 with Gardner as a team member. He went to Calumet, Mich., staying two seasons. In 1907, he moved on to Pittsburgh and after one season he returned to Montreal and played a season with the Shamrocks. He rejoined Wanderers just in time to be on his second Stanley Cup winner.

BERNARD GEOFFRION (Boom Boom) — Boomer, as he was often called, stepped from Montreal Nationals junior team to the Canadiens in 1951, scoring eight goals in 18 games. The five-foot, 11-inch, 185-pounder went on to register 393 goals before bowing out in the 1967–68 season, a total which ranked him fifth in league records at the time.

He won the Art Ross Trophy as league scoring champion twice (1954–55 and 1960–61), Hart Trophy as the most valuable player to his team (1960–61) and the Calder Trophy as top rookie during his first full season (1951–52). He was also only the second player to reach the 50-goal plateau in one season (1960–61), the year he achieved a personal high of 95 points.

E. G. GERARD (Eddie) turned professional with the Ottawa Senators in the 1913–14 season and became their captain in the 1920–21 campaign. During his ten years with the team he was on four Stanley Cup winners, although one was while he was on loan to Toronto St. Pats. Gerard's first victory in the Stanley Cup came in 1919–20 with a triumph over Seattle Metropolitans. This was followed by victories over Vancouver Millionaires in 1920–21 and over both Vancouver and Edmonton Eskimos in 1922–23.

H. L. GILMOUR (Billy) joined the Ottawa Silver Seven in the 1902–03 season from McGill University and stayed with the club for three consecutive Stanley Cup victories. His best season was 1902–03 when he collected ten goals in seven games. He also scored five goals in four games in the playoffs.

The Silver Seven repeated as winners of the Stanley Cup in 1903–04 and 1904–05, but lost their hold on the Cup in 1905–06. It was at the end of this season that Billy retired for one season.

F. X. GOHEEN (Moose) — It was said of Goheen that he was "the only individual three-man rush in hockey."

He was born in White Bear, Minn., Feb. 9, 1894, and was acknowledged as one of the truly great hockey players produced in the United States. He was an outstanding athlete in football, baseball and hockey, but it was the latter sport that rocketed him to international acclaim. He is credited with originating the wearing of helmets or head gear. Although primarily a defenseman, he was a prolific scorer and was noted for rink-length rushes.

E. R. GOODFELLOW (Ebbie) moved up to the NHL club in 1929–30 and scored 17 goals. The next season, Goodfellow led the American Division of the league with 25 goals.

Ebbie moved to defense in the 1934–35 season and continued to star. He was named to the NHL's second All-Star team in 1935–36 and twice to the first All-Star team, in 1936–37 and 1939–40. Goodfellow also won the Hart Trophy as the MVP to his team in 1939–40. He also played on three Stanley Cup-winning teams: 1935–36, 1936–37 and 1942–43.

He was captain of the Red Wings for five seasons, turning that post over to Sid Abel after the 1942–43 season when he retired. In all, Ebbie played 575 games with Detroit and scored 134 goals. Combined with 190 assists it gave him a points' total of 324.

MICHAEL GRANT (Mike) during his career played with three Montreal teams—the Crystals, Shamrocks and Victorias—and was the captain of each. When his career came to a close he had been the captain on three Stanley Cup victors. When he was not playing the sport, he often refereed games in the same league.

W. T. GREEN (Shorty) is often remembered as captain of the Hamilton Tigers who staged the first player strike in the history of the National Hockey League, but he had many other claims to fame.

Green joined the Hamilton Tigers and helped them win the Allan Cup in 1919, then returned to Sudbury and played there until the autumn of 1923 when he turned professional with Hamilton Tigers of the NHL. Tigers won league honors in 1925 and Shorty, as captain, was spokesman for the players who refused to participate in a playoff game unless the club paid a $200-per-player compensation. The owners refused to give in and Toronto and Canadiens played a series to decide the title.

S. S. GRIFFIS (Si) was a big man of 195 pounds but he became known as the fastest man in the game. Griffis started as a rover in the seven-man game of that era but later moved back to play cover-point (defense). In addition to the Stanley Cup triumph at Kenora, Griffis was captain of the Vancouver Millionaires that won it in 1914–15, although he did not play in the Cup series due to a broken leg sustained in the final game of the schedule.

Griffis was given a purse of gold by the citizens of Kenora and offered a fine home but moved to Vancouver after the Cup-winning season. He retired from hockey until 1911 when the Patricks started the Pacific Coast League. On his opening night with the Millionaires he played the full 60 minutes, scoring three goals and assisting on two others. He remained with the team until 1918 when he retired to stay.

GEORGE HAINSWORTH established two brilliant records during 11 seasons in the National Hockey League. Both came during the 1928–29 season. A goaltender, Hainsworth allowed only 43 goals in a 44-game schedule and recorded the remarkable total of 22 shutouts. Ironically, his team won 22 games that season.

He turned professional with Saskatoon in 1923–24 and remained with that team until shifting to Canadiens in 1926–27, where he was an immediate sensation. He won the Vezina Trophy in his first three seasons with Canadiens, playing behind such greats as Howie Morenz, Aurel Joliat, Battleship Leduc, Sylvio Mantha, Herb Gardiner and Pit Lepine.

GLENN H. HALL—One of the magical names in hockey was Glenn Henry Hall, veteran goalie who played 18 seasons in the NHL—four with Detroit,

Glenn Hall in action.

ten with Chicago and four with St. Louis. He was consistently one of the league's outstanding goaltenders, an All-Star selection for 11 years, finishing with a career goals-against average of 2.51.

He led the NHL in shutouts six seasons, including his rookie campaign when he won the Calder Trophy, and had 84 regular-season shutouts. He holds the NHL record for most consecutive games by a goaltender (502) and appeared in 906 league games. In Stanley Cup playoff records he had the most playoff games by a goalie (113) and most minutes played by a goalie in a career (6,899). His name appears three times on the Vezina Trophy and in his first season with St. Louis Blues he was awarded the Conn Smythe Trophy for his superior playoff record. Until the final half of his last active season Hall played without a mask.

J. H. HALL (Joe) played with the Quebec Bulldogs from 1910–11 through the 1915–16 season and was on two Stanley Cup championship teams—1911–12 and 1912–13—then finished his career with Montreal Canadiens. The Canadiens won the National Hockey League title in 1918–19 and went west to play for the Stanley Cup in Seattle. The series with Seattle, winners of the Pacific Coast League title, progressed through five games with each team winning two games and tieing one when the local Dept. of Health called it off because of an influenza epidemic.

Joe Hall was the most seriously stricken of several players who contracted influenza and died from it April 5, 1919.

315

DOUGLAS N. HARVEY (Doug) had 21 seasons in professional hockey, 14 of them with Montreal Canadiens where he played on six Stanley Cup championship teams. He also won the Norris Trophy seven times, virtually monopolizing this award to the National Hockey League's outstanding defenseman from the 1954–55 season through 1961–62. He was named ten times to the NHL's first All-Star team and once to the second team. His passing ability is shown in the 452 assists garnered in regular-season NHL games, plus 64 in play-offs.

Quite properly tagged as a "winning type" player, Harvey is always mentioned when the greatest defensemen of all time are being compared. But he seldom took himself seriously and often relieved dressing room tension with a well-timed amusing remark.

GEORGE W. HAY—Many experts called George William Hay the greatest stickhandler in hockey when he played in the National Hockey League during the 1920s. He had a poor season with Chicago, playing much of it with torn ligaments in his left shoulder, and he was dealt to Detroit prior to the 1927–28 season.

With the Cougars (later Red Wings), Hay led the club with 22 goals and 13 assists. The 10 NHL coaches selected an All-Star team that year and Hay was named on the forward unit with center Howie Morenz and rightwinger Bill Cook. King Clancy and Eddie Shore were the defensemen and Roy Worters the goalie.

W. M. HERN (Riley) had a record of playing on seven championship teams in his first nine years in hockey. Hern received much credit for Wanderers winning the Stanley Cup in 1906–07 and during the next five years he was one of the outstanding players on the team. Wanderers won the Stanley Cup again in 1907–08 and 1909–10 with Hern an outstanding drawing card.

BRYAN HEXTALL—On and off the ice, he has been a credit to the game of hockey. In the words of Hockey Hall of Fame member James Dunn: "He is a very clean-living individual and an excellent ambassador for professional hockey."

He led the National Hockey League in points in 1941–42 with 56 from 24 goals and 32 assists, was selected three times to the league's first All-Star team and twice to the second All-Star team. Other career highlights include scoring 20 or more goals in seven of his 12 NHL seasons and scoring the overtime winning goal of a 1939–40 Stanley Cup game against Toronto.

HARRY HOLMES (Hap)—If there had been a trophy for the leading netminder during the period that Holmes played, he would have won it eight times. After three seasons and one Stanley Cup in Toronto, Holmes moved to Seattle for two seasons and was a standout for the first team to take the Stanley Cup to a U.S. city. He appeared to be following the Cup around when he returned to Toronto and helped them win it the next year but he was lured back West again and for eight seasons was a standout in the PCHA, being the leading goalie six times against such outstanding rivals as Hugh Lehman and George Hainsworth. He was the Seattle goalie in the 1918–19 Cup series that finished without a winner, due to an influenza epidemic in Seattle.

With the windup of the WHL in 1926, players went en masse to the expanded NHL and Holmes shifted to Detroit where he played two years before retiring. The memory of this great goalie, who died in the summer of 1940 in Florida while vacationing, is perpetuated in the Harry Holmes Memorial Trophy, awarded annually since 1941 to the leading goalie of the American Hockey League.

C. T. HOOPER (Tom)—The team from Kenora, Ont., challenged three times for the Stanley Cup before they finally won it in January, 1907.

One of the key members of that Cup-winning team was Charles Thomas Hooper, a hometown boy who was to play on one other world championship team, the Montreal Wanderers of 1907–08. Hooper was born in Rat Portage (later changed to Kenora), Nov. 24, 1883, and played his first organized hockey with the high school team in 1900. That team was so good that it defeated the town's senior team in an exhibition contest.

G. R. HORNER (Red)—Few athletes can boast the unusual distinction of receiving the highest honor in the game despite holding the title of badman.

For the 12 seasons of his National Hockey League career with Toronto Maple Leafs, G. Reginald Horner was known as the "the badman of the league." An aggressive six-foot-one, 200-pounder, Horner led the NHL in penalties for eight successive seasons— 1932–33 through 1939–40. He set a league record for penalties in a single season, spending 167 minutes in the box in 43 games of the 1935–36 season, a record that was to stand for 20 years.

GORDON HOWE (Gordie) played one year of minor pro with Omaha of the U.S. League, then joined Detroit in the 1946–47 season. He had deceptive size for a six-footer and he used his 205 pounds to advantage with an ability to shoot with equal dexterity from either side, and an effortless skating style. He was tough, but not in a bullying way, and he was hardy. Howe also earned numerous nicknames, such as "Mr. Elbows" from opponents and "Power" from his teammates.

He could also have been called "The Most" as he established more records than any other NHL player. Just a few from his impressive list are: Most seasons played (25), most regular-season games (1,687), most Hart Memorial Trophies as the MVP to his team (6), most Art Ross Trophies as league scoring champion (6), most career goals in regular season (786), and most selections to NHL All-Star teams (21—12 times to the first team, nine to the second). Other mosts include: assists—1,023; points—1,809; winning goals—122; games including playoffs—1,841; goals including playoffs—853; assists including playoffs—1,114; points including playoffs—1,967; points in a playoff final series—12; and numerous other All-Star Game records.

Even before retirement from the NHL Gordie was a great ambassador of hockey off the ice, attending banquets, signing thousands of autographs and doing much little-publicized charitable work. For excellence and durability his career will probably never be matched.

Howe further proved his greatness by starring in the World Hockey League at an age when other athletes his age were long retired.

"Both on and off the ice, Gordie Howe's conduct . . has demonstrated a high quality of sportsmanship and competence which is an example to us all. He has earned the title: Mr. Hockey."   Lester B. Pearson,
former Prime Minister of Canada

S. H. HOWE (Syd) — The intangible but vital assets of a great hockey player are identified with the career of Sydney Harris Howe, an unselfish player who swung from center to wing or defense during 16 seasons in the National Hockey League. He followed a nomadic career for some time, being loaned to Philadelphia Quakers, then Toronto Maple Leafs, returning to Ottawa at the start of the 1932—33 season. Syd was with the Senators when they transferred to St. Louis in 1935. Then Jack Adams purchased him for the Detroit Red Wings and the late Jim Norris credits Howe as being the man who started the upsurge in attendance at Detroit.

Howe set a modern record Feb. 3, 1944, by scoring six goals in one game against Rangers at Detroit. And he was on the ice when Mud Bruneteau scored the goal that ended the longest game in Stanley Cup history. During his NHL career, Howe scored 237 goals and had 291 assists.

J. B. HUTTON (Bouse) played goal for the Ottawa team that won the Canadian Amateur Hockey Association intermediate title in 1898—99 and he also moved up to play two games with the Silver Seven. He stayed with that club for six seasons, averaging 2.9 goals-against in a recorded 36 games. He earned his only two shutouts of regular season play in 1901—02. Hutton also played in 12 games in Stanley Cup competition, allowing 28 goals.

HARRY HYLAND — Very few athletes can boast that they have played on two national championship teams in the same year but one of these is Harry Hyland, a very versatile performer. A prominent writer once said: "Hyland was one of the greatest

rightwingers of his day, and teamed with Dr. Gordon Roberts to form one of the best scoring combinations in the game."

J. D. IRVIN (Dick) was an outstanding player and coach. He played four seasons with Regina Caps before returning to Portland, where he scored 30 goals in 30 games. Irvin moved to Chicago for the 1926—27 season, was the first captain of the Hawks, collected 18 goals and 18 assists and was second to Bill Cook in the league scoring race. He fractured his skull in the 12th game of the next season, ending his playing career. After coaching Chicago he moved to Toronto in 1931 for a Stanley Cup-winning season. He also coached Montreal Canadiens from 1940—55, his teams winning three more Cups.

HARVEY JACKSON (Busher) — An excellent leftwinger, Jackson collected 241 goals and 234 assists in 633 National Hockey League games. In playoffs, he had 18 goals and 12 assists in 72 games. He carried 195 pounds on his five-foot, 11-inch frame.

He signed in 1930 with Charlie Conacher and was put with Joe Primeau to form the "Kid Line" that

The great Gordie Howe.

544

played so brilliantly for Toronto Maple Leafs. He was on Leaf teams that three times won the league championship and once (1931–32) won the Stanley Cup. He led the league in scoring with 28 goals and 25 assists in 1932–33 and was named five times to NHL All-Star teams.

ERNEST JOHNSON (Moose) turned professional with Montreal Wanderers and played with them on four Stanley Cup championship winners—1905–06, 1906–07, 1907–08 and 1909–10. He joined New Westminster Royals of the Pacific Coast League in 1912. This team moved to Portland at the beginning of World War I and he led it to a league title in 1915–16. He later played with Victoria Maroons, Los Angeles and other teams of the Western Hockey League. He finished his pro career in 1931.

I. W. JOHNSON (Ching)—From the fall of 1926 until the spring of 1938, he stood out as one of the most colorful defensemen in the National Hockey League. He spent 11 of those years with New York Rangers and was three times named to the first All-Star team and twice to the second team. Johnson's NHL career ended with the New York Americans in 1937–38. He had played in 463 games and acquired 969 minutes in penalties.

T. C. JOHNSON (Tom) played 15 seasons in the National Hockey League—978 games, 51 goals, 213 assists—and had his best season in 1958–59 when he won the Norris Trophy as the NHL's premier defenseman. Because of teammate Doug Harvey's great skill, Johnson never figured in the power play but he was a leader when the team was shorthanded. He had speed and skill in the corners, ability to wheel and lay a perfect pass, and didn't take foolish penalties. He frequently played center when his team needed a goal late in a game.

AUREL JOLIAT was called the Mighty Atom or the Little Giant, this man named Aurel Emile Joliat who spent 16 seasons as a member of the Montreal Canadiens in the National Hockey League. Despite six shoulder separations, three broken ribs, and routine injuries such as five nose fractures, Joliat went on to score 270 goals, tieing Morenz on the all-time list. He was also noted as an outstanding checker, capable of stopping an opponent, wheeling on a dime and starting a rush of his own. His playing weight was 135 pounds.

Joliat played on three Stanley Cup-winning teams—1923–24, 1929–30 and 1930–31—and won the Hart Trophy in the 1933–34 season. He was also on one first and three second All-Star teams.

G. B. KEATS (Duke)—It is doubtful that any great hockey player ever bounced around more teams and leagues than Gordon Blanchard Keats. Duke scored 119 goals in 128 games prior to playing in the NHL where, in two years, he added another 30 goals.

Aurel Joliat   *Ted Kennedy*

L. P. KELLY (Red) graduated to the NHL at the age of 19 from Toronto St. Michael's Majors, an Ontario Junior A team. He played with Detroit Red Wings 12½ seasons, mostly as a defenseman, then was traded to Toronto Maple Leafs where he completed his playing career.

During that span Kelly was a four-time winner of the Lady Byng Memorial Trophy, the first winner of the James Norris Memorial Trophy and he played on eight Stanley Cup-winning teams. Kelly also was named six times to the NHL's first All-Star team, twice to the second team, and played for nine Prince of Wales Trophy-winning clubs. He also competed in 19 Stanley Cup playoffs, a record, in 164 playoff games, another record, and was runner-up to Gordie Howe for most games played in NHL regular-season action, 1,316

T. S. KENNEDY (Ted)—His first Stanley Cup team was the 1944–45 Leafs and he became a dogged leader in their first triple triumph—1946–47 through 1948–49. He succeeded Syl Apps as team captain in 1948 and led the team to another Cup triumph in 1950–51.

Ted Kennedy is still remembered as one of the greatest face-off men in the game's history. In 696 league games, he scored 231 goals and collected 329 assists.

ELMER J. LACH turned professional in 1940–41 with Montreal Canadiens and in the ensuing 13 seasons, Lach ran up an enviable record of achievement. He played in 646 scheduled games and 76 playoff games. In league play he amassed 215 goals and 408 assists, adding 19 goals and 45 assists in playoffs.

Elmer was selected to five All-Star teams, making the first team in 1944–45, 1947–48 and 1951–52 and the second team in 1943–44 and 1945–46. He also played on three Stanley, Cup-winning teams, in 1943–44, 1945–46 and 1952–53. He led the league in scoring to win the Art Ross Trophy in 1944–45 with a total of 80 points – 26 goals and 54 assists in a 50-game schedule. Lach was also voted the Hart Trophy that season. In 1947–48 he again led the league in scoring.

EDOUARD LALONDE (Newsy) was a brilliant goal-scorer but Newsy also earned his name as one of the roughest players of his day. Feuds between Lalonde and Joe Hall, when the latter played with Quebec Bulldogs, helped fill Montreal's old Westmount Arena.

Newsy scored 441 goals in 365 games and he was a scoring champion five different times while playing in the National Association, Pacific Coast League and National Hockey League. He once scored 38 goals in an 11-game schedule and, while with Vancouver, he scored 27 goals in 15 games.

J. B. LAVIOLETTE (Jack) is one of only three athletes named to both the Hockey Hall of Fame and Canada's Sports Hall of Fame. He was named to the latter as a lacrosse player. He joined a team at Sault Ste. Marie, Mich., and was selected as an International League All-Star. When he formed Canadiens, Laviolette played point (defense) but he later moved up to play on a line with Didier Pitre and Newsy Lalonde. Jack had great speed and earned the nickname "Speed Merchant." He played on a Stanley Cup winner in 1915–16 and retired at the end of the 1917–18 season.

F. H. LEHMAN (Hughie) played on eight Stanley Cup challengers but was successful only once, with Vancouver in the 1914–15 season. He also shares a record with Percy LeSueur of having played for two different challenging teams within two months. He played for Galt against Ottawa and for Berlin against Wanderers in 1909–10.

PERCY LESUEUR — His hockey career spanned 50 years but he gained his fame as the goaltender for Ottawa Senators between 1906 and 1913. He acted in many capacities connected with hockey: player, coach, manager, referee, inventor, arena manager, broadcaster and columnist.

R. B. T. LINDSAY (Ted) played on the great Production Line with Sid Abel and Gordie Howe. That line played a major role in the phenomenal success of the Wings between 1948 and 1955 when they won seven straight league titles and the Stanley Cup four times.

Ted played 13 seasons with Detroit before being traded to Chicago prior to the 1957–58 season. He retired after the 1959–60 campaign but made a remarkable comeback with Detroit in 1964–65 and was an inspiration in their winning the Prince of Wales Trophy. He retired again, this time to stay,

after that season with a record of 379 goals in his 17 NHL seasons. Lindsay was named eight times to the first All-Star team and once to the second.

D. MACKAY (Mickey) was often called "The Wee Scot," but Duncan McMillan MacKay was a big star of professional hockey in its formative years. In the words of Frank Patrick, for whom MacKay was to play for several seasons: "MacKay was a crowd-pleaser, clean, splendidly courageous, a happy player with a stylish way of going. He was sensational in quick breakaways, a sure shot in alone with a goalie and could stickhandle. He was outstanding in every way."

M. J. MALONE (Joe) was a remarkable marksman who performed scoring miracles in both the National Hockey Association and the National Hockey League. Malone led the NHA in scoring in 1912–13, and he tied Frank Nighbor in 1916–17 with 41 goals in 20 games. He topped the NHL in its first season, 1917–18, with the phenomenal total of 44 goals in 20 games.

Some of his outstanding single-game performances include: nine goals, against the Sydney Millionaires in a 1913 Stanley Cup playoff game; eight goals, against Montreal Wanderers in 1917; seven goals, against Toronto in 1920.

SYLVIO MANTHA enjoyed 14 seasons in the National Hockey League as a hard-rock defenseman and during that span he played for nine first-place teams and three Stanley Cup winners. He joined Montreal Canadiens in 1923–24, the first year they won the Cup. They won it twice more with Mantha in the lineup, in 1929–30 and 1930–31.

He became a player-coach with Montreal in 1935–36, then moved to Boston Bruins where he finished his playing days in 1936–37.

J. C. MARSHALL (Jack) was associated with five Stanley Cup winners and two other teams that challenged for the Cup during a 17-year hockey career. An outstanding center, he played two seasons with Montreal AAA. He moved to Montreal Wanderers for two seasons but by 1906–07 he was playing for Montreal Montagnards. Jack was back with the Wanderers in 1907, switched to the Montreal Shamrocks for the following two seasons, then returned once again to the Wanderers where he stayed through 1912.

F. G. MAXWELL (Steamer) — In 1925–26, he coached Winnipeg Rangers to the Manitoba championship. Winnipeg Maroons of the American Professional Hockey League was his next stop and he coached them until the league terminated in 1927–28. Maxwell returned to coaching amateur teams, both junior and senior, and in 1929–30 he coached Elmwood Millionaires to both junior and senior Manitoba championships. He coached another World championship club in 1934–35 when Winnipeg Monarchs won the title at Davos, Switzerland.

FRANK McGEE–His name was written into the hockey record book in 1905 with one spectacular scoring splurge.

On Jan. 16, 1905, McGee scored 14 goals in a Stanley Cup game as Ottawa trounced a weary Dawson City, Yukon, team, 23-2. That, of course, is a Stanley Cup record but so are some of his other achievements in that game. Frank scored eight consecutive goals in eight minutes and 20 seconds. Three of these came in a span of 90 seconds and the fourth came 50 seconds later, Cup records for three-goal and four-goal outputs by an individual.

W. G. McGIMSIE (Billy)–Many of hockey's great players achieved their fame as members of several teams but William George McGimsie was the exception. He played all of his major league hockey with one team, the Kenora Thistles.

GEORGE McNAMARA was a big and rugged Irishman who knew only one way to go–forward. George and his equally strong brother Howard formed a powerful defense unit that became known throughout Ontario and other parts of Canada as "The Dynamite Twins."

RICHARD W. MOORE (Dickie) moved up to the Royals of the Quebec Senior League in 1951–52. Halfway through that season he was elevated to the pro Canadiens and played with them until retiring after the 1962–63 season. He twice led the NHL in scoring. His first title, in 1957–58, was achieved despite a broken left wrist incurred with three months left in the schedule. At his own request, a cast was placed on the wrist which enabled him to grip the stick and he never missed a game, topping the league with 36 goals and 48 assists. The next season he scored 96 points, breaking the existing record of 95 set by Gordie Howe.

PATRICK J. MORAN (Paddy) played top-level hockey for 16 seasons, all but one with Quebec Bulldogs, and although he retired the season before the National Hockey League was formed, he is regarded as one of the greatest standup goaltenders in the game.

H. W. MORENZ (Howie) was signed to a pro contract by Leo Dandurand of the Montreal Canadiens and joined that club for the 1923–24 season. Howie became almost immediately a million dollar box office attraction. He had reckless speed and his headlong rushes set turnstiles clicking wherever Canadiens played. He was nicknamed "the Babe Ruth of Hockey" by sportswriters in the United States.

Howie performed in the National Hockey League for 14 seasons and also earned at various times such tags as "the Canadien Comet," the "Hurtling Habi-

tant," the "Mitchell Meteor," and the "Stratford Streak." He had great stickhandling ability and a snapping shot. Morenz played with Canadiens for 11 seasons, then was traded to Chicago. He went to New York Rangers midway through 1935–36 and came back to Canadiens for the 1936–37 season. He broke his leg in a game Jan. 28, 1937, and it led to his death March 8, 1937. During his career, Morenz scored 270 goals and won the Hart Trophy three times–1927–28, 1930–31 and 1931–32. In 1928–29, he scored 40 goals in 44 games and in 1924–25 he scored 30 goals in 30 games. He was twice named to the first All-Star team and once to the second.

WILLIAM MOSIENKO (Bill)–Chicago Black Hawks had a great forward unit during the 1940s, known as the Pony Line. It was comprised of the Bentley brothers, Max and Doug, and rightwinger Bill Mosienko. During a 14-year stay in the National Hockey League, Mosienko was a very productive scorer, accounting for 258 goals and 538 points in 711 games. He spent a total of 20 years in professional hockey, playing in 1,030 games, and in that time he accumulated only 129 minutes in penalties.

Mosienko won the Lady Byng Trophy in 1944–45 and was twice named to the second NHL All-Star team–in 1944–45 and 1945–46. He also set the record for the fastest three goals in one game–21 seconds–against New York Rangers in New York, March 23, 1952.

FRANK NIGHBOR played the 1910–11 season in Port Arthur, Ont., and turned professional with Toronto in 1913. His first Stanley Cup triumph came with Vancouver Millionaires when they defeated Ottawa in the 1914–15 final. The next season, he returned to Ottawa and remained with them until

Howie Morenz, considered one of the fastest and most effective of all hockey players.

the last half of the 1928–29 season when he played for Toronto. That was his final season as a player.

While with the Senators, Nighbor played on four more Stanley Cup champions: 1919–20, 1920–21, 1922–23 and 1926–27. He was also the initial winner of two of the league's great trophies, the Hart and the Lady Byng. Nighbor won the Hart, awarded to the MVP on his team, in 1923–24, and the Lady Byng in 1924–25 and 1925–26.

REGINALD NOBLE (Reg) moved into professional hockey with Toronto in 1916–17 but the club disbanded part way through the season. He was sent to Montreal Canadiens but it was ruled that he came too late to play for them in the Stanley Cup playoffs. Canadiens lost the final to Seattle. The National Hockey League was organized the following season and Reg played for Toronto Arenas who won the Stanley Cup. He scored 28 goals in 22 games that season.

Toronto became the St. Patrick's in 1919–20 and Noble played for this team when it defeated Vancouver in the Cup final of 1921–22. He was traded to Montreal Maroons in 1924 and came out a winner again when Maroons won the Cup in 1925–26. A trade took him to Detroit Cougars and he played five years for them as a defenseman, returning to the Maroons early in 1933 to finish out his NHL playing career with a total of 170 goals.

HAROLD OLIVER (Harry) was born Oct. 26, 1898, in Selkirk, Man., and started his hockey career on the ponds of Selkirk. He went on to attain greatness with Boston Bruins and New York Americans in a National Hockey League career that spanned eleven years.

Oliver was considered in a class by himself, the ideal type of athlete of his day. Although he weighed only 155 pounds, he moved with the speed and grace of a thoroughbred and was called "smooth as silk" by the late Harry Scott, Sports Editor of the Calgary Albertan, who once performed with Montreal Canadiens. Oliver's appearance and deportment were exemplary, both on and off the ice.

LESTER PATRICK—It is impossible to describe fully the many contributions which Lester Patrick made to the game of hockey throughout his lifetime as a player, coach, manager, owner and National Hockey League governor.

He was one of hockey's real immortals and identified with many of the major developments in style of play, the organization and expansion of the game. He was one of the first rushing defenseman in the game. As a coach and executive, he inaugurated hockey's first major farm system. With his brother Frank, he devised the profitable playoff system still used and he was responsible for many rule improvements. He introduced pro hockey to British Columbia and was a guiding force behind its rise in the Eastern United States, especially New York.

THOMAS PHILLIPS (Tommy)—Hockey old-timers who could recall the game as it was played in the early 1900s were generally agreed that Thomas Neil Phillips was the greatest hockey player they have ever seen. He had everything a good player should have—whirlwind speed, bullet-like shot, stickhandling wizardry—and he was regarded as being without peer as a backchecker.

PIERRE P. PILOTE—A premier rushing defenseman, Pierre stood five-ten and weighed 178 lbs. He broke into the NHL with Chicago in 1956 after serving his pro apprenticeship at Buffalo and soon established himself as a regular. During his first five full seasons with Chicago he never missed a game but was finally forced out in 1962 with a shoulder separation. Pierre left the National Hockey League at the end of the 1968–69 season with a mark of 976 games (including playoffs), 559 points and 1,353 penalty minutes. He had also played on one Stanley Cup championship team, the Chicago Black Hawks of 1960–61, and in eight All-Star games.

DIDIER PITRE was the idol of French-Canadian hockey followers in the early, rough-and-ready days of the game. He weighed about 200 pounds, had a shot "like a cannonball," and could skate with tremendous speed for a big man.

When Laviolette formed Les Canadiens in 1909, Pitre was the first player he signed and he was to remain with the team until retirement in 1923, except for the 1913–14 season when he played for Vancouver. It was the style of Laviolette and Pitre, both very fast, that caused sportswriters to designate the team as the Flying Frenchmen.

WALTER PRATT (Babe) possessed three basic qualities of greatness: ability, leadership, and the rare knack of inspiring all those who played with him to a special effort.

Pratt turned pro with Philadelphia, the Rangers' farm club, and moved up to New York in January, 1936. He played on a Stanley Cup winner with the Rangers in 1939–40 and with the league championship team of 1941–42. In that Cup-winning season, Pratt teamed on defense with Ott Heller and they allowed only 17 goals-against over a 48-game schedule. He was traded to Toronto in November, 1942, and while a Leaf he won the Hart Trophy (1943–44) and was named once to each of the first and second All-Star teams.

A. J. PRIMEAU (Joe) wasn't merely a great hockey player, he was also a great coach. Prior to 1970, he was the only man to coach teams which won the Memorial Cup, Allan Cup and Stanley Cup. The former two represent the Canadian junior and senior hockey championships.

He became the center on Toronto's famous Kid Line with Charlie Conacher and Harvey Jackson on the wings, and although his linemates were more dazzling, Joe was the smooth-passing co-ordinator who made their glory possible. He was a tenacious checker and an extremely clean player, often referred to as "Gentleman Joe." He was also a strong penalty-killer. Primeau was fifth in the NHL scoring race in 1929–30, and second in both 1931–32 and 1933–34, being voted to the second All-Star team the latter year. He won the Lady Byng Trophy in 1931–32.

HARVEY PULFORD—Few men in the annals of Canadian sport can equal the great all-round record of athletic achievement set by Harvey Pulford. He was outstanding in many sports: hockey, football, lacrosse, boxing, paddling, rowing and squash. Although he was born in Toronto, in 1875, he spent most of his life in Ottawa where he won championships in virtually every sport in which he participated. He was a defense star of Ottawa's Silver Seven from 1893 to 1908 and played on Stanley Cup winners in 1902–03, 1903–04 and 1904–05.

Pulford is best-remembered in hockey as a clean but hard-hitting defenseman who helped make possible those Stanley Cup victories, particularly over Kenora and Dawson City.

FRANK RANKIN—In the early days of organized hockey, long before Howie Morenz came on the scene, Stratford, Ont., was a stronghold of the sport. And one of the most common names in the area was Rankin: Charlie, Gordon, Ramsay and Frank, to name but a few, were hockey standouts. Frank Rankin later went on to become a successful coach and in 1924 he directed the Toronto Granites to an Olympic championship, winning the world amateur title in a series played at Chamonix, France.

Maurice "Rocket" Richard

CLAUDE E. RAYNER (Chuck)—Although six-foot-one and weighing 205 pounds, Rayner was a very agile goalie. His goals-against average for ten seasons in the NHL was 3.50, a very respectable figure measured against the fact that the Rangers made the playoffs only twice. In the 1950–51 season Rayner won the Hart Trophy, awarded annually to the player adjudged most valuable to his team, and he was three times named to the league's second All-Star team.

KENNETH REARDON (Kenny) had a headlong, fearless style of play which accounted for many injuries during his National Hockey League career, but his dashing disregard for personal safety made him a favorite of the fans around the league. Reardon rejoined the Canadiens after World War II for the 1945–46 season and for the next five seasons was named to All-Star teams of the NHL. He made the first team in 1946–47 and 1949–50, the second team in the other three seasons. He played on a Stanley Cup winner in 1945–46.

MAURICE RICHARD (The Rocket)—Whenever the name of Maurice Richard is mentioned, it immediately conjures a vision of flashing skates and brilliant goal-scoring. He was known as The Rocket through an 18-year National Hockey League career that saw him score 544 goals in 978 league games.

He set many records, some of which will stand for a long time. Richard scored 83 winning goals and 28 tieing goals, and in 133 playoff games he had 82 goals and 44 assists. On Dec. 28, 1944, he spent the day moving into a new home, then went out and notched eight points—five goals, three assists—a record. He was named eight times to the NHL's first All-Star team and six times to the second.

GEORGE RICHARDSON—The Richardson name was well known in Kingston, Ont., around the turn of the century and George added further laurels in a brief but sensational hockey career. Like many other Canadians, Richardson entered the army during World War I. He went overseas as Officer Commanding No. 2 Company of the Canadian Expeditionary Force, Second Battalion, and was killed in action on the night of Feb. 9, 1916. The George Richardson Stadium, home grounds of Queen's University football teams at Kingston, was erected in his honor. George was an outstanding hockey player who never turned professional.

GORDON ROBERTS was a great leftwinger who managed to play professional hockey while acquiring his medical degree at McGill University in Montreal.

On graduation from McGill in 1916, he left for the West Coast where he practiced medicine and continued to play hockey. Roberts signed with Vancouver and was sensational with the Millionaires. In 1917 he established the all-time scoring record for the Pacific Coast Hockey Association by scoring 43 goals in 23 games. His hospital duties took him to Seattle the next year and he joined the Mets where he again starred. He didn't play the next season but returned to Vancouver in 1920.

ARTHUR H. ROSS (Art) was many things to the game of hockey. He was a pioneer, innovator, strategist, promotor, outstanding player, coach and manager. His name is indelibly etched into its history. He invented the Art Ross nets and Art Ross puck, both still in use today, and left his mark on the game in many other ways.

BLAIR RUSSEL played all of his major hockey with the Victorias. He scored 110 goals in 67 games and once registered seven in a game against the Shamrocks, in 1904. He also had a six-goal game and a five-goal game. Like many of the good players of his time, Blair was a very clean player who was equally adept at scoring or checking.

In a vote conducted by daily newspapers of Toronto and Montreal at that time, Blair Russel was named to an All-Star team along with such greats as Bowie, Harvey Pulford, Frank McGee, Alf Smith and Billy Gilmour. All of these players are members of the Hockey Hall of Fame.

ERNEST RUSSELL first appeared in senior hockey with the Winged Wheelers, in 1905, but the remainder of his playing career was spent with the Montreal Wanderers. This team won the Stanley Cup four times with Russell in the lineup—1905–06, 1906–07, 1907–08 and 1909–10. Although he played for the Wanderers, Ernie maintained membership in the MAAA for other sports. This didn't suit the membership who expelled him, and he didn't play during the 1908–09 season. When he returned in 1909–10, Russell and Newsy Lalonde engaged in a furious struggle for the scoring leadership, which Lalonde won by scoring nine goals in the last game of the season. He did win a scoring title, however, in 1906–07 with 42 goals and he also scored in ten consecutive games in the 1911–12 season.

J. D. RUTTAN (Jack) enjoyed a long and illustrious career in hockey, both as a player and coach, all of it in amateur ranks.

The Manitoba Varsity team of 1909–10 won the championship of the Winnipeg Senior Hockey League. Ruttan was a member of that team and he stayed with the Varsity through two more seasons, then played for the Winnipeg Hockey Club. That was the team that won everything in sight—the Winnipeg League for a start and the Allan Cup, symbolic of senior hockey supremacy in Canada, for a finish.

T. G. SAWCHUK (Terry) was one of the greatest goaltenders in hockey history—he played more seasons, more games, and recorded more shutouts than

Harvey Pulford   *Art Ross*

any other goalie in the history of the National Hockey League.

Terry was the first player to win the rookie award in three professional leagues—the old U.S. Hockey League in 1947–48, the American Hockey League in 1948–49 and the NHL in 1950–51. A career highlight was the 1952 Stanley Cup playoffs when he led Detroit to the Stanley Cup in a minimum eight games, collecting four shutouts and allowing only five goals.

FRED SCANLAN—One of the great forward lines around the turn of the century was comprised of three players who were to be elected into the Hockey Hall of Fame: Harry Trihey, Arthur Farrell and Frederick Scanlan. Fred Scanlan played in the era when forward passing was not allowed; in other words, all passes had to be lateral. The forwards usually advanced up the ice abreast while the rover trailed.

Frank J. Selke, a member of the Hockey Hall of Fame, once said of Scanlan: "He was the workhorse of the great Shamrock forward line, always ready for his share in the new-style combination attacks, combining heady play with an accurate shot."

M. C. SCHMIDT (Milt) was a powerful, hard-hitting center who never gave up the puck without a fight. He stood six feet tall and weighed 185 pounds. During his NHL career, Milt scored 229 goals and a total of 346 points. He won the league scoring title in 1939–40, won the Hart Trophy as the MVP to his team in 1951–52, and played for two Stanley Cup-winning teams, 1938–39 and 1940–41. He was also voted three times to the league's first All-Star team—1939–40, 1946–47 and 1950–51—and to the second team in 1951–52.

DAVID SCHRINER (Sweeney) was a celebrated hockey player who divided his National Hockey League career between two teams, the New York Americans and Toronto Maple Leafs. In eleven NHL seasons, Schriner scored a total of 201 goals. With the Americans he was twice scoring champion of the league, winning in 1935–36 with 45 points and in 1936–37 with 46 points. As a member of the Maple Leafs, Schriner played on two Stanley Cup winners, 1941–42 and 1944–45 when he scored six and three goals respectively. Sweeney was also named to the league's first All-Star team in 1935–36 and the second team in 1936–37.

EARL W. SEIBERT played 15½ seasons in the National Hockey League, and in that time he established himself as one of the all-time great defensemen. Earl was voted to NHL All-Star teams in ten consecutive seasons, making the first team in 1934–35, 1941–42, 1942–43 and 1943–44. He was noted for his rushing ability and accounted for 89 goals and a total of 276 points in scheduled league games, adding another 11 goals and eight assists in playoffs.

OLIVER L. SEIBERT was one of the first Canadians to play on artificial ice when his team played an exhibition game in St. Louis. Oliver used a pair of skates he made by cutting them out of a piece of solid steel. The blades turned up in front and were fastened to the shoes by wooden screws. He was also the first Berlin player to turn pro. After playing for Berlin Rangers, champions of the Western Ontario Hockey Association for six successive seasons (1900–1906). Oliver became a pro with Houghton, Mich. He also played pro with London and Guelph in the Ontario Pro League and Northwestern Michigan League.

Oldtimers like to recall the time Oliver skated against a trotter. The horse had a one-mile record of 2:13 but Oliver, wearing his old rocker skates, won a match race of one mile over a course laid on the ice of the Grand River. It was claimed he could skate as fast backward as forward. Oliver is the father of Earl, another Hall of Fame member.

E. W. SHORE (Eddie) broke into the NHL in 1926–27 with Boston Bruins and in subsequent seasons he was to personify the most vigorous aspects of a hard, rough and fast game. His great talent was to take over the offense and set up plays, literally knocking down any opponent in the way. This, of course, brought him an abundance of penalties and he became involved in many hard-fought fistic battles. During his 13-year stay with the Bruins, Shore scored 105 goals and added 179 assists. He wound up his NHL career with New York Americans in the 1939–40 season.

Eddie Shore is the only defenseman to win the Hart Trophy four times—1932–33, 1934–35, 1935–36 and 1937–38—a tremendous feat. He was also voted seven times to the NHL's first All-Star team and once to the second team. He also played on two Stanley Cup-winning teams, 1928–29 and 1938–39.

ALBERT SIEBERT (Babe)—A great hockey player, with a heart as big as his massive body, was lost Aug. 25, 1939, when Albert Siebert drowned at St. Joseph, Ont. National Hockey League fans of that era cherish the memory of Siebert as a great, broad-shouldered giant with cool and fearless eyes, a man who rode through his plays with the complete confidence of his own power.

Although still a junior, he moved up to play for Niagara Falls seniors in 1924–25 and made the jump into the National Hockey League the following season with Montreal Maroons.

H. J. SIMPSON, M. M. (Bullet Joe) was a man who proved himself outstanding, both on the ice and on the battlefield where he won the Military Medal. Returning to hockey following World War I, Simpson played a season with the Selkirk Fishermen in 1919–20. He joined the Edmonton Eskimos in 1921–22 and played four seasons with that club. Twice during his tenure with the Eskimos, the team won the Western Canada Hockey League championship and Simpson was given much of the credit for this achievement.

Joe joined the New York Americans of the National Hockey League in 1925–26. Edmonton had received many offers for Simpson from both Vancouver Maroons and the Ottawa Senators before finally selling him to the Americans. He remained with that team as a player until 1931, managed the

Eddie Shore one of the all-time greats

Americans from 1932 until 1935, then managed New Haven and Minneapolis before retiring from the game.

ALFRED E. SMITH joined Ottawa in 1895 and very early showed a penchant for rough play. After three seasons, Smith dropped out of hockey but returned, at the age of 30, after Ottawa won the Stanley Cup in 1902–03. He helped the team win the league championship and the Stanley Cup in the succeeding two seasons, playing right wing on a line that had Frank McGee at center.

Ottawa lost the Cup to the Wanderers in 1905–06. He and Harry Westwick joined Kenora in that team's unsuccessful bid to defend the Stanley Cup against Wanderers in March, 1907. Smith played the 1907–08 season with Ottawa, then returned the following season to Pittsburgh to play in a pro City League. That was his final playing year but he remained in the game as a coach, with Renfrew, Ottawa, New York Americans, Moncton, N.B., and North Bay, Ont.

REGINALD SMITH (Hooley) turned professional with Ottawa of the National Hockey League, playing right wing, and it was here that he developed a sweeping hook-check that made him a formidable two-way player.

Senators won the Stanley Cup in 1926–27. Ottawa dealt the five-foot-ten, 160-pounder to Montreal Maroons before the next season and once again his team was in the Cup final, although they lost to the Rangers. It was with Maroons that Smith combined with Nels Stewart and Babe Siebert to form the great "S" line, a trio combining great scoring power with aggressive play, and it was with this team that he played on his second Stanley Cup team, in 1934–35. Smith, captain of the team, the next year was voted All-Star center.

THOMAS J. SMITH joined Pittsburgh in the International League, led the team with 23 goals in 22 games, and in 1909 led the Ontario Professional Hockey league scoring, playing rover for Brantford. Typhoid fever kept him idle in 1910 but he again led the scoring in 1911, this time as a center for Galt which won the league title but lost to Ottawa in a challenge for the Stanley Cup.

In 1912 he moved to play with Moncton in the Maritime Pro League, the team winning the league title but losing to Quebec Bulldogs, NHA champs, in another Cup challenge. Smith played for Quebec the next season and from it came his only Stanley Cup triumph. He was on a line with Joe Malone and Jack Marks, finishing four goals behind Malone who scored 43 to win the scoring crown. The little bulldog—he was five-foot-four and 150 pounds—was dealt to Canadiens in 1917 and when the NHA dissolved the next year he quit hockey. Smith came back to play 10 games with Quebec in 1919 but was scoreless and retired as a player at age 35.

RUSSELL STANLEY (Barney)—In a 15-year professional hockey career, he played every position on the ice except goal. Strangely enough, his only Stanley Cup-winning team came in his first year as a pro. Barney came up through amateur ranks, playing for Paisley, the Edmonton Maritimers, Edmonton Dominions and Edmonton Albertas between 1909 and 1915. He joined Vancouver Millionaires on Feb. 15, 1915, and this club went on to win the coveted Cup.

J. S. STEWART (Black Jack) probably earned the nickname Black Jack because of his darkly handsome features but many who played against him in the National Hockey League might offer a different reason. Stewart was an outstanding defenseman who hit like a blackjack. He was a regular with Detroit through the 1949–50 season, then was dealt to Chicago where he finished his playing career at the end of the 1951–52 season.

Stewart played on two Stanley Cup-winning teams, 1942–43 and 1949–50, and was named five times to NHL All-Star teams. He was on the first All Star team in 1942–43, 1947–48 and 1948–49, and the second team in 1945–46 and 1946–47. He was also voted Detroit's most valuable player in the 1942–43 season.

NELS STEWART (Old Poison)—In the days that Nels Stewart, Babe Siebert and Hooley Smith played together as the famed S-line of the Montreal Maroons, they were looked upon as the most feared trio in hockey. A burly, 200-pounder, he skated with short, toddling steps and he used a stick with so flat a lie that he had to play the puck almost between his skates. But he was truly Old Poison, collecting a total of 324 goals and 191 assists in 653 league games. He was the first to score more than 300 goals in the NHL, a record that stood for many seasons.

BRUCE STUART, during his major league hockey career, played on three Stanley Cup champions. He played for the Montreal Wanderers when they won the Cup in 1907–08, and with Ottawa Senators for two Cup triumphs, in 1908–09 and 1910–11.

WILLIAM H. STUART (Hod)—A tragic diving accident in Belleville, Ont., June 23, 1907, ended the life of William Hodgson Stuart. It also ended the hockey career of a great defenseman.

Rated one of the best of his or any other time, Hod was born in Ottawa and rose up through minor ranks in that city. With his brother, Bruce, he broke into big-time hockey with the Ottawa Senators in the 1898–99 season. They moved together to the Quebec Bulldogs in 1900–01 and while Bruce returned to Ottawa after a season, Hod remained in Quebec. After the 1901–02 season he accepted an offer to play for Calumet in the International Professional Hockey League, where he also acted as captain and manager.

"Cyclone" Taylor

"Rocket" Richard (left) and "Cyclone" Taylor

FRED TAYLOR. O. B. E. (Cyclone) was a brilliant hockey player in every phase of the game and he starred at defense, center and rover. When he played defense for Ottawa and Renfrew, his furious rushes earned him the famous nickname Cyclone.

Cyclone's scoring feats are legend. He collected 194 goals in 186 league games and another 15 in 19 playoff games. Taylor seemed to be like old wine — he improved with age. He was 30 when he joined Vancouver and at the age of 35 he was in the process of winning two consecutive scoring titles, playing as a rover and center. In 18 games of the 1917–18 schedule, Taylor rapped home 32 goals. The previous season, he scored six goals in one game against Victoria. Taylor played on two Stanley Cup-winning teams, Ottawa in 1908–09 and Vancouver in 1914–15.

CECIL THOMPSON (Tiny) — In an era when great goaltenders were the rule, rather than the exception, Cecil Thompson didn't take a back seat to anyone. The tag of Tiny was something of a misnomer: he stood five-foot-ten and weighed around 170 pounds. His goaltending opposition at that time included such stalwarts as George Hainsworth, Roy Worters, Charlie Gardiner and Lorne Chabot, but he was still able to win the Vezina Trophy on four occasions: 1929–30, 1932–33, 1935–36 and 1937–38.

Boston purchased Thompson and Cooney Weiland before the 1928–29 season and Tiny took over as the No. 1 goalie from Hal Winkler, remaining with the Bruins for ten seasons. He played his final

two NHL seasons with Detroit, then retired. His lifetime average in league games was 2.27 and his playoff average of goals-against was a flat 2.0 per game In addition to his Vezina Trophy triumphs, Thompson was twice voted to the league's first All-Star team and twice to the second team.

H. J. TRIHEY (Harry) starred in hockey with McGill University of Montreal, and later with Montreal Shamrocks. He played rover and was captain of the Shamrocks when they won the Stanley Cup in 1898–99 and 1899–1900. He retired as a player in 1901. Trihey had a deadly shot and, although not noted for speed, was a clever skater.

GEORGES VEZINA is one of the most renowned goaltenders in the history of the National Hockey League and his name is perpetuated by the trophy presented annually to the goaltender(s) having played a minimum 25 games for the team with the fewest goals scored against it. Vezina was the nearest thing to the perfect athlete, never missing a scheduled or playoff game from the time he broke into the National Hockey League until he retired 15 years later. He was a strong competitor on the ice, and always a gentleman, seldom becoming excited in the heat of sustained goalmouth action.

Georges played on five championship teams and on Stanley Cup winners in 1915–16 and 1923–24. His final game was played Nov. 28, 1925, when he started against Pittsburgh despite severe chest pains. He had to retire after one period. This was the first indication of tuberculosis, which claimed him Mar. 26, 1926.

J. P. WALKER (Jack) played only two seasons in the National Hockey League, but he enjoyed 30 years of close association with the game and won many honors as a center and rover.

Detroit purchased his contract before the 1926–27 season and he played two seasons with them before returning west to join the Edmonton Eskimos. In 1931–32, Walker went on to play and manage the Hollywood Stars, then the Oakland team. He retired after that season to manage, coach and referee in the Pacific Coast League.

MARTIN WALSH (Marty) — In five seasons with Ottawa, Walsh played in 59 league games and scored 135 goals. He also had 26 goals in eight playoff games and played on Stanley Cup winners in 1908–09 and 1910–11. Other players on that first Cup winner included Percy LeSueur, Fred Lake, Cyclone Taylor, Bill Gilmour, Albert Kerr and Bruce Stuart.

Walsh had many games in which he scored a high number of goals, including: 10 against Port Arthur, March 16, 1911; seven against Montreal, March 7, 1908; six against Galt, Jan. 5, 1910; six against Renfrew, Jan. 24, 1911; five against Wanderers, Jan. 11, 1908; and five against Shamrocks, Jan. 15, 1910. He was the leading scorer in the National Hockey Association for three seasons.

H. E. WATSON (Moose) played for Toronto Dentals in 1919, then moved over to Toronto Granites the following year. Granites won the Allan Cup in 1921–22 and 1922–23, adding the Olympic championship in 1924. Watson was an outstanding player for Canada in the Olympics, scoring 13 of the 30 goals which were scored against Czechoslovakia.

A fast man for his huge size, Watson was offered a $30,000 contract to play the 1925–26 season with Montreal Maroons. He was regarded as the best amateur center in Canada at that time. Harry had previously been offered a pro contract by Toronto St. Pats, but he had turned it down.

RALPH WEILAND (Cooney) played eleven seasons in the National Hockey League with Boston, Detroit and the old Ottawa Senators, and was a member of two Stanley Cup championship teams — the Bruins of 1928–29 and 1938–39, his first and last seasons in the NHL.

A very slick stickhandler, Weiland came to the Bruins from Minneapolis and was put on a line with Dit Clapper and Dutch Gainor which became known as "The Dynamite Line." Cooney was sold to Ottawa for the 1932–33 season, then went to Detroit but he returned to Boston in 1935–36 in a trade for Marty Barry and he remained with Boston until retirement as a player. He coached the Bruins in 1939–40 and they won their third Stanley Cup under his guidance

in 1940–41 — their last until 1969–70. After leaving the Bruins he coached at Hershey and New Haven in the American League. Then he was named coach of the Harvard University team and he stayed with them until retiring in 1971.

HARRY WESTWICK (Rat) played goal for Ottawa Seconds but soon converted to rover and went on to become one of the game's outstanding competitors in this position. He played for Aberdeens of the Ottawa City League and graduated from that team to the Senators in 1895. He played for that team when it won three consecutive Stanley Cups, starting with the 1902–03 season. Westwick had his most productive season in 1904–05 when the Silver Seven won its final Stanley Cup, scoring a total of 24 goals in 13 games. Westwick retired before another Cup came to Ottawa in 1908–09.

FREDERICK WHITCROFT played for the Peterboro Colts in 1901 when they won the Ontario Hockey Association junior championship, defeating a good Stratford team in the final series. He played the 1905 season with Midland, Ont., but returned to Peterboro to captain the Intermediate club which won the OHA championship the following season. Then he shifted his services to Western Canada for a season and came back to Ontario to play for Kenora Thistles when they won the Stanley Cup in January, 1907.

At the end of the 1907 season, Whitcroft moved to Edmonton and became captain of the senior hockey club. He scored 49 goals that season and Edmonton challenged Ottawa for the Stanley Cup but lost in two straight games.

G. A. WILSON (Phat) — His first senior team was the Port Arthur War Veterans. He joined the club in 1918 and remained with it until 1920. The following season he played with Iroquois Falls of the Northern Ontario Hockey Association which defeated Soo Greyhounds for the league title.

He returned to Port Arthur and was a member of the Bearcats team that won the Allan Cup three times: 1925, 1926 and 1929. In 1930, Wilson played with the same team which won the Western Canada title. A flashy type of defenseman, Wilson starred with the Port Arthur club in many other seasons and was a member of the club that toured Western Canada in 1926 and 1928.

ROY WORTERS — One of the smallest goalies ever to play in the National Hockey League, he was the first of his trade to win the Hart Trophy. Worters was only five-foot-two and seldom weighed more than 130 pounds, but he starred in the NHL for 12 seasons, often with teams that gave him a minimum amount of protection. He won the Hart Trophy in 1928–29 and added the Vezina Trophy in 1930–31. Roy was also twice named to the league's second All-Star team.

CANADA

CANADA'S SPORTS HALL OF FAME

Toronto, Ontario

Canada's Sports Hall of Fame came into existence in 1955, when well-known sports representatives from each province were brought to Toronto by officials of the Canadian National Exhibition to discuss a plan to give permanent recognition to Canada's great athletes. Mr. Harry I. Price, then Chairman of the C.N.E. sports committee and Mr. L.C. Powell, then C.N.E. Publicity Director, were the prime movers of the project. The inaugural meeting was held on June 10th of that year.

As one of the oldest Halls of Fame on the continent, the purpose of Canada's Sports Hall of Fame is to honor Canadians who have contribut-

Thousands gathered in front of Canada's Sports Hall of Fame on August 23rd, 1975 to watch the parade of athletes and the Annual Induction Ceremonies.

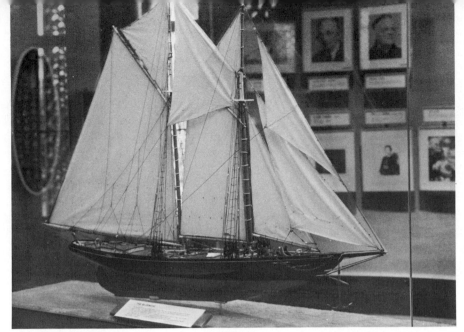

Model of the famed schooner, The Bluenose, which successfully beat all challengers in the 1920's and '30s.

The William Wrigley, Jr. Trophy awarded for the world's marathon swimming championship first won by Canadian George Young in 1927.

ed to sport in Canada, whether on the athletic field as a competitor or behind the scenes in a builder capacity. Photos and citations of the 264 Honored Members are displayed along with materials relevant to the history and heritage of sport in Canada. Any Canadian winning an Olympic gold medal is automatically admitted. Others are elected after consideration by a Selection Committee, which is made up of sportswriters representing every province in the country.

The Sports Hall of Fame is run by a Board of Governors made up of men active in government and business from across the country. Mr. Harry I. Price was the first Chairman of the Board. He was succeeded in 1968 by Mr. W. Harold Rea who in turn was succeeded by Mr. Harry E. Foster in 1975.

Canada's Sports Hall of Fame is funded jointly by the Canadian National Exhibition and by the Fitness Amateur Sport Branch of the Department of National Health and Welfare. It is a bilingual institution, its name in French being: "Le Temple de la Renommée des Sports du Canada." In 1974, it published a book of biographies entitled *Canada's Sporting Heroes*. This book, which has been called the best work currently available on Canada's sports history has been a publishing success. The Ontario Department of Education has established a course of study based on the book. Among its more recent activities has been the production of a film designed to promote Canada's Sports Hall of Fame.

The highlight of the year is the Annual Induction Ceremony of new Honored Members. This well attended event occurs in late August and receives extensive coverage by the sportsnews media.

Admission to the displays is free and the building is open to the public year round.

As Canada's only national sports hall of fame covering many sports, it acts as a source of inspiration to the thousands of young people who visit it every year and also plays an important role in preserving Canada's sports heritage.

Miss Supertest III, a mural and photos of various honorees in the Hall of Fame.

—All photographs in this chapter, courtesy Canada's Sports Hall of Fame

THE ORIGINAL INDUCTEES

Norman Baker

Lionel Conacher

NORMAN BAKER was named Canada's Outstanding Basketball Player during the First Half-Century, in a poll conducted by Canadian Press. Norm started at the age of 10 and played for Nanaimo as a midget-age competitor. In 1939, he returned to Victoria, his birthplace and was on Canadian championship teams in 1939–40, 1941–42 and 1945–46. He was on the RCAF championship team in 1942–43. He played professionally with Chicago Stags in 1946, then returned to Vancouver and played for the Hornets. In 1949, he joined the New York Celtics, after playing Whirlwinds and joined the Stars Of The World who toured Europe. His final season was 1951 with Boston.

LIONEL CONACHER excelled at hockey, football, lacrosse, boxing, track and field, swimming and rowing. He played for the Argonaut Grey Cup team of 1921. He played for Toronto Maple Leafs baseball team which won the Triple A championship in 1926. In 1921 he helped Toronto win the Ontario Lacrosse Association senior title and he also helped Aura Lee defeat Toronto Granites for the Sportsman Cup in hockey. He played professional hockey for Pittsburgh Pirates, New York Americans, Montreal Maroons and Chicago Black Hawks. He played on Stanley Cup winners with Chicago in 1933–34 and Montreal in 1934–35. He was named on the second all-star NHL team twice and to the first team once. He spent 11 seasons in the NHL as a defenseman and scored 80 goals and earned 105 assists.

EDOUARD (NEWSY) LALONDE was voted Canada's Outstanding Lacrosse Player of the Half-Century by Canadian Press in 1950. He started playing lacrosse in 1904 with Cornwall of the National League at age 16. He stayed on as the team's goalkeeper through the 1905–06 seasons. In 1910, he helped Montreal Nationals win the National League title. He joined New Westminster in 1911.

JIMMY McLARNIN won the world welterweight title, May 29, 1933, at Los Angeles by knocking out Young Corbett III in the first round. He lost the title to Barney Ross a year later, but regained it in a rematch at the Polo Grounds, New York, September 17, 1934, by out-pointing him in 15 rounds. In a later rematch, May 28, 1935, Ross regained the title.

HOWARD WILLIAM (HOWIE) MORENZ started playing in Stratford and signed with the Montreal Canadiens in 1923–24. He was nicknamed "the Babe Ruth of hockey" by U.S. sportswriters. He played for 14 seasons with Montreal Canadiens, Chicago Black Hawks, and New York Rangers in the National Hockey League. He was also known as The Canadian Comet, The Hurtling Habitant, The Mitchell Meteor and The Stratford Streak. He was a great stickhandler and had a hard shot, combined with reckless speed.

He played 11 seasons with Canadiens, one with Chicago, half a season with New York, then returned to Montreal and remained with them until, on Jan. 28, 1937, he broke his leg during an NHL contest. Six weeks later, on March 8, 1937, he died. Morenz scored 270 goals and won the Hart Trophy as the league's most valuable player (three times: 1927–28, 1930–31 and 1931–32). He scored 40 goals in 44 games during the 1928–29 season and 30 goals in 30 games in 1924–25. He also earned 197 assists during his career for a total of 467 points.

He was voted Canada's Outstanding Hockey Player of the Half-Century by a Canadian Press poll in 1950.

JACK PURCELL dominated badminton for 15 years. He played for the first time at Guelph, when he was 21, and was defeated in the first round of every event in the Canadian championships at Ottawa the next year. In the next five years he held every title in Ontario, winning the singles five times and the mixed doubles four consecutive times.

His first singles title came in 1928, and in 1930 he retained his title as well as defeating the four best British players who were on the tour at the time. He won the Surrey Doubles, but was defeated in the semifinals of the All-England singles. He was suspended in 1931 for writing instructional articles and engaging in the sports goods business. Then he turned professional and beat the best.

FANNY (BOBBY) ROSENFELD was born in Russia and became a Canadian citizen in 1920. She won the Olympic 400 metres at the Olympics in Amsterdam in 1928. She defeated the world 100-yard champion Helen Filkey of Chicago at the Canadian National Exhibition in 1923. She set a world record of 26 seconds for the 220 in 1925, at Varsity Stadium. In 1925, at the CNE, she equalled the world record of 11 seconds for the 100-yard dash and she still holds the Canadian record for the standing broad jump with eight feet, one inch. This was set in 1925 at Varsity Stadium. She won her first trophy at a War Veterans meet at Barrie in 1922.

Her major victory was being named Canada's Female Athlete of the Half Century, in a 1950 poll by the Canadian Press. She also ran the first leg for the Canadian relay team which set an Olympic record of 48.2 seconds in the 400 metres. She was also second in the 100-metre final. She coached the 1934 Canadian women's team at the British Empire Games at London. Earlier, in 1928, she set three Canadian records at Halifax: running broad jump, discus and standing broad jump.

C. ROSS "SANDY" SOMERVILLE went to the finals of the Canadian Amateur, only to be defeated; but in 1926, at the Kanawaki course, he defeated C. C. Fraser of the Toronto Golf Club 4 and 3 to become Canadian amateur champion for the first time. Over the next decade and more he repeatedly proved himself Canada's finest amateur golfer. He took the title again in 1928, 1930, 1931, 1935 and 1937. On three of these occasions he defeated American amateurs in the finals, including a lopsided 11 and 10 victory over J. W. Platt of Philadelphia on his home course, London Hunt in 1930. On two other occasions he lost to Americans in the finals — in 1934 to Albert Campbell of Seattle (the defending champion), one up, and in 1938 to Ted Adams of Columbia, Mississippi the 39th hole. His greatest victory occurred in the 1932 U.S. Amateur at the Five Farms course in Baltimore where he beat Johnny Goodman 2 and 1 for the U.S. championship.

DAVE TURNER learned soccer in Edmonton and set out on a career in the sport in 1922 after first teaching school. He played with Canadian West Coast and U.S. teams. He played for Cumberland, then St. Andrew's in the British Columbia League. He later played with Fall River, Mass., and then for Toronto (Ulster United) in 1926. After one year in Toronto he went back to the Pacific Coast to join New Westminster during the late 20's and 30's.

PERCY WILLIAMS was named Canada's outstanding track and field performer of the first half century, by a Canadian Press Poll in 1950. He is Canada's only double Olympic winner — at the 1928 Amsterdam Olympics. At the age of 19, he won the gold

Jimmy McLarnin

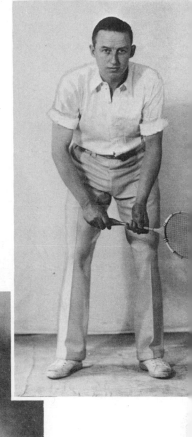

Jack Purcell

"Bobby" Rosenfeld

"Sandy" Somerville

medal in the 100 meters in 10.8 seconds and three days later, on August 1st, he captured the gold for the 200 meters in 21.8 seconds.

A year later, he defeated the best in the U.S., in competition at Madison Square Garden, to prove his victories were not flukes. In 1930, at the Hamilton, Ontario, British Empire Games, his track career ended when something clicked in his leg. He entered the 1932 Los Angeles Olympics but could do no better than fourth in the event.

JOE WRIGHT, SR. excelled in boxing, wrestling, track and field, baseball and football—but his mania was rowing. He became one of Canada's most famous rowing coaches. He stroked Toronto Argonauts to victory in the U.S. National, in 1885, at Albany.

Twenty years later he stroked the Double Blue to victory in the Royal Canadian Henley, at Port Dalhousie. At 42, in 1906, in England, he won the Grand Challenge. Wright was named Canada's Outstanding Oarsman of the Half-Century in the Canadian Press poll of 1950.

At 44, he played for the Argonaut senior football team—with his son. He piloted Pennsylvania University crews from 1916 to 1926. He won titles with Toronto Argonauts at the Royal Canadian Henley and the U.S. National championship. In 1928, he coached his son to the Diamond Sculls, against R. Lee.

DR. JACK WRIGHT was named Canada's Outstanding Lawn Tennis player of the Half-Century in

(Above) An interior view showing the main display area.
(At left) Joe Wright, Sr.

Ceremonies honoring thirty-five hockey and football stars on August 23, 1975.

the Canadian Press Poll of 1950. He represented Canada in Davis Cup play for 11 years and for seven years was first in Canada. He played most of his tennis in Montreal. Against Japan, at Montreal in 1927, he defeated Tacheichi Harada in Davis Cup matches. At one point he was ranked third in the world. He won the Canadian championship in 1927, 1929 and 1931. From 1923 to 1933 he was on every Canadian Davis Cup team and also represented Canada at zone matches between Cuba, U.S. and Japan.

GEORGE YOUNG won $25,000.00 on January 16, 1927 in the Catalina Marathon. In 1928, he and 198 others attempted the Toronto marathon, but no one completed it and so he and 13 others received part of the purse. In 1929, he was taken from the water with cramps and in 1930 he suffered temporary blindness and cramps. He won the 15-mile Canadian National Exhibition marathon in 1931. In 1950, he was voted the Greatest Swimmer of the Half-Century by the Canadian Press Poll.

Dr. Jack Wright

(At left)
George Young

333

INTERNATIONAL HOCKEY HALL OF FAME AND MUSEUM

Kingston, Ontario

The newest fan or the most dyed-in-the-wool hockey buff will find something of interest at the International Hockey Hall of Fame and Museum in Kingston, Ontario. The shrine, opened in 1965 after a 20-year campaign by local hockey officials, mixes a blend of the past and present in displays showing early sticks and equipment along with those used by today's heroes of the ice lanes.

The main feature of the hall is its gallery of more than 200 members who have been enshrined over the years. Included are players, builders of the sport and hockey's unsung heroes, the officials. Also included are pictures and accounts of the top amateur and professional stars of Canada and the United States.

With the game of hockey gaining international prominence, an attempt is being made to display not only North American items, but those from over 25 countries on five continents who play Canada's national winter sport. Displays including Russian, Swedish, Czechoslovakian, Norwegian and Japanese hockey items are on view. An up-to-date record of winners of the International Ice Hockey Federation's yearly world amateur hockey championships is kept, along with National Hockey League trophy and award winners.

The 40-foot by 65-foot hall attempts to show the hockey fan not only the stars of today, but offers a glimpse of the players of the past with their equipment and uniforms. A complete display case depicts the evolution of ice skates over the past 100 years, while another showcase contains the history of hockey sticks from one used in the first organized league in the world played on Kingston's harbor ice in 1886 to the curved blades of today.

Pictures and equipment from the historic hockey game played annually on Kingston's harbor are also on display. Every year a re-creation of the first Queen's College-Royal Military College game is staged. A replica of the field hockey type of stick used in that game is one of the most popular souvenir items sold at the hall.

—All photographs and art in this chapter, courtesy International Hockey Hall of Fame and Museum

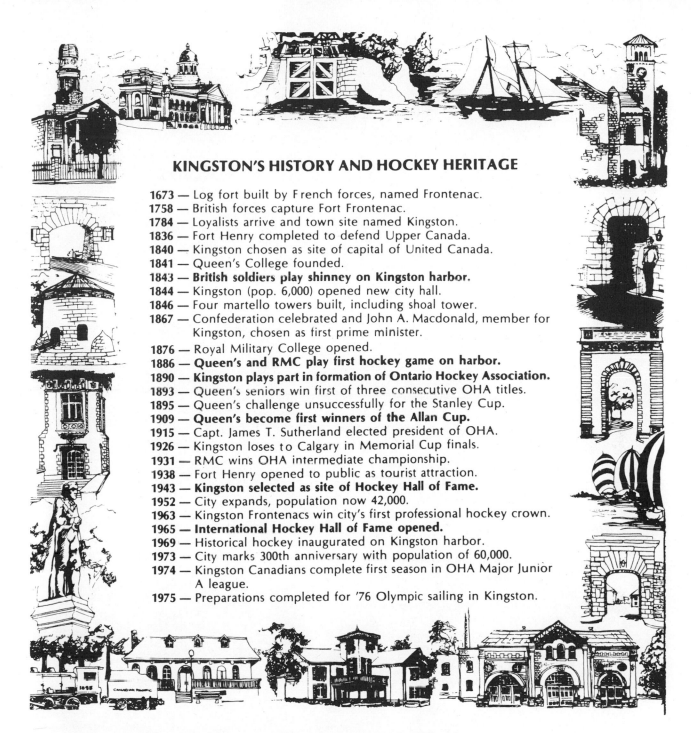

KINGSTON'S HISTORY AND HOCKEY HERITAGE

1673 — Log fort built by French forces, named Frontenac.
1758 — British forces capture Fort Frontenac.
1784 — Loyalists arrive and town site named Kingston.
1836 — Fort Henry completed to defend Upper Canada.
1840 — Kingston chosen as site of capital of United Canada.
1841 — Queen's College founded.
1843 — **British soldiers play shinney on Kingston harbor.**
1844 — Kingston (pop. 6,000) opened new city hall.
1846 — Four martello towers built, including shoal tower.
1867 — Confederation celebrated and John A. Macdonald, member for Kingston, chosen as first prime minister.
1876 — Royal Military College opened.
1886 — **Queen's and RMC play first hockey game on harbor.**
1890 — **Kingston plays part in formation of Ontario Hockey Association.**
1893 — Queen's seniors win first of three consecutive OHA titles.
1895 — Queen's challenge unsuccessfully for the Stanley Cup.
1909 — **Queen's become first winners of the Allan Cup.**
1915 — Capt. James T. Sutherland elected president of OHA.
1926 — Kingston loses to Calgary in Memorial Cup finals.
1931 — RMC wins OHA intermediate championship.
1938 — Fort Henry opened to public as tourist attraction.
1943 — **Kingston selected as site of Hockey Hall of Fame.**
1952 — City expands, population now 42,000.
1963 — Kingston Frontenacs win city's first professional hockey crown.
1965 — **International Hockey Hall of Fame opened.**
1969 — Historical hockey inaugurated on Kingston harbor.
1973 — City marks 300th anniversary with population of 60,000.
1974 — Kingston Canadians complete first season in OHA Major Junior A league.
1975 — Preparations completed for '76 Olympic sailing in Kingston.

Another display which attracts hockey fans of all ages is the collection of hockey cards from the four-team National Hockey Association, forerunner of today's National Hockey League. These 60-year-old cards were the first of the sport to be printed and are valued at over $5 each today. Other collections of hockey cards and pins are also on display.

Although the game of hockey is predominantly a male domain, women's teams from the early 1900s until today are also given places of prominence.

The International Hockey Hall of Fame and Museum is truly called "Hockey's Home" because of Kingston's historic past with the game. The displays and exhibits should appeal to every member of the family.

335

THE ORIGIN OF HOCKEY IN CANADA AND THE UNITED STATES

from a report submitted to the
Canadian Amateur Hockey Association
in 1942

The word "HOCKEY" is derived from the French word "Hoquet."

The first hockey was played by the Royal Canadian Rifles, an Imperial unit, stationed in Halifax and Kingston in 1855; it is quite possible that English troops stationed in Kingston from 1783 to 1855 played hockey, as there is evidence in old papers, letters, and legend that the men and officers located with the Imperial troops, as early as the year 1783, were proficient skaters and participated in field hockey. It is more than likely that the pioneers played their field hockey in those early days on skates but that is not an established fact. The playing of hockey games as early as 1855 in Kingston is certain. Early manuscripts, letters, and even the sticks and a puck used in the early days of hockey have been located. With ice conditions more favorable in Kingston harbor, which is situated at the terminus of the Great Lakes, than on the East coast, it is only logical that there was more actual hockey and skating in Cataraqui (the old Indian name for Kingston), than in Halifax.

Montreal makes a fair claim as the birthplace of hockey with records of games in 1874. Medals and pictures of the early games are on record but they are superseded by games in Kingston and Halifax; in fact, the first games played in Montreal used what are known as the Halifax rules.

Hockey popularity apparently spread across Eastern Canada after its introduction in Kingston and Halifax by the Imperial troops. R. F. Smith had records to prove that hockey was played at McGill in 1879. Mr. Smith and an associate, W. F. Robertson, who visited England the previous year, devised a set of rules for hockey games at McGill college, where they were both students. It was stated that Mr. Robertson had received his inspiration after having seen the game of field hockey played while he was in England. It is stated that about 30 participated in the first McGill game in Montreal. Hockey was also played at the winter ice carnivals held in Montreal in 1882–83.

The Victoria Hockey Club of Montreal was the senior hockey club of Canada, at that time. The Victorias were unquestionably one of the most genuinely amateur hockey clubs that has ever participated in Canada's great winter game. Their members were particularly proud of their amateur standing and there is no record of any member of the famous "Vics" having failed to live up to their high standing in sports.

Hockey appears to have been introduced into Ottawa in the early '80s. It was introduced by players who were former members of the early McGill college teams. One of the prominent figures in the introduction of hockey in Canada's National Capital was Dr. P. B. Ross, of the Ottawa Journal.

Introduced into the United States in the '90s

Hockey was introduced into the United States in the '90s and there are records showing that McGill and Queen's Universities played in New York in 1897, and strange to say, they played on artificial ice. W. F. Nickle, Kingston barrister, and formerly Attorney-General of Ontario, and who had been a member of the Ontario Hockey Association Executive for two years during the time that the late John Ross Robertson was president of that body, acted as manager of the Queen's team during that visit. Mr. Nickle tells a thrilling story of the difficulties that his team encountered while crossing the channel to Cape Vincent, N.Y., where the Queen's team entrained for New York.

The game of hockey probably dates back to the first time that men put runners on their feet to glide on ice, and the first really authentic story of ice skating is dated 1396 when a young woman in Scheidam, Holland, seriously injured while skating, lived so patient and beautiful a life that she was canonized as Saint Siedwi. This gives skating the only sport patron Saint.

It is certain that the first ORGANIZED league hockey was played in Kingston on the harbor ice, near Tete-De-Pont Barracks, built in 1672, and formerly known as Fort Frontenac, so called in honor of Count Frontenac, first Governor under the French regime. In this barracks the pioneer soldiers were stationed. The league comprised four clubs, the Royal Military College, Queen's University, Kingston Athletics and the Kingston Hockey Club. That league operated in 1885–86. The league was eventually merged into the Ontario Hockey Association when the provincial body was formed in 1890.

Canadian Military Records

Tracing back through early, authentic-military records, Edwin Horsey, a reliable Canadian historian, quotes facts from his father's diary as follows: "Desertions from the Imperial troops had become most prevalent, due to high civic wages being paid and attraction as regards living conditions across the border in the United States, so it was decided to form a regiment for service in Canada only, recruited by allowing men in regular Imperial regiments to volunteer into it, instead of leaving the colony for service abroad. The corps was commonly referred to as the 'Bull-Frogs.' The battalion was 1100 strong and was said to have been a fine body of men, with more medals than any other regiment in the services." Continuing, Mr. Horsey quotes from his father's diary: "It was not until 1855 that part of the Royal Canadian Rifles came to Kingston, when some 15 officers and 397 other ranks came here to relieve the 9th Imperial regiment, wanted for overseas service following the Crimean war.

The Royal Canadian Rifles were disbanded in 1870, and were succeeded by the present Royal Canadian Horse Artillery."

The military records are quoted as there is definite evidence that the soldiers played a group game of hockey. Historian Horsey's father also left the following reference to hockey in his diary under an earlier date—1846–47: "Most of the soldier boys were quite at home on skates. They could cut the figure eight and other fancy figures, but 'shinny' was their great delight. Groups would be placed at the Shoal tower (opposite City Buildings, in the harbor) and Point Frederick (the point of land where the Royal Military College stands) and fifty or more players on each side would be in the game." As the game of "Shinny" or "Shanty" as it is called in Scotland, and "Hurtling" as it is termed in Ireland, is undoubtedly the grandparent of our present game of hockey, brought up to its present form through the principal medium of the Ontario Hockey Association and other kindred associations during the past fifty-two years, it seems obvious that we have the connecting link thoroughly established.

It has been suggested in some quarters that the game of hockey was invented by Canadian Indians, but there has been nothing found to substantiate this claim, neither have we any record of any Indian hockey clubs.

The first hockey sticks used in Canadian hockey games were imported from England, and cost four shillings each. They were quite unlike the present-day Canadian sticks, being shorter and more like the type of stick used during the old indoor polo games that were so popular during the very early days of the "roller skate" epidemic, over 50 years ago. The first hockey nets to be used in Canada were introduced into a game in Montreal by none other than our own W. A. (Billy) Hewitt, who was Sporting Editor of the Montreal Herald during the winter of 1899. Mr. Hewitt believes that to the best of his knowledge the game was between the Shamrocks and the Victorias. Mr. Hewitt states that the late Francis Nelson had got the idea concerning the nets while in Australia. He also stated that they may have been in use in the O.H.A. prior to Mr. Hewitt's connection with that body. But your committee is of the opinion that nets were used for the first time in Montreal.

Curling

While peering into the past for hockey data, your committee unearthed the following interesting facts concerning a sister ice-game, Curling. It is stated that "The first curling on this continent was played by Wolfe's soldiers at Quebec in 1759–60 with irons melted from French cannon, used for stones, and the first record of Kingston's part in inter-city curling dates back to 1856, although there were games in Kingston long before that time," . . . and "that the same military men stationed in Halifax and Kingston, who are credited with starting hockey in Canada, brought curling to Canada, and now the Dominion has more curlers and more curling clubs than any other place in the world," and also more hockey players and hockey clubs than any other country in the world.

Sir Montagu Allan

Lord Stanley of Preston

The photographs, on pages 337 and 338, show early Hall of Fame inductees not appearing in other Hockey chapters in this volume.

Joseph (Joe) Malone

Frank Calder

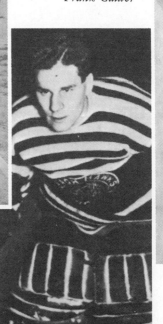

(At right) Charles (Chuck) Gardiner

Frank Nighbor

(At left)
Aubrey (Dit)
Clapper

Georges Vezina

The Future

What does the future hold for the International Hockey Hall of Fame?

If the aims and objectives of the present board of directors are carried out, the Kingston hall could emerge as a prominent sports edifice.

The building is presently being taxed to its capacity with the Hall of Fame located on the second floor and a public auditorium housed on the main floor. The directors foresee the need for an addition to the building to facilitate the increasing number of displays and artifacts which are painstakingly gathered every year. There are plans to enhance the present hall now being used as a hockey shrine. Better lighting and displaying techniques are to be utilized through the assistance of professional museology personnel. Financing of the independently-operated hall is expensive and monies will be realized through existing government grants and a prudent board of directors.

A display is being prepared to depict the evolution of the sport from the simple game of shinny to a highly-organized business throughout the world.

New exhibits are continuously being sought and the hall is at present making a concerted attempt to supply materials from five continents playing the game of ice hockey. It is hoped that artifacts and articles from all around the world will be forthcoming from this quest. It is also planned to induct members of the international community into the hall so they may be honored and remembered for their contributions.

Perhaps more than any other comparable hockey hall of fame, the Kingston facility is conscious of the historical segments of the game, and this aspect will be carried on during future years.

As long as the game of hockey is played, regardless of where and by whom, the International Hockey Hall of Fame will endeavor to display and promote Canada's national winter sport.

*   *   *

The enshrinees in the International Hockey Hall of Fame and Museum are identical with those in the Hockey Hall of Fame, Toronto, Ontario.

William A. Hewitt

Duncan (Mickey) MacKay

"MIGHTY MEN
WHICH WERE OF OLD
...MEN OF RENOWN"

THE HALL OF FAME
FOR GREAT AMERICANS

On the campus of
Bronx Community College
of the City University
of New York

Since 1900, long before numerous halls of fame devoted to athletic prowess appeared, the Hall of Fame for Great Americans has conducted regular elections to single out those American men and women whose lives have contributed significantly toward human advancement.

Here in a timeless setting of classical grandeur, designed by famed architect Stanford White, stand side by side in their niches of honor presidents and statesmen, scientists and inventors, artists and humanitarians. Each is commemorated by a specially commissioned bronze portrait bust and tablet bearing words that symbolize his or her remarkable vision and accomplishments.

In this Bicentennial Era you are invited to visit the Hall of Fame, to walk through the majestic Colonnade, and to become acquainted with the nearly one hundred Americans who merit recognition and enduring fame in future generations.

The site selected for the Hall of Fame stands on the ground that figured prominently in Revolutionary War history. It overlooks the Harlem and Hudson Rivers and the Palisades beyond, and was occupied during the War by the British army and used as a fort and lookout.

The process of selection of the first candidates for enshrinement began early in 1900, when the public was invited to submit nominations. Provisions were made to include up to 50 names in the initial election.

By May 1, 1900, more than 1,000 nominations had been received by the New York University Senate. Having designated some 100 prominent persons throughout the country as electors, the Senate submitted to them the 100 names which had received the greatest public support. To this number were added 100 nominees selected by the Senate. The electors themselves were invited to suggest other candidates. The final list contained a total of 234 names from which 29 were elected by the required majority vote.

The bust of Thomas Paine, revolutionary activist, showing plaque which reads: "Those who expect to reap the blessings of freedom must like men, undergo the fatigues of supporting it."

—Biographies and related information
are by courtesy of the Hall of Fame
for Great Americans

The exterior view of the Hall of Fame from the river view showing the colonnade with the busts of the electees.

Eight names were added in 1905, ten in 1910, nine in 1915, seven in 1920, two in 1925, four in 1930, three in 1935, one in 1940, four in 1945, six in 1950, three in 1955, three in 1960, and four in 1965.

In 1970 there were two new Hall of Fame members elected, namely, Lillian D. Wald and Albert Abraham Michelson. In 1973 four were honored: Louis Dembitz Brandeis, George Washington Carver, Franklin Delano Roosevelt, and John Philip Sousa. This brings the total number of enshrinees to 99.

Under the original constitution governing the Hall of Fame, no foreign-born citizen was eligible for election. To rectify this obvious injustice, the University Senate in 1904 decided to establish a Hall of Fame for foreign-born Americans. However, in 1914 the constitution was changed to strike out any distinction between native citizens and Americans of foreign birth.

One alien has been granted what might be considered "associate membership;" in recognition of the Marquis de Lafayette's service in the American Revolution, his bust occupies a special niche in the wall of an adjacent University building. From there the statue of the French soldier and statesman overlooks the colonnade where—but for an accident of birth—the bronze image would stand today.

Also in 1914, the University set apart a site in the colonnade for a Hall of Fame for Women. But eight years later, after seven names had been chosen, the University Senate decided to abolish in future elections any discrimination as to sex and to combine the names of the women with those of the men. Today, the colonnade displays bronze likenesses of eight women.

In 1922, the required period of time between the death of a prospective candidate and his eligibility for election was increased from ten years to twenty-five years.

It was a basic concept of its founders that the Hall of Fame be national rather than regional in character. To this end, the minimum number of electors has been fixed at 100, with all states represented. As Dr. Henry Mitchell MacCracken, originator of the Hall of Fame and at that time New York University's Chancellor, observed in 1901. "Local and temporary influence or the solicitations of interested supporters are not likely to weigh seriously with a tribunal so constituted." Today, approximately 125 electors represent all 50 states.

From the list of nominees submitted to them by the University Senate, the electors may choose a maximum of seven persons for admission to the Hall of Fame. Later, a committee of leading American artists selects an outstanding sculptor who will execute a bronze bust of each winning candidate. The bust must be made specifically for the Hall of Fame and must not be duplicated for exhibition elsewhere within 50 years of its execution.

The considerable cost of enshrinement, including the unveiling ceremony, is usually borne by private citizens or institutions dedicated to perpetuating the memory of the dignitary elected.

Marquis de Lafayette, the only alien, who occupies a special niche in the wall of a building adjacent to the colonnade in recognition of his service in the American Revolution.

A Visit to the Hall of Fame

As you pass through the great iron gates and start on your way around the graceful arc of the Hall of Fame Colonnade, you will come upon *Alexander Graham Bell*, inventor of the telephone. A few steps further will bring you to a buckskin-clad *John James Audubon*, the painter who aroused

The interior view showing busts of famous Americans.

William Cullen Bryant

worldwide interest in America's birds and their natural environment. Nearby are astronomer *Maria Mitchell, Dr. William C. Gorgas,* the man who conquered yellow fever, and the *Wright Brothers.*

Continue into the gallery that holds the Founding Fathers, then turn into the sweeping semicircle containing the portrait busts of outstanding lawyers and judges, military and naval heroes, artists and educators, scientists and humanitarians. Note the special alcove occupied by the *Marquis de Lafayette,* America's most distinguished honorary citizen.

Pause for a moment to gaze westward from this tranquil spot in a busy city. On the next hill sit the Cloisters, and beyond rise the Palisades of the Hudson. Here, only a short distance from midtown, you are enjoying one of New York City's most scenic vistas of natural beauty.

Proceed to the gallery of authors, where portraits of *Poe, Emerson, Walt Whitman, Harriet Beecher Stowe* and others await you.

As you retrace your steps to the entrance, reflect on the fact that America has not only been a land of opportunity. To many who have risen from humble origins it has also been a land of accomplishment and fulfillment.

Portraits in Bronze

The bronze busts in the Hall of Fame Colonnade constitute one of the nation's finest portrait collections. Nearly all were especially commissioned for the Hall of Fame. On permanent display are the works of over fifty master scupltors. Included among them are such artists as Daniel Chester French, sculptor of the Lincoln Memorial, Frederick Mac-Monnies, whose reliefs grace Fifth Avenue's Washington Arch, and James Earle Fraser, whose works include figures of "Justice" and "Law" for the U.S. Supreme Court and "End of the Trail." Larger than life-sized and reflecting the individual style of each sculptor, the bronze busts have been photographed many times for publication as true likenesses of the persons elected to the Hall of Fame.

The Hall of Fame Colonnade

The Colonnade is approximately 630 feet in length. Dedicated May 30, 1901, it was constructed in two stages and achieved its present form in 1914. At the outset bronze tablets alone were used to commemorate each person elected. In 1907 the first bronze bust was installed, a replica of Horace Mann, later replaced in 1930 by on original portrait by Adolph A. Weinman, designer of the Walking Liberty half-dollar and the Mercury dime.

The Colonnade and the three adjoining buildings were designed in Beaux Arts style by Stanford White, one of America's most imaginative architects at the turn of the century. The intricate and beautiful bronze doors of Gould Memorial Library, the domed building, honor the memory of this brilliant taste-maker. White also designed the Washington Arch in Greenwich Village and the Battle Monument at West Point. He also designed the Newport Casino, now the Tennis Hall of Fame.

HALL OF FAME

ARTISTS, MUSICIANS, ACTORS

Edwin Booth, 1833–1893. Elected 1925. Most popular American dramatic actor of mid-19th century. Excelled in Shakespearean tragedies. Founder and first president of the Players Club in New York City. *Sculptor: Edmond T. Quinn, 1926.*

Charlotte Saunders Cushman, 1816–1876. Elected 1915. Actress. Began stage career as opera singer, but switched to acting. Admired in America and England for Shakespearean roles. *Sculptor: Frances Grimes, 1925.*

Stephen Collins Foster, 1826–1864. Elected 1940. Composer of popular ballads and minstrel songs, among them "O Susanna," "Old Folks at Home" (Swanee River), and "Camptown Races." *Sculptor: Walker Kirtland Hancock, 1941.*

Edward Alexander MacDowell, 1861–1908. Elected 1960. Composer, pianist and music teacher. Acclaimed as concert performer. First professor of music at Columbia University. "To a Wild Rose" and other "Woodland Sketches" are among his best-known works. *Sculptor: C. Paul Jennewien, 1964.*

Augustus Saint-Gaudens, 1848–1907. Elected 1920. Sculptor of monumental figures accenting personality of the subject—Lincoln in Chicago's Lincoln Park, Farragut in New York's Madison Square, Sherman in Central Park. *Sculptor: James Earle Fraser, 1926.*

John Philip Sousa, 1854–1932. Elected 1970. Band leader and composer of many popular marches. He was first prominent as conductor of the United States Marine Band. He was a prolific composer of marches including "The Stars and Stripes Forever," "El Capitan" and about 130 others. He also wrote numerous songs, overtures and operettas. In addition to directing his own band, he joined the Navy as a lieutenant in 1917 at the age of 62 and organized 100 bands in 20 months. *Sculptor: Karl H. Gruppe, 1976*

Gilbert Charles Stuart, 1755–1828. Elected 1900. Portrait painter of many of the Founding Fathers and George Washington in particular. Influenced development of painting in the young nation. *Sculptor: Laura Gardin Fraser, 1922.*

James Abbott McNeill Whistler, 1834–1903. Elected 1930. Artist. Portrait painter, experimenter with color, and admirer of Oriental art. His most famous painting: "Portrait of My Mother—Arrangement in Grey and Black." *Sculptor: Frederick MacMonnies, 1931.*

AUTHORS

George Bancroft, 1800–1891. Elected 1910. Historian. Wrote 10-volume *History of the United States* from the discovery of America to the end of the Revolutionary War, the most popular American historical work of the 19th century. Saw American history as progressing from despotism to democracy. *Sculptor: Rudulph Evans, 1930.*

William Cullen Bryant, 1794–1878. Elected 1910. Poet and newspaper editor. His poetry celebrated beauty of nature. Edited *New York Evening Post* for 50 years. Favored workingmen's rights, opposed slavery and took part in founding the Republican party. *Sculptor: Herbert Adams, 1929.*

Samuel Langhorne Clemens (Mark Twain), 1835–1910. Elected 1920. Writer, lecturer and humorist. Created best known characters, Tom Sawyer and Huckleberry Finn, based upon youth in Missouri. Expressed uniquely American outlook in humorous, often cynical, philosophizing. *Sculptor: Albert Humphreys, 1924.*

Stephen Foster

Mark Twain

James Fenimore Cooper

Ralph Waldo Emerson

James Fenimore Cooper, 1789–1851. Elected 1910. Writer. Creator of epic tales of American frontier life. First American to receive international acclaim for fiction. Best known for the *Leatherstocking Tales,* which included *Last of the Mohicans* and *The Deerslayer. Sculptor: Victor Salvatore, 1930.*

Ralph Waldo Emerson, 1803–1882. Elected 1900. Philosopher, poet, essayist and lecturer. One of the founders of American transcendentalism, a philosophy that urged man to strive to employ his limitless capacities. The outstanding American philosopher of his age and a strong influence on Thoreau and Whitman. *Sculptor: Daniel Chester French, 1923.*

Nathaniel Hawthorne, 1804–1864. Elected 1900. Novelist and short-story writer. Best known works are *The Scarlet Letter* and *The House of the Seven Gables.* His writing considered the human tragedy that results from radical social change. *Sculptor: Daniel Chester French, 1929.*

Oliver Wendell Holmes, 1809–1894. Elected 1910. Poet, essayist and physician. Renowned for writing "Old Ironsides" and "The Autocrat of the Breakfast Table" before becoming a physician. Published statistical findings about contagion of childbed fever, confirmed by others' research 18 years later. *Sculptor: Edmond T. Quinn, 1929.*

Washington Irving, 1783–1859. Elected 1900. Satirist, historian and travel writer. Achieved international prominence with the *Sketch Book,* which included the story of Rip Van Winkle. Wrote about his travels in Spain and the Far West and biographies of Columbus and Washington. America's first man of letters. *Sculptor: Edward McCartan, 1927.*

Sidney Lanier, 1842–1881. Elected 1945. Poet, musician and literary critic in the post-Civil War South. Noted for writing melodic verse with great flair. *Sculptor: Hans Schuler, 1946.*

Henry Wadsworth Longfellow, 1807–1882. Elected 1900. Poet. Achieved popularity for such verse as "The Village Blacksmith," *Evangeline, The Song of Hiawatha, The Courtship of Miles Standish,* and "Paul Revere's Ride." First American author able to support himself through publication of poetry. *Sculptor: Rudulph Evans, 1929.*

James Russell Lowell, 1819–1891. Elected 1905. Poet, editor, teacher, diplomat, and political satirist. Active in antislavery movement. Wrote *The Biglow Papers* on the Mexican and Civil Wars. America's foremost man of letters and editor of *Atlantic Monthly* and *North American Review. Sculptor: Allan Clark, 1930.*

Washington Irving

Henry Wadsworth Longfellow

Harriet Beecher Stowe   *Henry Thoreau*

Thoreau's cabin at Walden Pond.
—From an 1854 edition of Walden

John Lothrop Motley, 1814–1877. Elected 1910. Historian. Wrote *The Rise of the Dutch Republic* (1856) and later *The History of the United Netherlands* (1860, 1867) in dramatic narrative style, comparing influences of political freedom vs. tyranny. *Sculptor: Frederick MacMonnies, 1930.*

Thomas Paine, 1737–1809. Elected 1945. Writer and political reformer. His pamphlet, "Common Sense," aroused Americans to declare independence in 1776. *Sculptor: Malvina Hoffman, 1952.*

Francis Parkman, 1823–1893. Elected 1915. Historian. Wrote narrative history of the frontier rich in description. Best known for *The Oregon Trail* and *Montcalm and Wolfe,* the latter dealing with French and Indian War. Noted for painstaking research. *Sculptor: Hermon A. MacNeil, 1929.*

Edgar Allan Poe, 1809–1849. Elected 1910. Poet, critic and short-story writer. Innovator in detective story genre and tales of horror and the supernatural. Master of lyric poetry, his work later influenced French symbolist poets. *Sculptor: Daniel Chester French, 1922.*

Harriet Beecher Stowe, 1811–1896. Elected 1910. Writer of antislavery novel *Uncle Tom's Cabin,* published in 1851–52. It sold 300,000 copies within a year and influenced the coming of the Civil War. *Sculptor: Brenda Putnam, 1925.*

Henry David Thoreau, 1817–1862. Elected 1960. Essayist, philosopher and poet. Originator of civil disobedience, which Gandhi and Martin Luther King, Jr. adopted in challenging injustice. *Sculptor: Malvina Hoffman, 1962.*

Walt Whitman, 1819–1892. Elected 1930. The poet of democracy. Wrote in free verse. Most famous works include *Leaves of Grass,* "O Captain! My Captain!," and "When Lilacs Last in the Dooryard Bloom'd," an elegy for Lincoln. *Sculptor: Chester Beach, 1931.*

John Greenleaf Whittier, 1807–1892. Elected 1905. Poet and journalist. Wrote fiery abolitionist poems and articles. A prolific writer and devout Quaker; many of his poems are sung as church hymns. *Sculptor: Rudulph Evans, 1928.*

345

Booker T. Washington

Daniel Boone

BUSINESSMEN, PHILANTHROPISTS

Peter Cooper, 1791–1883. Elected 1900. Inventor, manufacturer and philanthropist. Built first steam locomotive made in America, "Tom Thumb." Steel industry pioneer. His philanthropy and founding of Cooper Union set the pattern for later giving by Andrew Carnegie. *Sculptor: Chester Beach. 1924.*

George Peabody, 1795–1869. Elected 1900. Philanthropist, merchant and financier. First American to engage in philanthropy on a broad scale. The Peabody Education Fund pioneered in developing the foundation grant as an instrument of benefaction. *Sculptor: Hans Schuler. 1926.*

EDUCATORS

Mark Hopkins, 1802–1887. Elected 1915. Educator. Professor of philosophy and president of Williams College. A skilled teacher who used dialogue and personal approach with his students. *Sculptor: Hans Hoerbst. replica.*

Mary Lyon, 1797–1849. Elected 1905. Educator and feminist. Innovator in higher education for women. Founded Mt. Holyoke College for educating women of less affluent means. *Sculptor: Laura Gardin Fraser. 1927.*

Horace Mann, 1796–1859. Elected 1900. Education reformer. Led in development of public education in Massachusetts, a model for the nation. Helped organize state board of education, then directed it in devising reforms. Founded first public teacher training school in U.S. at Lexington, Mass. *Sculptor: Adolph A. Weinman. 1930.*

Alice Freeman Palmer, 1855–1902. Elected 1920. Educator. Graduate of U. of Michigan, professor and head of history department at Wellesley College. Appointed president of Wellesley and later dean of women at U. of Chicago. *Sculptor: Evelyn Longman. 1924.*

Sylvanus Thayer, 1785–1872. Elected 1965. Military engineer and educator. Graduate of West Point, he revitalized the academic structure. Later founded and endowed Thayer School of Engineering at Dartmouth College. *Sculptor: Joseph Kiselewski. 1966.*

Booker T. Washington, 1858–1915. Elected 1945. Educator. First head of Tuskegee Institute. Advocated vocational training and economic advancement for blacks. Adviser to Presidents Theodore Roosevelt and Taft. *Sculptor: Richmond Barthe. 1946.*

Emma Willard, 1787–1870. Elected 1905. Educator. Sought education for women comparable to that given men. Organized Troy Female Seminary in 1821, probably the first women's higher education institution in the U.S. *Sculptor: Frances Grimes. 1929.*

ENGINEERS, ARCHITECTS

James Buchanan Eads, 1820–1887. Elected 1920. Engineer and builder. Designed armored steamboats, built Mississippi River bridge at St. Louis, opened Mississippi River to deeper draft ships at its mouth. *Sculptor: Charles Grafly. 1924.*

EXPLORERS

Daniel Boone, 1734–1820. Elected 1915. Explorer. Led settlers into Kentucky through Cumberland Gap. A romantic figure to Americans of his own time and afterwards. *Sculptor: Albin Polasek. 1926.*

HUMANITARIANS

Jane Addams, 1860–1935. Elected 1965. Social worker. Established Hull House settlement in Chicago slums. A pacifist in World War I and afterward, she received a Nobel Peace Prize in 1931. *Sculptor: Granville W. Carter. 1968.*

Susan B. Anthony, 1820–1906. Elected 1950. Feminist reformer. As a young teacher, demanded equal pay for women teachers. Agitated for New York law to grant women equal property rights. Led women's suffrage movement for nearly fifty years. *Sculptor: Brenda Putnam, 1952.*

Lillian D. Wald, 1867–1940. Elected 1970. Social worker. Organized Henry Street Settlement in New York City. Originated visiting nurse and public school nurse systems. *Sculptor: Eleanor Platt, 1971.*

Frances Elizabeth Willard, 1839–1898. Elected 1910. Reformer and feminist. Educator, later president of the World Woman's Christian Temperance Union, and organizer of national Prohibition party in 1882. Worked for women's suffrage and better working conditions for women. *Sculptor: Lorado Taft, 1923.*

INVENTORS

Alexander Graham Bell, 1847–1922. Elected 1950. Invented the telephone, which he patented in 1876 and demonstrated at the Centennial Exhibition. *Sculptor: Stanley Martineau, 1951.*

Thomas Alva Edison, 1847–1931. Elected 1960. Inventor. Pioneered the revolution in technology by establishing the first industrial research laboratory from which came a multitude of inventions: the incandescent electric light, phonograph, motion-picture camera, storage battery, mimeograph and dictating machine. *Sculptor: Bryant Baker, 1961.*

Robert Fulton, 1765–1815. Elected 1900. Artist and engineer. Developed several improvements in transportation, most notably the steamboat. *Sculptor: Jean-Antoine Houdon, replica.*

Elias Howe, 1819–1867. Elected 1915. Patented the first sewing machine, but Isaac M. Singer's worked better and became a commercial success. *Sculptor: Charles Keck, 1930.*

Samuel Finley Breese Morse, 1791–1872. Elected 1900. Invented the telegraph, the first instrument capable of transmitting electrical signals across long distances. *Sculptor: Chester Beach, 1928.*

George Westinghouse, 1846–1914. Elected 1955. Inventor of air brake and electrically controlled signals for railroad trains. Innovator in development and use of alternating current. Founded Westinghouse Electric Co. *Sculptor: Edmondo Quattrocchi, 1957.*

Eli Whitney, 1765–1825. Elected 1900. Invented, but never patented, the cotton gin for cleaning seeds from cotton. *Sculptor: Chester Beach, 1926.*

Orville Wright, 1871–1948. Elected 1965. Aviation pioneer and inventor. Made the first piloted flight in a heavier-than-air craft, remaining aloft 12 sec. for a distance of 120 ft. at Kitty Hawk, N.C. in 1903. *Sculptor: Paul Fjelde, 1967.*

Wilbur Wright, 1867–1912. Elected 1955. Co-inventor of airplane with his brother Orville. Made longest flight of original four flights at Kitty Hawk, N.C. in 1903, 852 ft. in 59 sec. *Sculptor: Vincent Glinsky, 1967.*

LAWYERS, JUDGES

Louis Dembitz Brandeis, 1856–1941. Elected 1973. Born in Louisville, Kentucky, November 13, 1856. He graduated from Harvard University Law School in 1877 and practiced in Boston, Massachusetts, from 1879 until 1916. His liberal ideas caused him to take many public cases for which he was not paid. He was an expert on insurance law and railroad law, and he successfully fought rate increases and monopolies. He was appointed to the Supreme Court by President Wilson in 1916. He became famous on the Court for his dissenting opinions. Many of his opinions were later adopted

Thomas Edison

Elias Howe

Oliver Wendell Holmes   John Paul Jones

by the majority of the Court. Brandeis University, Waltham, Massachusetts, was named for him. *Sculpture not completed.*

Rufus Choate, 1799–1859. Elected 1915. Notable 19th century trial lawyer. Completed Webster's unexpired term in the Senate. *Sculptor: Herman A. MacNeil, 1928.*

Oliver Wendell Holmes, Jr., 1841–1935. Elected 1965. Associate Justice, U.S. Supreme Court. Came to prominence as a legal scholar. As Supreme Court justice, noted for dissents which later gained acceptance and for eloquent use of language. *Sculptor: Joseph Kiselewski, 1970.*

James Kent, 1763–1847. Elected 1900. New York Chancellor and legal scholar. His *Commentaries on American Law* became a standard text for educating lawyers. Along with Justice Story, he laid the cornerstone of American equity law. *Sculptor: Edmond T. Quinn, 1926.*

John Marshall, 1755–1835. Elected 1900. Chief Justice, U.S. Supreme Court. Established power of Supreme Court to declare federal and state laws unconstitutional. *Sculptor: Herbert Adams, 1925.*

Joseph Story, 1779–1845. Elected 1900. Associate Justice, U.S. Supreme Court. Favored federal government over the states. Opposed slavery. Later became an innovator in legal education at Harvard. *Sculptor: Herbert Adams, 1930.*

MILITARY

David Glasgow Farragut, 1801–1870. Elected 1900. Commander of Union Navy on Gulf Coast during Civil War. Despite Southern background, served Union cause. Captured New Orleans, blockaded Vicksburg, won control of Mobile Bay. Rank of Admiral in U.S. Navy created for him. *Sculptor: Charles Grafly, 1927.*

Ulysses Simpson Grant, 1822–1885. Elected 1900. Eighteenth president. Commander of Union Armies, which he led to victory in Civil War. His presidency was marred by scandals among high officials. *Sculptor: James Earle Fraser with Thomas Hudson Jones, 1923.*

Thomas Jonathan "Stonewall" Jackson, 1824–1863. Elected 1955. Confederate general in Civil War, called "Stonewall" for holding fast at First Battle of Bull Run. Died after being accidentally wounded. *Sculptor: Bryant Baker, 1957.*

John Paul Jones, 1747–1792. Elected 1925. Captain in Continental Navy during American Revolution. Noted for daring triumphs over the British. *Sculptor: Charles Grafly, 1928.*

Robert Edward Lee, 1807–1870. Elected 1900. General in command of Confederate Armies during Civil War. Led the South's forces at Gettysburg. After the war became president of Washington and Lee University. *Sculptor: George T. Brewster, 1923.*

William Tecumseh Sherman, 1820–1891. Elected 1905. General of Union Army which laid waste to conquered Confederate territory. His army's "march through Georgia" was the precursor of modern strategy to destroy the enemy's will to fight. In 1884, declined to run for president if nominated. *Sculptor: Augustus Saint-Gaudens, replica.*

Walter Reed

PHYSICIANS, SURGEONS

William Crawford Gorgas, 1854–1920. Elected 1950. Physician and sanitary engineer. Wiped out yellow fever in Cuba and Panama Canal Zone by eradicating mosquito carriers of the disease. *Sculptor: Bryant Baker, 1951.*

William Thomas Green Morton, 1819–1868. Elected 1920. Dentist. First to use ether as a general anesthetic in 1846. *Sculptor: Helen Farnsworth Mears, replica.*

Walter Reed, 1851–1902. Elected 1945. U.S. Army physician, surgeon and medical researcher. Discovered that yellow fever was caused by bacteria transmitted through mosquito bite. *Sculptor: Cecil Howard, 1948.*

SCIENTISTS

Robert E. Lee

Louis Agassiz, 1807–1873. Elected 1915. Zoologist, geologist, and science teacher. Advanced the theory of a glacial age in the earth's geologic history. *Sculptor: Anna Hyatt Huntington, 1928.*

John James Audubon, 1785–1851. Elected 1900. Painted America's birds from first-hand observation. His published pictures became world-famous. *Sculptor: A. Stirling Calder, 1927.*

George Washington Carver, c. 1864–1943. Elected 1973. Born in Diamond, Missouri, of slave parents. His early years were spent in poverty and in poor health. Having taken the name of George Carver, his master who freed him, he studied constantly and attended schools wherever possible, graduating from high school in Minneapolis, Kansas. He was rejected from college entrance because of his color and went west to homestead 160 acres where he built a sod house. The unproductive, barren land forced him back to Iowa, where he entered Simpson College from which he transferred to Iowa State. After graduation he was offered an assistant botanist's position specializing in hybridizing fruits. He was the first black to graduate from the college and the first to serve on the faculty. Using the peanut, he created more than 300 products which helped alleviate the food shortage in World War I. He finally received recognition for his work as a botanist and chemurgist. He contributed his life savings to a foundation for research at Tuskegee, where he had become, in 1896, the director of the department of agricultural research. *Sculptor: Richmond Barthé*

Josiah Willard Gibbs, 1839–1903. Elected 1950. Physicist. His theories of thermodynamics and statistical mechanics established foundations of modern fields of physical chemistry and chemical engineering. *Sculptor: Stanley Martineau, 1957.*

Asa Gray, 1810–1888. Elected 1900. Botanist, biologist, and Harvard professor. Early disciple of Darwinism in America. *Sculptor: Chester Beach, 1925.*

Joseph Henry, 1797–1878. Elected 1915. Physicist. Discoverer of induced current. Built first electric motor using electromagnets. First head of Smithsonian Institution. *Sculptor: John Flanagan, 1924.*

Matthew Fontaine Maury, 1806–1873. Elected 1930. Naval officer and oceanographer. Innovated in compilation and publication of navigational charts. *Sculptor: F. William Sievers, 1931.*

Albert Abraham Michelson, 1852–1931. Elected 1970. Experimental physicist who excelled in measurement of light and optics. First American to receive a Nobel Prize in science. *Sculptor: Elisabeth Gordon Chandler, 1973.*

Maria Mitchell, 1818–1889. Elected 1905. Self-taught astronomer and Vassar College professor. Pioneered in education and achieving recognition for women's scientific accomplishments. *Sculptor: Emma F. Brigham, replica.*

Simon Newcomb, 1835–1909. Elected 1935. Astronomer. Calculated planetary orbits and motion of the moon, gaining international esteem. *Sculptor: Frederick Mac Monnies, 1936.*

STATESMEN

John Adams, 1735–1826. Elected 1900. Statesman, lawyer and diplomat. First vice president and second president of the U.S. His resolution in the Continental Congress in May 1776 led the colonies to become independent states. As president, he risked his political future to preserve peace. *Sculptor: John Francis Paramino, 1924.*

John Quincy Adams, 1767–1848. Elected 1905. Statesman and diplomat; sixth president. As secretary of state, influenced drafting of Monroe Doctrine. After a single term as president, he served in Congress as an antislavery crusader, 1831–1848. *Sculptor: Edmond T. Quinn, 1930.*

Henry Clay, 1777–1852. Elected 1900. Statesman. Kentucky congressman, long-time speaker of the House of Representatives. Notable for promoting internal improvements and political compromises affecting slavery. *Sculptor: Robert Aitken, 1929.*

Grover Cleveland, 1837–1908. Elected 1935. Twenty-second and twenty-fourth president. Only president elected for two separate terms. Fought for governmental reform and financial honesty. *Sculptor: Rudulph Evans, 1937.*

Benjamin Franklin

Patrick Henry

John Adams

Alexander Hamilton

James Monroe

Benjamin Franklin, 1706–1790. Elected 1900. Printer, diplomat, scientist, statesman and inventor. His skillful diplomacy assured French support for the American Revolution. Just before his death he urged Congress to end slavery in America. *Sculptor: Robert Aitken, 1927.*

Alexander Hamilton, 1755–1804. Elected 1915. Statesman. First secretary of the treasury. Advocate of strong centralized government; master of finance and taxation. Killed in duel with Aaron Burr. *Sculptor: Giuseppe Ceracchi, replica.*

Patrick Henry, 1736–1799. Elected 1920. Statesman, patriot, orator. As a revolutionary leader, he argued eloquently for independence. Later influenced adoption of the Bill of Rights. *Sculptor: Charles Keck, 1930.*

Andrew Jackson, 1767–1845. Elected 1910. Seventh president. Victorious in Battle of New Orleans, 1815. A strong president, he upheld federal supremacy over the states and democratized officeholding. *Sculptor: Belle Kinney, 1924.*

Thomas Jefferson, 1743–1826. Elected 1900. Third president, author of Declaration of Independence, statesman and philosopher. As president, he made the Louisiana Purchase and dispatched the Lewis and Clark expedition to the Far West. *Sculptor: Robert Aitken, 1924.*

Abraham Lincoln, 1809–1865. Elected 1900. Statesman and lawyer; sixteenth president. Sought to preserve the Union and put an end to slavery. His magnanimity toward the defeated South was cut short by an assassin's bullet. *Sculptor: Augustus Saint-Gaudens, replica.*

James Madison, 1751–1836. Elected 1905. Statesman and lawyer; fourth president. A framer of the Constitution, he later secured adoption of the Bill of Rights. President during the War of 1812. *Sculptor: Charles Keck, 1929.*

James Monroe, 1758–1831. Elected 1930. Fifth president. His two terms called "era of good feelings." The Monroe Doctrine declared the Western Hemisphere closed to further European colonization. *Sculptor: Hermon A. MacNeil, 1931.*

William Penn, 1644–1718. Elected 1935. Religious leader, statesman and founder of Pennsylvania. Upholder of religious freedom and friendly relations with native American Indians. *Sculptor: A. Stirling Calder, 1936.*

Abraham Lincoln

Daniel Webster

Franklin Delano Roosevelt, 1882–1945. Elected 1973. Born in Hyde Park, New York, January 30, 1882, he graduated from Harvard University, studied law at Columbia University Law School, and was admitted to the bar to practice law in 1907. From 1913 to 1920 he was Assistant Secretary of the Navy under President Wilson. A permanently crippling attack of polio at the age of 39 did not deter him from becoming governor of New York in 1928, and in 1933, the thirty-second President, to which office he was elected four times. An inspiring and forceful personality, he revived the economy during the Great Depression, instigated a program of social change called the New Deal, and guided the strategy of winning World War II. He died suddenly at Warm Springs, Georgia, April 12, 1945. *Sculpture not completed.*

Theodore Roosevelt, 1858–1919. Elected 1950. Twenty-sixth president. Favored regulation of big business, conservation of environment, and strong American foreign policy. *Sculptor: Georg Lober, 1954.*

George Washington, 1732–1799. Elected 1900. First president, commander-in-chief of Continental Army in the American Revolution, landowner, agricultural experimenter, and statesman. He assured the establishment of a republic for which the revolution was fought. *Sculptor: Jean-Antoine Houdon, replica.*

Daniel Webster, 1782–1852. Elected 1900. Senator, constitutional lawyer, and secretary of state. Renowned as protector of the Constitution, preserver of the Union and upholder of compromise on slavery. *Sculptor: Robert Aitken, 1926.*

Woodrow Wilson, 1856–1924. Elected 1950. Twenty-eighth president, political scientist, president of Princeton. As president, achieved reforms to regulate business, banking and labor. Led U.S. to join Allied cause in World War I. Founded the League of Nations to preserve peace. *Sculptor: Walker Kirtland Hancock, 1956.*

THEOLOGIANS

Henry Ward Beecher, 1813–1887. Elected 1900. Clergyman, minister of Plymouth Congregational Church, Brooklyn, N.Y. Antislavery, but not abolitionist, before Civil War. Spellbinding preacher. *Sculptor: Massey Rhind, 1923.*

Phillips Brooks, 1835–1893. Elected 1910. Episcopal Bishop of Massachusetts. Renowned preacher at Trinity Church, Boston; distinguished orator. Wrote words to "O Little Town of Bethlehem." *Sculptor: Daniel Chester French, 1924.*

William Ellery Channing, 1780–1842. Elected 1900. Religious leader and theologian. Prominent in establishing Unitarianism. Called for development of distinctive American literature, and influenced literary flowering of New England. *Sculptor: Herbert Adams, 1927.*

Jonathan Edwards, 1703–1758. Elected 1900. Religious leader and theologian. Dynamic figure in the "Great Awakening" religious revival of mid-18th century. *Sculptor: Charles Grafly, 1926.*

Roger Williams, 1603–1683. Elected 1920. Religious leader. Exiled from Massachusetts for his belief in the separation of church and state. Founded Rhode Island Colony, which tolerated different religious groups and ordained a humane policy toward native American Indians. *Sculptor: Hermon A. MacNeil, 1926.*

Roger Williams

The Aviation Hall of Fame in Dayton, Ohio is in the Civic Auditorium where pioneers of aviation along with modern heroes are honored by plaques with portrait sketches by Milton Caniff, a native of Dayton. A feature of the Hall of Fame is a ceramic mural of the first flight by the Wright Brothers which can be seen in the reproduction of this watercolor through the doors of the auditorium.

*The National
Cowboy Hall of Fame and
Western Heritage Museum in
Oklahoma City, Oklahoma
is a very imposing
structure that was opened
in 1965 and has since
then entertained more
than 3,000,000 visitors
who have been thrilled
by the great variety
of displays including
the* END OF THE TRAIL,
*a well-known sculpture by
James Earle Fraser.*

FROM A
WATERCOLOR PAINTING
BY KAY SMITH

Kay Smith

The Hall of Fame of Great Americans, Bronx Community College, New York, formerly New York University, stands on the heights overlooking the Harlem and Hudson Rivers, that were prominent in Revolutionary War History. Designed by Stanford White, celebrated architect of that period (1900) who planned the graceful open-air colonnade 630 feet in length, the portion shown includes busts from left to right:
James Abbott McNeill Whistler, Stephen Collins Foster, Daniel Boone,
Edward Alexander MacDowell, David Glasgow Farragut, John Paul Jones,
Thomas Jonathan "Stonewall" Jackson and John Philip Sousa with
George Peabody in the foreground right.

THE AGRICULTURAL HALL OF FAME AND NATIONAL CENTER

Bonner Springs, Kansas

By R. Roger Harkins

Overlooked by all too many Americans during our recent Bicentennial celebration were the facts that it was "the embattled farmer" who first "fired the shot heard 'round the world" and that the venerable Minute Man, with trusty rifle in his right hand, has his other hand resting upon a plow.

It is really not surprising that this would happen. America has always taken its farmers and ranchers for granted. Indeed, if pressed, most urban children would probably insist that milk comes from the supermarket.

But there is one place where the accomplishments of the indomitable American Farmer have not been forgotten: The Agricultural Hall of Fame and National Center just north of Bonner Springs, Kansas. Dedicated to the marvel of the fast-disappearing American family-farm, the "Ag Hall," as it is known in the Heart of America, offers a nostalgic look at the pioneer accomplishments of that courageous band of farmers who built a nation one furrow at a time.

The American Farmer is the Hope of the World

And those accomplishments are worth memorializing: in 1776, a single American farm worker barely wrung enough from the soil to keep his own family fed; but, 200 years later, he produces enough food and fiber to meet his own needs and those of 60 other persons as well. His efforts are both the envy and the hope of a world, much of which is precariously balanced on the threshold of starvation.

The Hall of Fame lies between two major traffic arteries (Interstate 70 and U.S. Highways 24, 40 and 73) within 100 miles of the old geographical center of the 48 States and 12 miles of downtown Kansas City, Kansas. The 268-acre site is conveniently adjacent to the Wyandotte County Campground, the Wyandotte County Park (containing the county's historical museum, community center and tennis courts) and the Wyandotte County Golf Course.

McCormick's original reaper

—All photographs in this chapter,
courtesy The Agricultural
Hall of Fame and National Center

(Above) Each year the Hall of Fame
stages two live steam threshing shows,
giving its visitors a look at
grain production on the Great Plains
prior to the turn of the century.

The Blacksmith Shop in the basement
of the main building will one day be part
of a rural village.

(At right) Included in the Hall's exhibits
are this sleigh and horse-drawn rural mail coach.
In the background is the Hall's display
of state flowers.

Prime visionary behind the Agricultural Hall of Fame was the late Howard Cowden, founder of the agribusiness giant known today as Farmland Industries. Through Cowden's leadership — and that of many others active in the Co-op Movement, the Bonner Springs site was eventually selected over some 50 other locations that bid for the facility.

With the passage of Public Law 86-680 in 1960, the Congress granted an exclusive charter which describes the Hall as " . . . a non-profit corporation organized for . . . fostering . . . a greater sense of appreciation of the dignity and importance of agriculture, historically carried out through owner-operated farms, and the part it has played in developing those social, economic and spiritual values which are essential in maintaining the free and democratic institutions of our republic; and to maintain and operate a library and museum for the collection and preservation for posterity of agricultural tools, implements, machines, vehicles, pictures, paintings, books, papers, documents, data, relics, mementos, artifacts and other items and things relating to agriculture. Also to honor farmers, farm women, farm leaders, teachers, scientists, inventors, governmental leaders, and other individuals who have helped make this nation great by their outstanding contributions to the establishment, development, advancement or improvement of agriculture in the United States of America."

No Federal Aid

The Hall receives no Federal support. Its funds come from admission charges ($1.50 for adults and 50 cents for children), the sale of souvenirs, tax-deductible donations, the sale of Booster Club memberships ($25 per year) and bequests. Frankly, it has had its financial problems — a not un-

The Hall of Rural Living where nostalgia reigns king.

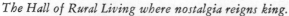

common occurrence among non-profit, educational organizations—but a fair appraisal of its current condition would seem to indicate that it is growing a bit stronger every day.

The first building, containing the administrative offices and the Hall of Rural Living, was opened in 1965. Another building, housing the Hall's comprehensive $1.5 million collection of rare and unique antique farm machinery, was added in 1967. Also included on the site are a one-mile nature trail and farm pond, an 8,000-volume agricultural library, a log-cabin, general store, harness repair shop, blacksmith's shop, veterinarian's office and a complete one-room country school.

Among the exhibits seen by the Hall's 60,000 visitors annually are collections of antique washing machines, china, sewing machines, spinning wheels, hand tools, a glass beehive with real, working, producing bees, rural handicrafts, a complete series of farm implements, a barbed wire collection, a combine with glassed-in sides so that you can see how it works and a quarter-mile model steam railroad that offers free rides to children on special events days. Those events include well-attended live steam threshing shows held each July and September and horse and tractor pulling contests.

Electing Hall of Fame Members

Members are elected to the Hall of Fame by a vote of the nationwide 170-member Board of Governors. A unique feature of the election process is that anyone may submit a name in nomination, provided that the agricultural contributor has been deceased for at least 10 years and never convicted of any crime involving moral turpitude. Prior to March 1 of each year, those suggested are screened by a Committee on Nominations. Candidates receiving a favorable vote of the majority of the committee members, together with all unsuccessful nominees from the previous year, are then submitted to a special 50-member Board of Elections chosen by the Board of Governors.

Ballots are returned by August 10 of each year and those elected are enshrined at the next following annual meeting of the Board of Governors, usually held in February or March.

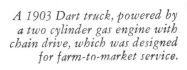

A 1903 Dart truck, powered by a two cylinder gas engine with chain drive, which was designed for farm-to-market service.

George Washington

orge Washington Carver

Cyrus Hall McCormick

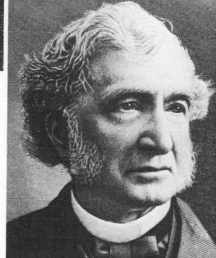

Justin Smith Morrill

Members of the Hall of Fame

The first election, held in 1963, enshrined five men whose contributions to American agriculture border on the legendary:

GEORGE WASHINGTON CARVER(1864–1943), the son of slave parents who changed the face of Southern agriculture through shifting its emphasis from cotton to peanuts and sweet potatoes and developing a variety of new products that could be produced from these commonplace crops. Working from his humble laboratory at Tuskegee Institute in Alabama, Carver attracted worldwide attention with his dedication to mankind. In the words of President Franklin Delano Roosevelt, his life "will for all time afford an inspiring example to youth everywhere."

GEORGE WASHINGTON (1732–1799), who is so well known for his military leadership and statesmanship that his primary agricultural accomplishment—that of demonstrating that American Farmers could be independent from traditional English markets—often has been overlooked. A successful farmer (7,000 bushels of wheat and 10,000 bushels of corn in 1770), Washington practiced crop rotation, diversified farming, tested manures, improved varieties of crops, developed conservation practices to reduce soil erosion, experimented with the breeding of horses and cattle and was responsible for the introduction of the use of mules to U.S. agriculture.

THOMAS JEFFERSON(1743–1826), the father of scientific agriculture in America. He invented a seed drill, a hemp brake, a threshing machine and the moldboard plow. Jefferson was one of the first to import Merino sheep to improve the American breed and worked out a rotation cycle for wheat, corn, peas, potatoes and clover that maintained the fertility of the land. He experimented with various types of fertilizers and promoted agricultural education throughout his life.

CYRUS HALL McCORMICK(1809–1884), inventor of the reaper, the single most important agricultural advancement of its era (one of the Hall of Fame's most prized exhibits is an original McCormick reaper, one of the few left in the world). McCormick was the first of the large-scale implement manufacturers and his business practices revolutionized agriculture.

JUSTIN SMITH MORRILL (1810–1898), the Vermont congressman known as "The Father of the Land-Grant Colleges," for his tireless work in both the U.S. House of Representatives and Senate resulting in the granting of public lands for the support of national agricultural schools.

Thomas Jefferson

357

The Kickapoo Indian Tribe stages a rain dance during a steam threshing show.

Horse pulling contests are among the special events staged by the Hall each year.

Since the initial election, three more persons have had their names engraved on the roll of honor as a part of the nation's Bicentennial celebration:

ELI WHITNEY (1765–1825), best known for his invention of the cotton gin, which enabled one man to clean the seeds from as much cotton in a single day as he formerly cleaned by hand in an entire winter. His machine increased U.S. cotton exports from 189,500 pounds in 1791 to 41 million pounds in 1803. In 1798, Whitney may have made an equally great contribution, establishing the principle of interchangeable parts—a forerunner of mass production—in firearms manufacture.

CONGRESSMAN DUDLEY M. HUGHES (1848–1927) and **SENATOR HOKE SMITH** (1855–1931), co-sponsors of the 1914 Smith-Hughes Act, which established vocational education—and particularly vocational agriculture—in the nation's high schools.

The Hall of Fame is open from 9 a.m. to 5 p.m. 362 days each year (exceptions are Thanksgiving, Christmas and New Year's Days).

Plans for expansion include a Memorial Hall of Honors, a Museum of Science and Technology and a Learning Center complete with a multimedia hemisphere.

Rural Values Represent the American Spirit

The most significant aspect of the Hall of Fame is sometimes not immediately evident to the casual visitor. Inextricably intertwined with all of its aging machinery and artifacts is a sense of those rural values which have pervaded the American Spirit from the beginning. There are no signs calling attention to them, but they are there nonetheless. By looking carefully, one can almost see the calloused hand that once guided the now rusted plow and feel the presence of that legion of faceless farmers who have defied—and continue to defy—the logic of capitalism by buying at retail and selling at wholesale.

Eli Whitney

Senator Hoke Smith

Congressman Dudley Hughes

359

THE AMERICAN INDIAN HALL OF FAME

Anadarko, Oklahoma

The American Indian has made an indelible imprint on our national character and culture. History is replete with names and deeds of hundreds of outstanding personalities and doubtless many more have gone unrecorded. All have contributed inestimably to the development of the social, economic, political and cultural well-being of the United States.

Indian woods and water lore, arts and handicraft are basic in the programs of all American patriotism-building youth groups. Outdoor enthusiasts, young and old, rely on Indian folkways for guidance.

Indian tactics in battlefield maneuvering were adopted early in America by our military strategists.

Indian language, meaningful and melodious, has enriched America's vocabulary with such names as Oklahoma, Alabama, Missouri, Mississippi, Suwannee, Chattanooga, Utah and many, many more.

A few American Indians have been honored by statuary and other memorials in the United States, including statues of Sequoyah, inventor of the Cherokee alphabet and contributor to the science of written language; Sacajawea, Shoshoni Indian woman leader of the Lewis and Clark Expedition to the Pacific Coast in 1804 - 6, thereby opening America's "Empire of the Golden West."

The Hall of Fame, located just east of the Southern Plains Indian Museum and Crafts Center on U.S. 62, was founded by the late Logan Billingsley of Katonah, N.Y., who thought of the idea while employed with the Indian service in Anadarko before Oklahoma statehood.

In 1953, a senate joint resolution was passed and signed by Governor Murray to set aside a 10-acre tract at Anadarko for the purpose of commemorating the contributions made by American Indians to their people and to the development of the American way of life.

Chiefs, Warriors, Educators, Athletes and Even a Vice President

The first statue to be dedicated in the Indian Hall of Fame was that of Black Beaver in 1954. Black Beaver was a Delaware Indian scout and

Sacajawea (Shoshoni)
—Sculptor: Leonard McMurry

—All photographs in this chapter, courtesy American Indian Hall of Fame

guide who served in the wagon train of gold seekers that blazed the path to California in 1849. Keating Donaho was the sculptor for the first statue.

Chief Joseph of the Nez Percé was next to be honored in 1957. Kenneth F. Campbell sculpted the bust of the Indian chief who displayed remarkable generalship in the war following the cession of tribal lands in the Treaty of 1863 but who was forced at last to surrender. He and his reduced band of 431 were then removed to Indian Territory and it was not until 1885 that they were allowed to return west.

In 1958, busts of Allen Wright and Osceola were added.

The Wright bronze was dedicated along with that of Black Beaver in the State Capitol at Oklahoma City. Wright, a Choctaw, was a minister, educator, translator and stateman, who originally suggested the name "Oklahoma" for the state.

Osceola was the Seminole war leader who resisted removal from Florida to the territory west of the Mississippi.

Campbell was the sculptor for the bust of Wright and Madeleine Park did the one of Osceola.

In the years that followed others were inducted into the Hall of Fame and their accomplishments are set forth in the biographies which incidentally include the date of induction.

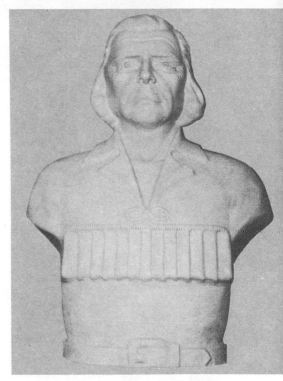
Black Beaver (Delaware)
—Sculptor: Keating Donahue

HALL OF FAME *In order of enshrinement*

BLACK BEAVER (Delaware)—Se-ket-Tu-Ma-Quah, renowned Delaware Indian scout and guide of many U.S. government exploring expeditions throughout the Southwest, made seven treks over different routes to the Pacific Coast. He was a guide with the military escort under the command of Captain R. B. Marcy that accompanied the famous wagon train of gold seekers to the California gold fields in 1849, charting the long used "California Road" west from Fort Smith, Arkansas. Black Beaver, born in 1806 on the site of Belleville, Illinois, came southwest as a young man, his band of Delaware living as neighbors to the Absentee Shawnee near the Oklahoma-Arkansas boundary. He was interpreter to Colonel Henry Dodge on the noted Leavenworth (or Dragoon) Expedition from Fort Gibson to the Wichita village on Red River in 1834, for the first council between the United States and the Plains Indians in Oklahoma. Delaware place names and old Indian village sites including old Camp Arbuckle—all south of the Canadian River in Oklahoma—are places where Black Beaver's band lived at different times before the Civil War. He and members of his band went to Kansas, and served as scouts in the Union Army during the War. He returned to the Washita River near Anadarko where he opened up a fine farm after the War. He became a preacher in the Baptist Church, and was counted as a leader among the Indians of the Wichita Agency until his death on May 8, 1880. Black Beaver's grave is in a government plot near his old home place west of Anadarko. (Inducted 1954)

CHIEF JOSEPH (Nez Percé)—Hinmaton-yalakit was an intrepid warrior and leader of the Nez Percé of Southwestern Oregon. In the war following the cession of their tribal lands in the Treaty of 1863 Chief Joseph, leading his small band in a 1,000-mile retreat, displayed such generalship as to inspire one historian to describe it as "worthy to be remembered with that of Xenophon's Ten Thousand." Chief Joseph was forced to surrender, and under military escort he and his band reduced to 431 were taken to Indian Territory.

Chief Joseph (Nez Percé)
—Sculptor: Kenneth F. Campbell

Allen Wright (Choctaw)
—Sculptor: Kenneth F. Campbell

Osceola (Seminole)
—Sculptor: Madeleine Park

*Charles Curtis
(Kaw)*
—Sculptor:
Madeleine Park

Eventually (1885), the Nez Percé were permitted to return to their beloved West, locating in the Colville Reservation in Washington, where Chief Joseph died in 1904. The Nez Percé are now located in Idaho. (Inducted 1957)

ALLEN WRIGHT (Choctaw)—Kiliahote, "Come, let's go and make a light." Principal Chief of the Choctaw Nation, 1866–1870. As minister of the Gospel, educator, translator and statesman, he was a great leader in the advancement of his people and the development of Oklahoma. One of the first Choctaw boys sent to an eastern college (1848), he graudated from Union College, Schenectady, N.Y. (1852), and from Union Theological Seminary, New York City (1855), the first Indian from the Indian Territory awarded the M.A. degree. He served his nation in many capacities and was a delegate in the making of the Choctaw-Chickasaw Treaty of 1866 at Washington after the Civil War, when he suggested the name "Oklahoma" for the proposed organization of the Indian Territory. He died on December 2, 1885, and was buried in the cemetery at Old Boggy Depot in Atoka County, Choctaw Nation, Indian Territory. (Inducted 1958)

OSCEOLA (Seminole)—Asi-Yahola was born in the Old Creek Country in the Chattahoochee River region about 1804. When a small child, his widowed mother brought him to Florida in company with a friendly band of the Lower Creeks to live among the Seminole that evenutally settled near Silver Springs, Florida. The United States Government wrote and signed the Treaty of Payne's Landing which would remove the Seminole to the territory west of the Mississippi. With Osceola as their warleader, the Seminoles began their resistance to removal. After an heroic stand against superior U.S. forces, Osceola agreed to a parley near Ft. Marion where General Jessup seized Osceola and the other chiefs, including "Wild Cat" who bore "a white plume and pipe." The Seminole leaders were transferred to Fort Moultrie, Charlestown, South Carolina. Catlin, the famous artist, painted a portrait of Osceola shortly before the Indian leader's death on January 30, 1838. (Inducted 1958)

CHARLES CURTIS (Kaw)—A member of the Kaw or Kansas Tribe, he received his allotment of land in the Kaw Reservation in Oklahoma. Attorney, statesman, diplomat, leader in 19th century Indian affairs, longtime Congressman and Senator from Kansas, Curtis was the first man of Indian descent to be elected Vice President of the United States. He was the running-mate of President Herbert Hoover in the campaign of 1928.

Following the creation of the Dawes Commission, a resultant of the opening of "the Oklahoma Country" in 1889 to white settlement, Curtis fathered the famous "Curtis Act" (finally approved June 28, 1898) which made sweeping changes in the affairs of the Five Civilized Tribes, substituting Federal courts for Indian courts, enrollment of Indian citizens by the Dawes Commission, and allotment of lands and many other provisions for the final closing of Indian governments.

Curtis was one of the most outstanding floor leaders of the United States Senate in history and had given more than 40 years devoted service to his government and to the Indian peoples when death came to him February 8, 1936, in Washington, D.C. (Inducted 1959)

QUANAH PARKER (Comanche)—Born on the Great Plains about 1845, son of Peta Noconi, Chief of the Quahadi band of Comanche, and his white wife, Cynthia Ann Parker. Quanah's name is from a Comanche word Kwania meaning "fragant." His mother had been captured by the Comanches in an attack on Parker's Fort, Texas, in 1835. She was reared by the Comanches, and many years later she was re-captured by some Texas troops in battle with the Quahadi, and taken to her white relatives in Texas where she pined for her Indian family and died a few years later in the 1860s. Quanah was living on the Kiowa, Comanche and Kiowa-Apache Reservation near Fort Sill when he visited his mother's family in Texas, and from that time bore her family name Parker.

Quanah took part in the Indian war on the Plains in the early 1870s as chief of the hostile Quahadi that finally surrendered in 1876 to Gen. R. M. McKenzie, and settled with the Kiowa and the Kiowa-Apache on their new reservation in what is now southwestern Oklahoma. Quanah was one of the most influential and prominent leaders of three confederated tribes on the Kiowa-Comanche Reservation for many years, and encouraged them in stock-raising and farming. He died on February 23, 1911. The remains of him and his mother, Cynthia Ann Parker, were taken from their original burial places, and re-interred in the Fort Sill Cemetery in 1957, where handsome stone monuments mark their graves. (Inducted 1959)

SACAJAWEA (Shoshoni)—Of the Shoshoni tribe that lived near the head-waters of the Missouri River, in the mountains of Western Montana, she is famous for her services as guide and interpreter for the Lewis and Clark Expedition to the Pacific in 1805–06, that charted the first pathway for the Americans in the Louisiana Purchase.

In April, 1805, Captains Lewis and Clark with a guard of U.S. soldiers set out west from St. Louis on the Expedition west, accompanied by the French trapper, Charbonneau with his young wife, Sacajawea and their infant son, Baptiste. She proved the dependable guide, and won the high regard of all on the Expedition for her bravery and resourcefulness in many difficult and dangerous places along the way to the Pacific Coast.

Several years after the return of the Expedition, Sacajawea left her home in St. Louis to return to her people far west. On her way, she met a band of Comanches (a tribe related to the Shoshoni), remaining with them on the western prairies of Oklahoma. When her Comanche husband died, she went back to her people on the headwaters of the Missouri River in the Northwest.

Sacajawea was one hundred years old when she died on April 9, 1884. Her grave is marked near the Shoshoni Agency on the Wind River Reservation in Wyoming.

Some time after the Expedition to the Pacific, Sacajawea was awarded a special medal by the United States for her great service to the American people. Many art works have memorialized her as one of the greatest American Indians. (Inducted 1959)

JIM THORPE (Sac and Fox)—Wa-tho-buck—"Bright Path" of the Sac and Fox tribe (also, part Potawatomi) is famous in history as the World's greatest athlete. He entered Carlisle Indian School in Pennsylvania in 1904, at the age of fifteen, and became noted on Carlisle's field of sports both as a star football player and all-around athlete. Jim stood 6 feet and 1 inch in height and weighed 188 pounds in his prime.

When the World's Olympic Games were held in Sweden in 1912, Jim was a member of the Olympic team from the United States, for he had won a place on the team during the American tryouts at New York in the spring. During the Games at Stockholm in July, Jim Thorpe won first in the Pentathlon—a 200-meter dash, running broad jump, throwing the discus, throwing the javelin and the 1,500-meter run. Next, in one afternoon Jim was winner of the Decathlon, a series of ten contests: 100-meter dash, running broad jump, 110-meter hurdle race, putting the 16-pound shot, 400-meter dash, running high jump, throwing the javelin, throwing the discus, pole vault, 1,500-meter run. Scoring in these ten events was by allowing 1,000 points for each performance, Jim scoring 8,413.95 points out of a possible 10,000 points, his nearest competitor scoring 7,742.49 points. Jim Thorpe's smooth, even development demonstrated by his marvelous performances had won the highest honors in the Olympic Games of 1912. The King of Sweden handed Thorpe the fine trophies as winner of the Decathlon and Pentathlon at the Olympic Games saying, "You sir, are the greatest athlete in the world."

Jim Thorpe, the World's great athlete, died at Los Angeles, California, March 28, 1953, at the age of 64 years. His grave has been enshrined near his old Carlisle school in Pennsylvania. (Inducted 1960)

Quanah Parker (Comanche)
—Sculptor: Jack Hill

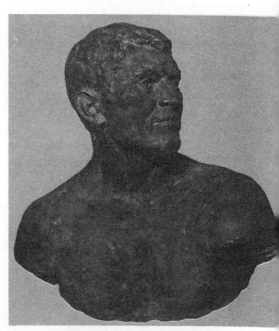

Jim Thorpe (Sac and Fox)
—Sculptor: Leonard McMurry

Pontiac (Chief of the Ottawa)
—Sculptor: Pietro Montana

PONTIAC (Chief of the Ottawa)—Born near Fort Defiance in the Maumee River country of present Ohio, around 1716–1726, he became the chief and leader of the confederated tribes of the Ottawa, Potawatomi and Ojibwa, with great influence among all the tribes throughout the Mississippi Valley. He was slightly over six feet tall, of heavy stature and with well shaped features. He had many noble qualities of character—great power and virtues of mind, a strong intellect and commanding energy. He was sometimes crafty, subtle and high tempered in his dealings with others yet there was the humanitarian about him that made him capable of magnanimous acts. He was honored and revered by the Indian people for these traits.

He led the Indian forces on the side of the French in the battle that saw the English victory in the fall of Quebec. French trading posts were soon in the hands of the English, the Indians finding themselves treated with contempt and neglect. The tribes resented these ways and suffered from want and deprivation of articles for which they had traded in nearly 150 years of friendship with the French.

Pontiac now rose as the Indian leader whose great genius as an organizer roused the tribes from the St. Lawrence River to the Gulf of Mexico, in a war against the English with the avowed purpose of saving this country for the Indian people. All the British posts were attacked suddenly on the same day by the tribes living in the vicinity of each. Only Fort Pitt and Detroit put up a defense that forced the Indians to raise the siege of battle. Pontiac's plans were finally crushed, and he was forced to sign a treaty with the English in 1765. He still held himself with dignity remembering the long friendship with the French.

Pontiac was assassinated in 1769—some say through an English plot against him, and others say through jealous partisanship of an Indian tribesman. Pontiac was buried where now stands the City of St. Louis, Missouri. (Inducted 1961)

SEQUOYAH (Cherokee)—Famous in history as the inventor of the alphabet for his people, the Cherokee, a contribution in letters made by no other single individual in the history of mankind. Born in the mountain country of now Eastern Tennessee about 1764, Sequoyah had no formal education, knew no English and spoke only his native Cherokee tongue. Yet in twelve years he completed at his home (then in Alabama) his great work on the Cherokee alphabet, bringing his people the gift of the written word.

A skilled silversmith in his earlier years, his English name "George Guess" (or "Gist") was the trademark of excellent workmanship.

He moved to Arkansas where he was a recognized leader of the Western Cherokees, and in 1828 signed the Treaty that gave present Northeastern Oklahoma to the Cherokee Nation. His log cabin home near Sallisaw, in Sequoyah County, is enclosed in a stone building that stands as one of Oklahoma's historic shrines. His burial place is unknown, somewhere in Northern Mexico where he died about 1843 while in search of a lost band of Cherokees. (Inducted 1962)

Little Raven (Arapaho)
—Sculptor: John Learned

LITTLE RAVEN (Arapaho)—Hosa, Chief of the Southern Arapaho was born about 1817 in the Platte River region where later a vast tract was assigned the Arapaho and their kindred tribe, the Cheyenne, by the United States in 1851. Parts of the two tribes moved south toward Bent's Fort on the Arkansas where they became known as the Southern Arapaho and Southern Cheyenne. Little Raven and their other chiefs signed a treaty with the Federal government in 1861, reducing their lands to a smaller reservation in Southeastern Colorado, with promises of implements, mills, livestock and schools for the development of their people. Chief Little Raven was pleased with these prospects for the Arapaho advocated agricultural living in the old traditional ways before they had secured horses (1750) and become buffalo hunters on the plains.

The Sioux and other Plains tribes arose in war on the frontier during the American Civil War yet Little Raven stood for peace with the United States. He was brave in defense of his Indian allies, a great orator and wise in counsel with U.S. Army officers. (Inducted 1962)

CHIEF TISHOMINGO (Chickasaw) — Born about 1737 in the old Chickasaw country, present Northeastern Mississippi, where the Chickasaws had been aligned with the earliest English trading interests and had been involved in the Indian wars on this Mississippi colonial frontier.

Tishomingo was noted as a great warrior with the victorious Chickasaws in their last war with the Cherokees about 1769. He was again with his victorious tribesmen in a war with the Creeks in 1793–95.

For his bravery, his strong character and good sense, he was esteemed by his people, and chosen as their tribal Tishomingo, "Assistant Chief," a title given a great leader who served ("Minco" or "mingo" — called "king" by the English) under the old, tribal form of government.

Chief Tishomingo (Chickasaw)
—Sculptor: Leonard McMurry

About 1815, though Tishomingo was opposed to the innovation, the Chickasaw country was divided into four districts by U.S. Indian Agent, to facilitate the payment of the tribal annuities. Tishomingo became chief of one of these districts, and was a signer of the treaties with the United States from this time. He was the real leader of the Chickasaws, in old tribal ways. He signed the Treaty of Pontotoc in 1832, providing for the sale of the Chickasaw country in Mississippi for cash so when the Chickasaws moved west a few years later they were the wealthiest of any of the Five Civilized Tribes. This treaty states that the Chickasaws felt grateful to their old chiefs for long attending to the business of the Nation, and especially requests their "beloved chief Tishomingo, who is now grown old and is poor," to receive a pension from them for the rest of his life "as a token of their kind feelings for him, on account of his long and valuable services." Chief Tishomingo was over 100 years old when he died on the road west to the Indian Territory. It is said that he was buried near Little Rock, Arkansas, in 1838. (Inducted 1963)

ALICE BROWN DAVIS (Seminole) — Chieftain of the Seminoles in Oklahoma, the only woman appointed to this position was an outstanding leader in education and Christian culture among her people in the history of this country. She was born near Park Hill, Cherokee Nation, on September 10, 1852, daughter of Dr. John Frippo Brown, a graduate of medicine in Scotland who was in U.S. government service when the Seminoles moved west from Florida, and his wife Lucy (Redbeard) Brown, member of the tribal clan of Seminole chiefs. Alice's first schooling was among the Cherokees. After the Civil War when all the Seminoles settled in their own nation (present Seminole County, Oklahoma), she attended the Presbyterian Mission school near present Wewoka. She served as a teacher before her marriage in 1874 to George R. Davis, a native of Indiana. They lived on a ranch near Arbeka post office in the Seminole Nation where they had a trading store. Mrs. Davis was left on her own resources when the youngest of her eleven children was three years old. Small in stature, capable and dignified, she managed the ranch, the store and post office at Arbeka, at the same time caring for and educating her children. (Inducted 1964)

Alice Brown Davis (Seminole)
—Sculptor: Willard Stone

POCAHONTAS (Powhatan) — Also called Mataoka, both names signifying *playful* or *amusing* in the Algonquian languages, was born in 1595 near the James River in Virginia, the "dearest" daughter of Powhatan, Chief of a confederation of Indian Tribes. She saved the life of Captain John Smith of Jamestown from death at the hands of Powhatan's warriors when she was only twelve years old. Her act of mercy at once made her important in the contest for power between Powhatan's tribes and the Jamestown colonists. Pocahontas herself at the head of a band of Indian warriors, or with a group of Indian girls took food to the starving colonists on several occasions.

The colonists later (1613) fearing Indian war abducted Pocahontas and held her as a hostage in Jamestown. She, however, made friends with the women

Sequoyah (Cherokee)
—Sculptor: Leonard McMurry

Pocahontas (Powhatan)
—Sculptor: Kenneth F. Campbell

Will Rogers (Cherokee)
—Sculptor: Electra Waggnor

Maj. Gen. Clarence Leonard Tinker (Osage)
—Sculptor: Leonard McMurry

there, showed them how to prepare the foods found in this country and helped nurse the sick. She was treated with kindness and became a Christian convert. John Rolf, an "honest and discrete" young colonist, asked Gov. Thomas Dale permission to marry Pocahontas. Their wedding was held with fine ceremony at the Parish Church in April, 1614. They made their home near Henrico where Rolf with Indian aid improved the growing of tobacco and learned how to cure the leaf for overseas shipping. He promoted the tobacco trade in England that soon flourished, thereby establishing the economic life of the Virginia colonists.

The Rolfs with their little son, Thomas and a party of Indian relatives visited England in 1616. Pocahontas gracious and dignified was entertained by royalty and everywhere acclaimed with honor. When the Rolfs were about to sail for home in America, Pocahontas died at the age of twenty-two, and was buried at Gravesend, England, March 21, 1617, in the chancel of St. George's Church. Her son, Thomas Rolf, educated in England, was later prominent and successful in Virginia. Generations of many old Virginia families trace their Indian ancestry to Pocahontas whose life was truly significant in the making of America. (Inducted 1965)

WILL ROGERS (Cherokee)—Of Cherokee descent, born November 4, 1879, on the family ranch near Oolagah, Indian Territory. He was the son of Clem V. Rogers, a successful business man, and his charming wife, Mary (Schrimsher) Rogers. Will finally attended Kemper Military Academy in Missouri where a two-year stay completed his formal education. Shown how to hold a lariat in his hands before he was five years old, he kept on playing with his rope through the years and learned to do fantastic tricks with it. He won the first prize in a roping contest (1899) at Claremore, the place he always called "home."

He rode his favorite horse over the country looking for work as a cowboy. Next, he set out for "big ranching business" in Argentina. Soon penniless and starving, he left South America with a job on a cattle boat shipping to South Africa.

Texas Jack's Wild West Show playing in Johannesburg offered him his first job in the show business (1902), and he was instantly a big hit as "The Cherokee Kid" in his rope act. His jokes about himself and others of the show as he twirled the rope with fast thinking and acting got a big laugh from his audience. He traveled far and wide in vaudeville. He had the leading part in stage shows and many motion pictures. It was in his act with Ziegfield's Follies (New York) in World War I that he began slanting quips on celebrities in his audience. (Inducted 1965)

MAJ. GEN. CLARENCE LEONARD TINKER (Osage)—Born on November 21, 1887, in the Osage country of Indian Territory, Clarence L. Tinker was part Osage Indian. He worked as a boy in his father's printing shop of the Osage News, an early day newspaper in Pawhuska. The boy learned the Osage language, something he never forgot throughout his long military career. Young Tinker began his Army career after his graduation from Wentworth Military Academy, Lexington, Missouri. He was sent (1908) to the Philippines Constabulary as Second Lieutenant, and there served four years before transferring to the regular U.S. Army. After World War I, he was captain and professor of military science at the Polytechnical high school and junior college at Riverside, California.

Tinker graduated from flying school, and was awarded the Soldier's Medal in 1921, for having demonstrated his daring and unselfishness in a flight over England when his plane crashed and caught fire. He pulled out his passenger, an American Naval officer, from the blazing wreckage. Early in 1942, he was appointed commander of the U.S. Air Forces in Hawaii, and promoted from brigadier to major general.

In the Battle for Midway on June 7, 1942, Major General Tinker was the pre-dawn flight leader in the perilous attack on the Japanese naval units in retreat toward Wake Island in the Pacific Ocean. His plane went out of control and dived out of formation into the sea. Major General Tinker (age 54) and his eight crewmen perished. (Inducted 1966)

ROBERTA CAMPBELL LAWSON (Delaware)—A granddaughter of Reverend Charles Journeycake, last chief of the Delaware tribe, was born October 31, 1878, in the family home at Alluwe in the Indian Territory. The story of the Delaware, or Leni-Lenape, is a part of the history of ten different states as the tribe moved west through a period of 200 years from Delaware and Pennsylvania, finally to settle in Oklahoma by Treaty with the Cherokee in 1867. Members of the Delaware tribe were prominent in the founding and development of the City of Bartlesville, Oklahoma. (Inducted 1968)

Roberta Campbell Lawson (Delaware)
—Sculptor: Leonard McMurry

JOSE MARIA (Anadarko)—"The brave José Maria is chief of the An-a-da-cos, and principal chief of the Associated bands of the Caddos, An-a-da-cos and Ionies, frequently designated by the general term of Caddos" are words of a testimonial signed by U.S. Indian Agent, Jesse Stem for the Indians of Texas in March, 1852. Known as Iesh among his people, the Anadarko chief was born in 1805, near the Sabine River in East Texas, where visiting Catholic missionaries christened him "Jose' Maria." He and other Associated Caddo chiefs living in Louisiana in 1835, signed a treaty providing that all these tribes should move away from U.S. Territory. The chiefs led their people west to the Trinity and Brazos rivers in the Republic of Texas, for many years a dark battleground. For his courage and honesty, Jose' Maria attained his place as chief of all the Associated Caddo bands and became a firm and loyal friend of many white families. He was among the signers of a treaty with the Texans in 1843 at Bird's Fort, Texas, promoted by Governor Sam Houston who spoke in defense of the Indians. Three years later, Jose' Maria was in Washington in behalf of the Caddo bands when he was presented another testimonial testifying his peace and friendship signed by President James K. Polk. Under the supervision of the U.S. Indian Agent in 1854, the Anadarko and Associated bands were assigned a reservation on the Brazos River in the State of Texas. Under the leadership of Jose' Maria, the tribes on the Brazos were soon prospering. They lived in good homes, sent their children to the reservation school, cultivated their farms and raised herds of fine horses for which the Caddo tribe had long been noted. Attacks on the Indians near the borders of the Brazos Reserve caused alarm. After counsel with the U.S. Indian Agent and U.S. army officers, the Caddos came north from the Brazos location to the Washita River in the Indian Territory. The site where the Caddo first encamped is now the City of Anadarko, Oklahoma, so named for the peace and friendship promoted by the great Chief Jose' Maria. At the outbreak of the Civil War, his name appeared on a treaty of friendship with the Confederate States. Jose' Maria died about 1862, during the Civil War. (Inducted 1969)

Jose' Maria (Anadarko)
—Sculptor: Leonard McMurry

HIAWATHA (Ojibway)—The long narrative poem by Henry Wadsworth Longfellow, first published on November 10, 1855 was based upon the adventures of Manabozho first reported by Henry Rowe Schoolcraft, American explorer, geologist and writer. Hiawatha, an Ojibway Indian reared by his grandmother, Nokomis, daughter of the Moon, became the leader of his people, married Minnehaha, and taught peace with the white man. (Inducted 1976)

The following Indians will be honored in the future as funds become available:

TECUMSEH	(Shawnee)	**JOHN ROSS**	(Cherokee)
PUSHMATAHA	(Choctaw)	**STAND WATIE**	(Cherokee)
MASSASSOIT	(Wampanoag)	**GERONIMO**	(Apache)
KEOKUK	(Sac and Fox)		

Hiawatha (Ojibway)
—Sculptor: Kenneth F. Campbell

THE AVIATION HALL OF FAME

Dayton, Ohio

In 1962, through the untiring efforts of several civic and aviation-minded members of the Aviation Committee of the Dayton Area Chamber of Commerce, the Aviation Hall of Fame was established. On July 14, 1964, Public Law 88-372 of the 88th Congress granted the Aviation Hall of Fame a Federal Charter, as a nationally recognized non-profit public foundation.

The objectives are to honor scientists, inventors, pilots, engineers and other individuals who have helped make this Nation great in the field of aviation; to perpetuate the memory of such persons and record their achievements and contributions by suitable memorials; to establish and maintain a library and display preserving for posterity the history of those honored by the Aviation Hall of Fame.

Organization

The affairs of the Aviation Hall of Fame are managed by a Board of Trustees comprised of thirty-six (36) members.

Membership

General membership is a membership open to persons of good character with a sincere interest in aviation, upon payment of annual dues as determined by the Board of Trustees. Organizational membership is a membership entered in the name of a company, corporation or any other legally designated group which has expressed an interest in the Aviation Hall of Fame program and aims of the organization, upon payment of annual dues as determined by the Board of Trustees. Such company, corporation, etc., shall designate one individual as a representative to exercise all rights of such company, corporation, etc.

Board of Nominations

Members of the Board of Nominations are elected by the Board of Trustees. The Board consists of persons who are members of the Aviation Hall of Fame. The Board of Nominations nominates those citizens or res-

—All photographs and portraits in this chapter, courtesy Aviation Hall of Fame

The "First Flight" mural, located in the Dayton Convention and Exhibition Center, depicts the historic achievements of Orville and Wilbur Wright at Kitty Hawk, North Carolina on December 17, 1903. On that day, these two brothers from Dayton, Ohio, liberated man forever from the limitations of the land and sea. This mural created from an intricate pattern of more than 163,000 ceramic tiles each portraying an aspect of the Wright Brothers accomplishment faces the entrance to the Hall of Fame.

idents of the United States who have contributed in an outstanding manner to aviation. Selections are made by secret mail ballot when authorized by the Board of Trustees. Each year, the Aviation Hall of Fame honors recipients of its Awards in absentia, in person, or posthumously at Enshrinement Ceremonies. No person is honored for achievement attained less than five (5) years prior to election to the Aviation Hall of Fame enshrinement.

Type of Award

A plaque with a statement of the recipient's accomplishments is the Award. This plaque is hung in the Aviation Hall of Fame. In addition, the recipient's portrait, created by world-famous Milton Caniff, is also hung in the Aviation Hall of Fame.

Physical Facilities

The Aviation Hall of Fame is presently housed in the Dayton Convention and Exhibition Center, Dayton, Ohio 45402 which was opened in January of 1973. Dominating the entrance hall of this beautiful and spacious building, is a 60' x 20' mosaic mural, sponsored by the Aviation Hall of Fame. The mural, which was begun in 1970, is a unique blend of fine art, photographic analysis, computer technology and a new printing technique, in which 163,000 one-inch square tiles were used to reproduce a photo of the historic first flight on December 17, 1903. Titled "The First Flight," the mosaic was created by nationally known designer Read Viemeister of Yellow Springs, Ohio, and its cost of $100,000 was made possible by the Rike Family Foundation of Dayton, Ohio. A display of the plaques of the aviation pioneers who have been enshrined is located on the third floor of the Convention Center, together with the Administrative Office of the organization.

Award Schedule

To provide for orderly progressive recognition of those citizens or residents who have made outstanding contributions to aviation in the past, an award schedule was established and used.

Selection Period

The schedule is now current and selections are made five (5) or more years after the achievement.

THE ROSTER OF ENSHRINEES

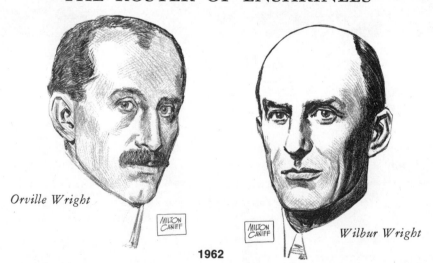

Orville Wright

Wilbur Wright

1962

ORVILLE WRIGHT for oustanding contribution to aviation by the co-invention of the first successful man carrying airplane

WILBUR WRIGHT for outstanding contribution to aviation by the co-invention of the first successful man carrying airplane

1963

OCTAVE CHANUTE for outstanding contributions to aviation through his compilation of the aeronautical accomplishments of the pioneers of flight, his demonstration of successful man carrying gliders, and his valuable counsel to others engaged in flight research

BENJAMIN DELAHUF FOULOIS for outstanding contributions to aviation by his dedicated advancement of military aviation, his vision of the need for improved long range military aircraft, and his inspirational leadership of the Army Air Corps

FRANK PURDY LAHM for outstanding contributions to aviation by his vision of the potential of aircraft for military purposes and his dedication to the task of organizing proper training facilities for the Army Air Corps

SAMUEL PIERPONT LANGLEY for outstanding contributions to aviation through his studies of air and space, his demonstrations of the practicability of mechanical flights and his inspirational guidance to others

1964

THOMAS SCOTT BALDWIN for outstanding contributions to aviation by early pioneering in balloons, by basically improving parachutes, by developing and demonstrating successful dirigibles, by improving airplanes and by instructing others in flight

GLENN HAMMOND CURTISS for outstanding contributions to aviation by developing lightweight engines, by improving airplanes and control systems, and by creating basic new forms of airplanes

THEODORE GORDON ELLYSON for outstanding contributions to aviation by dedicated pioneering and advancement of naval aviation, and by eminence as the first naval aviator

JOHN JOSEPH MONTGOMERY for outstanding contributions to aviation by research into the nature of the laws of flight, by building and testing a series of early gliders with flight control systems, and by bringing widespread attention to aeronautics by public demonstrations of gliders

CALBRAITH PERRY RODGERS for outstanding contributions to aviation by demonstrating the feasibility of transcontinental flight

HENRY W. WALDEN for outstanding contributions to aviation by conceiving, building and demonstrating manned flight in the first successful monoplane in the United States

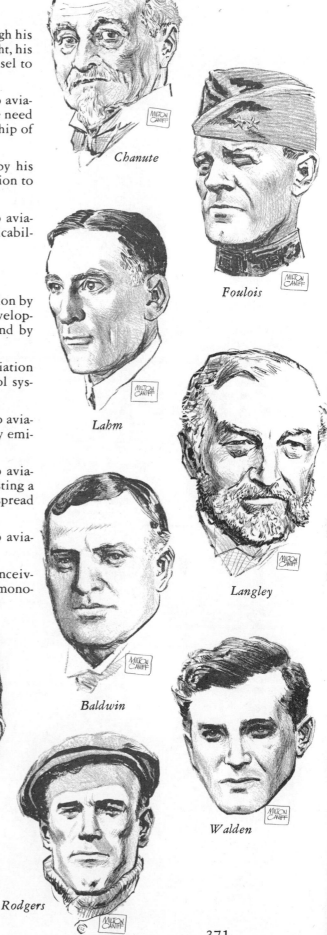

Chanute

Foulois

Lahm

Langley

Baldwin

Walden

Curtiss

Ellyson

Montgomery

Rodgers

371

1965

ALEXANDER GRAHAM BELL for outstanding contributions to aviation by research into principles of lift, propulsion, and control, and advancement of adequate scientific test facilities

ALFRED AUSTELL CUNNINGHAM for outstanding contributions to aviation by his untiring efforts to make aviation an integral part of the Marine Corps, and by distinction as the first Marine aviator

EUGENE BURTON ELY for outstanding contributions to aviation by skillful exhibition flights, and successfully demonstrating the operational use of airplanes with naval vessels thereby proving the practicability of aircraft carriers

A. ROY KNABENSHUE for outstanding contributions to aviation by early public demonstrations of balloons and steerable balloons, by designing, building and demonstrating early dirigibles, and by managing airplane exhibitions teams

ALBERT CUSHING READ for oustanding contributions to aviation as a naval aviator by participating in the first successful transatlantic flight and by devotion to advancing naval aviation

EDWARD VERNON RICKENBACKER for outstanding contributions to aviation by demonstrated skill as a combat pilot, and by capable direction and management of organizations, assisting immeasurably the vital growth of modern commercial aviation

THOMAS ETHOLEN SELFRIDGE for outstanding contributions to aviation by the design and development of airplanes, by pioneer flights, and by making the first ultimate sacrifice in aviation

CHARLES EDWARD TAYLOR for outstanding contributions to aviation by mechanical ability and skill in building the first successful engine, and by dedicated service in maintaining early airplanes in readiness for their historic flights

1966

LINCOLN BEACHEY for outstanding contributions to aviation by significant early demonstrations of the flight capabilities of aircraft, including the performance of important acrobatics

WILLIAM EDWARD BOEING for outstanding contributions to aviation by his successful organization of a network of airline routes and the production of vitally important military and commercial aircraft

Cunningham

Bell

Ely

Read

Knabenshue

Beachey

Rickenbacker

Taylor

Selfridge

Boeing

Goddard

Towers

Mitchell

Martin

Arnold

ROBERT HUTCHINGS GODDARD for outstanding contributions to aviation by his pioneering work in rocket technology which laid the foundation for man's travel in space

GLENN LUTHER MARTIN for outstanding contributions to aviation by important advances in aircraft design and manufacture

WILLIAM MITCHELL for outstanding contributions to aviation by his visionary theories and practical demonstrations of the tactical missions of an independent air force, and his martyrdom in the advancement of these concepts

JOHN HENRY TOWERS for outstanding contributions to aviation by his epic airplane flights and his dedicated effort in the ultimate recognition of airpower as a vital naval doctrine

1967

HENRY HARLEY ARNOLD for outstanding contributions to aviation by his pioneering flights, devotion to concepts of strategic airpower, and brilliant leadership of the air forces in World War II

JAMES HAROLD DOOLITTLE for outstanding contributions to aviation by his pioneering scientific advances in flight technology, military leadership and valued service to astronautics

CHARLES AUGUSTUS LINDBERGH for outstanding contributions to aviation by his historic transatlantic solo flight, pioneering of air routes and technical service to aeronautical organizations

CARL ANDREW SPAATZ for outstanding contributions to aviation by his life-long devotion to the advancement of the air forces, and commanding leadership in bringing victory in World War II through air power

1968

RICHARD EVELYN BYRD for outstanding contributions to aviation by pioneering use of airplanes in the polar regions, making flights over both poles, and devotion to the acquisition of scientific knowledge of these vast regions

JOHN ARTHUR MACREADY for outstanding contributions to aviation as an early test pilot, by participating in the first non-stop transcontinental fight and by pioneering in high altitude flight

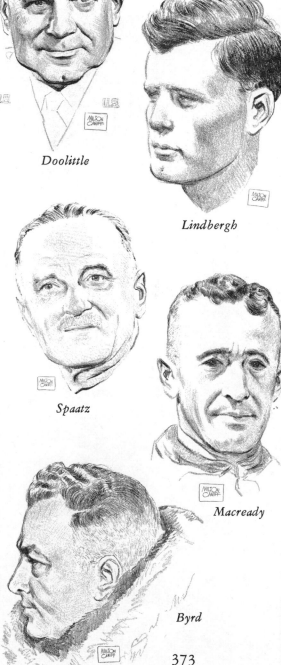

Doolittle

Lindbergh

Spaatz

Macready

Byrd

Loening

Post

Gross

de Seversky

Trippe

Earhart (Putnam)

Sikorsky

Douglas

Eaker

AMELIA EARHART PUTNAM for outstanding contributions to aviation by her dedicated promotion of the interests of women in flying, setting of numerous records in the air, and pioneering in transcontinental and transoceanic flights

IGOR IVAN SIKORSKY for outstanding contributions to aviation by his development of large multi-engine aircraft, including flying boats used in commercial transoceanic flights, and for developing the single-rotor helicopter

1969

DONALD WILLS DOUGLAS for outstanding contributions to aviation by the design and manufacture of military and commercial aircraft contributing to the Nation's safety and progress in the air

GROVER LOENING for outstanding contributions to aviation by his development of new forms of airplanes, and by distinguished service in furthering the utility of aircraft in both peace and war

WILEY HARDEMAN POST for outstanding contributions to aviation by his flights around the world that demonstrated the practicality of new flight-related equipment, and for conceiving and proving the feasibility of the fully pressurized flying suit

1970

ALEXANDER P. deSEVERSKY for outstanding contributions to aviation by his achievements as a pilot, aeronautical engineer, inventor, industrialist, author, strategist, consultant, and scientific advances in aircraft design and aerospace technology

IRA CLARENCE EAKER for outstanding contributions to aviation by his demonstrations of new flight techniques and devotion to developing and leading air forces that brought victory in World War II

ROBERT ELLSWORTH GROSS for outstanding contributions to aviation by his personal faith in aviation and his leadership in the manufacture of commercial and military aircraft and in programs of vital importance to national security and to space technology

JUAN TERRY TRIPPE for outstanding contributions to aviation by his creative development of the basic principles of airline operation, and pioneering leadership in international commercial aviation

1971

WILLIAM McPHERSON ALLEN for outstanding contributions to aviation by his dedicated leadership in the development and acceptance of commercial and military jet aircraft, and for the advancement of supersonic and space travel

JACQUELINE COCHRAN ODLUM for outstanding contributions to aviation by her devotion to the advancement of the role of women in all of its aspects, and by establishing new performance records that advanced aeronautics

HARRY FRANK GUGGENHEIM for outstanding contributions to aviation by his life-long devotion to the promotion of aeronautics, and for encouraging and supporting others in their vital developments

GEORGE CHURCHILL KENNEY for outstanding contributions to aviation by his development of new warplane armament and tactics, and exceptional leadership of United States air forces in war and peace

1972

CLAIRE LEE CHENNAULT for outstanding contributions to aviation by development of the science of pursuit aviation and by distinguished, personal leadership in the air struggle to preserve freedom throughout the world

LEROY RANDLE GRUMMAN for outstanding contributions to aviation through his engineering innovations, successful designs, and productive accomplishments that advanced aircraft for military and civilian use

JAMES HOWARD KINDELBERGER for outstanding contributions to aviation by his aeronautical designs and precision manufacturing techniques that helped to develop American air power, and for valuable contributions to the Nation's space efforts

CURTIS EMERSON LeMAY for outstanding contributions to aviation by his dedicated development of effective air power that helped to bring victory in World War II, building the Strategic Air Command into a force for peace, and leading the United States Air Force

1973

BERNT BALCHEN for outstanding contributions to aviation by his aerial explorations and his devotion to the establishment of the airplane as a vital means of transportation in the polar regions

HOWARD ROBARD HUGHES for outstanding contributions to aviation by his development of advanced design aircraft, by setting aerial records that demonstrated the capabilities of aircraft, and by development of domestic and international commercial aviation

Allen

Cochran (Odlum)

Kenney

Guggenheim

Chennault

Grumman

LeMay

Kindelberger

Hughes

Balchen

375

ELMER AMBROSE SPERRY, SR. for outstanding contributions to aviation by his development of gyroscopic instruments and flight control systems that added immeasurably to aircraft utility and safety

CHARLES ELWOOD YEAGER for outstanding contributions to aviation by his exceptional test flights resulting in the attainment of supersonic flight and his devotion to aerospace research and safety

1974

C. L. 'KELLY' JOHNSON for outstanding contributions to aviation by his innovative technical concepts that significantly advanced the science of aircraft design, performance, and reliability and helped achieve supersonic and space flight

JOHN KNUDSEN NORTHROP for outstanding contributions to aviation by his originality and ingenuity in aircraft construction and design, by producing aircraft vital to world peace and by creative development of missiles and their guidance systems

T. CLAUDE RYAN for outstanding contributions to aviation by his development of significantly advanced aircraft, his training of critically needed pilots during World War II, and development of electronic space navigational systems that enabled men to land on the moon

CYRUS R. SMITH for outstanding contributions to aviation by his creative advancements in developing domestic air transportation, his valuable service in organizing the Army Air Forces Air Transport Command and his devotion to the expansion of international aviation

LEIGH WADE for outstanding contributions to aviation by his flight testing of new and improved aircraft and equipment, his participation in the first Round-The-World flight, and his years of devotion to aeronautical advancements

1975

REUBEN HOLLIS FLEET for outstanding contributions to aviation by his leadership in military flight training, organizing the air mail service, developing successful training aircraft, flying boats for commercial and military use and multi-engine bombers

FRANK LUKE, JR. for outstanding contributions to aviation by his demonstrated extraordinary courage and skill as a pursuit pilot and his development of new tactical combat maneuvers by which he became America's second ranking ace during World War I

ROBERT CAMPBELL REEVE for outstanding contributions to aviation as a barnstormer, air mail pilot and bush pilot, and by his vital role in demon-

Sperry

Yeager

Johnson

Northrop

Smith

Ryan

Wade

Fleet

Luke

strating unique uses of the airplane that influenced the economic boom and cultural development of Alaska

ROSCOE TURNER for outstanding contributions to aviation by his participation in early commercial aviation and involvement in air racing leading to important technical advancement in design and performance of high speed aircraft and engines

1976

CLARENCE DUNCAN CHAMBERLIN for his pioneering work as a test and air race pilot, and for his endurance and long distance flights, including a non-stop flight from New York to Germany in 1927

JOHN HERSCHEL GLENN, JR. for his distinguished service as a military aviator in World War II and the Korean War, and for his epic contribution to the United States Space Program by orbiting the earth three times on February 20, 1962

GEORGE WILLIAM GODDARD for his pioneering contributions, while serving in the Army Air Service, to aerial photography as a means of improving aerial reconnaissance and mapping, and as the prime developer of the Air Force aerial strip camera used in nuclear tests and aerial surveillance overflights

ALBERT FRANCIS HEGENBERGER for his pioneering work in the development of early flight instruments and navigation equipment for the Army Air Service, as well as a practical flight instrument and radio beacon system which enabled him to make the first official solo blind flight and the first transoceanic flight to Hawaii, which earned him the "Mackay Trophy" and two "Collier Trophies"

EDWIN ALBERT LINK for his invention of mechanical flight simulators which have been used by military and civilian aviation to train pilots for solo flight, instrument flight, and aerial navigation; and also special simulators used for astronaut training in the space program

SANFORD ALEXANDER MOSS for his research in thermodynamics which brought into being the aircraft engine turbosupercharger, which enabled aircraft to maintain high speed flight at high altitude

WILLIAM ALLAN PATTERSON for four decades a central figure in the nation's air transport industry, for his effort in merging four fledgling airlines into a major transcontinental airline system, and for the introduction of numerous passenger conveniences and services now standard in the airline industry

NATHAN FARRAGUT TWINING for his outstanding service in the Army Air Force during World War II, including the distinction of commanding three combat air forces at one time, and for his guidance as Chief of Staff of the United States Air Force and his part in establishing its present structure

Reeve

Turner

Chamberlin

Glenn

Goddard

Twining

Link

Hegenberger

Moss

Patterson

377

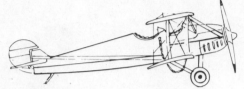

THE TETERBORO AVIATION HALL OF FAME

Teterboro, New Jersey

The tower at Teterboro

—All photographs in this chapter, courtesy Teterboro Aviation Hall of Fame

The idea of organizing an aviation hall of fame at Teterboro was first seriously discussed at the 50th Anniversary party commemorating Billy Diehl's first landing at the airfield, then operated by the Wittemanns, on August 13, 1920. The party, called a Wing Ding, was held in the Texaco hangar on August 14, 1970. It had been organized by Don Baldwin, Texaco's Chief Pilot, Hank Esposito of Atlantic Aviation, and H. V. Pat Reilly of Pan American.

In addition to Billy Diehl, the old-timers honored that evening were Clarence Chamberlin, Bernt Balchen, Aron "Duke" Krantz, Charles Lindbergh and Blanche Noyes. Well over 500 people were in attendance enjoying beef steak and beer and mingling with the old-timers present.

Among the guests were Mr. and Mrs. Donald Borg and their son, Gregory. The Borgs were long-time aviation buffs. Donald, the publisher of *The Record*, Bergen County's only daily newspaper, had flown with Floyd Bennett in the 1920s. As the evening progressed, the Borgs and Pat Reilly discussed the great interest shown by the guests in the aviation pioneers and the unique historical significance of Teterboro Airport. They agreed that Teterboro's aviation heritage was something that should be preserved for the edification of generations to come.

Almost a year and a half later, Reilly approached Don Borg with the idea of organizing a hall of fame. It was agreed that they would co-found an organization that would not only honor aviation pioneers but also help perpetuate aviation education.

On the original Executive Committee of the Board of Trustees were John Breslin, Jr., Horace F. Banta, Fairleigh Dickinson, Jr., Edward A. Jesser, Jr., Alexander Summer, Sr., Borg and Reilly. These men named the organization the Teterboro Aviation Hall of Fame, wrote by-laws and elected officers. Don Borg was named President, Alexander Summer, Sr., Vice President, and H. V. Reilly, Secretary-Treasurer.

The founding group of Trustees outlined the following purposes of the organization:

- To receive and maintain funds for charitable and educational purposes.

Billy Diehl

Charles Lindbergh

- To honor aviation leaders, pilots, teachers, engineers, inventors, governmental leaders and other individuals who contributed to the fame and development of Teterboro Airport.
- To perpetuate the memory of such persons and record their contributions and achievements by suitable memorials.
- To promote a better sense of appreciation of the origin and growth of Teterboro Airport and the part aviation in general has played in the changing aspects of community and nation.
- To establish and maintain a library and museum preserving for posterity the history of those honored by the Teterboro Aviation Hall of Fame.

By the end of the first year and a half, the organization had over 400 paying members and had gathered a great deal of aviation memorabilia.

The most significant gifts came from the Curtiss-Wright Corporation in Wood-Ridge. They contributed a jet engine and an experimental air cushion car. The Bergen County historical society, through the auspices of its President Marden Nystrom and with a nudge from Leonard Schiff, the President of the Air Force Association, contributed a propellor from Commander Byrd's transatlantic Fokker F-7, that had been damaged in a 1927 flight test accident at Teterboro. The students at the Teterboro School of Aeronautics carefully restored the jet engine and the air car under the direction of the school's director, Tony DiStefano.

Four highly successful and entertaining Hall of Fame induction dinners were held from 1973 through 1976 under the Chairmanship of Ned Jesser. Aviation pioneers were honored either for their contribution to the growth of the airport or the notoriety their history-making feats brought to Teterboro. Those elected into the Hall of Fame were: Charles A. Lindbergh, Clarence Chamberlin, Floyd Bennett, "Duke" Krantz, Billy Diehl, Clyde Pangborn, Fred L. Wehran, Amelia Earhart, Ed Gorski, the three Wittemann brothers, Charles, Paul and Walter, Anthony Fokker, Jack Webster, Bill Hartig, Fred Bohlander, Donald Borg, Bernt Balchen, Juan T. Trippe, Roger Q. Williams, O. P. "Ted" Hebert, Arthur Godfrey, Ivan Gates, Bert Acosta and George DeGarmo.

Donald Borg

Amelia Earhart (Putnam)

Bill Hartig and Clarence Chamberlin

Over the years additional Board of Trustees were elected, including Wilton T. Barney, Austin Drukker, Bennett H. Fishler, Jr., David Van-Alstyne, Edward Straus, William E. Shaughnessy, Fred Wehran, William McDowell, Henry Esposito, Frederick Scholz, Marden Nystrom, Edwin Boyle, Donald Hules, Charles Agemian, William Staehle, General Francis Gerard, Ben Rock, Caesar Pattarini, William Gott, Richard I. Brown, John P. Kennedy, Dr. Walter Hartung, James R. Sutphen, Joseph Muscarelle, Sr., Robert Coppenrath, Toshihiko Sakow, Alexander Summer, Jr., Walter Gates, Victor Williams, Ed Gorski and B. Michelle Reilly, who had been instrumental in the founding of the organization.

Due to failing health, Donald Borg stepped down as President at the end of the first year, and was succeeded by Wilton T. Barney. A year later Alexander Summer, Sr., retired and Bennett Fishler was elected Vice President. At the same time Pat Reilly was named Executive Vice President, Michelle Reilly Secretary and Lillian Terlizzi Executive Secretary. Mrs. Terlizzi works on a part time basis at the Hall of Fame office located in the Pan Am Building at Teterboro. She is a Past President of World Wings of New Jersey, Inc., an organization of former Pan Am flight attendants, who have volunteered endless hours in the development of the Hall of Fame.

At the 1975 induction dinner the first aviation scholarship was awarded by the Hall of Fame in conjunction with the Teterboro School of Aeronautics to a young Maywood resident, David Paotilla.

In November of that year, President Barney and John Kennedy, Vice President, Pan American, a strong supporter of Hall of Fame activities, signed a contract that would permit the Hall of Fame to use the top two floors of the old control tower on the Atlantic Aviation hangar for the first aviation museum in the State of New Jersey for a yearly rental of one dollar. As soon as the agreement was reached, Henry Esposito of Atlantic Aviation offered to supply heat and electricity to the museum, and Toshihiko Sakow, an industrial design consultant, agreed to design the interior of the building.

Then Afred Dellentash, who had just brought a new aircraft business to Teterboro named the Triple D Corp., stepped forward and volunteered to do the interior construction of the museum. Irv Koetting has donated his expertise in the electronic field.

The Teterboro Aviation Hall of Fame museum features memorabilia displays, photographs and other aviation artifacts. There are motion picture films of historic first flights that originated at Teterboro and an aviation library. On the top floor, which is the former FAA control tower, visitors have an opportunity to view the aircraft activity at the busy airport and listen to the FAA controllers direct aircraft takeoffs and landings.

The museum is the first of its kind in the State of New Jersey. It is a small beginning of what the visionary members of the Board of Trustees see as an outstanding tribute to aviation in New Jersey and an educational tool for the young of our communities.

INDUCTEES

See Aviation Hall of Fame (Dayton) for short biographies of these individuals.

BERT ACOSTA—Born 1895. A barnstorming air race champion in the 1920s, he established an endurance record with Chamberlin in 1920 at Teterboro and co-piloted Commander Byrd on third successful nonstop Atlantic flight. He flew in the Spanish Civil War in 1936. (Elected 1975)

*BERNT BALCHEN

FLOYD BENNETT—Born 1890. He received the Congressional Medal of Honor and world acclaim as pilot for the Byrd expedition from Spitzbergen to the North Pole and back. They were the first men to fly over either pole. Bennett built the Fokker F-7. While preparing for Byrd's transatlantic flight in 1927, he was seriously injured in a crash of the "America" during a test flight at Teterboro. On April 25, 1928 he died of pneumonia contracted on a mercy flight carrying needed spare parts to three stranded pilots of the aircraft "Bremen" at Greeneley Island, Newfoundland. (Elected 1972)

FRED W. BOHLANDER—Born 1908. An expert mechanic for the Fokker Aircraft Corporation from 1924 to 1931, he served 34 years as police chief of Teterboro. He was Teterboro Airport's guardian and greatest booster. (Elected 1973)

DONALD G. BORG—Born 1906. Publisher, philanthropist, civic leader, co-founder and first President of Teterboro Aviation Hall of Fame, his imaginative leadership established Teterboro Airport as a historic landmark in New Jersey. (Elected 1973)

*CLARENCE CHAMBERLIN

GEORGE DE GARMO—Born 1893. A pioneer in aerial photography in the 1930s, he owned the New Standard Flying Service at Teterboro. He flew in World Wars I and II and the Korean conflict. (Elected 1975)

WILLIAM DIEHL (Billy)—Born 1891. An aviation early bird, he was the first itinerant pilot to land at Teterboro Airport, on August 13, 1920. He was a civilian flight instructor for the Army Signal Corps during World War I, an inventor, a test pilot, and a stunt pilot in motion pictures, including Pearl White's famous serial, "Perils of Pauline." (Elected 1972)

*AMELIA EARHART PUTNAM

ANTHONY H. G. FOKKER (The Flying Dutchman)—Born 1890. A world-famous designer, builder and test pilot, his F-7 tri-motors made more historic first flights than any other type aircraft. His Teterboro-based aircraft company was the largest in the United States in the 1920s. (Elected 1973)

Fred Bohlander

George DeGarmo

Bert Acosta

Anthony Fokker

Floyd Bennett

381

Arthur Godfrey

(At left)
Ivan Gates

Aron "Duke" Krantz

Edward Gorski

O. P. "Ted" Hebert

IVAN R. GATES — Born 1890. Pilot and aviation promoter, he founded and operated the nationally famous Gates Flying Circus, aviation's most colorful group of flying daredevils, based at Teterboro Airport from 1926 to 1929. In 1927 and 1928 he promoted two National Air Show and Air Circus events at Teterboro. (Elected 1975)

ARTHUR GODFREY — Born 1903. Entertainer, pilot, environmentalist, and retired Colonel of the U.S. Air Force Reserve, he brought national attention the Teterboro Airport through his radio and television programs in 1952. He logged over 16,000 flying hours in every type of aircraft, from Pipers to the Boeing 747. (Elected 1975)

EDWARD GORSKI — Born 1906. From 1920 to 1940 he was a leading aviation figure at Teterboro. He began his career as a mechanic for Chamberlin, Fokker Aircraft and Amelia Earhart. Later he became a pilot, an instructor and a fixed-base operator. (Elected 1972)

WILLIAM A. HARTIG — Born 1895. Chief mechanic for Teterboro-based Wittemann Aircraft Company, Fokker Aircraft Corporation, and aviation pioneer Clarence Chamberlin, he was considered the greatest aircraft mechanic of his day. (Elected 1973)

O. P. HEBERT (Ted) — Born 1900. Pilot, instructor and aircraft distributor, as a Lieutenant, at Teterboro he accepted DH-4s modified by Fokker for the Army Air Service from 1923 to 1925. He co-founded the Pacific Seaboard Airline in 1933. He was awarded a mail route between Chicago and New Orleans in 1934. His Safair Flying Service is the oldest fixed-base operation at Teterboro, established in 1941. (Elected 1974)

ARON F. KRANTZ (Duke) — Born 1896. A daredevil aerial wing-walking acrobat with Gates Flying Circus from 1924 to 1929, he became a New York Daily News pilot in the 1930s. He was a B-24, B-29 test pilot in World War II and chief pilot for the Bendix Corporation in the 1950s. (Elected 1972)

*CHARLES A. LINDBERGH

CLYDE E. PANGBORN — Born 1893. He learned to fly with the U.S. Army Air Service in 1918. An acrobatic stunt pilot and chief pilot for Gates Flying

Circus, he was famous for flying upside down. In 1928 he made the first airmail pickup with hook and tackle at Teterboro. In 1929 he became owner of the New Standard Flying Service. In 1931, he and Hugh Herndon made the first nonstop transpacific flight—from Japan to Clyde's native state of Washington. (Elected 1972)

*JUAN T. TRIPPE

JACK ORDWAY WEBSTER—Born 1895. A U.S. Airmail test pilot from 1919 to 1923, he tested more than 300 modified DH-4 aircraft for the Wittemann Aircraft Corporation at Teterboro. In August 1921 he made a historic test airmail flight from Teterboro to San Francisco in a DH-M-2. (Elected 1973)

FRED L. WEHRAN—Born 1900. Airport developer, operator and pilot, he owned Teterboro Airport in the 1940s. He installed the first control tower, paved runways, and established at Teterboro the world's busiest air freight terminal. (Elected 1972)

ROGER Q. WILLIAMS—Born 1891. Barnstormer, engineer, author and lecturer, he began flying in 1914 and flew in World War I and World War II, where he earned the rank of Colonel. From 1919 to 1924 he worked for the Wittemann Aircraft Corporation. In 1928, with Clarence Chamberlin, he set a flight endurance record of 51 hours and 52 minutes over Mitchell Field, New York. In 1929, with Captain Lewis Yancey, he made the first flight from New York to Rome, setting a world's record for distance and time. In 1930 he made a record nonstop flight from New York to Bermuda and back. (Elected 1974)

WITTEMANN BROTHERS—Born: Charles 1884; Paul 1894; Walter 1896. As early as 1905, the Wittemanns founded the first airplane manufacturing plant in the United States on their family estate on Staten Island. As pioneer designers and builders, they established the first aircraft activity at Teterboro in 1918. They had a contract with the Post Office to convert surplus U.S. Army de Havilland DH-4 aircraft for the first airmail service. The Wittemann Corporation manufactured the largest World War I plane, the Barling Bomber. (Elected 1972)

Clyde Pangborn

Fred Wehran

Jack Webster

Roger Williams

Charles Wittemann

383

THE CIRCUS HALL OF FAME

Sarasota, Florida

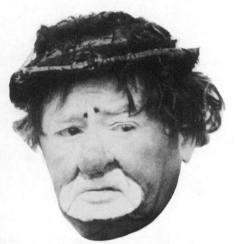

Otto Griebling, one of the greatest pantomine clowns of all time.

A Brief History

The Circus Hall of Fame is the vision of three men who had one thing in common. They all loved the circus. In 1954, when the Ringling Museums closed the Museum of the American Circus, these three men decided that Sarasota needed a circus museum—a museum that would house and exhibit all circus memorabilia and also keep future generations aware of circus history. These original owners brought their vast collections and mementos to start the museum.

These three circus buffs were: Colonel B. J. Palmer, who was already a celebrated citizen known as "The Father of Chiropractics." He had founded the College of Chiropractics in Davenport, Iowa. The second of these three circus buffs was: John L. Sullivan, a retired businessman from Syracuse, New York. He was the curator of The American Museum of the Circus until 1954. He was an original founder of the Sailor Circus at Sarasota Senior High School and one of its biggest boosters. The third was Dr. Chester H. Hoyt, a retired minister who was also connected with The American Museum of the Circus until 1954. Dr. Hoyt was the first curator of the Circus Hall of Fame. All three original founders are deceased.

After working on their dream for two years, they realized that in order to open the Museum they needed more capital. Several business and professional men in Sarasota were approached and a corporation was founded in 1956. Some of these men are still on the Board of Directors. Not only did they realize the dream, but it has become a true testament to the free enterprise system of the United States. It still operates on the free enterprise system, promoting and generating the funds which not only pay the taxes and operating expenses and satisfy the stockholders, but also help to continue to educate and preserve the circus for future generations.

Starting the Circus Hall of Fame

In the course of their planning, the idea of a Shrine for "Circus Greats" was conceived. The Circus Hall of Fame is to the circus what the Baseball Hall of Fame is to baseball. A National Awards Committee was formed, numbering thirteen persons from different parts of the country. They are, of course, circus buffs, but more important they are circus historians. There have been four changes in this committee since 1956. The committee accepts nominations from the general public each year. After very thorough research of the nominees, if elected by a majority of the committee, they will be permanently enshrined in the Circus Hall of Fame. Some nominees are not voted in on their first year; however, once nominated they are eligible for a second and third consideration.

Selecting Members of the Circus Hall of Fame

The two basic rules for eligibility for nomination to the Hall of Fame are: that the nominee must have been retired for at least five years, or he must be deceased. As of 1976, there are ninety-one persons in the Circus Hall of Fame. Some are circus owners, producers, or managers; however, most are performers. The Circus Hall of Fame represents all performers and all circuses whether living, dead or out of business. The National Awards Committee normally meets in Sarasota during the month of February. The awards are given to the electees during one of the circus performances the day after the committee has elected them.

In addition to the Hall of Fame Shrine, the four-acre complex maintains a Museum of the Circus, a Side Show Museum, and a Museum of Puppetry housed in the Puppet Theater. The collection of antique puppets, some dating back to the 18th century, is considered one of the finest in the world. The puppets are kept in working order and several shows are given daily.

Antoinette Concello, the first woman to do a flying trapeze somersault.

Aerial view of the Circus Hall of Fame.

As the recipient of many fine collections of international circusiana, as well as individual donations from circus "greats" or their families, the Circus Hall of Fame now has one of the largest collections of circus memorabilia in the world. It has become a mecca for circus buffs from all over the world. The collection of circus lithographs and posters is so vast that they must keep exchanging them every six months in order to display them all.

Among the many wagons, there are the largest and the smallest bandwagons ever built. The Two Hemispheres bandwagon was built for P. T. Barnum in 1903 at a cost of $40,000.00. This wagon weighs ten tons and when used by P. T. Barnum in his street parades was drawn by a forty-horse hitch. The Two Hemispheres bandwagon has become the cornerstone of the complex and is displayed at the front entrance. The Sig Sautelle bandwagon has been fully restored and is used by the Circus Hall of Fame in parades within a fifty-mile radius of Sarasota. A special hitch has been devised for an elephant to pull this beautiful wagon. They have a coach that was given to General Tom Thumb by Queen Elizabeth. This coach is a tiny replica of coaches used by the royal family in England during the 18th century.

The Circus Hall of Fame was under the direction of Colonel W. W. Narramore for fifteen years. Upon his retirement, G. Herb Garrido,

Jules Jacot, wild animal trainer.

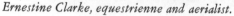

Ernestine Clarke, equestrienne and aerialist.

The Rieffenach Sisters, equestrian act.

formerly of St. Louis, Missouri, was selected to fill this position. He has introduced many innovations. One of these is the return to the old-fashioned European one-ring circus under canvas. All circus performances are now held under a blue and white Big Top. For the past two years the George Hanneford Family Circus has been performing during both winter and summer seasons. The Hanneford family has been performing in European and American circuses for seven generations.

The Shrine for "circus greats" has been completely remodeled. Many of the exhibits throughout both museums have either been done over or replaced with other names relating to contemporary circus performers. The puppet theater has been completely remodeled and new plays have been written.

Edwin "Poodles" Hanneford, an expert horseman, one of the all-time great clown riders.

The thinking for the future is to inaugurate a magic and illusion show to be performed between circus performances.

The objectives at the Circus Hall of Fame are:
1. To Publicly Honor Circus Stars of All Times
2. To Collect and Display Mementos of the Stars
3. To Maintain a Circus Historical Library
4. To Develop and Train Stars of the Future
5. To Create a True Understanding for the Educational and Recreative Value of the Circus

The Circus Hall of Fame is open every day of the year from 9 a.m. until 5 p.m. The circus acts for the Winter Season begin one week before Christmas and end one week after Easter. The Summer Season begins the second week in June and ends on Labor Day.

387

Con Colleano, toreador of the tight wire

HALL OF FAME

	ELECTED		ELECTED
Lillian Leitzel, Aerialist	1958	Sig Sautelle, Management	1962
James A. Bailey, Management	1960	Charles T. Hunt, Management	1962
William Cameron Coup, Management	1960	Adam Forepaugh, Management	1962
Fred Bradna, Ringmaster	1960	Antoinette Concello, Flyer	1962
Phineas Taylor Barnum, Showman	1960	Henry B. Gentry, Management	1962
Dan Rice, Showman-Clown	1960	Lucia Zora, Performer-Trainer	1962
Bird Millman, Wire Walker	1961	Roy James McDonald, "Mickey the Clown"	1962
John Ricketts, Father of American Circus (Lost at sea with the circus)	1961	James Robinson, Management	1962
Bill "Cap" Curtis, Management	1961	Victor Pepin, Equestrian Performer	1962
Charles McGee Sparks, Management	1961	Issac A. Van Amburgh, First American Animal Trainer	1963
Ringling Brothers-5, Management-Owners	1961	May Wirth, Equestrian Bareback	1963
Orin Davenport, Equestrian Acrobat	1961	Philip Astley, Circus Founder	1963
Thomas Pool, Management	1962	Lindeman Brothers-3, Management-Performers	1964
Philip Lailson, Management	1962	Dexter W. Fellows, Press Agent	1964
Clarke Family, Equestrians	1962	Albert Jerome Powell, Trapeze-Contortionist	1964
Jacob Bates, Equestrian Shows	1962	Oscar Lowande, Equestrian	1964
Irene Ledgett, Performer	1962		
Roland Butler, Press Agent Artist	1962		

	ELECTED
Clyde Beatty, Animal Trainer	1965
Charlie Siegrist, Greatest All Round Circus Performer	1965
Con Colleano, Tight Wire Artist	1965
Lalo Codona, Catcher	1965
Alfredo Codona, Flyer	1965
Jorgen Christiansen, Equestrian Trainer	1966
Ernestine Clarke, Equestrian Acrobat	1966
Matthew Buckley, Management-Performer	1966
Ernest Millette, Flyer	1967
Captain William Heyer, Equestrian Trainer	1967
Elly Ardelty, Aerialist	1967
Edwin "Poodles" Hanneford, Equestrian-Clown	1967
Mabel Stark, Lion Tamer	1968
Rudy Rudynoff Troupe, Equestrians	1968
The Pallenbergs, Bear Trainers	1968
Edna Curtis Christiansen, Equestrian	1968
Charles Bell, Clown	1968
Nelson Family, Acrobats	1968
Billy Smart, Management	1970
Rieffenach Sisters, Equestrian Acrobats	1970
Mayme Fay Ward, Aerialist-Trapeze	1970
Ira George Millette, Comb. Balancing Act	1970
Jules Jacot, Animal Trainer	1971
Felix Adler, Clown	1971
Pat Valdo, Clown-Management	1971
George Hamid Sr., Performer	1971
Captain Jack Bonavita, Animal Trainer (John F. Genter)	1971
Hans Jahn, Equilibrist	1972
Otto Griebling, Clown	1972
Damoo G. Dhotre, Animal Trainer	1973
Buffalo Bill Cody, Wild West Performer	1973
Karl L. King, Musician-Composer-Bandleader	1973
Arthur Konyot, Equestrian	1974
Tom Mix, Equestrian-Management	1974
Tosca Canestrelli, Bounding Rope Act	1975
Merle S. Evans, Musical Director	1975
Zacchini Brothers, Human Cannonballs	1975
Alfred Court, Animal Trainer	1975
Winifred Colleano, Solo Trapeze	1975

(Above) Mayme Fay Ward, great flyer. (Below) Catherine and Emil Pallenberg with one of their trained bears.

(Above) "The Sources of Country Music," the last painting by the famed Missouri artist and muralist Thomas Hart Benton.This was painted for the Hall of Fame and completed just before the artist's death. (Below) One of nine dioramas depicting historic scenes and moments in country music, this one the first recordings of the Carter Family and Jimmie Rodgers in Bristol, Tennessee by Ralph Peer, in August of 1927. The figures, each about 5" high, are Ralph Peer, Maybelle Carter, Jimmie Rodgers, Sara Carter and A. P. Carter.

THE COUNTRY MUSIC HALL OF FAME AND MUSEUM

Nashville, Tennessee

By Douglas B. Green

No form of American music is as dominated by, interested in, and obsessed with its own tradition as is country music. Scholars and admirers of all types of music tend to revere influential figures of the past, but in no other native musical form is there the unbroken link of centuries of folk-music tradition for the scholar, and a devotion to stars of the past by the fan.

It is really not surprising, in this light, that the first and only Hall of Fame dedicated to an American musical form should have been the Country Music Hall of Fame. It is also fitting that the parent organization—the Country Music Foundation—should be the foremost scholarly/archival resource on country music in the world, and that the Country Music Hall of Fame and Museum should be similarly dedicated to preservation and presentation of artifacts from the music's past.

Country music draws from a number of rich veins, the longest and richest going to medieval England, Scotland and Ireland, where the lonely unaccompanied ballad and the haunting strain of the bagpipe make up the basis upon which modern country music is founded. Here ballads and tunes were passed from parent to child, generation after generation, and great respect was given the family member who was the balladeer and musician, for in a time and a place where one might go no further in a lifetime than five or ten miles from his birthplace, these ballads and tunes were nearly the only means of entertainment.

Country Music Came with the First Settlers

Country music—this music of rural Great Britain—came to North America with the first English settlers, and the same ballads and tunes (usually played on the fiddle, not the bagpipes, in the colonies) became as much a part of American life as they had been in the Old World.

—All photographs in this chapter, courtesy Country Music Hall of Fame and Museum

391

This, then, helps explain the concern for tradition which so characterizes country music, its students and its fans, for a significant part of the music's repertoire in the age of moon landings is still made up of songs and tunes composed hundreds of years ago. It is really no surprise at all that such a deep commitment to tradition exists in the country music community among performers, business men, scholars and fans alike.

The Country Music Hall of Fame stands at the head of Nashville's 16th Avenue South, recently renamed Music Square East by the City Council in recognition that this area has long been called "Music Row" informally, because most of the major record labels and music publishers have offices — and usually recording studios as well — on 16th or 17th Avenue South, in what was, in the 1940s, a quiet residential area of a pretty, medium-sized southern city.

In the early 1950s more and more singers and their producers began travelling to Nashville to record, and by 1967, when the Country Music Hall of Fame opened its doors to the public, the "Music Row" area had become one of the financial and artistic centers of the music world, and a major tourist attraction in and of itself.

Yet, interestingly enough, this building which hosts over a third of a million visitors each year was somewhat late in coming, for the idea of a hall of fame itself was proposed several years before a building of its own was even planned on. The original hall of fame, such as it was, consisted of the plaques of the early members displayed in the crowded setting of the Tennessee State Museum near the state capitol in downtown Nashville.

The Idea Becomes a Reality

In 1961 — significantly, a period when country music was just beginning to recover from the shock waves of the massive phenomenon called

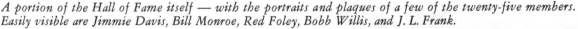

A portion of the Hall of Fame itself — with the portraits and plaques of a few of the twenty-five members. Easily visible are Jimmie Davis, Bill Monroe, Red Foley, Bobb Willis, and J. L. Frank.

"rock & roll"—an executive from the music trade paper *Cash Box* named Allen Bergofsky suggested and formally proposed that the music industry and other concerned Nashville business donate the money to build a Country Music Hall of Fame and Museum. In 1963, an influential Washington D. C. area show promoter and broadcasting executive named Connie B. Gay donated $10,000 and the project progressed thanks to the efforts of industry magnates and recording artists, including RCA's Steve Sholes, Decca Records (now called MCA) Owen Bradley, booking agent Hubert Long, Capitol Records' Ken Nelson, Acuff-Rose Publishing and Hickory Records' head Wesley Rose, singer and actor Tex Ritter, Cedarwood Music's Bill Denny, Vice President of Broadcast Music Inc. (BMI) Frances Preston, Columbia Records' Frank Jones, Harold Hitt, and longtime Grand Ole Opry star Roy Acuff.

The Nashville community at large—both business and private—were quick to respond to this lead, and enough money was raised to build the Country Music Hall of Fame within a few years. Today, virtually the entire operation—Hall of Fame and Museum upstairs and Library and Media Center and offices downstairs—are supported by the $2.00 admissions fee of the visitors who tour the facility annually.

It is significant that as early as 1964 it became clear to the industry leaders who directed the setting up of the Hall of Fame that the wide-ranging educational activities planned for the newly formed Country Music Foundation could not be pursued through the operation of a Hall of Fame and Museum alone. A library facility designed to serve the needs of the specialized researcher was thus included in the basic plans of the Hall of Fame building. Initially located in a balcony area, the rapid rate of acquisition of material quickly exhausted available space, and construction was soon begun on a large area in the basement of the building which was completed in 1971, and dedicated in June, 1972.

Expanding the Facilities

Within three years it was apparent that the collection was rapidly outgrowing even the 4,000 square feet allotted to it in the basement library area, and in addition far-sighted directors of the museum had ambitious plans for dramatic new exhibits, and it was ultimately decided to expand the Hall of Fame and Museum upstairs and down, doubling the space currently available. Construction was begun late in 1975, and the spacious structure—futuristically barn-like in design—was completed in the early part of 1977.

It is the long central portion of the "barn" which contains the Hall of Fame itself, the plaques and portraits of each member surrounding a central row of display cases which contain artifacts which once belonged to a Hall of Famer: the first guitars of Chet Atkins and Eddy Arnold, Fred Rose's sheet music, Jimmie Rodgers's brakeman's uniform, Tex Ritter's gunbelt and other memorabilia of the stars.

The museum itself is located in two large wings which enter into the Hall of Fame itself, and while there are artifacts here which once belonged to country music pioneers and stars, there is much more as well: the most dramatic being a multi-screened slide show delineating in music, photography and narrative, the roots of country music.

Popular Special Exhibits

Other popular exhibits are a re-creation of a recording session, which studies have shown to be the single most interesting aspect of Nashville's music business to the average Hall of Fame patron, as well as a series of nine dioramas, depicting historic moments in country music's history in miniature, honoring industry pioneers for their struggles to both make country music popular and to give it respectability and dignity as well.

A guitar exhibit, featuring an "exploded" view of a guitar so that the tourist can understand the many components which go into the construction of the instrument, and a valuable collection of performers' rare guitars has proven to be extremely popular. There is a rotating exhibit of costumes — from the floppy hats and bib-overalls of the early years to the rhinestones, spangles, and fringe of the flashy fifties to the sometimes tasteful, sometimes exotic outfits of today — which gives an insight into the mood and self-image of country music through the years.

The long needed expansion afforded the opportunity for the museum to add several exciting new exhibits, again with the emphasis on patron participation. One such exhibit is a walk-through demonstration of a "star's" touring bus, in which he or she travels with a band between personal appearances. These lavishly outfitted homes-on-the-road are a part of country music folklore, and to experience — even if only for a few moments — being on such a glamorous land cruiser is a fascinating thrill for the average country music fan.

Similarly, a sixteen-track recording apparatus — which is called the "board" in recording studios — has been rigged up to simulate its function in the recording studio, and the Hall of Fame visitor is able to get a firsthand look at the mechanical methods by which the mysterious process of recording is done.

Elvis Presley's gold-plated 1958 Cadillac is yet another new exhibit. This garish automobile is a tribute to one of many publicity stunts dreamed up for the pioneer rockabilly singer by his famous manager Colonel Tom Parker.

Dominating both the Museum and the Hall of Fame itself is a huge mural painted by the famous Missouri artist Thomas Hart Benton, entitled "The Sources of Country Music." The striking mural was, ironically, Benton's last painting in a long and highly respected career, and he put the final touches to the work only hours before his death at the age of eighty-six.

In addition, the museum area contains a sizeable and recently enlarged souvenir shop, "The Country Store," which contains a wide variety of wares, from T-shirts and corn cob pipes to scholarly books on the subject of country music and reissues of rare records on long play albums. A "walkway of stars" — not dissimilar to Hollywood's — greets entering

*An exhibit of guitars
with the boots of
some of the country music stars
in the barn shaped display case
symbolic of the Hall of Fame.*

visitors who may look upon the names of those entertainers who have contributed to country music and to the Country Music Foundation in innumerable ways.

Special Features for Scholarly Research

The basement of the Hall of Fame contains both the Library and Media Center and the offices of the Country Music Foundation, and houses the extensive collection of this unique and complete archive. Stored here for the use of scholars and students of the music are over 60,000 records, from Edison cylinders to Loretta Lynn's latest hit album, and thousands of books, magazines, newspapers, periodicals, songbooks, and printed materials from a century ago to the present.

The archives of the Country Music Foundation Library also include complete and near-complete issues of major and minor trade papers, periodicals and fan club journals, with some, including *Billboard* and *Variety* stretching back to the turn of the century. In addition, there is a growing collection of audio-visual resources, including a collection of film and television prints, and videotapes and a large number of interview tapes with country music pioneers recorded under the Country Music Foundation's Oral History Project.

The resources of the Library and Media Center are open to serious students and researchers by appointment only, and here they are able to pursue their particular field of inquiry through a number of avenues in this most complete archive of country music. Those interested in a particular artist may consult extensive vertical files, where newspaper clippings, publicity material, and a large number of photographs are stored, filed by the particular personality in which the researcher may be interested.

The offices of the Country Music Foundation Press are located in the basement area of the Hall of Fame building. With over half a dozen books in print to its credit, and a scholarly quarterly called the *Journal of Country Music,* published for the benefit of libraries and researchers, the fledgeling press is well on its way to disseminating to scholars worldwide the information housed in the vast resources of the Country Music Foundation Library.

Method of Selecting Members of the Hall of Fame

Election of members of the Country Music Hall of Fame is a somewhat complicated and often confusing procedure, not only because of the care which goes into the selection of new members, and the extremely limited number of members enshrined, but because the important trade organization which does the actual voting and awarding is called the Country Music Association, and is frequently mistakenly identified with the Country Music Foundation and its activities. Yet the election of Hall of Fame members is the only connection between the two otherwise unrelated organizations.

This is how it's done: A panel of 250 electors from all regions of the nation has been chosen, composed of longtime industry leaders and knowledgeable experts, the minimum requirement being activity in the field of country music for at least ten years. The panel is composed of entertainers, songwriters, historians, disc jockeys, businessmen, a wide and knowledgeable range of those who are intimately familiar with the music and its history.

A lengthy ballot, composed of well over one hundred names (with ample room for write-in votes) is mailed annually to the panel, and from this list the five names receiving the greatest number of votes are chosen for a second round of balloting.

From these five names, the board of electors votes again, choosing the one each feels most deserving of Hall of Fame induction. The winner of this round of balloting is announced as part of the nationally televised Country Music Association Awards Show every October. Frequently more than one member is elected. Once (1974) because of a mathematically highly improbable tie between Pee Wee King and Owen Bradley, two were selected. Usually however, because of a rule which insists that a deceased person be elected at least every third year, there are two selected at that time. This rule is designed to prevent only the "hottest" new singers from being elected based on a couple of years of successes. The committee is very aware of the historical significance of the pioneers of this form of entertainment, but future committees may not be so versed in the knowledge of past performers. The rule assures a continuing touch with the past.

Frank "Pee Wee" King

Owen Bradley

If on a third year of election there has not been a deceased person being enshrined, the electors are presented two final nomination lists, one consisting of living candidates and the other a list of deceased pioneers. The nominee with the greatest number of votes in *each* category being elected to membership in the Country Music Hall of Fame.

Individuals who have contributed enormously to country music have been elected since 1961—long before a building was erected to house their plaques, portraits and memorabilia—and this extremely limited method of selection has kept membership small. Only twenty-nine members have been elected to the Country Music Hall of Fame in the sixteen years since the process was begun.

A brief look at the members of the Country Music Hall of Fame gives an insight into the broad spectrum covered by membership, for neither artist nor businessman is particularly favored on that basis alone—the deciding factor has been the individual's (or in some cases group's) contribution to the development, growth, and shaping of the music and its popularity. The members of the Hall of Fame have helped to bring country music from its position as an anachronistic mountain music before the advent of radio and records, to the musical phenomenon which is now enjoying continuing and growing world-wide popularity.

Members of the Hall of Fame and Their Contributions

The first elections, held in 1961, enshrined a triumverate of men who have, almost without question, done more to shape and popularize country music than any others: **Fred Rose** (1897 - 1954), one of the alltime great songwriters who went from Broadway to Hollywood to write countless hits for Gene Autry and other before coming to Nashville to become legendary in guiding the songwriting and recording careers of Hank Williams, Roy Acuff, and literally dozens of others. He and Acuff formed the first publishing company in the south—Acuff-Rose Music—in 1943, and built it into an international concern.

Intimately entwined—as a performer and a songwriter—with Fred Rose was **Hank Williams** (1923 - 1953), the skinny kid from Alabama whose life was a spinning kaleidoscope of hit records, bouts with alcoholism, hit songs, a painful marriage and divorce, and a roller coaster career until his death at the age of twenty-nine. For many people the lonely wailing voice of Hank Williams is the voice of country music, and his songs such as "Your Cheating Heart," "I Can't Help It If I'm Still in Love With You," "Jambalaya," and "Cold Cold Heart" are country music classics.

Also elected that year was **Jimmie Rodgers** (1897 - 1933), another legendary performer who died young. Widely known as the Singing Brakeman, he was the first country music singer to achieve widespread popularity on record, and to have the trapping of "stardom" decorate his life and his career in the early days of sound recording. Combining the black blues of his native Mississippi with sentimental songs of the white tradition, Rodgers was tremendously popular in the six short years he re-

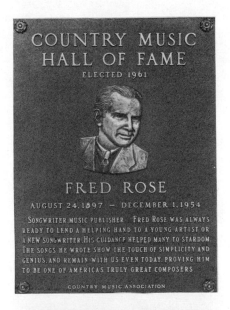

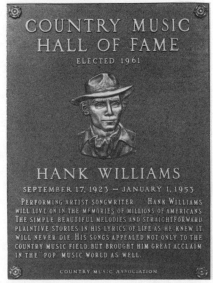

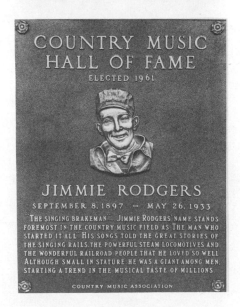

corded, and left an indelible imprint on country music style, as well as a strong influence on a score of influential performers who followed him.

Roy Acuff (1903 -   ) became the first living member of the Country Music Hall of Fame upon his election in 1962. A popular and influential performer in the "old-time" southeastern style, he is not only still popular as a performer (a 1974 minor hit for him gave Acuff the distinction of being the oldest performer ever to make the "charts"), he also has been a shrewd businessman, and has watched the Acuff-Rose firm he co-founded grow into an international giant.

Tex Ritter (1905 - 1974), an actor, singer, and singing cowboy of international repute, was elected in 1964. Ritter was, over and above his considerable musical achievements, a scholar and student of western music, and was a staunch supporter of the Country Music Hall of Fame and especially the Foundation Library and Media Center.

Ernest Tubb (1914 -   ), the tall leathery-faced Texan, became the next member in 1965. Famous for his biggest hit "Walking The Floor Over You," Tubb still travels some 100,000 miles a year on tour, and is considered a pioneer in mating the lonesome sound of the southeast mountains with the more modern cowboy sounds of the southwest. When he came to the Grand Ole Opry in 1943, he was one of the first to introduce electric instruments to that stage.

Because of rules no longer in effect, there were four electees in 1966, with **Eddy Arnold** (1918 -   ) heading the list. One of the record industry's biggest alltime sellers — regardless of field — in history, Arnold is credited with establishing the smoother sound which enabled country music to shed some of the "hillbilly" image which impeded its progress for so long. Yet the same year one of the greatest of the pure old-time musicians, Uncle Dave Macon (1870 - 1952) was elected. A superb comedian, banjo player, and entertainer, Macon came from the old school of showmen — he could do it all — and although he didn't begin a professional career until he was fifty-two years old, he performed regularly up until about a month before his death at the age of eighty-one.

George D. Hay (1895 - 1968) was also elected that year. Hay, an unyielding advocate of simple old time music who went by the title "The Solemn Old Judge," helped found the two most important radio barn dances in country music history: The WLS National Barn Dance in 1924, and WSM's Grand Old Opry the following year, and he remained at the helm of the Opry for three decades. Finally, Jim Denny (1911 - 1963) — a publisher, businessman, and promoter — was elected in 1966; his behind-the-scenes guidance shaped the careers of many entertainers, and he built the Cedarwood Music Company nearly single-handed.

A bumper crop of four men were elected in 1967. Those selected included two influential businessmen: **J. L. Frank** (1900 - 1952), a pioneer show promoter and powerful influence on the careers of Roy Acuff, Minnie Pearl, Pee Wee King and others; and **Steve Sholes** (1914 - 1968), who championed country music in a long career at RCA, signing Eddy Arnold, Jim Reeves and an almost unknown Mississippi boy, Elvis Presley.

COUNTRY MUSIC HALL OF FAME

ELECTED 1962

ROY ACUFF

SEPTEMBER 15, 1903

"THE SMOKY MOUNTAIN BOY"..."FIDDLED" AND SANG HIS WAY INTO THE HEARTS OF MILLIONS THE WORLD OVER. OFTENTIMES BRINGING COUNTRY MUSIC TO AREAS WHERE IT HAD NEVER BEEN BEFORE. "THE KING OF COUNTRY MUSIC"... HAS CARRIED HIS TROUP OF PERFORMERS OVERSEAS TO ENTERTAIN HIS COUNTRY'S ARMED FORCES AT CHRISTMASTIME FOR MORE THAN TWENTY YEARS. MANY SUCCESSFUL ARTISTS CREDIT THEIR SUCCESS TO A HELPING HAND AND ENCOURAGING WORD FROM ROY ACUFF.

COUNTRY MUSIC ASSOCIATION

COUNTRY MUSIC HALL OF FAME

ELECTED 1964

TEX RITTER

JANUARY 12, 1907

BORN PANOLA COUNTY, TEXAS.... ALUMNUS UNIVERSITY OF TEXAS. ONE OF AMERICA'S MOST ILLUSTRIOUS AND VERSATILE STARS OF RADIO, TELEVISION, RECORDS, MOTION PICTURES, AND BROADWAY STAGE. UNTIRING PIONEER AND CHAMPION OF THE COUNTRY AND WESTERN MUSIC INDUSTRY. HIS DEVOTION TO HIS GOD, HIS FAMILY, AND HIS COUNTRY IS A CONTINUING INSPIRATION TO HIS COUNTLESS FRIENDS THROUGHOUT THE WORLD.

COUNTRY MUSIC ASSOCIATION

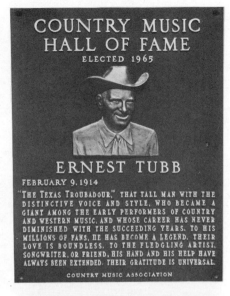

COUNTRY MUSIC HALL OF FAME

ELECTED 1965

ERNEST TUBB

FEBRUARY 9, 1914

"THE TEXAS TROUBADOUR," THAT TALL MAN WITH THE DISTINCTIVE VOICE AND STYLE, WHO BECAME A GIANT AMONG THE EARLY PERFORMERS OF COUNTRY AND WESTERN MUSIC, AND WHOSE CAREER HAS NEVER DIMINISHED WITH THE SUCCEEDING YEARS. TO HIS MILLIONS OF FANS, HE HAS BECOME A LEGEND. THEIR LOVE IS BOUNDLESS. TO THE FLEDGLING ARTIST, SONGWRITER, OR FRIEND, HIS HAND AND HIS HELP HAVE ALWAYS BEEN EXTENDED. THEIR GRATITUDE IS UNIVERSAL.

COUNTRY MUSIC ASSOCIATION

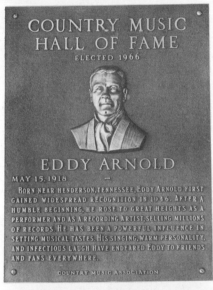

COUNTRY MUSIC HALL OF FAME

ELECTED 1966

EDDY ARNOLD

MAY 15, 1918   —

BORN NEAR HENDERSON, TENNESSEE, EDDY ARNOLD FIRST GAINED WIDESPREAD RECOGNITION IN 1946. AFTER A HUMBLE BEGINNING, HE ROSE TO GREAT HEIGHTS AS A PERFORMER AND AS A RECORDING ARTIST, SELLING MILLIONS OF RECORDS. HE HAS BEEN A POWERFUL INFLUENCE IN SETTING MUSICAL TASTES. HIS SINGING, WARM PERSONALITY, AND INFECTIOUS LAUGH HAVE ENDEARED EDDY TO FRIENDS AND FANS EVERYWHERE.

COUNTRY MUSIC ASSOCIATION

COUNTRY MUSIC HALL OF FAME

ELECTED 1966

UNCLE DAVE MACON

OCTOBER 7, 1870   —   MARCH 22, 1952

"THE DIXIE DEWDROP," FROM SMART STATION, TENNESSEE, WAS A MAN WHOSE DELIGHTFUL SENSE OF HUMOR AND STERLING CHARACTER ENDEARED HIM TO MILLIONS. A PROFESSIONAL PERFORMER ON THE GRAND OLE OPRY FOR 26 YEARS, HE WAS A "MINSTREL OF THE COUNTRYSIDE" PRIOR TO THAT. HE WAS A COUNTRY MAN WHO LOVED HUMANITY AND ENJOYED HELPING OTHERS. A PROFICIENT BANJOIST, HE WAS A SINGER OF OLD-TIME BALLADS AND WAS, DURING HIS TIME, THE MOST POPULAR COUNTRY MUSIC ARTIST IN AMERICA.

COUNTRY MUSIC ASSOCIATION

COUNTRY MUSIC HALL OF FAME

ELECTED 1966

GEORGE D. HAY

NOVEMBER 9, 1895

"THE SOLEMN OLD JUDGE," A MEMPHIS NEWSPAPERMAN-TURNED-RADIO ANNOUNCER, GEORGE D. HAY CARRIED HIS LOVE OF COUNTRY MUSIC TO RADIO—FIRST IN CHICAGO AND THEN NASHVILLE, AS THE MAN WHO ORIGINATED THE GRAND OLE OPRY. HE APPEARED AS MASTER OF CEREMONIES FOR NEARLY 30 YEARS ON THE OPRY UNTIL HIS RETIREMENT AND WAS INSTRUMENTAL IN FURTHERING THE CAREERS OF HUNDREDS OF PERFORMERS.

COUNTRY MUSIC ASSOCIATION

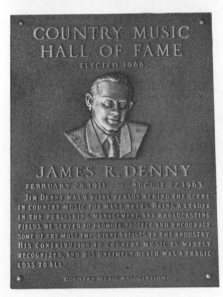

COUNTRY MUSIC HALL OF FAME

ELECTED 1966

JAMES R. DENNY

FEBRUARY 28, 1911   —   AUGUST 27, 1963

JIM DENNY WAS A VITAL PERSON BEHIND THE SCENE IN COUNTRY MUSIC FOR MANY YEARS. BEING A LEADER IN THE PUBLISHING, MANAGEMENT, AND BROADCASTING FIELDS, HE SERVED TO PROMOTE, PROTECT, AND ENCOURAGE SOME OF THE MOST IMPORTANT ARTISTS IN THE INDUSTRY. HIS CONTRIBUTION TO COUNTRY MUSIC IS WIDELY RECOGNIZED, AND HIS UNTIMELY DEATH WAS A TRAGIC LOSS TO ALL.

COUNTRY MUSIC ASSOCIATION

COUNTRY MUSIC HALL OF FAME

ELECTED 1967

J. L. (JOE) FRANK

APRIL 15, 1900   —   MAY 4, 1952

PIONEER PROMOTER OF COUNTRY & WESTERN SHOWS. HIS METHOD OF COMBINING BROADCASTING AND PERSONAL APPEAR-ANCES MOVED COUNTRY ENTERTAINERS FROM RURAL SCHOOL-HOUSES INTO CITY AUDITORIUMS AND COLISEUMS. INSPIRED AND HELPED TO DEVELOP THE CAREERS OF ROY ACUFF, GENE AUTRY, EDDY ARNOLD, PEE WEE KING, MINNIE PEARL, ERNEST TUBB, AND MANY MORE. THIS UNSELFISH, COMPASSIONATE MAN WAS ONE OF THE INDUSTRY'S MOST LOVED MEMBERS.

COUNTRY MUSIC ASSOCIATION

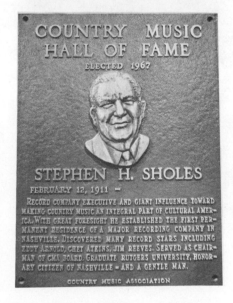

COUNTRY MUSIC HALL OF FAME

ELECTED 1967

STEPHEN H. SHOLES

FEBRUARY 12, 1911   —

RECORD COMPANY EXECUTIVE AND GIANT INFLUENCE TOWARD MAKING COUNTRY MUSIC AN INTEGRAL PART OF CULTURAL AMER-ICA. WITH GREAT FORESIGHT HE ESTABLISHED THE FIRST PER-MANENT RESIDENCE OF A MAJOR RECORDING COMPANY IN NASHVILLE. DISCOVERED MANY RECORD STARS INCLUDING EDDY ARNOLD, CHET ATKINS, JIM REEVES. SERVED AS CHAIR-MAN OF CMA BOARD. GRADUATE RUTGERS UNIVERSITY, HONOR-ARY CITIZEN OF NASHVILLE — AND A GENTLE MAN.

COUNTRY MUSIC ASSOCIATION

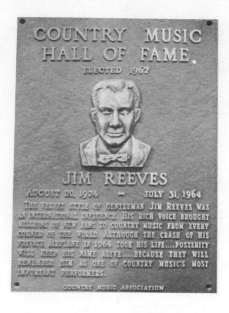

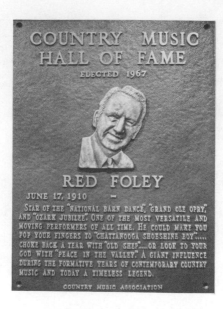

Bob Wills

Gene Autry and Art Satherley

Two performers were elected in 1967 as well: **Jim Reeves** (1924 - 1964), the smooth-voiced singer who bridged both country and popular music, and who was killed in a plane crash at the height of his career; and **Red Foley** (1919 - 1968), a country boy from Blue Lick, Kentucky, who was able to bridge all musical gaps, having tremendous records in country, pop, rhythm and blues, and had the first million-selling gospel record, "Peace In The Valley," yet who never lost the country identity which endeared him to millions of fans.

Bob Wills (1905 - 1975), the fiddling creator of an entire style of music called "western swing" was 1968's electee. Famous for "San Antonio Rose" and hundreds of other country classics, Wills merged the songs and styles of country music with the danceable big-band sound and the "hot" solos of New Orleans jazz to create one of the most distinct and exciting of country music's sub-genres.

Gene Autry (1907 -   ), the singing cowboy whose music and screen presence shaped a whole form of country music was elected to the Hall of Fame in 1969. Now famous as a multimillionaire businessman, it is all too easy to overlook the tremendous contributions Autry made to country music as a singer, songwriter, and as one of the top record sellers in country music's history; all in addition to defining the screen character of the singing cowboy and fostering the careers of many singing cowboys who followed his lead.

One of country music's handful of true pioneers, the original **Carter Family,** was elected in 1970. They first recorded their plaintive mountain ballads and gospel songs for Victor Records in 1927, setting the definitive style for singers and groups in the Appalachian tradition from that time to the present, and featuring the revolutionary guitar style of Maybelle Carter, who is still actively performing with the Johnny Cash road show.

Bill Monroe (1911 -) was also elected that year; he, like Wills, created an entire substyle in country music almost singlehanded, and today bluegrass music (derived from the name of Monroe's band, the Blue Grass Boys), is one of the most popular and easily distinguished music styles in the world. Rarely a day goes by that one doesn't hear the sounds of a driving five string banjo or a wailing fiddle in some commercial, some film or television sound track, or recording.

Pioneer recording man **Arthur E. Satherley** (1889 -) was elected to the Country Music Hall of Fame the following year. A hale and hearty man in his mid-eighties, "Uncle Art's" crisp memory spans the entire history of commercial country music, from his days with Thomas Edison, recording on cylinders, to the height of his career in the 1940s, when he was recording the biggest-selling artists for Columbia: Autry, Acuff, Wills, Monroe and literally scores of others.

Politician, singer, actor, songwriter and businessman, Governor **Jimmie Davis** (1902 -) was elected in 1972. Twice elected governor of Louisiana, Davis first made his mark on country music in the early 1930s, but became known worldwide with "You Are My Sunshine" in 1939.

In 1973 **Chet Atkins** (1923 -) was elected, honoring the man who changed the course of country music not only through his unique and tremendously popular guitar stylings, but through his creativity as a producer and an executive with RCA Records. **Patsy Cline** (1932 - 1963) was also elected that year, in memory of her short but brilliant and influential career which ended in a tragic plane crash which killed her and three other prominent country stars en route to a benefit performance.

The first tie in the balloting occurred in 1974 as has been previously mentioned. This was a mathematical improbability of high order, which allowed two important figures to be inducted: **Pee Wee King** (1914 -), a bandleader and developer of talent who co-wrote such classics as "Slow-Poke," "You Belong To Me," "Bonaparte's Retreat,"

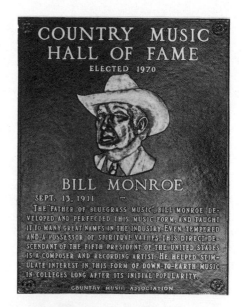

Jimmie Davis

Chet Atkins

Patsy Cline

The Carter Family

The former entrance of the Hall of Fame showing the graceful barn-like structure and one of the fountains as it appeared before the extensive remodeling and construction of the new addition which approximately doubled the size of the building and changed the public entrance.

and the all-time most popular song in country music, "Tennessee Waltz" and **Owen Bradley** (1915 -), a musician and composer. He not only began and helped develop the "Music Row" area in Nashville and guided much of the recording which was to come to Music City, but he also recorded a galaxy of hitmakers for Decca (now MCA) records, including Foley, Cline, Monroe, Davis and many others.

In 1975 the first comedian (or in this case comedienne) was elected to the Country Music Hall of Fame in the person of **Minnie Pearl** (1912 -). Her dimestore hat with its dangling price tag and her shrill "How-dee!" have become world-wide trademarks for country music and for country humor, which has always been an extremely important part of country music on stage and on radio and television.

1976 saw both a deceased and living member inducted once again. **Paul Cohen** (1908 - 1971), a pioneer record executive, was one of the first to utilize Nashville facilities to record, and was instrumental in developing Nashville as a national music center in years to come. As a producer and executive for Decca Records he guided the recordings of fellow Hall of Famers Red Foley, Ernest Tubb, Bill Monroe, Jimmy Davis, Patsy Cline, and, coincidentally, the living member inducted with him that Bicentennial year: **Kitty Wells** (1919 -   ).

Born right in Nashville, Muriel Deason used the name of an old folk song, "Sweet Kitty Wells," as a stage name while touring with her husband's popular band, Johnny and Jack. The astonishing success of her record "It Wasn't God Who Made Honky-Tonk Angels" vaulted to national stardom, however, and her sweet, plaintive voice has continued to embody the essence of traditional country music, and earned her long-held title "Queen of Country Music."

Other stars are sure to follow in succeeding years: the names Merle Travis, Vernon Dalhart, Bradley Kincaid, the Sons of the Pioneers, Lefty Frizzell, Johnny Cash, Merle Haggard and Loretta Lynn and many others will no doubt enter the pantheon of the greats in the not too distant future, each honored for his or her unique contribution to the growth, the sound, and the style of country music as a vital, growing business and as a uniquely American artistic entity.

Significance of the Country Music Hall of Fame

Yet it is important to see the Country Music Hall of Fame, impressive and meaningful as it is, as just a part of an organization which has had as its sole purpose from its inception the preservation of the history of this unique musical form, from the rudest beginnings through the early age of record and radio on up to the international scope of the present. The Country Music Foundation encompasses the Hall of Fame, the Museum, the Library and Media Center, the Foundation Press, and all their activities, both separate and interrelated, for two basic objectives: first, to become the repository for as much information on country music and its history as possible; and second, to share and communicate this information to a growing public which is becoming increasingly interested in the history of this most history-conscious of American musical forms. Whether through visual display in the Museum, printed matter from the press, recordings or rare documents from the Library, or any other resource available, the Country Music Foundation has and will continue to look toward gaining knowledge of country music's past and present, and presenting it — and the insight gained in and from the search — to those who wish to share in this knowledge.

The Country Music Hall of Fame, then, is much more than a hallway filled with the plaques and portraits of stars and pioneers: in the museum which surrounds it and the library and archive which rest beneath it, it is a unique and remarkable commitment by an industry to its own heritage. That such a museum and library and archive exists tells a lot about the people — both businessmen and entertainers — who make up the world of country music. It, in fact, tells a lot about country music.

MOVIELAND
WAX MUSEUM

Buena Park, California

I n this wax museum there are 232 stars of the movies — past and present — in 79 simulated situations from famous movies. In the strict
sense it is not a hall of fame. However, since this entertainment medium
has thrilled three or four generations of fans, the stars whose scenes have

*This exciting set of "Ben Hur" recreates
the chariot race scene from the 1959 Academy-award winning motion picture starring Charlton Heston.*

(Above) Exterior view, of the Movieland Wax Museum in Buena Park, (Los Angeles) California. (At right) A view of the entrance at night.

been selected for this book, which pays tribute to the super achievers in all fields, must constitute a Hall of Fame of the Movie industry.

This museum was dedicated May 4, 1962, at which time Mary Pickford said: "Dedicated this day to the artists of the entertainment industry who, through their talents and efforts, have contributed so much to the enjoyment and understanding of the peoples of the world."

(Below) Edward G. Robinson, accompanied by his granddaughter, as he attended the dedication ceremony of the set in the Museum featuring him as "Little Caesar".

405

Roy Rogers, Dale Evans and Trigger on the set in a scene from "Don't Fence Me In".

(Above) A scene from "Guns of Navarone", starring Gregory Peck, David Niven, Anthony Quinn and Gia Scala.

Robert Redford and Paul Newman as they appear on the Museum set in a scene from "Butch Cassidy and the Sundance Kid".

Authenticity is the key throughout Movieland. Most sets include original costumes donated by the stars or duplicates made from the original patterns found on file in movie archives. Fantastic and meticulous craftsmanship combines with special animation and extensive sound and sight effects to make the movies come alive for visitors. To complete the atmosphere, sets are equipped with props and artifacts like those used in the films—klieg lights, microphones, wind machines and cameras ready to roll. It all adds to the mystique.

Going back to the real beginnings of moving pictures, Movieland houses one of America's finest collections of original movie machines, Mutoscopes and Biographs with "flys-card" films starring favorites from Tom Mix to Rin Tin Tin. There is also a magnificent display of rare movie stills and elaborate posters.

(At right) The Pieta, originally carved by Michelangelo for St. Peter's in Rome, has been copied for the Movieland Wax Museum by Pietrasanta artisans from one flawless piece of Carrara marble taken from Michelangelo's own quarry. (Below) The crew on the bridge of the United Star Ship Enterprise on the Star Trek set as they appeared in person, DeForest Kelley (Dr. "Bones" McCoy), William Shatner (Captain Kirk), Leonard Nimoy (Mr. Spock) and Nichelle Nichols (Lt. Uhura).

THE NATIONAL COWBOY HALL OF FAME AND WESTERN HERITAGE CENTER

Oklahoma City, Oklahoma

Anyone who has ever been thrilled by a western movie or story, or admired the western scenes of Frederic Remington, Charles M. Russell, Charles Schreyvogel, Thomas Moran, Frank Tenney Johnson, Joseph Sharp, Albert Bierstadt, and others, will be enthusiastic about this combination hall of fame, museum, art gallery and reference center. All of this is housed in an imposing group of buildings immaculately maintained on Route # 66 in Oklahoma City on thirty-seven acres known as Persimmon Hill. The acreage permits enough space for a nature trail as an added feature of the educational program that is one of the primary goals of this western cultural center.

The architectural design resulted from a national competition, participated in by two hundred fifty-seven architects, which was won by Harold Jack Begrow and Jack Brown of Birmingham, Michigan, with a very daring but functional design that is extremely modern, but symbolic of the west. The high slanted ceilings are reminiscent of the tents used by the pioneers around a campfire coming from the glow of light reflected from fountains in the center of the buildings. The fountains represent the importance of water to the early settlers.

The exciting memorial building including the Payne-Kirkpatrick Building which houses the breathtaking statue the *End of the Trail,* cost $3,300,000 and have collections valued at $10,000,000.

The idea for the center dedicated to the west and its heroes originated in 1952 with a visit to the Will Rogers memorial at Claremore, Oklahoma, by Chester A. Reynolds, a Kansas City manufacturer. He thought that there should be a shrine to honor many of the outstanding men who developed the west. He personally visited the governors of the seventeen western states represented here and sold them on the idea of cooperating in the program to finance and build the center.

Rodeo Hall with a bronze of Bill Linderman in the foreground and a painting of Phil Lyne, the 1971 and 1972 all-around Rodeo champ in the background.

The saddle shop display with various saddles, stirrups, bits, etc.

By an act of Congress of August 5, 1957, the center became a national memorial dedicated to the courageous men and women who pioneered the vast and rich empire known as the American West. It is a living lesson in initiative and free enterprise which has given our generation and many generations yet unborn the richest heritage ever given a free people.

The seventeen western states represented here, Arizona, California, Colorado, Idaho, Kansas, Montana, Nebraska, Nevada, New Mexico, North Dakota, Oklahoma, Oregon, South Dakota, Texas, Utah, Washington, and Wyoming, accepted a quota of money to raise based on population to finance the project. Through various means each state, with the efforts of interested individuals and organizations, succeeded in making its quota and reaching the goal of paying for this marvelous learning center.

In truth this represents the indomitable spirit of the pioneers. On June 26, 1965, the Center was dedicated and opened to the public. In June of 1975 the Cowboy Hall of Fame received its three millionth visitor.

The location of the Hall of Fame was the result of competition between more than one hundred cities. The selection was narrowed first to ten, and then, to three cities with the final selection going to its present site atop beautiful Persimmon Hill, surrounded by thirty-seven acres.

The expressed purpose of the Center as stated in the official information sheet is as follows:

No era in the history of this nation stands so dramatically apart as the incomparable saga of development of the West. For here, on the sprawling prairies and rugged terrain they loved so well, our forefathers stood together, regardless of background or race, and fought for a concept of life known to few others. If our country is to survive as a free nation, the coming generations of American youth must realize their heritage . . .

the hardships and struggles, the ideals and inspirations of these indomitable pioneers who carved our civilization from a rugged wilderness. To this heritage is the National Cowboy Hall of Fame and Western Heritage Center dedicated—the first gesture of a grateful America to honor the noble men and women of dauntless spirit who pioneered the vast empire known as the American West—to make its development one of the great epochs of world history to bequeath to this and to the many generations yet unborn the richest heritage ever given a free people.

Some of the Special Attractions at the National Cowboy Hall of Fame

There is an impressive collection of Western Art by Albert Bierstadt, Henry Farny, Nicolai Fechin, Robert Henri, Thomas Hill, William R. Leigh, Alfred Jacob Miller, Thomas Moran, Frederic Remington, Carl Rungius, Charles M. Russell, Charles Schreyvogel, Joseph Henry Sharp, Willard Stone and others.

The art exhibits include bronzes, wood sculptures, oils, watercolors, pastels and pen and ink drawings. The collection of the Charles M. Russell bronzes is the most nearly complete collection in existence. There are seven illustrated letters by C. M. Russell and also a Russell sketch book containing 87 original sketches. There is a 35 calibre 1895 Winchester rifle with C. M. Russell engravings done with a penknife on each side of the breach.

The art gallery

A recent acquisition of great importance was the donation of the Albert K. Mitchell collection of Remington and Russell material valued at $1,800,000. Three of Remington's most famous paintings are included in this exciting collection including *In From the Night Herd*. A Remington bronze of great interest and value on exhibit is *Bronco Buster*. Other important bronzes on display include *The Last Drop* by Charles Schreyvogel, and *Meat for Wild Men, The Buffalo Runner, Counting Coup, The Bronc Twister* by Charles M. Russell.

The National Rodeo Hall of Fame

One area of this collection of western memorabilia is devoted to the rodeo performers. Situated in the center of the Hall of Great Westerners is the National Rodeo Hall of Fame honoring the all around champion cowboys each year beginning with 1929. Twenty two exhibit spaces contain saddles, trophies, buckles, boots, and other personal effects of the world's all-around champions. In addition there are 14 display cases featuring photographs of the All-Around Champion Cowboys and the men elected as honorees in the Rodeo Hall of Fame.

Two pylons, each 14 feet high, are covered with plaques containing names of the All-Around Champion Cowboys and the men elected as honorees in the Rodeo Hall of Fame.

The Great Map of the West

This is a unique feature of this educational center. Dean Krakel, Managing Director of the Hall, felt that a map of the continental United States to show visually the early settlement and expansion of the nation was essential to tie together for the visitors all the wonderful exhibits that are a part of Americana, as displayed there.

Chief Curator Juan Menchaca and his staff developed a thirty-two by forty-eight foot relief map of the United States. The map is tilted toward the viewers and curved to suggest the curvature of the earth's surface. A tape recording is coordinated with multi-colored lights to show in historical sequence the development of settlements, trails and railroads across the country.

The End of the Trail

This massive alabaster white sculpture by the late James Earle Fraser is certainly one of the great attractions of this museum. It is eighteen feet high, two and one-half times life size, portraying a defeated Indian warrior slumped over his weary war pony. The statue and portions of the studio collection of Fraser and his wife Laura Gardin Fraser are exhibited in a special wing.

This exhibit includes commemorative medals and coins including the original casts for the Buffalo-Indian head nickel, sculptures of historic figures, ten-foot high bas reliefs of American history scenes, sculpting tools, photographs, sketches and personal items of this famous American sculptor team.

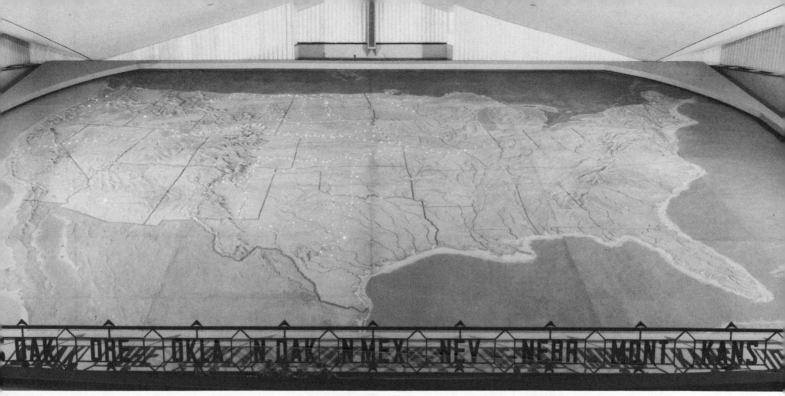

The Great Map of the West

Hambrick Garden

Shade trees, a stream splashing over waterfalls, flowers, and western plants make Hambrick Garden a beautiful experience in your visit. Walkways take you through the garden. In Hambrick Garden are the graves and markers of famous bucking horses. Beautification of the museum grounds was made possible by Miss Freda Hambrick of Colorado Springs, Colorado. Miss Hambrick is a member of the Board of Directors.

Founders Hall

This section of the Western Heritage Center honors the industrialists, merchants, editors, teachers and others who brought civilization to the western range.

Ackerman Garden

This refreshing beauty spot is located at the entrance to the Payne-Kirkpatrick Memorial which holds the *End of the Trail* and other sculpture by James Earle Fraser and Laura Gardin Fraser.

West of Yesterday

This series of exhibits begins with the American Indians. Then there are trappers, prospectors, the U.S. Cavalry, cowboys, homesteaders, and finally a pioneer town. There are nickelodeons in the Silver Dollar Saloon, the Stockyard Hotel, the old gunshop, saddle shop and, of course, the blacksmith shop. Other reminders of the old west are the lawyer's office and the newspaper shop, doctor's office, general store, photo studio, chapel and finally—the jail.

413

Aerial view of the Cowboy Hall of Fame

HONOREES

MANNER OF SELECTION

The usual manner of nominating persons for the Hall of Fame of Great Westerners comes from within the various states. A Biography and letter should be sent to the Trustees of the particular state where the nominee is from, stating reasons why the person should be considered. Ordinarily, this person should have been deceased for at least five years. Nomination Biographies submitted must be typewritten, double spaced, and be not more than three pages in length. Then, Trustees from that particular State jointly consider the matter, referring or declining to refer the Biography to the Nominating Committee of the National Cowboy Hall of Fame and Western Heritage Center for further consideration. They must have this information no later than January 1st of each year. Then, the Nominating Committee brings the matter before the Board of Directors at its Annual Meeting for final consideration.

The manner of electing persons to the Hall of Great Western Performers is much the same.

Nominees to the Rodeo Hall of Fame are screened by vote of the Rodeo Historical Society, with approval of the Rodeo Cowboys' Association of Denver, Colorado. Final ratification is made by the Directors of the National Cowboy Hall of Fame and Western Heritage Center.

Captain William Clark

HALL OF GREAT WESTERNERS

AT LARGE

EDWARD F. BEALE (1822–1893), California, trailblazer of empire, developer of state's largest ranch.

WARREN L. BLIZZARD (1888–1954), Oklahoma, world known animal husbandman.

FRANK S. BOICE (1894–1956), Arizona, rancher, national cattle industry leader.

JOHN EDWARD BOREIN (1873–1945), California, working cowboy and western artist.

CHRISTOPHER 'KIT' CARSON (1809–1868), guide for Fremont and Kearny expeditions that helped overthrow Spanish control and open the West.

JESSE CHISHOLM (1805–1868), Frontiersman, Guide, Trader, Trail Blazer, Peace Maker. It is said that no one ever left his home cold or hungry. The Chisholm Trail was named for him.

JEAN PIERRE CHOUTEAU (1758–1849), Oklahoma, fur trader and Indian agent for the Osage. He established the first permanent white settlement in 1796 near what is now Salina, Oklahoma.

CAPTAIN WILLIAM CLARK (1770–1838), distinguished army officer who was co-leader of Lewis and Clark Expedition.

JOHN CLAY (1851–1934), a native Scot who became one of America's leading ranch managers and founder of businesses dealing with agriculture and livestock.

WILLIAM F. 'BUFFALO BILL' CODY (1846–1917), Nebraska, express rider, scout, showman.

CHARLES F. CURTISS (1863–1947), Iowa, famed dean of agriculture, breeder of better livestock.

FATHER PIERRE-JEAN DE SMET (1801–1873), Jesuit missionary who spent his life among the Indians of the Northwest, to whom he was known as 'Blackrobe' — outstanding mediator among the tribes and between Indians and whites.

GENERAL GRENVILLE MELLEN DODGE (1831–1916), merchant, banker, Civil War officer, Congressman; chief engineer in building of Union Pacific and other railroads.

DWIGHT D. EISENHOWER (1890–1969), Kansas, internationally famous soldier, statesman, farmer-stockman, Army 5-Star General, 34th President of the United States.

JOHN WARNE GATES 1855–1911), Promoter, speculator, captain of industry. One of the most vigorous and colorful figures in American finance.

CHARLES GOODNIGHT (1836–1929), Texas, trail blazer beneficial cattle king.

JAMES J. HILL (1838–1916), Minnesota, founder of Great Northern railroad, colonizer, empire builder, land improver.

CYRUS K. HOLLIDAY (1826–1900), Kansas, founder of the Santa Fe railway system; a developer of the West.

SAM HOUSTON (1793–1863), soldier, statesman, first president of Texas Republic, governor of Tennessee and Texas.

CHIEF JOSEPH (c. 1840–1904), Oregon, a Nez Percé Chief who rose to greatness as a leader and spokesman, never ceasing his efforts to win fair and just treatment for his people.

RICHARD KING (1824–1885), river boat captain who founded the great King ranch of South Texas and helped build a regional culture.

CAPTAIN MERIWETHER LEWIS (1774–1809), leader of famed Lewis and Clark Expedition, Virginia land owner, Governor of Louisiana Territory.

Youthful portrait of Father De Smet

Captain Meriwether Lewis

415

— Illustration by Frederic Remington

ABRAHAM LINCOLN (1809–1865), Illinois, 16th President of the United States who signed into law many Acts from which all states benefited, mainly the Homestead Act — probably the most important single factor in the settlement of the West.

JAKE McCLURE (1903–1940), New Mexico rancher, world champion roper, rodeo judge.

HENRY MILLER (1827–1916), California, immigrant butcher boy who became great land developer and rancher on a giant scale.

GENERAL WILLIAM JACKSON PALMER (1836–1909), Colorado, Civil War General, builder of Denver and Rio Grande railroad, industrialist, philanthropist.

WILLIAM MacLEOD RAINE (1871–1954), dean of Western novelists with 80 books in 19 million copies.

FREDERIC REMINGTON (1861–1909), painter, sculptor, whose Western work has true fidelity to subject and scene.

EUGENE MANLOVE RHODES (1869–1934), New Mexico, writer whose western fiction was fact.

WILL ROGERS (1879–1935), Oklahoma, cowboy humorist, actor, writer, humanitarian.

THEODORE ROOSEVELT (1858–1919), North Dakota, rancher, interpretive Western author, conservationist, President of the United States.

CHARLES M. RUSSELL (1864–1926). Montana, unequalled Western artist.

SACAJAWEA (1787–1884), the talented Shoshone woman who guided the Lewis and Clark Expedition from Dakota to the Pacific.

JEDEDIAH STRONG 'JED' SMITH (1799–1831), explorer who opened trails and fur-trading contracts with the Indians to be used by other Western pioneers.

ALEXANDER H. SWAN (1831–1905), Wyoming, creator of great ranches in intermountain area, importer of purebreds, builder of stockyards industry.

BRIGHAM YOUNG (1801–1877), Utah, colonizer, state builder, Mormon exodus leader.

ARIZONA

RAMON AHUMADO (1868–1926), superb horseman, roundup boss and rancher.

WILL C. BARNES (1858–1936), pioneer cowman, territorial legislator, range official, writer, recipient of Congressional Medal of Honor.

WILLIAM FLAKE (1839–1932), colonizer, stabilizer of northern region, area builder.

COLONEL HENRY C. HOOKER (1828–1907), founder of oldest continuous ranch in state, livestock breeder.

EUSEBIO FRANCISCO KINO (1645–1711), the famed Father Kino, Jesuit missionary, leader in development of agriculture and livestock raising.

GEORGE C. RUFFNER (1862–1933), freighter, peace officer in territory and state, rancher.

JOHN H. SLAUGHTER (1842–1922), pioneer cattleman and sheriff of Cochise County who rid the Tombstone area of outlaws during boom days.

FRANK WALLACE (1860–1946), early-day trail driver who helped in development of many large ranches and the livestock industry of his state.

CALIFORNIA

WILLIAM HUGH BABER (1893–1968), one of the outstanding men in California's livestock and farming industry, civic leader, rancher.

FRED HATHAWAY BIXBY (1875–1952), huge ranch operator, philanthropist, farm and livestock official.

HENRY C. DAULTON (1829–1893), overland trail maker, miner, rancher, public servant.

W. C. 'WES' EADE (1874–1961), rancher, cattle organization official, supporter of farm youth program.

AMADEO PETER GIANNINI (1870–1949), founder and developer of the famous Bank of America—a builder of men, inspiring them with his tireless vitality and tempering them with his kindness.

COLONEL W. W. HOLLISTER (1818–1886), transcontinental drover, rancher, developer of vast areas.

COLLIS POTTER HUNTINGTON (1821–1900), railroad builder, industrialist and financier who helped build first transcontinental railroad.

DR. CHARLES BRUCE ORVIS (1858–1955), pioneer veterinarian and stockman, improver of beef cattle.

RICHARD ROY OWENS (1881–1953), stockman, noted contributor to better livestock.

JOSEPH RUSS (1825–1886), pioneer livestock grower, business and political leader, philanthropist.

HUBBARD S. RUSSELL, SR. (1885–1963), rancher, Western cattle producer, politician and oil pioneer.

COLORADO

WILLIAM BENT (1810–1869), frontiersman, Indian trader, fort builder.

CHARLES BOETTCHER (1852–1948), Prussian immigrant whose far flung business interests included hardware, banking, beet sugar factories, cement plants, electric light and power, meat packing, real estate and ranching.

CHARLES E. COLLINS (1869–1944), trail hand, cowboy, outstanding cattleman, official.

Amadeo Giannini

417

John Evans

Frank Gooding

JOHN EVANS (1841–1897), a medical doctor who, after outstanding career as physician, church and educational leader in Indiana and Illinois, was appointed territorial governor of Colorado to become one of the greatest advocates of the state and the city of Denver.

JOHN W. ILIFF (1831–1878), cattle king, business leader, stockmen's official.

OTTO MEARS (1840–1931), Russian immigrant who was called 'Pathfinder of the Western Slope' for building toll roads and railroads through mountains and plains.

NATHAN MEEKER (1817–1879), author, pioneer settler, Indian Agent, philanthropist.

HENRY M. PORTER (1840–1937), outstanding industrialist, banker, cattleman, civic leader and philanthropist who contributed greatly to the building of Denver.

JOHN WESLEY PROWERS (1838–1884), early day wagon train freighter who later became outstanding cattle breeder, merchant and legislator.

WINFIELD S. STRATTON (1848–1902), gold prospector who struck it rich at Cripple Creek and used his millions to help develop his home town, Colorado Springs.

MAHLON DANIEL THATCHER (1839–1916), a pioneer businessman, banker and philanthropist who contributed much to the state's development.

IDAHO

FRANK R. GOODING (1859–1929), pioneer builder, governor, U. S. Senator, stockman.

JOHN HAILEY (1835–1921), Indian fighter, Oregon trail driver, cattleman, state builder.

KANSAS

DAN D. CASEMENT (1868–1953), blue ribbon breeder and feeder, stock association builder.

CALVIN W. FLOYD (1872–1955), cattleman, association official, banker, leading example of service.

GEORGE GRANT (1822–1878), immigrant from Scotland who built a cattle empire, importer of first Angus bulls.

JESSE CLAIRE HARPER (1883–1961), veteran coach of many sports, succeeded Rockne as athletic director at Notre Dame, prominent rancher and cattleman.

CHARLES J. 'BUFFALO' JONES (1844–1919), naturalist who turned from slaying wild animals to preserving them.

DR. L. L. JONES (1879–1954), famed veterinarian, cattle breeder and rancher who contributed much to the development of the Garden City area.

EMIL C. KIELHORN (1876–1946), German immigrant who became successful rancher, banker and legislator, diligent in betterment of his community.

JOSEPH G. McCOY (1837–1915), constructed the stock yards at railhead in Abilene and started the development of the Chisholm Trail.

WILLIAM D. POOLE (1829–1911), founder of one of the oldest continuous ranches, developer.

MONTANA

CHARLES M. BAIR (1857–1943), 'King of Western Wool Growers.' Helped organize irrigation projects, coal and oil production in Montana.

ROBERT S. FORD (1842–1914), overland trail boss, territorial official, rancher who had first cattle north of the Missouri.

JOHN M. HOLT (1848–1913), rancher, livestock official, community builder.

MYRON D. JEFFERS (1833–1900), overland freighter, one of first to trail herds from Texas, rancher and inspiring leader.

ADKIN W. KINGSBURY (1842–1924), early pioneer, sheep herder, farmer, placer miner and stockman.

CONRAD KOHRS (1835–1920), modest hero of a great immigrant saga; beaten down by nature, he rose to be 'king of cattlemen.'

MORTIMER HEWLETT LOTT (1827–1920), miner and stockman who pioneered the settlement and development of southwest Montana.

CHARLES HERBERT McLEOD (1859–1946), early-day merchant who played an important role in the state's political maturity and its community development.

PETER PAULY (1871–1953), one of Montana's greatest cattle and sheep growers later well known as industrialist and banker.

HENRY SIEBEN (1847–1937), nationally recognized stockman, financier and civic leader.

NELSON STORY, SR. (1838–1926), miner, rancher, cattleman who took the first Texas trail herd to Montana in 1866.

GRANVILLE STUART (1834–1918), prospector who helped discover the gold fields of Montana, later outstanding as cattleman, legislator, diplomat and historian.

JOHN SURVANT (1864–1951), cattleman, businessman, State Senator, grubstaker of less fortunate.

WILLIAM WISEHAM TERRETT (1847–1922), outstanding livestock leader of southeastern Montana—developer of the great JO Ranch.

NEBRASKA

JOHN BRATT (1842–1918), territorial and state leader and developer.

WILLA SIBERT CATHER (1876–1947), American novelist and teacher. One of the country's foremost writers of the 20th Century whose novels about the West and Southwest are noted for their insight into character and the period.

CHARLES F. COFFEE (1847–1935), rancher and banker who was one of the leaders in the development of the great Omaha stockyards.

JAMES H. COOK (1857–1942), trail driver, scout, Indian fighter, rancher.

EDWARD CREIGHTON (1820–1874), builder of first transcontinental telegraph line, rancher, developer of plains country.

JAMES C. DAHLMAN (1856–1930), Omaha's cowboy mayor—a cattleman and former sheriff of Dawes County who contributed much to the development of his community and state.

GEORGE WARD HOLDREGE(1847–1926), railraod builder and rancher who promoted better agriculture in his area.

Willa Cather

James Dahlman

419

"End of the Trail" by James Earle Fraser

MORELL CASE KEITH (1823–1899), early-day stage and freight operator, one of the first large scale ranchers in Western Nebraska.

MOSES PIERCE KINKAID (1854–1922), lawyer, jurist, congressman whose 'Kinkaid Act' allowed 640-acre homestead.

FRANK J. NORTH (1840–1885), scout, first Sand Hills rancher, showman, stabilizer of wild country.

WILLIAM A. PAXTON (1837–1907), early railroad building contractor, legislator, business and civic leader.

BARTLETT RICHARDS (1859–1911), rancher, cattleman, banker, civic leader.

NEVADA

PEDRO ALTUBE (1827–1904), 'father' of Basques in America, rancher and cattleman, Spanish Ranch founder.

LEWIS R. BRADLEY (1806–1879), second governor of state, builder and leader.

HENRY HOLLOWELL CAZIER(1885–1963), civic-minded rancher and electric power developer whose enterprise contributed to development of his state.

WILLIAM H. MOFFATT (1875–1963), a native Californian who owned extensive ranching and packing interest in both Nevada and California, and is called the guiding spirit in development of Nevada's livestock industry.

JOHN SPARKS (1843–1908), rancher on vast scale, twice governor, states' right fighter in western expansion.

WILLIAM MORRIS STEWART (1827–1909), attorney who helped form Territorial government and the state's constitution, counsel for great mining interests, served as Nevada's attorney general and six years as state's first U.S. Senator, wrote the 15th amendment to U.S. Constitution and led fight for remonetization of silver.

DANIEL C. WHEELER (1840–1915), a rancher, early purebred breeder, renowned civic worker.

William Moffatt

NEW MEXICO

HOLM OLAF BURSUM(1867–1953), well known rancher who led statehood movement and was chairman of Constitutional Convention.

JOHN S. CHISUM (1824–1884), trail blazer, trail driver, creator of a fabulous empire in free range days.

VICTOR CULBERSON (1863–1930), cattleman whose skill built a vast spread, national stockmen's official.

JAMES FIELDING HINKLE (1862–1951), a cattleman and banker who served his community and state as mayor, legislator and governor.

SOLOMON LUNA (1858–1912), large scale cattle, horse and sheep rancher, generous in community support.

LUCIEN B. MAXWELL (1818–1875), first of the cattle barons from a small but adventurous beginning.

THOMAS EDWARD MITCHELL (1863–1934), pioneer cattleman and horse breeder, introduced first registered Herefords to New Mexico.

BURTON C. MOSSMAN (1867–1956), handler of a million cattle, noted free enterpriser, state builder.

Charles O'Donel

Edward Gaylord

Thomas Gilcrease

CHARLES M. O'DONEL (1860–1933), manager of great Bell Ranch for 34 years—one of the most staunch cattlemen of New Mexico history serving as leader of both state and national cattlemen's associations.

CHARLES SPRINGER (1858–1933), rancher, lawyer, principal writer of New Mexico Constitution, pioneer road builder.

NORTH DAKOTA

J. M. 'MURT' BUCKLEY (1878–1962), early-day cowboy, horseman and foreman of the great HT ranch who later, as owner of his own ranch, contributed much to his community's development—famed for his fairness and good humor.

WILLIAM CONNOLLY (1861–1946), charitable rancher who encouraged better ranching and self-reliance, his faith and ingenuity 'turned desert into paradise.'

MATT CROWLEY (1875–1955), ranchman, conservationist, official who left an indelible mark in his community.

ALEX CURRIE (1859–1937), famed horse and cattle breeder, prophet of balanced agriculture.

JAMES WILLIAM (BILL) FOLLIS (1865–1950), rancher who left a heritage of courage, honesty, generosity and integrity—loved and emulated by all who knew him.

JOHN W. GOODALL (1857–1931), rancher, frontier sheriff, philanthropist.

FRANK KEOGH (1877–1955), well-known early-day rancher who did much to organize and advance the welfare of his region.

DANIEL MANNING (1845–1914), horse breeder, rancher, pillar in area civic affairs and range industry.

WILSE L. RICHARDS (1862–1953), for 60 years leader of the cattle industry, depression burned in 1923, he built again on the ashes.

DR. VICTOR H. STICKNEY (1855–1927), pioneer doctor, first and only physician for years in western Dakotas who also left his mark as stockman, banker and civic leader.

ANDREW VOIGHT (1867–1939), pioneer rancher noted for hospitality to Indians and whites alike.

OKLAHOMA

OTTO BARBY (1865–1954), homesteader in 'No Man's Land' who stayed when weaklings burned out, conservationist.

JAMES A. CHAPMAN (1881–1966), oil pioneer of the Southwest whose philanthropies have greatly advanced educational, charitable and health institutions of the region.

CHARLES F. COLCORD (1859–1934), rancher, town and city builder, civic leader.

EDWARD KING GAYLORD (1873–1974), editor, publisher, founder of a business empire— devoted builder of Oklahoma whose career parallels Oklahoma's growth from 1903 onward.

THOMAS GILCREASE (1890–1962), oil man, founder of Gilcrease Institute of American History and Art in Tulsa, farmer, rancher, real estate dealer, banker, philanthropist.

HENRY CHARLES HITCH, SR. (1884–1967), cattle rancher, wheat farmer, stock investor, successful entrepreneur.

The relief column

FREDERIC REMINGTON

JAMES K. HITCH (1855–1921), cattleman, farmer, developer of Oklahoma panhandle, pillar of stability for the region.

BEN JOHNSON (1896–1962), ranch operator, champion roper, a living link between historical events that tied old west into the new.

LYNN RIGGS (1899–1954), author and playwright, whose play 'Green Grow The Lilacs' was the basis for the famous musical 'Oklahoma' that has contributed much to Western American folklore.

SEQUOYAH (George Gist) (1760–1844), Cherokee Indian who, although completely unschooled, invented the syllabary (alphabet) which made his people literate.

WILLIAM M. TILGHMAN (1854–1924), cattleman, frontier peace officer in Kansas and Oklahoma for fifty years.

CHARLES H. TOMPKINS (1873–1957), driver up the long trail, champion roper, showman, highway planner.

REVEREND SAMUEL AUSTIN WORCESTER (1798–1859), missionary to Cherokees in Georgia and Indian Territory—founded and made Park Hill Mission an Indian cultural center.

William Tilghman

OREGON

PETER FRENCH (1849–1897), pioneer cowman who started the purebred cattle business in southestern Oregon, a leader in the natural conflict between the homesteaders and stockmen.

WILLIAM (BILL) KITTREDGE (1876–1958), his ability and integrity built a cattle empire, his interests included agriculture, reclamation, land and wildlife conservation and improved breeding methods.

FRED A. PHILLIPS (1869–1964), stockman, reclamationist who helped draft nation's farm credit program and headed it in his area for years.

Bill Kittredge

SOUTH DAKOTA

BEN C. ASH (1851–1946), frontiersman, trail blazer, peace officer.

TOM BERRY (1879–1951), cattleman, legislator, as governor rescued state from depression and drouth.

AL CLARKSON (1866–1957), horse breeder and cattleman, area developer and stabilizer, active in government and civic affairs.

JAMES TAYLOR CRAIG (1863–1930), stalwart leader of his area in ranching, banking and civic affairs.

NEWTON EDMUNDS (1819–1908), second governor of Dakota Territory whose policy of 'negotiation not gunpowder' brought about favorable treaties

Stephen Austin

Charles Schreiner

with the Indians which closed the 'War of the Outbreak' and whose utmost faith in Dakota in darkest days encouraged settlers to hang on, thus laying the foundation of a great state.

JOHN D. HALE (1847–1929), early-day ox team freighter who later distinguished himself as a stockman.

TOM JONES (1868–1949), pioneer cattleman, leader in community and state affairs.

G. E. LEMMON (1857–1946), peace maker with the Indians, operator of one of the world's largest ranches, civic official.

JAMES PHILIP (1857–1911), Scot born freighter, cowboy, scout, prospector, buffalo preserver who left a lasting imprint in his new land.

TEXAS

STEPHEN F. AUSTIN (1793–1836), colonizer, secretary of the Republic, state builder and rancher.

SAMUEL BURK BURNETT (1849–1922), pioneer cattleman, founder of the Four Sixes Ranch, intermediary between the Kiowa-Comanche Indians and stockmen, friend of Quanah Parker, banker and businessman.

J. FRANK DOBIE (1888–1964), widely known Western author and historian.

MIFFLIN KENEDY (1818–1895), rancher, cattleman, railroad builder, developer of South Texas.

ROBERT JUSTUS KLEBERG, JR. (1896–1974). Through his genius for livestock breeding and ranch management, he contributed to developing world wide sources of food by improving production of protein.

EDWARD C. LASATER (1860–1930), rancher, dairyman, area developer, originator of new hybrid breed of cattle.

OLIVER LOVING (1812–1867), trail blazer and dean of trail drivers, one who helped open the West.

CAPTAIN JOHN T. LYTLE (1844–1907), early-day trail driver and rancher who directed millions of longhorns and other cattle over the trails to Kansas and other points north.

JOHN MARCELLUS 'TEX' MOORE (1865–1950), cowboy, artist, author and Texas Ranger whose brush and pen preserved the heritage of the rugged life in early Texas history and brought him the title of 'Official Cowboy Artist of Texas.'

DAVID D. PAYNE (1871–1960), cowman, conservationist, and patriot who wholeheartedly subscribed to the principle of free enterprise.

GEORGE THOMAS REYNOLDS (1844–1925), Pioneer Texas trail driver—builder of a fabulous cattle empire—banker and businessman.

CAPTAIN CHARLES ARMAND SCHREINER (1838–1927), French immigrant who, starting from scratch, at one time owned more than a half million acres of Texas range land, trailed herds of up to 2500 head of cattle to Kansas railheads.

SVANTE MAGNUS SWENSON (1816–1896), pioneer, banker, business leader, one of Austin's leading citizens, rancher, colonizer, public official, philanthropist.

DANIEL WAGGONER (1828–1902), rancher who built cattle empire, civic worker.

UTAH

JOSHUA REUBEN CLARK, JR. (1871–1961), farmer, cattleman, lawyer, churchman, state and federal government official, served as Under Secretary of State and Ambassador to Mexico.

JACOB HAMBLIN (1819–1886), colonizer, developer of a state, pacifier of warring Indians, humanitarian.

ANTHONY W. IVINS (1852–1931), pioneer cattleman, peace officer, banker, church official.

JESSE KNIGHT (1845–1921), developer of great ranches and other business enterprises who believed that wealth had no meaning except in terms of its ultimate social use—and for him the welfare of the people around him was the only legitimate goal of business.

JOHN A. SCORUP (1872–1959), pioneer cattleman, builder of empire, public official.

Jesse Knight

WASHINGTON

ARTHUR ARMSTRONG DENNY (1822–1899), one of the founders of Seattle, pioneer business leader, legislator, congressman.

FRANK MILES ROTHROCK (1870–1957), miner, purebred breeder, stockyards builder.

HIRAM F. 'OKANOGAN' SMITH (1829–1893), pioneer settler, miner, cattleman, territorial official, developer.

BENJAMIN E. SNIPES (1835–1906), a true, self made cattle king, ruined in panic of '93, he built again.

ANDREW J. SPLAWN (1843–1908), a developer of the Northwest, first purebred breeder, organizer of industry.

ISAAC INGALLS STEVENS (1818–1862), first governor of Washington Territory, instrumental in establishing Territorial government and working out treaties with the Indians.

Isaac Stevens

WYOMING

JOSEPH M. CAREY (1845–1924), territorial and state official, U. S. Senator, author of reclamation laws, rancher.

WILLIAM C. 'BILLY' IRVINE (1852–1924), pioneer stockman, civic and state leader.

JOHN B. KENDRICK (1857–1933), governor, U. S. Senator, rancher, stockmen's organizer.

ESTHER HOBART MORRIS (1814–1902), established the first women's suffrage law in the United States, first woman in the world to hold judicial office—was Justice of the Peace.

JOHN W. MYERS (1825–1901), pioneer trader, ranchman, creator of first water right still in use.

WILLIS M. SPEAR (1862–1936), rancher, cattleman, State Senator; a rugged pioneer stockman who was instrumental in bringing stability and order to the West.

FRANCIS E. WARREN (1844–1929), last territorial governor, first elected governor, U. S. Senator, civic developer.

ELIAS W. WHITCOMB (1838–1915), free-lance trader, one of the two earliest landowners in Wyoming territory, shrewd businessman.

Esther Morris

A painting of John Wayne by Norman Rockwell

Tom Mix

HALL OF GREAT WESTERN PERFORMERS

GENE AUTRY — Native of Texas and Oklahoma. Famous Cowboy Singer. Will Rogers' discovery, he has written over 250 songs, starred in 82 Western feature pictures, and has completed 52 half-hour television programs. Elected in 1972 to the Board of Trustees of the National Cowboy Hall of Fame.

AMANDA BLAKE — Beloved by millions of television fans as 'Miss Kitty', the red-haired proprietress of Dodge City's 'Long Branch Saloon' on the GUNSMOKE series. A native New Yorker, she has been a star performer of stage, screen and television since her teens. An active advocate of preserving our Western traditions.

WALTER BRENNAN (1894–1974) Three generations of movie and television fans know his famous voice, limp and scowl. Played 'Grandpa' in THE REAL McCOYS, and 'Will Sonnett' in THE GUNS OF WILL SONNETT television series. Great movie roles include THE WESTERNER, THE FAR COUNTRY, and BAD DAY AT BLACK ROCK. Was a three-time academy award winner, elected in 1971 to the Board of Trustees of the National Cowboy Hall of Fame.

HARRY CAREY (1880–1947) — Experienced the life of a cowboy before beginning his screen career in 1910. He became a star when Director John Ford cast him in the lead in the CHEYENNE HARRY series. His acting career continued into the 1940's as a character actor in excellent major Westerns including SEA OF GRASS, DUEL IN THE SUN, and RED RIVER.

GARY COOPER (1901–1961), native Montanan whose personal life and great roles in movies like HIGH NOON, THE HANGING TREE, and THE VIRGINIAN, epitomized to the world the best kind of American. His manly, taciturn, and gentlemanly ways earned for him the title of The Tall American.

WILLIAM S. HART (1870–1946), originally a Shakespearean actor, he won public acclaim for his stage version of BEN HUR in 1899. Loved the Western frontier life and was the first western star to feature his horse 'Fritz.' A noted individualist, he worked in the days of silent films; producing, directing, writing, and acting in his films of frontier life.

CHARLES 'BUCK' JONES (1891–1942) — Became a stunt man for the Fox Studios where he graduated to stardom. Buck starred in films for several Studios. Among the most appealing features of his pictures was the presence of his white stallion, Silver.

COLONEL TIM McCOY — Translator-interpreter for the Bureau of Indian Affairs. U. S. Indian agent. Made history in a movie called THE THUNDERING HERD, a film based on one of Zane Grey's best novels. Organized his own Circus and Wild West Show. Did some T.V. work.

JOEL McCREA — One of Hollywood's most famous cowboys, both on and off the screen. Star of many Westerns since the 30's in such roles as THE VIRGINIAN, STARS IN MY CROWN, WELLS FARGO, and UNION PACIFIC. A leading California and Nevada rancher, his fans intuitively know he is a real cowman. Elected an officer of the Board of Trustees of the National Cowboy Hall of Fame in 1970.

TOM MIX (1880–1940), one of the most popular stars of all time who set the pattern for Western movies loved by people the world over. He was cowboy, soldier of fortune, law officer, rodeo hand, and top Hollywood performer — a Western hero on and off the screen.

ROY ROGERS and DALE EVANS — "King of the Cowboys and Queen of the West" — Roy was born in Ohio and worked on a New Mexico ranch where he developed the skills of roping, riding and playing the guitar. In

Barbara Stanwyck

Walter Brennan

Joel McCrea

California during the early 1930's, Roy, along with Hugh Farr, Tim Spencer and Bob Nolan, formed The Sons of the Pioneers which led Roy to the movies. At Republic Pictures, Roy met a Texas-born girl by the name of Dale Evans who traveled to Hollywood as a popular vocalist. She was cast opposite Roy in numerous pictures and the couple was married New Years Eve in 1947 on a ranch near Davis, Oklahoma.

RANDOLPH SCOTT — An all-time western favorite. Became a star when cast in a very successful Zane Grey series. Played a variety of roles from straight drama to light comedy but is best remembered as the strong silent type of Western hero. His last film was a western classic, RIDE THE HIGH COUNTRY, in 1962 which co-starred Joel McCrea.

BARBARA STANWYCK — Native of Brooklyn, New York. She performed in eleven western movies, including the very first ANNIE OAKLEY, and in numerous television roles. Every phase of her career has been characterized by uncompromising professionalism. Miss Stanwyck says: 'I love westerns — I always have. I think historically women played a tremendous role in the winning of the West.'

JIMMY STEWART — Native of Indiana, Pennsylvania. One of Hollywood's leading motion picture stars. Among his outstanding Western films are MAN FROM LARAMIE, BROKEN ARROW, and THE FAR COUNTRY.

ROBERT TAYLOR (1911–1969), one of Hollywood's most glamorous actors, especially well known in adventure and Western roles such as WESTWARD THE WOMAN, THE LAST HUNT, QUO VADIS and IVANHOE. Star of THE DETECTIVES and DICK POWELL shows and DEATH VALLEY DAYS host on television, rancher, conservationist, and proponent of preserving Western ideals.

JOHN WAYNE — Known to his friends as 'Duke.' One of the all-time greats among motion picture stars. Since 1949, he has been among the first ten money-makers in the industry and has appeared in numerous films that have kept him at the top of the list for 19 consecutive years. When he is not making pictures, he lives a rugged life similar to the one he portrays on the screen.

NATIONAL RODEO HALL OF FAME HONOREES

DOFF ABER (1908–1946), Wyoming—Twice World Champion Bronc Rider. Influential in organization of professional Rodeo.

TEX AUSTIN (1885–1938), New Mexico—Rodeo's foremost promoter. Promoted more big rodeos, including the first Madison Square Garden Rodeo, than any other man.

BERTHA BLANCETT (1884–   ), Oregon—one of the earliest and greatest pioneer cowgirls.

L. E. 'ED' BOWMAN (1886–1961), Colorado—Relay Race Rider, Calf Roper, Cutting Horse man, owning and riding a national champion.

CLYDE BURK (1913–1945), Oklahoma—Four times World Champion Calf Roper.

CHESTER BYERS (1892–1945), Texas—World Champion Trick and Fancy Roper, Steer Roper, Calf Roper, Author of book, 'Roping.'

LEE CALDWELL (1892–1952), Oregon—Three times World Champion Saddle Bronc Rider.

Display cases in Rodeo Hall with saddles and trophies of rodeo greats

YAKIMA CANUTT (1895–   ). Washington—the most famous "contest hand" of his era, later became the foremost innovator in Western motion picture production.

PAUL CARNEY (1912–1950), Colorado—World Champion Bareback Bronc Rider and All-Around Champion Cowboy, competed in four events.

J. ELLISON CARROLL (1862–1942), Texas—the first steer roper recognized as the World's Champion in the 1880's and one of the greatest ropers of all time.

BOB CROSBY (1897–1947), New Mexico—All-around cowboy, Steer Roping Champion, permanent holder of Roosevelt Trophy, Pendleton, Oregon and Cheyenne, Wyoming.

EDDIE CURTIS (1908–1965), Oklahoma—All-around cowboy, competed in four events. One of the founders of the Cowboys Turtle Association, original cowboy organization. Rodeo Producer and rancher.

VERNE ELLIOTT (1890–1962), Colorado—Cowboy, Rodeo Producer; produced first indoor Rodeo.

GEORGE L. "KID" FLETCHER (1914–1957), Colorado—World Champion Bull Rider, All-around Cowboy, competed in four events.

MIKE HASTINGS (1892–1965), Wyoming—Steer wrestler and bronc rider. He was a behind-the-scenes maker of champions.

C.B. IRWIN (1875–1934), Wyoming—steer roper, rodeo producer, probably influenced the course of rodeo more than any other man. Owned the great bucking horse, "Steamboat".

PETE KNIGHT (1903–1937), Alberta, Canada—Four times World Champion Saddle Bronc Rider, permanent holder of Prince of Wales Trophy, Calgary, Canada.

BILL LINDERMAN (1920–1965), Montana—Twice World Cahampion All-Around Cowboy, President of Rodeo Cowboys Association and later Secretary-Treasurer. He is credited with the ultimate strengthening of the Association; five-event competitor.

EDDIE McCARTY (1887–1946), Wyoming—Champion Bronc Rider and Steer Roper who later became a prominent Rodeo Producer.

CLAY McGONAGILL (1879–1921), New Mexico—from the turn of the century, he was for twenty years the biggest winner in roping.

LUCILLE MULHALL (1884–1940), Oklahoma—the first and most famous cowgirl of all time.

JOHNNIE MULLINS (1884–   ), Arizona—bronc rider, steer roper, rodeo producer, great bucking horse man and one of rodeo's foremost innovators.

VICENTE OROPEZA (1858–1923), Mexico—introduced trick and fancy roping north of the border. Was one of the greatest trick ropers of all time.

BILL PICKETT (1870–1932), Oklahoma—Range cowboy, originator of the standard Rodeo sport of steer wrestling.

SAMUEL THOMAS "BOOGER RED" PRIVETT (1858–1926), Texas—was the most famous bronc rider for longer than any other man. Pioneered and did more than any other man to promote bronc riding as a spectator attraction.

COKE T. ROBERDS (1870–1960), Colorado—Cowboy bronc rider, roper, breeder of Steel Dust horses, founder of a Quarter Horse dynasty.

Bill Linderman

Another interior view of the museum featuring western sculpture.

LEE ROBINSON (1891–1927), Texas—Range cowboy, Champion Calf Roper, inventor of low-cantle saddle tree known as the Lee Robinson Saddle.

IKE RUDE (1894–   ), Oklahoma—First living inductee elected in 1974. Won third world steer roping title in 1953 at the age of 59.

DICK SHELTON (1901–1970), Texas—a top all around cowboy, maybe the best bulldogger of all time.

MARTIN T. 'THAD' SOWDER (1874–1831), Colorado—Winner of first recognized World's Championship in 'Bronco Riding' at Festival of Mountain and Plain, Denver, Colorado in 1901 and 1902.

FANNIE SPEERY STEELE (1887–   ) Montana—one of the greatest cowgirl bronc riders of all time. Always rode "slick".

HUGH STRICKLAND (1888–1941), Idaho—Champion Bronc Rider and Steer Roper, Arena Director, all-around cowboy.

LEONARD STROUD (1893–1961), Colorado—Great Trick Rider and Trick Roper, Champion Bronc Rider, Rodeo Producer.

JACKSON SUNDOWN (1863–1923), Idaho—one of the greatest bronc riders of all time. Rode an A fork saddle. Was proclaimed the World's Champion bronc rider at Pendleton, Oregon at the age of 50 in 1916.

FRITZ TRUAN (1916–1945), California—(Born Frederick Gregg Truran); World Champion All-Around Cowboy and World Champion Bronc Rider; U.S. Marine. Killed in heroic action on Iwo Jima in World War II.

GUY WEADICK (1885–1953), Canada—was the first to preach big prize money as the key to cowboy contests' success. Promoted the Calgary Stampede in 1912, one of the most important milestones in rodeo history.

ORAL ZUMWALT (1903–1962), Montana—All-around cowboy, rancher and horse breeder, Rodeo Producer.

(All of the past All-Around Champions are given recognition in the Hall, whether or not elected as Honorees. Only one Honoree in the Rodeo Hall of Fame is elected each year by the Board of Trustees and under present policy only deceased persons are eligible. Nominations may be made by individuals and groups.)

NATIONAL POLICE MUSEUM HALL OF FAME

North Port, Florida

The National Police Officers Association of America began a program in 1955 to establish a suitable memorial building to honor the members of their profession. By October 15, 1960, they had achieved their goal in dedicating the National Police Hall of Fame memorial on the south Tamiami Trail on Florida's West Coast. This is the only national shrine paying tribute to law enforcement officers.

Police officers throughout the United States who have met death in the line of duty are honored with an engraved plaque in the center of the building flanked by the National Colors, a memorial wreath, the flags of

—All photographs in this chapter, courtesy National Police Museum Hall of Fame

Exterior view of the National Police Museum Hall of Fame.

NOVEMBER 22, 1963

DIED IN THE LINE OF DUTY

JOHN F. KENNEDY

J. D. TIPPIT

POSTHUMOUS
MEDAL
OF
VALOR

Dick Tracy, always with the lawman.

*(At left) A special tribute
to President John F. Kennedy and
Officer J. D. Tippit, who was slain
attempting to apprehend the
assassin of the President.*

(Below) Display of general police equipment.

Old wall posters

Display of some of the interesting equipment in the Police Museum Hall of Fame.

each state draped in their honor along with the official flag of the National Police Officers Association of America.

There are many interesting displays, such as the most modern scientific equipment to help police solve crimes. Finger printing equipment is on display and large diagrams show in detail how "prints" are made and read. There are historic exhibits of the weapons and tools used by such famous criminals as John Dillinger, Ma Barker and others.

Modern firearms powerful enough to penetrate a car's motor block are displayed along with implements of human restraint. Leg irons, handcuffs, a straight jacket and belts are all displayed.

Examples of the latest police vehicles, fully equipped, along with normal firearms, billy clubs, blackjacks and other regular police equipment of the simplest and most sophisticated type create a lot of interest for children and adults alike.

There are uniforms of law enforcement organizations of England, Turkey, France, Germany, China, Sweden, Israel, Chile, Luxembourg, Iran and Nigeria showing that crime is an international problem. Hundreds of shoulder insignia make a very colorful display.

There is an exhibit of counterfeit money, narcotic displays showing the tools of the drug user and a picture of a typical narcotic user that will convince anyone that this is a horrible path to take.

Crime prevention and the importance of law and order are the central themes throughout this memorial museum. It is open seven days a week and has attracted thousands of visitors since the opening.

Drugs must be defeated.

433

THE SONGWRITERS' HALL OF FAME

New York City, New York

The Songwriters' Hall of Fame in New York City was established in 1968 to honor America's most significant popular songs and the gifted composers and lyricists who created them. The "founding fathers" included major lyricists, composers, music publishers, record rights and senior music journalists. Publisher Howard Richmond spearheaded the effort, and provided the leadership and initial funding which converted years of talk about how to celebrate our songwriters from conversation to a living entity.

It was logical, overdue and inevitable. Jazz and musical theatre have long been recognized as uniquely American gifts to world entertainment, and for many years the extraordinary impact of other forms of U.S. popular music had been a joyful global phenomenon. At home, our songwriters have fueled an awesome "music explosion" that has made popular

Hoagy Carmichael playing the late Fats Waller's piano, on loan from his son Tom Waller, Jr., at the opening ceremony of the Songwriters' Hall of Fame Museum on January 18, 1977 at One Times Square, NYC.

music and records the most dynamic, influential and successful — both creatively and financially — area of entertainment. The Songwriters' Hall of Fame was organized to honor these achievements in a variety of ways, and has already won international status in the music community.

The impossible dream has come true, and today the Songwriters' Hall of Fame is a lively, growing reality. Its first awards dinners in New York and Beverly Hills inducted some forty-eight writers into the Hall of Fame. This group includes men and women of diverse racial, religious and geographic origin, and reflects the many streams that have joined in the great river that is American popular music. Many of the talents are still with us, but quite a few of the highly prized "pianola" trophies of membership have gone to the heirs of writers who live on vigorously in the "standards" — a term applied to hits that have survived time and trend to become part of the standard repertory. In addition to the creators, some twenty individual songs were honored during the Hall's first five years.

Even before the first awards dinner, the Board of Directors had unanimously voted into the Hall of Fame two world-famous giants of popular song — Richard Rodgers and Irving Berlin. The Board, which sets the basic policies and plays a key role in selecting those to be inducted into the prestigious Hall, is composed of fifteen dedicated and prominent music men and women of national stature. One of these is the late Johnny Mercer, who served with distinction as First President from 1968

Steuben glass bowl presented to Sigmund Romberg in appreciation of his presidency of the Songwriters' Protective Association, now called the American Guild of Authors and Composers (AGAC). The framed photo is signed by all the members, including Oscar Hammerstein who wrote the text of the inscription to "Romy". It is on loan from AGAC.

—All photographs in this chapter, courtesy Songwriters Hall of Fame

435

to 1973, when he retired. In September 1973, the Board of Directors elected his successor, lyricist Sammy Cahn, whose contributions have won four "Oscar" awards from the Motion Picture Academy, an "Emmy" from the Television Academy, and many kudos.

Other officers include a Vice President, Treasurer and Secretary, and there is a Board of Trustees and an Advisory Council. It is the Managing Director and the Executive Committee of the Board of Directors who are most closely involved in daily operations and decisions. Since the HALL is committed to the celebration of all forms of popular song from all parts of the country, it is hardly surprising that the Board of Directors and other bodies represent a national and distinguished cross section of the world of U.S. popular music.

It is particularly important for the Board of Directors to be truly and conscientiously representative. Utilizing research facilities available through special committees of knowledgeable experts, the Board draws up each year a list of composers and lyricists who — in the collective opinion of the Board — are most deserving of election to the Hall of Fame. It is a major honor, and not to be granted lightly. The lyricists and composers who are considered must have been engaged in the profession of popular music for at least twenty years prior to their nomination. This is no mere popularity contest, but sober judgment by a group of experienced professional peers.

After the Board of Directors has nominated a slate of qualified candidates, the actual voting is done by the full membership of the National Academy of Popular Music which confirms the candidates for the Hall of Fame. It is an organization of professionals. To join the Academy, a composer or lyricist must have achieved membership status in "one of the three recognized American performing rights organizations," (ASCAP, BMI, or SESAC) or, "have at least one musical work issued in printed or recorded form." Yearly dues for the Academy have been set at $10.00, while a life membership involves a single $100.00 payment.

Those elected during the first five years include most of the top American songwriters who have created the "standards", and the younger creators who have produced lasting hits more recently will undoubtedly be honored similarly in due course. The Hall of Fame recognizes the achievements of writers who have made substantial contributions to popular song over a period. Additional songwriters become eligible every year, and will be welcomed.

Every kind of popular song is eligible for enshrinement.

Main Objective

The Songwriters' Hall of Fame and the Academy are committed to a variety of important goals and projects. Two have already been mentioned.
1) Yearly election of outstanding writers into the Hall of Fame, and honoring important individual songs.
2) Annual award presentations honoring the elected.

Leaning on Victor Herbert's desk (on loan from the Library of Congress) are l. to r.: Abe Olman ("Oh! Johnny Oh! Johnny Oh!!") Managing Director of the Songwriters' Hall of Fame — holding the Pianola Songwriter Award; Oscar Brand ("A Guy Is A Guy") Vice President & the Museum's curator; and Leonard Whitcup ("Frenesi") its treasurer, holding a red sequined slipper — the 1st Annual Children's Hall of Fame Award given by the Center of Films for Children to Harold Arlen for "The Wizard of Oz".

There are several others:

3) The establishment of a permanent and appropriate home for the Hall of Fame and its collection and research library.

4) Collection and preservation of original manuscripts, memorabilia, photos, rare sheet music, books, letters, records and other biographical data relating to the men and women who have contributed significant American songs. This collection will cover both the past and present writers, and will be an invaluable reference and research center for teachers, students, historians, journalists, and the public. More than 5,000 pieces of music and original manuscripts of scores have already been assembled and the collection is growing.

The initial focus has been on writers and songs honored thus far, but the scope is being widened to cover the whole of U.S. popular song.

5) Establishment of scholarships for deserving and talented students, today's apprentice writers who may create tomorrow's standards. This program will run in collaboration with music conservatories and other academic institutions.

All this and other programs under consideration will require funds substantially larger than those derived from the dues income of the National Academy of Popular Music. The Hall of Fame hopes to generate significant sums through associate membership for firms that publish or record music, as well as philanthropic gifts from individuals, business firms, organizations and foundations—including those not directly involved in the music world.

George Gershwin's desk, which he designed and had built to his specifications, was presented to the Library of Congress by his brother and collaborator Ira Gershwin in 1953. It is on loan to the Songwriters' Hall of Fame from the Library of Congress for this exhibit.

Songs and Writers Receiving Special Citation

"ALL OF ME" .... GERALD MARKS/SEYMOUR SIMONS
"AS TIME GOES BY" .... HERMAN HUPFELD
"BE MY LITTLE BABY BUMBLEBEE" .... HENRY MARSHALL/STANLEY MURPHY
"DARKTOWN STRUTTERS BALL" .... SHELTON BROOKS
"HOW HIGH THE MOON" .... NANCY HAMILTON/MORGAN LEWIS
"I'M JUST WILD ABOUT HARRY" .... NOBLE SISSLE/EUBIE BLAKE
"I WONDER WHO'S KISSING HER NOW" ...... HOUGH ADAMS/HOWARD ORLOG
"HAPPY BIRTHDAY TO YOU" .... PATTY SMITH HILL/MILDRED J. HILL
"OH JOHNNY, OH JOHNNY, OH" .... ED ROSE/ABE OLMAN
"POPEYE THE SAILOR MAN" .... SAMUEL LERNER
"PUT ON YOUR OLD GREY BONNET" ...... STANLEY MURPHY/PERCY WENRICH
"POOR BUTTERFLY" .... JOHN GOLDEN/RAYMOND HUBBELL
"RUDOLPH THE RED-NOSED REINDEER" .... JOHNNY MARKS
"SMILES (There are)" .... LEE ROBERTS
"TENNESSEE WALTZ" .... PEE WEE KING/REDD STEWART
"WHAT A DIFFERENCE A DAY MADE" .... STANLEY ADAMS/MARIA GREVER
"WHEN IT'S SLEEPY TIME DOWN SOUTH" .... CLARENCE MUSE/LEON RENE/
OTIS RENE, JR.
"WHEN IRISH EYES ARE SMILING" .... ERNEST R. BALL/GEORGE GRAFF/
CHAUNCEY OLCOTT
"WHISPERING" .... JOHN SHONBERGER/VINCENT ROSE
"WON'T YOU COME HOME, BILL BAILEY" .... HUGHIE CANNON

HALL OF FAME
Elected by Members During the First Six Years • 1969- 1975

LIVING WRITERS

HAROLD ADAMSON
MILTON AGER
LOUIS ALTER
HAROLD ARLEN
BURT BACHARACH
KATHERINE LEE BATES
IRVING BERLIN
LEONARD BERNSTEIN
JERRY BOCK
IRVING CAESAR
SAMMY CAHN
HOAGY CARMICHAEL
J. FRED COOTS
SAM COSLOW
HAL DAVID
MACK DAVID

BENNY DAVIS
HOWARD DIETZ
EDWARD ELISCU
RAY EVANS
SAMMY FAIN
IRA GERSHWIN
BUD GREEN
JOHN GREEN
E.Y. HARBURG
SHELDON HARNICK
EDWARD HEYMAN
BURTON LANE
JACK LAWRENCE
ALAN J. LERNER
JAY LIVINGSTON
FREDERICK LOEWE

JOSEPH MEYER
MITCHELL PARISH
LEO ROBIN
RICHARD RODGERS
ARTHUR SCHWARTZ
PETE SEEGER
CARL SIGMAN
STEPHEN SONDHEIM
JULE STYNE
JIMMY VAN HEUSEN
HARRY WARREN
NED WASHINGTON
MABEL WAYNE
PAUL FRANCIS WEBSTER
JACK YELLEN

DECEASED WRITERS

FRED AHLERT
ERNEST BALL
WILLIAM BECKET
WILLIAM BILLINGS
JAMES BLANK
CARRIE JACOBS BOND
JAMES BROCKMAN
LEW BROWN
NACIO HERB BROWN
ALFRED BRYAN
JOE BURKE
ANNE CALDWELL
HARRY CARROLL
SIDNEY CLARE
WILL D. COBB
GEORGE M. COHAN
CON CONRAD
HART P. DANKS
REGINALD DE KOVEN
PETER DE ROSE
BUDDY DE SYLVA
MORT DIXON
WALTER DONALDSON
PAUL DRESSER
DAVE DREYER
AL DUBIN
VERNON DUKE
GUS EDWARDS
RAYMOND EGAN
DUKE ELLINGTON
DANIEL DECATUR EMMET
DOROTHY FIELDS
TED FIORITO
FRED FISHER
STEPHEN FOSTER
ARTHUR FREED
RUDOLPH FRIML
GEORGE GERSHWIN
L. WOLFE GILBERT

HAVEN GILLESPIE
PATRICK S. GILMORE
MACK GORDON
FERDE GROFE
WOODY GUTHRIE
OSCAR HAMMERSTEIN
LOU HANDMAN
W. C. HANDY
OTTO HARBACH
CHARLES K. HARRIS
LORENZ HART
RAY HENDERSON
JULIA WARD HOWE
HOWARD JOHNSON
JAMES P. JOHNSON
JAMES WELDON JOHNSON
ARTHUR JOHNSTON
ISHAM JONES
IRVING KAHAL
GUS KAHN
BERT KALMAR
JEROME KERN
FRANCIS SCOTT KEY
TED KOEHLER
HUDDIE LEDBETTER
EDGAR LESLIE
SAM LEWIS
FRANK LOESSER
BALLARD MAC DONALD
ED MADDEN
JIMMY MC HUGH
JOHNNY MERCER
JIMMY MONACO
NEIL MORET
ETHELBERT NEVIN
JACK NORWORTH
SCOTT JOPLIN
CHAUNCEY OLCOTT
JOHN HOWARD PAYNE

J. S. PIERPONT
LOU POLLACK
COLE PORTER
RALPH RAINGER
ANDY RAZAF
HARRY REVEL
EBEN E. REXFORD
JIMMIE RODGERS
SIGMUND ROMBERG
GEORGE F. ROOT
BILLY ROSE
VINCENT ROSE
HARRY RUBY
BOB RUSSELL
JEAN SCHWARTZ
HARRY B. SMITH
SAMUEL FRANCIS SMITH
TED SNYDER
JOHN PHILIP SOUSA
ANDREW STERLING
SEYMOUR SIMONS
CHARLES TOBIAS
EGBERT VAN ALSTYNE
ALBERT VON TILZER
HARRY VON TILZER
FATS WALLER
SAMUEL A. WARD
KURT WEILL
RICHARD WHITING
CLARENCE WILLIAMS
HANK WILLIAMS
SPENCER WILLIAMS
SEPTIMUS WINNER
HENRY C. WORK
ALLIE WRUBEL
VINCENT YOUMANS
JOE YOUNG
RITA JOHNSON YOUNG
VICTOR YOUNG

STARS
HALL OF FAME

Orlando, Florida

The theme of this facility is memory moments from the world of entertainment featuring life-size, lifelike figures of 180 stars of motion pictures, television and song "on stage" in memorable scenes from their careers. There are one hundred elaborate sets in four separate areas, the silent and golden age of motion pictures and the modern age of the movies. The best of television and the sounds of the stars are the other two areas.

Visitors first enter a theatre lobby reminiscent of the elaborate theatres of the '20's and '30's. Then there is the Multi Motion Theatre, a special slide presentation designed to sweep visitors along on a trip through the various emotions generated in the whole spectrum of motion pictures— hate, love, anger, disappointment, pathos, surprise, happiness and on and on.

—All photographs in this chapter, courtesy Stars Hall of Fame

Katharine Hepburn and Humphrey Bogart in one of the classic movies of all time, "African Queen" as shown at the Stars Hall of Fame in one of the sets that recreate famous scenes.

The Stars Hall of Fame Wax Museum, Orlando, Florida.

Sophisticated audio-visual equipment and special effects techniques are used to reinforce rapidly changing moods and to recreate major milestones in the history of entertainment.

After the theatre presentation, guests journey through a flashing, quadrophonic time tunnel. Surrounding them in their journey back through time are dramatic and ever-changing audio visual walls that will mark each step back to the days of the Golden Era of Motion Pictures.

One of the first stops at the end of the tunnel is a lifelike Charlie Chaplin in the set from the 1938 film, "Gold Rush," as guests embark on their journey through the glamorous and exciting world of motion pictures, television and song.

Guests actually have the feeling of being a part of the show, standing face to face with such greats of the entertainment world as Rudolph Valentino, Humphrey Bogart, Clark Gable, Greta Garbo, Gloria Swanson, Flip Wilson, the Beatles, Tyrone Power, Burt Reynolds, Sophia Loren and Judy Garland.

"Abracadabra" . . . Art of Sculpting and Set Decorating Creates "You Are There" Realism

Their eyes sparkle with the zest of life. If you look long enough and hard enough, you might even think you see them blink.

But that's absurd . . . . isn't it? After all, they're wax?

But, then, there's the way their arms and hands freeze in gestures far too lifelike to ignore. Their physical proportions and characteristics—from their toes to their nose—are exact.

The celebrities in residence, featured on 100 separate and elaborate stage sets, do more than simply create an illusion of the world of entertainment.

They put visitors to Stars Hall of Fame right on center stage with them during a unique entertainment experience in the nation's number one tourist state. The attraction is themed on great moments from the world of entertainment, featuring the wax figures of motion picture, television and singing stars recaptured in memorable moments from their careers.

The lifelike and life-size duplication is made possible through the intricate and skilled art of sculpting. Once the stars are selected for enshrinement, their physical statistics have to be obtained.

In many instances a photographer is granted an actual sitting with the star in order to shoot posture photos and to take measurements for the sculptor. Color slides also are taken for a study of body "depth." The stars' height, weight, complexion tone, shoulder width, color of hair and eyes and even the length of the ears are detailed.

Multi-angle shots of the star in the actual scene to be duplicated in the Stars Hall of Fame also are studied. In some cases, as with Barbra Streisand, the star's agent is contacted to help provide information.

Then the sculptor begins, designing first a clay head in the likeness of the star. The head, complete with moles and dimples, is then approved by the creative personnel and a plaster mold is made to serve as the form when the hot wax is poured. Next, thousands of strands of hair are rooted in, one at a time; beards, mustaches, eyelashes and brows also are implanted. The glass eyes are made from finely ground glass, colored originally to the exact tone of the stars' eyes—one of the reasons for the startling realism. Teeth also are positioned in the head.

An artist then applies base, flesh tones of paint to the figure. This step of the process is critical since every star has a different skin tone, and matching it requires a dual talent. Not only must the artists paint from a heavy base up to the proper skin tone, but they also must project how that color will look under the set lights that will later illuminate the figure to produce the desired realism.

Meanwhile, the figure is sent to the costumer, where an authentic replica of the original set costume is prepared, even if it means weaving cloth specifically for the garment.

In some cases, an original costume—or parts of it—is donated by the star.

The set has been designed and executed simultaneously with the sculpting. Working from approved sketches, designers build sets outside the attraction, placing the final touches later when the props are added.

Finally, the figures are placed on the set. A series of pin beams are subtly cast on the forehead, each side of the body, and from the bottom and top for the eyes. Each pin beam is brightened or dimmed, according to the dramatics of the set. The set design may also include a speaker, providing theme music or dialogue from that particular movie.

Mae West in a scene from the 1933 Paramount movie "She Done Him Wrong," one of the 100 sets at the Stars Hall of Fame.

441

Description of the Sets Featured at the Stars Hall of Fame

SET	DATE	FIGURES
Mad Wednesday	1947	Harold Lloyd
Awful Tooth	1937	Spanky, Darla, Buckwheat, Alfalfa, Dentist
Perfect Day	1929	Stan Laurel, Oliver Hardy
Summerville/Pitts	—	Slim Summerville, Zazu Pitts
Animal Crackers	1930	Harpo Marx, Groucho Marx, Chico Marx
Sherlock Jr.	—	Buster Keaton
Gold Rush	1925	Charlie Chaplin
Will Rogers	1931	Will Rogers
Don't Fence Me In	1945	Roy Rogers, Dale Evans
Wolves of the Rail	1918	William S. Hart
Branded Men	1931	Ken Maynard
Rustlers Roundup	1933	Tom Mix
Bright Eyes	1934	Shirley Temple
Rasputin & the Empress	1932	Lionel Barrymore, Ethel Barrymore, John Barrymore
The Taming of the Shrew	1929	Mary Pickford, Douglas Fairbanks
Merry Widow	1934	Maurice Chevalier, Jeannette MacDonald
Marie Antoinette	1938	Norma Shearer
Queen Christina	1933	Greta Garbo, John Gilbert
Private Life of Henry VIII	1933	Charles Laughton, (4) Maidens
She Done Him Wrong	1933	Mae West
Son of the Shiek	1926	Rudolph Valentino
Blood and Sand	1941	Tyrone Power
Dinner at Eight	1933	Jean Harlow
Min and Bill	1930	Wallace Beery, Marie Dressler
Poppy	1936	W. C. Fields
Top Hat	1935	Fred Astaire, Ginger Rogers
Sunset Boulevard	1950	Gloria Swanson, William Holden, Eric Von Stroheim, Camera Man, Boom Man
Gone with the Wind	1939	Clark Gable, Vivien Leigh, Olivia DeHavilland, Leslie Howard, Hattie McDaniels
The Thin Man	1934	Myrna Loy, William Powell
Angels with Dirty Faces	1938	James Cagney, Pat O'Brien
Little Caesar	1931	Edward G. Robinson
Trader Horn	1931	Harry Carey, Native
African Queen	1951	Humphrey Bogart, Katharine Hepburn
Wizard of Oz	1939	Judy Garland, Bert Lahr, Ray Bolger, Jack Haley
Lady of the Tropics	1939	Hedy Lamarr, Robert Taylor
House of Wax	1953	Vincent Price, Girl
Dracula	1931	Bela Lugosi, Helen Chandler
Hunchback of Notre Dame	1923	Lon Chaney
Frankenstein	1931	Boris Karloff, Dwight Frye
Dr. Jekyll & Mr. Hyde	1932	Fredric March
Transition Zone	—	Frankenstein Photo Gallery
Dr. Zhivago	1965	Omar Sharif, Julie Christie, Rod Steiger, Coachman

A recreation of the all-time fun classic "The Wizard of Oz" by L. Frank Baum showing the Tin Man (Jack Haley), Dorothy (Judy Garland), Scarecrow (Ray Bolger) and Cowardly Lion (Bert Lahr).

Laurel and Hardy who for years were one of the favorite comedy teams of the country, as they are shown at the Stars Hall of Fame.

(Below) Glenn Ford posing next to the museum portrayal of his appearance in "Teahouse of the August Moon."

Charlie Chaplin as he appeared in "The Gold Rush," one of the comedy classics.

SET	DATE	FIGURES
Love Story	1970	Ryan O'Neal, Ali MacGraw
West Side Story	1961	Natalie Wood, Richard Beymer
The Nutty Professor	1963	Jerry Lewis
The Singing Nun	1966	Debbie Reynolds
The Absent Minded Professor	1961	Fred MacMurray
The King and I	1956	Yul Brynner, Deborah Kerr
Si Yo Fuera Diputado	1951	Cantinflas, Customer
Flesh and the Woman	1958	Gina Lollobrigida
Wild Angels	1966	Nancy Sinatra
And God Created Woman	1957	Brigitte Bardot
Gentlemen Prefer Blondes	1953	Marilyn Monroe
Cleopatra	1963	Richard Burton, Elizabeth Taylor, Rex Harrison
Spartacus	1960	Jean Simmons, Woody Strode, Kirk Douglas, Laurence Olivier, Nina Foch
Ben Hur	1959	Charlton Heston, Stephen Boyd, (6) Extras
Butch Cassidy & the Sundance Kid	1969	Robert Redford, Paul Newman

SET	DATE	FIGURES
The Sting	1973	Robert Redford, Paul Newman
Hondo	1954	John Wayne
Shane	1953	Alan Ladd
High Noon	1952	Gary Cooper, Grace Kelly
The French Connection	1971	Gene Hackman
Teahouse of the August Moon	1956	Glenn Ford, Geisha Girl
Guns of Navarone	1961	David Niven, Gia Scala, Gregory Peck, Anthony Quinn
Two Women	1961	Sophia Loren, Eleanor Brown
Patton	1970	George C. Scott
PT 109	1963	Cliff Robertson, (4) Extras
Deliverance	1972	Burt Reynolds
Psycho	1960	Anthony Perkins
On the Waterfront	1964	Marlon Brando
The Godfather	1971	Marlon Brando
Planet of the Apes	1968	Roddy McDowall, Maurice Evans, Kim Hunter
Transition Zone	—	Peter Falk (Columbo)
Laugh-In	1972	Dan Rowan, Dick Martin
Beverly Hillbillies	1966	Buddy Ebsen, Irene Ryan, Donna Douglas, Max Baer, Jr.
The Flip Wilson Show	1970	Flip Wilson, Geraldine
Bob Hope/Jack Benny		Bob Hope, Jack Benny
All in the Family	1971	Carroll O'Connor, Jean Stapleton
The Lucy Show	1954	Lucille Ball
The Untouchables	1959	Robert Stack
Wagon Train	1957	Ward Bond
Bonanza	1965	Lorne Greene, Dan Blocker, Michael Landon
The Rifleman	1958	Chuck Connors
Ben Casey	1961	Vince Edwards, Bettye Ackerman, Sam Jaffe
Star Trek	—	Leonard Nimoy, Nichelle Nichols, DeForest Kelley, William Shatner
Transition Zone		Nimoy Photo Gallery
Funny Girl		Barbra Streisand
Cabaret		Liza Minnelli
Tom Jones		Tom Jones
Lady Sings the Blues		Diana Ross
Ray Charles		Ray Charles
Liberace		Liberace
Nat "King" Cole		Nat "King" Cole
Camelot		Julie Andrews
White Christmas		Bing Crosby
Fitzgerald/Armstrong		Ella Fitzgerald, Louis Armstrong
Beatles		George Harrison, Ringo Starr, Paul McCartney, John Lennon
Student Prince		Mario Lanza
Sammy Davis, Jr.		Sammy Davis, Jr.
Country Western		Roy Clark, Johnny Cash

444 STARS

NATIONAL STATUARY HALL

The Nation's Capitol, Washington, D.C.

The concept of a National Statuary Hall began in the middle of the nineteenth century. The completion of the present House wing in 1857 allowed the House of Representatives to move into its new and larger chamber. The old, vacant, semicircular, marble columned chamber became a cluttered thoroughfare between the Rotunda and the House wing.

Suggestions for the use of the old chamber were made as early as 1853 by Gouverneur Kemble, a former member of the House, who pressed for its use as a gallery for historical paintings. The space between the columns seemed too limited for such a purpose, but was considered more suited for the display of busts and statuary.

On April 19, 1864, the Honorable Justin S. Morrill in the House of Representatives proposed: "To what end more useful or grand, and at the same time simple and inexpensive, can we devote it [the Chamber] than to ordain that it shall be set apart for the reception of such statuary as each State shall elect to be deserving of in this lasting commemoration?"

This proposal was enacted into the law creating the National Statuary Hall, July 2, 1864 (sec. 1814 of the Revised Statutes), the essential part of which provides:

> And the President is hereby authorized to invite each and all the States to provide and furnish statues, in marble or bronze, not exceeding two in number for each State, of deceased persons who have been citizens thereof, and illustrious for their historic renown or for distinguished civic or military services such as each State may deem to be worthy of this national commemoration; and when so furnished the same shall be placed in the Old Hall of the House of Representatives, in the Capitol of the United States, which is set apart, or so much thereof as may be necessary, as a national statuary hall for the purpose herein indicated.

By 1933, 65 statues were crowded into Statuary Hall. In some places they were lined three deep which was esthetically displeasing. More important, however, the structure of the chamber would not accommodate the excessive weight and there were statues yet to come.

Interior view of National Statuary Hall in the Capitol, Washington, D.C.
—Photograph by Kay Smith

— Unless indicated otherwise, all photographs in this chapter courtesy Architect of the Capitol

On February 24, 1933, Congress passed House Concurrent Resolution No. 47 to provide for the relocation of statues and to govern the future reception and location of statues.

Resolved by the House of Representatives (the Senate concurring), That the Architect of the Capitol, upon the approval of the Joint Committee on the Library, with the advice of the Commission of Fine Arts, is hereby authorized and directed to relocate within the Capitol any of the statues already received and placed in Statuary Hall, and to provide for the reception and location of the statues received hereafter from the States.

Under authority of this resolution, it was decided that only one statue from each State should be placed in Statuary Hall. The others are prominently located in designated areas and corridors of the Capitol.

Ninety-one statues, 45 marble and 46 bronze, have been contributed by 50 States. Two statues have been contributed by 41 States. One statue has been received from each of the following 9 States: Alaska, Colorado, Montana, Nevada, New Mexico, North Dakota, Utah, Washington and Wyoming.

The basis for selection was different in each state, and the selections were made over a period of many years, so that the standards which appeared important to one state legislature were completely different from those considered thirty years later by another state. The conditions and problems of the state and national governments and the lives of the people changed so much from one generation to another that values and measures of greatness hardly relate to each other.

It is said that National Statuary Hall epitomizes the story of America. Massachusetts selected John Winthrop with this description of his contribution to the state. "He gave all his strength, devotion and fortune to the American colonies." He was a Puritan of English culture. Yet, California chose the early Spanish missionary Junipero Serra, and Wisconsin chose Father Marquette, a French missionary. Vermont selected Ethan Allen, the "Robin Hood of the Revolution," and Louisiana selected Huey P. Long, controversial senator of the 1930s — certainly a wide divergence of choices. This is typical of the ninety-one selections made for the honor of perpetual recognition in this hallowed hall.

(Below) The National Statuary Hall attracts many tour groups in the Capitol.
—Photograph by Kay Smith

ALPHABETICAL LIST OF THE 91 STATUES
IN THE NATIONAL STATUARY HALL COLLECTION

Statue	State	Sculptor	Medium	Unveiling or congressional proceedings	Location
*Adams, Samuel	Massachusetts	Anne Whitney	Marble	Congressional Proceedings 1876	Statuary Hall
Allen, Ethan	Vermont	Larkin G. Mead	Marble	Congressional Proceedings 1876	Statuary Hall
Allen, William	Ohio	Charles H. Niehaus	Marble	Placed 1887	Statuary Hall
Austin, Stephen F.	Texas	Elisabet Ney	Marble	Congressional Proceedings 1905	Small House rotunda
*Aycock, Charles Brantley	North Carolina	Charles Keck	Bronze	Unveiled 1932	Hall of Columns
Bartlett, E. L. "Bob"	Alaska	Felix W. de Weldon	Bronze	Unveiled 1971	House connecting corridor
Beadle, William H. H.	South Dakota	H. Daniel Webster	Bronze	Unveiled 1938	Statuary Hall
Benton, Thomas H.	Missouri	Alexander Doyle	Marble	Congressional Proceedings 1899	Statuary Hall
Blair, Francis P., Jr.	Missouri	Alexander Doyle	Marble	Congressional Proceedings 1899	Hall of Columns
Borah, William E.	Idaho	Bryant Baker	Bronze	Unveiled 1947	Senate connecting corridor
Bryan, William Jennings	Nebraska	Rudulph Evans	Bronze	Unveiled 1937	Statuary Hall
*Burke, John	North Dakota	Avard Fairbanks	Bronze	Unveiled 1963	Statuary Hall
*Calhoun, John C.	South Carolina	Frederic W. Ruckstull	Marble	Unveiled 1910	Statuary Hall
*Carroll, Charles, of Carrollton	Maryland	Richard E. Brooks	Bronze	Congressional Proceedings 1903	Statuary Hall
Cass, Lewis	Michigan	Daniel Chester French	Marble	Congressional Proceedings 1889	Statuary Hall
Chandler, Zachariah	Michigan	Charles H. Niehaus	Marble	Unveiled 1913	Hall of Columns
*Chavez, Dennis	New Mexico	Felix W. de Weldon	Bronze	Unveiled 1966	Vestibule north of Rotunda
Clarke, James P.	Arkansas	Pompeo Coppini	Marble	Placed 1921	Hall of Columns
Clay, Henry	Kentucky	Charles H. Niehaus	Bronze	Unveiled 1929	Statuary Hall
Clayton, John M.	Delaware	Bryant Baker	Marble	Unveiled 1934	Senate connecting corridor
Clinton, George	New York	Henry Kirke Brown	Bronze	Placed 1873	Small House rotunda
Collamer, Jacob	Vermont	Preston Powers	Marble	Congressional Proceedings 1881	Hall of Columns
Curry, Jabez Lamar Monroe	Alabama	Dante Sodini	Marble	Congressional Proceedings 1908	Hall of Columns
*Damien, Father	Hawaii	Marisol Escobar	Bronze	Unveiled 1969	Hall of Columns
Davis, Jefferson	Mississippi	Augustus Lukeman	Bronze	Unveiled 1931	Statuary Hall
Fulton, Robert	Pennsylvania	Howard Roberts	Marble	Congressional Proceedings 1889	Statuary Hall
Garfield, James A.	Ohio	Charles H. Niehaus	Marble	Congressional Proceedings 1886	Rotunda
George, James Z.	Mississippi	Augustus Lukeman	Bronze	Unveiled 1931	Hall of Columns
Glick, George W.	Kansas	Charles H. Niehaus	Marble	Congressional Proceedings 1914	Hall of Columns
Gorrie, John	Florida	C. A. Pillars	Marble	Unveiled 1914	Statuary Hall
*Greene, Nathanael	Rhode Island	Henry Kirke Brown	Marble	Congressional Proceedings 1870	Vestibule north of Rotunda
Greenway, John C.	Arizona	Gutzon Borglum	Bronze	Unveiled 1930	Statuary Hall

*Statue was relocated to the Main Hall, first floor, east central front of the Capitol, January, 1976.

Statue	State	Sculptor	Medium	Unveiling or congressional proceedings	Location
Hamlin, Hannibal	Maine	Charles E. Tefft	Bronze	Unveiled 1935	Statuary Hall
Hampton, Wade	South Carolina	Frederic W. Ruckstull	Marble	Unveiled 1929	House connecting corridor
Hanson, John	Maryland	Richard E. Brooks	Bronze	Congressional Proceedings (1903)	Senate connecting corridor
Harlan, James	Iowa	Nellie V. Walker	Bronze	Installed 1910	Hall of Columns
Houston, Samuel	Texas	Elisabet Ney	Marble	Congressional Proceedings 1905	Statuary Hall
Ingalls, John J.	Kansas	Charles H. Niehaus	Marble	Congressional Proceedings 1905	Statuary Hall
Jackson, Andrew	Tennessee	Belle Kinney Scholz and Leopold F. Scholz	Bronze	Unveiled 1928	Rotunda
* Kamehameha I	Hawaii	Thomas R. Gould	Bronze	Unveiled 1969	Statuary Hall
Kearny, Philip	New Jersey	Henry Kirke Brown	Bronze	Congressional Proceedings 1888	Hall of Columns
Kenna, John E.	West Virginia	Alexander Doyle	Marble	Placed 1901	Hall of Columns
King, Thomas Starr	California	Haig Patigian	Bronze	Unveiled 1931	Hall of Columns
King, William	Maine	Franklin Simmons	Marble	Congressional Proceedings 1878	House connecting corridor
* Kino, Eusebio F.	Arizona	Suzanne Silvercruys	Bronze	Unveiled 1965	Hall of Columns
Kirkwood, Samuel J.	Iowa	Vinnie Ream	Bronze	Placed 1913	Statuary Hall
La Follette, Robert M., Sr.	Wisconsin	Jo Davidson	Marble	Unveiled 1929	Statuary Hall
Lee, Rev. Jason	Oregon	Gifford Proctor [1]	Bronze	Unveiled 1953	Statuary Hall
Lee, Robert E.	Virginia	Edward V. Valentine	Bronze	Unveiled 1934	Statuary Hall
* Livingston, Robert R.	New York	Erastus Dow Palmer	Bronze	Placed 1875	Statuary Hall
* Long, Dr. Crawford W.	Georgia	J. Massey Rhind	Marble	Unveiled 1926	Senate connecting corridor
Long, Huey P.	Louisiana	Charles Keck	Bronze	Unveiled 1941	Statuary Hall
Marquette, Pere Jacques	Wisconsin	Gaetano Trentanove	Marble	Congressional Proceedings 1896	House connecting corridor
McCarran, Patrick A.	Nevada	Yolande Jacobson	Bronze	Unveiled 1960	Statuary Hall vestibule north
McDowell, Dr. Ephraim	Kentucky	Charles H. Niehaus	Bronze	Unveiled 1929	Senate connecting corridor
McLoughlin, Dr. John	Oregon	Gifford Proctor [1]	Bronze	Unveiled 1953	House connecting corridor
* Morris, Esther H.	Wyoming	Avard Fairbanks	Bronze	Unveiled 1960	Statuary Hall vestibule north
Morton, J. Sterling	Nebraska	Rudulph Evans	Bronze	Unveiled 1937	Hall of Columns
Morton, Oliver P.	Indiana	Charles H. Niehaus	Marble	Congressional Proceedings 1900	Hall of Columns
Muhlenberg, John P. G.	Pennsylvania	Blanche Nevin	Marble	Congressional Proceedings 1889	Small House rotunda
Pierpont, Francis H.	West Virginia	Franklin Simmons	Marble	Unveiled 1910	Statuary Hall
Rice, Henry Mower	Minnesota	Frederick E. Triebel	Marble	Unveiled 1916	Statuary Hall

[1] *Joint commission for the Oregon statues was given to A. Phimister Proctor and his son, Gifford, Phimister died before the models were completed and the statues were executed by Gifford (G. MacG.).*

448 STATUARY HALL

Statue	State	Sculptor	Medium	Unveiling or congressional proceedings	Location
*Rodney, Caesar	Delaware	Bryant Baker	Marble	Unveiled 1934	Statuary Hall
Rogers, Will	Oklahoma	Jo Davidson	Bronze	Unveiled 1939	House connecting corridor
Rose, Uriah M.	Arkansas	Frederic W. Ruckstull	Marble	Placed 1917	Statuary Hall
*Russell, Charles M.	Montana	John B. Weaver	Bronze	Unveiled 1959	Statuary Hall
*Sabin, Dr. Florence R.	Colorado	Joy Buba	Bronze	Unveiled 1959	Statuary Hall
*Sanford, Maria L.	Minnesota	Evelyn Raymond	Bronze	Unveiled 1958	Senate connecting corridor
Sequoyah (Sequoya)	Oklahoma	Vinnie Ream (completed by G. Julian Zolnay)	Bronze	Unveiled 1917	Statuary Hall
Serra, Junipero	California	Ettore Cadorin	Bronze	Unveiled 1931	Statuary Hall
Sevier, John	Tennessee	Belle Kinney Scholz and Leopold F. Scholz	Bronze	Unveiled 1931	Statuary Hall
*Sherman, Roger	Connecticut	Chauncey B. Ives	Marble	Congressional Proceedings 1872	Statuary Hall
Shields, Gen. James	Illinois	Leonard W. Volk	Bronze	Unveiled 1893	Hall of Columns
Shoup, George L.	Idaho	Frederick E. Triebel	Marble	Congressional Proceedings 1910	Statuary Hall
Smith, Gen. E. Kirby	Florida	C. Adrian Pillars	Bronze	Congressional Proceedings 1922	Hall of Columns
Stark, John	New Hampshire	Carl Conrads	Marble	Congressional Proceedings 1894	Vestibule north of Rotunda
Stephens, Alexander H.	Georgia	Gutzon Borglum	Marble	Unveiled 1927	Statuary Hall
*Stockton, Richard	New Jersey	Henry Kirke Brown (completed by H. K. Bush-Brown)	Marble	Congressional Proceedings 1888	Statuary Hall
Trumbull, Jonathan	Connecticut	Chauncey B. Ives	Marble	Congressional Proceedings 1872	House connecting corridor
Vance, Zebulon Baird	North Carolina	Gutzon Borglum	Bronze	Unveiled 1916	Statuary Hall
Wallace, General Lew	Indiana	Andrew O'Connor	Marble	Unveiled 1910	Statuary Hall
Ward, Joseph	South Dakota	Bruno Beghé	Marble	Unveiled 1963	Hall of Columns
Washington, George	Virginia	Antoine Houdon	Bronze	Unveiled 1934	Rotunda
Webster, Daniel	New Hampshire	Carl Conrads (after Thomas Ball)	Marble	Congressional Proceedings 1894	Statuary Hall
Wheeler, General Joseph	Alabama	Berthold Nebel	Bronze	Unveiled 1925	Statuary Hall
White, Edward Douglass	Louisiana	Arthur C. Morgan	Bronze	Unveiled 1955	Senate connecting corridor
Whitman, Marcus	Washington	Avard Fairbanks	Bronze	Unveiled 1953	Statuary Hall
Willard, Frances E.	Illinois	Helen Farnsworth Mears	Marble	Congressional Proceedings 1905	Statuary Hall
**Williams, Roger	Rhode Island	Franklin Simmons	Marble	Congressional Proceedings (1872)	Statuary Hall
Winthrop, John	Massachusetts	Richard S. Greenough	Marble	Congressional Proceedings 1876	Hall of Columns
Young, Brigham	Utah	Mahonri Young	Marble	Unveiled 1950	Statuary Hall

*Statue was relocated to the Hall of Columns, January, 1976.

Roger Williams

(At right)
John Winthrop

Junipero Serra

HONOREES SELECTED BY THE STATES
IN THE NATIONAL STATUARY HALL

From the First Settlements to the Pre-Revolutionary Years, 1607–1770

FATHER JAMES MARQUETTE, Wisconsin, 1637–1675. He braved the untrodden wilderness and risked all for God and King.

JUNIPERO SERRA, California, 1713–1784. He led the forces of Spanish civilization and Christianity in subduing California.

JOHN STARK, New Hampshire, 1728–1822. Surviving two wars, he lived long to enjoy the land he helped to free.

GEORGE WASHINGTON, Virginia, 1732–1799. First in war, first in peace and first in the hearts of his countrymen.

ROGER WILLIAMS, Rhode Island, 1604–1683. He colonized Rhode Island, befriended the Indians and fathered religious liberty.

JOHN WINTHROP, Massachusetts, 1588–1649. He gave all his strength, devotion and fortune to the American colonies.

Signers of the Declaration of Independence

SAMUEL ADAMS, Massachusetts, 1722–1803. He managed the details of the "Boston Tea Party" and was the firebrand of the American Revolution.

CHARLES CARROLL, Maryland, 1737–1832. He outlived all other signers of the Declaration of Independence.

BENJAMIN FRANKLIN, Pennsylvania, 1706–1790. A Founding Father, author, inventor, diplomat, printer and inspirational spirit.

JOHN HANCOCK, Massachusetts, 1737–1793. He dared to speak and act courageously against the tyranny of George III.

THOMAS JEFFERSON, Virginia, 1743–1826. Peerless founder and leader of America's Democratic Party.

CAESAR RODNEY, Delaware, 1728–1784. A signer of the Declaration of Independence, a member of the Continental Congress 1774–1776, and a major general in the Revolutionary Army.

ROGER SHERMAN, Connecticut, 1721–1793. The only Founding Father who signed all four of America's first State Papers: The Declaration of 1774 (a non-trade pact); The Declaration of Independence, 1776; The Articles of Confederation, 1777; the United States Constitution, 1787.

RICHARD STOCKTON, New Jersey, 1730–1781. One of the distinguished and able men of the Colonial Period, an early financial adviser of Princeton University.

Leaders in the Revolutionary War

ETHAN ALLEN, Vermont, 1737–1789. He was the leader of the Green Mountain Boys. He impressed Washington with his fortitude and firmness.

GEORGE CLINTON, New York, 1739–1812. He was Vice President under Jefferson, also under Madison, and was the first governor of New York State.

NATHANAEL GREENE, Rhode Island, 1742–1786. He was a leading general in the Revolutionary War, led the army in the southern campaign and was given a plantation by the state of Georgia in gratitude.

ALEXANDER HAMILTON, New York, 1757–1804. A great soldier and patriot, a gifted orator, he was an aide-de-camp of Washington, and later he was the first Secretary of the Treasury under President Washington.

JOHN HANSON, Maryland, 1715–1783. He was President of the Continental Congress in 1781 and 1782.

ROBERT R. LIVINGSTON, New York, 1746–1813. He served as minister to France under Jefferson and made the arrangements with the French that led to the Louisiana Purchase.

JOHN P. G. MUHLENBERG, Pennsylvania, 1746–1807. He was a soldier, a Lutheran minister, and a statesman who served in both houses of Congress.

JONATHAN TRUMBULL, Connecticut, 1710–1785. A trusted adviser of Washington, he was a champion of the rights and liberties of the American people. He was the father of John Trumbull, the painter.

Colonizers and Pioneers

WILLIAM ALLEN, Ohio, 1803–1879. He served as a senator from Ohio, 1837–1849, and was governor of Ohio, 1874–1876.

STEPHEN F. AUSTIN, Texas, 1793–1836. He won Texas independence in 1836.

THOMAS HART BENTON, Missouri, 1782–1852. He was a leading senator from Missouri, serving for thirty years, 1821–1851.

JOHN C. CALHOUN, South Carolina, 1782–1852. As a member of the United States Senate, as Secretary of War under Monroe and Secretary of State under Tyler, he led public thought by appeals to reason and by the honesty and purity of his own life.

Father James Marquette

John Hanson

HENRY CLAY, Kentucky, 1777–1852. As United States senator from Kentucky and as a candidate for President, he was respected for his parliamentary skills and for his gifted oratory.

SAM HOUSTON, Texas, 1793–1863. He was the first president of the Texas Republic, served as United States senator from Texas, 1846–1859, was the seventh governor of Texas and resigned rather than take the oath of loyalty to the Union.

ANDREW JACKSON, Tennessee, 1767–1845. His career as a citizen, as a statesman, as a builder of the Republic, as a congressman, senator, judge and as President was an inspiration to men for all time.

WILLIAM KING, Maine, 1768–1852. The first governor of Maine and a leader in advancing the rights of labor.

REV. JASON LEE, Oregon, 1803–1845. He combined the fervor of a missionary, the foresight of a seer, and the patriotism of a loyal citizen.

DR. JOHN McLOUGHLIN, Oregon, 1784–1857. He was very influential in the early settlement of Oregon.

JOHN SEVIER, Tennessee, 1745–1815. He served with distinction in the Revolutionary War and was the first governor of Tennessee.

MARCUS WHITMAN, Washington, 1802–1847. He and his wife built the first American home on the west coast. They were Christian missionaries who were massacred by Indians in one of the widely publicized atrocities of that period.

Sam Houston

Andrew Jackson

John Sevier

BRIGHAM YOUNG, Utah, 1801–1877. He led his people to the promised land and founded the state of Utah.

Progress in Science and Education

JOHN M. CLAYTON, Delaware, 1796–1856. He served his state as one of its greatest chief justices, served with distinction in the United States Senate and, as Secretary of State, under President Taylor.

JACOB COLLAMER, Vermont, 1792–1865. He gave a half century of service to Vermont and served the nation as Postmaster General under President Taylor.

ROBERT FULTON, Pennsylvania, 1765–1815. By his successful application of steam to water navigation he revolutionized the commerce and trade of the world and changed military history.

DR. JOHN GORRIE, Florida, 1802–1855. He developed the first process for air conditioning.

DR. CRAWFORD W. LONG, Georgia, 1815–1878. He was the first to use ether in surgery, in 1842.

DR. EPHRAIM McDOWELL, Kentucky, 1771–1830. As a country doctor, he was the first surgeon ever to perform an ovariotomy, in 1809.

DR. FLORENCE R. SABIN, Colorado, 1871–1953. A teacher at Johns Hopkins, 1905–1925, and elected to the National Academy of Sciences in 1925, the subjects of her special studies were tuberculosis, the lymphatic system and the brain.

SEQUOYA, Oklahoma, 1770–1844. He invented an alphabet for the Cherokee Indian Nation and taught his people to read and write.

DANIEL WEBSTER, New Hampshire, 1782–1852. There is no military halo around his mighty head. No names of battles tell his fame, but he set forth and explained in living and burning words, as no other did or could, the immortal principles of American government, to defend which navies were built, armies were raised, and our great military leaders and their men fought and bled and gave up their lives.

Leaders of the Confederacy

JEFFERSON DAVIS, Mississippi, 1808–1889. He was United States senator, Secretary of War under President Pierce, 1853–1857, and President of the Confederacy.

GEN. WADE HAMPTON, South Carolina, 1818–1902. He raised and commanded "Hampton's Legion" for the Confederacy, and after the war he served as United States senator from South Carolina, 1879–1891.

GEN. ROBERT E. LEE, Virginia, 1807–1870. He was the son of Revolutionary War hero "Light-Horse Harry" Lee, served as superintendent of West Point, and left the army to join the Confederate forces in 1861. He commanded that army throughout the Civil War.

GEN. E. KIRBY SMITH, Florida, 1824–1893. His was the last Confederate force to surrender.

ALEXANDER H. STEPHENS, Georgia, 1812–1883. Vice President of the Confederacy and a former member of the House of Representatives and governor of Georgia, Stephens was steadfast in supporting causes that he regarded as true and just.

GEN. JOSEPH WHEELER, Alabama, 1836–1906. He fought in the Indian, Civil, and Spanish-American Wars with great distinction.

Jefferson Davis

Leaders in the Struggle to Save the Union

GEN. EDWARD D. BAKER, Oregon, 1811–1861. He died at Balls Bluff, Virginia, dedicated to the cause of freedom as set forth in the Constitution.

JAMES A. GARFIELD, Ohio, 1831–1881. He served in the Civil War as a major general in the Union forces, in the House of Representatives, 1863–1880, and was President from March 4, 1881, until he died from an assassin's bullet on September 19, 1881.

GEN. ULYSSES S. GRANT, Illinois, 1822–1885. He commanded the Union forces in the Civil War, was promoted to "General of the Armies" in 1866 by a grateful Congress, and served as President of the United States, 1869–1877.

HANNIBAL HAMLIN, Maine, 1809–1891. He served Abraham Lincoln as Vice President during the Civil War and was a member of the Senate from Maine, 1869–1881.

GEN. PHILIP KEARNEY, New Jersey, 1814–1862. He fought with Gen. Winfield Scott and was wounded in the Mexican War (1848), was a major general on the Union side of the Civil War, and was killed at Chantilly, Virginia, while commanding troops.

THOMAS STARR KING, California, 1824–1864. He saved California for the Union during the Civil War by riding day and night from town to town, kindling the spirit of one Union indivisible.

SAMUEL J. KIRKWOOD, Iowa, 1813–1894. He was governor of Iowa during the Civil War and pledged his personal fortune to the Union cause.

ABRAHAM LINCOLN, Illinois, 1809–1865. He saved the Union and abolished slavery in the United States. Along with George Washington, he was one of the two most celebrated Americans of the first century after the Declaration of Independence.

OLIVER P. MORTON, Indiana, 1823–1877. He was governor of Indiana during the Civil War and was instrumental in equipping 200,000 soldiers for the Union cause.

FRANCIS H. PIERPONT, West Virginia, 1814–1899. "Father of West Virginia," he was loyal to the Union cause in his support of President Lincoln and was noted as a patriot, statesman and Christian.

GEN. JAMES SHIELDS, Illinois, 1810–1879. He had the unique distinction of serving as United States senator for three different states: Illinois, Minnesota, and Missouri.

GEN. LEW WALLACE, Indiana, 1827–1905. He was a soldier and a lawgiver, author and idealist, dreamer of beautiful dreams for better things for his fellowmen, and wielder of sword and pen which helped those dreams come true.

General Lew Wallace

Prominent Statesmen-Leaders in Promoting States Rights

FRANCIS P. BLAIR, Missouri, 1821–1875. His career is unique in that he was born of Democratic parents, served in the House of Representatives as a Republican, in the Senate as a Democrat, and wound up his career as a Democrat.

JOHN BURKE, North Dakota, 1859–1937. After serving as North Dakota state senator in 1893–1895, he served as governor from 1907 to 1912. Under President Wilson, Burke, a Democrat, served as Secretary of the Treasury, 1913–1921.

Lewis Cass

(At left) Ulysses S. Grant

J. Sterling Morton

LEWIS CASS, Michigan 1782–1866. He served five Presidents—Madison, Monroe, Adams, Jackson and Buchanan—in high office, including Secretary of War, Secretary of State, and Ambassador.

ZACHARIAH CHANDLER, Michigan, 1813–1879. He was prominent in helping to organize the Republican Party and was Secretary of the Interior under President Grant.

JOHN J. INGALLS, Kansas, 1833–1900. He was a great orator, which talent served him well in his eighteen years as a United States senator.

JOHN E. KENNA, West Virginia, 1848–1893. He served his state for sixteen years in Congress as senator and representative before an untimely death at the age of 45.

ZEBULON B. VANCE, North Carolina, 1830–1894. He served as governor and United States senator for North Carolina in the reconstruction years.

The Expansionist Group

WILLIAM JENNINGS BRYAN, Nebraska, 1860–1925. He was an unsuccessful candidate for the office of President in 1896, 1900, and 1908, and was noted for his eloquence.

JAMES P. CLARKE, Arkansas, 1854–1916. He served as Arkansas senator for twelve years and was respected for many years of public service.

GEORGE W. GLICK, Kansas, 1827–1911. More than any other man, he was responsible for the construction of the important railroads in Kansas.

J. STERLING MORTON, Nebraska, 1832–1902. He was acting governor of Nebraska and helped plant 1,000,000 trees in Nebraska before serving as Secretary of Agriculture under President Cleveland. He inspired Arbor Day as a national observance.

John Campbell Greenway   *Maria L. Sanford*

HENRY M. RICE, Minnesota, 1817–1894. He was influential in establishing peace with the Indian tribes and founding the state of Minnesota.

GEORGE L. SHOUP, Idaho, 1836–1904. He was governor of the territory of Idaho and a member of the United States Senate during the formative years of Idaho.

Improving Education

CHARLES B. AYCOCK, North Carolina, 1859–1912. He set forth the great value of education to North Carolina and the nation, putting it above the needs for fine roads and other public improvements.

WILLIAM H. H. BEADLE, South Dakota, 1838–1915. He was a crusader for conservation, and through his efforts twenty million acres of school lands and recreational land in South Dakota, North Dakota, Montana, Washington, Idaho and Wyoming were reserved for future use.

J. L. M. CURRY, Alabama, 1825–1903. He was devoted to the cause of general education in the South.

JAMES Z. GEORGE, Mississippi, 1826–1897. He served as United States senator from Mississippi, 1881–1897, and was respected as a great commoner in his concern for others.

JOHN CAMPBELL GREENWAY, Arizona, 1872–1926. He was an engineer who helped to build the Southwest.

JAMES HARLAN, Iowa, 1820–1899. He was an educator who went to the United States Senate, 1855–1865, was Secretary of the Interior in 1865, and senator, 1866–1872. His daughter married Robert Todd Lincoln.

URIAH M. ROSE, Arkansas, 1834–1913. He was a charter member of the American Bar Association, and a great legal scholar.

MARIA L. SANFORD, Minnesota, 1836–1920. A professor at the University of Minnesota for thirty years, she was one of the first woman professors in the United States and a leading educator of Negroes and Indians.

The New Style Politician

WILLIAM E. BORAH, Idaho, 1865–1940. He was a United States senator, 1907–1940, and a candidate for the Republican nomination for President in 1936.

ROBERT M. LaFOLLETTE, SR., Wisconsin, 1855–1925. He lived a life reflected by a statement of his: "Each one should count it a patriotic duty to build at least a part of his life into the life of his country, to do his share in the making of America according to the plan of the fathers."

HUEY P. LONG, Louisiana, 1893–1935. He served Louisiana as a colorful but controversial senator from 1931 until his death by assassination in 1935.

National Image Builders

WILL ROGERS, Oklahoma, 1879–1935. He was the big brother of the world, whose wholesome humor always boosted the fellow who needed a lift. His humor took the sting out of political strife and poured oil on the troubled waters of international discord.

CHARLES M. RUSSELL, Montana, 1864–1926. A distinguished painter and sculptor, he is widely known as the "cowboy artist" through his superb portrayal, on canvas and in bronze, of cowboys, Indians, frontiersmen and scenes of the Old West.

Robert M. LaFollette, Sr.

Will Rogers   *Charles M. Russell*

Kamehameha I

Frances E. Willard

(At right)
Father Damien

The Reformers

DENNIS CHAVEZ, New Mexico, 1888–1962. He was senator from New Mexico from 1935 to 1962 and supported liberal causes to benefit the Spanish-speaking and Indian constituents in his state.

FATHER DAMIEN, Hawaii, 1840–1889. He devoted his life to the care of lepers in a colony on Molokai Island in Hawaii. He went to Hawaii from Belgium as a resident priest, but because of a shortage of doctors he treated the patients along with performing his religious duties. He contracted leprosy himself in 1885.

KAMEHAMEHA I, Hawaii, c. 1758–1819. King of the island of Hawaii after 1790 and later conqueror of all the Hawaiian Islands, he brought law, order and prosperity to the islands, dealing cordially with the traders who visited Hawaii.

EUSEBIO F. KINO, Arizona, c.1644–1711. Spanish missionary, mathematician, cartographer and explorer, he made innumerable expeditions, often accompanied only by Indian guides, from his mission base in Sonora while colonizing the Southwest.

ESTHER H. MORRIS, Wyoming, 1814–1902. A leader in the struggle for woman suffrage, she became the first woman justice of the peace in the United States in 1870. A law which was passed in the territory of Wyoming in 1869 through her efforts became a model for later suffrage laws.

FRANCES E. WILLARD, Illinois, 1839–1898. She dedicated her life to the cause of temperance.

WOMEN'S HALL OF FAME, INC.

Seneca Falls, New York

Since time began, women have had a tremendous impact on the course of history. However, only in modern times have women been recognized for their talents on a broad scale. Given the opportunity, they have distinguished themselves in such widely varied fields as music and business, science and social welfare, politics and education. Never has adequate recognition been given to them for their contributions. To provide a permanent place of honor for America's most outstanding women of achievement, a national museum for contemporary and historical figures will be erected on the 270-acre campus of Eisenhower College in Seneca Falls, N.Y.

American women, of the past or present, are elected to the Women's Hall of Fame by the National Honors Committee, a 25-member panel of eminent authorities achieving a balance of occupational specializations and geographic representation. The National Honors Committee makes its selection from nominations submitted by the public, national organizations, and newspaper and magazine editors. The First Honors Ceremony was held on August 26, 1973, with 20 of the country's most outstanding women proclaimed for permanent honor.

The Seneca Falls area of New York State is steeped in the tradition of women's rights. It was in Seneca Falls on July 19 and 20 in 1848 that Elizabeth Cady Stanton and Lucretia Mott convened the first Women's Rights Convention. It was this convention which sparked the long but eventually successful battle for woman suffrage — the nucleus from which the recognition of women's rights emerged.

Membership in the Women's Hall of Fame corporation, which entitles a person to attend the annual meeting each September and have full vote in the corporation's affairs, is obtained by paying annual dues of $5.00. Tax-deductible contributions to support the first and only national Women's Hall of Fame are welcome. And persons wishing to submit nominations for future elections may do so by requesting a nomination form from the Women's Hall of Fame, Inc., P.O. Box 335, Seneca Falls, N.Y. 13148.

—All sketches in this chapter, courtesy Women's Hall of Fame

National Honors Committee

HONOREES

JANE ADDAMS (1860–1935): Became one of the nation's most noted social reformers and a Nobel Peace Prize Winner in 1931. Founded Hull House in the neediest neighborhood of Chicago. Started day nurseries, kindergartens, boys' clubs, and many more programs. Cultural activities were included such as book bindery, an art studio and a music school. Battled for abolishment of child labor.

MARIAN ANDERSON (1908–   ): One of the most honored artists in the world of music, a famous contralto. Received the Bok Award in 1941 and established a scholarship fund for promising young musicians. Delegate to the United Nations in 1957. Winner of numerous honorary degrees and decorated by Kings of Denmark and Sweden.

SUSAN B. ANTHONY (1820–1906): Poured into her battles against vice and injustice, a devotion, loyalty, and self-sacrifice that most women channel into their families. Only through equal rights could women become effective workers for social change. Crusaded the hardest for a law allowing voting by women. Her long battle for woman's equality had not been a futile one.

CLARA BARTON (1822–1912): A woman of large vision and great heart. For her efforts during the Civil War, she became known as the "Angel of the Battlefield." In 1881 she organized the American Association of the Red Cross. She supervised relief work in many disasters and not only emergency relief but the rehabilitation of victims. During her leadership of the American chapter, it aided people during the massacre perpetrated by the Turks in Armenia and also during the Spanish American War.

MARY McLEOD BETHUNE (1875–1955): An outstanding woman, a legend in her own time, a symbol of Black Americans' heritage. Organizer and Director of Division of Negro Affairs of the National Youth Administration. Founder and for 38 years President of the Bethune-Cookman College. It has served as a center of culture for the community, of interracial good will and of racial integrity. "I Leave you Love, I Leave you Hope, I Leave you Faith, . . ."

Jane Addams

Marian Anderson

Susan B. Anthony

Clara Barton

Mary McLeod Bethune

ELIZABETH BLACKWELL (1821–1910): Overcame great prejudice to become the first woman in this country to obtain a medical degree. Her concern for all people was the driving force which dominated her whole life. In a long and memorable career she founded the New York Infirmary for Women and Children and aided in the creation of the Medical College there. Returning to England, she became professor of gynecology in the newly established London School of Medicine for Women.

PEARL S. BUCK (1892–1973): Most translated of all American authors, a Pulitzer Prize winner and the only American woman Nobel Laureate for literature for her portrayal of Chinese life. Founded the East-West Association to encourage cultural exchanges. A deep interest in children led her to Welcome House, a non-profit organization which provides care for Amerasians.

RACHEL LOUISE CARSON (1907–1964): Biologist and writer, her writing skills combined with her keen interest in marine biology produced much-acclaimed articles and books. Served with the United States Bureau of Fisheries. Three years of work and research resulted in the author's last major and most controversial work, "The Silent Spring," which awakened the nation to dangers of pesticides.

MARY CASSATT (1845–1926): America's first and probably greatest woman painter and etcher. Greater part of her life was spent on the Continent of Europe, especially in Paris. Her fame rests upon pictures and prints depicting the world-old theme of motherhood. Her work is represented in Luxembourg Palace and in the leading galleries and museums of America. French critics noted, "she remains exclusively of her people. Hers is a direct and significant expression of the American character."

EMILY DICKINSON (1830–1886): One of America's leading poets lived and died unnoticed while America was embarked on the greatest era of national expansion. Decades later, Americans have come to realize that this poet represented the last flowering of nineteenth century New England culture. The poet's garden in particular was a universal from which she drew quantities of her material. Only after her death were her poems published and her position in American and world literature assured.

AMELIA EARHART (1898–1937): Aviatrix, "First Lady of the Air." Her life moved in only one direction—flying. At the rim of her stream of consciousness lurked an unshakable quiet complex that she did not truly deserve the tributes accorded her. Making the transatlantic flight solo and the crossing twice in the air, purged her of the feeling of dissatisfacton that had so long annoyed her. Awarded the United States Distinguished Flying Cross and the French Legion of Honor Cross.

ALICE HAMILTON (1869–1970): Pioneer doctor in American industrial medicine. Started Chicago's first baby health center. With Jane Addams' permission the doctor lived at the Hull House and her activities brought her into contact with the neighborhood's immigrant workers where she conducted investigations in industrial plants which led to state laws to protect workers from dust, gases, fumes, lead and mercury poisoning. She led crusade in field of industrial toxicology. First woman to be appointed to the faculty of the Harvard Medical School.

HELEN HAYES (1900–   ): The most satisfying culmination of long weeks of sacrifice for an actor is to see a marquee aglow with the letters of his name. In 1955 this coveted honor was extended to the "First Lady of the American Stage." During her active career, she made countless performances on stage, screen, radio and television. The acclaimed actress also took time to work as National chairman of the women's division of the Infantile Paralysis Foundation. One of her outstanding performances was that of Queen Victoria in "Victoria, Regina."

Elizabeth Blackwell

Pearl S. Buck

Rachel Louise Carson

Mary Cassatt

Emily Dickinson

Amelia Earhart

Alice Hamilton

Helen Hayes

461

Helen Keller

Eleanor Roosevelt

Florence Sabin

Margaret Chase Smith

Elizabeth Cady Stanton

Helen Brooke Taussig

Harriet Tubman

HELEN KELLER (1880–1968): Both a humanitarian and writer, this incredible blind and deaf woman mastered five foreign languages. She lectured on behalf of the American Foundation for the Blind. She strove constantly to improve the understanding of blindness and conditions of the blind. At the outbreak of World War II, she spent most of her time in the service of war-blinded and educated the blind in protecting themselves against air raid dangers. Her contributions are great to the many socially-minded organizations. Her life was an inspiration to many who are handicapped today.

ELEANOR ROOSEVELT (1884–1962): As America's first lady, she worked to overcome discriminatory practices against minority groups. She served as a delegate to the first session of the United Nations and defended the right of war refugees to choose whether or not to return to their homelands. As first chairman of the United Nations' Rights Commission, she played a leading role in formulating and passing the historic Declaration of Human Rights. Nothing is more unimpregnable in the annals of American history than the assumption that she earned her place on her own merits and by virtue of her own acumen.

FLORENCE SABIN (1871–1953): As an eminent scientist and researcher, she was particularly noted for her studies of the lymphatic system, of the blood vessels, and tuberculosis. She was one of the key figures in the 20th century movement to change the aim of medical study from the cure of disease to the maintenance of health. She was awarded numerous prizes meaningful only to members of the medical profession.

MARGARET CHASE SMITH (1897–   ): After thirty-two years on Capitol Hill, the distinguished, soft-spoken Republican Senator from Maine finally relinquished her seat with the advent of the November 1972 elections. Maintaining a highly independent position, she had the courage of her convictions. While she won the respect of the Democrats, she sometimes frustrated her fellow Republicans. She did much to advance the status of women in the Armed Services. She was a watchdog on matters pertaining to national defense, having served on various committees.

ELIZABETH CADY STANTON (1815–1902): After seeing the cruel and unjust treatment of women before the law, in the office of her father, Judge Cady, she vowed, even as a child, to find a way to help change these laws. Her marriage to the abolitionist leader, Henry B. Stanton, swept her swiftly into the current of national politics. This laid a firm foundation for the political experience to wage the battle for woman's rights in which she was to become a most inspiring leader. Together with friends, she planned and executed the first Woman's Rights Convention in Seneca Falls, New York, July 19th and 20th, 1848. Her life story is truly the history of the Woman's Rights Movement.

HELEN BROOKE TAUSSIG (1898–   ): After years of study and research, the persistent doctor developed viable theories about the source of the condition resulting in the "blue baby" and developed the curative operation. After visiting Germany, she published a report, pointing out the dangers of the thalidomide drug, preventing the widespread use of this drug in our country. Her fundamental concepts have made possible the modern surgery of the heart which enables countless children to lead productive lives.

HARRIET TUBMAN (1826–1913): "The Moses of her people." She became the leading "conductor" of the underground railroad in this country. She herself escaped into New York State from slave bondage in 1849. During the Civil War, she served as nurse, spy and scouting guide for the Union. She led her people to freedom, liberating thousands of slaves from bondage. In her own words, "I was free and I couldn't believe it. There was such a glory all around and the sun was shining through the trees and on the hills. I was free!"

OTHER SPORTS HALLS OF FAME IN THE UNITED STATES

Arkansas Hall of Fame
P. O. Box 5152, Hillcrest Station
Little Rock, Arkansas 72205

Atlanta Sports Hall of Fame, Inc.
Hotel Internationale
Atlanta, Georgia 30312

Black Athletes Hall of Fame
165 West 46th Street
New York, New York 10036

Collegiate Hall of Fame
P. O. Box 1745, 645 South Acoma Boulevard
Lake Havasu, Arizona 86403

Christopher Norris Cricket Library
McGill Library, Haverford College
Haverford, Pennsylvania 19041

International Fishing Hall of Fame
Tampa, Florida

World Sport-Fishing Hall of Fame
Pier 66, Drawer 9177
Fort Lauderdale, Florida 33310

Florida Sports Hall of Fame
Cypress Gardens, Florida 33880

Georgia Athletic Hall of Fame
Georgia State Archives Building
Atlanta, Georgia 30312

Green Bay Packers Hall of Fame
Green Bay, Wisconsin

The Hunting Hall of Fame
New Canaan, Connecticut 06840

State of Michigan Sports Hall of Fame, Inc.
Cobo Hall — One Washington Boulevard
Detroit, Michigan 48226

Southern New Jersey's Sports Hall of Fame
and Museum
Bridgeport, New Jersey 08302

North Carolina Sports Hall of Fame
P.O. Box 395
Linville, North Carolina 28646

Oregon Sports Hall of Fame
Portland, Oregon

National Polish-American Sports Hall of Fame
9131 Grayfield Avenue
Detroit, Michigan 48239

Sailing Hall of Fame
United States Naval Academy
Annapolis, Maryland 21402

Speed Skating Hall of Fame
Recreation Center
Newburgh, New York 12550

Frankfort-Elberta National Soaring Hall of Fame
403 Main Street
Frankfort, Michigan 49635

International Softball Congress Hall of Fame
9800 South Sepulveda Boulevard
Los Angeles, California 90045

International Palace of Sports
Camelot Square
North Webster, Indiana 46555

National Art Museum of Sport, Inc.
Madison Square Garden Center Gallery of Art
Pennsylvania Plaza
New York, New York 10001

St. Louis Sports Hall of Fame
100 Stadium Plaza — Busch Stadium
St. Louis, Missouri 63102

United States Track and Field Hall of Fame
P. O. Box 297
Angola, Indiana 46703

A.T.A. Hall of Fame and Trapshooting Museum
Vandalia, Ohio 45377

Water Ski Museum - Hall of Fame
Winter Haven, Florida 33880

OTHER HALLS OF FAME IN CANADA

Lacrosse Hall of Fame
New Westminster, British Columbia, Canada

Houdini Magical Hall of Fame
4983 Clifton Hill
Niagara Falls, Ontario, Canada

National Sport and Recreation Center
Ottawa, Canada

(continued on next page)

(continued)

OTHER HALLS OF FAME IN THE UNITED STATES

Accounting Hall of Fame
Ohio State University
1775 College Road
Columbus, Ohio 43210

Advertising Hall of Fame
1225 Connecticut Avenue
Washington, D. C. 20036

United States Air Force Museum
Wright Patterson Air Force Base, Ohio 45433

82nd Airborne Division Museum
Fort Bragg Military Reservation
North Carolina

Art Directors Club Hall of Fame
488 Madison Avenue
New York, New York 10022

International Best Dressed Hall of Fame
Eleanor Lambert, Inc.
32 East 57th Street
New York, New York 10022

National Broadcasters Hall of Fame
Freehold, New Jersey 07728

Hall of Fame for Business Leadership
Time and Life Building, Rockefeller Center
New York, New York 10020

Candy Hall of Fame
5 Jupiter Street
Hershey, Pennsylvania 17033

Composers' Showcase Big Band Hall of Fame
Holiday Inn
Lakewood, Ohio 44107

Coty Hall of Fame
Eleanor Lambert, Inc.
32 East 57th Street
New York, New York 10022

Gospel Music Hall of Fame and Museum
Nashville, Tennessee

Hollywood Walk of Fame
6324 Sunset Boulevard
Hollywood, California 90028

Inventors Hall of Fame
Patent Office
Washington, D. C.

Jazz Hall of Fame
311 West 74th Street
New York, New York 10023

Newport Jazz Hall of Fame
Newport, Rhode Island

Jewish American Hall of Fame
Judah Magnes Museum
2911 Russell Street
Berkeley, California 94705

Labor's International Hall of Fame
19268 Grand River Avenue
Detroit, Michigan 48223

Miss America Hall of Fame
Atlantic City, New Jersey

Henry R. Luce Hall of News Reporting
Smithsonian Institution
1000 Jefferson Drive, S. W.
Washington, D. C. 20560

International Museum of Photography
900 East Avenue
Rochester, New York 14607

National Academy of Recording
Arts and Sciences Hall of Fame
6430 Sunset Boulevard
Hollywood, California 90028

Ringling Brothers Museum of Art
Sarasota, Florida

Rose Bowl Hall of Fame
Pasadena, California

International Space Hall of Fame
Alamagordo, New Mexico

Museum of Surgical Science and Hall of Fame
1524 North Lake Shore Drive
Chicago, Illinois 60610

Theater Hall of Fame
Uris Theater
1633 Broadway
New York, New York 10019

West Point Museum
West Point, New York